KU-739-176

Scotland:
The Autobiography

Scotland:
The Autobiography

2,000 Years of Scottish History
By Those Who Saw It Happen

ROSEMARY GORING

VIKING
an imprint of
PENGUIN BOOKS

VIKING

Published by the Penguin Group

Penguin Books Ltd, 80 Strand, London WC2R ORL, England
Penguin Group (USA) Inc., 375 Hudson Street, New York, New York 10014, USA
Penguin Group (Canada), 90 Eglinton Avenue East, Suite 700, Toronto, Ontario, Canada M4P 2Y3
(a division of Pearson Penguin Canada Inc.)
Penguin Ireland, 25 St Stephen's Green, Dublin 2, Ireland
(a division of Penguin Books Ltd)
Penguin Group (Australia), 250 Camberwell Road, Camberwell, Victoria 3124, Australia
(a division of Pearson Australia Group Pty Ltd)
Penguin Books India Pvt Ltd, 11 Community Centre, Panchsheel Park, New Delhi – 110 017, India
Penguin Group (NZ), 67 Apollo Drive, Rosedale, North Shore 0632, New Zealand
(a division of Pearson New Zealand Ltd)
Penguin Books (South Africa) (Pty) Ltd, 24 Sturdee Avenue, Rosebank, Johannesburg 2196, South Africa

Penguin Books Ltd, Registered Offices: 80 Strand, London WC2R ORL, England

www.penguin.com

First published 2007
1

Copyright © Rosemary Goring, 2007
The moral right of the author has been asserted

Grateful acknowledgement is made for permission to reproduce
an extract from Direadh 1, from Hugh MacDiarmid's
Complete Poems, published by Carcanet Press Ltd

Further permissions can be found on pages 450–62
which represent a continuation of this copyright page

All rights reserved
Without limiting the rights under copyright
reserved above, no part of this publication may be
reproduced, stored in or introduced into a retrieval system,
or transmitted, in any form or by any means (electronic, mechanical,
photocopying, recording or otherwise), without the prior
written permission of both the copyright owner and
the above publisher of this book

Set in 11.25/13.75pt Monotype Bembo
Typeset by Rowland Phototypesetting Ltd, Bury St Edmunds, Suffolk
Printed in Great Britain by Clays Ltd, St Ives plc

A CIP catalogue record for this book is available from the British Library

ISBN 978-0-670-91657-3

www.greenpenguin.co.uk

Penguin Books is committed to a sustainable future
for our business, our readers and our planet.
The book in your hands is made from paper
certified by the Forest Stewardship Council.

Mixed Sources
Product group from well-managed
forests and other controlled sources
www.fsc.org Cert no. SA-COC-1592
© 1996 Forest Stewardship Council

FSC

For Tom and Marie

Epigraph

Scotland small? Our multiform, our infinite Scotland *small*?
Only as a patch of hillside may be a cliché corner
To a fool who cries 'Nothing but heather!'

Hugh MacDiarmid

Contents

Introduction

In a spartan study on the north side of St Andrews, in the days of Margaret Thatcher's political reign, one of the most important figures in the making of modern Scotland could be found at work at his desk in a gloomy bay window rattled by sea winds. Though he was usually dressed in jeans and trainers, his hair tousled, his expression owlishly vague, there was no mistaking the rapier mind behind the genial personality and gentle voice. Unlike the Prime Minister, this man did believe in society. He believed in it so passionately that he spent his career unearthing evidence that would illuminate the lives of people at every level of the social scale.

This man was Professor T. C. Smout, godfather of Scottish social and economic history, who in 1980 had moved from Edinburgh University to St Andrews, thereby establishing its reputation as a cradle of progressive Scottish history in the latter part of the twentieth century. There could hardly be a better location to inspire the exploration of Scotland's past than this rocky east coast outpost. Few places are more steeped in dramatic event and blood. A short distance from Smout's study was the spot where the mild and forgiving George Wishart was hanged and burned, after kissing his executioner on the cheek; only a few miles away was the moor where turncoat Archbishop Sharp was dragged from his coach and run through by Covenanting extremists. John Knox had taken shelter in St Andrews Castle, a short sprint from Smout's door, while the story of golf, which found its spiritual home here under the Victorians, unfolded almost within earshot of the history department. Here too, a future king, William Windsor, came to study, leaving the town reeling in the wake of paparazzi and blonde-haired and gleaming-toothed fortune-hunters, not to mention a legacy of manholes sealed like tombs.

For a year in the early 1980s I was a student of T. C. Smout, one of only a handful studying for a degree in social and economic history, and one of only two – the other was a Scouser – who had chosen to take the course he ran on original sources for Scottish history. Here we discovered that while history has largely been written by those in positions of authority, it was possible to discover what those without power thought and how they behaved. Church and court records, for instance, offered a trove of insight into the lives of ordinary people, whether it was the servant indicted for fornication, the husband charged with his wife's murder, or the pauper unwanted in any parish. Read between the lines of a farmer's will, and you'd hear the farmer himself. Presented with material such as this, it's not surprising one came away from tutorials with curiosity well and truly piqued. After taking this course, Scotland looked different.

And so it might. When, in 1969, Smout published *A History of the Scottish People 1560–1830*, the nature of Scottish history shifted on its axis. A groundbreaking work of deep research and reflection, it represented a turning point not only in historiography, but, as its influence percolated into the mainstream, in the way Scots viewed themselves and their heritage. Though there had been distinguished social and economic historians at work in Scotland long before Smout, none had attempted such a comprehensive recalibrating of the country's history from a social perspective, that of trying to understand the experiences and environment of ordinary Scots rather than merely their governing elite, and of their ordinary lives, rather than only the rarefied habits of their social superiors. In this Smout was part of the new wave of historical research sweeping Europe and America, in which the little man's history, the seemingly unimportant person's tale, was finally to be given its place on the stage. Those who formed the bedrock of history were at last being exhumed.

In the decades since, ranks of younger historians have assiduously trawled for evidence that illuminates the social history of our nation, thereby beginning to fill in the wasteland of silence and ignorance. That it took an Englishman to effect this revolution is not the least fascinating aspect of Smout's influence within the academic community. Since followed by an array of eminent successors, pre-eminent among them Professor Tom Devine, he and his fellow historians have arguably done more in their time for the Scots than any other discipline or establishment. History may be going out of fashion in schools, but as publishers' lists and TV documentaries plainly show, hunger for understanding the past, especially from a social and economic perspective, cannot be satisfied. As newspaper editors are perhaps too well aware, the power of the human voice telling its own story never loses its appeal.

Before T. C. Smout, with only a few exceptions such as H. G. Graham's magnificent *The Social Life of Scotland in the Eighteenth Century*, the history of Scotland used to be the history of its royalty and rulers – principally

William Wallace, Mary, Queen of Scots and Bonnie Prince Charlie – of its aristocracy, its politicians, and of a handful of national disasters that affected the common people, such as the famines of the late seventeenth century, or the Highland (never the Lowland) Clearances. The subject was dominated by so-called victim history, a trend perpetuated in schools in the hope that the gorier the material, the more appealing it would be to a generation unfairly presumed to start from a point of zero interest in the past.

With the approach of Devolution, however, the telling of the past as a perpetual dirge was deemed unhelpful. People began to yearn for a rewriting of history, of the sort offered by the American historian Arthur Herman, who argued that with the flowering of the Scottish Enlightenment Scots effectively 'made' the modern world, offering a framework for philosophical thought, economic know-how and scientific exploration that other nations eagerly embraced. This up-beat, can-do, top-of-the-class version of events was particularly popular with nationalists: those, for instance, who like to point to the plethora of Scots today running Britain, not just Scotland. Many take justifiable delight in the fact that arguably the two most important inventions of modern times – the telephone and the television – were the brainchildren of Scots, while the first successful steps in the world-changing process of cloning took place on the outskirts of Edinburgh in a part of the country previously better known as the home of Rosslyn Chapel and the sort of religious superstition that later fuelled the Da Vinci Code.

Depending on what lens you choose, it would be possible to portray the past as nothing more than a litany of poverty and misery; or to see it as an ever-boiling stew of religious bigotry and fanaticism; to point only to the glowing roll-call of innovation, or focus more upon those who left, from explorers to novelists and entrepreneurs. One could narrow the frame to an inspiring list of intellectual genius and educational excellence, or imagine the past as a tale of unrelenting oppression and stoicism.

Scotland's history, of course, contains all of the above. This anthology has to represent all these histories, and more besides. Indeed, to keep an already broad canvas within the frame I have had to exclude the Scottish diaspora, those who made their names once they had left the country, among them some of the world's best-known Scots, such as environmentalist John Muir and the founder of the American Navy, John Paul Jones. The only exception is philanthropist Andrew Carnegie, whose endowment of many public libraries in his homeland has had an

incalculably beneficial effect on generations of Scots. The role of Scots
sent abroad on professional business, however, has not been excluded,
and includes armies, explorers, plant collectors and missionaries, all of
whom played a significant part in the expansion of Scotland's international profile.

The guiding premise of this book, to show history as it happened
by those who were there, allows it to present a vivid and immediate
rendering of the past. Many of the accounts here were made in good
faith at the time of events, or in more reflective hindsight, yet they
contain inevitable biases or inaccuracies. Indeed, one of the delights of
history is assessing how true or fair a representation an eyewitness account
offers. Though the testimonies here don't avoid your eye or blush on
the page, the hardest ones to assess for truth are those where the teller is
deliberately lying, a practised practitioner of revision rather than an
inadvertent distorter. Thus you have Mary, Queen of Scots' adviser Sir
James Melville keener to record that he had cautioned her against
showing such blatant favouritism towards David Riccio than to elaborate
on the manner of his murder; or the unthinking jingoism of the *Times*'s
account of the sinking of the *Arandora Star*, during the Second World
War, when the squabbling between German and Italian POWs was
claimed to have cost other passengers their lives.

Despite the awareness today of the rich history that lies buried or
newly revealed in archives and records, an anthology such as this, which
is driven by the need for flowing narratives of some length, can make
relatively little use of these sources for the earlier periods. As a result, for
several long centuries the commentators on events chosen here are those
to whom historians have traditionally turned, such as the great Latin
chroniclers – Ailred of Rievaulx and William of Malmesbury, Walter
Bower and Matthew Paris – although where possible I have looked to
them for evidence of what the commoner was experiencing in these
sparsely recorded eras.

With many of the earliest official documents and with translations
from Latin of the first historians, one runs into the difficulty literary
critic Henry Mackenzie found with the young Robert Burns's work –
the relative impenetrability of the Scots language. To make the densest
of these passages more readable, I have put them into simpler English,
but for those who wish to read them in their original state, they are
included in an appendix. The surprisingly modern English of some of
the earliest accounts reflects a recent spate of translation from the Latin.

The original autobiography of Scotland, albeit mute, lies in its rock formations and mountain ranges, its volcanic plugs and sandstone cliffs. These are followed by the standing stones, place names, and outlines or ruins of the earliest habitations, the first places where human voices were heard. Runes scratched at Maes Howe by passing Viking pilgrims read like graffiti: 'Hermund of the hard axe carved these runes', 'Ingibiord is the loveliest of the girls', 'Jerusalem-farers broke in here'. One can speculate endlessly about the character of the men who scratched these messages. Such snippets, however, are little more than whispers from those who passed this way before us. Like the outlines of long-lost ancient buildings, they are tantalizing, but unsatisfying.

By the time of the chroniclers, events are frequently being recorded by those drawing on the testimony of second- or third-generation relatives of witnesses. To some extent they offer nothing more than a kernel of fact, wrapped in an entertaining coating of make-believe. Sometimes an overtly unfactual medium such as poetry has almost as much historical validity. The Border Ballads, represented here by the haunting 'Sir Patrick Spens' – written after the Maid of Norway's ship sank within sight of the Scottish coastline – express the intense feelings and events of their time; if nothing else can be certain, one can be pretty sure that the mood they convey accurately reflects popular opinion.

Inevitably, the chroniclers concentrated more on battles than on domestic matters which, though they would be intriguing for us, were of no importance to them. Since the history of Scotland is riddled with conflicts settled at the point of a sword or by a hangman's noose, I have offered these accounts as sparingly as possible; otherwise the perpetual clashing of steel would be deafening. Not every significant battle or disaster, therefore, is covered. In fact, far from it.

Even so, there is a harrowing amount of bloodshed. There is no avoiding the conclusion that Scottish life, be it in the doll's-house environment of Skara Brae, or the palace of Holyroodhouse, was often a brutal affair. Naturally, also, people have tended to record the exceptional rather than the mundane. They are far less likely to turn to their diary or write to their mother to record another quiet day of hoeing or shodding – even assuming they could write or had the time to write – than they are to unburden themselves during times of great stress or drama.

As the clergy were among the most educated (and prolix) Scots, with leisure to sit at a desk, it's not surprising that events of religious importance have been heavily recorded, be it the trials of heretics and witches, or the Great Disruption of 1843. Indeed, few episodes have been chronicled in greater detail than the travails and triumphs of the Covenanters, when ministers picked at their consciences as if they were half-healed scabs, and used their diaries and letters almost as a form of confessional.

Since bad news is usually more colourful than good, and certainly generates far more in the way of documents, an anthology such as this has drawn heavily on the frequently grisly high points of history. Indeed, if one did not know that the majority of the population lived peaceful existences for centuries on end, with the greatest threat to life coming from starvation, disease, childbirth and overwork rather than heavily armed invaders, much of the selection here would suggest a history of almost constant warfare and conflict. That would, of course, be a gross distortion of facts. By comparison with England, for instance, medieval Scottish royalty enjoyed relatively untroubled reigns – only two were murdered in comparison with England's five or six; and until 1939, as many wars were fought abroad by Scots as at home. But while town and country life went on in relative tranquillity for years on end, the lives of these almost invisible citizens could be as hard to survive on a day-to-day basis as if they were under constant flak attack.

At no time was this more evident than in newly industrialized Scotland. Up until this point large swathes of the population remain invisible to the historian, especially women, children and those – the majority – who could not write. Their lives are glimpsed only when championed, found in court, or mentioned by others. Thus, at the turn of the nineteenth century, when the engineer Robert Bald witnessed the conditions of women working in the mines, he wrote a level-headed yet impassioned account of what they endured. As so often in his era, his work is overlaid with a note of moralizing, but the outrage he felt at the suffering of this community is molten. Yet, when women from the mines are finally found on record, nearly thirty years later, the rawness of their voices casts Bald's account into the shade. Even so, it was probably not these chilling first-hand accounts that moved the authorities to act, but the pen-and-ink sketches of conditions underground that were published alongside them. These showed women and children jack-knifed almost to their knees under panniers that were strapped across their foreheads, the tunnel they were navigating barely large enough to accommodate their painful passage. Sometimes words are not enough for those who would prefer to keep their imaginations in the dark, much like these virtual slaves. As Fleet Street editors learned during the Vietnam War, an image reaches the heart faster than the printed word. It's worth noting, therefore, that it was a collaboration of pioneering Scots – Hill and Adamson – who led the field in the art of the photographic portrait.

The overriding principle behind the selection of the pieces in this book has been readability. It would be an exaggeration to say that almost as much has been read and discarded as has been included, but not much of an exaggeration. Promising avenues have frequently narrowed into blind alleys. A reference to the outspoken Protestant George Buchanan's self-defence before the Portuguese Inquisition in Lisbon, for instance, looked hugely promising. How many had faced such an ordeal and emerged unscathed? But even though Buchanan was fighting for his life, the theological complexity of his argument proved indigestible. In tribute to his survival, I have instead included his lively description of Highlanders from his idiosyncratic history of Scotland.

Diaries, which are often one of the most immediate conduits to events, can also be disappointing. One such was the incredibly detailed journal kept by an eighteenth-century Orcadian farmer, Patrick Fea, over a period of nearly forty years. If one was interested in the shifting patterns of weather in that period, or the number of sheep he sent to market, this might be riveting: '19 April, 1769: A severe Rain all day nothing done to the Labg only got some dung to the potatoe ground'. As a record of Orkney life, however, it is strangely unilluminating, and people get shorter shrift than livestock. Fea's wife, for example, merits a mention only when she is stricken with illness, and then in passing. More recently, Jimmy Boyle's prison diaries are a little too self-conscious. His first book, *A Sense of Freedom*, is far more powerful.

Historical records are naturally riven with posturing. Why would they be otherwise? Who wouldn't try to mould history in the way that presents what they have done in the best light, before others write their version? Even supposedly objective recording of facts, as in newspapers, can be wildly distorted. At their best, however, journalists' accounts – fabled as the first draft of history – are an honourable attempt to grasp the essentials of a situation, and put it into context without prejudice. Though their currency is purportedly hard fact, one might see the best of them as a latter-day form of the Border Ballads: a succinct, colourful recording of happenings that includes emotion as well as statistics. Hence the number of newspaper accounts drawn on here for the twentieth and twenty-first centuries, many of them unwittingly revealing in their tone. Total dispassion, it seems, is almost impossible, even among unsentimental news reporters. The telling of history is all the better for that.

A book such as this could not have been compiled without the help of the many previous anthologies in whose steps it follows. Of these, three are outstanding. The first, in every sense, is the late Agnes Mure Mackenzie's *Scottish Pageant*, a superb four-volume record of the nation from the coming of the Romans to the start of the nineteenth century as found in a plethora of original sources, many of which she translates for those of us whose Latin is inadequate. Tribute must be paid to *Scottish Voices, 1745–1960* by T. C. Smout and Sydney Wood, which picks up the Scottish story at the point where the working classes begin to take a substantially well-recorded part in it; and lastly to Louise Yeoman's *Reportage Scotland*, an enthusiastic, scholarly account of Scotland's history, from the time of Agricola's campaigns to Devolution.

A considerable debt is owed to these, and to many other books. The aim, however, with *Scotland: The Autobiography*, has been to gather a sufficiently fresh range of voices and perspectives to make it feel as if Scotland's tumultuous history were being told for the first time.

Rosemary Goring
April 2007

Discovering Skara Brae

PROFESSOR VERE GORDON CHILDE

In 1850 shifting sand dunes revealed a hidden stone settlement on the Bay of Skaill on the Orkney mainland. It was only after a further dislodging of sand in 1924, however, that full excavation took place. Starting in 1928, the work was led by Professor Vere Gordon Childe from the University of Edinburgh. The world looked on with amazement as he revealed the most complete Neolithic settlement in Europe, featuring superbly preserved domestic interiors with stone cupboards, dressers and box beds, cooking utensils and jewellery-like beads. This windswept village, it was calculated, had been occupied for 600 or so years. Human remains were also discovered, showing that despite the low doors and ceilings of these dwellings, the inhabitants had not been pygmies, as first suggested, but were at least 5 feet 3 inches tall. In his description of the revelations thrown up in the second year of excavation, Childe conjures a vivid picture of the life of some of the earliest farmers in Scotland.

Last year's work had familiarized us with the general plan of the unique agglomeration of stone huts linked by narrow covered alleys that lie buried under the sand dunes by the Bay of Skaill. Then, too, we obtained a vivid glimpse into a domestic interior as it had been hastily left by its prehistoric inhabitants.

This year's work has given us some insight into another aspect of the community's life. The majority of the huts previously known opened on to a narrow flagged passage, running east and west. We pursued this land in a westerly direction. As before, we found that the villagers must have lived upon the street roofs during fair weather, leaving there a substantial deposit of kitchen refuse, broken pottery, and lost implements. But the street led to no further dwellings.

Instead it was barred by a double gateway, the inner portal being flanked by massive jambs with holes in the wall behind, in which the bar that fastened the door once slid. Traversing the gates one debouched upon a sort of open square. This had never been roofed and was filled with clean sand when we reached it. But it had been carefully paved with neatly fitting pieces of slate resting on a substratum of heavier flag stones, which in turn had been bedded on blue clay.

This was no dwelling place, for it lacked a hearth and all those puzzling pieces of stone furniture that are so conspicuous in the huts. It was even comparatively clear of the broken bones and limpet shells left over from feasts that the villagers dropped everywhere indiscriminately. Perhaps the paved area served as a market place. In any case four entries opened on to it in addition to the main street from which we emerged.

One of the two openings on the west side proved to be the door of a cruciform porch that had once been roofed by a single large slate. Two arms of the cross were blind recesses corbelled over in one of which stood the familiar cooking pot full of sheep and limpet stew – or rather the shells and bones left therefrom.

But the fourth gave access to a hut of a new type, pear-shaped instead of roughly square. It boasted a well-built central hearth, the last fire upon which had consumed a huge mass of whale bone whose charred remains were spread over a wide area of the floor. Food debris, particularly the inevitable limpet shells, too, were strewn about everywhere, but all the normal furnishings of a dwelling-hut were missing.

In fact this chamber seems rather to have served as a workshop. The northern end was occupied by bins of clay, perhaps the raw material of the village potter, and nearly four hundred pieces of flint were found scattered about on the floor. Clearly the flint knapper laboured here, sitting by the fire, and his products were so numerous and well wrought that one can scarcely believe the villagers were acquainted with iron or even bronze. They were living in a genuine stone age, however belated that may have been in such remote isles.

Another feature of the new hut was that several of the stones in its walls and a pillar near the hearth had been carved. Such markings are clearly to be correlated with the numerous flint implements lying about and show that the Skara Brae carvings were normally executed with stone rather than metal blades. Though some of the markings discovered this year constitute definite patterns, they are all so casual that they might well be explained as the efforts of the flint knapper trying the edge of his products when resting from labour.

Even more startling results were forthcoming in another direction: many of the existing huts have been built on the ruins of older structures. Under the floor of the newly uncovered 'market square' we had to dig down eight feet before reaching the intact virgin soil. Save for a foot of sand immediately below, and again just above the natural clay, the floor of the whole accumulation was the result of human occupation – broken bones and shells mingled with fragments of pottery and implements.

Again, three feet beneath the central fireplace of one of the old huts the walls of an earlier structure came to light. It seems to have been a circular chamber, roofed perhaps with a beehive vault, but entered in any case by a narrow roofed passage, quite like the familiar alley-ways of the later settlement. Yet it passed beneath the wall of the more recent hut.

Similar previous structures and deposits certainly exist beneath the floors of the remaining huts with the exception of the splendid chamber cleared last year. It is built on virgin soil-rock covered by a shallow deposit of sand. The material gathered from all the deep deposits so far explored agrees so completely with that found on the later hut floors and on the passage roofs that one must assume the deeper remains were left merely by an older generation of the same folk. The occurrence of blown sand below as well as above the oldest deposits shows that even the first settlements must have been established among the dunes.

The curious practice of roofing the streets was no doubt dictated by the necessity for preventing the hut entries being blocked with drifting sand. At a place like the Bay of Skaill, exposed to all the furies of northerly and westerly gales, one might easily wake in the morning to find one's door entirely choked with drifted sand, and to be constantly digging oneself out with shovels made from the shoulder-blades of oxen (such as we know the villagers used) would be at least tedious!

Agricola Sails around Scotland, AD c. 80

TACITUS

As Roman Governor of Britain, Agricola sent his fleet north to confirm that the land he was attempting to subjugate was indeed an island. In doing so, he came upon the Orkneys, described here by his son-in-law Tacitus, who acted as his chronicler. As for so many subsequent visitors to Scotland, weather dominates his first impressions.

The vast and boundless extent of land, running out in the farthest shore, contracts as it were in a wedge. The Roman fleet, having sailed for the first time the coast of this last-found sea, made certain that Britain was an island: and at the same time it discovered and subdued islands till then unknown, called Orcades. And Thule was seen, though even yet snow and winter hid it away. But they say that the sea was sluggish and heavy to the rowers, therefore not ever to be raised by winds. I think this must be because lands and mountains, the cause and matter of storms, are rare, and the deep mass of the high seas is stirred more slowly. One thing I will add: the sea nowhere has wider dominion. In divers places there are many currents, and not only against the shore does it rise or fall, but it flows in deeply, winding and piercing among hills and mountains, as if in its own habitation . . . The sky is foul with frequent rain and clouds: harshness of cold there is not. The length of their days is beyond the measure of our world: the night is clear, and in the farthest part of Britain so short one can scarcely tell the twilight from the dawn. But if clouds do not hinder, they say that the sun's brightness is seen all night, and nor sets nor rises but passes across the sky . . . The earth is fertile and fit for fruits, save for the olive and vine and those which are accustomed to warmer lands. They spring quickly, but ripen slowly, for the same cause, much moisture of earth and sky.

Death of St Columba, 597

ADAMNAN

St Columba's life is known largely through the posthumous biography of his successor Adamnan. A highly-charged and emotional work, it shows the depth of affection and reverence in which the indefatigable yet peace-loving monk was held. After being banished from Ulster in 563 Columba was granted the tiny Scottish island of Iona, where he founded a monastery and, with his companions, began to convert the Picts. His legacy is carried on in the Iona Community, an ecumenical movement founded in 1938 by the Church of Scotland minister George MacLeod with the aim of emulating Columba's spiritual compassion and pacifism.

As the end of the four years above-mentioned approached, after whose completion the truthful seer long in advance foreknew that the end of his present life would be, he went, drawn in a cart, since he was an old man wearied with age, to visit the brethren at work; on a certain day in the month of May. . . . And to those that were labouring in the western part of the island of Iona he began that day to speak thus, saying: 'In the celebration of Easter lately past, in the month of April I desired with desire to depart to Christ the Lord, even as he would have granted me, had I chosen. But lest the festival of joy should have been turned for you to sorrow, I have preferred to postpone a little longer the day of my departure from the world.'

Hearing him speak these sad words his friends the monks became very sorrowful; and he began to cheer them in so far as he could by consolatory words. After concluding, while he was sitting in his waggon he turned his face to the east, and blessed the island with those that dwelt in it; and from that day . . . even to the present time the venom of three-forked tongues of snakes has been powerless to hurt either men or cattle. After pronouncing this benediction the saint drove back to his monastery.

Then after a few days, while the celebration of mass was held upon the Lord's day, according to custom, he raised his eyes, and the venerable man's face appeared to be suffused with a glowing flush; because, as it is written, the countenance glows when the heart is glad. For he alone in that hour saw an angel of the Lord flying above, within the walls of the chapel . . .

At the end of the same week, therefore, that is on the Saturday, the venerable man himself and his faithful attendant Diarmait went to bless the nearest barn. After entering it and blessing it and two separated heaps of corn in it, the saint pronounced these words with his rendering of thanks, saying, 'I much congratulate my friends the monks, that this year, even if I must depart anywhere from you, you will have a sufficient year's supply.'

Hearing these words, Diarmait his attendant began to be sorrowful and spoke thus: – 'Thou saddenest us very often, father, this year, because thou remindest us frequently of thy departure.'

And the saint gave him this answer: 'I have some little secret speech which, if thou promise me truly to disclose it to none before my death, I may communicate to thee somewhat more clearly, concerning my departure.' And when the attendant bending his knees had concluded such a promise as the saint wished, the venerable man proceeded to speak: 'In holy books, this day is called Sabbath, which means rest: and truly this day is Sabbath to me, because it is my last day of this present laborious life, and I hold Sabbath in it after my painful labours; and in the middle of this following venerated night of the Lord I shall, in the language of the Scriptures, go the way of the fathers. For already my Lord Jesus Christ deigns to invite me; and at his invitation, in the middle of this night, I say, I shall pass to him. For so it has been revealed to me by the Lord himself.' . . .

Hearing these sad words, his attendant began to weep bitterly. And the saint endeavoured as best he could to console him.

After this the saint left the barn; and returning toward the monastery he sat down mid-way, in a place where afterwards a cross, fixed into a mill-stone and still standing, is seen at the side of the road. And while the saint rested there, sitting for a little while, wearied with age, as I have said above, behold a white horse met him, the obedient drudge that had been accustomed to carry the milk-vessels between the byre and the monastery; and coming to the saint, strange to say placed its head in his bosom (being inspired as I believe by God, by whose will every animal is [made] wise with such perception of things as the Creator himself has decreed); and knowing that its master was soon to depart from it, and that it should see him no more, began to lament, and like a human being to pour tears copiously into the saint's lap, and to foam much and weep. And seeing this the attendant began to drive away the tearful mourner; but the saint forbade him, saying, 'Permit this our lover to pour the torrents of its bitterest grief onto my bosom. See thou, man as thou art, and with a rational soul, thou couldst know nothing of my death except what I myself have recently disclosed to thee; but to this brute and irrational beast the Creator has clearly revealed, in whatever way he wished, that its master is about to depart from it.' And so speaking he blessed his servant the horse, as it turned sadly from him.

And he departed thence and climbed a little hill above the monastery. He stood for a little while upon its summit, and standing raised both palms, and blessed his monastery, saying: 'Upon this place, small and mean though it be, not only kings of the Scots with their peoples, but even rulers over strange and barbarous nations, with the peoples subject to them, will bestow great and especial honour; especial reverence will be bestowed also by saints even of other churches.'

After these words he descended from the little hill and returned to the monastery, and sat in his hut writing a psalter; and reaching the verse of the thirty-third psalm where it is written 'They that seek the Lord shall not lack any good thing,' he said: 'Here at the end of the page I must cease; let Baithine write what follows.' . . .

After finishing the writing of this verse above-mentioned at the end of the page, the saint entered the church for evening mass of the Lord's night; which presently concluded he returned to his little dwelling, and rested over-night in his bed, where in place of bedding he had a bare rock, and for pillow a stone which also today stands as some kind of monument beside his grave. Thus resting there he gave his last commands to the brethren, his attendant alone for audience, saying, 'I commit these last words to you, my children, that between you you have mutual and not pretended charity, with peace; and if you observe this, after the example of the holy fathers, God, the gladdener of the good, will aid you, and I, dwelling with him, will intercede for you; and not only will the necessaries of this life be sufficiently provided by him, but also the prizes of eternal good things will be assigned, prepared for those that uphold what is divine . . .'

Thus far have been brought the last words, related briefly, of the venerable father, as of one passing over from this weary pilgrimage to the heavenly country.

After this, his happy last hour gradually approaching, the saint was silent.

Thereafter when the bell that struck at midnight resounded, he rose quickly and went to the church, and running faster than the rest he entered alone, and, kneeling in prayer before the altar, lay back. Diarmait the attendant, following more slowly, at the same moment saw from afar the whole church within filled for the saint with angelic light; but as he approached the door, the same light very quickly vanished: but a few others also of the brethren, also at a distance, had seen it. So Diarmait entered the church, and cried in a tearful voice, 'Where art thou, father?' And feeling in the darkness, because the lanterns of the brethren had not yet been brought, he found the saint lying on his back before the altar; and he raised him a little, and sitting beside him placed the holy head in his lap. And meanwhile the company of monks running up with lights saw their father dying, and began to lament.

And, as we have learned from some who were present there, before his soul departed the saint opened his eyes and looked about to either side with a countenance of wonderful joy and gladness, for he saw the holy angels coming to him.

Then Diarmait raised [Columba's] holy right hand to bless the saintly man's choir of monks; and the venerable father himself also, so far as he could, moved his hand at the same time, so that he appeared to bless the brethren even by the movement of his hand, since in the departure of his soul he could not do it in speech. And after the holy benediction thus signified he presently breathed out his spirit.

And after he had left the tabernacle of the body, his face remained so glowing, and marvellously made joyous by the vision of angels, that it appeared not as of one dead, but as of one asleep and living.

Viking Invaders, 870

MATTHEW PARIS

Viking invaders were terrifyingly brutal, but sometimes they met their match.
Abbess Ebba of Coldingham monastery was one. Matthew Paris was a Benedic-
tine monk at St Albans. One of the finest chroniclers in medieval England, he
was famed for his knowledge of foreign countries.

In the year of the Lord 870 an innumerable host of Danes landed in
Scotland; and their leaders were Inguar and Hubba, men of terrible
wickedness and unheard-of bravery. And they, striving to depopulate
the territories of all England, slaughtered all the boys and old men whom
they found, and commanded that the matrons, nuns and maidens should
be given up to wantonness.

And when such plundering brutality had pervaded all territories of
the kingdoms, Ebba, holy abbess of the cloister of Coldingham, feared
that she too, to whom had been instructed the care of government and
the pastoral care, might be given up to the lust of pagans and lose her
maiden chastity, along with the virgins under her rule; and she called
together all the sisters into the chapter-house, and burst into speech in
this wise, saying, 'Recently have come into our parts the wickedest
pagans, ignorant of any kind of humanity; and roaming through every
part of this district they spare neither the sex of woman nor the age of
child, and they destroy churches and churchmen, prostitute nuns, and
break up and burn everything they come upon. Therefore if you decide
to acquiesce in my advice, I conceive a sure hope that by divine mercy
we may be able both to escape the fury of the barbarians and to preserve
the chastity of perpetual virginity.'

And when the whole congregation of virgins had undertaken with
sure promises that they would in all things obey the commands of their
mother, that abbess of admirable heroism showed before all the sisters
an example of chastity not only advantageous for those nuns but also
eternally to be followed by all succeeding virgins: she took a sharp knife
and cut off her own nose and upper lip to the teeth, offering a dreadful
spectacle of herself to all beholders. And since the whole congregation
saw and admired this memorable deed, each one performed a similar act
upon herself, and followed the example of her mother.

And after this had so taken place, when next morning dawned, the most wicked brigands came upon them, to give up to wantonness the holy women, and devoted to God; as also to plunder the monastery itself and burn it down in flames. But when they saw the abbess and each of the sisters so horribly mutilated, and saturated with their blood from the soles of their feet to their crowns, they retired from the place with haste, for it seemed to them too long to stay even for a short space there. But as they retired thence the aforesaid leaders commanded their evil satellites to set fire to and burn down the monastery with all its offices and with the nuns themselves.

And so the execution was fulfilled by the servants of iniquity, and the holy abbess and all the virgins with her attained most holily to the glory of martyrdom.

Battle between the Saxons and Northmen, 937

THE ANGLO-SAXON CHRONICLE

The Battle of Brunanburgh, which took place in Dumfriesshire, was provoked by the Scots under Constantine II because of their incursions into Northumbria. As the Anglo-Saxon Chronicle *delights in describing, the Northmen, as they were known, were trounced.*

In this year King Ethelstan, lord of earls, ring-giver to men, and his brother also Prince Edmund won life-long glory in conflict with the sword's edges around Brunnanburgh. They clove the shield-wall, hewed the war-lindens with hammered blades; so was it natural to them, the sons of Edward, from their ancestors that against every foe they defended their land, hoard and homes.

The foe gave way; the folk of the Scots and the ship-fleet fell death-doomed. The field was slippery with the blood of warriors, from the time when the sun, glorious star, glided up in morning tide over the world, the eternal Lord God's candle bright, till the noble creature sank to rest.

There lay many a warrior by darts laid low; many a northern man over the shield shot, and many a Scot beside, weary, war-sated. The West Saxons in companies continuously all the day long pressed after the hostile peoples, hewed the fugitives from behind cruelly with swords mill-sharpened. The Mercians refused not the hard hand-play to any of the heroes who for battle, death-doomed, sought land in ship's bosom, over the mingling waves, with Olaf.

There lay on the battle-field five young kings, by the swords put to sleep; and also seven earls of Olaf: of the army untold numbers, of the fleet and of Scots.

There was put to flight the Northmen's lord, driven by need to his ship's prow, with a small band: the boat drove afloat; the king fled out upon the fallow flood; he saved his life.

So there also the aged Constantin came north to his country by flight, hoary warrior. No need had he to exult in the intercourse of swords. He was bereft of his kinsmen, deprived of his friends on the meeting-place, bereaved in the battle. And he left his son in the slaughter-place, mangled with wounds, young in warfare.

He had no need to boast, the grizzly-haired man, of the bill-clashing, the old malignant; nor Olaf the more, with their remnants of armies. They had no cause to laugh, that they in works of war were the better, on the battle-field of the conflict of banners, of the meeting of spears, of the assemblage of men, of the contest of weapons; that on the slaughter-field they played with Edward's sons.

The Northmen retired, bloody remnant from the spears, in their nailed boats on the sounding sea. Over deep water they sought Dublin and Ireland again, with minds cast down.

So too the brothers, both together – king and prince – sought their country, the West Saxons' land, rejoicing in the war.

They left behind them to share the carrion the dusky-coated, the swart raven, of horny beak; and the grey-coated, the white-tailed eagle: to enjoy the meat the greedy war-hawk, and the grey beast, wolf in the weald.

Before this, greater slaughter of folk was never yet made in this island by the sword's edges.

The King of Scots Insults the English King, c. 971–975

WILLIAM OF MALMESBURY

William of Malmesbury was a Benedictine monk from Wiltshire who preferred to remain as librarian and chronicler at Malmesbury Abbey rather than take higher office. This account of a bumptious Scottish king being brought to heel gives an indication of the manners and politics of the times.

Moreover, although, as is said, [Edgar] was puny of stature and form yet the favour of nature had planted so great strength in his small body that he readily challenged to combat whomsoever he knew to be presumptuous; fearing this chiefly, that he should be feared in such sport.

Indeed it is reported that once in a feast, where the sarcasm of fools usually displays itself more openly, Kenneth, king of the Scots, said jestingly that it seemed strange that so many provinces were subject to so insignificant a manikin. And this was taken up perversely by a jester, and afterwards cast in Edgar's face at a formal banquet.

But he, concealing the matter from his followers, summoned Kenneth as if to consult him about a great secret; and taking him far aside into a wood gave him one of two swords which he carried with him. 'And now,' said he, 'thou mayest try thy strength, since we are alone. For now I shall have caused it to appear which should rightly be subject to the other. Thou also, shrink not from disputing the matter with me. For it is base that a king should be witty at the feast, and unready in conflict.'

[Kenneth] was confused, and dared utter no word: he fell at the feet of his lord king, and besought pardon for his innocent jest; and immediately obtained it.

English Fashion, Eleventh Century

SCOTICHRONICON

Animosity between Scotland and England has taken many forms. Possibly the least worrying was mild ridicule, as in this poem where the author, an early McGonagall, looks with disdain on the peculiarities of English style and implies that those who have time to think about such fripperies are of a lower moral standing.

A Poem on English Style of Fashion

The variety of their garments is a source of amazement to me.
Some of them are short – they could not be shorter,
scarcely touching the wrists – not to be raised by the hand.
Why are the clothes so short? Times change and clothes change with
   them . . .

Overcoats have sleeves reaching down to the heels
which you could easily wind three times round your arms.
You could wipe your bottom with them instead of rags
in the privy without doubt.
Alas! the leather skins would be badly worn away by their backsides . . .

A cap like an earthenware pot covers each head.
It is secured with a red cord.
Tubes form the clasp of its band. Every servant
that lives and serves
has a head the same as a gentleman.

If you see any lady fully dressed,
you will perceive her trailing behind her a dress with a tail
two ells long, like the wild beasts.
Flee from her as from death.
Thus she bears an acceptable gift to her lord.

The English race is like some kind of monkey.
It apes all the others daily, as it sees them.
Idleness produces more and more frivolity and worldliness
in their licentious minds
May the king of all grant to *us* the kingdom of heaven.

English Invective against the Scots, Eleventh Century

AILRED OF RIEVAULX

In a time of almost perpetual conflict, from border raids and skirmishes to fullblown battle, feelings between England and Scotland ran high. This highly coloured piece of invective is typical of accusations between mortal enemies, and was designed as much to incite violence towards the Scots as to offer useful facts.

So that execrable army, savager than any race of heathen, yielding honour to neither God nor man, harried the whole province and slaughtered everywhere folk of either sex, of every age and condition, destroying, pillaging and burning the vills, churches and houses. For they slaughtered by the edge of the sword or transfixed with their spears the sick on their pallets, women pregnant and in labour; the babes in their cradles, and other innocents at the breast or in the bosom of their mothers, with the mothers themselves; and worn-out old men and feeble old women, and the others who were for any reason disabled, wherever they found them. And the more pitiable a form of death they could destroy them by, the more did they rejoice . . .

It is even reported that in one place they slew many little children gathered together, and draining their blood collected it in a stream which they had previously dammed up, and thus drank that bloody water, – nay, now for the most part blood . . .

Capture of William I by the English, 1174

WILLIAM OF NEWBURGH

The English could scarcely believe their luck when the King of Scotland, William the Lion, whose raids on the north of England had been driving them to despair, fell into their hands. This account is recorded by the Yorkshire Augustinian canon William of Newburgh, who was a highly respected historian, working in the tradition of the Venerable Bede.

While things were thus in the northern parts of England the king's nobles in the province of York were frankly enraged that Scots should infest English territories; and they gathered with a strong force of cavalry at Newcastle upon the river Tyne. For, as the matter pressed, they could not collect forces of infantry. And they came thither on the sixth day of the week, wearied by their long and arduous journey.

Now when they discussed in common there what was to be done, the more prudent alleged that much had been done already, since the king of Scotland had retired very far, through fore-learning their approach; that for the present this ought to suffice for their moderate strength; it was not safe for them, nor of use to the king of the English, that they should advance further; lest perchance they should seem to expose their small number like a loaf of bread to be devoured by the endless host of the barbarians. They had not more than four hundred horsemen, while in the enemy's army were estimated more than eighty thousand men-at-arms.

To this the more eager replied that their most wicked foes ought by all means to be attacked; that they should not despair of victory, which without doubt would follow justice.

At last the opinion of the latter prevailing, because God so willed that the event should be ascribed rather to the divine will than to the power or prudence of man, the men of valour . . . somewhat refreshed by the night's rest advanced in the earliest morning with such speed – as though hastening by propulsion of some power – that before the fifth hour they had traversed twenty-four miles; although that seemed scarcely within the endurance of men laden with the weight of their arms.

And while they went a mist, so it is said, covered them so densely that they scarcely knew whither they were going. Then the more prudent, arguing the journey dangerous, asserted that extreme hazard surely threatened them unless they immediately turned and went back.

To this said Bernard de Balliol, a man noble and high spirited: 'Let him go back who will, but I will go on even if no one will follow; and not brand myself with a perpetual stain.'

So while they proceeded, suddenly the mist cleared away; and they, having the castle of Alnwick before their eyes, joyfully considered that it would be safe shelter for them if the enemy pressed upon them.

And behold the king of Scots was on the watch, with a troop of horse, about sixty or a few more, not far away, in the open fields; as if secure, and fearing nothing less than an attack of our men: the host of barbarians with part of the cavalry being scattered widely for the spoil.

And indeed at first when he saw our men he thought they were some of his own returning from the spoil. But presently noticing carefully the standards of our men, he at last understood that they had dared what he could not have guessed they would dare.

Nevertheless he was not dismayed, surrounded as he was by his army, so vast, although ill concentrated; and esteemed it certain that these few, being surrounded, must be easily swallowed up by the host spread out around them.

Immediately he struck his arms fiercely together, and aroused his men both by word and example, saying, 'Now it will appear who knows how to be a knight.'

And, the rest following, he rushed first upon the enemy, and was immediately intercepted by our men; and, his horse being killed, he was thrown to the ground and taken, with almost all his troop.

For even those who were able to escape by flight, when he was taken refused to flee; and, that they might be taken with him, yielded themselves voluntarily into the hands of the enemy.

Certain nobles also who chanced to be absent at the time but were not far away learned what had happened, and came presently at their horses' highest speed; and throwing themselves rather than falling into the hands of the enemy thought it honourable to share in the peril of their lord.

But Roger de Mowbray, who was there at the time, slipped away and escaped when the king was taken, and fled back into Scotland.

And our chief men carried away with rejoicing a noble prey, and returned in the evening to Newcastle, whence in the morning they had departed; and caused him to be most carefully guarded at Richmond, so as to send him in good time to their lord the illustrious king of the English.

Guidelines for the Clergy, Thirteenth Century

SCOTTISH ECCESIASTICAL STATUTES

It was not just commoners and the ungodly who needed to be given guidelines about propriety. Clearly the clergy had to be kept in line as well.

The Habit of Clerics

We ordain that rectors and vicars of churches and also those in positions of dignity, priests as well as clerics who are below sacred orders, be marked by decency both in mind and outward attire, that they wear not garments of red, green, or striped colours, nor garments ('panni') that would attract attention by their excessive shortness; that vicars also and priests wear their gowns ('Indumenta') close, and wear a becoming tonsure, and that those who ought to be an example to others offend not the gaze of beholders. But if, warned by their Ordinaries, they should not amend, let them be suspended from office and be subjected to the discipline of the Church.

Religious Houses, 1207

GERVASE OF CANTERBURY

A list of religious houses in Scotland by the chronicler Gervase of Canterbury shows how significant the Church's presence was.

IN LOTHIAN, of the king of Scotland, [are]: –

The abbacy of Newbattle, St Mary's; white monks
The abbacy of Melrose, St Mary's; white monks
The abbacy of Dryburgh; white canons
The abbacy of Kelso, St Mary's; grey monks
The abbacy of Coldstream; black nuns
The priory of Coldingham; black monks
The abbacy of Jedburgh; black canons
The priory of Haddington; white nuns
The abbacy of Edinburgh; black canons
The priory of South Berwick; white monks
The priory of North Berwick; black nuns
The priory of Eccles; white nuns

In the earldom of Fife in Scotland: –
The bishopric of St Andrews; black canons and culdees
The abbacy of holy Trinity, of Dunfermline; black monks
The abbacy of Stirling; black canons
The priory of May; black monks, of Reading
In the isle of St Columba; black canons
The abbacy of Lindores; monks of Tiron
The priory of Perth; black monks
The abbacy of Scone; black canons
The abbacy of Cupar; white monks
The priory of Roslin; black canons
The abbacy of Arbroath; monks of Tiron
The bishopric of Dunkeld, of St Columba; black canons and culdees
The bishopric of Brechin; culdees
The bishopric of Aberdeen
The bishopric of Moray
The priory of Urquhart; black monks of Dunfermline

The abbacy of Kinloss; white monks
The bishopric of Ross; culdees
The bishopric of Glasgow; secular canons
The abbacy of St Kinewin; monks of Tiron
The bishopric of Galloway: the abbacy of Whithorn; white monks
The bishopric of Dunblane; culdees
In Iona, an abbacy; culdees

Total, twenty-two

The Burning of a Bishop, 1222

ANNALS OF DUNSTABLE

The extreme measures taken by an angered nobleman show on one hand the outlandish brutality of medieval Scotland and, on the other, the rather contradictory need for penance that wrongdoers seem to have felt.

In the same year [1222] a certain bishop of the kingdom of Scotland, of the diocese of Caithness, sought from his subjects the tithes of hay concerning which both he and the earl of Caithness had made promise to the king of Scotland. And while decreeing as bishop he caused his decree to be fortified by both the royal seal and the seal of the earl.

But afterwards the earl was wroth [angry] about this, and went to the bishop in his country and, moved by rage, asked from him that the charter of the decree should be returned to him.

And because the bishop refused to do this, [the earl] slew [the bishop's] chaplain, a monk to wit, in his presence; and wounded to death in his sight a nephew of the bishop. And seeing this, the bishop said: 'Even if thou slay me, I will never resign to thee the instruments of my church.'

Then the earl was roused to anger, and ordered the said bishop to be bound to the door-post in the kitchen; and shutting the [outer] door, ordered the house to be set on fire.

And when it had been wholly fired the bishop's chains were loosened, and he came to the [outer] door, as if unhurt, to go out; but the earl, waiting outside to see the end, when he saw this caused the bishop to be cast into the fire, and ordered the two bodies of those previously slain to be thrown upon him. And so the three said martyrs for the defence of the right of the church departed to the Lord.

And the most Christian king of the Scots would not leave so great sacrilege unpunished, but set out with an army to take the earl.

But the earl heard this, and fled from the king's realm; and in the manner of Cain wandering and in exile roamed about among the isles of the sea. And at last he made these terms with the king: – first, that he and his heirs and his men would pay the tithes of hay; and that within six months he would bring to the king's feet the cut-off heads of all those who had taken part in the said crime. He resigned also the half of his earldom into the king's hands. He also bestowed certain lands upon that church whose bishop he had slain. Moreover also he promised to go on foot to Rome, and to obey the mandate of the chief pontiff concerning these things.

Church Corruption, 1271

THE CHRONICLE OF LANERCOST

Corruption in the medieval Church was widespread and, it seems, generally accepted. The bishop in question here, however, appears to have been spectacularly hypocritical even by the standards of his day. The colourful and biased Chronicle of Lanercost *was compiled at Lanercost Priory, in the English Borders, from oral and written material, and covered the period of the Scottish Wars of Independence.*

And so in the year of the Consecration of this Pope [Gregory X], there arose, as is reported, a great dispute in the [Papal] Curia over the election of William Wishart [to the see of St Andrews in 1271] many of them raising so many objections that the Head of the Church himself, having examined the objections set forth in writing, vowed by Saint Peter that if a moiety [a fraction] of the allegations were brought against himself, he never would seek to be Pope. At length, by intervention of the grace and piety of Edward he [Wishart] was consecrated under the Pope's dispensation. For the sake of example I do not hesitate to insert here what befell him later when he applied himself to his cure. Indeed, it is an evil far too common throughout the world that many persons, undertaking the correction of others, are very negligent about their own [conduct], and, while condemning the light offences of simple folk, condone the graver ones of great men.

There was a certain vicar, of a verity lewd and notorious, who, although often penalized on account of a concubine whom he kept, did not on that account desist from sinning. But when the bishop arrived to his ordinary visitation, the wretch was suspended and made subject to the prelate's mercy. Overcome with confusion, he returned home and beholding his doxy [mistress], poured forth his sorrows, attributing his mishap to the woman. Enquiring further, she learnt the cause of his agitation, and became bitterly aware that she was about to be cast out. 'Put away that notion,' quoth she to cheer him up, 'and I will get the better of the bishop.'

On the morrow as the bishop was hastening to his [the vicar's] church, she met him on the way laden with pudding, chickens and eggs, and, on his drawing near, she saluted him reverently, with bowed head. When the prelate enquired whence she came and whither she was going, she replied: 'My lord, I am the vicar's concubine, and I am hastening to the bishop's sweetheart, who was lately brought to bed, and I wish to be as much comfort to her as I can.' This pricked his conscience; straightaway he resumed his progress to the church, and, meeting the vicar, desired him to prepare for celebrating. The other reminded him of his suspension, and he [the bishop] stretched out his hand and gave him absolution. The sacrament having been performed, the bishop hastened away from the place without another word.

The Death of Alexander III, 19 March 1286

THE CHRONICLE OF LANERCOST

This colourfully prejudiced account of Alexander's (1241–86) death shows a man whose will would not be thwarted by commonsense, and who brought misfortune upon himself simply because, after a bibulous evening's enjoyment, he could not bear to spend the night apart from his new wife.

When they had sat down to dinner, he [the king] sent a present of fresh lampreys to a certain baron, bidding him by an esquire to make the party merry, for he should know that this was the Judgment Day. He [the baron], after returning thanks, facetiously replied to his lord: 'if this be Judgment Day, we shall soon rise with full bellies.'

The protracted feast having come to an end, he [Alexander] would neither be deterred by stress of weather nor yield to the persuasion of his nobles, but straightaway hurried along the road to Queensferry, in order to visit his bride, that is to say Yoleta, daughter of the Comte de Dru, whom shortly before he had brought from over the sea, to his own sorrow and the perpetual injury of the whole province. For she was then staying at Kinghorn. Many people declare that, before her engagement beyond the sea, she had changed her dress in a convent of nuns, but that she had altered her mind with the levity of a woman's heart and through ambition for a kingdom.

When he arrived at the village near the crossing, the ferrymaster warned him of the danger, and advised him to go back; but when [the King] asked him in return whether he was afraid to die with him: 'By no means,' quoth he, 'it would be a great honour to share the fate of your father's son.' Thus he arrived at the burgh of Inverkeithing, in profound darkness, accompanied only by three esquires. The manager of his saltpans, a married man of that town, recognizing him by his voice, called out: 'My lord, what are you doing here in such a storm and such darkness? Often have I tried to persuade you that your nocturnal rambles will bring you no good. Stay with us, and we will provide you with decent fare and all that you want till morning light.' 'No need for that,' said the other with a laugh, 'but provide me with a couple of bondmen, to go afoot as guides to the way.'

And it came to pass that when they had proceeded two miles, one and all lost all knowledge of the way, owing to the darkness; only the horses, by natural instinct, picked out the hard road. While they were thus separated from each other, the esquires took the right road; [but] he, at length (that I may make a long story short), fell from his horse, and bade farewell to his kingdom in the sleep of Sisara. To him Solomon's proverb applies: 'Wo unto him who, when he falls, has no man to raise him up.' He lies at Dunfermline alone in the south aisle, buried near the presbytery. Whence [comes it] that, while we may see the populace bewailing his sudden death as deeply as the desolation of the realm, those only who adhered to him most closely in life for his friendship and favours, wet not their cheeks with tears?

The Death of the Maid of Norway, c. 26 September 1290

ANONYMOUS

Margaret, Maid of Norway, the daughter of Alexander III and Margaret, by King Erik of Norway, was about seven when, on her way to Scotland to marry Prince Edward of England, her ship sank off Orkney. There's a strong note of feudal resentment in the popular ballad that marks the occasion, whose grief is not for the young woman but for the noblemen sent to fetch her, whose fate was bound up with hers.

'Sir Patrick Spens'

The King sits in Dunfermline town,
Drinking the blude-red wine;
'O whare will I get a skeely skipper,
To sail this new ship of mine?'

O up and spake an eldern knight,
Sat at the King's right knee, –
'Sir Patrick Spens is the best sailor
That ever sailed the sea.' –

Our King has written a braid letter,
And seal'd it with his hand,
And sent it to Sir Patrick Spens,
Was walking on the strand.

'To Noroway, to Noroway,
To Noroway o'er the faem;
The King's daughter of Noroway,
'Tis thou maun bring her hame.'

The first word that Sir Patrick read,
Sae loud loud laughed he;
The neist word that Sir Patrick read,
The tear blinded his ee.

'O wha is this has done this deed,
And tauld the King o' me,
To send us out, at this time of year,
To sail upon the sea?

'Be it wind, be it weet, be it hail, be it sleet,
Our ship must sail the faem;
The King's daughter of Noroway,
'Tis we must fetch her hame.' –

They hoysed their sails on Monenday morn,
Wi' a' the speed they may;
They hae landed in Noroway,
Upon a Wodensday.

They hadna been a week, a week,
In Noroway, but twae,
When that the lords o' Noroway
Began aloud to say, –

'Ye Scottishmen spend a' our King's gowd,
And a' our Queenis fee.' –
'Ye lie, ye lie, ye liars loud!
Fu' loud I hear ye lie;

'For I brought as much white monie
As gane my men and me,
And I brought a half-fou of gude red gowd,
Out o'er the sea wi' me.

'Make ready, make ready, my merrymen a'.
Our gude ship sails the morn.' –
'Now ever alake, my master dear,
I fear a deadly storm!

'I saw the new moon, late yestreen,
Wi' the auld moon in her arm;
And if we gang to sea, master,
I fear we'll come to harm.'

They hadna sail'd a league, a league,
A league but barely three,
When the lift grew dark, and the wind blew loud,
And gurly grew the sea.

The ankers brak, and the topmasts lap,
It was sic a deadly storm;
And the waves cam o'er the broken ship,
Till a' her sides were torn.

'O where will I get a gude sailor,
To take my helm in hand,
Till I get up to the tall top-mast,
To see if I can spy land?' –

'O here am I, a sailor gude,
To take the helm in hand,
Till you go up to the tall top-mast;
But I fear you'll ne'er spy land.' –

He hadna gane a step, a step,
A step but barely ane,
When a bout flew out of our goodly ship,
And the salt sea it came in.

'Gae, fetch a web o' the silken claith,
Another o' the twine,
And wap them into our ship's side,
And let nae the sea come in.' –

They fetch'd a web o' the silken claith,
Another o' the twine,
And they wapp'd them round that gude ship's side,
But still the sea cam in.

O laith, laith, were our gude Scots lords
To weet their cork-heel'd shoon!
But lang or a' the play was play'd
They wat their hats aboon.

And mony was the feather bed,
That flatter'd on the faem;
And mony was the gude lord's son,
That never mair cam hame.

The ladyes wrang their fingers white,
The maidens tore their hair,
A' for the sake of their true loves;
For them they'll see nae mair.

O lang, lang, may the ladyes sit,
We' their fans into their hand,
Before they see Sir Patrick Spens
Come sailing to the strand!

And lang, lang, may the maidens sit,
With their gowd kaims in their hair,
A' waiting for their ain dear loves!
For them they'll see nae mair.

Half-owre, half-owre to Aberdour,
'Tis fifty fathoms deep,
And there lies gude Sir Patrick Spens,
Wi' the Scots lords at his feet.

The Rise and Fall of William Wallace, 1297–1305

BLIND HARRY AND ANONYMOUS

Regarded as the father of Scottish nationalism, William Wallace was one of the most inspirational figures in the country's history. As a young man he made a name resisting the occupying English forces, and by leading the rout of the English at Stirling Bridge in 1297 he not only assured his place in his countrymen's hearts, but made the English rethink their attitude towards their northern neighbour. More than a century and a half later the epic poet Blind Harry captured the popular imagination with The Wallace, *his depiction of the hopeful, but ultimately tragic life of this courageous and far-sighted man. Here he evokes the excitement felt when Wallace was chosen as the country's leader.*

Quhen Scottis hard thir fyne tithingis of new	[heard this excellent news]
Out of all part to Wallace fast thai drew,	[From all over]
Plenyst the toun quhilk was thar heritage.	[Settled]
Thus Wallace straiff agayne that gret barnage.	[strove against; barons]
Sa he begane with strength and stalwart hand	[So]
To chewys agayne sum rowmys of Scotland.	[recover; parts]
The worthi Scottis that semblit till him thair	[flocked to]
Chaesit him for cheyff, thar chyftayne and ledar.	[Chose]

The Execution of William Wallace, 23 August 1305

ANONYMOUS

*Appointed Guardian of Scotland in the name of John Balliol in 1298, Wallace
began to make overtures to Europe in the hope of overthrowing English
domination. Severely rattled, Edward I sent his forces north in 1298 and overpowered Wallace's men at Falkirk. Wallace escaped to France where he tried,
unsuccessfully, to raise allies. On his return to Scotland he was captured and
taken to London, where he was tried for treason. It was an unfair charge since,
unlike many Scottish nobles, he had never conceded power to the English king.
His execution on 23 August 1305 is one of the most brutal in British history.
This account of it is a translation from a contemporary Latin record of the trial.*

It is considered that the aforesaid William, for the open sedition which
he had made to the same lord the King by felonious contriving, by
trying to bring about his death, the destruction and weakening of the
crown and of his royal authority and by bringing his standard against his
liege lord in war to the death, should be taken away to the palace of
Westminster as far as the Tower of London, and from the Tower as far
as Allegate, and thus through the middle of the city as far as Elmes, and
for the robberies, murders and felonies which he carried out in the
kingdom of England and the land of Scotland he should be hanged there
and afterwards drawn. And because he had been outlawed and not
afterwards restored to the king's peace, he should be beheaded and
decapitated.

And afterwards for the measureless wickedness which he did to God
and to the most Holy Church by burning churches, vessels and shrines,
in which the body of Christ and the bodies of the saints and relics of the
same were wont to be placed together, the heart, liver, and lung and all
the internal [parts] of the same William, by which such evil thoughts
proceeded, should be dispatched to the fire and burned. And also because
he had committed both murders and felonies, not only to the lord the
King himself but to the entire people of England and Scotland, the body
of that William should be cut up and divided and cut up into four
quarters, and that the head thus cut off should be affixed upon London
bridge in the sight of those crossing both by land and by water, and one
quarter should be hung on the gibbet at Newcastle upon Tyne, another

quarter at Berwick, a third quarter at Stirling, and a fourth quarter at St John's town [Perth] as a cause of fear and chastisement of all going past and looking upon these things.

The Battle of Bannockburn, 23–24 June 1314

JOHN BARBOUR

John Barbour's epic poem The Brus *celebrates Scotland's resounding victory against Edward II's army at Bannockburn on Midsummer's Day under the command of Robert I. This was a defining event in Scottish history, striking a fatal blow to England's wars of attrition against Scottish independence. John Barbour, who was born in 1320, was Archdeacon of Aberdeen, and composed his work in 1375 from the memories of men who had fought with or known Robert the Bruce. One early verse encapsulates the idealism that lay behind the Scots' need to defend their country. Its first line has become almost a national slogan.*

A! fredome is a noble thing!
Fredome mayss man to haiff liking,
Fredome all solace to man giffis:
He levys at ess that frely levys.
A noble hart may haiff name ess,
Na ellys nocht that may him pless,
Gyff fredome failyhe: for fre liking
Is yharnyt our all othir thing.
Na he that ay hass levyt fre
May nocht knaw weill the propyrte,
The anger, na the wretchyt dome
That is couplyt to foul thyrldome.

Bot gyff he had assayit it,
Than all perquer he suld it wyt;
And suld think freedom mar to pryss
Than all the gold in warld that is . . .

Ah! Freedom is a noble thing!
Freedom gives man pleasure,
Freedom gives all solace to man:
He lives at ease who freely lives.
A noble heart may have no comfort,
Nor anything else that will please him,
If freedom fails: for free decision
Is yearned for above any thing.
No, he who has always lived free
May not well know the property,
The anger, no the wretched doom
That is coupled to foul thraldom.

But if he had experienced it,
Then he would know it in his soul;
And would think freedom more to be prized
Than all the gold in the world . . .

The Battle of Bannockburn: an Englishman's View, 23–24 June 1314

ROBERT BASTON

Edward II was so certain of defeating the Scots that he brought along Carmelite friar and poet Robert Baston to record England's triumph. When the English were defeated, Baston was captured and told he would only be released if he honoured the Scots' success and England's humiliation in a poem. This he did, without any sycophancy or cringing, highlighting rather the beastliness of any war, whoever the victor. This translation from the Latin is by Edwin Morgan.

It is June Thirteen Fourteen, and here I set the scene,
The Baptist's head on a tureen, the battle on Stirling green.
Oh I am not glued to ancient schism and feud,
But my weeping is renewed for the dead I saw and rued.
Who will lend me the water I need to baptize these forays?

[. . .]

The Scottish king forms and informs his potent throng,
Infantry and cavalry. Oh what an array, so ordered and strong!
The king's voice is heard, inspiring the nobility,
Giving the measured but fiery word to the men of quality.
He checks and directs the formation of his eager troops.
Others are worthless, he reckons, and their star droops.
He incites and delights the multitude of his men.
He flytes and derides the English – their treaties not worth a hen.
He said, and he led; all fingers must be firm to the end.
Never swerve from a serf of the shameless Saxon blend!
The masses are sassy, they relish the royal rousing.
They will stand like a band and give the Saxons a sousing!

[. . .]

Black Monday gives a new life to the deadly plague.
Scots blow the plague by lucky force upon the English flag.

The Angles are like angels glittering high and proud,
But valorous and vassal both are labouring under a cloud.
English eyes scan the skies for Scots ambushes to arise,
But Scots are near, are here, full size, surprise surprise!

The plebs are roaring and swearing, but when things get scary
They wilt and are weary, they crack under the fury.
The ogre is mediocre, the Scots are stockier.
Who will be known as victor? The Dutiful Doctor.
A reckless raid pretends to be robustly arrayed.
Deep sobs escalade from the face's palisade,
Scots find a route to rush fast forward on foot,
Brandishing boot on boot, fielding loot for loot.

[. . .]

What snatching and catching, what bruising and broostling, what grief!
What warhorns and warnings, what winding and wirrying, no relief!
What slashing and slaughtering, what wounding and wailing, what a
     rout!
What lurking and lunging, what grabbing and groaning, what a
     turnabout!
What roaring and rearing, what shrinking and shaking, what lassooing!
What cloaking and collecting, what snipping and snecking, what
     undoing!
Bellies will be empty. Both broadswords and bodies are booty.
So many fatherless children to clutch at futurity!

The Declaration of Arbroath, 6 April 1320

This succinct, uncompromising and heart-felt plea can be considered the cornerstone of Scottish political thought and an influence on countless democracies since, notably as the model for the American Constitution. It was written on 6 April 1320 to Pope John XXII by the Scottish barons who were growing weary with fending off English attempts to subjugate their country, and is the first time that the authority of a king is defined by his willingness to grant the reasonable demands of his people. Even Robert the Bruce is given a clear warning that if he doesn't do as his subjects wish – i.e. if he capitulates to the English – he will be got rid of.

Declaration of Arbroath

Thus our nation under their [Pope's predecessors] protection did indeed live in freedom and peace up to the time when that mighty prince the King of the English, Edward, the father of the one who reigns today, when our kingdom had no head and our people harboured no malice or treachery and were then unused to wars or invasions, came in the guise of a friend and ally to harass them as an enemy. The deeds of cruelty, massacre, violence, pillage, arson, imprisoning prelates, burning down monasteries, robbing and killing monks and nuns, and yet other outrages without number which he committed against our people, sparing neither age nor sex, religion nor rank, no one could describe nor fully imagine unless he had seen them with his own eyes.

But from these countless evils we have been set free, by the help of Him Who though He afflicts yet heals and restores, by our most tireless Prince, King and Lord, the Lord Robert. He, that his people and his heritage might be delivered out of the hands of our enemies, met toil and fatigue, hunger and peril, like another Maccabaeus or Joshua and bore them cheerfully. Him, too, divine providence, his right of succession according to our laws and customs which we shall maintain to the death, and the due consent and assent of us all have made our Prince and King. To him, as to the man by whom salvation has been wrought unto our people, we are bound both by law and by his merits that our freedom may be still maintained, and by him, come what way, we mean to stand.

Yet if he should give up what he has begun, and agree to make us or our kingdom subject to the King of England or the English, we should exert ourselves at once to drive him out as our enemy and a subverter of his own rights and ours, and make some other man who was well able to defend us our King; for, as long as but a hundred of us remain alive, never will we on any conditions be brought under English rule. It is in truth not for glory, nor riches, nor honours that we are fighting, but for freedom – for that alone, which no honest man gives up but with life itself.

Therefore it is, Reverend Father and Lord, that we beseech your Holiness with our most earnest prayers and suppliant hearts, inasmuch as you will in your sincerity and goodness consider all this, that, since with Him Whose vice-regent on earth you are there is neither weighing nor distinction of Jew and Greek, Scotsman or Englishman, you will

look with the eyes of a father on the troubles and privations brought by
the English upon us and upon the Church of God. May it please you to
admonish and exhort the King of the English, who ought to be satisfied
with what belongs to him since England used once to be enough for
seven kings or more, to leave us Scots in peace, who live in this poor
little Scotland, beyond which there is no dwelling-place at all, and covet
nothing but our own. We are sincerely willing to do anything for
him, having regard to our condition, that we can, to win peace for
ourselves . . .

Robert Bruce's Epitaph, 1329

WALTER BOWER

*Several years after Robert the Bruce's death, on 7 June 1329, the chronicler and
poet Walter Bower composed this overblown but moving tribute. As well as
likening Bruce to the greatest names of biblical and mythological history, he
also recorded his signal achievements, among them his victory at the Battle of
Bannockburn, his defeat of Edward II at Byland, and the shortlived peace treaty
of Edinburgh in 1328.*

Robert Bruce, the nation's virtue, lies in the earth;
Bold and righteous prince of joy, in all his ways most sure.
A Paris he was in shapeliness, a Hector renowned for his sword,
Royal rose of soldiery, a Socrates, Maro or Cato in his words.

[. . .]

Lamenting the loss of the royal rights of Scots-born men,
postponing idle pleasures, he left his old sweet life for a bitter regimen.
Cold he suffered, and for sleep he lay in dens of wild beasts,
while for his food he did not refuse the fruit of acorn-laden trees.

[. . .]

For the protection of his rights he placed his only hope in Christ,
hiding himself in the thorny bush, drinking water, never wines.
With his strong comrades in the assault, he seemed a fierce wild boar,
And thus he earned his royal throne, wore down the enemy's spear.

At this man's warrior-thrust a host of evil-doers falls;
on their iron-armoured backs of men his wounds are cruel.
He sharpens the weapons of war, sword raging at a host of knights:
this one falls, that one dies, and their king is put to flight.

In good order the king of Scots brings his standard forth,
fighting mightily he bears it through a thick-packed host.
To boundless praise he triumphs mightily over the foe,
and sent him homewards, the English king, as our new lyric goes.

When he is made lord of Byland, joyful victory is prepared,
The host in flight is ravaged, and the slaughter multiplied.
A solemn truce is covenanted, but the peace agreed is false.
After the death of the reverend king, peace suffers a reverse.

O what grief among the people! Alas, our grief is doubled.
Every eye is given to weeping while disorder multiplies.
He who in the royal roll was counted flower of kings,
now in a muddy little place is laid as food for worms.

This outstanding king was like a bracelet on our arms
A previous ring or a jewel in the ear of noble men,
A twisted torque which folk may wear around their throats –
Now he lies below, stripped of towering glory's robes.

Bird Flu, or Similar, 1344

JOHN OF FORDUN

In the year 1344 there was so great a pestilence among the fowls, that men utterly shrank from eating, or even looking upon, a cock or a hen, as though unclean and smitten with leprosy; and thus, as well as from the aforesaid cause, nearly the whole of that species was destroyed . . .

The Black Death, 1350

JOHN OF FORDUN

This horrifyingly swiftly transmitted disease swept Europe in waves in the fourteenth and fifteenth centuries. Scotland, being less densely populated, was less severely affected than more urbanized countries, but it did not escape unscathed, and it's thought that about a third of the population died.

In the year 1350, there was, in the kingdom of Scotland, so great a pestilence and plague among men (which also prevailed for a great many years before and after, in divers parts of the world – nay, all over the whole earth), as, from the beginning of the world even unto modern times, had never been heard of by man, nor is found in books, for the enlightenment of those who come after. For, to such a pitch did that plague wreck its cruel spite, that nearly a third of mankind were thereby made to pay the debt of nature. Moreover, by God's will, this evil led to a strange and unwonted kind of death, insomuch that the flesh of the sick was somehow puffed out and swollen, and they dragged out their earthly life for barely two days. Now this everywhere attacked especially the meaner sort and common people; – seldom the magnates. Men shrank from it so much that, through fear of contagion, sons, fleeing as from the face of leprosy or from an adder, durst not go and see their parents in the throes of death.

The Auld Alliance, 1385

JEAN FROISSART

The relationship between Scotland and France was not always the fond partnership of popular myth. The French chronicler Jean Froissart conveys the strong feelings on both sides of the treaty during a campaign in 1385 when a small band of French soldiers arrived to help their allies repel the English.

News was soon spread through Scotland that a large body of men-at-arms from France were arrived in the country. Some began to murmur and say, 'What devil has brought them here? or who has sent for them? Cannot we carry on our wars with England without their assistance?

We shall never do any effectual good as long as they are with us. Let them be told to return again, for we are sufficiently numerous in Scotland to fight our own quarrels, and do not want their company. We neither understand their language nor they ours, and we cannot converse together. They will very soon eat up and destroy all we have in this country, and will do us more harm, if we allow them to remain amongst us, than the English could do in battle . . .' Such was the conversation of the Scots on the arrival of the French: they did not esteem them, but hated them in their hearts, and abused them with their tongues as much as they could, like rude and worthless people as they are.

I must, however, say that, considering all things, it was not right for so many of the nobility to have come at this season to Scotland: it would have been better to have sent twenty or thirty knights from France than so large a body as five hundred or a thousand. The reason is clear. In Scotland you will never find a man of worth: they are like savages, who wish not to be acquainted with anyone, and are too envious of the good fortune of others, and suspicious of losing anything themselves, for their country is very poor. When the English make inroads thither, as they have very frequently done, they order their provisions, if they wish to live, to follow close at their backs; for nothing is to be had in that country without great difficulty. There is neither iron to shoe horses, nor leather to make harness, saddles or bridles: all these things come ready made from Flanders by sea; and, should these fail, there is none to be had in the country . . .

The Earls of Douglas and Moray were the principal visitants to the lords of France. These two lords paid them more attention than all the rest of Scotland. But this was not the worst, for the French were hardly dealt with in their purchases; and whenever they wanted to buy horses, they were asked, for what was worth only ten florins, sixty and a hundred: with difficulty could they be found at that price . . . besides, whenever their servants went out to forage, they were indeed permitted to load their horses with as much as they could pack up and carry, but they were waylaid on their return, and villainously beaten, robbed and sometimes slain, insomuch that no varlet dared go out foraging for fear of death. In one month, the French lost upwards of a hundred varlets; for when three or four went out foraging not one returned, in such a hideous manner were they treated.

The French and the Scots marched back [from invading England] the way they had come. When they arrived in the lowlands, they found the whole country ruined; but the people of the country made light of it, saying that with six or eight stakes they would soon have new houses, and find cattle enow for provision . . .

The Scots said, the French had done them more mischief than the English; when asked 'In what manner?' they replied, 'By riding through their corn, oats and barley, on their march, which they trod underfoot, not condescending to follow the roads, for which damages they would have a recompense before they left Scotland; and they should neither find vessel nor mariner who would dare to put to sea without their permission.' . . .

When the admiral, with his barons, knights and squires, were returned to the neighbourhood of Edinburgh, they suffered from famine, as they could scarcely procure provision for their money. . . . Upon this many knights and squires obtained a passage to France, and returned through Flanders, or wherever they could land, famished, and without arms or horses, cursing Scotland, and the hour they had set foot there. They said they had never suffered so much in any expedition, and wished the King of France would make a truce with the English for two or three years, and then march to Scotland and utterly destroy it: for never had they seen such wicked people, nor such ignorant hypocrites and traitors . . .

Acts of Parliament

JAMES I, JAMES II AND JAMES III

A sample from half a century's worth of Acts of Parliaments gives a glimpse of the concerns of these times.

1427, The Whelps of Wolves

It is statute and ordained by the King, with consent of his whole council, that each baron within his barony at the proper time of the year shall cause his servants to seek the whelps of the wolves and cause them to slay them. And the baron shall give to the man that slays one in his barony and brings the baron his head ii shillings. And when the baron ordains to hunt and chase the wolves, the tenants shall rise with the baron under the pain of a wether [fine] to each man not rising with the baron. And that the barons hunt in these baronies and chase the wolves four times in the year and as often as any wolf is seen within the barony.

And that no man seek the wolves with shooting except only in the times of hunting them.

1427, Lepers

(It is ordained) that no leper folk, neither man nor woman, from hence-forth enter or come into any burgh of the realm except thrice in the week – that is to say, each Monday, each Wednesday, each Friday, from ten o'clock to two afternoon; and where fairs and markets fall on these days that they delay their entering the burghs and go on the morrow to get their living. Also that no leprous folk sit to beg neither in kirk nor in kirkyard, nor in any other place within the burghs except at their own hospital and at the port of the town and other places without the burghs.

1436, Drinking in Taverns

The King and the three estates have ordained that no man in burghs be found in taverns at wine, ale, or beer after the stroke of nine o'clock, and the bell that shall be rung in the said burgh – the which being sounded, the aldermen and baillies shall put them in the King's prison, the which, if they do not, they shall pay for each time that they be found culpable before the chamberlain one shilling.

1447

James II was fearful that the art of archery was being neglected for the craze for golf and football.

Wapinschawings [muster of men under arms]

It is decreed and ordained that wapinschawings be held by the lords and barons, spiritual and temporal, four times in the year, and that football and golf be utterly cried down and disused, and that the bowmarks be made at each parish kirk, a pair of butts, and shooting be made each Sunday. And that each man shoot six shots at the least under the pain to be raised upon them that come not; at the least 2d. to be given to them that come to the bowmark to drink. And this to be used from Christmas to Allhallowmass after . . . And as touching the football and the golf we ordain it to be punished by the baron's fine.

1471, The Preservation of Wild Birds

Anent the preservation of birds and wild fowls that are fit to eat for the sustenation of man, such as partridge, plovers, wild ducks, and such like fowls, it is ordained that no man destroy their nests nor their eggs, nor yet slay wild birds in moulting time when they may not fly; and that all men according to their power destroy nests, eggs, and young birds of prey.

Rooks' Nests

Anent rooks, crows, and other birds of prey, as herons, buzzards, and *myttals* [type of hawk], the which destroy both corn and wild birds, such as partridges, plovers, and others, and as to the rooks and crows building in orchards, kirkyards, or other places, it is seen speedful that they to whom such trees pertain prevent them from building, and destroy them with all their power, and in no wise let the birds fly away. And where it is proved that they build and that the birds are flown and the nests found in the trees, at Beltane the trees shall be forfeit to the king, except they be redeemed again, and they that own the said trees [shall be mulcted] in v shillings fine to the king. And that the said birds of prey be utterly destroyed by all manner of means, by all ingenuity and manner of way that may be found thereto, for the slaughter of them shall cause great multitude of divers kinds of wild birds for man's sustenance.

The Murder of James I, 20 February 1437

? ONE OF QUEEN JOAN'S ATTENDANTS

James I, second son of Robert III, was taken prisoner as a boy by the English King Henry IV, and kept for eighteen years in the Tower of London. On his release, in 1423, he returned to Scotland with his wife Joan, determined to reinstate royal authority over the country's powerful nobles. In so doing he created

serious enemies, but his murder was as much to do with claims to the throne by
the progeny of his father's second marriage as with resentment at his harsh
behaviour. His murderers came for him when he was staying at Blackfriars, the
royal lodging in Perth. This account is a translation by the scribe John Shirley of
the original Latin version, which was probably given by one of the Queen's
companions.

. . . Thus after this can fast approach the night in the which the said
James Stewart, King of Scots, should falsely, him unwitting, suffer his
horrible death by murder; this which is pity that any gentle or good man
to think upon. So both after supper and long into quarter of the night,
in the which the Earl of Athol and Robert Stewart were about the King,
where they were occupied at the playing of the chess, at the tables, in
reading of romances, in singing and piping, in harping, and in other
honest solaces of great pleasure and disport . . .

. . . the King asked for the voidee [parting cup] and drank . . . and
every man departed and went to rest. Then Robert Stewart that was
right familiar with the King and had all his commandments in the
chamber, was the last departed: and he knew well the false purveyed
treason and was consented thereto, and therefore left the King's Chamber
doors open, and had bruised and blundered the locks of them in such
wise that no man might shut them. And about midnight he laid certain
planks and hurdles over the ditches of the ditch that environed the
garden of the chamber, upon which the said traitors entered. That is to
say the foresaid Sir Robert Graham, with other of his coven unto the
number of three hundred persons: the King that same time standing in
his nightgown, all unclothed save his shirt, his cap, his comb, his kerchief,
his furred pinsons [slippers], upon the form and the foot-sheet, so standing afore the chimney, playing with the Queen and other ladies and
gentlewomen with her, cast off his nightgown for to have gone to bed.
But he harkened and heard great noise without and great clattering
of harness, and men armed, with great sight of torches. Then he remembered him, and imagined anon that it should be the false traitorous
knight, his deadly enemy, Sir Robert Graham: and suddenly the Queen,
with all the other ladies and gentlewomen, ran to the chamber door and
found it open; and they would have shut it but the locks were so
blundered that they neither could nor might shut it. The King prayed
them to keep the said door as well as they might, and he would do all
his might to keep him to withstand the false malice of his traitors and
enemies, he supposing to have brasten [broken] the ferments of the

chamber windows, but they were so square and so strongly soldered in the stones with molten lead that they might not brasten for him without more and stronger help. For which cause he was ugly astonished and in his mind could think on no other succour but start to the chimney and take the tongs of iron that men righted the fire with in time of need, and under his feet he mightily brast up a plank of the chamber floor and therewithal covered him again and entered low down among the ordure of the privy, that was all of hard stone and none window nor issue thereupon save a little square hold even at the side of the bottom of the privy, that at the making thereof of old time was left open to cleanse the said privy, by the which the King might well have escaped, but he made to let stop it well three days afore, hard with stone, because that when he played there at the paume the balls that he played with oft ran in at that foul hole, for there was ordained without a fair playing place for the King.

And so there was for the King no rescue nor remedy, but there he must abide, alas the while! The traitors without laid at the chamber doors with crows, with levers, and with axes, that at the last they brake up all and entered, because the door was not fast shut, with swords, axes, glaives, bills, and other terrible and fearful weapons. Among the great press of which traitors there was a fair lady sore hurt in the back, and other gentlewomen hurt and sore wounded. With the which the ladies and all the women made a sorrowful skyre [scream] and ran away for the hideous fear of those boistous [sic] and merciless men of arms. The traitors furiously passed forth into the chamber, and found the Queen so dismayed and abashed of that horrible and fearful governance that she could neither speak nor withdraw her; and as she stood there sore astonished, like a creature that had lost her kindly reason, one of the traitors wounded her villainously and would have slain her, had not been one of Sir Robert Graham's sons, that thus spake to him and said, 'What will ye do, for shame of yourself, to the Queen? She is but a woman. Let us go and fetch the King.' And then, not witting well what she did or should do for that fearful and terrible affray, fled in her kirtle [underdress], her mantle hanging about her; the other ladies in a corner of the chamber crying and weeping all distrait, made a piteous and lamentable noise with full heavy looking and cheer.

And there the traitors sought the King in all the chamber about, in the withdrawing chambers, in the litters, and under the presses, the forms, the chairs, and all other places; but long they busily sought the King, but they could not find him, for they neither knew nor remembered the privy. The King, hearing of long time no noise nor stirring of the traitors, weened and deemed that they had all been gone, and cried to the women that they should come with sheets and draw him up out of that unclean place of the privy. The women at his calling came fast to the privy door that was not shut, and so they opened it with labour, and as they were aboutward to help up the King, one of the ladies, called Elizabeth Douglas, fell into the privy to the King. Therewith, one of the false traitors, called Robert Chambers, supposed verily since they could not find in none of the said chambers the King, that he had of necessity hidden him in the privy: and therefore he said to his fellows, 'Sirs,' quoth he, 'whereto stand we thus idle and lose our time, as for the cause that we be come for hither. Come on forth with me, and I shall readily tell you where the King is.' For this same Robert Chambers had been afore right familiar with the King, and therefore he knew all the privy corners of these chambers; and so he went forth straight to the same privy where the King was, and perceived and saw how a plank of the floor was broken up, and lift it up with a torch and looked in, and saw the King there and a woman with him. Saying to his fellows, 'Sirs, the spouse is found wherefore we be come and all this night have carolled here.' Therewithal, one of the said tyrants and traitors, cleped [called] Sir John Hall, descended down to the King, with a great knife in his hand, and the King, doubting him sore of his life, caught him mightily by the shoulders and with great violence cast him under his feet, for the King was of his person and nature right manly strong. And seeing another of that Hall's brethren that the King had the better of him, went down also for to destroy the King: and anon as he was there descended, the King caught him manly by the neck and cast him above that other, and so he defouled them both under him that all a long month after men might see how strongly the King had holden them by the throats, and greatly the King struggled with them for to have bereaved them of their knives, by the which labour his hands were all for-cut. But an the King had been in any wise armed, he might well have escaped this matter, by the length of his fighting with those two false traitors: for if the King might any while longer have saved himself, his servants and much other people of the town by some fortune should have had some knowledge thereof, and so have come to his succour with help. But alas the while, it will not be. Fortune was to him adverse, as in preserving his life any longer.

Therewithal that odious and false traitor Sir Robert Graham, seeing the King laboured so sore with those two false traitors which he had cast under his feet, and that he waxed faint and was weary, and that he was weaponless, the more pity was, descended down also unto the King, with an horrible and mortal weapon in his hand. And then the King cried him mercy. 'Thou cruel tyrant,' quoth Graham to him. 'Thou hadst never mercy of lords born of thy blood, ne of none other gentlemen that came in they danger, therefore no mercy shalt thou have here.' Then said the King, 'I beseech thee that for the salvation of my soul, ye will let me have a confessor.' Quoth the said Graham, 'Thou shalt never have other confessor but this same sword.' And therewithal he smote him through the body, and therewithal the good King fell down. And then the said Graham, seeing his King and sovereign lord infortuned with so much disease, anguish, and sorrow, would have so left, and done him no more harm. The other traitors above, perceiving this, said unto Sir Robert, 'We behote thee faithfully, but if thou slay him or thou depart, thou shalt die for him on our hands doubtless.' And then the same Sir Robert, with the other two that descended first down, fell upon that noble prince, and in full horrible and cruel wise they murdered him. Alas for sorrow that so immeasurably cruelty and vengeance should be done to that worthy prince, for it was reported by true persons that saw him dead, that he had sixteen deadly wounds in his breast, without many another in divers places of his body.

The Battle of Flodden, 9 September 1513

THOMAS RUTHALL

James IV entreated his brother-in-law Henry VIII not to attack the Scots' ally, France, but when he refused to listen, scoffing that 'I am the very owner of Scotland', James felt obliged to fight. His army met the English at Flodden, near the Scottish border. Despite their sophisticated weaponry and the weary state of the English, the Scots were annihilated, James among them. For this some blame the Scots' long spears which were useless when pitted against the shorter English bill, which could simply chop them to pieces, thus reducing them to hand-to-hand conflict in which, since they were kept at a distance by the English weapons, the Scottish soldiers had no chance. Thomas Ruthall, Bishop of Durham, who was present, wrote shortly afterwards to Thomas Wolsey with this account of the conflict.

On the 9th day of this present month, after a terrible battle the King of Scots, with most of the lords and nobles of his realm, were vanquished and overthrown and slain. During this battle my Lord Treasurer like a noble, brave and powerful captain, by his great wisdom, boldness and experience, and with the assistance, good conduct and vigour of his son the Lord Howard, Admiral of England, acquitted himself so well that for this most famous act his realm and subjects deserved as much praise, renown and gratitude as ever any nobleman did. All the more so considering that the number of their enemy was far greater than the King's army, and also considering the great number of awesome large weapons, 17 in all, besides many other small pieces. And not forgetting the strength of the Scots, being as well furnished with armour, weapons and other equipment of war as ever men were, with their abundance of food, wines of all sorts, bread, beer and ale, tents and pavilions far beyond ours, which had to be seen and tasted to be believed, as they were by our people, which greatly refreshed them.

And compare the courage and swift attack of the Scots with the discomfort and feebleness of our people who were low on food and had had nothing to drink except water for three days and not much of that, and with the great pain and hard work that they endured in going 8 miles that day on foot by dangerous and painful ways over hills and dales and yet, most dangerous of all, in ascending and climbing high and steep hills to meet and give battle to the King of Scots, who was camped there with his weapons set to his best advantage and to the annoyance of our army.

And since the Scots had possession of the hill, the wind and the sun were with them against our people; considering these impediments, dangers and perils, it is to be thought that this victory came more from the hand of God, with the help of the glorious Confessor Saint Cuthbert, than by any strength or power of men, although after such pain and labour they did not lack courage, strength and heart, as was plain from their actions.

For as well as the King of Scots, all the lords of Scotland, except for five, and the most part of the noblemen of Scotland which that day died, there were 10 thousand Scots killed, and as some of them affirm they do not have 15 thousand in the whole country.

The said Scots were so heavily defended, with complete armour, coats of mail, shields, and other equipment that arrows could not harm them, and when it came to hand-to-hand blows of bills and halberds they were so mighty, large, strong and great men that they would not fall when

4 or 5 bills struck on one of them at once; yet even so our bills quietened them very well and did more good that day than bows for they soon deprived the Scots of their long spears in which they put their greatest trust, and when they came to hand-to-hand combat, though the Scots fought hard and bravely with their swords, they could not fend off the bills that rained so thick and fast upon them.

That day there were many good and dutiful captains who played their parts well, yet the Lord Howard was the first attacker and energetically led the vanguard of our army to whom Saint Cuthbert's banner was joined with the whole retinue of the bishopric; and even though the Scots had the greatest disrespect for the banner and set fearlessly upon it, yet by the grace of God, the assistance of Saint Cuthbert and the courage of the captains and others under the banner, they gained no advantage but instead suffered great loss and damage of their people, and yet few or none who had been under the banner were killed, although many were hurt. So it is that with great honour Saint Cuthbert's banner is returned again to his church, bringing with it the King of Scots' banner for which a memorial now stands beside the shrine there. And the said King was not far from his banner when he was killed.

And as well as this, all the great weaponry of Scotland were taken and are at Berwick, with several prisoners, but not many, for our people, intending to make all things certain, took little notice of taking prisoners, but disposed of all that came to hand, both King, bishops, lords, knights, nobles, or whoever else, who were no sooner killed than immediately stripped of their armour and clothes and left lying naked in the field where men might have seen a remarkable number of well-off, well fed and fat men, among whom the King of Scots' body was found, with many wounds and naked, and was brought to my Lord Treasurer, who was in Berwick, in whose keeping the same body still is.

And yet when our captains and people had thus acquitted themselves so well, they were hugely annoyed, for while away from their tents and occupied with the Scots, all their goods, horses and belongings were stolen. But whether this was done by Scots or by Borderers, I cannot say, but the rumour is that the borderers did their worst. I pray God makes amends for as a result of this treatment our people were more discouraged on leaving than by all the harm done to them by the Scots, and such treatment has, and shall, make them less willing to return there again if required.

[modified version, see Appendix I, p. 435]

A Paen to Oatcakes, 1521

JOHN MAJOR

The staple of the Scottish larder so impressed the chronicler John Major that he grew almost poetic in its praise.

Wheat will not grow in every part of the island; and for this reason the common people use barley and oaten bread. And as many Britons are inclined to be ashamed of things nowise to be ashamed of, I will here insist a little. And first I say this: that though the soil of all Britain were barren, no Briton need blush for that . . . Just such bread were Christ and his apostles wont to eat . . . Pliny, too, makes mention in his thirtieth book of meal made from oats, and there is in Normandy, near to Argentolium, a village called Pain d'Aveine. But you may object that it is so called in derision, and because such meal is an uncommon thing among the Gauls. I say, for my part, that I would rather eat that British oaten bread than bread made of barley or of wheat. I nowhere re- member to have seen on the other side of the water such good oats as in Britain, and the people make their bread in the most ingenious fashion. For those who may be driven to use it, I will explain their method.

The oats having been grown in a soil of a middling richness, they roast the grain thus: a house is built in the manner of a dove-cot, and in the centre thereof, crosswise from the wall, they fix beams twelve feet in height. Upon these beams they lay straw, and upon the straw the oats. A fire is then kindled in the lower part of the building, care being taken that the straw, and all else in the house, be not burnt up. Thus the oats are dried, and thereafter carried to the mill, where, by a slight elevation of the upper millstone, the outer husk gets shaken out. The flour alone then remains, dried, and in good condition, more excellent by far than the flour that is used by confectioners in any part of the world. From this dried grain, which from its resemblance to lentil flour they call by that name, after it has been ground small in the manner of meal, the oaten bread is made.

As the common people use it both leavened and unleavened, oats are very largely grown. Just eat this bread once, and you shall find it far from bad. It is the food of almost all the inhabitants of Wales, of the northern English . . . and of the Scottish peasantry; and yet the main strength of the Scottish and English armies is in men who have been tillers of the soil – a proof that oaten bread is not a thing to be laughed at.

The Burning of George Wishart, 1 March 1546

JOHN KNOX

George Wishart, a schoolteacher from Angus who had been charged with heresy for teaching the Greek New Testament, left the country to spend some years in Switzerland. There he absorbed the theology of the Swiss reformers. On his return to Scotland, he widely preached the Lutheran doctrine of justification by faith, which led to his arrest on the orders of Cardinal Beaton. He was tried and condemned to death at the stake. Wishart was by all accounts a gentle and very likeable man, and his beliefs were the inspiration for John Knox. Knox's account of his execution is followed by that of the murder, in retribution, of Cardinal Beaton. With these acts, the full force of the Reformation in Scotland was unleashed.

When he came to the fire, he sat down upon his knees, and rose again; and thrice he said these words, 'O Thou Saviour of the world, have mercy upon me: Father of Heaven, I commend my spirit into Thy holy hands.' When he had made this prayer, he turned to the people, and said these words: 'I beseech you, Christian brethren and sisters, that you be not offended at the word of God for the affliction and torments which you see already prepared for me. But I exhort you, that you love the word of God, your salvation, and suffer patiently, and with a comfortable heart, for the word's sake, which is your undoubted salvation and everlasting comfort. Moreover, I pray you, show my brethren and sister, which have heard me often before, that they cease not nor leave off to learn the word of God, which I taught them, after the grace given me, for no persecutions nor troubles in this world, which lasts not. And show unto them that my doctrine was no wives' fables, after the constitutions made by men; and if I had taught men's doctrine, I had not greater thanks by men. But for the word's sake, and true Evangel, which was given to me by the grace of God, I suffer this day by men, not sorrowfully, but with a glad heart and mind. For this cause I was sent, that I should suffer this fire for Christ's sake. Consider and behold my face, you shall not see me change my colour. This grim fire I fear not; and so I pray you for to do, if any persecution come to you for the word's sake; and not to fear them that slay the body, and afterward have no power to slay the soul . . .'

Then, last of all, the hangman, that was his tormentor, sat down upon his knees and said, 'Sir, I pray you, forgive me, for I am not guilty of your death.' To whom he answered, 'Come hither to me.' When he was come to him he kissed his cheek and said, 'Lo! Here is a token that I forgive you. My heart, do thine office.' And then, by and by, he was put upon the gibbet, and hanged, and there burnt to powder. When the people beheld the great tormenting of that innocent, they could not hold back piteous mourning and complaining of the innocent lamb's slaughter.

[modified version, see Appendix II, p. 437]

The Murder of Cardinal David Beaton, 29 May 1546

JOHN KNOX

But early on the Saturday morning, the 29 May, they were with several groups of people in the Abbey kirk-yard, not far from the Castle. First, the gates being open, and the drawbridge let down, for receiving lime and stone, and other things necessary for building (for Babylon was almost finished) – first, we say, William Kirkcaldy of Grange, younger, and six people with him, tried, and gaining entrance, asked the porter 'If my Lord was awake?' who answered, 'No'.

While William and the porter talked, Norman Leslie approached with his men; and because there were not many of them, they easily got in. They went to the middle of the courtyard, and immediately John Leslie arrived, rather roughly, and four men with him. The frightened porter would have drawn up the bridge; but John, who was on his way in, leapt in. And while the porter prepared to defend himself, he was knocked on the head, the keys were taken from him, and he was thrown into the ditch; and so the place was seized.

A shout went up: the workmen, more than a hundred of them, ran off the walls and, without being harmed, were sent out of the gate. First, William Kirkcaldy stood guard at the back door, fearing that the fox had escaped. Then the rest went to the gentleman's rooms, and without hurting anyone, they put more than fifty people out of the gate. The number who did this was only sixteen people. The Cardinal, woken by the shouting, asked from his window, what the noise was about? It was answered that Norman Leslie had taken his Castle. Understanding this, he ran to the back door; but seeing the passage taken, he returned quickly to his room, took his two-handled sword, and made his chambermaid drag chests and other obstacles against the door.

Then John Leslie came to the door, and asked him to open it. The Cardinal asking, 'Who calls?' he answers, 'My name is Leslie.' He asks again, 'Is that Norman?' The other says, 'No, my name is John.' 'I want Norman,' says the Cardinal 'for he is my friend.' 'Content yourself with such as are here; for you won't get anyone else.'

Accompanying John there were James Melville, a man well acquainted with Master George Wishart, and Peter Carmichael, a stout gentleman. In the meantime, while they push at the door, the Cardinal hides a box of gold under the coals that were laid in a secret corner. At length he asked, 'Will you save my life?' John answered, 'It may be that we will.' 'No,' says the Cardinal, 'swear to me by God's wounds and I will open to you.' Then John answered, 'That which was said, is unsaid'; and so cried, 'Fire, fire,' (for the door was very sturdy); and so a scuttle of burning coals was brought. Seeing which, the Cardinal or his chambermaid (it is uncertain which), opened the door, and the Cardinal sat down in a chair and cried, 'I am a priest; I am a priest; you will not kill me.'

John Leslie (according to his former vows) struck him first, once or twice, and so did Peter. But James Melville (a gentle and modest man) seeing them both enraged, drew them aside, and said, 'This work and judgment of God (although it is secret) ought to be done with greater gravity'; and pointing the sword at him, said, 'Repent of your former wicked life, but especially the shedding of the blood of that notable instrument of God, Master George Wishart, who although he was consumed by the flame of the fire before men, yet asks for a vengeance upon you, and we are sent from God to revenge it: For here, before my God, I protest, that neither the hatred of your person, the love of your riches, nor the fear of any trouble you could have done to me in particular, moved, nor moves me to strike you; but only because you have been, and remain an obstinate enemy of Christ Jesus and his holy Evangel'. And so he struck him twice or thrice through with a stog sword; and so he fell, never word heard out of his mouth but 'I am a priest: fie, fie: all is gone.'

[modified version, see Appendix III, p. 438]

John Knox Apologizes to Queen Elizabeth I, 1559

JOHN KNOX

In his pamphlet 'The First Blast of the Trumpet against the Monstrous Regiment of Women', John Knox railed against the unnaturalness of women ruling a country. He adopted a more conciliatory tone in reply to Queen Elizabeth I's unfavourable response to this political squib.

To Elizabeth, Queen of England
Edinburgh 1559

As your Grace's displeasure with me, most unfairly conceived, has been a great and almost intolerable worry to my wretched heart; so is my clean conscience a comfort, so that I do not become despairing, however strong the temptation: for in God's presence, my conscience bears witness that I never maliciously or on purpose offended your Grace, nor your realm; and therefore, however I am judged by man, I am certain of being absolved by Him who alone knows the secrets of hearts.

I cannot deny writing a book against the usurped Authorities and unjust Regiment of Women; nor am I inclined to retract, or call back any main point or proposition of the same. But why either your Grace or any who honestly favour England's liberty, should be offended at the author of such a work, I can see no good reason: For, firstly, my book does not touch on your Grace's person in particular, nor, if my writing is fairly considered, is it prejudicial to any liberty of the realm.

How could I be an enemy to your Grace's person, for whose deliverance I studied and strove more than any of those that now accuse me? And, so far as your regiment is concerned, how could I, or can I envy that which I have thirsted for, and for which I give thanks unreservedly to God? That is, it has pleased Him, in his eternal goodness, to exalt you (who was once in danger), to the manifestation of his glory and rooting out of idolatry?

God is witness that I sincerely both love and revere your Grace; indeed, I pray that your reign be long prosperous and quiet; and that because of the peace which Christ's members, previously persecuted, have enjoyed under you . . .

[modified version, see Appendix IV, p. 439]

Schooldays, 1560s

JAMES MELVILLE

James Melville's nostalgic account of his schooldays reveals the intellectual rigour expected of young boys, a regimen of study that Melville took in his stride. The nephew of the famous Presbyterian reformer Andrew Melville, he later became a noted scholar, a proponent of religious reform, and, above all, an entertaining autobiographer.

My father put my eldest and only brother David, about a year and a half above me, and me together, to a relative and brother in the ministry of his, to school, a learned, kind man, who out of gratitude I name, Mr William Gray, minister at Logie Montrose. He had a sister, a godly and honest woman, ruler of his house, who often reminded me of my mother and was a very loving mother to me indeed. There were a good many of the country's gentle and honest men's children at the school, well trained both in letters, godliness, and exercises of honest games.

There we learned to read the Catechism, Prayers, and Scripture; to rehearse the Catechism and Prayers by heart; and there I first found (blessed be my God for it!) that spirit of holiness beginning to work in my heart, even when I was about eight and nine; to pray going to bed and rising, and being in the fields alone to say over the prayers I had learned, with a sweet moving in my heart; and to abhor swearing and rebuke and complain about those I heard swear. In which the example of that godly matron, who was sickly and given to reading and praying in her bed, did benefit me greatly; for I lay in her room and heard her devotions.

There we learned the rudiments of Latin grammar, with Latin and French vocabulary; also some French speech, with the correct reading and pronunciation of that language. We went further, to the Etymology of Lillius and his Syntax, and also a little of the Syntax of Linacer; to that was added Hunter's Nomenclature, the Minora Colloquia of Erasmus, and some of the Eclogues of Virgil and Epistles of Horace; also Cicero's Epistolis ad Terentiam . . .

There we also had good fresh air, and were taught by our master to handle the bow for archery, the club for golf, the sticks for fencing, also to run, to jump, to swim, to wrestle, to take part in competitions, every one having his match and antagonist, both in our lessons and games.

A happy and golden time indeed, if our negligence and ingratitude had not moved God to shorten it, partly because of the reduction of numbers, which caused the master to grow weary, and partly because of a disease which the Lord, for sin and contempt of his Gospel, sent upon Montrose, which was only two miles from Over Logie; so that the school dispersed, and we were all sent for and brought home.

I was at that school for almost five years, in which time, of public news, I remember I heard of the marriage of Henry and Mary, King and Queen of Scots, Seigneur David's slaughter, of the King's murder at the Kirk of Field, of the Queen's taking at Carberry, and the Langside field . . . Also I clearly remember how we went to the top of the moor to see the fire of joy burning on the steeple head of Montrose on the day of the King's birth.

[modified version, see Appendix V, p. 440]

Mary, Queen of Scots, Arrives in Scotland, 19 August 1561

JOHN KNOX

The return of Mary, Queen of Scots, to Scotland saw the beginning of one of the most momentous and colourful episodes in Scottish political history. Her arrival is recalled here by John Knox, writing after the murder of David Riccio, with more than a little venom and hindsight.

On the nineteenth of August, 1561, between seven and eight in the morning, Mary Queen of Scotland arrived, a widow, with two galleys, from France . . . At her arrival the sky itself plainly told what comfort she brought for this country, namely sorrow, pain, darkness, and all impiety. For, in living memory, the skies were never darker than at her arrival, which for two days thereafter continued like that; for, besides the excessive wet, and the foulness of the air, the mist was so thick and so dark that no man could see another much beyond the length of two pairs of boots. The sun was not seen to shine two days before, nor two days after. God gave us that warning; but, alas, most were blind.

[modified version, see Appendix VI, p. 441]

The Murder of Riccio, 9 March 1566

SIR JAMES MELVILLE

The murder of Mary, Queen of Scots's secretary, and possibly lover, David Riccio, by her husband Darnley and his friends was a turning point in the Queen's already turbulent affairs. This description of Riccio's brutal death, when the Queen was heavily pregnant, comes from one of her most trusted counsellors, the diplomat and soldier Sir James Melville, who became page to Mary at the age of fourteen, and was later appointed privy councillor and a gentleman of the bedchamber. Most interesting is his portrait of Riccio and of Mary's flagrant favouritism towards him, despite his advice to her to be more prudent.

Now there came here, with the ambassador of Scavoy, one David Riccio, from Piemont, who was a merry fellow and a good musician; and her Majesty had three valets of her chamber who sang three parts and wanted a bass to sing the fourth part; therefore they told her Majesty of this man who could be their fourth mate, and so he was brought to sing sometimes with the rest; and later, when his master the ambassador went back, he stayed in this country, and was kept in her Majesty's service as a valet of her chamber.

And later, when her French secretary went back to France, this David obtained this post, and thereby got into a better position, and got her Majesty's attention, sometimes in the presence of the nobility, and when there were great conventions of the estates, which caused him to be so envied and hated that some of the nobility would frown at him, and some of them would cold-shoulder him, and ignore him, when they came into the chamber, and found him always speaking with her Majesty.

Therefore, not without some fear, he complained to me about his situation, and asked my advice about how to behave. I told him, that strangers were often envied when they interfered too much in the affairs of foreign countries. I also said that it was thought that most of the business of the country passed through his hands, and advised him, when the nobility were present, to give them their place, and ask the Queen's Majesty to be content with that. He did this, and later said to me that the Queen would not allow him to do this; but carried on using him in the old manner. Later, seeing the envy against the said David increase even further, and that by his ruin her Majesty would incur much displeasure, I took the opportunity to tell her what advice I had given to Seigneur David, as is outlined above. Her Majesty said that he did not interfere in any way except in her French writing and affairs, just as her other French secretary had done; and whoever found fault with this, she would not allow to carry out her ordinary duties. She thanked me for my continual care, and promised to take good care from then on, as was required.

The King, Darnley, probably gave his consent too easily to the slaughter of seigneur David, which the Lords of Morton, Ruthven, Lindsay and others had devised, so that they could be masters of the court and hold the parliament. The King was still very young, and not very experienced with the nature of this nation. It was also thought that the Earl of Lennox knew of the plan, for he had his chamber within the palace; and so had the Earls of Atholl, Bothwell, and Huntly, who both escaped by jumping out of a window, towards the little garden where the lines are encamped. This vile act was done upon a Saturday (9th) of March in the year 1565 [by the old Scots calendar] at around six o'clock.

When the Queen was at her supper in her room, a number of armed men entered within the courtyard before the closing of the gates, and took the keys from the porter. And some of them went up through the King's chamber, led by the Lord Ruthven and George Douglas the postulate bishop; the rest remained in the courtyard with drawn swords in their hands, crying 'a Douglas, a Douglas' for their slogan; for it was in the gloaming of the evening.

The King had gone up to the Queen earlier, and was leaning upon her chair when the Lord Ruthven entered with his headpiece upon his head, and George the postulate came in with him and various others, so roughly and irreverently that the table fell, the candles and meat and plates fell. Seigneur David clutched the Queen about the waist, and cried for mercy; but George Douglas drew out the King's dagger that was behind his back, and struck him first with it, leaving it sticking in him. He gave great screams and cries, and was roughly removed from the Queen, who could not get him safe, neither by threat or entreaty. He was forcibly dragged out of the room, and slain in the outer hall, and her Majesty kept as captive.

[modified version, see Appendix VII, p. 441]

Mary, Queen of Scots, Appeals to Elizabeth I for Help, 1 May 1568

MARY, QUEEN OF SCOTS

Mary's fortunes spiralled into chaos after the murder of her husband Darnley in 1567, and her marriage to the chief suspect, the Earl of Bothwell, a mere three months later. She lost all credibility as a monarch, and after an abortive attempt to pitch her troops against her outraged Scottish nobles, she was obliged to concede defeat. She was captured, and imprisoned on Lochleven, where she was forced to abdicate in favour of her son, James. On the eve of her shortlived escape, Mary contacted her cousin in a letter written in a hasty scrawl.

1 May 1568

Madame my good sister, the slow passing of time in my weary prison, and the wrongs received from those to whom I have done so many benefits, is less weariful to me than to be unable to tell you the truth of my evil fortune, and of the hurts which have been done to me from many airts [quarters]; wherefore, having found the means, by a good servant here, to send you this word, I have delivered all my thought to the bearer, praying you to believe him as myself.

You remember that it has pleased you, divers times, to assure me that if you should see the ring which you sent me, you would help me in all my afflictions. You know how my brother Moray has all I own. Those who have anything agree to send me nothing: Robert Melvin at least says he dare not send it me, though I entrusted him with it secretly as my dearest jewel. For which cause I beg you, seeing these presents, to have pity on your good sister and cousin, and to be assured that you will never have a more near and loving kinswoman in this world. You can also consider the significance of the example practised against me, not only as a king or a queen, but as one of the meanest subjects.

I beg you to have a care lest anyone should know that I have written to you, for that would cause me to be worse treated: and they boast that they are warned by their friends of all you say and do. Believe the bearer like myself. God keep you from misfortune and give me patience and grace that I may one day mourn to you my fortune, and say to you more than I dare write, which may serve you no little.

From my prison this 1st May,
Your most obliged and affectionate good sister and cousin,
MARIE R.

Act against Luxury, 1581

THE PARLIAMENT OF SCOTLAND

There were economic reasons for insisting that the populace wore clothes made from materials made in Scotland, but the main reason for this act appears to have been one of sheer elitism. Nobody but royalty and nobility, it seems, was allowed to dress themselves in finery.

The king's majesty and estates of this parliament considering the great abuse among his subjects of the lower order presuming to imitate his highness and the nobility in the use and wearing of costly clothing of silks of all sorts, wool, cambric, fringes and edging of gold, silver and silk and woollen cloth made and brought from other foreign countries as a result of which the prices of these are grown so exorbitant that it cannot be any longer sustained without great injury and inconvenience of the commonweal, given that God has granted this realm sufficient resources for clothing its inhabitants if the people were virtuously employed in working at this at home, whereby great numbers of poor people now wandering begging might also be released to the benefit and wealth of the country.

For the remedy of which it is statute and ordained that none of his highnesses subjects man or woman being under the degrees of dukes, earls, lords of parliament, knights, or landed gentlemen, that has or may spend two thousand merks of free yearly rent or fifty chalders victual at least, or their wives, sons, or daughters shall after the first day of May next, use or wear in their clothing or apparel or lining thereof any cloth of gold or silver, velvet, satin, damask, taffeta or any trimmings, fringes, edging or embroidery of gold, silver or silk, nor wool, cambric or woollen cloth made and brought from any foreign countries under the pain of a hundred pounds of every landed gentleman, a hundred pounds of every yeoman for every day that his wife, son or daugher transgresses this act. And also that the poor people may be the better kept in work through the working of the country's wool, therefore it is statute and ordained that no type of wool be transported out of this realm in time coming under the pain of confiscation for the same wool and of all the remaining movable goods of the persons, owners and transports thereof to our sovereign lord's use.

[modified version, see Appendix VIII, p. 443]

The Habits of Highlanders, 1582

GEORGE BUCHANAN

Scholar, high-ranking Protestant, and one-time tutor to Mary, Queen of Scots (whom he later accused of complicity in her husband Darnley's murder), George Buchanan wrote a biased but entertaining history of Scotland, which includes this description of Highlanders.

In their food, clothing, and in the whole of their domestic economy, they adhere to ancient parsimony. Hunting and fishing, supply them with food. They boil the flesh with water poured into the paunch or the skin of the animal they kill, and in hunting sometimes they eat the flesh raw, merely squeezing out the blood. They drink the juice of the boiled flesh. At their feasts they sometimes use whey, after it has been kept for several years, and even drink it greedily; that species of liquor they call bland, but the greater part quench their thirst with water. They make a kind of bread, not unpleasant to the taste, of oats and barley, the only grain cultivated in these regions, and, from long practice, they have attained considerable skill in moulding the cakes. Of this they eat a little in the morning, and then contentedly go out a hunting, or engage in some other occupation, frequently remaining without any other food till the evening.

They delight in variegated garments, especially striped, and their favourite colours are purple and blue. Their ancestors wore plaids of many different colours, and numbers still retain this custom, but the majority, now, in their dress, prefer a dark brown, imitating nearly the leaves of the heather, that when lying upon the heath in the day, they may not be discovered by the appearance of their clothes; in these, wrapped rather than covered, they brave the severest storms in the open air, and sometimes lay themselves down to sleep even in the midst of snow.

In their houses, also, they lie upon the ground; strewing fern, or heath, on the floor, with the roots downward and the leaves turned up. In this manner they form a bed so pleasant, that it may vie in softness with the finest down, while in salubrity it far exceeds it; for heath, naturally possessing the power of absorption, drinks up the superfluous moisture, and restores strength to the fatigued nerves, so that those who lie down languid and weary in the evening, arise in the morning vigorous and sprightly.

They have all, not only the greatest contempt for pillows, or blankets, but, in general, an affectation of uncultivated roughness and hardihood, so that when choice or necessity induces them to travel in other countries, they throw aside the pillows, and blankets of their hosts, and wrapping themselves round with their own plaids, thus go to sleep, afraid lest these barbarian luxuries, as they term them, should contaminate their native simple hardiness.

The Morning of Mary, Queen of Scots's Execution, 8 February 1587

MARY, QUEEN OF SCOTS

After Mary's escape from Lochleven her troops were defeated at Langside by the Regent Moray, and she fled to seek her cousin's support. Instead of offering protection, however, Elizabeth consigned Mary to nineteen years' incarceration in various gilded prisons, from Carlisle to Fotheringay. Since her presence created a potential rallying point for a Catholic restoration, she was a perpetual thorn in the English Queen's side, but it was not until Mary was – fairly or unfairly – implicated in a plot to assassinate Elizabeth that her execution was ordered. This letter to her brother-in-law Henri III, King of France, was written in the early hours of the morning of her execution. The original is in French.

Monsieur my brother-in-law, having by God's permission – for my sins as I think – come to throw myself into the arms of this Queen my cousin, where I have had many weary troubles and passed near twenty years, I am at last, by her and her Estates, condemned to death: and having claimed my papers, by them removed, in order to make my will, I have not been able to recover anything which would serve, nor to win leave to make one freely, nor that after death my body should be borne, as I desire, into your kingdom, where I have had the honour to be Queen, your sister, and your ally from of old.

Today, after dinner, my sentence has been announced to me, of being executed tomorrow as a criminal, at eight in the morning. I have not had leisure to give you a full account of all that has happened: but if you will please to believe my physician and these others my forlorn servants, you will hear the truth: as, thanks be to God, I despise death, and faithfully protest that I receive it innocent of all crime, even supposing I were in their jurisdiction. The Catholic religion, and the upholding of the right to this Crown which God has given me, are the two causes of my condemnation: none the less they will not let me say that it is for the Catholic religion I die, but for fear of a change in theirs: and for proof of this they have taken away my chaplain, whom, though he is in the house, I could not make them let me have to confess me, or to give me the Last Sacrament: but they have strongly urged me to receive the consolation and doctrine of a minister of theirs brought here on purpose. The bearer of this, and his companions, mostly your own subjects, will witness to you how I bear myself in this my last action.

It remains for me to beg you, as Most Christian King, my brother-in-law and old ally, who have always protested your affection for me, that you now make proof in all these points of your goodness, as much in Christian charity, easing my mind in the discharging of my conscience, which without you I cannot achieve: which is to reward my forlorn servants, leaving them their wages, and further to obtain prayers for a Queen who has once borne the title of Most Christian, and who dies a Catholic, stripped of all her goods. As for my son, I recommend him to you as he shall deserve, for I cannot answer for him. I have ventured to send you two rare stones, good for the health, desiring that for you with long and happy life. You will accept them as from your most affectionate good-sister, who dying bears witness of her good heart to you. Once more I recommend to you my servants. You will order, if you please, that for my soul's good I shall be paid a part of what you owe me, and that in honour of Jesus Christ, Whom tomorrow, at my death, I shall pray for you, you will leave me as much as will found an obit [as will create a legacy], and will make the needful alms.

This Wednesday, at two hours after midnight.
Your most affectionate and good sister,
MARIE R.

The Execution of Mary, Queen of Scots, 8 February 1587

ROBERT WINGFIELD

This eyewitness account of Mary's execution at Fotheringay, written for Lord Burghley, the Lord High Treasurer, was probably by courtier – and hired assassin – Robert Wingfield.

First, the said Scottish Queen, carried by two of Sir Amyas Paulett's gentlemen, the Sheriff going before her, came most willingly out of her

chamber into an entry next the hall, at which place the Earl of Shrewsbury and the Earl of Kent, Commissioners for the execution, with the
two governors of her person and divers knights and gentlemen did meet
her, where they found one of the Scottish Queen's servants, named
Melvin, kneeling on his knees, who uttered these words with tears to
the Queen of Scots his mistress: 'Madam, it will be the sorrowfullest
message that ever I carried, when I shall report that my Queen and
dearest mistress is dead.' Then the Queen of Scots, shedding tears,
answered him, 'You ought rather to rejoice than weep, for that the end
of Mary Stewart's troubles is now come. Thou knowest, Melvin, that
all this world is but vanity and full of troubles and sorrows: carry this
message from me to my friends, that I die a true woman to my religion,
and like a true Scottish woman and a true French woman. But God
forgive them that have long desired my end; and He that is the true
judge of all secret thoughts knoweth my mind, how that ever it hath been
my desire to have Scotland and England united together. Commend me
to my son, and tell him that I have not done any thing that may prejudice
his kingdom of Scotland: and so, good Melvin, farewell,' and kissing
him, she bade him pray for her.

Then she turned her to the Lords, and told them that she had certain
requests to make of them. One was for a sum of money which she said
Sir Amyas Paulett knew of, to be paid to one Curle her servant; next all
her poor servants might enjoy that quietly which by her will and testament she had given unto them; and lastly that they might be all well
intreated, and sent home safely and honestly into their countries. 'And
this I conjure you, my lords, to do.'

Answer was made by Sir Amyas Paulett, 'I do well remember the
money Your Grace speaketh of, and Your Grace need not to make any
doubt of the not performance of your requests, for I do surely think
they shall be granted.'

'I have,' said she, 'one other request to make unto you, my lords, that
you will suffer my poor servants to be present about me at my death,
that they may report when they come into their countries that I died a
true woman unto my religion.'

Then the Earl of Kent, one of the Commissioners, answered, 'Madam,
it cannot well be granted, for that it is feared lest some of them would
with speeches both trouble and grieve Your Grace, and disquiet the
company, of which we have already had some experience, or seek to
wipe their napkins in some of your blood, which were not convenient.'
'My lord,' said the Queen of Scots, 'I will give my word and promise

for them that they should not do any such thing as your lordship hath named. Alas, poor souls, it would do them good to bid me farewell. And I hope your mistress, being a maiden Queen, in regard of womanhood will suffer me to have some of my own people about me at my death. And I know she hath not given you so strict a commission but that you may grant me more than this, if I were a far meaner woman than I am.' And then (seeming to be grieved) with some tears uttered these words: 'You know that I am cousin to your Queen, and descended from the blood of Henry VII, a married Queen of France, and the anointed Queen of Scotland.'

Wherefore, after some consultation, they granted that she might have some of her servants, according to Her Grace's request, and therefore desired her to make choice of half a dozen of her men and women. Who presently said that of her men she would have Melvin, her apothecary, her surgeon, and one other old man besides, and of her women, those two that did use to lie in her chamber.

After this, she being supported by Sir Amyas' two gentlemen aforesaid, and Melvin carrying up her train, and also accompanied with all the lords, knights, and gentlemen aforenamed, the Sheriff going before her, she passed out of the entry into the great hall, with her countenance careless, importing rather mirth than mournful cheer, so she willingly stepped up to the scaffold which was prepared for her in the hall, being two feet high and twelve feet broad, with rails round about, hanged and covered with black also. Then, having the stool brought to her, she sat her down; by her, on the right hand, sat the Earl of Shrewsbury and the Earl of Kent, and on the left hand stood the Sheriff, and before her the two executioners; round about the rails stood knights, gentlemen, and others.

Then silence being made, the Queen Majesty's Commission for the execution of the Queen of Scots was openly read by Mr Beale, Clerk of the Council, and these words pronounced by the assembly, 'God save the Queen.' During the reading of which Commission the Queen of Scots was silent, listening unto it with as small regard as if it had not concerned her at all, and with as cheerful a countenance as if it had been a pardon from Her Majesty for her life; using as much strangeness [indifference] in word and deed as if she had never known any of the assembly, or had been ignorant of the English language.

Then one Dr Fletcher, Dean of Peterborough, standing directly before her, without the rail, bending his body with great reverence, began to utter this exhortation, following, 'Madame, the Queen's most excellent majesty, etc.,' and iterating these words three or four times, she told him, 'Mr Dean, I am settled in the ancient Catholic Roman religion, and mind to spend my blood in defence of it.' Then Mr Dean said, 'Madame, change your opinion and repent of your former wickedness, and settle your faith only in Jesus Christ, by Him to be saved.' Then she answered again and again, 'Mr Dean, trouble not yourself any more, for I am settled and resolved in this my religion, and am purposed therein to die.' Then the Earl of Shrewsbury and the Earl of Kent, perceiving her so obstinate, told her that since she would not hear the exhortation begun by Mr Dean, 'We will pray for Your Grace, that it stand with God's will that you may have your heart lightened, even at this last hour, with the true kingdom of God, and so die therein.' Then she answered, 'If you will pray for me, my lords, I will thank you: but to join in prayer with you I will not, for that you and I are not of one religion.'

Then the lords called for Mr Dean, who kneeling on the scaffold stairs began this prayer, 'O most gracious God and merciful Father, etc.,' all the assembly, saving the Queen of Scots and her servants, saying after him. During the saying of which prayer, the Queen of Scots sitting upon a stool, having about her neck an Agnus Dei, in her hand a crucifix, at her girdle a pair of beads with a golden cross at the end of them, a Latin book in her hand, began with tears and with loud and fast voice to pray in Latin; and in the midst of her prayers she slided off from her stool, and kneeling, said divers Latin prayers, and after the end of Mr Dean's prayer, she, kneeling, prayed in English to this effect, for Christ His afflicted Church, and for an end of their troubles; for her son, and for the Queen's Majesty, that she might prosper and serve God aright. She confessed that she hoped to be saved by and in the blood of Christ, at the foot of whose crucifix she would shed her blood. Then said the Earl of Kent, 'Madam, settle Christ Jesus in your heart, and leave these trumperies.' Then she, little regarding or not at all, went forward with her prayers, desiring that God would avert His wrath from this Island, and that he would give her grief and forgiveness for her sins. These with other prayers she made in English, saying she forgave her enemies with all her heart that had long sought her blood, and desired God to convert them to the truth; and in the end of her prayer she desired all saints to make intercession for her to Jesus Christ, and so kissing the crucifix of her also, said these words, 'Even as Thy arms, O Jesu, were spread here upon the Cross, so receive me into Thy arms of mercy, and forgive me all my sins.'

Her prayer being ended, the executioners kneeling desired Her Grace to forgive them her death, who answered, 'I forgive you with all my heart, for now, I hope, you shall make an end of all my troubles.' Then they, with her two women, helping of her up, began to disrobe her of her apparel; then she laying the crucifix upon the stool, one of the executioners took from her neck the Agnus Dei, which she laying hands of, gave it to one of her women, and told the executioner he should be answered money for it. Then she suffered them, with her two women, to disrobe her of her chain of pomander beads and all other her apparel most willingly, and with joy rather than sorrow helped to make unready [undress] herself, putting on a pair of sleeves with her own hands which they had pulled off, and that with some haste, as if she had longed to be gone.

All this time they were pulling off her apparel, she never changed her countenance, but with smiling cheer she uttered these words, that she never had such grooms to make her unready, and that she never put off her clothes before such a company.

Then she being stripped of all her apparel saving her petticoat and kirtle, her two women beholding her made great lamentation, and crying and crossing themselves, prayed in Latin. She turning herself to them, embracing them, said these words in French, 'Ne criez vous, j'ai promis pour vous,' and so crossing and kissing them, bade them pray for her and rejoice, and not weep, for that now they should see an end of all their mistress' troubles.

Then she, with a smiling countenance, turned to her men servants, as Melvin and the rest, standing upon a bench nigh to the scaffold, who sometimes weeping, sometimes crying out aloud, and continually crossing themselves, prayed in Latin, and crossing them with her hand bade them farewell, wishing them to pray for her even until the last hour.

This done, one of the women, having a Corpus Christi cloth lapped up three-corner-ways, kissing it, put it over the Queen of Scots' face, and pinned it fast to the caul of her head. Then the two women departed from her, she kneeling down upon the cushion most resolutely and without any token or fear of death, she spake aloud this psalm in Latin, 'In te Domine confide, non confundar in aeternum, etc.' Then groping for the block, she laid down her head, putting her chin over the block with both her hands, which holding there still, had been cut off had they not been spied. Then lying upon the block most quietly, and stretching out her arms, cried, 'In manu tuas, Domine,' three or four times. Then she lying very still upon the block, one of the executioners holding of her slightly with one of his hands, she endured two strokes of the other executioner his axe, she making very small noise or none at all, and not stirring any part of her from where she lay; and so the executioner cut off her head, saving one little gristle, which being cut in sunder, he lift up her head to the view of all the assembly, saying 'God save the Queen'.

Then her dressing of lawn falling off from her head, it appeared as grey as one of three score and ten years old, polled very short, her face in a moment by so much altered from the form she had when she was alive, as few could remember her by her dead face. Her lips stirred up and down for a quarter of an hour after her head was cut off.

Then Mr Dean said with a loud voice, 'So perish all the Queen's enemies,' and afterwards the Earl of Kent came to the dead body, and standing over it, said with a loud voice, 'Such end of all the Queen's and the Gospel enemies.'

Then one of the executioners, pulling off her garters, espied her little dog, which was crept under her clothes, which could not be got forth by force, yet afterwards would not depart with the dead corpse, but came and lay between her head and her shoulders, which being imbrued with her blood was carried away and washed, as all things else were that had any blood was either burned or clean washed, and the executioners sent away with money for their fees, not having any one thing that belonged to her. And so, every man being commanded out of the hall, except the Sheriff and his men, she was carried by them up into a great chamber, lying ready for the surgeons to embalm her.

The North Berwick Witches, 1591

NEWS FROM SCOTLAND

In 1590, James VI and his bride Anne of Denmark were believed to have fallen victim to a coven of witches gathered at North Berwick, who had tried to sink James's ship by raising a storm. For a king who believed his own courtiers were plotting against him, it was presumably easier to deal with supernatural agents than genuinely threatening ones. The anonymous pamphlet, News from Scotland, *from which this extract comes, was probably published in late 1591, following the alleged witches' trials, and is thought to have been written by James Carmichael, minister of Haddington, who was possibly present at the proceedings. It is a fine piece of propaganda, prurience and prejudice, and shows the anxious atmosphere in which preposterous witchcraft accusations could be taken seriously.*

Some of it is fiction, but much is taken from the victims' depositions and testimonies, and it is the main piece of written evidence of the varieties of torture used to extract confessions, most awful of which was 'the boots'. Such details were absent from court records. In showing how Geillis Duncan was made to confess, it offers the only account of the origin of the protracted North Berwick witchhunt.

Within the town of Tranent in the kingdom of Scotland there dwelleth one David Seton, who, being deputy bailiff in the said town, had a maidservant called Geillis Duncan, who used secretly to be absent and to lie forth of her master's house every other night. This Geillis Duncan took in hand to help all such as were troubled or grieved with any kind of sickness or infirmity, and in short space did perform many matters most miraculous. Which things, forasmuch as she began to do them upon a sudden, never having done the like before, made her master and others to be in great admiration, and wondered thereat. By means whereof the said David Seton had his maid in some great suspicion that she did not those things by natural and lawful ways, but rather supposed it to be done by some extraordinary and unlawful means.

Whereupon her master began to grow very inquisitive, and examined her which way and by what means she was able to perform matters of so great importance; whereat she gave him no answer. Nevertheless, her master, to the intent that he might be better try and find out the truth of the same, did with the help of others torment her with the torture of the pilliwinks [thumbscrews] upon her fingers, which is a grievous torture, and binding or wrinching her head with a cord or rope, which is a most cruel torment also, yet would she not confess anything. Whereupon they, suspecting that she had been marked by the devil (as commonly witches are), made diligent search about her, and found the enemy's mark to be in her fore-crag, or forepart of her throat; which being found, she confessed that all her doings was done by the wicked allurements and enticements of the devil, and that she did them by witchcraft.

After her confession, she was committed to prison where she continued for a season; where immediately she accused these persons following to be notorious witches, and caused them forthwith to be apprehended one after another: viz. Agnes Sampson, the eldest of them all, dwelling in Haddington, Agnes Tompson of Edinburgh, Doctor Fian, alias John Cunningham, master of the school at Saltpans in Lothian . . . with innumerable others in those parts . . . of whom some are already executed, the rest remain in prison to receive the doom of judgement at the king's Majesty's will and pleasure . . .

This aforesaid Agnes Sampson, which was the elder witch, was taken and brought to Holyroodhouse before the king's Majesty and sundry other of the nobility of Scotland, where she was straitly examined; but all the persuasions which the king's Majesty used to her with the rest of his council might not provoke or induce her to confess anything, but stood stiffly in the denial of all that was laid to her charge. Whereupon they caused her to be conveyed away to prison, there to receive such torture as hath been lately provided for witches in that country.

And forasmuch as by due examination of witchcraft and witches in Scotland it hath lately been found that the devil doth generally mark them with a privy mark, by reason the witches have confessed themselves that the devil doth lick them with his tongue in some privy part of their body before he doth receive them to be his servants; which mark commonly is given them under the hair in some part of their body whereby it may not easily be found out or seen, although they be searched. And generally so long as the mark is not seen to those which search them, so long the parties that hath the mark will never confess anything. Therefore by special commandment this Agnes Sampson had all her hair shaven off in each part of her body, and her head thrawn with a rope according to the custom of that country, being a pain most grievous, which she continued almost an hour, during which time she would not confess anything, until the devil's mark was found upon her privities [genitals]; then she immediately confessed whatsoever was demanded of her, and justifying those persons aforesaid to be notorious witches.

Item, the said Agnes Sampson was after brought again before the king's Majesty and his council, and being examined of the meetings and detestable dealings of those witches, she confessed that upon the night of Allhollon Even last [Halloween], she was accompanied as well with the persons aforesaid as also with a great many other witches to the number of two hundred; and that all they together went to sea each one in a riddle or sieve, and went in the same very substantially with flagons of wine, making merry and drinking by the way in the same riddles or sieves, to the kirk of North Berwick in Lothian . . .

Item, the said Agnes Sampson confessed that the devil being then at North Berwick kirk attending their coming in the habit or likeness of a man, and seeing that they tarried over long, he at their coming enjoined them all to a penance, which was that they should kiss his buttocks in sign of duty to him; which being put over the pulpit bare, everyone did as he had enjoined them. And having made his ungodly exhortations, wherein he did greatly inveigh against the king of Scotland, he received their oaths for their good and true service towards him, and departed; which done they returned to sea, and so home again . . .

The said witches being demanded how the devil would use them when he was in their company, they confessed that when the devil did receive them for his servants, and that they had vowed themselves unto him, then he would carnally use them, albeit to their little pleasure, in respect of his cold nature; and would do so at sundry other times.

As touching the aforesaid Doctor Fian, alias John Cunningham, the examination of his acts since his apprehension declareth the great subtlety of the devil and therefore maketh things to appear the more miraculous. For being apprehended by the accusation of the said Geillis Duncan aforesaid, who confessed he was their register [clerk], and that there was not one man suffered to come to the devil's readings but only he, the said doctor was taken and imprisoned and used with the accustomed pain provided for those offences, inflicted upon the rest as is aforesaid.

First, by thrawing of his head with a rope, whereat he would confess nothing. Secondly, he was persuaded by fair means to confess his follies, but that would prevail as little. Lastly, he was put to the most severe and cruel pain in the world, called 'the boots'; who after he had received three strokes, being enquired if he would confess his damnable acts and wicked life, his tongue would not serve him to speak. In respect whereof the rest of the witches willed [suggested] to search his tongue, under which was found two pins thrust up into the head, whereupon the witches did say, 'Now is the charm stinted [stopped]', and showed that those charmed pins were the cause he could not confess anything. Then he was immediately released of the boots, brought before the king, his confession was taken, and his own hand willingly set thereunto, which contained as followeth.

First, that at the general meetings of those witches he was always present; that he was clerk to all those that were in subjection to the devil's service bearing the name of witches; that always he did take their oaths for their true service to the devil, and that he wrote for them such matters as the devil still pleased to command him . . .

After that the depositions and examinations of the said Doctor Fian alias Cunningham was taken, as already is declared, with his own hand willingly set thereunto, he was by the master of the prison committed to war, and appointed to a chamber by himself, where, forsaking his wicked ways, acknowledging his most ungodly life, showing that he had too much followed the allurements and enticements of Satan, and fondly practised his conclusions by conjuring, witchcraft, enchantments, sorcery, and such like, he renounced the devil and all his wicked works, vowed to lead the life of a Christian, and seemed newly converted towards God . . .

Nevertheless, the [following] night he found such means that he stole the key of the prison door and chamber in the which he was, which in the night he opened and fled away to the Saltpans . . . of whose sudden departure when the king's Majesty had intelligence, he presently commanded diligent inquiry to be made for his apprehension and for the better effecting thereof he sent public proclamations into all parts of his land to the same effect. By means of whose hot and hardy pursuit he was again taken and brought to prison, and then being called before the king's Highness he was re-examined, as well touching his departure as also touching all that had before happened. But this doctor, notwithstanding that his own confession appeareth remaining in record under his own handwriting . . . yet did he utterly deny the same.

Yet for more trial of him to make him confess, he was commanded to have a most strange torment which was done in this manner following. His nails upon all his fingers were riven and pulled off with an instrument called in Scottish a 'turkas', which in England we call a pair of pincers, and under every nail there was thrust in two needles over even up to the heads. At all which torments notwithstanding the doctor never shrunk any whit, neither would he then confess it the sooner for all the tortures inflicted upon him. Then was he with all convenient speed, by commandment, conveyed again to the torment of the boots, wherein he continued a long time and did abide so many blows in them that his legs were crushed and beaten together as small as might be, and the bones and flesh so bruised that the blood and marrow spouted forth in great abundance, whereby they were made unserviceable for ever. And notwithstanding all these grievous pains and cruel torments he would not confess anything; so deeply had the devil entered into his heart, that he utterly denied all that which he had before avouched, and would say nothing thereunto but this: that what he had done and said before was only done and said for fear of pains which he had endured . . .

The said Doctor Fian was soon after arraigned, condemned, and adjudged by the law to die, and then to be burned according to the law of that land provided in that behalf. Whereupon he was put into a cart and, being first strangled, he was immediately put into a great fire, being

ready provided for that purpose, and there burned in the castle hill of
Edinburgh on a Saturday in the end of January last past, 1591. The rest
of the witches which are not yet executed remain in prison till further
trial, and knowledge of his Majesty's pleasure.

No Pipe-playing on Sundays, 1593

THE PRESBYTERY OF GLASGOW

*The reputation of the Scottish authorities as cheerless and punitive was formed
by such joyless edicts as the following.*

The Presbytery of Glasgow statutes and ordains that if Mungo Craig
shall play on his pipes on the Sunday from the sun rising till the sun
going to, in any place within the bounds of the Presbytery, that he
immediately thereafter shall be summarily excommunicated.

[modified version, see Appendix IX, p. 444]

Grammar School Mutiny, 1595

ROBERT BIRREL

*Edinburgh burgess Robert Birrel noted this violent escapade in the city when a
pack of grammar school boys were refused their customary 'rights', although it's
not clear what these were.*

The 15 of September, John Macmorrane was killed by the shot of a
pistol fired from the school. This John Macmorrane being Baillie for the
time, the bairns of the said grammar school came to the town's council
as they did every year, to seek the privilege, which was refused; at which,
a number of scholars, being gentlemen's bairns, made a mutiny, and
came in the night and took the school, and provided themselves with
meat, drink and ancient firearms, pistol, and sword: they reinforced the
doors of the school, so that they refused to let in their master or any
other man, unless they were granted their privilege as usual.

The Provost and Baillies and Council hearing of this, they ordered
John Macmorrane Baillie to go to the grammar school and reinstate

order. The said John, with some officers, went to the school, and requested the scholars to open the doors: they refused. The said Baillie and officers took a beam of wood and ran at the back door with the beam. A scholar asked him to desist from battering the door, otherwise, he vowed to God, he would shoot a pair of bullets through his head. The said Baillie, thinking he dared not shoot, he, with his assistants, ran with the beam at the door. There came a scholar called William Sinclair, son to William Sinclair chancellor of Caithness, and with a pistol shot out of a window, and shot the said Baillie through the head, so that he died. Shortly after all of the townsmen ran to the school, and took the said bairns and put them in the tolbooth: but all the bairns were let free without hurt done to them for the same, within a short time thereafter.

[modified version, see Appendix X, p. 444]

Border Reivers Defy Capture, 14 April 1596

THE LORD TREASURER OF ENGLAND

The Scottish–English border was rife with violence, theft and confrontations. Some considered the Borderers a race distinct from the rest of their nations. Here, in a letter to the Privy Council, the embittered march warden Thomas Scrope (whose role it was to patrol and maintain order at the border) relays a description by the Lord Treasurer of the audacious rescue from Carlisle Castle of 'Kinmont Willie', a reiver (plunderer) from the notoriously wild Armstrong family. His rescuer was Scott of Buccleugh.

I thought it my duty to inform you of 'the proud attempt' which the Scots have made on this her Majesty's castle and chief strength here, praying you to move her Majesty for such redress as may please her. The ground of it proceeds from the cause which I formerly told you of, and will now be imparted to you by my Lord Treasurer, to whom to avoid tediousness I refer you.

'Yesterday evening, in the dead of night, Walter Scott of Hardinge, Buccleugh's chief man, accompanied with 500 horsemen of Buccleugh's and Kinmont's friends, came armed with crowbars, handpicks, axes and scaling ladders, to an outer corner of the base court of this castle, and to the back gate of the same – which they undermined speedily and quietly and made themselves possessors of the base court, broke into the room where Will of Kinmont was, carried him away, and when they were discovered by the watch, left for dead two of the watchmen, hurt a servant of mine, one of Kinmont's keepers, and were out of the back door before they were seen by the watch of the inner court, and before resistance could be made.

'The watch, it seems, because of the stormy night, were either asleep or had got under some cover to protect themselves from the violence of the weather; as a result of which the Scots carried out their plan with less difficulty. The place where Kinmont was kept, in respect of the manner of his taking, and the assurance he had given that he would not escape, I assumed to enforce the bond, and did not expect that any would have dared to attempt to breach in time of peace any of her Majesty's castles, a place of such great strength. If Buccleugh himself has been the captain of this proud attempt, since some of my servants tell me they heard his name called out (the truth whereof I shall shortly find out), then I humbly beseech, that her Majesty will be pleased to send to the King, to call for and find that the nature of his offence shall merit retaliation, for it will be a dangerous example to leave this outrageous attempt unpunished . . . In revenge for which, I intend that something shall shortly be brought against the principals of this action for reparation.'

[modified version, see Appendix XI, p. 445]

The Scottish Diet, 1598

FYNES MORYSON

Fynes Moryson, an educated traveller from Lincolnshire who had been in Asia Minor and Palestine as well as all over Europe, offers his unflattering view of Scottish food and eating habits.

Touching their diet: They eate much red Colewort and Cabbage, but little fresh meate, using to salt their Mutton and Geese, which made me more wonder, that they used to eate Beefe without salting. The Gentlemen reckon their revenewes, not by rents of monie, but by chauldrons of victuals, and keepe many people in the Families, yet living most on Corne and Rootes, not spending any great quantity on fleshe. My selfe was at a Knights House, who had many servants to attend him, that brought in his meate with their heads covered with blew [blue] caps, the Table being more then halfe furnished with great platters of porredge, each having a little peece of sodden meate: And when the Table was served, the servants did sit downe with us, but the upper messe in steede of porredge, had a Pullet with some prunes in the broth. And I observed no Art of Cookery, or furniture of Houshold stuffe, but rather rude neglect of both . . . They vulgarly eate harth Cakes of Oates, but in Cities have also wheaten bread, which for the most part was bought by Courtiers, Gentlemen, and the best sort of Citizens . . . They drinke pure Wines, not with sugar as the English, yet at Feasts they put Comfits in the Wine . . . Their bedsteads were then like Cubbards in the wall, with doores to be opened and shut at pleasure, so as we climbed up to our beds. They used but one sheete, open at the sides and top, but close at the feete, and so doubled . . .

The First New Year's Day, 1600

THE PRIVY COUNCIL

Scotland finally came into line with the rest of Europe in 1600, by starting the new year on 1 January instead of on 25 March. It is a date that Scots have since taken very fondly to heart.

The King's Majesty and Lords of his Secret Council, understanding that in all other well governed commonwealths and countries the first day of the year begins yearly upon the first day of January, commonly called New Year's Day, and that this realm only is different from all others in the count and reckoning of the years, and His Majesty and Council willing that there shall be no discrepancy between His Majesty's realm and lieges and other neighbouring countries in this particular, but that they shall adjust themselves to the order and custom observed by all other countries, especially seeing the course and season of the year is most proper and answerable thereto, and that the alteration thereof imports no hurt nor prejudice to any party: thereof His Majesty, with advice of the Lords of his Secret Council, statutes and ordains that henceforth, the first day of the year shall begin yearly upon the first day of January, and the present document they intend shall come into force on the first day of January next to come, which shall be the first day of them and six hundredth year of God . . .

[modified version, see Appendix XII, p. 446]

The Union of the Crowns, 24 March 1603

ROBERT CAREY

A few hours after the death of Elizabeth I, Robert Carey, a Warden of the Marches, set out from London to bring the news to her nephew James VI that he was now King of England as well as Scotland.

The Queen grew worse and worse. . . . There was no hope of her recovery, because she refused all remedies. On Wednesday, the twenty-third of March, she grew speechless. That afternoon, by signs, she called for her Council, and by putting her hand to her head, when the King of Scots was named to succeed her, they all knew he was the man she desired should reign after her . . .

About six at night she made signs for the Archbishop and her Chaplains to come to her, at which time I went in with them, and sat upon my knees full of tears to see that heavy sight. . . . I went to my lodging, and left word with one in the Cofferer's chamber to call me, if that night it was thought she would die, and gave the porter an angel [a coin] to let me in any time when I called. Between one and two of the clock on Thursday morning, he that I left in the Cofferer's chamber brought me word the Queen was dead . . .

The Friday night I came to my own house at Witherington, and presently took order with my deputies to see the borders kept in quiet, which they had much to do: and gave order the next morning the King of Scotland should be proclaimed King of England, and at Morpeth and Alnwick. Very early on Saturday I took horse for Edinburgh, and came to Norham about twelve at noon, so that I might well have been with the King at supper time: but I got a great fall by the way, and my horse with one of his heels gave me a great blow on the head that made me shed much blood. It made me so weak that I was forced to ride a soft pace after, so that the King was newly gone to bed by the time that I knocked at the gate.

I was quickly led in, and carried up to the King's chamber. I kneeled by him, and saluted him by his title of England, Scotland, France and Ireland. He gave me his hand to kiss, and bade me welcome. After he had long discoursed of the manner of the Queen's sickness and of her death, he asked what letters I had from the Council? I told him, none: and acquainted him how narrowly I escaped from them [they had not wanted him to take the news to James]. And yet I had brought him a blue ring from a fair lady, that I hoped would give him assurance of the truth that I had reported. He took it and looked upon it, and said, 'It is enough: I know by this you are a true messenger.' Then he committed me to the charge of my Lord Home, and gave straight command that I should want nothing. He sent for his chirurgeons [surgeons] to attend me, and when I kissed his hand at my departure he said to me these gracious words: 'I know you have lost a near kinswoman, and a loving mistress; but take here my hand, I will be as good a master to you, and will requite this service with honour and reward.'

So I left him that night, and went with my Lord Hume to my lodging, where I had all things fitting for so weary a man as I was. After my head was dressed, I took leave of my Lord and many others that attended me, and went to my rest . . .

Upon the report of the Queen's death the East border broke forth into great unruliness, insomuch as many complaints came to the King thereof. I was desirous to go to appease them, but I was so weak and ill of my head that I was not able to undertake such a journey, but I offered that I would send my two deputies that should appease the trouble and make them quiet, which was by them shortly after effected.

The Evils of Tobacco, 1604

JAMES VI AND I

There were many things King James VI and I disliked beyond witches; one was tobacco. Despite his abhorrence, however, it quickly became popular at all levels of society, with both men and women.

Shall we that disdain to imitate the manners of our neighbour France (having the style of the first Christian King) and that cannot endure the spirit of the Spaniards (their King being now comparable in largeness of dominions to the great Emperor of Turkey), shall we, I say . . . abase ourselves so far as to imitate those beastly Indians, slaves to the Spaniards, refuse to the world, and as yet aliens from the covenant of God? Why do we not as well imitate them in walking naked as they do? In preferring glasses, feathers, and such toys to gold and precious stones, as they do? Yea, why do we not defy God and adore the Devil, as they do?

. . . Is it not both great vanity and uncleanness, that at the table, a place of respect, of cleanliness, of modesty, men should not be ashamed to sit tossing of tobacco pipes and puffing of the smoke of tobacco one to another, making the filthy smoke and stink thereof to exhale athwart the dishes and infect the air, when very often men that abhor it are at their repast? . . .

A custom loathesome to the eye, hateful to the nose, harmful to the brain, dangerous to the lungs, and in the black, stinking fume thereof nearest resembling the horrible Stygian fume of the pit that is bottomless.

Ben Jonson Walks to Scotland, 1618–1619

WILLIAM DRUMMOND OF HAWTHORNDEN

One of the most famous encounters in literary history was that between the eminent playwright Ben Jonson and the reclusive Scottish poet William Drummond. The overweight, over-opinionated Jonson set out to walk to Scotland from London in the summer of 1618 and probably reached Hawthornden Castle, where Drummond lived, around Christmas. The reason for his gruelling trip is uncertain, although some suggest he was asked to make the journey by the King, who had perhaps commissioned him to write an account of Scotland. He spent some days with Drummond, who kept notes of their conversations. Offering his trenchant views on the great writers of their day, Jonson proved himself great company, if disconcertingly critical. Even his young host was not spared: 'He said to me, that I was too good and simple, and that oft a mans modestie made a fool of his witt,' wrote Drummond, uncomplainingly.

Certain informations and maners of Ben Johnsons to W. Drumond

1. That he had ane intention to perfect ane Epick poeme intituled Hero-ologia, of the Worthies of his Country, rowsed by Fame, and was to dedicate it to his Country, it is all in Couplets, for he detesteth all other Rimes . . .

2. He recommended to my reading Quintilian (who (he said) would tell me the faults of my Verses as if he had lived with me) and Horace, Plinius 2dus Epistles, Tacitus, Juvenall, Martiall; whose Epigrame Vitae quae faciunt beatiorem etc. he heth translated.

3. His Censure of the English poets was this, that Sidney could not keep a Decorum in making every one speak as well as himself.

Spencers stanzas pleased him not, nor his matter, the meaning of which Allegorie he had delivered in papers to Sir Walter Raughlie . . .

That Dones Anniversarie was profane and full of Blasphemies: that he told Mr Donne, if it had been written of the Virgin Marie it had been something; to which he answered, that he described / the Idea of a Woman, and not as she was.

That Done, for not keeping of accent, deserved hanging.

That next himself only Fletcher and Chapman could make a Mask.

That Shakespear wanted Arte . . .

6. His censure of my verses was that they were all good, especiallie my Epitaph of the Prince, save that they smelled too much of the Schooles, and were not after the fancie of the tyme; for a child sayes he may writte after the fashion of the Greeks and Latine verses in running; yet that he wished, to please the King, that piece of Forth Feasting had been his owne.

7. He esteemeth John Done the first poet in the World, in some things: his verses of the Lost Chaine he heth by heart; and that passage of the Calme, That dust and feathers doe not stirr, all was so quiet. Affirmeth Done to have written all his best pieces ere he was 25 years old.

A Visitor's Impression of Edinburgh, 6 June 1634

SIR WILLIAM BRERETON

Fifteen years after the Privy Council strenuously tried to make the capital cleaner, the English Puritan and soldier Sir William Brereton arrived, and was unimpressed. Reaching the city late at night 'because of the foot-boy's negligences', he was forced to put up in a 'mean and nasty lodging', which may explain some of his revulsion and bad temper. The rest was, it seems, the fault of the city's disregard for hygiene.

This city is placed in a dainty, healthful pure air, and doubtless were a most healthful place to live in, were not the inhabitants most sluttish, nasty, and slothful people. I could never pass through the hall, but I was constrained to hold my nose; their chambers, vessel, linen and meat, nothing neat. But very slovenly; only the nobler and better sort of them brave, well-bred men, and much reformed. This street, which may indeed deserve to denominate the whole city, is always full thronged with people, it being the market-place, and the only place where the gentlemen and merchants meet and walk, wherein they may walk dry under foot though there hath been abundance of rain. Some few coaches are here to be found for some of the great lords and ladies, and bishops . . .

The sluttishness and nastiness of this people is such, that I cannot omit the particularizing thereof, though I have more than sufficiently often touched upon the same: their houses, and halls, and kitchens, have such a noisome taste, a savour, and that so strong, as it doth offend you so soon as you come within their wall; yea, sometimes when I have light from my horse, I have felt the distaste of it before I have come into the house; yea, I never came to my own lodging in Edenborough, or went out, but I was constrained to hold my nose, or to use wormwood, or some such scented plant.

Their pewter, I am confident, is never scoured; they are afraid it should too much wear and consume thereby; only sometimes, and that but seldom, they do slightly rub them over with a filthy dish-clout, dipped in the most sluttish greasy water. Their pewter pots, wherein they bring wine and water, are furred within, that it would loathe you to touch anything which comes out of them. Their linen is as sluttishly and slothfully washed by women's feet, who, after their linen is put into a great, broad, low tub of water, then (their clothes being tucked up above their knees) they step into the tub and tread it, and trample it with their feet (never vouchsafing a hand to nett or wash it withal) until it be sufficiently cleansed in their apprehensions, and then it looks as nastily as ours doth when it is put unto and designed to the washing, as also it doth so strongly taste and smell of lant [smoke] and other noisome savours, as that when I came to bed I was constrained to hold my nose and mouth together. To come into their kitchen, and to see them dress their meat, and to behold the sink (which is more offensive than any jakes [privy]) will be a sufficient supper, and will take off the edge of your stomach.

The National Covenant, 1638

JOHN LIVINGSTONE

The signing of the National Covenant in 1638 and, in 1643, the Solemn League and Covenant, were critical events in the evolution of Scottish religious and political history. When Charles I imposed the Book of Common Prayer on Scotland, fears about the Anglicization of Scotland came to a head. This prompted the formulation in 1638 of an updated version of the Covenant of 1581, which made it clear that the Scottish Kirk rejected the concept of the divine right of kings, and would not tolerate the merest whiff of papacy in its worship. It is estimated that over 300,000 signed the Covenant of 1638. When they were declared rebels, Covenanters held outdoor services, with lookouts posted to watch for informants. John Livingstone, a staunch Covenanter whose views caused him lifelong trouble, had served with the Scottish army during the civil wars in Ireland and England. He was one of the small party of commissioners who went to Holland to negotiate with Charles II in 1649. Since Presbyterianism was not legalized until 1690, he died in exile in Rotterdam. Here he describes his risky journey to sympathizers in London with the National Covenant, and its reception in Scotland.

Throughout the summer of 1637 I had as much work in preaching in public and devotions in private as at any time before, partly in Lanark and partly in the west, and at Communions at various places, and in the Stewartry of Kircudbright and the Presbytery of Stranraer while I was waiting at the port for my wife to arrive from Ireland. This summer several ministers of Scotland were charged with letters of horning to buy and receive the Service book which stirred up great emotions throughout the land. Apart from a disturbance in Edinburgh begun by some of the common people at the first reading of the Service book the true rise of that blessed reformation in Scotland began with two petitions against the Service book, one from the west and the other from Fife, which met together at the Council door in Edinburgh, the one now knowing the other.

After that on the 20 September a great many petitions from several parts were presented against the Service book; these being denied by the king the number of the petitioners and their demands increased for they desired not only exemption from the Service book but from the five ceremonies of Perth and the High Commission Court, and these things being denied they at last also asked for freedom from episcopacy and a free parliament and General Assembly. When these things were still denied, and their number had so increased that in a way they were the whole body of the land and considering that the lords' controversy with them was the breach of Covenant, in the beginning of March 1638, they renewed the national Covenant which had formerly been sworn several times by the authority of king and parliament. I was immediately sent to go swiftly to London with several copies of the Covenant and letters to friends at Court of both nations; to avoid discovery I rode in a gray coat and a gray Montero cape.

One night riding late, the horse and I fell to the ground where I lay for about a quarter of an hour as if dead . . . Yet it pleased the Lord that I recovered, and got to Ferrybrigs where after a day or two's stay I came to London. But one of my eyes and part of my cheek being bloodshot I did not go out, but Mr Eleasar Borthwick delivered the letters for me. Some friends and some of the English nobility came to my chamber to be told how matters went, and told that the Marquess of Hamilton had sent him to me to report that he had overheard the king saying, I was arrived, but he would endeavour to put a pair of fetters about my feet, at which, fearing to be waylaid on the main road, I bought a horse, and came home by St Albans and the wester way.

I was present at Lanark and at several other parishes when on a Sabbath after the forenoon sermon the Covenant was read and sworn, and may truly say that in all my life, except one day in the kirk of Shotts I never saw such motions from the Spirit of God, all the people generally and most willingly concurring where I have seen above a thousand people all at once lifting up their hands, and the tears dropping down from their eyes, so that through the whole land except the professed papists and some few who for base ends adhered to the prelates, the people univer-sally entered into the Covenant of God for reformation of religion against prelates and ceremonies.

[modified version, see Appendix XIII, p. 446]

The Battle of Dunbar, 3 September 1650

OLIVER CROMWELL

At the Battle of Dunbar Oliver Cromwell's Puritan army faced Scottish Coven-anting troops outraged by the execution of Charles I. The encounter turned into such a cruel and unnecessary rout that historian Thomas Carlyle dubbed it the Dunbar Drove. Cromwell's army was ill, hungry and in a far inferior position, but the Covenanting clergy urged their commander General David Leslie to abandon his stand on the top of Doon Hill, and thus led their men into disaster. As well as those killed, ten thousand or more were taken prisoner and suffered appalling conditions as they were marched south or shipped abroad. Cromwell wrote to Parliament the day after the battle to inform them of the outcome of the battle.

For the Honourable William Lenthal, Speaker of the Parliament of England, These.
Dunbar, 4th September, 1650

Sir . . .

We having tried what we could to engage the Enemy, three or four miles West of Edinburgh; that proving ineffectual, and our victual failing, – we marched towards our ships for a recruit of our want. The Enemy did not at all trouble us in our rear; but marched the direct way towards Edinburgh, and partly in the night and morning slips-through his whole Army; and quarters himself in a posture easy to interpose between us and our victual. But the Lord made him to lose the opportunity. And the morning proving exceeding wet and dark, we recovered, by that time it was light, a ground where they could not hinder us from our victual: which was an high act of the Lord's Providence to us. We being come into the said ground, the Enemy marched into the ground we were last upon; having no mind either to strive to interpose between us and our victuals, or to fight; being indeed upon this 'aim of reducing us to a' lock, – hoping that the sickness of your Army would render their work more easy by the gaining of time. Whereupon we marched to Musselburgh, to victual, and to ship away our sick men; where we sent aboard near five-hundred sick and wounded soldiers.

And upon serious consideration, finding our weakness so to increase, and the Enemy lying upon his advantage, – at a general council it was thought fit to march to Dunbar, and there to fortify the Town. Which (we thought), if anything, would provoke them to engage. As also, That the having of a Garrison there would furnish us with accommodation for our sick men, 'and' would be a good Magazine, – which we exceedingly wanted; being put to depend upon the uncertainty of weather for landing provisions, which many times cannot be done though the being of the whole Army lay upon it, all the coasts from Berwick to Leith having not one good harbour. As also, To lie more conveniently to receive our recruits of horse and foot from Berwick.

Having these considerations, – upon Saturday, the 30th of August, we marched from Musselburgh to Haddington. Where, by that time we had got the van-brigade of our horse, and our foot and train, into their quarters, the Enemy had marched with that exceeding expedition that they fell upon the rear-forlorn of our horse, and put it in some disorder; and indeed had like to have engaged our rear-brigade of horse with their whole Army, – had not the Lord by His providence put a cloud over the Moon, thereby giving us opportunity to draw off those horse to the rest of our Army. Which accordingly was done without any loss, save of three or four of our aforementioned forlorn; wherein the Enemy, as we believe, received more loss.

The Army being put into a reasonable secure posture, – towards midnight the Enemy attempted our quarters, on the west end of Haddington: but through the goodness of God we repulsed them. The next morning we drew into an open field, on the south side of Haddington; we not judging it safe for us to draw to the Enemy upon his own ground, he being prepossessed thereof; – but rather drew back, to give him way to come to us, if he had so thought fit. And having waited about the space of four or five hours, to see if he would come to us; and not finding any inclination in the Enemy so to do, – we resolved to go, according to our first intendment, to Dunbar.

By that time we had marched three or four miles, we saw some bodies of the Enemy's horse draw out of their quarters; and by that time our carriages were gotten near Dunbar, their whole Army was upon their march after us. And indeed, our drawing back in this manner, with the addition of three new regiments added to them, did much heighten their confidence, if not presumption and arrogancy. – The Enemy, that night, we perceived, gathered towards the Hills; labouring to make a perfect interposition between us and Berwick. And having in this posture a great advantage, – through his better knowledge of the country, he effected it: by sending a considerable party to the strait Pass at Copperspath; where ten men to hinder are better than forty to make their way . . .

The Enemy lying in the posture before mentioned, having those advantages; we lay very near him, being sensible of our disadvantages; having some weakness of flesh, but yet consolation and support from the Lord himself to our poor weak faith, wherein I believe not a few amongst us stand: That because of their numbers, because of their advantages, because of their confidence, because of our weakness, because of our strait, we were in the Mount, and in the Mount the Lord would be seen; and that He would find out a way of deliverance and salvation for us: – and indeed we had our consolations and our hopes.

Upon Monday evening, – the Enemy's whole numbers were very great; about Six-thousand horse, as we heard, and Sixteen-thousand foot at least; ours drawn down, as to sound men, to about Seven-thousand five-hundred foot, and Three-thousand five-hundred horse, – 'upon Monday evening,' the Enemy drew down to the right wing about two-thirds of their left wing of horse. To the right wing; shogging [moving] also their foot and train much to the right; causing their right wing of horse to edge down towards the sea. We could not well imagine but that the Enemy intended to attempt upon us, or to place themselves in a more exact condition of interposition. The Major-General and myself coming to the Earl Roxburgh's House, and observing this posture, I told him I thought it did give us an opportunity and advantage to attempt upon the Enemy. To which he immediately replied, That he had thought to have said the same thing to me. So that it pleased the Lord to set this apprehension upon both of our hearts, at the same instant. We called for Colonel Monk, and shewed him the thing: and coming to our quarters at night, and demonstrating our apprehensions to some of the Colonels, they also cheerfully concurred.

We resolved therefore to put our business into this posture: That six regiments of horse, and three regiments and an half of foot should march in the van; and that the Major-General, the Lieutenant-General of the horse, and the Commissary-General, and Colonel Monk to command the brigade of foot, should lead on the business; and that Colonel Pride's brigade, Colonel Overton's brigade, and the remaining two regiments of horse should bring up the cannon and rear. The time of falling-on to be by break of day; – but through some delays it proved not to be so; 'not' till six o'clock in the morning.

The Enemy's words was, *The Covenent*; which it had been for divers days. Ours, *The Lord of Hosts*. The Major-General, Lieutenant-General Fleetwood, and Commissary-General Whalley, and Colonel Twistleton, gave the onset; the Enemy being in a very good posture to receive them, having the advantage of their cannon and foot against our horse. Before our foot could come up, the Enemy made a gallant resistance, and there was a very hot dispute at sword's point between our horse and theirs. Our first foot, after they had discharged their duty (being overpowered with the Enemy), received some repulse, which they soon recovered. For my own regiment, under the command of Lieutenant-Colonel Goffe and my Major, White, did come seasonably in; and, at the push of pike, did repel the stoutest regiment the Enemy had there, merely with the courage the Lord was pleased to give. Which proved a great amazement to the residue of their foot; this being the first action between the foot. The horse in the meantime did, with a great deal of courage and spirit, beat back all oppositions; charging through the bodies of the Enemy's horse, and of their foot; who were, after the first repulse given, made by the Lord of Hosts as stubble to their swords. – Indeed, I believe I may speak it without partiality: both your chief Commanders and others in their several places, and soldiers also, acted with as much courage as ever hath been seen in any action since this War. I know they look not to be named; and therefore I forbear particulars.

The best of the Enemy's horse being broken through and through in less than an hour's dispute, their whole Army being put into confusion, it became a total rout: our men having the chase and execution of them near eight miles. We believe that upon the place and near about it were about Three-thousand slain. Prisoners taken: of their officers, you have this enclosed List; of private soldiers near Ten-thousand. The whole baggage and train taken, wherein was good store of match, powder and bullet; all their artillery, great and small, – thirty guns [cannons]. We are confident they have left behind them not less than Fifteen-thousand arms. I have already brought in to me near Two-hundred colours, which I herewith send you. What officers of theirs of quality are killed, we yet cannot learn; but yet surely divers are: and many men of quality are mortally wounded, as Colonel Lumsden, the Lord Libberton and others. And, that which is no small addition, I do not believe we have lost twenty men. Not one Commission Officer slain as I hear of, save one Cornet; and Major Rooksby, since dead of his wounds; and not many mortally wounded: – Colonel Whalley only cut in the handwrist, and his horse (twice shot) killed under him; but he well recovered another horse, and went on in the chase . . .

A Good Use for the Plantations, 1665

REGISTER OF THE PRIVY COUNCIL

This request to the Privy Council for authority to ship beggars and other undesirables such as prostitutes and gypsies out of sight shows what some Scots thought, not only of social outcasts but also of the newly colonized plantations in the West Indies.

Supplication by George Hutcheson, merchant in Edinburgh, for himself and in name and behalf of his copartners, merchants of the ship bounding for Jamaica and Barbados, as follows: Out of a desire to promote the Scottish and English plantations in Jamaica and Barbados for the honour of their country, as well as to free the kingdom of the burden of many strong and idle beggars, Egyptians, common and notorious whores and thieves and other dissolute and loose persons banished or stigmatized for gross crimes, they have been by former acts of Council authorized to seize upon such persons and transport them to the said plantations; and though of late they have by warrant from the sheriffs, justices of peace and magistrates by burghs where the said persons haunt, apprehends some of them, yet without authority of the Council they may meet with some opposition in this good work. The Lords, having considered the petition, grant warrant to the petitioned to transport all such persons delivered to them by the magistrates, providing always that you bring the said persons before the Lord Justice Clerk, to whom it is hereby recommended to try and take notice of the persons that they be justly convicted for crimes or such vagabonds as by the laws of the country may be apprehended to the effect the country may be disburdened of them.

Murder of Archbishop Sharp, 3 May 1679

JAMES RUSSELL

James Sharp, Archbishop of St Andrews, was particularly loathed by radical Covenanters for having switched loyalties at the time of the Restoration and thus reneging on his belief in the need to get rid of all trappings of Church hierarchy. He had seriously compromised himself, as they saw it, by accepting a bishopric, and would have to pay the price for his betrayal. This account of his murder on Magus Muir is by James Russell, one of his murderers. We join the story when the nervous group of conspirators are told that the Archbishop's coach has been spied.

... whereupon all the 9 rode what they could to Magusmuir, the hills at the nearest, and Andrew Henderson riding afore, being best mounted, and saw them when he was on the top of the hill, and all the rest came up and rode very hard, for the coach was driving hard; and being come near Magus, George Fleman and James Russell riding into the town, and James asked at the goodman if that was the bishop's coach? He fearing, did not tell, but one of his servants, a woman, came running to him and said it was the bishop's coach, and she seemed to be overjoyed; and James riding towards the coach, to be sure, seeing the bishop looking out at the door, cast away his cloak and cried, Judas be taken!

The bishop cried to the coachman to drive; he firing at him, crying to the rest to come up, and the rest throwing away their cloaks except Rathillet, . . . fired into the coach driving very fast about half a mile, in which time they fired several shots in at all parts of the coach, and Alexander Henderson seeing one Wallace having a cock'd carrabine going to fire, gript him in the neck, and threw him down and pulled it out of his hand. Andrew Henderson outran the coach, and stroke the horse in the face with his sword; and James Russell coming to the postiling [postilion], commanded him to stand, which he refusing, he stroke him on the face and cut down the side of his shine, and striking at the horse next brake his sword, and gripping the ringeses [harness] of the foremost horse in the farthest side: George Fleman fir'd a pistol at the north side of the coach beneath his left arm, and saw his daughter dight of the furage [brush off the wad (of a gun)]; and riding forward, gripping the horses' bridles in the nearest side and held them still, George Balfour fired likewise, and James Russell got George Fleman's sword and lighted of his horse, and ran to the coach door, and desired the bishop to come forth, Judas.

He answered, he never wronged a man: James declared before the Lord that it was no particular interest, nor yet for any wrong that he had done to him, but because he had betrayed the church as Judas, and had wrung his hands these 18 or 19 years in the blood of the saints, but especially at Pentland . . . and they were sent to execute his vengeance on him this day, and desired him to repent and come forth; and John Balfour on horseback said, Sir, God is our witness that it is not for any wrong thou hast done to me, nor yet for any fear of what thou could do to me, but because thou has been a murderer of many a poor soul in the kirk of Scotland, and a betrayer of the church, and an open enemy and persecutor of Jesus Christ and his members, whose blood thou hast shed like water on the earth, and therefore thou shalt die! And fired a pistol; and James Russell desired him again to come forth and make him for death, judgement, and eternity; and the bishop said, Save my life, and I will save all yours.

James answered, that he knew it was not in his power either to save or to kill us, for there was no saving of his life, for the blood that he had shed was crying to heaven for vengeance on him, and thrust his shabel [rusty old sword] at him. John Balfour desired him again to come forth, and he answered, I will come to you, for I know you are a gentleman and will save my life; but I am gone already, and what needs more? And another told him of keeping up of a pardon granted by the king for 9 persons at Pentland, and then at the back side of the coach thrust a sword at him, threatening him to go forth; whereupon he went forth, and falling upon his knees, said, For God's sake, save my life; his daughter falling on her knees, begging his life also. But they told him that he should die, and desired him to repent and make for death.

Alexander Henderson said, Seeing there has been lives taken for you already, and if ours be taken it shall not be for nought; he rising of his knees went forward, and John Balfour stroke him on the face, and Andrew Henderson stroke him on the hand and cut it, and John Balfour rode him down; whereupon he, lying upon his face as if he had been dead, and James Russell hearing his daughter say to Wallace that there was life in him yet, in the time James was disarming the rest of the bishop's men, went presently to him and cast of his hat, for it would not cut at first, and haked his head in pieces.

Having thus done, his daughter came to him and cursed him, and called him a bloody murderer; and James answered they were not murderers, for they were sent to execute God's vengeance on him; and presently went to the coach, and finding a pair of pistols, took them, and then took out a trunk and brake it up, and finding nothing but women's furniture, asked what should be done with it; and it was answered, that they would have nothing but papers and arms; and Andrew Henderson lighted, and took a little box and brake it up, and finding some papers, which he took; and opening a cloak-bag they found more papers and a Bible full of porterers [portraits], with a little purse hung in it, a copper dollar, two pistol ball, two turners, two stamps, some coloured thread, and some yellow coloured thing like to pairings of nails, which would not burn, which they took.

At this time James Russell was taking the rest of his men's arms, and Wallace, as he would have resisted, came roundly forward, and James Russell smote him on the cheek with his shabel and riped all their pockets, and got some papers and a knife and fork, which he took; and crying to the rest to see that the bishop be dead, William Danziel lighted, and went and thrust his sword into his belly, and the dirt came out; turning him over, ript his pockets, and found a whinger and knifes conform, with some papers, which he took. James Russell desired his servants to take up their priest now.

The Battle of Killiecrankie, 27 July 1689

THE EARL OF BALCARRES

This was the first significant Jacobite rising, and was followed by more than a half century of abortive attempts to bring James II and VII or his heirs back to the throne. On hearing of the expulsion of James and his replacement with William of Orange, and of the government's plan to set up a garrison in Inverlochy, Viscount Dundee, John Graham of Claverhouse, gathered his supporters and prepared for confrontation. The Government's men were led by General Hugh Mackay, who met them at the narrow pass of Killiecrankie in Perthshire. Dundee was killed in the action and although the victory lay with his party, both sides suffered dreadful losses. Colin, the third Earl of Balcarres, tells the story in a letter to James.

As the Viscount was marching to Atholl, Major-General Cannon arrived from Ireland; he brought about three hundred new-raised men with him. Their arrival had been seasonable if two accidents had not happened, which made their coming do the Viscount more prejudice than all the good could be expected from so few men; he had been often promised by the Earl of Melfort, that a considerable body should be sent over, both of horse and foot, with ammunition and all other necessaries, which they were in great want of, (insomuch that many of the best gentlemen who had followed him for many weeks had seen neither bread, salt, or drink, except water;) instead of this hope from Ireland, the Clans saw all their expectations reduced to this three hundred men, who were in as great misery as themselves, which discouraged them extremely; next, the loss of some provisions, as beer, cheese, &c., which was coming to them in ships, which General Cannon detained so long at Mull, that an English frigate came and took them. But, notwithstanding all these discouragements, the Viscount resolved to secure the Castle of Blair, and, about the end of July, marched down to Atholl.

When he came to the Castle of Blair, he called a Council of War, having intelligence that Mackay was entering by the narrow pass of Killicrankie into that country. Many of the Clans and other officers were for maintaining that pass, because they thought not themselves strong enough to encounter him, and as their general rendezvous was to be in two days, when they should become considerably stronger. But the Viscount convinced them that, in all appearance, they never could have so fair an opportunity, Mackay having then only two troops of horse with him, but, if they delayed, he would soon bring up all the English horse and dragoons, which the Highlanders of all things most fear. This determined them, and it was resolved to suffer Mackay to enter the pass, and to fight him with half his number, rather than stay till his cavalry had joined him. Mackay, having entered the pass without resistance, formed his army, of above four thousand men, upon a plain, having a small river in his rear, upon the further side of which he placed his baggage.

The Viscount of Dundee encamped upon a heath the night before the battle, and was desirous, before so bold an undertaking, to have some symptoms that his Highlanders (after so long a peace) still retained the courage of their ancestors, so manifest upon former occasions. For this end, while his men slept in their plaids, near the break of day, he caused a loud alarm be made the enemy was at hand. The Highlanders instantly were roused, threw away their plaids, seized their arms, and ran to the front of their camp, drew up into order, then calmly stood, expecting the enemy. When the Viscount perceived this, and that not a man of them had retired, with full assurance he instantly began his march to meet the enemy. When he came to a height that overlooked the plain where Mackay was, he was much pleased to observe them drawn up in but one line, and without any reserve; he assured his men they should beat them if they observed his orders.

The posture of the enemy made him change the order of his battle; he formed his small army, of near two thousand, into three divisions, deep in file, with large intervals between them, that he might not be outflanked by Mackay, who was more than double his number, and of veteran troops. Having completed his disposition, which took some time, in the afternoon he marched down to the attack. The Highlanders suffered their fire with courage, – then, when nearer them, delivered their own, and with sword and targe rapidly broke through their line and fell upon their flanks and rear, so that, in a moment, the whole intervals of this extended front gave way and fled. The Viscount put himself at the head of his small body of horse; Sir William Wallace had produced a commission from your Majesty, that morning, to command them, to the great mortification of the Earl of Dunfermline, and even of others who thought themselves injured, yet had that respect for your service that no dispute was made at so critical a time. The Viscount advanced to attack their cannon, but thought Sir William advanced too slowly; he called them to march, but Sir William not being so forward, the Earl of Dunfermline and some others left their ranks and followed the Viscount; with these he took their cannon before the rest came up.

When he observed the foot beaten and horse fled, he rode towards a body of Macdonalds in the rear, intending to make use of them to attack the regiments of Hastings and Leven, who were retiring unbroken from not being fronted; but unhappily, while doing this, he was, by a distant shot, mortally wounded; he attempted to return, but fell from his horse. – Although the Highlanders had acted with order and intrepidity, yet unluckily, when they came to the enemies' baggage, it stopped their pursuit, and lost them part of the fruits of their victory, for Mackay and these two regiments got off, – yet many of them were killed next day by the Atholl men, as they were repassing at Killiecrankie.

General Mackay fled to Stirling, and arrived the next day, with not above two hundred of his army; he had two thousand men killed upon the field, and near five hundred made prisoners. The victory was complete, but, I must own, your Majesty's affairs were undone by the irreparable loss of the Viscount of Dundee. Your friends who knew him best were in doubt if his civil or military capacities were most eminent. None of this nation so well knew the different interests, tempers, and inclinations of the men most capable to serve you; none had more the ability to insinuate and persuade; he was extremely affable, and, although a good manager of his private fortune, yet had no reserve when your service and his own reputation required him to be liberal, which gained him the hearts of all who followed him, and brought him into such reputation, that, had he survived that day, in all probability he had given such a turn to your affairs, that the Prince of Orange could neither have gone nor sent into Ireland, so your Majesty had been entirely master of that kingdom, and in a condition to have landed with what forces you pleased in Scotland, which of all things your friends most desired.

The Massacre of Glencoe, 13 February 1692

A GENTLEMAN IN SCOTLAND

Fear of Jacobites plotting against him led William of Orange to demand an oath of allegiance from the leaders of all the clans in the Highlands. The chief of the Macdonalds left it late to take his oath and missed by a day the deadline of 1 January 1692. The King decided to make an example of him, but as the following letters show, Macdonald had played into his hands by giving him the excuse he had been looking for. The massacre – of thirty-eight, to which were added forty women and children who died of exposure – caused outrage throughout Britain, and later that year a piece of protest propaganda was published, offering a colourful description of what had happened, and demanding justice, which was never done.

Extracts from Letters of the Master of Stair:

2 December 1691 (to the Earl of Breadalbane)

. . . I think the clan Donell must be rooted out, and Lochiel. Leave the McLeans to Argyll . . . God knows whether the 12,000 l. sterling had been better employed to settle the Highlands, or to ravage them; but, since we will make them desperate, I think we should root them out before they can get that help they depend upon . . .

3 December 1691 (to Lt-Col. Hamilton, the subordinate to Hill at Fort William)

. . . The McDonalds will fall in this net. That's the only popish clan in the kingdom, and it will be popular to take severe course with them. Let me hear from you with the first whether you think that this is the proper season to maul them in the cold long nights, and what force will be necessary . . .

11 January 1692 (to Sir Thomas Livingston, Commanding in the Highlands)

. . . Just now, my Lord Argile tells me that Glenco hath not taken the oaths, at which I rejoice, it's a great work of charity to be exact in rooting out that damnable sect, the worst in all the Highlands . . .

Extracts from the King's instructions:

11 January 1692 (to Sir Thomas Livingston)
Sic supra scribitur, William R

1. You are hereby ordered and authorized to march our troops, which are now posted at Inverlochy and Inverness, and to act against these Highland rebels who have not taken the benefit of our indemnity, by fire and sword,

and all manner of hostility; to burn their houses, seiz [sic] or destroy their goods
or cattell, plenishing or cloaths, and to cutt off the men . . .

4. . . . If McKean or Glencoe, and that tribe, can be well separated from the
rest, it will be a proper vindication of the publick justice to extirpate that sect
of thieves . . .

A Letter from a Gentleman in Scotland to his friend at London, who desir'd a Particular Account of the Business of Glenco.

Edinburgh April 20 1692
Sir

The Account you desir'd of that strange and surprising Massacre of Glenco,
take as follows: – Mac-jan Mac-donald, Laird of Glenco, a Branch of the
Mackdonalds, one of the greatest Clans (or Tribes) in the North of Scotland,
came with the most considerable Men of his Clan to Coll. Hill, Governour of
Fort William at Inverlochy, some few days before the Expiring of the time for
receiving the Indemnity appointed by Proclamation, which as I take it, was the
First of January last, entreating he would administer unto him the Oaths which
the foresaid Proclamation requir'd to be taken; that so submitting himself to
the Government, he might have its Protection. The Colonel receiv'd him with
all Expressions of Kindness; nevertheless shifted the administring the Oaths to
him, alledging that by the Proclamation it did not belong to him, but to the
Sheriffs, Bailyffs of Regalities, and Magistrates of Burghs, to administer them.
Mac-jan Complaining that by this Disappointment he might be wrong'd, the
Time being now near the Expiring, and the Weather so extreme, and the ways
so very bad, that it was not possible for him so soon to reach any Sheriff, &c,
got from Coll. Hill, under his Hand, his Protection; and withal he was assur'd,
that no Orders from the Government against him should be put in Execution,
until he were first advertis'd, and had time allow'd him to apply himself to King
or Council for his Safety. But the better to make all sure (tho' this might have
seem'd Security enough for that time) with all dispatch imaginable he posted
to Inverary, the Chief Town of Argyleshire, there he found Sir Collin Campbell
of Arakinlis, Sheriff of that Shire, and crav'd of him the Benefit of the Indemnity,
according to the Proclamation, he being willing to perform all the Conditions
requir'd. Sir Collin at first scrupled to admit him to the Oaths, the Time which
the Proclamation did appoint being elapsed by one day, alledging it would be
of no use to him then to take them: But Mac-jan represented that it was not
his Fault, he having come in time enough to Colonel Hill, not doubting but

he could have administred the Oaths to him, and that upon his refusal he had made such hast [sic] to Inverary, that he might have come in time enough, had not the extremity of the Weather hinder'd him; and even as it was, he was but one day after the Time appointed; and that would be very unbecoming the Government to take Advantage of a Man's coming late by one Day, especially when he had done his utmost to have come in time. Upon this, and his threatening to protest against the Sheriff for the Severity of this Usage, he administred to him and his Attendants the Oaths, Mac-jan depending upon the Indemnity granted to those who should take them; and having so done, he went home, and lived quietly and peaceably under the Government, till the day of his Death.

In January last, a Party of the Earl of Argile's Regiment came to that Country: the Design of their coming was then suspected to be to take course with those who should stand out, and not submit, and take the Oaths. The Garison of Inverlochy being throng'd, and Glenco being commodious for quartering, as being near that Garison, those Soldiers were sent thither to Quarter; they pretended they came to extract Arrears of Cess and Hearth-Money . . . e'er they entred Glenco, that Laird, or his Sons, came out to meet them, and asked them if they came as Friends or as Enemies? The Officers answer'd as Friends, and gave their Paroll of Honour, that they would do neither him nor his Concerns any harm; upon which he welcom'd them, promising them the best Entertainment the Place could afford. This he really performed, as all the Soldiers confess. He and they lived together in mutual Kindness and Friendship fifteen days or thereabouts; so far was he from fearing any Hurt from them. And the very last Day of his Life he spent in keeping Company with the Commander of that Party, Capt. Campbell of Glenlyon, playing at Cards with him till 6 or 7 at Night, and at their parting mutual Protestations of Kindness were renew'd. Some time that very day, but whether before or after their parting, I know not, Capt. Campbell had these Orders sent him from Major Duncanson, a Copy whereof I here send you.

Ballacholis, Feb 12. 1692

Sir

You are hereby ordered to fall upon the Rebels the Mac-Donalds of Glenco, and put all to the Sword under 70. You are to have especial Care, that the Old Fox and his Sons do upon no account escape your Hands; You are to secure all the Avenues, that no Man escape; This you are to put in Execution at five a Clock in the Morning precisely, and by that time or very shortly after it, I'll strive to be at you with a stronger Party; If I do not come to you at five, you are not to tarry for me, but to fall on. *This is by the King's SPECIAL COMMAND*, for the Good and Safety of the Country that these Miscreants may be cut off, Root and Branch. See that this be put in Execution without Feud or Favour, else you may expect to be Treated as not true to the King or Government, nor a Man fit to carry Commission in the King's Service. Expecting you will not fail in the fulfilling hereof, as you love your self. I subscribe these with my Hand,

Robert Duncanson.
For Their Majesties Service, to Capt. Robert Campbell of Glenlyon.

[. . .]

The soldiers being disposed five or three in a House, according to the Number of the Family they were to Assassinate, had their Orders given them secretly. They had been all receiv'd as Friends by these poor People, who intended no Evil themselves, and little suspected that their Guests were design'd to be their Murtherers. At 5 o'Clock in the Morning they began their bloody work, Surpris'd and Butcher'd 38 Persons, who had kindly receiv'd them under their Roofs. Mac-jan himself was Murther'd, and is much bemoaned; He was a stately well-favour'd Man, and of good Courage and Sense: As also the Laird Archintrikin, a Gentleman of more than ordinary Judgment and Understanding, who had submitted to the Government, and had Coll. Hill's Protection in his Pocket, which he had got three Months before. I cannot without Horror represent how that a Boy about Eight Years of Age was murthered; he seeing what was done to others in the House with him, in a terrible Fright ran out of the House, and espying Capt. Campbell, grasp'd him about the Legs, crying for Mercy, and offering to be his Servant all his Life. I am informed Capt. Campbell inclined to spare him; but one Drummond, an Officer, barbarously ran his Dagger through him, whereof he died immediately. The rehearsal of Several Particulars and Circumstances of this Tragical Story, makes it appear most doleful; as that Mac-jan was killed as he was drawing on his Breeches, standing before his Bed, and giving Orders to his Servants for the good Entertainment of those who murthered him; While he was speaking the Words, he was shot through the Head, and fell dead in his Ladies Arms, who through the Grief of this and other bad Usages she met with, died the next day. It is not to be ommitted, that most of these poor People were killed when they were asleep, and none was allowed to pray to God for Mercy. Providence ordered it so, that that Night was most boisterous; so as a Party of 400 Men, who should have come to the other End of the Glen, and begun the like work there at the same Hour, (intending that the poor Inhabitants should be enclosed, and none of them escape) could not march at length, until it was 9 o'Clock, and this afforded to many an Opportunity of escaping, and none were killed but those in whose Houses Campbell and Glenlyon's Men were Quartered, otherwise all the Males under 70 Years of Age, to the number of 200, had been cut off, for that was the Order; and it might have been easily executed, especially considering that the Inhabitants had no Arms at that time; for upon the first hearing that the Soldiers were coming to the Glen, they had conveyed them all out of the way: For though they relyed on the promises which were made them for their Safety; yet they thought it not improbable that they might be disarmed. I know not whether to impute it to difficulty of distinguishing the difference of a few Years, or to the fury of the Souldiers, who being once glutted with Blood, stand at nothing, that even some above Seventy Years of Age were destroyed. They set all the Houses on Fire, drove off all the Cattle to the Garison of Inverlochy, Viz. 900 Cows, 200 Horses, and a great many Sheep and Goats, and there they were divided amongst the Officers. And how dismal may you imagine the Case of the poor Women and Children was then! It was lamentable, past expression; their Husbands and Fathers, and near Relations were forced to flee for their Lives; they themselves almost stript, and nothing left them, and their Houses being burnt, and not one House nearer than six Miles; and to get thither they were to pass over Mountains, and Wreaths of Snow, in a vehement Storm, wherin the greatest part of them perished through Hunger and Cold. It fills me with horror to think of poor stript Children and Women, some with Child, and some giving Suck, wrestling against a Storm in Mountains, and heaps of Snow, and at length to be overcome, and give over, and fall down and die miserably.

You see . . . in Duncanson's Order to Capt. Campbell of Glenlyon, That the old Fox nor none of his Sons escape; but notwithstanding all this wicked Caution, it pleas'd God that the two young gentlemen, Mac-jan's Sons escap'd: For it happen'd that the younger of these Gentlemen trusted little to the fair promises of Campbell, and had a more watchful eye over him than his Father or Brother, who suffered themselves by his reiterated Oaths to be deluded into a belief of his Integrity: He having a strong Impression on his Spirit, that some mischievous Design was hidden under Campbell's specious Pretences, it made him, after the rest were in Bed, remain in a retired Corner, where he had an advantageous Prospect into their Guard. About midnight perceiving several Souldiers to enter it, this encreased his Jealousy; so he went and communicated his fears to his Brother, who could not for a long time be persuaded there was any bad Design against them, and asserted, That what he had seen, was not a doubling their Guards in order to any ill design, but that being in a strange place, and at a distance from the Garison, they were to send out Centinels far from the Guard, and because of the Extremity of the Weather relieved them often, and the Men he saw could be no more but these. Yet he persisting to say, That they were not so secure, but that it was fit to acquaint their Father with what he had seen, he prevailed with his Brother to rise, and go with him to his Father who lay in a Room contiguous to that they were in. Though what the younger Son alledged made no great Impression on his Father, yet he allowed his Sons to try what they could discover. They well knowing all Skulking places there, went and hid themselves near to a Centinel's Post, where instead of one they discovered eight or ten Men; this made them more inquisitive, so they crept as near as they could without being discovered, so near that they could hear one say to his Fellows, That *he liked not this Work, and that had he known of it he would have been very unwilling to have come there; but that none, except their Commanders, knew of it until within a quarter of an hour.* The Soldier added, That he was willing to fight against the Men of the Glen, but it was base to murder them. But to all this was answered, *All the blame be on such as gave the Orders; we are free, being bound to obey our Officers.* Upon hearing of these words the young Gentlemen retired as quickly and quietly as they could towards the House, to inform their Father of what they had heard, but as they came nigh to it, they perceived it surrounded, and heard Guns discharged, and the People shrieking; whereupon, being unarm'd, and totally unable to rescue their Father, they preserved their own Lives in hopes yet to serve their King and Country, and see Justice done upon those Hell-Hounds, treacherous Murtherers, the Shame of their Country, and Disgrace of Mankind.

I must not forget to tell you, That there were two of these officers who had given their Paroll of Honour to Mac-jan, who refused to be concerned in that Brutal Tragedy, for which they were sent Prisoners to Glasco [Glasgow], where if they remain not still, I am sure they were some Weeks ago.

Thus, Sir, in obedience to your Commands, I have sent you such Account as I could get of that monstrous and most inhuman Massacre of the Laird of Glenco, and others of his Clan. You desire some Proofs of the truth of the Story; for you say there are many in England who cannot believe such a thing could be done, and publick Justice not executed upon the Ruffians: For they take it for granted that no such order could be given by the Government; and you say they will never believe it without a downright Demonstration . . . But to put you out of all doubt, you will e'er long have my Lord Argyle's Regiment with you in London, and there you may speak with Glenlyon himself, with Drummond and the rest of the Actors in that dismal Tragedy; and on my life, there is never a one of them will deny it to you; for they know that it is notoriously known all over Scotland, and it is an Admiration to us that there should be any one in England who makes the least doubt of it. Nay, Glenlyon is so far from denying it, that he brags of it, and justifies the Action publicly: He said in the Royal Coffee-House in Edinburgh, that he would do it again; nay, That he would stab any man in Scotland or in England, without asking the Cause, if the King gave him Orders, and that it was every good Subject's duty so to do; and I am credibly inform'd, that Glenlyon and the rest of them have address'd themselves to the Council for a Reward for their good Service in destroying Glenco, pursuant to their Orders.

There is enough of this mournful subject: If what I have said satisfy you not, you may have what farther Proof, and in what manner you please to ask it, Sir

Your Humble Servant, &c,

A Gael's View of the Islands, 1695

MARTIN MARTIN

A Gaelic-speaker from Skye, where he was factor to MacLeod of MacLeod, Martin Martin wrote a colourful and detailed travelogue, Description of the Western Islands of Scotland, *which combined his interest in the people and their customs with a clear-sighted scientific outlook. It's said that this book was the inspiration for Dr Johnson's trip to the Highlands and Islands, on the grounds that 'No man now writes so ill as Martin's account of the Hebrides is written.' What he lacks in Johnson's wit and style, Martin gains in his lack of prejudice. These are a handful of his descriptions, drawn from the islands.*

Island of Lewis
Illnesses and cures

They are generally of a sanguine constitution: this place hath not been troubled with epidemical diseases, except the small-pox, which comes but seldom, and then it sweeps away many young people. The chin-cough afflicts children too: the fever, diarrhoea, dysentery, and the falling down of the uvula, fevers, jaundice and stitches, and the ordinary coughs proceeding from cold are the diseases most prevalent here. The common cure used for removing fevers and pleurisies, is to let blood plentifully

... When the uvula falls down, they ordinarily cut it, in this manner – They take a long quill, and putting a horsehair double into it, make a noose at the end of the quill, and putting it about the lower end of the uvula, they cut off from the uvula all that is below the hair with a pair of scissors; and then the patient swallows a little bread and cheese, which cures him. This operation is not attended with the least inconvenience, and cures the distemper so that it never returns. They cure green wounds with ointment made of golden-rod, all-heal, and fresh butter. The jaundice they cure two ways – the first is by laying the patient on his face, and pretending to look upon his backbones, they presently pour a pail-full of cold water on his bare back; and this proves successful. The second cure they perform by taking the tongs, and making them red-hot in the fire; then pulling off the clothes from the patient's back, he who holds the tongs gently touches the patient on the vertebrae upwards of the back, which makes him furiously run out of doors, still supposing the hot iron is on his back, till the pain be abated, which happens very speedily, and the patient recovers soon after.

Whisky

In Lewis their plenty of corn was such as disposed the natives to brew several sorts of liquors, as common usquebaugh [whisky], another called trestarig, *id est, acqua vitae* [a strong spirit] three times distilled, and this by the natives is called usquebaugh baul, *id est*, usquebaugh which at first taste affects all the members of the body. Two spoonfuls of this last is a sufficient dose, and if any man exceed this, it would presently stop his breath and endanger his life. The trestarig and usquebaugh baul are both made of oats.

Island of Harris
Rats

I have seen a great many rats in the village Rowdil, which became very troublesome to the natives, and destroyed all their corn, milk, butter, cheese, etc. They could not extirpate these vermin for some time by all their endeavours. A considerable number of cats was employed for this end, but were still worsted, and became perfectly faint, because overpowered by the rats, who were twenty to one. At length one of the natives, of more sagacity than his neighbours, found an expedient to renew his cat's strength and courage, which was by giving it warm milk after every encounter with the rats; and the like being given to all the other cats after every battle, succeeded so well, that they left not one rat alive, notwithstanding the great number of them in the place.

Island of St Kilda

One of the inhabitants of St Kilda, being some time ago wind-bound in the isle of Harris, was prevailed on by some of them that traded to Glasgow to go thither with them. He was astonished at the length of the voyage, and of the great kingdoms, as he thought them, that is isles, by which they sailed; the largest in his way did not exceed twenty-four miles in length, but he considered how much they exceeded his own little native country.

Upon his arrival at Glasgow, he was like one that had dropped from the clouds into a new world, whose language, habit, &c., were in all respects new to him; he never imagined that such big houses of stone were made with hands; and for the pavements of the streets, he thought it must needs be altogether natural, for he could not believe that men would be at the pains to beat stones into the ground to walk upon. He stood dumb at the door of his lodging with the greatest admiration; and when he saw a coach and two horses, he thought it to be a little house they were drawing at their tail, with men in it; but he condemned the coachman for a fool to sit so uneasy, for he thought it safer to sit on the horse's back. The mechanism of the coach wheel, and its running about, was the greatest of all his wonders.

When he went through the streets, he desired to have one to lead him by the hand. Thomas Ross, a merchant, and others, that took the diversion to carry him through the town, asked his opinion of the High Church? He answered that it was a large rock, yet there were some in St Kilda much higher, but that these were the best caves he ever saw; for that was the idea which he conceived of the pillars and arches upon which the church stands. When they carried him into the church, he was yet more surprised, and held up his hands with admiration, wondering how it was possible for men to build such a prodigious fabric, which he supposed to be the largest in the universe. He could not imagine what the pews were designed for, and he fancied the people that wore masks (not knowing whether they were men or women) had been guilty of some ill thing, for which they dared not show their faces. He was amazed at women wearing patches, and fancied them to have been blisters. Pendants seemed to him the most ridiculous of all things; he condemned periwigs mightily, and much more the powder used in them; *in fine*, he condemned all things as superfluous he saw not in his own country.

He looked with amazement on every thing that was new to him. When he heard the church bells ring he was under a mighty consternation, as if the fabric of the world had been in great disorder. He did not think there had been so many people in the world as in the city of Glasgow; and it was a great mystery to him to think what they could all design by living so many in one place. He wondered how they could all be furnished with provision; and when he saw big loaves, he could not tell whether they were, bread stone, or wood. He was amazed to think how they could be provided with ale, for he never saw any there that drank water. He wondered how they made them fine clothes, and to see stockings made without being first cut, and afterwards sewn, was no small wonder to him. He thought it foolish in women to wear thin silks, as being a very improper habit for such as pretended to any sort of employment. When he saw the women's feet, he judged them to be of another shape than those of the men, because of the different shape of their shoes. He did not approve of the heels of shoes worn by men or women; and when he observed horses with shoes on their feet, and fastened with iron nails, he could not forbear laughing, and thought it the most ridiculous thing that ever fell under his observation. He longed to see his native country again, and passionately wished it were blessed with ale, brandy, tobacco and iron, as Glasgow was.

Famine, 1698

PATRICK WALKER

Towards the end of the seventeenth century seven years of bad weather and failed crops resulted in a famine so severe that a fifth of the Scots population – about 200,000 people – were reduced to begging. The death toll was staggering. Some believed the country had been cursed because of the persecution of the Covenanters, others that they were being punished because James VII had been ousted from the throne. The writer Patrick Walker recorded the scene.

These not unheard-of manifold Judgements continued seven Years, not always alike, but the Seasons, *Summer* and *Winter*, so cold and barren, and the wonted Heat of the Sun so much withholden, that it was discernible upon the Cattle, flying Fowls and insects decaying, that seldom a Fly or Gleg was to be seen: Our Harvests not in the ordinary Months; many shearing in *November* and *December*, yea, some in *January* and *February*; The Names of the Places I can instruct: Many contracting their Deaths, and losing the use of their Feet and Hands sharing and working amongst it in Frost and Snow; and after all some of it standing still, and rotting upon the Ground, and much of it for little Use either to Man or Beast, and which had no Taste or Colour of Meal.

Meal became so scarce, that it was at Two Shillings a Peck, and many could not get it. It was not then with many, *Where will we get Silver?* But, *Where will we get Meal for Silver?* I have seen, when Meal was all sold in Markets, Women clapping their Hands, and tearing the Clothes off their Heads, crying, *How shall we go home and see our Children die in Hunger? They have got no Meat these two Days, and we have nothing to give them.*

Through the long Continuance of these manifold Judgements, Deaths and Burials were so many and common, that the Living were wearied in the Burying of the Dead. I have seen Corpses drawn in Sleds, many got neither Coffin nor Winding-sheet . . .

The Darien Venture, 25 December 1699

REVEREND ARCHIBALD STOBO

The disastrous Darien expedition was one of the lowest points of Scottish economic and political history. So much money was lost that the country faced ruin, and its vulnerability hastened calls for a union with England, which followed in 1707. The Company of Scotland Trading to the Indies and Africa, better known as the Scottish Darien Company, had promised prosperity by opening up trade with central America and Africa. Raising £400,000 for the scheme, which accounted for about half of the accessible capital in Scotland, the Company set sail to stake out its first post, on the Darien coast on the Panama isthmus. Five ships carrying 1,200 Scots landed in November 1698, but by the summer of the following year they had fled, 300 already dead, 150 more to die as they made for home or America. They had faced hostile Spanish colonists, English neighbours who were forbidden to trade with them, and above all chronic illness and lack of provisions.

Shortly after the first settlers had fled, a second fleet arrived, bringing food and manpower, swiftly followed by a third and final party. On board this last arrival, on a ship called the Rising Sun, *was the Reverend Archibald Stobo, one of four ministers in the party. He had left Scotland on 20 August 1699, and arrived to discover that the rumours about the desertion of the colony, and the conditions faced, had been all too true. Stobo later deserted the* Rising Sun *in Carolina, and never returned to Scotland.*

. . . Upon the 20 day [of October] we came within the tropicks, where each one that had never passed the tropicks, according to the custom of those that goe unto the East or West Indies payed ther bottle of brandie & pound of sugar, which proved fatall to some through ther excessive drinking. Upon the 9 November we discovered land which was very refreshing unto us (being out of sight of it for six weeks). The islands were these, Antego possessed by the English, Monserat possessed by the same, Rockdundo [Redonda] possessed by none, Navis possessed by the English also. Our Counsellors thought it fitt to wreat [write] from Monserat unto the Directors & other kynd frinds in Scotland to let them know of our preservatione & safety hitherto, and since they were going ashore upon this account, they thought it convenient to carry along some casks to bring aboard some fresh water. The Governor by noe means would suffer them to bring one bottle of water telling them he was discharged to give any aid or assistance to the Scots Collony, but there being some particular gentlemen upon that island which were intimately acquaint with some of owr officers which went ashore entertained them kyndly & complemented them with some oranges, rum and sugar & lykways told them the Collony was deserted & dispersed themselves among the Dutch, France and English plantations which was not at all beleeved by us.

Having passed all these islands we saw noe more land until the 18 of this instant that we discovered the land of Carthagine upon the coasts of America about 50 leagues from Darien. Upon the 17 of this instant, it pleased the Lord to call Mr Allexander Dallgleish one of the ministers who dyed on the 15 day of his sickness, being ane hecktick fever. And the self same day we lost the *Litle Hope* in the night tyme & did not sie her until the 26 day. Upon the 27 [possibly 29] day, ther came two indians aboard of us in one of ther canows, we were very kind unto them & keeped them aboard all night, but we could not well understand them . . .

Upon the last day of November we arrived in Calledonia Bay; wher instead of being comforted after owr long voage we mett with greater sound of sorrow then ever hitherto, finding the Collony deserted & owr country men gone. But by the good providence of God ther was two English sloupes here, one from New England in which was Capt Thomas Drumond, one of the late Councellors, & some of owr country men which had come along with him expecting to meet us heir. The other from Jamaica which he mett with by the way & perswaded to come heir with him from whom he [we] got ane account of the Collony's desertions, both tyme & reasons. The tyme of its desertions was upon the 20 day of June 1699. The reasons whereof (as Capt Drumond said) was (1) great sickness, having noemen to work. (2) want of provisione. (3) never from the tyme of ther aryvall heir hearing any word from Scotland, for all the letters they had sent. (4) The threatned invasione of the Spaniards, which is owr own case at present. (5) The great divisione that fell among the Counsellors which gave occasione of many inconveniencies amongst themselves & to the Collony, such as seasing upon the ships &c., but was severall tymes prevented until they came all at length to goe togither. He gave us ane account of the ships also. One of them called the *Snow* [it was actually the *Dolphin*] was lost upon this coast. The *St Andrew* was gone to Jamaica and as some say was arrested ther for debt. The *Unicorn* and *Calledonia* were at New England. The *Unicorn* was outerly disabled for goeing to sea, & the *Calledonia* was bound for Scotland. These two sloups were lodden with provisione, which owr Councellors bought, together with the Jamaica sloup.

There were also 5 men heir which came with Jamieson's ship and Stark's, who gave us account what was become of these two ships & the men. They landed heir about the 10 of August 1699. Jamieson's ship was brunt heir in this bay, the wrack of which is to be seen to this day. Her burning was occasioned by a whore which Jamiesone had brought along with him, she making a complaint of his Mait unto him, who had the charge of drawing the oyl, brandy &c. Jamieson caused lay him in confinemen[t], then the couper had his charge, and being one night when he was drawing brandy, he lets the candle fall among the brandy, but all their might could not quench it, so ship and provisions were all lost, but no men. It is said he thought to have brunt Stark's ship also. When his ship was on fyre he cut her cables & sett her straight upon Stark's wher she was rideing. But he escaped with great difficulty. Mr Starck went unto Jamaica wher the officers sold ther men (as it is said) at a very base rate for sugar & brandy &c. This in short about those that were before us.

As for our selvs, the day after owr landing, which was the first of December 1699, Scots colours was sett up wher owr men had been, which was done with great solemnity, shutting of guns, drinking &c. Then after that ther was a generall court called both of Counsellars & officers to sie if they would resettle the place, and after much consultatione it was voted resettle. Then ther was ane account taken of the provisions which came to about 6 moneths provisione at sharp allowance, each man half pund of bread, as much of beef and the third part of a gill of brandy per diem, and the want of provisione made them send away with the ships all the men that were thought unfit for work. The sharp allowance & word of sending some away to Jamaica occasioned a ploatt designed by some to sease upon the provissions & the ships, then to make the best of ther way for ther own hands. This was tymously discovered, and one of the men was hanged upon the 20 of December 1699. At this executione the first peece of worship was performed ashoar in Calledonia by the ministers. The last day of December, being the Sabbath, was the first day of preaying ashoar, and, upon the Wednesday after, we had a Fast and Thanksgiving in one. If ther come not speedy recreets from Scotland we will be obleidged to desert the place as those before us did, owr provisions ar both scarcer then was expected & growen very bade, which occasions much sicness unto owr men.

As for the place & country wher we are, it is very comodius for fortificatione but not soe good for plantatione . . . The neck that owr Collony is settled upon is full of litle hills except a litle peece wher the fort is made, and this is not fit for planting, it being very marishy ground, & full of crabs that destroyes all that is planted in it. Besydes, it is thought to be very unwholsome for people's health. Ther is noe kynd of fruit in this place for use unless we goe 3 or 4 miles in the countrey into the indians' plantations. Ther indeed is a very pleasant countrey & such fruits as the countrey yields such as plantines, bonanes, potates &c. and befor owr people can get them it costs them twice ther worth. Ther is a great deall of fowls, wild hogs, munkies &c. in this place but very ill to get, it being such a woody place & noe passage can be had through these woods unless we fall upon a small foot road made by the indians, and this is very rare to find. In short it may be called a countrey of wonders . . .

There are exceeding great thunderings & lightenings & showers that comes doun almost lyke whole water. This is the only temperall tyme in the year. But they say from the latter end of March untill the first of December it is always great heat & rain . . .

As for the nativs, they are a very insignificant people, both for poverty & paucity. They provyde nothing but for the present tyme. They live in fruits they hav in ther plantations . . . & now & then shuts a fowl or a wild hogg, and that they hing above ther fire till it be as tastles as a widered loaf [leaf?]. This is all the mens' work; the women makes the meal ready & spins some cotine and barks of tress to be hangmakes to ly in, which they ty betwixt two trees & this is all ther beds. They have noe cloaths but what they have gott & does get from owr people, only the women hat a bit brale [?brate, an apron] of ther own making wrapt about their middle. Ther women are very modest . . .

They are a very greedy & covetous people, especially of linnen cloath. They have a very strange language & difficule. Some words of it scarce any man would be able to get letters for expressing it. They are & which is most of all lyke to learn, & hes already learned, of owr people wicked ways. When anything angers or offends them, they will say God dam you for a son of a bich.

Ther were about ane 160 men dyed upon the voage besyds what hath dyed since we came heir . . .

Upon the first day of the new year the drums were allowed to go through the gentlemen's hutts ashore for the new year's gift, & after that they came aboard of the ships & being all drunk with the brandy they had got, when they came to owr ship two of them fell overboard, one of which perished cursing & swearing most hardily.

The Run-up to the Union of the Scottish and English Parliaments, 1707

DANIEL DEFOE, STIRLING TOWN COUNCIL AND GEORGE LOCKHART OF CARNWATH

It was widely believed at the time that a handful of landed and affluent Scots took Scotland into a Union of Parliaments with England purely for their own advantage. Even though it has since proved to have been a mainly benign and often beneficial political twinning for Scotland as well as England, the Union remains a painful subject in certain quarters, and some nationalists still gnaw over its bones. What is not in doubt is that there was an unprecedented degree of popular opposition to it in the months leading up to it, a wave of well-argued dissent – and some mob activity – that the authorities ought to have taken into consideration.

The writer and government agent Daniel Defoe was sent by the English parliament to act as a spy in Scotland in the run-up to the Union of the Parliaments. His role was to mingle widely, in disguise, and urge the Scots to back the proposal, which he genuinely thought would benefit their country as well as his own. He was taken aback to discover the strength of feeling against the proposed merger, as witnessed here in Edinburgh.

I had not been Long There but I heard a Great Noise and looking Out Saw a Terrible Multitude Come up the High street with A Drum at the head of Them shouting and swearing and Cryeing Out all Scotland would stand together, No Union, No Union, English Dogs, and the like.

I Can Not Say to you I had No Apprehensions, Nor was Monsr *De Witt* quite Out of my Thoughts [the Dutch statesman had been killed by a mob in The Hague], and perticulary when a part of This Mob fell upon a Gentleman who had Discretion little Enough to say something that Displeased them just Undr my Window.

He Defended himself bravely and Call'd Out lustily also for help to the Guard who being within Hearing and Ready Drawn up in Close Ordr in the street, advanc't, Rescued the Gentleman, and took the person he was Grappld with prisoner.

The City was by this time in a Terrible fright. The Guards were Insulted and stoned as they stood, the Mob put out all the lights, no body could stir in the streets, and not a light be seen in a windo' for fear of stones.

A petition from Stirling Town Council against the proposed Union is typical of the widespread civic outcry.

18 November 1706

To His Grace Her Majesties high Commissioner and the Estates of Parliament. The Address of the provost Baillies Town Councill and other Inhabitants of the Burgh of Stirling.
Humbly Sheweth

That having deliberated upon the great affair of the union of the two nations, as contained in the printed articles, we judged it our indispens- able duty to the nation, to this place, indeed to posterity, with all imaginable deference to your Grace and Honourable Estates of parliament humbly to represent, That although we desire that true peace and friendship be perpetually Cultivated with our neighbours in England . . ., yet we judge your going into this treaty as it now lies before you will bring an insupportable burden of taxations upon this land, which all the grants of freedom of trade will never counterbalance being so uncertain and precarious while still under the regulations of the English in the parliament of Britain, who may if they please discourage the most considerable branches of our trade, if any way considered to interfere with their own.

That it will prove ruinous to our manufacturers, that it will expose our religion, church government as established by law, our claim of right, laws, liberties and consequently all that's valuable. To be encroached upon, indeed wholly subverted by them, whose principles do, and supposed interest may lead thereunto, that it will deprive us and the rest of the royal burghs in this nation, in a great measure of our fundamental right of being represented in the legislative power, that thereby one of the most ancient nations so long and so gloriously defended by our worthy patriots will be suppressed. Our parliament is the very hedge of all that is dear to us, extinguished and we and our posterity brought under a lasting yoke which we will never be able to bear, the fatal consequences of which we tremble to think upon . . .

[modified version, see Appendix XIV, p. 447]

Jacobite and anti-Unionist George Lockhart of Carnwath describes the scene in Edinburgh in 1706 during the final debates on the Union.

During this time . . . the Parliament Close and the Outer Parliament House were crowded every day when the Parliament was met, with an infinite number of people, all exclaiming against the Union and speaking very free concerning the promoters of it: the Commissioner [Queensberry] as he passed along the street was cursed and reviled to his face, the Duke of Hamilton [official leader of the National or Federal Party] huzza'd and convoyed every night with a great number of apprentices and younger sort of people from the Parliament House to the Abbey, exhorting him to stand by the country, and assuring him of his being supported. And before the 23rd of October, above three or four hundred of them, being thus employed, did as soon as they left His Grace hasten in a body to the house of Sir Patrick Johnston (their late

darling Provost, one of the Commissioners of the Treaty, a great pro-
moter of the Union in Parliament, where he sat as one of the representatives of the town of Edinburgh), threw stones at his windows, broke
open his doors, and searched his house for him, but he having narrowly
escaped prevented his being torn in a thousand pieces. From thence the
mob, which was increased to a great number, went through the streets,
threatening destruction to all the promoters of the Union, and continued
for four or five hours in this temper, till about three next morning a
strong detachment of the Foot Guards was sent to secure the gate called
the Netherbow Port, and keep guard in the Parliament Close. 'Tis not
to be expressed how great the consternation was that seized the Courtiers
on this occasion. Formerly they did, or pretended, not to believe the
disposition of the people against the Union: but now they were
thoroughly convinced of it, and terribly afraid of their lives, this passage
making it evident that the Union was crammed down Scotland's throat.
For not only were the inclinations of the elder and wiser known by the
actions of the rasher and younger, but even the very soldiers, as they
marched to seize the Port, were heard to say to one another, 'Tis hard
we should oppose those that are standing for the country, 'tis what we
can't help just now, but what we won't continue at. The mob being
once despatched, guards of regular forces were placed in the Parliament
Close, Weighhouse, and Netherbow Port, and the whole army, both
horse and foot, was drawn together near Edinburgh, and continued so
all the session of Parliament: nay, the Commissioner (as if he had been
led to the gallows) made his parade every day after this from the Parliament House to the Cross (where his coach waited him) through two
lanes of musketeers, and went from thence to the Abbey, the Horse
Guards surrounding his coach, and if it was dark, for the greater security
a part of the Foot Guards likewise . . .

The Government were not fond of any such amusements, and therefore the next day after it happened, the Privy Council met and ordained
those guards to be continued, and emitted a proclamation against
tumultous meetings, wherein they commanded all persons to retire off
the street whenever the drum should beat and give warning, ordered
the guards to fire upon such as would not obey, [and] granted an
indemnity to such as should upon that occasion kill any of the lieges . . .
The Courtiers, being deadly afraid of their bones, gave no ear to decency,
reason, or justice, but pressed a vote, and the motion was approved . . .
yet His Grace was constantly saluted with curses and imprecations as he
passed through the streets, and if the Parliament sat till towards evening,

then to be sure he and his guards were all well pelted with stones . . . so that often he and his retinue were obliged to go off at a top gallop and in great disorder.

A Jacobite Escapes from the Tower of London, 23 February 1716

THE COUNTESS OF NITHSDALE

The 1715 Jacobite Rising, following the accession of George I, was led by the disaffected Earl of Mar and had so much popular support in Scotland it ought to have succeeded. It did not, however, and before the Old Pretender had even landed in Scotland, events had been sealed by the inconclusive Battle of Sheriffmuir on 13 November, when the inept Mar's vastly larger contingent were held at bay by the king's men. One of the defeated rebels was William Maxwell, fifth Earl of Nithsdale, who was captured at Preston and sent to the Tower of London to await his execution, which was scheduled for 24 February 1716. In a letter to her sister, his doughty wife Winifred describes how she carried out an audacious plan for his escape after learning that of all the prisoners, her husband was the one for whom there was no hope of reprieve.

I immediately left the House of Lords, and hastened to the Tower, where, affecting an air of joy and satisfaction, I told all the guards I passed by, that I came to bring joyful tidings to the prisoners. I desired them to lay aside their fears, for the petition had passed the House in their favour. I then gave them some money to drink to the Lords and his Majesty, though it was but trifling; for I thought, that if I were too liberal on the occasion, they might suspect my designs, and that giving them something would gain their good humour and services for the next day, which was the eve of the execution.

The next morning I could not go to the Tower, having so many things in my hands to put in readiness; but in the evening, when all was ready, I sent for Mrs Mills, with whom I lodged, and acquainted her with my design of attempting my Lord's escape, as there was no prospect of his being pardoned; and this was the last night before the execution. I told her that I had everything in readiness, and I trusted that she would not refuse to accompany me, that my Lord might pass for her. I pressed her to come immediately as we had no time to lose. At the same time I sent for Mrs Morgan, usually known by the name of Hilton, to whose acquaintance my dear Evans [the Countess's maid] had introduced me, which I looked upon as a very singular happiness. I immediately communicated my resolution to her. She was of a very tall and slender make, so I begged her to put under her own riding-hood, one that I had prepared for Mrs Mills, as she was to lend her's to my Lord, and that in coming out he might be taken for her. Mrs Mills was then with child; so that she was not only of the same height, but nearly of the same size as my Lord. When they were in the coach, I never ceased talking, that they might have no leisure to reflect. Their surprise and astonishment, when I first opened my design to them, had made them consent, without ever thinking of the consequences. On our arrival at the Tower, the first I introduced was Mrs Morgan; for I was only allowed to take in one at a time. She brought in the clothes that were to serve Mrs Mills, when she left her own behind her. When Mrs Morgan had taken off what she had brought for my purpose, I conducted her back to the staircase; and, in going, I begged her to send me in my maid to dress me; and that I was afraid of being too late to present my last petition that night if she did not come immediately. I despatched her safe, and went partly down stairs to meet Mrs Mills, who had the precaution to hold her handkerchief to her face, as was very natural for a woman to do when she was going to bid her last farewell to a friend on the eve of his execution. I had indeed desired her to do it, that my Lord might go out in the same manner. Her eye-brows were rather inclined to be sandy, and my Lord's were dark and very thick; however, I had prepared some paint of the colour of her's to disguise his with. I also brought an artificial head-dress of the same coloured hair as her's; and I painted his face with white and his cheeks with rouge, to hide his long beard, as he had not time to shave. All this provision I had before left in the Tower.

The poor guards, whom my slight liberality the day before had endeared to me, let me go quietly with my company, and were not so strictly on the watch as they usually had been; and the more so, as they were persuaded, from what I had told them the day before, that the prisoners would obtain their pardon. I made Mrs Mills take off her own hood, and put on that which I had brought for her; I then took her by the hand and led her out of my Lord's chamber; and in passing through the next room, in which there were several people, with all the concern imaginable, I said, 'My dear Mrs Catherine, go in all haste, and send me my waiting maid; she certainly cannot reflect how late it is; she forgets that I am to present a petition tonight, and, if I let slip their opportunity

I am undone, for tomorrow will be too late. Hasten her as much as possible, for I shall be on thorns till she comes.'

Every body in the room, who were chiefly the guards' wives and daughters, seemed to compassionate me exceedingly, and the sentinel very officiously opened the door to me. When I had seen her out, I returned back to my Lord, and finished dressing him. I had taken care that Mrs Mills did not go out crying, as she came in, that my Lord might better pass for the Lady who came in crying and afflicted, and the more so, because he had the same dress she wore. When I had almost finished my dressing my Lord in all my petticoats, excepting one, I perceived that it was growing dark, and was afraid that the light of the candles might betray us, so I resolved to set off; I went out leading him by the hand, and he held his handkerchief to his eyes; I spoke to him in the most piteous and afflicted tone of voice, bewailing bitterly the negligence of Evans who had ruined me by her delay.

Then said I, 'My dear Mrs Betty, for the love of God run quickly, and bring her with you; you know my lodging, and if ever you made dispatch in your life, do it at present; I am almost distracted with this disappointment.' The guards opened the doors, and I went down stairs with him, still conjuring him to make all possible dispatch. As soon as he had cleared the door, I made him walk before me, for fear the sentinel should take notice of his walk, but I still continued to press him to make all the dispatch he possibly could.

At the bottom of the stairs, I met my dear Evans, into whose hands I confided him. I had before engaged Mr Mills to be in readiness, before the Tower, to conduct him to some place of safety, in case we succeeded. He looked upon the affair so very improbable to succeed, that his astonishment, when he saw us, threw him into such consternation, that he was almost out of himself, which Evans perceiving, with the greatest presence of mind, without telling him any thing, lest he should mistrust them, conducted him to some of her own friends, on whom he could rely, and so secured him, without which we should have been undone. When she had conducted him, and left him with them, she returned to find Mr Mills, who, by this time, had recovered himself from his astonishment. They went home together, and, having found a place of security, they conducted him to it.

In the mean while, as I had pretended to have sent the young lady on a message, I was obliged to return up stairs and go back to my Lord's room, in the same feigned anxiety of being too late, so that every body seemed sincerely to sympathize with my distress. When I was in the room, I talked to him, as if he had been really present, and answered my own questions in my Lord's voice, as nearly as I could imitate it. I walked up and down, as if we were conversing together, till I thought they had time enough thoroughly to clear themselves of the guards. I then thought proper to make off also.

I opened the door, and stood half in it, that those in the outward chamber might hear what I said, but held it so close, that they could not look in. I bid my Lord a formal farewell for that night, and added, that something more than usual must have happened to make Evans negligent on this important occasion, who had always been so punctual in the smallest trifles; that I saw no other remedy than to go in person; that, if the Tower were still open when I finished my business, I would return that night; but that he might be assured I would be with him as early in the morning as I could gain admittance into the Tower, and I flattered myself I should bring favourable news.

Then, before I shut the door, I pulled through the string of the latch, so that it could only be opened on the inside. I then shut it with some degree of force, that I might be sure of its being well shut. I said to the servant as I passed by, who was ignorant of the whole transaction, that he need not carry in candles to his master till my Lord sent for him, as he desired to finish some prayers first. I went down stairs, and called a coach. As there were several on the stand, I drove home to my lodgings, where poor Mr Mackenzie had been waiting to carry the petition, in case my attempt had failed. I told him there was no need of any petition, as my Lord was safe out of the Tower, and out of the hands of his enemies, as I hoped; but that I did not know where he was . . .

Manners, 1720

REVEREND ADAM PETRIE

A minister who had spare time on his hands because he was for a long period without a charge, Adam Petrie wrote a manual of manners as a guide for young people. On the subject of seemly conduct, he believed that 'Art corrects what is bad, and helps to perfect what is good; without which a Man is clownish in every Thing he sets about.' He took manners very seriously indeed, suggesting that, as seen in one example he offers, they could be a matter of life and death.

If one be sleeping in the Fields, you are not to go near him, except he be your Acquaintance, lest some hath been before you that hath exercised too much familiarity with his Pocket, and you be suspected by him. If you pass by one easing Nature, you should turn your Face another Way, and should not so much as notice him. If you can evite [avoid] passing by him, it is better.

If you be to travel in a Coach, let your Superiors enter first; and when you enter, take the worst Place. . . . If you are about to travel on Horseback, let your Superiors be first mounted, and the Inferiors should first dismount to be ready to give Assistance.

In travelling keep a little behind your Superior; if your Station be such as that you may ride up with him, then place yourself on his left Hand; and if there be three in Company, let the next eminent Person place himself on his right Hand, and the other on the left. If he be to pass a River where there may be Danger, go first; and if after, keep some Distance from him, that so you may not dirty him.

It is civil not to sit too long in a Room with Ladies, and to leave them a little after they have come off a Journey, or when they are to take a Journey: Neither is it convenient to suffer them to ride too far, and not to have Access to be alone; for if there be no Houses on the Way, then they may cause them light at some Place where they may conveniently retire from the Company, that so they may have their own Freedom; tho I am not for Men's shewing them the Reason of making them light, for this would put them to the Blush. Some such Expression may be used, as, *Let us allow the Horses to breath a little.* I have heard of a modest Lady, who in riding with an inconsiderate Person lost her Life . . .

Do not smell at what you eat or drink; and it is most rude to do it to what another eats or drinks . . .

If it be enquired what you are for? you must answer, *What you please.* If there be Ladies, let them have a Share of all that's presented. If a Lady with Child long for any thing, she may frankly desire the same (but modestly) wherever she is; for some have smarted severely for their Folly . . .

Make no Noise with your Spoon or Knife. It is rude to suck your Meat out of the Spoon with an ungratefull Noise.

Do not bite your Bread into Pieces, nor Fruit, &c. but cut or break the same: Neither must you keep your Knife always in your Hand.

It is indecent to fill the Mouth too full; such cramming is more suitable to a Beast than a rational Creature.

Put not both your Hands to your Mouth at once. Be sure to throw nothing in the Floor, 'tis uncivil and disobliging . . .

It is clownish to pick the Shells of an Egg with your Fingers: Pair it with your Knife. It is little better to pick out an Egg from the Shell with Bread.

Do not lick your Fingers, nor dirty your Napkin.

If you have occasion to wipe your Nose, or the Sweat from your Face, hold up your Napkin betwixt you and the Company, and do it with as little Noise as possible with your Handkerchief. To wipe the Nose or Sweat of the Face with a Table Napkin is most rude . . .

Be sure to wipe your Mouth before you drink, and when you drink hold in your Breath till you have done. I have seen some colour the Glass with their Breath, which is certainly very loathsome to the Company to think that they must drink out of the same Glass . . .

It is unbecoming in Church to have their Eyes running hither and thither. It shows an unstable Heart. Nor must you move your Body in an unseemly Manner.

It is rude to laugh, sleep, or whisper others in the Ear in Time of divine Worship, or in Time of Sermon.

It is rude to come to Church in a gawdy Dress. A grave decent Apparel is most suitable for the House of GOD. I do not plead but that Persons may be arranged according to their Rank and Station; but that they should not have a light Dress, such as bare shoulders and bare Breasts, or any Thing that is indecent.

It is uncivil for Persons to seek out the weak Places of a Sermon to expose the Preacher. This is no Sign of Piety or Wit.

The Aftermath of the Union of Parliaments, 1723

DANIEL DEFOE

Fifteen or so years after the Union of Parliaments, Daniel Defoe travelled through Scotland and concluded that the influence of the Union of Parliaments following on from the Union of Crowns, had not been as universally beneficial as he had expected. His picture of Kirkudbright illustrates his point.

I take the decay of all these seaport towns, which 'tis evident have made a much better figure in former times, to be owing to the removing of the Court and nobility of Scotland to England: for it is most certain, when the Court was at home, they had a confluence of strangers, residence of foreign ministers, being of armies, etc., and consequently their nobility dwelt at home [and] spent the means of their estates and the product of their country among their neighbours. The return of their coal and salt and corn and fish brought them in goods from abroad, and perhaps money. They sent their linen and other goods to England, and received the return in money: they made their own manufactures, and though not so good or cheap as from England, yet they were cheaper to public stock, because their own poor were employed. Their wool which they had over and above went to France, and returned ready money. Their lead went to Holland, and their cattle and sheep to England, and brought back in that one article over £100,000 per annum.

Then it was the seaport towns had a trade, their Court was magnificent, their nobility built fine houses and palaces which were richly furnished and nobly finished within and without. They had infinitely more value went out than came back in goods, and therefore the balance was evidently on their side; whereas now their Court is gone, their nobility and gentry spend their time, and consequently their estates, in England. The Union opens the door to all English manufactures, and suppresses their own, prohibits their wool from going abroad, and yet scarcely takes it off at home. If the cattle go to England, the money is spent there too. The troops raised there are in English service, and Scotland receives no premio for the levies, as she might have done abroad, and as the Swiss and other nations do at this time . . .

Galloway, as I hinted before, begins even from the middle of the bridge of Dumfries; the first town on the coast, of any note, is Kirkubright [sic], or, as vulgarly call'd, Kirkubry. It must be acknowledg'd this very place is a surprize to a stranger, and especially one whose business is observation, as mine was.

Here is a pleasant situation, and yet nothing pleasant to be seen. Here is a harbour without ships, a port without trade, a fishery without nets, a people without business; and, that which is worse than all, they do not seem to desire business, much less do they understand it. I believe they are very good Christians at Kirkubry, for they are in the very letter of it, they obey the text, and are contented with such things as they have. They have all the materials for trade, but no genius to it; all the opportunities for trade, but no inclination to it. In a word, they have no notion of being rich and populous, and thriving by commerce. They have a fine river, navigable for the greatest ships to the town-key; a haven, deep as a well, safe as a mill-pond; 'tis a meer wet dock, for the little island of Ross lyes in the very entrance, and keeps off the west and north west winds, and breaks the surge of the sea; so that when it is rough without, 'tis always smooth within. But, alas! there is not a vessel, that deserves the name of a ship, belongs to it; and, though here is an extraordinary salmon fishing, the salmon come and offer themselves, and go again, and cannot obtain the privilege of being made useful to mankind; for they take very few of them. They have also white fish, but cure none; and herrings, but pickle none. In a word, it is to me the wonder of all the towns of North-Britain; especially, being so near England, that it has all the invitations to trade that Nature can give them, but they take no notice of it. A man might say of them, that they have the Indies at their door, and will not dip into the wealth of them; a gold mine at their door, and will not dig it.

It is true, the reason is in part evident, namely, poverty; no money to build vessels, hire seamen, buy nets and materials for fishing, to cure the fish when it is catch'd, or to carry it to market when it is cur'd; and this discourages the mind, checks industry, and prevents all manner of application. People tell us, that slothfulness begets poverty, and that is true; but I must add too, that poverty makes slothfulness, and I doubt not, were two or three brisk merchants to settle at Kirkubry, who had stock to furnish out ships and boats for these things, they would soon find the people as industrious, and as laborious as in other places; or, if they did not find them so, they would soon make them so, when they felt the benefit of it, tasted the sweet of it, had boats to fish, and merchants to buy it when brought in; when they found the money coming, they would soon work. But to bid men trade without money, labour without wages, catch fish to have them stink, when they had done, is all one as to bid them work without hands, or walk without feet; 'tis the poverty of the people makes them indolent.

Again, as the people have no hands (that is, no stock) to work, so the gentry have no genius to trade; 'tis a mechanism which they scorn; tho' their estates are not able to feed them, they will not turn their hands to business or improvement; they had rather see their sons made foot soldiers, (than which, as officers treat them now, there is not a more abject thing on earth), than see them apply to trade, nay, to merchandize, or to the sea, because those things are not (forsooth) fit for gentlemen.

In a word, the common people all over this country, not only are poor, but look poor; they appear dejected, and discourag'd, as if they had given over all hopes of ever being otherwise than what they are. They are, indeed, a sober, grave, religious people, and that more, ordinarily speaking, than in any other part of Scotland, far from what it is in England; conversation is generally sober, and grave; I assure you, they have no assemblies here, or balls; and far from what it is in England, you hear no oaths, or prophane words in the streets; and, if a mean boy, should be heard to swear, the next gentleman in the street, if any happen'd to be near him, would cane him, and correct him; whereas in England, nothing is more frequent, or less regarded now, than the most horrid oaths and blasphemies in the open streets, and that by the little children that hardly know what an oath means.

But this we cannot cure, and, I doubt, never shall; and in Scotland, but especially in this part of Scotland, you have none of it to cure.

The Porteous Riot, 14 April 1736

REVEREND ALEXANDER CARLYLE

At the execution of Andrew Wilson, a smuggler with whom the public had great sympathy (his crime was to steal from a customs officer), an armed guard was placed at the gibbet in the Grassmarket in Edinburgh in case of trouble. When Wilson was hanged, the gathering grew rowdy and Captain John Porteous, who led the guard, ordered his men to fire on the crowd. Around thirty were killed and wounded, and Porteous was imprisoned, tried and sentenced to death. He was reprieved at the last moment, but the mob broke into the Tolbooth prison, dragged him out, and executed their own justice. Alexander Carlyle, later minister of Inveresk, was a schoolboy at the time, and was present at the riot.

I was witness to a very extraordinary scene that happened in the month of February or March [sic] 1736, which was the escape of Robertson, a condemned criminal, from the Tolbooth Church in Edinburgh. In those days it was usual to bring the criminals who were condemned to death into that church to attend public worship every Sunday after their condemnation, when the clergyman made some part of his discourse and prayers to suit their situation; which, among other circumstances of solemnity which then attended the state of condemned criminals, had no small effect on the public mind. Robertson and Wilson were smugglers, and had been condemned for robbing a custom-house, where some of their goods had been deposited; a crime which at that time did not seem, in the opinion of the common people, to deserve so severe a punishment. I was carried by an acquaintance to church to see the prisoners on the Sunday before the day of execution. We went early into the church on purpose to see them come in, and were seated in a pew before the gallery in front of the pulpit. Soon after we went into the church by the door from the Parliament Close, the criminals were brought in by the door next the Tolbooth, and placed in a long pew, not far from the pulpit. Four soldiers came in with them, and placed Robertson at the head of the pew, and Wilson below him, two of themselves sitting below Wilson, and two in a pew behind him.

The bells were ringing and the doors were open, while the people were coming into the church. Robertson watched his opportunity, and, suddenly springing up, got over the pew into the passage that led in to the door in the Parliament Close, and no person offering to lay hands on him, made his escape in a moment – so much the more easily, perhaps, as everybody's attention was drawn to Wilson, who was a stronger man, and who, attempting to follow Robertson, was seized by the soldiers, and struggled so long with them that the two who at last followed Robertson were too late. It was reported that he had maintained his struggle that he might let his companion have time. That might be his second thought, but his first certainly was to escape himself, for I saw him set his foot on the seat to leap over, when the soldiers pulled him back. Wilson was immediately carried out to the Tolbooth, and Robertson, getting uninterrupted through the Parliament Square, down the back stairs, into the Cowgate, was heard of no more till he arrived in Holland. This was an interesting scene, and by filling the public mind with compassion for the unhappy person who did not escape, and who was the better character of the two, had probably some influence in producing what followed: for when the sentence against Wilson came to be executed a few weeks thereafter, a very strong opinion prevailed that there was a plot to force the Town Guard, whose duty it is to attend executions under the order of a civil magistrate.

There was a Captain Porteous, who by his good behaviour in the army had obtained a subaltern's commission, and had afterwards, when on half-pay, been preferred to the command of the City Guard. This man, by his skill in manly exercises, particularly the golf, and by gentlemanly behaviour, was admitted into the company of his superiors, which elated his mind, and added insolence to his native roughness, so that he was much hated and feared by the mob of Edinburgh. When the day of execution came, the rumour of a deforcement at the gallows prevailed strongly; and the Provost and Magistrates (not in their own minds very strong) thought it a good measure to apply for three or four companies of a marching regiment that lay in the Canongate, to be drawn up in the Lawnmarket, a street leading from the Tolbooth to the Grassmarket, the place of execution, in order to overawe the mob by their being at hand. Porteous, who, it is said, had his natural courage increased to rage by any suspicion that he and his Guard could not execute the law, and being heated likewise with wine – for he had dined, as the custom then was, between one and two – became perfectly furious when he passed by the three companies drawn up in the street as he marched along with his prisoner.

Mr Baillie had taken windows in a house on the north side of the Grassmarket, for his pupils and me, in the second floor, about seventy or eighty yards westward of the place of execution, where we went in due time to see the show; to which I had no small aversion, having seen one at Dumfries . . . which shocked me very much. When we arrived at the house, some people who were looking from the windows were displaced, and went to a window in the common stair, about two feet below the level of ours. The street is long and wide, and there was a very great crowd assembled. The execution went on with the usual forms, and Wilson behaved in a manner very becoming his situation. There was not the least appearance of an attempt to rescue; but soon after the executioner had done his duty, there was an attack made upon him, as usual on such occasions, by the boys and blackguards throwing stones and dirt in testimony of their abhorrence of the hangman. But there was no attempt to break through the guard and cut down the prisoner. It was generally said that there was very little, if any, more violence than had usually happened on such occasions. Porteous, however, inflamed with wine and jealousy, thought proper to order his Guard to fire, their muskets being loaded with slugs; and when the soldiers showed reluctance, I saw him turn to them with threatening gesture and an inflamed countenance. They obeyed, and fired; but wishing to do as little harm as possible, many of them elevated their pieces, the effect of which was that some people were wounded in the windows; and one unfortunate lad, whom we had displaced, was killed in the stair window by a slug entering his head . . . We had seen many people, women and men, fall on the street, and at first thought it was only through fear, and by their crowding on one another to escape. But when the crowd dispersed, we saw the lying dead or wounded, and had no longer any doubt of what had happened. The numbers were said to be eight or nine killed, and double the number wounded; but this was never exactly known.

This unprovoked slaughter irritated the common people to the last; and the state of grief and rage into which their minds were thrown, was visible in the high commotion that appeared in the multitude. Our tutor was very anxious to have us all safe in our lodgings, but durst not venture out to see if it was practicable to go home. I offered to go; went, and soon returned, offering to conduct them safe to our lodgings, which were only half-way down the Lawnmarket . . .

The sequel of this affair was, that Porteous was tried and condemned to be hanged; but by the intercession of some of the Judges themselves, who thought his case hard, he was reprieved by the Queen-Regent. The Magistrates, who on this occasion, as on the former, acted weakly, designed to have removed him to the Castle for greater security. But a plot was laid and conducted by some persons unknown with the greatest secrecy, policy, and vigour, to prevent that design, by forcing the prison the night before, and executing the sentence upon him themselves, which to effectuate cost them from eight at night till two in the morning; and yet this plot was managed so dexterously that they met with no interruption, though there were five companies of a marching regiment lying in the Canongate.

The Battle of Prestonpans, 21 September 1745

REVEREND ALEXANDER CARLYLE

The 1745 Jacobite Rebellion, led by Prince Charles Edward Stuart, the Young Pretender, started with a flourish. One of its high points was the Battle of Prestonpans, early in the campaign, when General Cope's men were annihilated. Alexander Carlyle, who was to become minister of Inveresk, was a volunteer in the militia, and took part in the city of Edinburgh's ineffectual attempts to protect the city from the advancing Jacobite army. The volunteers were not a hardy bunch. One party of dragoons were terrified into decamping by what they thought was the enemy approaching. It had, in fact, been the cries of a dragoon who had fallen into a coal-pit who made 'such a noise, as alarmed a body of men, who, for two days, had been completely panic-struck'. On the eve of the Jacobites' arrival, Edinburgh's troops camped out at Prestonpans, to await events. Carlyle slept in his father's manse at Prestonpans, eager for action the following day.

I directed the maid to awake me the moment the battle began, and fell into a profound sleep in an instant. I had no need to be awaked, though the maid was punctual, for I heard the first cannon that was fired, and started to my clothes; which, as I neither buckled nor gartered, were on in a moment, and immediately went to my father's, not a hundred yards off . . . my father had been up before daylight, and had resorted to the steeple. While I was conversing with my mother, he turned to the house, and assured me of what I had guessed before, that we were completely defeated. I ran into the garden where there was a mount in the south-east corner, from which one could see the fields almost to the verge of that part where the battle was fought. Even at that time, which could hardly be more than ten or fifteen minutes after firing the first cannon, the whole prospect was filled with runaways, and Highlanders pursuing them. Many had their coats turned as prisoners, but were still trying to reach the town in hopes of escaping. The pursuing Highlanders, when they could not overtake, fired at them, and I saw two fall in the glebe. By-and-by a Highland officer whom I knew to be Lord Elcho passed with his train, and had an air of savage ferocity that disgusted and alarmed. He inquired fiercely of me where a public-house was to be found; I answered him very meekly, not doubting but that, if I had displeased him with my tone, his reply would have been with a pistol bullet.

The crowd of wounded and dying now approached with all their followers, but their groans and agonies were nothing compared with the howlings, and cries, and lamentations of the women, which suppressed manhood and created despondency. Not long after the Duke of Perth appeared with his train, who asked me, in a very different tone, the way to Collector Cheap's, to which house he had ordered our wounded officers. Knowing the family were from home, I answered the questions of victorious clemency with more assurance of personal safety, than I had done to unappeased fury. I directed him the way to the house, which was hard by that where I had slept.

The rebel army had before day marched in three divisions, one of which went straight down the wagon-way to attack our cannon, the other two crossed the Morass near Seaton House; one of which marched north towards Port Seaton, where the field is broadest, to attack our rear, but overmarched themselves, and fell in with a few companies that were guarding the baggage in a small enclosure near Cockenzie. The main body marched west through the plains, and just at the break of day attacked our army. After firing once, they run on with their broadswords, and our people fled. The dragoons attempted to charge, under Colonel Whitney, who was wounded, but wheeled immediately, and rode off through the defile between Preston and Bankton, to Dolphingston, half a mile off. Colonel Gardiner, with his division, attempted to charge, but was only followed by eleven men, as he had foretold, Cornet Kerr being one. He continued fighting, and had received several wounds, and was at last brought down by the stroke of a broadsword over the head. He was carried to the minister's house at Tranent, where he lived till next forenoon . . . Some of the dragoons fled as far as Edinburgh, and one stood all day at the Castlegate, as General Guest would not allow him to be taken in. A considerable body of dragoons met at Dolphingston immediately after the rout, little more than half a mile from the field, where Cope joined them; and where it was said Lord Drummore offered to conduct them back, with assurance of victory when the Highlanders were busy with booty. But they could not be prevailed on by his eloquence no more than by the youthful ardour of Earls Home and Loudon. After a short halt, they marched over Falside Hill to Lauder. Sir Pater Halket, a captain in Lee's regiment, acted a distinguished part on this occasion; for after the rout he kept his company together; and getting behind a ditch in Tranent Meadow, he kept firing away on the rebels till they were glad to let him surrender on terms.

In the mean time my father became very uneasy lest I be ill treated by the rebels, as they would discover that I had been a Volunteer in Edinburgh; he therefore ordered the horses to be saddled, and telling me that the sea was out, and that we could escape by the shore without being seen, we mounted, taking a short leave of my mother and the young ones, and took the way he had pointed out. We escaped without interruption till we came to Portseton harbour, a mile off, where we were obliged to turn up on the land, when my father observing a small party of Highlanders, who were pursuing two or three carts with baggage that were attempting to escape, and coming up with the foremost driver, who would not stop when called to, they shot him on the spot. This daunted my father, who turned immediately, and took the way we came. We were back again soon after, when, taking off my boots and putting on shoes, I had the appearance of a person who had not been abroad. I then proposed to go to Collector Cheap's house, where I understood there were twenty-three wounded officers, to offer my assistance to the surgeons, Cunningham and Trotter, the first of whom I knew . . . When I went in, I told Cunningham (afterwards the most eminent surgeon in Dublin) that I had come to offer them my services, as, though no surgeon, I had better hands than a common servant. They were obliged to me; but the only service I could do to them was to try to find one of their medicine-chests among the baggage, as they could do nothing for want of instruments. I readily undertook this task, provided they would furnish me with a guard. This they hoped they could do; and knocking at the door of an inner room, a Highland officer appeared, whom they called Captain Stewart. He was good-looking, grave, and of polished manners. He answered that he would soon find a proper conductor for me, and despatched a servant with a message. In the mean time I observed a very handsome young officer lying in an easy-chair in a faint, and seemingly dying. They led me to a chest of drawers, where there lay a piece of his skull, about two fingers' breadth and an inch and a half long. I said, 'This gentleman must die.' 'No,' said Cunningham, 'the brain is not affected, nor any vital part: he has youth and a fine constitution on his side; and could I but get my instruments, there would be no fear of him.' This man was Captain Blake. Captain Stewart's messenger arrived with a fine, brisk, little, well-dressed Highlander, armed cap-a-pie with pistol, and dirk, and broadsword. Captain Stewart gave him his orders, and we set off immediately . . .

It was not long before we arrived at Cockenzie, where, under the protection of my guard, I had an opportunity of seeing this victorious army. In general they were of low stature and dirty, and of a contemptible appearance. The officers with whom I mixed were gentleman-like, and very civil to me, as I was on an errand of humanity. I was conducted to Lochiel, who was polished and gentle, and who ordered a soldier to make all the inquiry he could about the medicine-chests of the dragoons. After an hour's search, we returned without finding any of them, nor were they ever afterwards recovered. This view I had of the rebel army confirmed me in the prepossession that nothing but the weakest and most unaccountable bad conduct on our part could have possibly given them the victory. God forbid that Britain should ever again be in danger of being overrun by such a despicable enemy, for, at the best, the Highlanders were at that time but a raw militia, who were not cowards.

The Battle of Culloden, 16 April 1746

COLONEL KER OF GRADYNE

The Battle of Culloden, where the Duke of Cumberland's army demolished the Jacobite troops, marked the end of the rebellion. Thoroughly defeated, Prince Charles's supporters limped home while their leader lay low until he could be smuggled to safety. Appreciating the significance of the rebellion, Robert Forbes, a bishop of the Episcopal Church in Scotland, gathered first-hand testimony from those involved in the rising (see pages 131–3). There is considerable bias in some accounts, and also misremembering of facts, but the following account of the Battle of Culloden, by Colonel Ker of Gradyne, who was close to the Prince and was prized as a reliable witness, is thought to come very near the truth. One of the disadvantages of being an honest and unhistrionic witness, however, is that Ker's account seems strangely dull considering the events it describes.

Tuesday, being April 15th, the whole army marched up to the muir, about a mile to the eastward of Culloden House, where they were all drawn up in order of battle, to wait the Duke of Cumberland's coming. Keppoch's men joined in the field, from Fort William, and the whole was reviewed by the Prince, who was very well pleased to see them in so good spirits, though they had eaten nothing that day but one single biscuit a man, provisions being very scarce, and money too.

The Prince (being informed that the Duke of Cumberland had halted that day at Nairn, to refresh his men, and that the ships with the provisions were coming into the bay of Inverness, that evening) called a council of war; and, after great debates, (although that neither the Earl of Comarty [sic], who by this time was prisoner, though not known, nor the MacPhersons, nor a great many of the Frazers was come up,) it was resolved to march, and endeavour to surprise the Duke in his camp at Nairn, about twelve miles distance.

Accordingly, the march was begun betwixt seven and eight o'clock at night; the first column commanded by Lord George Murray, the second by the Prince. The night being dark, occasioned several halts to be made, for bringing up the rear. When about half way, Lord George Murray ordered Colonel Ker, one of the Prince's aides-de-camp, to go from front to rear, and to give orders to the respective officers to order their men to make the attack, sword in hand; which was thought better, as it would not alarm the enemy soon, and that their fire arms would be of use to them afterwards.

When he returned to the front, to inform Lord George Murray of his having executed his orders, he found they were halted a little to the eastward of Kilravock House, deliberating whether or not they should proceed, (having then but four miles to march to Nairn, where the enemy was encamped,) or return to Culloden, as they had not at most, or thereabouts, one hour to daylight; and if they could not be there before that time, the surprise would be rendered impracticable and the more so, as it was not to be doubted that the enemy would be under arms before day-light, as they were to march that morning, to give the Prince battle.

The Duke of Perth, and his brother, Lord John Drummond, who had been sent to advise the Prince, returned to Lord George Murray. Lochiel and others, that were in the front, hearing that there was a great interval betwixt the two lines, which would take up most of the time to day-light to join, it was resolved to return to Culloden, which was accordingly done, which, some say, was contrary to the Prince's inclination. They marched the shortest way back, by the church of Croy, which, though but scarce two miles from the place where the halt was made, yet it was clear day-light before the front arrived there; which makes it clear there was no possibility of surprising the enemy before day-light, as was designed.

The march continued to Culloden, from whence a great many, both officers and soldiers, went to Inverness, and other places, in quest of provisions, which were very much wanted. The Prince, with great difficulty, having got some bread and whiskey at Culloden, where reposing himself a little, after having marched all that night on foot, had intelligence brought, that the enemy were in sight; whereupon those about Culloden were ordered to arms, and several officers sent to Inverness and places adjacent, to bring up what men they could meet with. While those about Culloden were marching to the muir above the house, where they were joined with about three hundred of the Frazers, just then coming, Colonel Ker went out to reconnoitre the enemy. When he came back, he told the Prince and Lord George Murray, that their foot were marching in three columns, with their cavalry on their left; so that they could form their line of battle in an instant.

The Prince ordered his men to draw up in two lines, and the few horse he had in the rear towards the wings, and the cannon to be dispersed in the front, which was brought up with great difficulty, for want of horses. As there was no time to march to the ground they were on the day before, they were drawn up a mile farther westward, with a stone enclosure on the right of the first line, and the second at a proper distance behind. After having reconnoitred the enclosure, which ran down to the water of Nairn, on the right, so that no body of men could pass without throwing down the walls; and to guard against any attempts that might be made on this side, there were two battalions placed, facing outwards, which covered the right of two lines, and to observe the motions of the enemy, if they should make any attempt that way.

The Duke of Cumberland formed his line at a great distance, and marched in battle order till he came within cannon shot, where he halted, and placed his cannon in different places, at some distance, in the front, which outwinged the Prince's both to right and left, without his cavalry, which were mostly on the left, some few excepted who were sent to cover the right.

As soon as the Duke's cannon were placed, he began cannonading, which was answered by the Prince's, who rode along the lines to encourage his men, and posted himself in the most convenient place, (where one of his servants was killed by his side,) to see what passed, not doubting but the Duke would begin the attack, as he had both the wind and the weather on his back – snow and hail falling very thick at the same time. Here it is to be observed, that neither those that had been with the Earl of Cromarty . . . nor the MacPhersons, nor between two and three thousand men that had been on the field the day before, were come up. Notwithstanding these disadvantages, and the Duke's cannon playing with great execution, Lord George Murray, who commanded the right, sent Colonel Ker to know if he should begin the attack, which the Prince accordingly ordered.

As the right was farther advanced than the left, Colonel Ker went to the left, and ordered the Duke of Perth, who commanded there, to begin the attack, and rode along the line till he came to the right, where Lord George Murray was, who attacked, at the head of the Atholl men . . . with all the bravery imaginable, as indeed did the whole line – breaking the Duke's line in several places, and making themselves masters of two pieces of the enemy's cannon. Though they were both fronted and flanked by them, they, notwithstanding, marched up, under a close firing from right to left, to the very points of their bayonets, which they could not see till they were upon them, for the smoke. At the beginning of the attack, the Campbells threw down a great deal of the wall of the enclosure, for the dragoons on the Duke's left to pass to the rear of the Prince's army, which they were suffered to do, without receiving one shot from the two battalions that were placed to observe their motions. This being observed, and the constant fire kept up by the Duke's foot in the front, put the Prince's people in disorder, and rendered the defeat of his army complete.

The Prince retired in good order, with some few of his men, and crossed the water of Nairn at the ford, on the highway between Inverness and Corribreigh, without being pursued by the enemy, where he parted with them, taking only a few of Fitzjames's horse and some gentlemen along with him up that river, the rest taking the highway to Ruthven of Badenoch, where they stayed some days, expecting an answer of a letter that was sent to the Prince; but it not coming in the time expected, they all separated, every man to do the best for himself he could.

The Aftermath of Culloden, April 1746

ROBERT FORBES

But the most shocking part of this woful story is yet to come, – I mean the horrid barbarities committed in cold blood, after the battle was over. I do not now precisely remember how many days the dead bodies lay upon the field to glut the eyes of the merciless conqueror; but certain it is, that there they lay, till the stench obliged him to cause bury them. In the meantime, the soldiers, like so many savages, went up and down, knocking such on the head as had any remains of life in them, and, except in a very few instances, refusing all manner of relief to the wounded, many of whom, had they been properly taken care of, would undoubtedly have recovered. A little house into which a good many of the wounded had been carried, was set on fire about their ears, and every soul in it burnt alive; of which number was Colonel Orelli, a brave old gentleman, who was either in the French or Spanish service.

One Mr Shaw, younger of Kinrara, in Badenoch, had likewise been carried into another hut with other wounded men, and amongst the rest a servant of his own, who, being only wounded in the arm, could have got off, but chose rather to stay, in order to attend his master. The Presbyterian minister at Petty, Mr Laughlan Shaw, being a cousin of this Kinrara's, had obtained leave of the Duke of Cumberland to carry off his friend, in return to the good services the said Mr Laughlan had done the government; for he had been very active in dissuading his parishioners and clan from joining the Prince, and had likewise, as I am told, sent the Duke very pointed intelligence of all the Prince's motions. In consequence of this, on the Saturday after the battle, he went to the place where his friend was, designing to carry him to his own house. But as he came near, he saw an officer's command, with the officer at their head, fire a platoon at fourteen of the wounded Highlanders, whom they had taken all out of that house, and bring them all down at once; and when he came up, he found his cousin and his servant were two of that unfortunate number.

I questioned Mr Shaw himself about this story, who plainly acknowledged the fact, and was indeed the person who informed me of the precise number; and when I asked him if he knew of any more that were murdered in that manner on the same day, he told me that he believed there were in all two-and-twenty. At the same time, they were busy at Inverness hanging up the poor men, whom they called deserters, many of whom had been obliged to list in the Highland army for mere subsistence, the government never vouchsafing to send any relief to such of their men as were taken, well knowing what a merciful enemy they had to do with. And so great was the pleasure they took in looking at these unhappy creatures, that they never buried any of them till the gallows was full, so that, I am credibly informed, there were sometimes fourteen hanging in it altogether . . .

Their treatment of their prisoners may easily be guessed at, from what I have already said; and indeed history, I believe, can scarce afford a parallel to it. For some days it was dangerous for any person to go near them, or to pretend to give them the least relief; so that all of them, especially the wounded, were in a most dismal state. And after they were put on board the ships, numbers of them died every day, and were thrown over board like so many dogs; and several of them, I'm told, before they were really dead: yea, one of them, 'tis said, came alive to shore near Kessack, though, as to this last circumstance, I will not be quite positive. But the best idea I can give you of their usage, is by transcribing part of a letter from one of themselves, an authentic copy of which lies just now before me. The writer was one William Jack, sometime a merchant, and after that a messenger at Elgin, who had been with the Prince, and was taken prisoner some weeks after the battle, and sent aboard one of their ships from Inverness to London . . .

'Gentlemen, – This comes to acquaint you, that I was eight months and eight days at sea, of which time, I was eight weeks upon half a pound and twelve ounces oat-meal, and a bottle of water in the twenty-four hours, which was obliged to make meal and water in the bottom of an old bottle. There was one hundred and twenty-five put on board at Inverness, on the *James and Mary of Fife*. In the latter end of June, we was put on board of a transport of four hundred and fifty ton, called the *Liberty and Property*, in which we continued the rest of the eight months, upon twelve ounces of oat sheelin as it came from the mill. There was thirty-two prisoners more put on board of the said *Liberty and Property*, which makes one hundred and fifty-seven: and when we came ashore, there was only in life forty-nine, which would been no great surprise if there had not been one, conform to our usage. They would taken us from the hold in a rope, and hoisted us up to the yard-arm, and let us fall in the sea in order for ducking of us; and tying us to the mast and whipping us if we did any thing however innocent, that offended them: this was done to us when we was not able to stand. I will leave it to the readers to judge, what condition they might be in themselves with the above treatment. We had neither bed nor bed-clothes, nor clothes to keep us warm in day time. The ship's ballast was black earth and small stones, which we was obliged to dig holes to lie in to keep us warm, till the first of November last, that every man got about three yards of gross harn [sacking] filled up with straw, but no bed-clothes. I will not trouble you no more till I see you. There is none in life that went from Elgin with me, but William Innes in Fochabers . . .'

(signed) Will. Jack
Tilbury Fort, March 17th, 1747

Jacobite Orphans, 1746

JOHN MACDONALD

The memoirs of the son of a Highland Jacobite who died at Culloden offer an unusual perspective on the period. John Macdonald was the second youngest of a family of five. When their mother died, their father joined Prince Charles's army, and was last heard of by letter from Goolen's Inn and Livery Stables in the Canongate in Edinburgh. One child was taken in by a local family, but the other four were left in the care of a maid who soon went off with her lover.

My sister had it in her head to go to Edinburgh, to see my father. She got all the money she could get together, which was fourteen pounds Scots, or twenty-three shillings and four-pence English. With this, the letter from my father in her bosom, and her three brothers in her hand, out she sets for Edinburgh, from the parish of Urquhart, about the middle of September, 1745. Now our ages were as follows: Kitty, fourteen; Duncan, that was left with Boyd, between ten and eleven; Daniel, seven; I, four and a half; and my brother Alexander, two years and a half. She chose for her departure a moonlight night, that the people should not stop her; and so she got into Inverness about breakfast, having travelled nine miles. My sister carried the child on her back, Daniel carried the bundle, and I ran along side of both. In this manner we travelled from Inverness to Edinburgh, which is one hundred and fifty measured miles, in the pace of two months.

Now you shall see the providence of God towards helpless orphans that are left to his care alone. As we travelled, we were the surprise of every one, as we were so young. Our money being expended, we were obliged to beg our bread. We were kindly used by some and harshly by others that were against the Prince. One kind woman equipped us with a little bag for oatmeal, for people that would not take us in would give us a handful of meal. She gave us a round wooden dish also, which my sister put our pottage in when she met with good people that would let her bake it or bake cakes of oatmeal on their grid-iron. The chief of our food was pottage and milk, or cakes and milk; and sometimes, if we met with good friends at a farmhouse, we got a bit of meat. If it rained, we waited at a farmhouse sometimes for two or three days. On the journey we had two things to recommend us, although begging from house to house: the things we had on were all plaid, and of the finest kind, for an extravagant father cares not what he buys. Our apparel looked like that of a gentleman's children, and we had a great share of beauty . . .

We never marched when it rained, if it had been two or three days; and, on a fine sun-shining day, we played on the road till near night, when we continued to shuffle forward. If we could not reach a house, my sister would cover us with our plaids, and cut the tops of brooms with her knife to lay on and cover our plaids. In this manner we lay at nights for weeks, and always set off in the morning. When we had any brook to cross, or small river, my sister would carry over my young brother, then come for me, and afterwards come back to take my brother's hand. One time, as she was wading a river with Alexander, when she came near the other side, the water overpowered her and carried her and my brother into a whirlpool, where they floated, till a man who was digging potatoes at a little distance saw her distress, and ran to her relief . . .

When it was fine weather and we came to a rivulet, my sister washed our second shirt and stockings, for we either had no more at first, or else she did not chuse to bring any more with her. When we came to a river where was a ferry-boat, we begged our passage over. Then we came to Perth, where we stayed a week or two. The letter from my father was now so worn, with fretting and chaffing, that it was scarce legible; but a gentleman made shift to copy it for us afresh. From Perth we travelled to Kinghorn, where we staid a few days till we could get our passage to Leith. A gentleman who was a passenger in the same boat with us, paid our fare. Before we left the boat the same gentleman made a collection for us. He raised half-a-crown. As we passed through Leith we went into an eating-house, and had plenty of bread, meat and broth, for five-pence. In those days a working-man could dine well for two-pence. After dinner, we set out for Edinburgh on a fine walk, a mile and a half in length.

Now, my readers, let me tell you, that for what I have wrote hitherto I have been obliged to my sister; for I was too young to remember it. As we were passing onward to Edinburgh by Leith Walk, a country-woman of ours spoke to us, and asked my sister where we were going and from whence we came. My sister told her. She answered that Prince Charles was gone from Edinburgh, and all his army with him. On hearing this, we sat down and cried; and the woman cried out of pity. Then she took us to Goolen's Inn. Mr Goolen and every one in the house was surprised and sorry to see us in such a situation. Mr Goolen gave us some victuals, and told my sister he would get us into the workhouse. . . . My sister would not hear of the workhouse, nor of any confinement, but took us away immediately. We strayed down towards the bottom of the Canongate, staring at the signs, coaches, and fine horses. At the house below the Duke of Queensberry's, in the Canongate, a woman who stood at the door, seeing us strangers, and in the Highland dress, took us in, and asked us several questions concerning our situation. . . . She was a widow and let lodgings; her husband, before he died was a master-chairman, of the name of Macdonald, born near the place where we were born. The woman let us sleep in a lumber garret on an old mattress, and gave us an old blanket or two.

Next morning we set out again, and returned at night; and in this manner continued to live for some time. . . . Brother Daniel and I, when we got up one day in the morning, went out to play with the boys, and would not be kept under command by my sister, who had the young child to take care of; so that, in the day-time, we were seldom together. We went on in this manner for some time, till an unlucky accident happened, which separated us all. One day, as the Countess of Murray, who resided in the Canongate, was returning from an airing with her coach-and-six, my sister and the child on her back, crossing the street, were both run over by the carriage. My sister and brother screaming for fear, and the people calling 'Stop! stop!', made the Countess faint away. Kitty and Alexander were taken from under the horses, and, as God would have it, no bones were broken. They were both taken into the lady's house, and duly taken care of. When they recovered, the boy was put to nurse by Lady Murray; and one Mr Vernon, an Englishman who had been butler to Lord Murray and by him placed in a good office in the Excise, took my sister for a servant, and clothed her. Thus my sister and Alexander were done for. As to Daniel and me, we both of us begged, and played our time away; strolling round the country, and stopping sometimes in the barnyards, and at other times in a barn. In town we lay in the stairs; for about Edinburgh, as in Paris and Madrid, many large families live upon one staircase. They shut their own door, but the street-door is always open. There was an opinion at that time very prevalent amongst us poor children, of whom, after the Rebellion there were a great many, that the doctors came at night to find poor children asleep, and put sticking-plasters to their mouth, that they might not call out, and then to take them away to be dissected. . . . So when we passed the night in a stair or at a door one slept and the other kept watch.

John Macdonald went on to serve as a valet, footman and hairdresser to the nobility throughout Europe. He made his name as the pioneer of the umbrella in London.

Superstition and Punishment, 1754–1777

REVEREND JOHN MILL

A stern Shetland minister, John Mill kept a diary in which he talks about the devil as casually as if he were one of his parishioners. The second entry here is even more chilling.

I left my wife at Lerwick till the manse was got in order for her reception; supposing a married state would ease me in a great measure of worldly cares. But I soon found it rather increased them. The charge of repairing the manse straitened a little, but we soon got over it. The greatest plague was with cross-grained naughty servants, being thievish and mischievous, and liker wild beasts than Christians. My wife being of a delicate constitution couldn't bear the fatigues of a labouring and obstinacy of such wretches as neither feared God or regarded man. However, providentially, I was put upon a better method of setting of my land in halvers and keeping only one servant in the house, whereby I had more profit and less trouble. I endeavoured through grace to deal faithfully with the consciences of all sorts, which was not without effect, though not in a saving manner. I found a strong stress laid upon ordinances, especially the Sacrament of the Lord's Supper, as if it was a charm to save them, though they lived in sin; and the strongest arguments tending to prove the contrary, that it rather increased and aggravated their guilt, yet can't beat this delusion out of their heads. Nay, though God struck a healthy young man suddenly dead, who presumed to come to the Lord's table while he was living in whoredom, as afterwards appeared, and the people were publickly warned to take heed of sinning in like manner.

Meantime Satan raged exceedingly, and got actual possession of two poor women and a man. One of the women was mute, and made no answer to what I said; and a friend asking her quietly the reason, she said Satan would not suffer her to speak, which indeed I suspected. Then Satan seemed to make use of her tongue and said – The pulpit was upon the South Side of the Kirk. I said it would continue there as long as God pleased. He said I made lies upon him, for which I called him (as indeed he was) a damned rascal for his lying impudence, and that I spoke the truth, which he cared not for. While I spoke to the poor woman, he said I had no business with her, – that she was Satan's. I told him he could be assured of none till they were actually damned. While I was praying, he contradicted, saying – Grant not that. But at last became mute after a few sentences. The poor woman came to her senses and was much concerned when they told her she had spoken rudely to me, not being aware that it was more the speech of the enemy of souls than hers. Another poor woman was much in the same case, and during the possession brought forth a child without any sense of pain.

(1777)

In June, a son of Mr James Spence in Mid Yell, while attending the school at Sumburgh, went off alone, though only about 7 or 8 years old, and climbing the rocks in Sumburgh Head for birds' nests and slipping his hold, tumbled into the sea below, and couldn't be found, carried off it seemed by the tide; and as this fell out on the Sabbath day might serve for warning both to young and old, especially to that family, where little regard is paid to the Sabbath or Gospel ordinances.

Taking a Play to London, 1755

REVEREND ALEXANDER CARLYLE

Playwright John Home's tragedy Douglas *took the theatrical world by storm in 1756 when it was produced in London and became the favourite of the actress Mrs Siddons. Its fame, however, was not achieved overnight. In this extract from his autobiography, Home's friend Alexander Carlyle, minister of Inveresk, accompanies him with it part of the way to London to give it to the great impresario, Garrick. Carlyle recounts it as a mild comedy of mishaps but his championing of the play later led to him facing a gruelling inquiry from his outraged Church superiors, while Home, who was also a minister, was brought before the General Assembly of the Church of Scotland and suspended from his post.*

Six or seven Merse ministers ... set out for Woolerhaughhead in a snowy morning in February. Before we had gone far we discovered that our bard had no mode of carrying his precious treasure, which we thought enough of, but hardly foresaw that it was to be pronounced a perfect tragedy by the best judges ... The tragedy in one pocket of his greatcoat, and his clean shirt and nightcap in the other, though they balanced each other, was thought an unsafe mode of conveyance; and our friend ... had neglected to buy a pair of leather bags as he passed through Haddington. We bethought us that possibly James Landreth, minister of Simprin, and clerk of the Synod, would be provided with such a convenience for the carriage of his Synod records; and having no wife, no *altra cura*, to resist our request, we unanimously turned aside half a mile to call at James's; and, concealing our intention at first, we easily persuaded the honest man to join us in this convoy to his friend Mr Home, and then observing the danger the manuscript might run in a greatcoat-pocket on a journey of 400 miles, we inquired if he could lend Mr Home his valise only as far as Wooler, where he could purchase a new pair for himself. This he very cheerfully granted. But while his pony was preparing, he had another trial to go through; for Cupples, who never had any money, though he was a bachelor too, and had twice the stipend of Landreth, took the latter into another room, where the conference lasted longer than we wished for, so that we had to bawl out for them to come away. We afterwards understood that Cupples, having only four shillings, was pressing Landreth to lend him half-a-guinea, that he might be able to defray the expense of the journey. Honest James, who knew that John Home, if he did not return his own valise, which was very improbable, would provide him in a better pair, had frankly agreed to the first request; but as he knew Cupples never paid anything, he was very reluctant to part with his half-guinea. However, having at last agreed, we at last set out . . . By good luck the river Tweed was not come down, and we crossed it safely at the ford near Norham Castle; and, as the day mended, we got to Woolerhaughhead by four o'clock, where we got but an indifferent dinner, for it was but a miserable house in those days; but a happier or more jocose and merry company could hardly be assembled.

John Home and I, who slept in one room, or perhaps in one bed, as was usual in those days, were disturbed by a noise in the night, which being in the next room, where Laurie and Monteith were, we found they had quarrelled and fought, and the former had pushed the latter out of bed. After having acted as mediators in this quarrel, we had sound sleep till morning. Having breakfasted as well as the house could afford, Cupples and I, who had agreed to go two days' journey further with Mr Home, set off southwards with him, and the rest returned by the way they had come to Berwickshire again . . .

Cupples and I attended Home as far as Ferryhill, about six miles, where, after remaining all night with him, we parted next morning, he for London, and we on our return home. Poor Home had no better success on this occasion than before, with still greater mortification; for Garrick, after reading the play, returned it with an opinion that it was totally unfit for the stage.

A Scot Meets Voltaire, 24 December 1764

JAMES BOSWELL

James Boswell, later to become Johnson's biographer, was typical of a certain breed of intellectual Scot. As a young man, open to ideas and influences beyond his country, he travelled throughout Europe, and while doing so, invited himself into Voltaire's house at Ferney.

I was in true spirits; the earth was covered with snow; I surveyed wild nature with a noble eye. I called up all the grand ideas which I have ever entertained of Voltaire. The first object that struck me was his church with the inscription: 'Deo erexit Voltaire MDCCLXI.' His château was handsome, I was received by two or three footmen, who showed me into a very elegant room. I sent by one of them a letter to Monsieur de Voltaire which I had from Colonel Constant at the Hague. He returned and told me, 'Monsieur de Voltaire is very much annoyed at being disturbed. He is abed.' I was afraid that I should not see him. Some ladies and gentlemen entered, and I was entertained for some time. At last Monsieur de Voltaire opened the door of his apartment, and stepped forth. I surveyed him with eager attention, and found him just as his print had made me conceive him. He received me with dignity, and that air of the world which a Frenchman acquires in such perfection. He had a slate-blue, fine frieze night-gown, and a three-knotted wig. He sat erect upon his chair, and simpered when he spoke. He was not in spirits, nor I neither. All I presented was the 'foolish face of wondering praise'.

We talked of Scotland. He said the Glasgow editions were 'très belles'. I said, 'An Academy of Painting was also established there, but it did not succeed. Our Scotland is no country for that.' He replied with a keen archness, 'No; to paint well it is necessary to have warm feet. It's hard to paint when your feet are cold.' Another would have given a long dissertation on the coldness of our climate. Monsieur de Voltaire gave the very essence of raillery in half a dozen words . . .

I told him that Mr Johnson and I intended to make a tour through the Hebrides, the Northern Isles of Scotland. He smiled, and cried, 'Very well; but I shall remain here. You will allow me to stay here?' 'Certainly.' 'Well then, go. I have no objections at all.'

I asked him if he still spoke English. He replied, 'No. To speak English one must place the tongue between the teeth, and I have lost my teeth.' . . .

I returned yesterday to this enchanted castle. The magician appeared a little before dinner. But in the evening he came into the drawing room in great spirits. I placed myself by him. I touched the keys in unison with his imagination. I wish you had heard the music. He was all brilliance. He gave me continued flashes of wit. I got him to speak English, which he does in a degree that made me now and then start up and cry, 'Upon my soul this is astonishing!' When he talked our language he was animated with the soul of a Briton. He had bold flights. He had humour. He had an extravagance; he had a forcible oddity of style that the most comical of our *dramatis personae* could not have exceeded. He swore bloodily, as was the fashion when he was in

England. He hummed a ballad; he repeated nonsense. Then he talked of our Constitution with a noble enthusiasm. I was proud to hear this from the mouth of an illustrious Frenchman. At last we came upon religion. Then did he rage. The company went to supper. Monsieur de Voltaire and I remained in the drawing room with a great Bible before us; and if ever two mortal men disputed with vehemence, we did. Yes, upon that occasion he was one individual and I another . . . I demanded of him an honest confession of his real sentiment. He gave it me with candour and with a mild eloquence which touched my heart. I did not believe him capable of thinking in the manner that he declared to me was 'from the bottom of his heart'. He expressed his veneration – his love – of the Supreme Being, and his entire resignation to the will of Him who is All-wise. He expressed his desire to resemble the Author of Goodness by being good himself. His sentiments go no further. He does not inflame his mind with grand hopes of the immortality of the soul. He says it may be, but he knows nothing of it. And his mind is in perfect tranquillity. I was moved; I was sorry. I doubted his sincerity. I called to him with emotion, 'Are you sincere? are you really sincere?' He answered, 'Before God, I am.' Then with the fire of him whose tragedies have so often shone on the theatre of Paris, he said, 'I suffer much. But I suffer with patience and resignation; not as a Christian – but as a man.'

The New Town Is Conceived, 1767

THE SCOTS MAGAZINE

The announcement that architect James Craig's plan for the development of the New Town of Edinburgh had won the prize set by the city for the best new design signalled the birth of modern Edinburgh, and Scotland.

The project of enlarging of the city of Edinburgh begins now to take effect. An act of parliament was passed, May 20., for extending the royalty of the city; on the 3d of June the magistrates complimented Mr James Craig, architect, with a gold medal, and with the freedom of the city in a silver box, as an acknowledgement of his merit in having designed the best plan of the new town; the ground was afterwards marked out into proper plots for building; and by the end of July the magistrates and council had finally adjusted the plan, and notice was given, that it was to lie open at the council chamber for a month from the 3d of August, for the inspection of such as inclined to become feuers, where also were to be seen the terms on which feus would be granted. Several purchases have already been made; and as the bridge of communication, which is now well advanced, is to be finished in about two years, it is probable the building will be soon begun, so as the houses may be habitable by the time the bridge is finished.

The Invention of the Steam Engine, 1769

JAMES WATT

James Watt's invention of the condensing steam engine in 1769, which was conceived while he was mending the very basic Newcomen steam engine, was a crucial element in the advance of the industrial revolution and the railways and ships that were central to it. Towards the end of his life he was involved in various patent disputes, and in the following letter to his friend John Robison, railing against one such battle, he neatly summarizes the steps that led to his groundbreaking invention.

Heathfield, Birmingham, 24 October 1796

My Dear Sir . . .

I have been obliged to trouble many of my friends with these abominable law affairs but have hitherto, have only called those who lived near London, but now these scoundrels, – the Hornblowers and others have leagued against us we must call all who are willing to help us . . .

You will see from the papers sent you the objections and consequently the proper answers, I propose to send you my own general reply for your government, as soon as copy can be made. – The point is to establish that I was the inventor that the invention was perfect as to the *saving steam and fuel* at the time of the patent 1769, and that the specification is sufficient to enable a Mechanick understanding Newcomens Engine to have constructed one with these properties.

I did not invent this method piece meal but all at once in a few hours in 1765 I believe. The first step was the idea from the elastic nature of steam of condensing in a seperate [sic] vessel, 2d the getting out the water by a long pipe and the air by a pump, 3d that the pump would extract the water also 4th that grease might be used in place of water to keep the piston tight, 5th that Steam might be employed to press upon the piston in place of air 6 to keep the Cylinder warm.

The next day I set about it. The boiler was ready, I took a large syringe of Tom Hamiltons 2 inches diar [diameter] and a foot long that was the Cylinder. I made two tin ends to it with a pipe to convey steam to both of them. I made a tin Condenser consisting of a pump about an inch diar, and two small pipes about 10 inches long and 1/8 diar immersed in a small round cistron, which I still have. I placed the Cylr [cylinder] inverted tied a weight to the piston rod, blew out the air and condensed water through the piston rod, which was hollow, and when I judged the Cylr filled with steam, I drew up the piston of the pumps and the weight immediately followed, to my great Joy, all this was done in a day or two after I had contrived it . . .

The Encyclopaedia Britannica, *1771*

WILLIAM SMELLIE

One offshoot of the Enlightenment spirit was the Encyclopaedia Britannica, *a compendium of information arranged in a wholly original manner to reflect the widening knowledge and increasingly scientific interests of the late eighteenth century. Compiled by 'a society of Gentlemen in Scotland', its first editor was the Edinburgh printer and publisher William Smellie. The first volume was published in 1768, and the first three-set series completed in 1771. The second edition was printed in a ten-volume set, in 1777–84. Smellie's introduction to the three-volume work typifies the sometimes overweening confidence of the intellectual and critical Scottish man of letters.*

The method of conveying knowledge by alphabetical arrangement, has of late years become so universal, that Dictionaries of almost every branch of literature have been published, and their number still continues to increase. The utility of this method is indeed obvious; and experience has given it the stamp of approbation.

Among the various publications of this class, those of the greatest importance are General Dictionaries of Arts and Sciences: But it is to be regretted, that these, of all other kinds of Dictionaries, have hitherto fallen shortest of their purpose and yielded the least satisfaction. . . . The systematic nature of the Sciences will not admit of their being dismembered, and having their parts subjected to such fortuitous distributions: Yet they have suffered this violence in all the Dictionaries hitherto published . . .

In a work of this kind, the Sciences ought to be exhibited entire, or they are exhibited to little purpose. The absurdity and inefficacy of the contrary method, which has hitherto obtained, will be evident from an example or two. Supposing then, you want to obtain some knowledge of AGRICULTURE: You reasonably expect to be gratified by consulting one or other of these Dictionaries; as in all their Prefaces or Introductions the reader is taught to believe, that they contain the whole circle of Science and Literature, laid down in the most distinct, and explained in the most familiar manner. Well, how are you to proceed? The science is scattered through the alphabet under a multitude of words, as Vegetation, Soil, Manure, Tillage, Fallowing, Plough, Drain, Sowing, Marle, Chalk, Clay, Loam, Sand, Inclosure, Hedge, Ditch, Wheat, Barley, Harrow, Seed, Root, &c &c. After consulting a few of these articles, ignorant at the same time in what order you should have taken them, new references unexpectedly spring up, and multiply so thick, that you suddenly find yourself bewildered as in a labyrinth, without a clue to direct your course; and if haply you get through all the windings, you are still as far from the end of your inquiry as ever. To think of collecting a distinct or connected Whole from such a farrago, is vain: As well might you hope to acquire the idea of an edifice, the form of which is entirely demolished, from being shewn the scattered stones which once composed it. – But is there nothing to the purpose under the leading word, Agriculture, itself? No. After a definition of the word, the signification of which nobody is supposed to be ignorant of, you have a descant on the uses of the science, which every person must be sensible of, and then a few words upon its origin, which scarce any body can be at a loss to trace, without the help of a Dictionary. But nothing to the main point; no elements of the science, no particulars relating to the practice: But to complete the mortification of the wearied inquirer, he is at last given to understand, that he must for satisfaction have recourse to such and such authors who have written upon the subject; and these he must be at the expense of purchasing, or find other means than what his Dictionary affords of attaining the desired information.

Such are the defects of the old plan with regard to the Sciences: And so fond do the Compilers seem of derangement and demolition wherever it can be effected, that instead of giving a connected detail even of such subjects as according to their own plan naturally admit of being treated fully under one word, they industriously split them into many. For example, you want to know the history of BEES, their oeconomy and various operations. You therefore look out the word BEE, and are told it is 'An insect of which there are a great many species, &c. See APIS.' Upon turning to APIS, 'APIS, in zoology, a genus of four-winged insects, having their tails furnished with a sting, &c. See BEE, SWARM, HIVE, HONEY, WAX &c.' Well, you turn to the next word referred to, 'SWARM *of BEES*. See HIVE.' Upon consulting HIVE, you are told it is 'A convenient receptacle for bees. See BEE.' Then mention is made of two or three sorts of them, of which no other account is given, but that some are made with willow, others with straw; some of wood, others of glass; and that their usual form is conical. And so, with much the same satisfaction, you are carried through *Hiving, Honey, Honey-comb, Wax*, &c; and after being referred back from the last article to *Honey-comb, Honey, Hive, Bee, Apis*, you perhaps throw down the book in the heat of disappointment . . .

With a view to remedy these defects, and render a distinct knowledge of the Sciences attainable, the following Work has been planned. Being the first attempt of the kind, extensive in its nature, and difficult in the execution, it is offered to the Public with the utmost diffidence, and under a full sense of its requiring their utmost candour and intelligence.

Dr Johnson Arrives in Scotland, 14 August 1773

JAMES BOSWELL

In 1773 Dr Samuel Johnson finally accepted his acolyte James Boswell's invitation to visit Scotland and sent a note to say he had arrived. Thus began the most famous literary jaunt in Scotland's history. Here Boswell shows his anxiety that Johnson will form a good opinion of his country.

On Saturday the fourteenth of August, 1773, late in the evening, I received a note from him, that he was arrived at Boyd's inn, at the head of the Canongate. I went to him directly. He embraced me cordially; and I exulted in the thought, that I now had him actually in Caledonia. Mr Scott's [Johnson's friend from Oxford] amiable manners, and attachment to our Socrates, at once united me to him. He told me that, before I came in, the Doctor had unluckily had a bad specimen of Scottish cleanliness. He then drank no fermented liquor. He asked to have his lemonade made sweeter; upon which the waiter, with his greasy fingers, lifted a lump of sugar, and put it into it. The Doctor, in indignation, threw it out of the window. Scott said, he was afraid he would have knocked the waiter down. Mr Johnson told me, that such another trick was played him at the house of a lady in Paris. He was to do me the honour to lodge under my roof. I regretted sincerely that I had not also a room for Mr Scott. Mr Johnson and I walked arm-in-arm up the High Street, to my house in James's court: it was a dusky night: I could not prevent his being assailed by the evening effluvia of Edinburgh. I heard a late baronet, of some distinction in the political world in the beginning of the present reign, observe, that 'walking the streets of Edinburgh at night was pretty perilous, and a good deal odoriferous'. The peril is much abated, by the care which the magistrates have taken to enforce the city laws against throwing foul water from the windows; but, from the structure of the houses in the old town, which consist of many stories, in each of which a different family lives, and there being no covered sewers, the odour continues.

A Visitor's Impressions of Scotland, 1773

SAMUEL JOHNSON

By the year 1773, when Johnson and Boswell travelled through the Highlands and Islands, Highland emigrants were already sailing for America and the colonies. Yet while the Scotland they were to see was in some ways a new and beleaguered country, given the hostile political climate in the wake of the 1745 rebellion, some aspects of the Highland way of life had altered little for centuries.

A hut is constructed with loose stones, ranged for the most part with some tendency to circularity. It must be placed where the wind cannot act upon it with violence, because it has no cement; and where the water will run easily away, because it has no floor but the naked ground. The wall, which is commonly about six feet high, declines from the perpendicular a little inward. Such rafters as can be procured are then raised for a roof, and covered with heath, which makes a strong and warm thatch, kept from flying off by ropes of twisted heath, of which the ends, reaching from the center of the thatch to the top of the wall, are held firm by the weight of a large stone. No light is admitted but at the entrance, and through a hole in the thatch, which gives vent to the smoke. This hole is not directly over the fire, lest the rain should extinguish it; and the smoke therefore naturally fills the place before it escapes. Such is the general structure of the houses in which one of the nations of this opulent and powerful island has been hitherto content to live. Huts however are not more uniform than palaces; and this which we were inspecting was very far from one of the meanest, for it was divided into several apartments; and its inhabitants possessed such property as a pastoral poet might exalt into riches.

When we entered, we found an old woman boiling goats-flesh in a kettle. She spoke little English, but we had interpreters at hand; and she was willing enough to display her whole system of economy. She has five children, of which none are yet gone from her. The eldest, a boy of thirteen, and her husband, who is eighty years old, were at work in the wood. Her two next sons were gone to Inverness to buy meal, by which oatmeal is always meant. Meal she considered as expensive food, and told us, that in Spring, when the goats gave milk, the children could live without it. She is mistress of six goats, and I saw many kids in an enclosure at the end of her house. She had also some poultry. By the lake we saw a potatoe-garden, and a small spot of ground on which stood four shucks, containing each twelve sheaves of barley. She has all this from the labour of their own hands, and for what is necessary to be bought, her kids and her chickens are sent to market.

With the true pastoral hospitality, she asked us to sit down and drink whisky. She is religious, and though the kirk is four miles off, probably eight English miles, she goes thither every Sunday. We gave her a shilling and she begged snuff; for snuff is the luxury of a Highland cottage . . .

In Sky [sic] I first observed the use of brogues, a kind of artless shoes, stitched with thongs so loosely, that though they defend the foot from stones, they do not exclude water. Brogues were formerly made of raw hides, with the hair inwards, and such are perhaps still used in rude and remote parts; but they are said not to last above two days. Where life is somewhat improved, they are now made of leather tanned with oak bark, as in other places, or with the bark of birch, or roots of tormentil, a substance recommended in defect of bark, about forty years ago, to the Irish tanners, by one to whom the parliament of that kingdom voted a reward. The leather of Sky is not completely penetrated by vegetable matter, and therefore cannot be very durable.

The American Independence War, 19 June 1776

COLONEL ARCHIBALD CAMPBELL

Scottish soldiers played a major role in the American Independence War. Indeed, there was such enthusiasm to join up to fight that some unenlisted men stowed away so they could take part. What they encountered, however, was far from the glorious Royalist triumph they had perhaps expected. One of the many setbacks encountered was the Siege of Boston, in which the American rebels under General George Washington bluffed the British General Howe into evacuating the city. He did so without posting a warning to incoming British ships. In the letter below, a colonel in the 71st Royal Highlanders describes how he and his men sailed into Boston harbour, unaware that they would receive no aid from any quarter.

Sir

I am sorry to inform you that it has been my unfortunate lot to have fallen into the hands of the Americans in the middle of Boston harbour; but when the circumstances which have occasioned this disaster are understood, I flatter myself no reflection will arise to myself or my officers on account of it. On the 16th of June the *George* and *Annabella* transports, with two companies of the Seventy-First Regiment of Highlanders, made the land off Cape Ann, after a passage of seven weeks from Scotland, during the course of which we had not the opportunity of speaking to a single vessel that could give us the smallest information of the British troops having evacuated Boston. On the 17th, at daylight, we found ourselves opposite to the harbour's mouth at Boston; but, from contrary winds, it was necessary to make several tacks to reach it. Four schooners (which we took to be the pilots, or armed vessels in the service of his Majesty, but which were afterwards found to be four American privateers, of eight carriage-guns, twelve swivels, and forty men each) were bearing down upon us at four o'clock in the morning. At half an hour thereafter two of them engaged us, and about eleven o'clock the other two were close alongside. The George transport (on board of which were Major Menzies and myself, with one hundred and eight of the Second Battalion, the Adjutant, the Quarter-master, two Lieutenants, and five volunteers, were passengers) had only six pieces of cannon to oppose them; and the *Annabella* (on board of which was Captain McKenzie, together with two subalterns, two volunteers, and eighty-two private men of the First Battalion) had only two swivels for her defence. Under such circumstances, I thought it expedient for the *Annabella* to keep ahead of the *George*, that our artillery might be used with more effect and less obstruction. Two of the privateers having stationed themselves upon our larboard quarter and two upon our starboard quarter, a tolerable cannonade ensued, which, with very few intermissions, lasted till four o'clock in the evening, when the enemy bore away, and anchored in Plymouth harbour. Our loss upon this occasion was only three men mortally wounded on board the *Annabella*. As my orders were for the port of Boston, I thought it my duty, at this happy crisis, to push forward into the harbour, not doubting I should receive protection either from a fort or some ship of force stationed there for the security of our fleet.

Towards the close of the evening we perceived the four schooners that were engaged with us in the morning, joined by the brig *Defence*, of sixteen carriage-guns, twenty swivels, and one hundred and seventeen men, and a schooner of eight carriage guns, twelve swivels, and forty men, got under way and made towards us. As we stood up for Nantasket Road, an American battery opened upon us, which was the first serious proof we had that there could scarcely be many friends of ours at Boston; and we were far too embayed to retreat, especially as the wind had died away, and the tide of flood not half expended. After each of the vessels had twice run aground, we anchored at George's Island, and prepared for action; but the *Annabella* by some misfortune, got aground so far astern of the *George* we could expect but feeble support from her musketry. About eleven o'clock four of the schooners anchored right upon our bow, and one right astern of us. The armed brig took her station on our starboard side, at the distance of two hundred yards, and hailed us to strike the British flag. Although the mate of our ship and every sailor on board (the Captain only excepted) refused positively to fight any longer, I have the pleasure to inform you that there was not an officer, non-commissioned officer, or private man of the Seventy-First but what stood to their quarters with a ready and cheerful obedience. On our refusing to strike the British flag, the action was renewed with a good deal of warmth on both sides, and it was our misfortune, after the sharp combat of an hour and a half, to have expended every shot that we had for our artillery. Under such circumstances, hemmed in as we were with six privateers, in the middle of an enemy's harbour, beset with a dead calm, without the power of escaping, or even the most distant hope of relief, I thought it became my duty not to sacrifice the lives of gallant men wantonly in the arduous attempt of an evident impossibility. In this unfortunate affair Major Menzies and seven private soldiers were killed, the Quartermaster and twelve private soldiers wounded. The Major was buried with the honours of war at Boston.

Since our captivity, I have the honour to acquaint you that we have experienced the utmost civility and good treatment from the people of power at

Boston, insomuch, sir, that I should do injustice to the feelings of generosity did I not make this particular information with pleasure and satisfaction. I have now to request of you that, so soon as the distracted state of this unfortunate controversy will admit, you will be pleased to take an early opportunity of settling a cartel for myself and officers.

I have the honour to be, with great respect, sir, your most obedient and most humble servant.

Archibald Campbell, Lieut. Col. 2s Bat. 71st Regiment

Campbell's good treatment at the hands of his captors did not last, and his release was not procured until May 1778.

The Wealth of Nations, *March 1776*

DAVID HUME

The publication of Adam Smith's An Inquiry into the Nature and Causes of the Wealth of Nations *was a landmark in economic and political thought. Smith's great friend, the philosopher David Hume, was one of the first to record his verdict.*

Edinburgh, 1 Apr. 1776
Euge! Belle! Dear Mr Smith: I am much pleas'd with your Performance, and the Perusal of it has taken me from a State of great Anxiety. It was a Work of so much Expectation, by yourself, by your Friends, and by the Public, that I trembled for its Appearance; but am now much relieved. Not but that the Reading of it necessarily requires so much Attention, and the Public is disposed to give so little, that I shall still doubt for some time of its being at first very popular: But it has Depth and Solidity and Acuteness, and is so much illustrated by curious Facts, that it must at last take the public Attention. It is probably much improved by your last Abode in London. If you were here at my Fireside, I should dispute some of your Principles. I cannot think, that the Rent of Farms makes any part of the Price of the Produce, but that the Price is determined altogether by the Quantity and the Demand. It appears to me impossible, that the King of France can take Seigniorage of 8 per cent upon the Coinage. No body would bring Bullion to the mint: It woud [sic] be all sent to Holland or England, where it might be coined and sent back to France for less than two

per cent. Accordingly, Necker says, that the French King takes only two per cent of Seigniorage. But these and a hundred other Points are fit only to be discussed in Conversation; which, till you tell me the contrary, I shall still flatter myself with soon. I hope it will be soon: For I am in a very bad State of Health and cannot afford a long Delay . . .

DH

Death of David Hume, 25 August 1776

ADAM SMITH

Some time after the philosopher's death, Adam Smith wrote to Hume's publisher William Strahan to describe Hume's last weeks. In this affectionate tribute Hume comes across as an enormously likeable and humane man, yet his unconventional and challenging views had so angered certain parties that, as Smith later wrote, 'A single, and as, I thought a very harmless Sheet of paper, which I happened to Write concerning the death of our late friend Mr Hume, brought upon me ten times more abuse than the very violent attack I had made upon the whole commercial system of Great Britain.'

Kirkcaldy, Fifeshire, 9 Nov. 1776

Dear Sir,

It is with a real, though a very melancholy pleasure, that I sit down to give you some account of the behaviour of our late excellent friend, Mr Hume, during his last illness . . .

His cheerfulness was so great, and his conversation and amusements run so much in their usual strain, that, notwithstanding all bad symptoms, many people could not believe he was dying. 'I shall tell your friend, Colonel Edmondstone,' said Doctor Dundas to him one day, 'that I left you much better, and in a fair way of recovery.' 'Doctor,' said he, 'as I believe you would not chuse to tell any thing but the truth, you had better tell him, that I am dying as fast as my enemies, if I have any, could wish, and as easily and cheerfully as my best friends could desire.' . . .

Mr Hume's magnanimity and firmness were such, that his most affectionate friends knew, that they hazarded nothing in talking or writing to him as to a dying man, and that so far from being hurt by this frankness, he was rather pleased and flattered by it. I happened to come into his room while he was reading this letter, which he had just received, and which he immediately showed me. I told him, that though I was sensible how very much he was weakened, and that appearances were in many respects very bad, yet his cheerfulness was still so great, the spirit of life seemed still to be so very strong in him, that I could not help entertaining some faint hopes.

He answered, 'Your hopes are groundless. An habitual diarrhoea of more than a year's standing, would be a very bad disease at any age: at my age it is a mortal one. When I lie down in the evening, I feel myself weaker than when I rose in the morning; and when I rise in the morning, weaker than when I lay down in the evening. I am sensible, besides, that some of my vital parts are affected, so that I must soon die.' 'Well,' said I, 'if it must be so, you have at least the satisfaction of leaving all your friends, your brother's family in particular, in great prosperity.'

He said that he felt that satisfaction so sensibly, that when he was reading a few days before, Lucian's Dialogues of the Dead, among all the excuses which are alleged to Charon for not entering readily into his boat, he could not find one that fitted him; he had no house to finish, he had no daughter to provide for, he had no enemies upon whom he wished to revenge himself. 'I could not well imagine,' said he, 'what excuse I could make to Charon in order to obtain a little delay. I have done every thing of consequence which I ever meant to do, and I could at no time expect to leave my relations and friends in a better situation than that in which I am now likely to leave them; I, therefore, have all reason to die contented.'

He then diverted himself with inventing several jocular excuses, which he supposed he might make to Charon, and with imagining the very surly answers which it might suit the character of Charon to return to them. 'Upon further consideration,' said he, 'I thought I might say to him, Good Charon, I have been correcting my works for a new edition. Allow me a little time, that I may see how the Public receives the alterations.' But Charon would answer, 'When you have seen the effect of these, you will be for making other alterations. There will be no end of such excuses; so, honest friend, please step into the boat.' But I might still urge, 'Have a little patience, good Charon, I have been endeavouring to open the eyes of the Public. If I live a few years longer, I may have the satisfaction of seeing the downfal [sic] of some of the prevailing systems of superstition.' But Charon would then lose all temper and decency. 'You loitering rogue, that will not happen these many hundred years. Do you fancy I will grant you a lease for so long a term? Get into the boat this instant, you lazy loitering rogue.' . . .

The conversation which I mentioned above, and which passed on Thursday the 8th of August, was the last, except one, that I ever had with him. He had now become so very weak, that the company of his most intimate friends fatigued him; for his cheerfulness was still so great, his complaisance and social disposition were still so entire, that when any friend was with him, he could not help talking more, and with greater exertion, than suited the weakness of his body. At his own desire, therefore, I agreed to leave Edinburgh, where I was staying partly upon his account, and returned to my mother's house here, at Kirkcaldy, upon condition that he would send for me whenever he wished to see me; the physician who saw him most frequently, Doctor Black, undertaking, in the mean time, to write me occasionally an account of the state of his health.

On the 22nd of August, the Doctor wrote me the following letter:

'Since my last, Mr Hume has passed his time pretty easily, but is much weaker. He sits up, goes down stairs once a day, and amuses himself with reading, but seldom sees any body. He finds that even the conversation of his most intimate friends fatigues him and oppresses him; and it is happy that he does not need it, for he is quite free from anxiety, impatience, or low spirits, and passes his time very well with the assistance of amusing books.'

I received the day after a letter from Mr Hume himself, of which the following is an extract.

Edinburgh, 23rd August, 1776

'My Dearest Friend,
I am obliged to make use of my nephew's hand in writing to you, as I do not rise today . . . I go very fast to decline, and last night had a small fever, which I hoped might put a quicker period to this tedious illness, but unluckily it has, in a great measure, gone off. I cannot submit to your coming over here on my account, as it is possible for me to see you so small a part of the day, but Doctor Black can better inform you concerning the degree of strength which may from time to time remain with me. Adieu, &c.'

Three days after I received the following letter from Doctor Black.

Edinburgh, Monday, 26th August, 1776

'Dear Sir,
Yesterday about four o'clock afternoon, Mr Hume expired. The near approach of his death became evident in the night between Thursday and Friday, when his disease became excessive, and soon weakened him so much, that he could no longer rise out of his bed. He continued to the last perfectly sensible, and free from much pain or feelings of distress. He never dropped the smallest

expression of impatience; but when he had occasion to speak to the people about him, always did it with affection and tenderness. . . . When he became very weak, it cost him an effort to speak, and he died in such a happy composure of mind, that nothing could exceed it.'

Thus died our most excellent, and never to be forgotten friend; concerning whose philosophical opinions men will, no doubt, judge variously, every one approving or condemning them, according as they happen to coincide or disagree with his own; but concerning whose character and conduct there can scarce be a difference of opinion. His temper, indeed, seemed to be more happily balanced, if I may be allowed such an expression, than that perhaps of any other man I have ever known. Even in the lowest state of his fortune, his great and necessary frugality never hindered him from exercising, upon proper occasions, acts both of charity and generosity. It was a frugality founded, not upon avarice, but upon the love of independency. The extreme gentleness of his nature never weakened either the firmness of his mind, or the steadiness of his resolutions. His constant pleasantry was the genuine effusion of good-nature and good-humour, tempered with delicacy and modesty, and without even the slightest tincture of malignity, so frequently the disagreeable source of what is called wit in other men. It never was the meaning of his raillery to mortify; and therefore, far from offending, it seldom failed to please and delight, even those who were the objects of it. . . . And that gaiety of temper, so agreeable in society, but which is so often accompanied with frivolous and superficial qualities, was in him certainly attended with the most severe application, the most extensive learning, the greatest depth of thought, and a capacity in every respect the most comprehensive. Upon the whole, I have always considered him, both in his lifetime and since his death, as approaching as nearly to the idea of a perfectly wise and virtuous man, as perhaps the nature of human frailty will permit.

I ever am, dear Sir,
Most affectionately your's,
Adam Smith

A Jamaican Sugar Plantation, 1784

ZACHARY MACAULAY

Zachary Macaulay was born in Inverary, the son of a minister. He was sent to work in a Glasgow merchant's house at the age of fourteen, but to evade the problems he faced as a result of too much good company and high living among the students of Glasgow university, he left to work as a clerk on the plantations when he was sixteen. His description of the circumstances in which he and other white men lived among slaves is grim. Unlike many, Macaulay's conscience could not be silenced indefinitely, and he returned to Britain to become one of the foremost champions of the abolition of slavery.

Towards the end of the year 1784 a circumstance happened which gave a temporary suspension to my career, and led to a few sober reflections. I then saw that the only way that remained to extricate myself from the labyrinth in which I was involved was going abroad. I made known my wish to my father, and it was determined that I should try my fortunes in the East Indies. [*At the suggestion of a friend, however, his father sends him instead to the West Indies*] . . .

During the voyage to Jamaica I had a good deal of time for reflection, and I endeavoured to fortify myself, by previous resolutions, against the evils to which I felt myself prone. Company I had found my greatest snare, and I resolved to guard against it; and though every reformation proceeding on such grounds as mine then did must be partial and inadequate, yet one good effect arising from it was a resolution of abstaining from all excess in drinking, which I afterwards adhered to.

At this time I had not yet reached the age of seventeen, and found myself, on landing at Jamaica, without money, or without a single friend to whom I could turn for assistance. The letters of recommendation to persons in high position . . . were entirely neglected. The visions which had been presented to me of rapidly increasing wealth and honours now vanished entirely, but the disappointment did not seriously affect my spirits. I felt certainly indignation and resentment at the coldness and indifference shown me by men, from whom I thought I had a right to expect different treatment. But I recollect feeling a degree of self-complacency in finding myself able to reconcile my mind to very considerable hardships, rather than submit to repeat the humiliating applications which I had already made to those persons.

My trials, however, were not of long duration. One or two private gentlemen to whom a friend of mine had written to introduce me, soon found me out, and showed me great kindness. Through their exertions I obtained the situation of under-manager or book-keeper on a sugar plantation.

Here I entered upon a new mode of life which waged war with all my tastes and feelings. My position was laborious, irksome, and degrading, to a degree of which I could have formed no previous conception, and which none can imagine fully who have not, like me, experienced the vexatious, capricious, tyrannical, and pitiless conduct of a Jamaica overseer. To this, however, I made it a point of honour to reconcile my mind. Indeed I saw there was no medium for me, under the circumstances, between doing so and starving.

While my health remained good, I therefore submitted with cheerfulness to all the severe toil and painful watchings which were required of me. What chiefly affected me at first was, that by my situation I was exposed not only to the sight, but also to the practice of severities over others, the very recollection of which makes my blood run cold. My mind was at first feelingly alive to the miseries of the poor slaves, and I not only revolted from the thought of myself inflicting punishment upon them, but the very sight of punishment sickened me.

The die, however, was now cast; there was no retreating. I should gladly indeed have returned to Europe, but I had not the means. I had no friend at home to whom I could apply except my father, and I would almost sooner have died than have added any more pressure of that anxiety which a numerous family necessarily caused him. In the West Indies, I was bound, if I would not forfeit the regard of all whom were disposed to serve me, even to give no vent to those feelings which would have seemed to reproach them with cruelty. As the only alternative, therefore, I resolved to get rid of my squeamishness as soon as I could, as a thing which was very inconvenient. And in this I had a success beyond my expectations.

Virgil's expression, 'Easy is the descent to Hell,' is a bold, but perfectly just representation of the rapidity with which we move downwards in the scale of moral rectitude when once we have made a voluntary declension from the path of duty. I soon satisfied myself that the duty which I owed to my employers, for I used still to moralize, required the exact fulfilment of their orders; and that the duty which I owed myself, my father, and my friends, required that I should throw no obstacles, which the voice of all in the world whom I had hitherto known was so far from sanctioning, that it condemned them as foolish, childish, and ridiculous, in the way of my fortune.

At this time, that is in the year 1785, I find myself writing thus to a friend at home: 'But far other is now my lot, doomed by my own folly to toil for a scanty subsistence in an inhospitable clime. The air of this island must have some peculiar quality in it, for no sooner does a person set foot on it than his former ways of thinking are entirely changed. The contagion of an universal example must indeed have its effect. You would hardly know your friend, with whom you have spent so many hours in more peaceful and more pleasant scenes, were you to view me in the field of canes, amidst perhaps a hundred of the sable race, cursing and bawling, while the noise of the whip resounding on their shoulders, and the cries of the poor wretches, would make you imagine that some unlucky accident had carried you to the doleful shades.'

This picture, shocking as it is, owes nothing to fancy; but my mind was now steeled, and though some months before this period, in writing to the same friend I had had a heart to draw in very lively colours, and with pathetic touches which I really felt, the miseries of the negroes, yet now I was callous and indifferent, and could allude to them with a levity which sufficiently marked my depravity. I had indeed raised for myself an imaginary standard of justice in my dealings with them, to which I thought it right to conform.

But the hour of retribution seemed to be at hand. Dangerous, and repeated, and long-continued attacks of illness brought me frequently to the very borders of the grave. My sufferings were extreme; and they were aggravated by the most cruel neglect and the most hard-hearted unkindness. There was a kind of high-mindedness about me which kept me from complaining even in my lowest extremity of wretchedness, nor did the hope of better days ever forsake me. Nay, when stretched upon a straw mattress, with 'tape-tied curtains, never meant to draw,' burning with fever, pining under the want of every necessary comfort, shut out from the sight or converse of any one whom I could call a friend, unable to procure even a cup of cold water for which I did not myself crawl to the neighbouring rivulet, I maintained an unbroken spirit.

I tremble to think on the stupid insensibility, nay the desperate harness, with which at times I stood tottering upon the brink of eternity. Surely had I died then my place would have been where mercy is clean gone for ever, and where even God forgets to be gracious. May I not regard myself emphatically as a brand plucked out of the burning? These judgments, however, like those which visited Pharaoh, served only to harden my heart. Indeed this is the effect which appears, if we consult our Bible and experience, to be the necessary result of afflictions when they do not lead the mind to God.

When health returned my sufferings were soon forgotten; and better prospects opening upon me, and friends rising up daily who showed a willingness to serve me as soon as I was master of my business, I began to like my situation. I even began to be wretch enough to think myself happy.

My outward conduct indeed, for a West Indian planter, was sober and decorous, for I affected superiority to the grossly vulgar manners and practices which disgrace almost every rank of men in the West Indies, but my habits and dispositions were now fundamentally the same. In these I was quite assimilated to my neighbours, and this is a part of my life of which I scarce like either to speak or think. It was a period of most degrading servitude to the worst of masters.

A Bagpipe Competition, 1784

B. FAUJAIS ST FOND

Scotland's distinctive musical instrument makes a strong impression on an unprepared visitor.

A few moments later, a folding door opened at the bottom of the room, and to my great surprise, I saw a Scottish Highlander enter . . . playing upon the bagpipe, and walking up and down an empty space with rapid steps and a military air, blowing the noisiest and most discordant sounds from an instrument which lacerates the ear. The air he played was a kind of sonata, divided into three parts. Smith begged me to give it my whole attention, and to tell him afterwards the impression it made on me.

But I confess at first I could not distinguish neither air nor design. I only saw the piper marching away with rapidity, and with the same warlike countenance. He made incredible efforts both with his body and his fingers to bring into play at once the different pipes of his instrument, which made an unsupportable uproar.

He received nevertheless great applause from all sides. A second musician followed into the arena, wearing the same martial look and walking to and fro with the same martial air . . .

After having listened to eight pipers in succession, I began to suspect that the first part was connected with a warlike march and military evolutions: the second with a sanguinary battle, which the musician sought to depict by the noise and rapidity of his playing and by his loud cries. He seemed then to be convulsed; his pantomimical gestures resembled those of a man engaged in combat; his arms, his hands, his head, his legs, were all in motion; the sounds of his instrument were all called forth and confounded together at the same moment. This fine disorder seemed keenly to interest every one. The piper then passed, without transition, to a kind of andante; his convulsions suddenly ceased; the sounds of his instrument were plaintive, languishing, as if lamenting the slain who were being carried off from the field of battle. This was the part which drew tears from the eyes of the beautiful Scottish ladies. But the whole was so uncouth and extraordinary; the impression which this wild music made upon me contrasted so strongly with that which it made upon the inhabitants of the country, that I am convinced we should look upon this strange composition not as essentially belonging to music, but to history . . .

The same air was played by each competitor, of whom there was a considerable number. The most perfect equality was maintained among them; the son of the laird stood on the same footing with the simple shepherd, often belonging to the same clan, bearing the same name, and having the same garb. No preference was shown here save to talent, as I could judge from the hearty plaudits given to some who seemed to excel in that art. I confess it was impossible for me to admire any of them. I thought them all of equal proficiency: that is to say, the one was as bad as the other; and the air that was played as well as the instrument itself involuntarily put me in mind of a bear's dance.

Robert Burns Is Hailed as a Genius, 1786

HENRY MACKENZIE

Robert Burns was a little-known poet, living a life of hard labour as a farmer in Ayrshire, when he had his first collection printed in Kilmarnock in 1786. At this point he was reeling from a broken love affair, and was so discouraged by his life in Scotland that he was planning to emigrate to the West Indies. Publication of the poems was intended to raise funds for the journey. The reception of this edition, however, changed his plans by bringing him to the notice of the country's literati, among them the novelist Henry Mackenzie, whom he met when he visited

Edinburgh. Mackenzie wrote the following glowing review in his magazine, The
Lounger, *and in so doing established Burns's fame. As a result of this piece,
the list of subscribers to a new edition of his work, published by William Creech
the following year, ran across thirty-eight pages.*

I know not if I shall be accused of . . . enthusiasm and partiality when I
introduce to the notice of my readers a poet of our own country, with
whose writings I have lately become acquainted; but if I am not greatly
deceived, I think I may safely pronounce him a genius of no ordinary
rank. The person to whom I allude is Robert Burns, an Ayrshire ploughman, whose poems were some time ago published in a country town in
the west of Scotland, with no other ambition, it would seem, than to
circulate among the inhabitants of the country where he was born, to
obtain a little fame from those who had heard of his talents. I hope I
shall not be thought to assume too much, if I endeavour to place him
in a higher point of view, to call for a verdict of his country on the merit
of his works, and to claim for him those honours which their excellence
appears to deserve . . .

One bar [his lowly origins] have opposed to his fame, the language
in which the poems were written. Even in Scotland the provincial dialect
which [Allan] Ramsay and he have used is now read with a difficulty
which greatly damps the pleasure of the reader: in England it cannot be
read at all without such a constant reference to a glossary as nearly to
destroy the pleasure.

Some of his productions, however, especially those of the graver style,
are almost English . . . [He has] a power of genius not less admirable in
tracing the manners than in painting the passions or in drawing the
scenery of nature. That intuitive glance with which a writer like Shakespeare discerns the characters of men . . . forms a sort of problem in the
science of the mind, of which it is easier to see the truth than assign the
cause. Though I am very far from meaning to compare our rustic bard
with Shakespeare, yet whoever will read his lighter and more humorous
poems . . . will perceive with what uncommon penetration and sagacity
this Heaven-taught ploughman, from his humble and unlettered station,
has looked on men and manners . . .

Burns possesses the spirit as well as the fancy of a poet. That honest
pride and independence of soul which are sometimes the Muse's only
dower, break forth on every occasion in his works. It may be, then, that
I shall wrong his feelings while I indulge my own in calling the attention
of the public to his situation and circumstances. The condition, humble

as it was, in which he found content and wooed the Muses, might not have been deemed uncomfortable; but grief and misfortunes have reached him there; and one or two of his poems hint, what I have learned from some of his countrymen, that he has been obliged to form the resolution of leaving his native land, to seek under a West Indian clime that shelter and support that Scotland has denied him. But I trust means may be found to prevent this resolution from taking place, and that I do my country no more than justice when I suppose her ready to stretch out her hand to cherish and retain this native poet . . . To repair the wrongs of suffering or neglected merit, to call forth genius from the obscurity in which it has pined indignant, and place it where it may profit and delight the world; these are exertions which give to wealth an enviable superiority, to greatness and to patronage a laudable pride.

The Age of the Earth Is Proved by James Hutton, 1788

JAMES HUTTON AND JOHN PLAYFAIR

One of the brightest stars of the Enlightenment was geologist James Hutton, whose wholly original work proved that the world was massively older than the 6,000 years generally assumed at that time. After years of exhaustive work, much of it derided by his contemporaries, he proved the theory that old rocks weather with age and new rocks are formed from their sediment. Some of the rock formations he used to confirm his theory were found at Siccar Point on the coast of East Lothian. Below he describes taking his companions John Playfair and Sir James Hall to show them his evidence. Playfair's recollections of the day follow his.

Hutton:

Having taken [a] boat at Dunglass burn, we set out to explore the coast. At Siccar Point, we found a beautiful picture of this junction washed bare by the sea. The sandstone strata are partly washed away, and partly remaining upon the ends of the vertical schistus [chrystalline foliated metamorphic rock]: in many places, points of the schistus are seen standing up through among the sandstone, the greatest part of which is worn away. Behind this again we have a natural section of those sandstone strata, containing fragments of the schistus. Most of the fragments of the schistus have their angles sharp; consequently they have not travelled far, or been worn by attrition.

★

Playfair:

On us who saw these phenomena for the first time, the impression made will not easily be forgotten. The palpable evidence presented to us, of one of the most extraordinary and important facts in the nature history of the earth, gave a reality and substance to those theoretical speculations, which, however probable, had never till now been directly authenticated by the testimony of the senses. We often said to ourselves, What clearer evidence could we have had of the different formation of these rocks, and of the long interval which separated their formation, had we actually seen them emerging from the bosom of the deep? We felt ourselves necessarily carried back to the time when the schistus on which we stood was yet at the bottom of the sea, and when the sandstone before us was only beginning to be deposited, in the shape of sand or mud, from the waters of a superincumbent ocean. An epoch still more remote presented itself, when even the most ancient of these rocks, instead of standing upright in the vertical beds, lay in horizontal planes at the bottom of the sea, and was not yet disturbed by that immeasurable force which has burst asunder the solid pavement of the globe. Revolutions still more remote appeared in the distance of this extraordinary perspective. The mind seemed to grow giddy by looking so far into the abyss of time; and while we listened with earnestness and admiration to the philosopher who was now unfolding to us the order and series of these wonderful events, we became sensible how much further reason may sometimes go than imagination may venture to follow.

Robert Burns Meets Walter Scott, 1787

SIR WALTER SCOTT

As a bashful sixteen-year-old, Walter Scott encountered the by now legendary Robert Burns in the Edinburgh home of Adam Ferguson, Professor of Moral Philosophy. In the following account, Scott shows his precocious talent for observation.

I saw him one day at the late venerable Professor Ferguson's, where there were several gentlemen of literary reputation, among whom I remember the celebrated Mr Dugald Stewart. Of course, we youngsters sat silent, looked and listened. The only thing I remember which was remarkable in Burns's manner, was the effect produced upon him by a print of Bunbury's, representing a soldier lying dead on the snow, his dog sitting in misery on one side – on the other his widow, with a child in her arms. These lines were written beneath:

> Cold on Canadian hills, or Minden's plain,
> Perhaps that mother wept her soldier slain;
> Bent o'er her babe, her eye dissolved in dew,
> The big drops mingling with the milk he drew
> Gave the sad presage of his future years,
> The child of misery baptised in tears.

Burns seemed much affected by the print, or rather by the ideas which it suggested to his mind. He actually shed tears. He asked whose the lines were; and it chanced that nobody but myself remembered that they occur in a half-forgotten poem of Langhorne's called by the unpromising title of 'The Justice of Peace'. I whispered my information to a friend present; he mentioned it to Burns, who rewarded me with a look and a word, which, though of mere civility, I then received and still recollect with very great pleasure.

His person was strong and robust; his manners rustic, not clownish; a sort of dignified plainness and simplicity, which received part of its effect perhaps from one's knowledge of his extraordinary talents. His features are represented in Mr Nasmyth's picture: but to me it conveys the idea that they are diminished, as if seen in perspective. I think his countenance was more massive than it looks in any of the portraits. I should have taken the poet, had I not known who he was, for a very sagacious country farmer of the old Scotch school, i.e., none of your modern agriculturalists who keep labourers for their drudgery, but the douce gudeman who held his own plough. There was a strong expression of sense and shrewdness in all his lineament; the eye alone, I think, indicated the poetical character and temperament. It was large, and of a dark cast, which glowed (I say literally glowed) when he spoke with feeling or interest. I never saw such another eye in any human head, though I have seen the most distinguished men of my time. His conversation expressed perfect self-confidence, without the slightest presumption. Among the men who were the most learned of their time and country, he expressed himself with perfect firmness, but without the least intrusive forwardness; and when he differed in opinion, he did not hesitate to express it firmly, yet at the same time with modesty. I have only to add, that his dress corresponded with his manner. He was like a farmer dressed in his best to dine with the laird. I do not speak in malam partem, when I say, I never saw a man in company with his superiors in station or information more perfectly free from either the reality or the affectation of embarrassment.

Smallpox, 1791

THOMAS POLLOCK

The Reverend Thomas Pollock was appalled at what he saw as primitive behaviour among his parishioners in Kilwinning in Ayrshire, who not only refused to protect their children from smallpox by inoculation, but seemed keen that their children were exposed to the disease at the earliest opportunity.

Small Pox – This disease . . . rages here, at times, with the utmost violence, and is often extremely fatal. In the summer and autumn of 1791, upwards of 90 children had the natural small pox, and more than one half of them died. The chin-cough and natural small pox not unfrequently prevail at the same time. When this happens, as was the case at the above period, the ravages committed by this last disease are truly dreadful. The coincidence of these diseases might, in a great measure, be prevented by inoculation. But though in this, and in every other respect, inoculation is attended with the happiest consequences, it is only practised here in two or three families. From ignorance, and the most superstitious prejudices, the parents, regardless, or insensible of consequences, instead of inoculating their children, crowd into those houses in which the disease is of the most malignant nature, and at a time when it is the most infectious. The very worst kind of this dangerous and loathsome disease is, in this manner, communicated and spread, and thousands of valuable lives are lost to the community. This impious presumption, these illiberal and groundless prejudices, are not peculiar to this parish; in every other country parish in Scotland, the great bulk of the people think and act pretty much in the same way. It is well known, at least to the clergy, that every argument in support of inoculation, however conclusive or self-evident, makes no impression upon their minds. To make a law, obliging all persons, without distinction, to inoculate their children, would be thought inconsistent with the liberty of British subjects, and even with the common principles of humanity. But as the prosperity, nay the very existence of every country, is inseparably connected with the number of its inhabitants, something certainly ought to be attempted, to render, if possible, inoculation in Scotland more general than it is at present.

Twenty Years of Dramatic Change, c. 1792

WILLIAM CREECH

The Statistical Account of Scotland, *culled from responses to a series of questions by Church of Scotland ministers in every county, was first published between 1791 and 1799 in twenty-one volumes. In this first edition were three letters, by the bookseller and publisher William Creech, demonstrating the great changes Edinburgh had seen in the space of twenty years. A selection of his main points follows:*

In 1763 – There were two stage-coaches, with three horses, a coachman, and postilion to each coach, which went to the port of Leith (a mile and a half distant) every hour from eight in the morning, till eight at night, and consumed a full hour upon the road. There were no other stage-coaches in Scotland, except one, which set out once a month for London, and it was from twelve to sixteen days upon the journey.

In 1783 – There were five or six stage-coaches to Leith every half-hour, which ran it in fifteen minutes. Dunn, who opened the magnificent hotels in the New Town, was the first person who attempted a stage-coach to Dalkeith, a village six miles distant. – There are now stage-coaches, flies, and diligences, to every considerable town in Scotland, and to many of them two, three, four, and five: To London there were not less than sixty stage-coaches monthly, or fifteen every week, and they reached the capital in four days.

In 1763 – The number of boys at the grammar school was not more than 200.

In 1783 – The number of boys at the grammar school was 500. It is believed the most numerous school in Britain.

In 1763 – There was no such profession known as a Haberdasher.

In 1783 – The profession of a haberdasher (which includes many trades, the mercer, the milliner, the linen-draper, the hatter, the hosier, the glover, and many others), was nearly the most common in town; and they have multiplied greatly.

In 1763 – There was no such profession known as a perfumer: barbers and wigmakers were numerous, and were in the order of decent burgesses! Hairdressers were few, and hardly permitted to dress hair on Sundays; and many of them voluntarily declined it.

In 1783 – Perfumers had splendid shops in every principal street: Some of them advertised the keeping of bears, to kill occasionally, for greasing ladies and gentlemen's hair, as superior to any other animal fat. Hairdressers were more than tripled in number; and their busiest day was Sunday. There was a professor who advertised a Hair dressing Academy, and gave lectures on that noble and useful art.

In 1763 – The wages to maid-servants were generally from L.3 to L.4 a year. They dressed decently in blue or red cloaks, or in plaids, suitable to their stations.

In 1783 – The wages are nearly the same; but their dress and appearance are greatly altered, the maid-servants dressing almost as fine as their mistresses did in 1763.

In 1763 – A stranger coming to Edinburgh was obliged to put up at a dirty and uncomfortable inn, or to remove to private lodgings. There was no such place as an hotel; the word, indeed, was not known, or was only intelligible to persons acquainted with the French.

In 1783 – A stranger might have been accommodated, not only comfortably, but most elegantly, at many public hotels; and the person who, in 1763, was obliged to put up with accommodation little better than that of a waggoner or a carrier, may now be lodged like a prince, and command every luxury of life. His guinea, it must be acknowledged, will not go quite so far as it did in 1763.

In 1763 – It was fashionable to go to church, and people were interested about religion. Sunday was strictly observed by all ranks as a day of devotion; and it was disgraceful to be seen on the streets during the time of public worship . . .

In 1783 – Attendance on church was greatly neglected, and particularly by the men. Sunday was by many made a day of relaxation; and young people were allowed to stroll about at all hours. Families thought it ungenteel to take their domestics to church with them: The streets were far from being void of people in the time of public worship; and, in the evenings, were frequently loose and riotous; particularly owing to bands of apprentice boys and young lads.

In 1763 – There were five or six brothels, or houses of bad fame, and a very few of the lowest and most ignorant order of females sculked about the streets at night. A person might have gone from the Castle to Holyroodhouse, (the then length of the city), at any hour in the night, without being accosted by a single street-walker. Street-robbery, and pocket-picking were unknown.

In 1783 – The number of brothels has increased twenty-fold, and the women of the town more than a hundred-fold. Every quarter of the city and suburbs was infested with multitudes of females abandoned to vice, and a great many at a very early period of life, before passion could mislead, or reason teach them right from wrong. Street-robbers, pick-pockets, and thieves, had much increased.

In 1763 – In the best families in town, the education of daughters was fitted, not only to embellish and improve their minds, but to accomplish them in the useful and necessary arts of domestic economy. The sewing-school, the pastry-school, were then essential branches of female education; nor was a young lady of the best family ashamed to go to market with her mother.

In 1783 – The daughters of many tradesmen consumed the mornings at the toilet, or in strolling from shop to shop, &c. Many of them would have blushed to have been seen in a market. The cares of the family were devolved upon a housekeeper; and the young lady employed those heavy hours when she was disengaged from public or private amusements, in improving her mind from the precious stores of a circulating library; – and all, whether they had taste for it or not, were taught music at a great expense.

In 1763 – Young ladies (even by themselves) might have walked through the streets of the city in perfect security at any hour. No person would have interrupted, or spoken to them.

In 1783 – The mistresses of boarding-schools found it necessary to advertise, that their young ladies were not permitted to go abroad without proper attendants.

In 1791 – Boys, from bad example at home, and worse abroad, had become forward and insolent. They early frequented taverns, and were soon initiated in folly and vice, without any religious principle to restrain them. It has been an error of twenty years, to precipitate the education of boys, and make them too soon men.

The Trial of 'the Pest of Scotland', 30–31 August 1793

THOMAS MUIR

Thomas Muir, a Glasgow advocate, alarmed the authorities by his association with French revolutionaries and his outspoken anti-establishment views. He was declared a rebel after visiting France in 1793, and when he returned to Scotland he was imprisoned on various charges, including making public speeches vilifying the King and Constitution, and spreading such seditious books and pamphlets as Thomas Paine's The Rights of Man. *Tried by the notoriously harsh judge, Lord Braxfield, he was sentenced to fourteen years' deportation to Botany Bay, but escaped. He settled in France where he died at the age of thirty-four in 1799. At his trial Muir defended himself with great aplomb. No doubt anticipating the outcome, he told the jury, 'When our ashes shall be scattered by the winds of heaven, the impartial voice of future times will rejudge your verdict.'*

Gentlemen of the Jury, Let us this night throw away vain pretext: Let us act fairly and candidly. I smile at the charge of sedition. You yourselves are conscious that no sedition has existed in this country, and in your own minds you decried the accusation. I know for what I am brought to this bar, it is for having strenuously and actively engaged in the course of Parliamentary Reform; for having exerted every effort, by constitutional measures, to procure an equal representation of the people, in the House of the People.

Let not the Prosecutor skulk in darkness: Let him come manfully forward, and avow the cause which has impelled him to bring me here. I will give you little trouble: I will prevent the lassitude of the Judges: I will save you, the Jury, from the wretched mockery of a trial, the sad necessity of condemning a man, when the cause of his condemnation must be concealed, and cannot be explained.

Yes, I plead guilty. I openly, actively, and sincerely embarked in the cause of Parliamentary Reform, in the vindication and in the restoration of the rights of the people. Nor will I blush to unfold to you my motives;

they are supported by their own intrinsic strength, but they are likewise held up by the great and the venerable names of the living and of the dead. I contended for an equal representation of the people, in what I shall ever call the House of the People, because I considered it a measure essentially necessary to the salvation of the State, and to the stability of your boasted constitution.

Wherein then consists the excellency of that time-tried fabric, cemented by the blood of your fathers, flowing from the field and from the scaffold? I will tell you: It consists in the due balance of its three impelling powers, KING, LORDS, and COMMONS; if one of these powers loses its vigour, the constitution in proportion loses its vigour; if one of these powers becomes only a shadow of what it ought to be, if it becomes merged and absorbed into any of the other two, your constitution then also becomes a shadow, and it is annihilated. And do you not know, and does all the world not know that if any where the proud structure of the constitution has suffered the ravages of time or of corruption, it is in its popular branch.

Is it not a fact indisputable, that the representation of the people is not such as it once was, and is not such, as I trust in God, one day it shall be. The man then who sounds the alarm, when he discovers the approach of danger, who summons all who may be concerned in its reparation, is surely no enemy to the country, no foe to the constitution, because he labours in its preservation and protection.

Such were the motives of my conduct. If I am guilty, I have in my guilt many associates, men who now enjoy the repose of eternity, whom your fathers admired while living, and to whom you, their children, have erected statues. I have no time to run over all the venerable catalogue. But, is there a man ignorant of the illustrious Locke? And was not this sage in philosophy, this advanced champion in the cause of liberty, and of man; this friend to the British constitution, who wrote his Treatise on Government in its defence . . . was not he an advocate for a reform in Parliament, for a more equal representation of the Commons in the House of Commons? Will you venture to tear the records of *his* fame, to stigmatize *his* memory, and to brand *him* with the epithet of seditious? . . .

But if the attempt to procure a Reform in Parliament be criminal, your accusation must extend far and wide. It must implicate the Ministers of the Crown and the lowest subjects. Have you forgotten that in the year 1782, the Duke of Richmond, the present Commander of the forces, was a flaming advocate for the universal right of suffrage? Do you not know, that he presided in societies, and like Mr Pitt, advised an universal formation of such societies all over the kingdom? Have you never read his famous letter to Colonel Sherwin; in which his principles, his testimony, to a full and complete representation of the people, are indelibly recorded? Is guilt the passing insubstantial fashion of the day? Does it vary according to times, and to seasons, and to circumstances? Shall what was patriotism in 1782 be criminal in 1793?

African Exploration, 1796

MUNGO PARK

Explorer, and doctor from the Yarrow valley in the Borders, Mungo Park spent a gruelling eighteen months in the interior of Africa on behalf of the African Association of London, who had commissioned him to trace the course of the Niger. In so doing, he discovered that it flowed east. A remarkably stoical and self-effacing young man, when he returned unannounced to Britain from this trip, having long been given up for dead, he arrived at his brother-in-law's house so early in the morning that, not wishing to waken him, he passed time walking around his garden until a more sociable hour. Although Park married and set up practice in Peebles, his desire to return to Africa became too strong to resist. On a second exploratory visit to the Niger, on behalf of the government, he drowned, in 1806, after an ambush at the rapids of Bussa.

Just before it was dark, we took up our lodging for the night at a small village, where I procured some victuals for myself, and some corn for my horse, at the moderate price of a button; and was told that I should see the Niger (which the Negroes call Joliba, or *the great water*) early the next day. The lions are here very numerous: the gates are shut a little after sunset, and nobody allowed to go out. The thoughts of seeing the Niger in the morning, and the troublesome buzzing of musketoes, prevented me from shutting my eyes during the night; and I had saddled my horse, and was in readiness before daylight; but, on account of the wild beasts, we were obliged to wait until the people were stirring, and the gates opened. This happened to be a market-day at Sego, and the roads were everywhere filled with people, carrying different articles to sell. We passed four large villages, and at eight o'clock saw the smoke over Sego.

As we approached the town, I was fortunate enough to overtake the fugitive Kaartans, to whose kindness I had been so much indebted in my journey through Bambarra. They readily agreed to introduce me to the king; and we rode together through some marshy ground, where, as I was anxiously looking around for the river, one of them called out, *geo affilli* (see the water); and looking forwards, I saw with infinite pleasure the great object of my mission; the long sought for, majestic Niger, glittering to the morning sun, as broad as the Thames at Westminster, and flowing slowly *to the eastward* . . .

I heard somebody holloa; and looking behind, saw those I had taken for elephant hunters, running after me, and calling out to me to turn back. I stopped until they were all come up; when they informed me that the King of the Foulahs had sent them on purpose to bring me, my horse, and everything that belonged to me, to Fooladoo; and that therefore I must turn back, and go along with them. Without hesitating a moment, I turned round and followed them, and we travelled together near a quarter of a mile, without exchanging a word: when coming to a dark place in the wood, one of them said, in the Mandingo language, 'this place will do'; and immediately snatched my hat from my head. Though I was by no means free of apprehension, yet I resolved to show as few signs of fear as possible, and therefore told them, that unless my hat was returned to me, I should proceed no further. But before I had time to receive an answer, another drew his knife, and seizing upon a metal button which remained upon my waistcoat, cut it off, and put it into his pocket. Their intentions were now obvious: and I thought that the easier they were permitted to rob me of everything, the less I had to fear. I therefore allowed them to search my pockets without resistance, and examine every part of my apparel, which they did with the most scrupulous exactness. But observing that I had one waistcoat under another, they insisted that I should cast them both off; and at last, to make sure work, they stripped me quite naked. Even my half boots (though the sole of one of them was tied on to my foot with a broken bridle-rein) were minutely inspected. Whilst they were examining the plunder, I begged them, with great earnestness, to return my pocket compass; but when I pointed it out to them, as it was lying on the ground, one of the banditti, thinking I was about to take it up, cocked his musket and swore that he would lay me dead upon the spot if I presumed to put my hand upon it. After this, some of them went away with my horse, and the remainder stood considering whether they should leave me quite naked, or allow me something to shelter me from the sun. Humanity at last prevailed: they returned me the worst of the two shirts, and a pair of trousers; and, as they went away, one of them threw back my hat, in the crown of which I kept my memorandums; this was probably the reason they did not wish to keep it. After they were gone, I sat for some time, looking around me with amazement and terror. Whichever way I turned, nothing appeared but danger and difficulty. I saw myself in the midst of a vast wilderness, in the depth of the rainy season; naked and alone; surrounded by savage animals, and men still more savage. I was five hundred miles from the nearest European settlement. All these circumstances crowded at once on my recollection; and I confess that my spirits began to fail me.

Henry Raeburn, Early 1800s

ALLAN CUNNINGHAM AND ANONYMOUS

Henry Raeburn is arguably the greatest portraitist Scotland has produced. Orphaned young, he began as a jeweller's apprentice, started painting miniatures, and was taken under the wing of David Martin, then Edinburgh's pre-eminent portrait painter. After a short spell in Italy, Raeburn returned to Scotland to become its most celebrated artist. In the following recollections gathered by the Victorian essayist John Brown, his habits and technique are described, first by his friend Allan Cunningham, and then by an anonymous sitter, whose knowledge of other artists puts him among the wealthier of the country's citizens.

The following is Cunningham's account of him:

Though his painting-rooms were in York Place, his Dwelling-house was at St Bernard's, near Stockbridge, overlooking the Water of Leith – a romantic place. The steep banks were then finely wooded; the garden grounds varied and beautiful; and all the seclusion of the country could be enjoyed, without the remoteness. The motions of the artist were as regular as those of a clock. He rose at seven during summer, took breakfast about eight with his wife and children, walked up to his great room in 32 York Place . . . and was ready for a sitter by nine; and of sitters he generally had, for many years, not fewer than three or four a day. To these he gave an hour and a half each. He seldom kept a sitter more than two hours; unless the person happened – and that was often the case – to be gifted with more than common talents. He then felt himself happy, and never failed to detain the party till the arrival of a new sitter intimated that he must be gone.

For a head size he generally required four or five sittings: and he preferred painting the head and hands to any other part of the body: assigning as a reason that they required least consideration. A fold of drapery, or the natural ease which the casting of a mantle over the shoulder demanded, occasioned him more perplexing study than a head full of thought and imagination. Such was the intuition with which he penetrated at once to the mind, that the first sitting rarely came to a close without his having seized strongly on the character and disposition of the individual. He never drew in his heads, or indeed any part of the body, with chalk . . . but began with the brush at once.

The forehead, chin, nose, and mouth were his first touches. He always painted standing, and never used a stick for resting his hand on; for such was his accuracy of eye, and steadiness of nerve, that he could introduce the most delicate touches, or the utmost mechanical regularity of line, without aid, or other contrivance than fair off-hand dexterity. He remained in his painting-room till a little after five o'clock, when he walked home, and dined at six.

One of his sitters thus describes him:

He spoke a few words to me in his usual brief and kindly way – evidently to put me into an agreeable mood; and then, having placed me in a chair on a platform at the end of his painting-room, in the posture required, set up his easel beside me with the canvas ready to receive the colour. When he saw all was right, he took his palette and his brush, retreated back step by step, with his face towards me, till he was nigh the other end of his room; he stood and studied for a minute more, then came up to the canvas, and, without looking at me, wrought upon it with colour for some time. Having done this, he retreated in the same manner, studied my looks at that distance for about another minute, then came hastily up to the canvas and painted a few minutes more.

I had sat to other artists; their way was quite different – they made an outline carefully in chalk, measured it with compasses, placed the canvas close to me, and looking me almost without ceasing in the face, proceeded to fill up the outline with colour. They succeeded best in the minute detail – Raeburn best in the general result of the expression; they obtained by means of a multitude of little touches what he found by broader masses; they gave more of the man – he gave most of the mind.

Highland Emigration, 1806

JAMES CRAIG

An entry in the Statistical Account of Scotland *in 1805 for the parish of Strachur gives a flavour of official attitudes towards Highlanders in certain quarters: 'If a Highlander is forced or induced to leave the small circle which occupied his first affections, he cares not how far he goes from home. Going to another parish, or the district of another clan, is to him an entire banishment; and when he has resolved to set out, whether from necessity or choice, he would as soon cross the Atlantic as he would cross an arm of the sea.' In the same year, the Earl of Selkirk, who was planning to establish colonies in Canada, manned by emigrants, published a pamphlet extolling the benefits of Highland emigration and wondering, of those displaced from their land, 'why do they quarrel with that which is so beneficial to them?' His attitude provoked a series of indignant letters by the advocate James Craig, published in the* Edinburgh Herald and Chronicle *in 1806.*

. . . I cannot, as a friend to the country which contains me, but condemn a work of which the scope of ten out of twelve chapters is directly calculated to remove those apprehensions, which either the most discontented or the most sanguine Highlander, must entertain (but for such assurances) against so vast an adventure as emigration. Domestic dissatisfaction is a cheerless and dangerous sentiment; and yet, can there be a keener edge laid to the root of domestic peace, than those glowing pictures of independence, security, congenial society, and every blessing a Highlander has been taught to prize, which the Earl of Selkirk has pencilled under the term Emigration. Does he not turn to the peasant and say, 'Leave your country; leave a land which has no longer use for you; a land where you may have bread indeed, but where you can only earn that bread by a dereliction of every habit which could sweeten the morsel. Emigrate therefore; and if you will but turn towards the colony which I protect, and clear a few acres of its forests, you will become affluent and happy beyond the condition of all your fathers.' And does he not look towards the Legislature and plead – 'Encourage emigration – drain off your superfluous people – depopulate your mountains, and send your hardiest sons to foreign climes, there to become the sure and steady friends of the country which turned them from her bosom.' – Such, I contend, is the true import of the Noble Earl's advice; and if the particulars of its detail are embellished with the persuasives both of precept and example, still the object of all this is nothing else than to render his favourite emigration more palatable to the people, and less odious to the government . . .

I would not, in the present condition of Europe, speak the language of despondency; but, as a lover of my country, I cannot but advise the champions of emigration to look well to the ranks of our armies, and the demands of our navy; to regard the state of wages of domestic labour, and the calls of our manufacturers, mechanics, and farmers, before they proceed farther in their experimental schemes of depopulation; I would have them regard the thousands of waste acres in our own land before they thus struggle to drain the scanty population it possesses; and I would earnestly remind them that, until the days of Lord Selkirk, the doctrine of most philosophers was, that the life's blood of this nation was her inhabitants – her peasantry – nay, sir, I will add (without meaning offence to any class of subjects) her Highlanders . . .

He has told you, that the Highlander, inactive and indolent on his own shore, is no sooner transplanted to his Lordship's colony, than he becomes active and energetic, an industrious husbandman, and a promising warrior. The constitution of the man undergoes, it seems, a total revolution by the mere act of emigration, and the very hereditary vices of his nature are, by this single step, transformed into their opposite virtues . . .

The Noble Earl has argued, that any change of scene to a Highlander, is emigration; that to remove him across the Clyde is tantamount to removal across the Western Ocean; that Glasgow and Paisley are to him as foreign as the shores of Labrador, or St John's; that to be happy, he must have land; and that to have land, he must be an emigrant. . . . I would only request of Lord Selkirk and his admirers, generally to ask themselves these questions; – Granting that the Highland climate is boisterous, Is it not at least nearer to that of 'Glasgow and Paisley,' than the climate of the Back Settlements of North America; admitting that the manners of Lanark or Renfrew may at first surprise a native of Argyle or Inverness, are these manners more difficult for a Scotchman to imbibe, than the customs which pervade the banks of the Mississippi or the Oronooko? . . .

The Ossian Fraud, 1806

SIR WALTER SCOTT

There was great excitement throughout literary Europe when in 1762, 1765 and 1773 the young Scottish schoolmaster and poet James Macpherson published translations of an extraordinary series of epic poems he claimed to have found by an ancient Gaelic bard called Ossian. Romantic and emotional, they proved a huge success, and were widely translated. Samuel Johnson was the first to cast doubt on their authenticity, and after Macpherson's death, a report in 1805 concluded that the works were founded only on scraps of Gaelic originals which he had embellished. That he had done so with masterly ingenuity was also accepted. Walter Scott added his stern views on the subject in a letter to his friend Anna Seward.

Ashestiel September 1806

. . . As for the great dispute I should be no Scottish man if I had not very attentively considered it at some period of my studies & indeed I have gone to some length in my researches for I have beside me translations of some twenty or thirty of the unquestioned originals of Ossians poems. After making every allowance for the disadvantages of a literal translation & the possible debasement which those *now collected* may have suffered in the great & violent change which the Highlands have undergone since the researches of Macpherson I am compelled to admit that incalculably the greater part of the English Ossian must be ascribed to Macpherson himself and that his whole introductions notes &c &c is an absolute tissue of forgeries . . .

The Highland Society have lately set about investigating, or rather, I should say collecting materials to defend the authenticity of Ossian. Those researches have only proved that there were no real originals using that word as is commonly understood to be found for them. The oldest tale they have found seems to be that of Darthula but it is perfectly different both in diction & story from that of Macpherson – it is, however, a beautiful specimen of Celtic poetry & shews that it contains much which is worthy of preservation – indeed how should it be otherwise when we know that till about fifty years ago the Highlands contained a race of hereditary poets. Is it possible to think that perhaps among many hundreds who for such a course of centuries have founded their reputation & rank on practising the art of poetry in a country where scenery & manners gave such effect & interest & imagery to their productions, there should not have been some who have attained excellence? In searching out those genuine records of the Celtic Muse & preserving them from oblivion with all the curious information which they must doubtless contain I humbly think our Highland antiquaries would merit better of their country than confining their researches to the fantastic pursuit of a chimera . . .

Building the Bell Rock Lighthouse, 2 September 1807

ROBERT STEVENSON

The Stevenson family of engineers, from whom Robert Louis was descended, pioneered the art of modern lighthouse-building and in so doing established themselves as one of the most important families in the country. Among their earliest ventures was the Bell Rock lighthouse, an astonishing feat of engineering led by Robert Stevenson. The Bell Rock, lying about 11 miles south-east of Arbroath, was, in Robert's words, 'a sunk reef . . . so situated as to have long proved an object of dread to mariners on the eastern coast of Scotland'. Because of the lowness of the reef, work could only be carried out between tides for periods of a few hours. The construction crew experienced several alarming episodes, but few were more terrifying than this occasion, early in its construction, when one of their three boats drifted away. The Smeaton *was the boat assigned to the lighthouse crew, which had drifted off with the third boat in tow.*

In this perilous predicament, indeed, he found himself placed between hope and despair . . . situate upon a sunken rock in the middle of the ocean, which, in the progress of the flood-tide, was to be laid under water to the depth of at least twelve feet in a stormy sea. There were this morning thirty-two persons in all upon the rock, with only two boats, whose complement, even in good weather, did not exceed twenty-four sitters; but to row to the floating-light with so much wind, and in so heavy a sea, a complement of eight men for each boat, was as much as could, with propriety, be attempted, so that, in this way, about one-half of our number was unprovided for. Under these circumstances, had the writer ventured to dispatch one of the boats in expectation of either working the *Smeaton* sooner up towards the rock, or in hopes of getting her boat brought to our assistance, this must have given an immediate alarm to the artificers, each of whom would have insisted upon taking to his own boat, and leaving the eight artificers belonging to the *Smeaton* to their chance. Of course, a scuffle might have ensued, and it is hard to say, in the ardour of men contending for life, where it might have ended. It has even been hinted to the writer, that a party of *pickmen* were determined to keep exclusively to their own boat against all hazards.

The unfortunate circumstance of the *Smeaton* and her boat having drifted, was, for a considerable time, only known to the writer, and to the landing-master, who removed to the farther point of the rock, where he kept his eye steadily upon the progress of the vessel. While the artificers were at work, chiefly in sitting or kneeling postures, excavating the rock, or boring with the jumpers, and while their numerous hammers, and the sound of the smith's anvil continued, the situation of things did not appear so awful. In this state of suspense, with almost certain destruction at hand, the water began to rise upon those who were at work on the lower parts of the sites of the Beacon and Lighthouse. From the run of sea upon the rock, the forge fire was also sooner extinguished this morning than usual, and the volumes of smoke having ceased, objects in every direction became visible from all parts of the rock. After having had about three hours work, the men began, pretty generally, to make towards their respective boats for their jackets and stockings, when, to their astonishment, instead of three, they found only two boats, the third being adrift with the *Smeaton*.

Not a word was uttered by any one, but all appeared to be silently calculating their numbers, and looking to each other with evident marks of perplexity depicted in their countenances. The landing-master, conceiving that blame might be attached to him for allowing the boat to leave the rock, still kept at a distance. At this critical moment, the author was standing upon an elevated part of Smith's Ledge, where he endeavoured to mark the progress of the *Smeaton*, not a little surprised that her crew did not cut the praam [a flat-bottomed boat] adrift, which greatly retarded her way, and amazed that some effort was not making to bring at least the boat, and attempt our relief. The workmen looked steadfastly upon the writer, and turned occasionally towards the vessel, still far to leeward. All this passed in the most perfect silence, and the melancholy solemnity of the group made an impression never to be effaced from his mind.

The writer had all along been considering of various schemes, – providing the men could be kept under command, – which might be put in practice for the general safety, in hopes that the *Smeaton* might be able to pick up the boats to leeward, when they were obliged to leave the rock. He was, accordingly, about to address the artificers on the perilous nature of their circumstances, and to propose, That all hands should unstrip their upper clothing, when the higher parts of the rock were laid under water; that the seamen should remove every unnecessary weight and encumbrance from the boats; that a specified number of men should go into each boat, and that the remainder should hang by the gunwales, while the boats were to be rowed gently towards the *Smeaton*, as the course to the Pharos or floating-light lay rather to windward of the rock.

But when he attempted to speak, his mouth was so parched, that his tongue refused utterance, and he now learned by experience that the saliva is as necessary as the tongue itself for speech. He then turned to one of the pools on the rock and lapped a little water, which produced immediate relief. But what was his happiness, when, on rising from this unpleasant beverage, some one called out 'A boat, a boat!' and, on looking around, at no great distance, a large boat was seen coming through the haze making towards the rock. This at once enlivened and rejoiced every heart. The timeous visitor proved to be James Spink, the Bell Rock pilot, who had come express from Arbroath with letters. Spink had, for some time, seen the *Smeaton*, and had even supposed, from the state of the weather, that all hands were on board of her, till he approached more nearly, and observed people upon the rock; but not supposing that the assistance of his boat was necessary to carry the artificers off the rock, he anchored on the lee-side and began to fish, waiting, as usual, till the letters were sent for, as the pilot-boat was too large and unwieldy for approaching the rock, when there was any roughness or run of the sea at the entrance of the landing creeks.

Upon this fortunate change in circumstances, sixteen of the artificers were sent, at two trips, in one of the boats . . . the remaining sixteen followed in the two boats belonging to the service of the rock. Every one felt the most perfect happiness at leaving the Bell Rock this morning, though a very hard and even dangerous passage to the floating-light still awaited us, as the wind, by this time, had encreased to a pretty hard gale, accompanied with a considerable swell of the sea.

Conditions in the Mines, 1808

ROBERT BALD

Robert Bald, a civil engineer and factor to the Earl of Mar, wrote a scientific treatise on the mining industry, but included a heart-felt appendix on the conditions of women who worked in mines. Despite his harrowing descriptions, it took a government inquiry in 1840 into child labour to change the practice of using women and children in pits.

. . . We conceive it proper to bring into view the condition of a class in the community, intimately connected with the coal-trade, who endure a slavery scarcely tolerated in the ages of darkness and of barbarism. The class alluded to is that of the women who carry coals underground, in Scotland, – known by the name of Bearers. . . . The women are not only employed to carry the coals from the wall-face to the pit bottom, but also to ascend with them to the hill; no doubt this was the practice in the very early periods in collieries; and it is only wonderful, that such a custom should remain to the present day, in the midst of all our refinements.

This latter mode is unknown in England, and is abolished in the neighbourhood of Glasgow. . . . It is, however, a certain fact, that severe and laborious as this employment is, still there are young women to be found, who, from early habits, have no particular aversion to the work, and who are as cheerful and light in heart as the gayest of the fair sex; and as they have it in their power to betake themselves to other work if they choose, the carrying of coals is a matter of free choice; and therefore, no blame can be particularly attached to the coalmaster. Yet, still it must, even in the most favourable point of view, be looked upon as a very bad, old and disgraceful custom.

But, as married women are also as much engaged in this servitude as the young, it is in this instance that the practice is absolutely injurious and bad, even although they submit to it without repining . . .

In those collieries where this mode [using people not horses] is in practice, the collier leaves his house for the pit about eleven o'clock at night (attended by his sons, if he has any sufficiently old) when the rest of mankind are retiring to rest. Their first work is to prepare coals, by hewing them down from the wall. In about three hours after, his wife (attended by her daughters, if she has any sufficiently grown) sets out for the pit, having previously wrapped her infant child in a blanket and left it to the care of an old woman who, for a small gratuity, keeps three or four children at a time, and who, in their mothers' absence, feeds them with ale or whisky mixed with water. The children who are a little more advanced, are left to the care of a neighbour; and under such treatment, it is surprising that they ever grow up or thrive.

The mother, having thus disposed of her younger children, descends the pit with her older daughters, when each, having a basket of a suitable form, lays it down, and into it the large coals are rolled; and such is the weight carried, that it frequently takes two men to lift the burden upon their backs: the girls are loaded according to their strength. The mother sets out first, carrying a lighted candle in her teeth; the girls follow, and in this manner they proceed to the pit bottom, and with weary steps and slow, ascend the stairs, halting occasionally to draw breath, till they arrive at the hill or pit top, where the coals are laid down for sale; and in this manner they go for eight or ten hours almost without resting. It is no uncommon thing to see them, when ascending the pit, weeping most bitterly, from the excessive severity of the labour; but the instant they have laid down their burden on the hill, they resume their cheerfulness, and return down the pit singing.

The execution of work performed by a stout woman in this way is beyond conception. For instance, we have seen a woman, during the space of time above mentioned, take on a load of at least 170 lbs. avoirdupois, travel with this 150 yards up the slope of the coal below ground, ascend a pit by stairs 117 feet, and travel upon the hill 20 yards more to where the coals are laid down. All this she will perform no less than twenty-four times as a day's work. . . . The weight of coals thus brought to the pit top by a woman in a day, amounts to 4,080 pounds, or above thirty-six hundred-weight English, and there have been frequent instances of two tons being carried. The wages paid them for this work, are *eightpence per day!* . . .

The collier, with his wife and children, having performed their daily task, return home, where no comfort awaits them; their clothes are frequently soaked with water, and covered with mud; their shoes so very bad as scarcely to deserve the name. In this situation they are exposed to all the rigours of winter, the cold frequently freezing their clothes.

On getting home, all is cheerless and devoid of comfort; the fire is generally out, the culinary utensils dirty and unprepared, and the mother naturally first seeks after her infant child, which she nurses even before her pit clothes are thrown off.

From this incessant labour of the wife, the children are sadly neglected, and all those domestic concerns disregarded, which contribute to render the life of the labourer comfortable and happy. It is presumed, that it is from this habit of life that infectious diseases make in general greater havock among the children of colliers than among those of any other class of labourers, so much so, that we have seen the number of deaths in one year exceed the number of births. Enter their houses; these will afford ample demonstration of all that is adduced.

This habit of life is also the cause of the money which they earn being spent, without economy; hence they are always in want. No doubt, there are many exceptions to the contrary; but the case now brought forward is too frequently to be found . . .

Besides the wives and daughters of the colliers, there is another class of women attached to some collieries, termed Framed Bearers, or, more properly, Fremit Bearers, that is, women who are nowise related to those who employ them. These are at the disposal of the oversman below ground, and he appoints them to carry coals for any person he thinks proper, so that they sometimes have a new master every day: this is slavery complete; and when an unrelenting collier takes an ill-natured fit, he oppresses the bearer with such heavy loads of coal, as are enough to break, not only the spirit, but the back of any human being.

That the women are fully sensible, and feel the severity of their labour, is but too evident, especially to all those who have been accustomed to travel below ground. One case, for example, we shall mention, which occurred.

In surveying the workings of an extensive colliery below ground, a married woman came forward, groaning under an excessive weight of coals, trembling in every nerve, and almost unable to keep her knees from sinking under her. On coming up, she said in a most plaintive and melancholy voice: 'O SIR, THIS IS SORE, SORE WORK. I WISH TO GOD THAT THE FIRST WOMAN WHO TRIED TO BEAR COALS HAD BROKE HER BACK, AND NONE WOULD HAVE TRIED IT AGAIN.'

The Historical Novel Is Born, 1814

HENRY COCKBURN

Sir Walter Scott's Waverley novels were published anonymously initially because he feared jeopardizing his reputation as a lawyer and poet. They created an immediate sensation, being a wholly new sort of fiction, combining thrilling romance and adventure with a strong historical narrative. Although they have since been criticized for their twisting of facts and shameless myth-making, their influence on the course of literature has been incalculable. Henry Cockburn, the advocate, recalls the speculation the first volume caused. It was more than ten years before Scott publicly owned up to the authorship which, by then, was an open secret.

The unexpected newness of the thing, the profusion of original characters, the Scotch language, Scotch scenery, Scotch men and women, the simplicity of the writing, and the graphic force of the descriptions, all struck us with an electric shock of delight. I wish I could again feel the sensations produced by the first year of these two Edinburgh works. If the concealment of the authorship of the novels was intended to make mystery heighten their effect, it completely succeeded. The speculations and conjectures, and nods and winks, and predictions and assertions were endless, and occupied every company, and almost every two men who spoke in the street. It was proved by a thousand indications, each refuting the other, that they were written by old Henry Mackenzie, by George Cranstoun, by William Erskine, by Jeffrey, and above all, by Thomas Scott, Walter's brother, a regimental paymaster, then in Canada. But 'the Great Unknown,' as the true author was then called, always took good care, with all his concealment, to supply evidence amply sufficient for the protection of his property and his fame; so much so that the suppression of the name was laughed at in his presence as a good joke not merely by select friends, but by himself . . .

The Battle of Waterloo, 18 June 1815

SERGEANT-MAJOR DICKSON

The performance of the Royal Scots Greys at the Battle of Waterloo was crucial in clinching the British victory. As the entire French army gathered in sight of the Scots Greys, they marched to meet them. Napoleon was impressed by their courage, but believed that his army would destroy them in a mere half hour. As he retreated from the field some time later, he is said to have commented, 'These terrible Greys how they fight!' The following is an account of the action given by Sergeant-Major Dickson nearly forty years afterwards.

We had hardly reached our position when a great fusillade commenced just in front of us, and we saw the Highlanders moving up towards the road to the right. . . . Immediately after this, the General of the Union Brigade, Sir William Ponsonby, came riding up to us on a small bay hack. . . . Beside him was his aide-de-camp, De Lacy Evans. He ordered us forward to within fifty yards of the beech-hedge by the roadside. I can see him now in his long cloak and great cocked hat as he rode up to watch the fighting below. From our new position we could descry the three regiments of Highlanders, only a thousand in all, bravely firing down on the advancing masses of Frenchmen. These numbered thousands. . . . Then I saw the Brigadier, Sir Denis Pack, turn to the Gordons and shout out with great energy, 'Ninety-second, you must charge! All in front of you have given way.' The Highlanders, who had begun the day by solemnly chanting 'Scots wha hae' as they prepared their morning meal, instantly, with fixed bayonets, began to press forward through the beech and holly hedge to a line of bushes that grew along the face of the slope in front. They uttered loud shouts as they ran forward and fired a volley at twenty yards into the French.

At this moment our General and his aide-de-camp rode off to the right by the side of the hedge; then suddenly I saw De Lacy Evans wave his hat in the air, and immediately our colonel, Inglis Hamilton, shouted out, 'Now then, Scots Greys, charge!' and, waving his sword in the air, he rode straight at the hedges in front, which he took in grand style. At once a great cheer rose from our ranks, and we too waved our swords and followed him. I dug my spurs into my brave old Rattler and we were off like the wind . . .

All of us were greatly excited, and began crying, 'Hurrah, Ninety-second! Scotland for ever!' as we crossed the road. For we heard the Highland pipers playing among the smoke and firing below, and I plainly saw my old friend Pipe-Major Cameron standing apart on a hillock coolly playing 'Johnny Cope, are ye waukin' yet?' in all the din . . .

As we tightened our grip to descend the hillside among the corn we could make out the feather bonnets of the Highlanders, and heard the officers crying out to them to wheel back by sections.

They were all Gordons, and as we passed through them they shouted, 'Go at them, the Greys! Scotland for ever!' My blood thrilled at this, and I clutched my sabre tighter. Many of the Highlanders grasped our stirrups, and in the fiercest excitement dashed with us into the fight. The French were uttering loud, discordant yells. Just then I saw the first Frenchman. A young officer of Fusiliers made a slash at me with his sword, but I parried it and broke his arm; the next second we were in the thick of them. We could not see five yards ahead for the smoke . . .

The French were fighting like tigers. Some of the wounded were firing at us as we passed. . . . Then those in front began to cry out for 'quarter', throwing down their muskets and taking off their belts. The Gordons at this rushed in and drove the French to the rear. I was now in the front rank, for many of ours had fallen . . .

We now came to an open space covered with bushes, and then I saw [Sergeant] Ewart, with five or six infantry men about him, slashing right and left at them. . . . I was just in time to thwart a bayonet thrust that was aimed at the gallant sergeant's neck. . . . Almost single-handed, Ewart had captured the Imperial Eagle of the Forty-fifth 'invincibles,' which had led them to victory at Austerlitz and Jena. . . . We cried out, 'Well done, my boy!' and as others had come up, we spurred on in search of a like success . . .

We were saluted with a sharp fire of musketry, and again found ourselves beset by thousands of Frenchmen. We had fallen upon a second column; they were also Fusiliers. . . . We at once began a furious onslaught on this obstacle, and soon made an impression; the battalions seemed to open out for us to pass through, and so it happened that in five minutes we had cut our way through as many thousands of Frenchmen.

We had now reached the bottom of the slope. There the ground was slippery with deep mud. Urging each other on, we dashed towards the batteries on the ridge above, which had worked such havoc on our ranks. The ground was very difficult, and especially where we crossed the edge of a ploughed field, so that our horses sank to the knees as we struggled on. My brave Rattler was becoming quite exhausted, but we dashed ever onwards.

At this moment Colonel Hamilton rode up to us crying, 'Charge the guns!' and went off like the wind up the hill towards the terrible battery that had made such deadly work among the Highlanders. It was the last we saw of our colonel, poor fellow! His body was found with both arms cut off. His pockets had been rifled . . .

Then we got among the guns, and we had our revenge. Such slaughtering! We sabred the gunners, lamed the horses, and cut their traces and harness. I can hear the Frenchmen yet crying '*Diable!*' when I struck at them, and the long-drawn hiss through their teeth as my sword went home. Fifteen of their guns could not be fired again that day. The artillery-drivers sat on their horses weeping aloud as we went among them; they were mere boys, we thought.

Rattler lost her temper and bit and tore at everything that came in her way. She seemed to have got new strength. I had lost the plume of my bearskin just as we went through the second infantry column; a shot had carried it away. The French infantry were rushing past us in disorder on their way to the rear. [Someone] shouted to me to dismount, for old Rattler was badly wounded. I did so just in time, for she fell heavily the next second. I caught hold of a French officer's horse and sprang on her back and rode on . . .

But you can imagine my astonishment when down below, on the very ground we had crossed, appeared at full gallop a couple of regiments of Cuirassiers on the right, and away to the left a regiment of Lancers. I shall never forget the sight. The Cuirassiers, in their sparkling steel breastplates and helmets, mounted on strong black horses, with great blue rugs across the croups, were galloping towards me, tearing up the earth as they went, the trumpets blowing wild notes in the midst of the discharges of grape and canister shot from the heights.

Around me there was one continuous noise of clashing arms, shouting of men, neighing and moaning of horses. What were we to do? Behind us we saw masses of French infantry with tall fur hats coming up at the double, and between us and our lines these cavalry. There being no officers about, we saw nothing for it but to go straight at them and trust to Providence to get through. There were half-a-dozen of us Greys and about a dozen of the Royals and Enniskillens on the ridge. We all shouted, 'Come on, lads; that's the road home!' and, dashing our spurs into our horses' sides, set off straight for the Lancers.

But we had no chance. . . . The crash as we met was terrible; the horses began to rear and bite and neigh loudly, and then some of our men got down among their feet, and I saw them trying to ward off the lances with their hands . . .

Here again I came to the ground, for a Lancer finished my new mount, and I thought I was done for. We were returning past the edge of the ploughed field, and then I saw a spectacle I shall never forget. There lay brave old Ponsonby, the General of our Union Brigade, beside his little bay, both dead. His long, fur-lined cloak had blown aside, and at his hand I noticed a miniature of a lady and his watch; beyond him, our Brigade-Major, Reignolds of the Greys. . . . My heart filled with sorrow at this, but I dared not remain for a moment. It was just then I caught sight of a squadron of English Dragoons making straight for us. The Frenchmen at that instant seemed to give way, and in a minute more we were safe! The Dragoons gave us a cheer and rode on after the Lancers . . .

How I reached our lines I can hardly say, for the next thing I remember is that I was lying with the sole remnants of our brigade in a position far away to the right and rear of our first post. I was told that a third horse that I caught was so wounded that she fell dead as I was mounting her. Wonderful to relate, Rattler had joined the retreating Greys, and was standing in line riderless when I returned. . . . There were scarcely half a hundred of the Greys left out of the three hundred who rode off half-an-hour before . . .

It was not till afterwards that we soldiers learned what the Union Brigade had done that day, for a man in the fighting-ranks sees little beyond the sweep of his own sword. We had pierced three columns of fifteen thousand men, had captured two Imperial Eagles, and had stormed and rendered useless for a time more than forty of the enemy's cannon. Besides, we had taken nearly three thousand prisoners, and, when utterly exhausted, had fought our way home through several regiments of fresh cavalry.

Law and Justice in the Highlands, c. 1816–1826

JOSEPH MITCHELL

Joseph Mitchell was born in Forres in 1803, and, like his father, worked for the great engineer Thomas Telford. He became Superintendent and Engineer of Highland Roads, Bridges and Railways, and wrote a memoir in which he evokes the Inverness and Highlands of his childhood and early working life.

Public Executions

The hangman was a distinguished and awful functionary. The official who then held the appointment was a person condemned for sheep-stealing, which was at this time a capital crime; but he received a pardon on condition that he agreed to act as hangman, an office very unpopular. The former hangman, Taylor, had died from severe treatment by a mob. The office was no sinecure, as there was generally a hanging at every circuit in April and August. The man, however, was well to do. He had a comfortable house, £60 a year, and some control over the fish and meal markets. He rang the 'bell' when there was fish in town, and had a perquisite of a haddock out of every creel, and a handful of meal out of every sack that came into the market for sale.

The penal laws were then very severe. Theft and sheep-stealing as well as murder were capital offences. To add to the misery of the unhappy criminals, the penalty was delayed for six weeks after sentence. The execution was conducted with great solemnity. The gallows was erected at the Longman, a green on the sea-shore about two miles from the town. Round the gallows, twelve feet from the ground, was a raised platform on which the clergy and magistrates stood, the culprit on the drop.

According to my recollection the procession between the jail and the place of execution was very dreadful. A company of soldiers was generally required from Fort George as a guard. First came the town's officers with their red coats and halberds; then the magistrates and council. The culprit followed, attended by either one or two clergymen. He was clothed in a white robe, with bare neck, over which the noose of the rope hung loose, the upper end being borne by the hangman, who walked behind. Then followed respectable citizens. The military formed a guard on each side. Some of the culprits were worked up into a state of enthusiasm and prayed aloud, while at other times praise and prayer were conducted by the clergymen. When a man was hanged for sheep-stealing (and this was frequent) it was very sad to see his relatives weeping in deep distress at the foot of the gallows – poor, ignorant people.

Lunatics

There was no Lunatic Asylum or Poor House in the North, and five or six half-witted creatures used to go about the streets, tormented often by idle boys. A poor creature was kept for many years in the jail, who was said to have committed murder in a fit of insanity, and was condemned to confinement for life. He was placed in a cell with a small grated aperture for air and light, a pallet of straw for his bed, and bread and water for food. He lay there for many years, the community perfectly indifferent to his condition, till in 1816 he was removed to the Lunatic Asylum of Dundee, where in a few years he died. We children were told that if we were not good we would be sent to 'Trochter'; such was the name he was called, being the Gaelic for murderer. He used, in a stentorian voice, which was heard a long way off, up and down the street, to cry out in Gaelic, 'Oh yea, yea, Thighearna nan gras dean trochair orm', translated 'O Lord of Grace, have mercy on me.' The people became so accustomed to the cry that they thought nothing of it; but in the middle of the night, when the shouts were frequent, the noise was very appalling.

Smuggling

The Highlanders seem to have liked the idle, risky, and adventurous trade, and they felt they had the public sympathy in their favour. There was a romance about it. The still was generally placed in some secluded spot, in the ravine of a Highland burn, or screened by waving birch and natural wood, so that the smoke of the fire could scarcely be observed. There were scouts placed around, often three or four savage-looking men, sometimes women and boys. I have witnessed such a wild and romantic scene, a fit subject for an artist.

So general was smuggling that at Inverness there were two or three master coppersmiths who had a sign about their shops of a whisky still, indicating their employment. I recollect the mysterious manner in which my mother got her supply of whisky, and in perfect safety, although the collector of Excise lived some six doors away. Everybody declared 'small still' or smuggled whisky was the only spirit worth drinking. The Highland smugglers baffled the Government . . .

One morning as I was driving up Glenmoriston before breakfast, and taking a turn in the road of that beautiful valley, I saw before me at some little distance about twenty-five Highland horses tied to each other, and carrying two kegs of whisky each. They were attended by ten or twelve men, some in kilts and all with bonnets and plaids, and carrying large bludgeons. When they saw me approach two of them fell back until I came up with them. They scrutinized me sharply and said, 'It is a fine morning, sir;' to which I responded. Then one turned to the other and said, 'Ha rickh shealess ha mach Mitchell fere rate – mohr;' the literal translation of which is, 'You need not mind; it is the son of Mitchell, the man of the high roads.'

He then turned to me and said, 'Would you took a dram?' and on my assenting he took out of his pocket a round tin snuff-box, then common, but without the lid, holding about a large wine-glassful, and filled it with whisky from a bottle which he took from his side-pocket.

After some kindly greeting and talk and drinking my dram, I passed on, the other men politely touching their bonnets as I left. This was another scene for an artist, and is not likely to be seen again.

Almost all wines, spirits, and foreign commodities supplied to the Highlands were smuggled, chiefly from Holland.

I recollect, while visiting tacksmen on the west coast, being brought to a cave where a whole cargo of kegs of foreign spirits was piled up. The last cargo from Holland 'run' in the Moray Firth was in 1825, brought by one Donald MacKay, the fishermen of Campbelltown assisting.

I happened, with a friend, to be visiting an official of the fort, who had a cottage on the moor outside; and on our admiring the brandy (although being lads, twenty-one years of age, my friend and I were no great judges), he said if we liked we might have a supply; it was part of the cargo lately 'run' on the adjoining beach. His gardener placed two kegs (which with others were buried in the garden) in my gig, in which they were triumphantly carried to Inverness, notwithstanding the proximity of the collector of Excise.

An Experiment in Humanity, 1816

ROBERT OWEN

The custom-built cotton-spinning village of New Lanark on the banks of the Clyde was a landmark in philanthropy, begun in 1785 by David Dale and Robert Arkwright, and taken to even greater heights by Dale's son-in-law Robert Owen, who bought New Lanark from him in 1800. Because of the fiddly nature of work in the mills, a large percentage of the workforce were children, but unlike many millchildren they were well looked after, and given a good education. On buying the mills, Owen raised the minimum working age for children in the mills from six to ten. He was widely considered to be a prince among philanthropists, and many people visited to see how his system worked. Here he is interviewed by a Parliamentary Commission on the working conditions in his factory:

26 April 1816, Sir Robert Peel, Bart, in the Chair: examination of Mr Robert Owen

What is your situation in life? – I am the principal proprietor and sole acting partner of the establishment of New Lanark, in Scotland.

How many persons, young and old, are immediately supported by the New Lanark manufactory and establishment? – About 2,300.

To how many out of that number do you give employment? – This number varies occasionally, but upon the average about sixteen or seventeen hundred.

The remainder of the 2,300 are the women and children? – Children too young, and persons too old, of the same families; some of the wives are employed.

At what age do you take children into your mills? – At ten and upwards.

What are the regular hours of labour per day, exclusive of meal times? – Ten hours and three quarters.

What time do you allow for meals? – Three quarters of an hour for dinner, and half an hour for breakfast.

Then your full time of work per day is twelve hours, out of which time you allow the mills to cease work for an hour and a quarter? – Yes.

Why do you not employ children at an earlier age? – Because I consider it would be injurious to the children, and not beneficial to the proprietors.

What reason have you to suppose it is injurious to the children to be employed in regular manufactories at an earlier age? – The evidence of very strong facts.

What are these facts? – Seventeen years ago, a number of individuals, with myself, purchased the New Lanark establishment from the late Mr Dale, of Glasgow. At that period I find that there were 500 children, who had been taken from poor-houses, chiefly in Edinburgh, and those children were generally from the age of five and six, to seven and eight; they were so taken because Mr Dale could not, I learned afterwards, obtain them at a more advanced period of life; if he did not take them at those ages he could not obtain them at all. The hours of work at that time were thirteen, inclusive of meal times, and an hour and a half was allowed for meals. It [was] very soon discovered that although those children were very well fed, well clothed, well lodged, and very great care taken of them when out of the mills, their growth and their minds were materially injured by being employed at those ages within the cotton mills for eleven hours and a half per day. It is true that those children, in consequence of being so well fed and clothed and lodged, looked fresh, and to a superficial observer, healthy in the countenances; yet their limbs were generally deformed, their growth was stunted, and although one of the best school-masters upon the old plan was engaged to instruct those children regularly every night, in general they made but a very slow progress, even in learning the common alphabet . . .

In consequence, then, of your conviction that children are injured by being employed the usual daily hours in manufactories, when under ten years of age, you have for some time refused to receive children into your works till they are ten years of age? – Yes.

Do you think the age of ten the best period for the admission of children into full and constant employment for ten or eleven hours per day, within woollen, cotton or other mills or manufactories? – I do not.

What other period would you recommend for their admission to full work? – Twelve years.

How, then, would you employ them from ten to the age of twelve? – For the two years preceding, to be partially instructed; to be instructed one half the day, and the other half to be initiated into the manufactories by parties employing two sets of children in the day, on the same principle that two sets of children were employed when proprietors thought it their interest to work day and night.

Do you think ten hours and three quarters a day the proper time for children to be employed in manufactories? – I do not.

What time do you recommend? – About ten hours of actual employment, or at the most, ten hours and a half.

Do you give instructions to any part of your population? – Yes, to the children from three years old, upwards; and to every other part of the population that chuse to receive it.

Will you state the particulars? – There is a preparatory school, into which all the children, from the age of three to six, are admitted at the option of the parents; there is a second school, in which all the children of the population, from six to ten, are admitted; and if any of the parents, from being more easy in their circumstances, and setting a higher value upon instruction, wish to continue their children at school for one, two, three, or four years longer, they are at liberty to do so; they are never asked to take the children from the school to the works.

Will you state who supports the schools? – The schools are supported immediately at the expense of the establishment; they are indeed literally and truly supported by the people themselves.

Will you explain how that is? – New Lanark was a new settlement formed by Mr Dale; the part of the country in which these works were erected was very thinly inhabited, and the Scotch peasantry generally were disinclined to work in cotton mills; it was necessary that great efforts should therefore be made to collect a new population in such a situation, and such population was collected before the usual and customary means for conveniently supplying a population with food were formed, the work people therefore were obliged to buy their food and other articles at a very high price, and under many great disadvantages; to counterbalance this inconvenience, a store was opened at the establishment, into which provisions of the best quality, and clothes of the most useful kind, were introduced, to be sold at the option of the people, at a price sufficient to cover prime-cost charges, and to cover the accidents of such a business, it being understood at the time that whatever profits arose from this establishment, those profits should be employed for the general benefit of the work people themselves; and those school establishments have been supported, as well as other things, by the surplus profits, because in consequence of the pretty general moral habits of the people, there have been very few losses by bad debts, and although they have been supplied considerably under the price of provisions in the neighbourhood, yet the surplus profits have in all cases been sufficient to bear the expense of these school establishments; therefore, they have literally been supported by the people themselves.

The Sutherland Clearances, 1816

DONALD MACLEOD

Few episodes in Scottish history have cast so long a shadow as the forced removal of large swathes of the crofting community from their land in the Highlands. Donald MacLeod, a Sutherlander, wrote an uncompromising account of the protracted and sometimes vicious eviction of crofters, which began at the end of the eighteenth century, and lasted beyond the middle of the nineteenth. His home county attracted particular attention for the harshness of its treatment of tenants, notably by its reviled factor, Patrick Sellar, at whose name some women had been known to fall into a panic, or 'lose their reason'. MacLeod's piece begins shortly after tenants have received letters of eviction.

In about a month after the factors had obtained this promise of removal, and thirteen days before the May term the work of devastation was begun. They commenced by setting fire to the houses of the small tenants in extensive districts – part of the parishes of Farr, Rogart, Golspie, and the whole parish of Kildonan. I was an eye-witness of the scene. This calamity came on the people quite unexpectedly. Strong parties, for each district, furnished with faggots and other combustibles, rushed on the dwellings of this devoted people, and immediately commenced setting fire to them, proceeding in their work with the greatest rapidity till about three hundred houses were in flames!

The consternation and confusion were extreme; little or no time was given for removal of persons or property – the people striving to remove the sick and the helpless before the fire should reach them – next, struggling to save the most valuable of their effects. The cries of the women and children – the roaring of the affrighted cattle, hunted at the same time by the yelling dogs of the shepherds amid the smoke and the fire – altogether presented a scene that completely baffles description; it required to be seen to be believed.

A dense cloud of smoke enveloped the whole country by day, and even extended far on the sea; at night an awfully grand, but terrific scene presented itself – all the houses in an extensive district in flames at once! I myself ascended a height about eleven o'clock in the evening, and counted two hundred and fifty blazing houses, many of the owners of which were my relations, and all of whom I personally knew; but whose present condition, whether in or out of the flames, I could not tell. The conflagration lasted six days, till the whole of the dwellings were reduced to ashes or smoking ruins. During one of these days a boat lost her way in the dense smoke as she approached the shore; but at night she was enabled to reach a landing place by the light of the flames!

It would be an endless task to give a detail of the sufferings of families and individuals during this calamitous period; or to describe its dreadful consequences on the health and lives of the victims. I will, however, attempt a very few cases. While the burning was going on, a small sloop arrived, laden with quick-lime, and while discharging her cargo, the skipper agreed to take as many of the people to Caithness as he could carry, on his return. Accordingly, about twenty families went on board, filling deck, hold, and every part of the vessel. There were childhood and age, male and female, sick and well, with a small portion of their effects, saved from the flames, all huddled together in heaps.

Many of these persons had never been on sea before, and when they began to sicken a scene indescribable ensued. To add to their miseries, a storm and contrary winds prevailed, so that instead of a day or two, the usual time of passage, it was *nine days* before they reached Caithness. All this time, the poor creatures, almost without necessaries, most of them dying with sickness, were either wallowing among the lime, and various excrements in the hold, or lying on the deck, exposed to the raging elements! This voyage soon proved fatal to many, and some of the survivors feel its effects to this day.

During this time, also, typhus fever was raging in the country, and many in a critical state had to fly, or were carried by their friends out of the burning houses. Among the rest, a young man, Donald MacKay of Grumbmor, was ordered out of his parents' house; he obeyed, in a state of delirium, and (nearly naked) ran into some bushes adjoining, where he lay for a considerable time deprived of reason; the house was immediately in flames, and his effects burned. Robert MacKay, whose whole family were in the fever, or otherwise ailing, had to carry his two daughters on his back a distance of about twenty-five miles. He accomplished this by first carrying one, and laying her down in the open air, and returning, did the same with the other, till he reached the sea-shore, and then went with them on board the lime vessel before mentioned.

An old man of the same name, betook himself to a deserted mill, and lay there unable to move; and to the best of my recollection, he died there. He had no sustenance but what he obtained by licking the dust and refuse of the meal strewed about, and was defended from the rats and other vermin, by his faithful *collie*, his companion and protector. A number of the sick, who could not be carried away instantly, on account of their dangerous situation, were collected by their friends and placed in an obscure, uncomfortable hut, and there, for a time, left to their fate. The cries of these victims were heart-rending – exclaiming in their anguish, 'Are you going to leave us to perish in the flames?' However, the destroyers passed near the hut, apparently without noticing it, and consequently they remained unmolested, till they could be conveyed to the shore, and put on board the before-mentioned sloop.

George Munro, miller at Farr, residing within 400 yards of the minister's house, had his whole family, consisting of six or seven persons, lying in a fever; and being instantly to remove, was enabled, with the assistance of his neighbours to carry them to a damp kiln, where they remained till the fire abated, so that they could be removed. Meantime the house was burnt.

It may not be out of place here to mention generally, that the clergy, factors, and magistrates, were cool and apparently unconcerned spectators of the scenes I have been describing, which were indeed perpetrated under their immediate authority. The splendid and comfortable mansions of these gentlemen, were reddened with the glare of their neighbours' flaming houses, without exciting any compassion for the sufferers; no spiritual, temporal, or medical aid was afforded them; and this time they were all driven away without being allowed the benefit of their outgoing crop!

Nothing but the sword was wanting to make the scene one of as great barbarity as earth ever witnessed; and in my opinion, this would, in a majority of cases, have been mercy, by saving them from what they were afterwards doomed to endure. The clergy, indeed, in their sermons, maintained that the whole was a merciful interposition of Providence to bring them to repentance, rather than to send them all to hell, as they so richly deserved!

The Scotsman *Is Launched, January 1817*

HENRY COCKBURN

The founding of the Scotsman *newspaper, which dared to express opinions that ran counter to establishment views, marked a new era of public information and discourse and saw the birth of a distinctive brand of Scottish journalism. Its arrival delighted the advocate Henry Cockburn.*

The change which was taking place in the character of our population is now evinced by an occurrence which was remarkable both as an effect and as a cause. The first number of the *Scotsman* newspaper was published in January 1817. The incalculable importance of this event can only be understood by those who recollect that shortly before this the newspaper press of Edinburgh, though not as much fettered as in St Petersburg (as it has been said to have been), was at least in as hampered a condition as any press that is legally free could be. Most candid men who knew Scotland before the peace of 1814 will probably agree, that if the most respectable London opposition newspaper had been published in Edinburgh, the editor would have been better acquainted with the Court of Justiciary than he would have found comfortable. The undisturbed continuance of the *Edinburgh Review* would be inconsistent with this statement, were it not that there is no analogy between a work of which the politics are dignified by general literature, and which only appears quarterly, at the price of five shillings, and the provocations of a cheap and purely political and generally accusative publication, tormenting every week or every day. When John Cartwright, the itinerant political reformer, lectured here about 1812, he was attended by considerable audiences; yet because he advocated universal suffrage and annual parliaments, no editor of any Edinburgh newspaper, though offered payment as for an advertisement, had courage to allow any account whatever of the lectures to appear in his paper. An editor who attended them told me that, though he differed from the lecturer, what he said was a good and perfectly lawful defence of the doctrines espoused, and that he would have liked to have published their substance, but that he could not ruin his paper.

The appearance, therefore, of a respectable opposition newspaper was hailed and condemned according to people's tastes: but they all saw in it a sign. Though only published once a week, and taking only literary advertisements, it soon attained a large circulation. The *Scotsman* is now flourishing in a vigorous manhood, immeasurably the best newspaper that exists, or has ever existed, in Scotland. Its only defect has been heaviness; a defect, however, inseparable from provincial locality, particularly in Scotland, where the people are grave, and too far out of the world to acquire smartness and tact.

Radicals in the Playground, 1819

ALEXANDER SOMERVILLE

*Alexander Somerville was a self-taught labourer from East Lothian, who as a
young man became famous for being flogged in the army almost to the point of
death. Later in life he became a journalist. This account of his schooldays shows
how the politics of the day, in which economic tensions were running high and
the government was afraid of a radical uprising, reached as far as the playground.*

But to return to the time of the radicals of 1819, and the rumours that
came to Birnyknows school, that 'they were coming'. The term 'ragged
radicals' was a common one in newspapers of that time, and the boys
who heard their father read the newspapers or talk of the news, brought
this name of reproach to the school. It was suggested one day by some
of them, that an excellent play might be got up in the Eel Yards, a
meadow with some large trees in it, if the scholars divided themselves
into soldiers and radicals. As the soldiers were the most respectable in
the eyes of the better dressed sons of farmers and tradesmen, and as they
took the lead in everything, they made themselves soldiers; and, in
addition to that, took upon themselves to pick out those who were to
be radicals. This was done according to the quality of the clothes worn,
and I, consequently, found myself declared to be radical. The first day's
play passed with no greater disasters to me than the brim torn from an
infirm hat which I wore, my trousers split up, all the buttons torn
from my waistcoat, and my neck stretched considerably on the way to
strangulation. For being a radical who seemed inclined to look upon the
treatment I received as too serious for play, I was condemned to be
hanged. It happened that the clothes I wore were not of the usual
corduroy worn by the sons of farm labourers and always worn by me,
save in that year. Mine had been remade the year before from some
cast-off clothes given a year or two before that to the brother next to
me in age by his master. . . . These clothes having been old when I got
them, and having been worn by me all the summer in the woods herding
the cows, and all the autumn, they were not in sound condition. But
my poor mother always kept them patched up; and I never once went
out then or any time, with an open rent or a worn hole in my clothes.
As she spun wool for stockings, and lint for shirts, herself, and my father
knitted stockings at night, and my sisters made shirts, I was equal in

those articles to any one in the school; and I was only so badly clothed otherwise because the second year was running on between my father and a master for whom he then worked without a settlement of accounts . . .

When I went home on that first evening of my ragged radicalship, my poor mother stood aghast, lifted her hands, and said, in a tone of despair, 'What shall I do with those rags?' They were stripped off, I got an early supper and was sent to bed, while she began to mend them. . . . So I went to the school [the next day], my mother begging of me, with tears in her eyes, not to get my clothes torn again, else it would kill her to see me in such rags, and to have to sit up every night to mend them. But 'soldiers and radicals' was again the play, and again I was the radical upon whom the greatest number of the soldiers concentrated their warfare. They had seen me thrashed by the schoolmaster until I was blistered, without crying or shedding a tear, which made them think I could stand any amount of punishment or torment, without feeling it; in short, I was believed to be a great stubborn lad, who had no feeling in him. Had they seen me after leaving my mother that morning, and carrying her injunction with me, in a heart that was bursting with her words, they would have seen whether I had tears in me or not, and whether they would not come out.

As soon as I made my appearance, the cry of the 'ragged radical' was raised; the soldiers charged on me, and knocked my infirm hat over my eyes with my head through the crown of it. Some laid hold of me by the feet to carry me off to be hanged and beheaded, *as the real law upon the real radicals had taught them to imitate in play*. I made a violent effort to free myself, and the rents of yesterday, which my mother had so carefully sewed, broke open afresh. The hat I raised from where it had sunk over my face, and saw part of the brim in the hands of a lad who was a kind of king of the school, or cock of the walk, with some of my poor mother's threads hanging from it. He was older than I, and was a fighter. I had never fought, nor had heard of two human creatures going together to fight, until I came to that school. Yet neither had I heard of the divine principle of forbearance and forgiveness, as regards blows upon the body, and the laceration of feelings worse than blows upon the body – my father, who gave me many good precepts, never having contemplated the possibility of my being a fighting boy. . . . But I was a strong boy for my age, and I had received very bad treatment. My honour and the remembrance of my affectionate mother's toils made me feel like a giant. I amazed the king of the school by giving him a blow in the face that laid him flat on his back, and amazed the onlookers by giving several of them as much with the same results. Not that I escaped without blows myself. I got many, but they were returned with principle and interest. Some one ran to the schoolmaster and told that I was thrashing 'Master' Somebody, for he being a gentleman's son was called 'Master', while I had to submit to a nick-name, derived from the state of my clothes. The school was summoned in at once, it being near the schoolhour in the morning . . .

The schoolmaster stood with the *taws* ready to flagellate the moment I entered the school. He inquired who began the fight, and every one named me. He at once ordered me to hold up my right hand, which I did, and received a violent cut on the edge of it, given with his whole strength. He ordered my left hand up, and up it went and received a cut of the same kind; then my right, which got what it got before; next my left, which also got what it got before; and so on he went until I had got six cuts (skults we called them) on each hand. He had a way of raising himself upon his toes when he swung the heavy *taws* round his head, and came down upon his feet with a spring, giving the cuts slantingly on the hand. He saw me resolved to take all he could give without a tear, whereupon he began to cut at the back of my hands. I drew them behind me to save them, which seeing, cut at the open places of my torn clothes, where my skin was visible; and always as I wriggled to one side to save those bare places, I exposed other bare places on the other side, which he aimed at with terrible certainty. After a time he pushed me before him, still thrashing me on the bare places, and on the head, until he got me to the farther end of the school, where the coals lay in a corner. Here he ordered me to sit down and remain until he gave me liberty to leave that place, which he did not do until evening. The day was piercing cold. The house was an old place, with no furniture nor partition in it. I sat at the end farthest from the fire-place, and near to the door, which was an old door that did not fit its place, and which allowed the wind to blow freely through. It blew through and about me as if it had been another school-master, and was as partial to farmers' sons, and as cruel to the ragged boys of farm labourers, as he was.

George IV Visits Scotland, 14 August 1822

JOHN GIBSON LOCKHART

The arrival of George IV in Scotland was an event of great significance, at least for the people of Edinburgh, who were bedazzled by the man's attempt to emulate Scottish style with his tartan hose and jaunty kilt. Sir Walter Scott, whose only flaw, one friend confessed, was an overfondness for his social superiors, had arranged the visit, and was rowed out to his ship to welcome him. Writer and biographer John Gibson Lockhart, who recorded this event, was Scott's son-in-law.

On receiving the poet on the quarter-deck, his Majesty called for a bottle of Highland whisky, and having drunk his health in this national liquor, desired a glass to be filled for him. Sir Walter, after draining his own bumper, made a request that the King would condescend to bestow him the glass out of which his Majesty had just drunk his health; and this being granted, the precious vessel was immediately wrapped up and carefully deposited in what he conceived to be the safest part of his dress. So he returned with it to Castle Street; but, to say nothing at this moment of graver distractions, on reaching his house he found a guest established there of a sort rather different from the usual visitors of the time. The poet Crabbe, to whom he had been introduced when last in London by Mr Murray of Albemarle Street, after repeatedly promising to follow up the acquaintance by an excursion to the north, had at last arrived in the midst of these tumultuous preparations for the royal advent. Notwithstanding all such impediments, he found his quarters ready for him, and Scott entering, wet and hurried, embraced the venerable man with brotherly affection. The royal gift was forgotten – the ample skirt of the coat within which it had been packed, and which he had hitherto held cautiously in front of his person, slipped back to its more usual position – he sat down beside Crabbe, and the glass was crushed to atoms. His scream and gesture made his wife conclude that he had sat down on a pair of scissors, or the like; but very little harm had been done except the breaking of the glass, of which alone he had been thinking.

Child Worker in a Dundee Factory, 1824

JAMES MYLES

James Myles was born near Glamis, the son of a shoemaker who was imprisoned for murder. His near-destitute mother moved to Dundee to find employment, and seven-year-old James was sent to work at a mill. Conditions were harsh. As punishment for an error, he was once dangled by his ear out of the window. It was three storeys from the ground.

It was on a Tuesday morning in the month of 'Lady June' that I first entered a spinning mill. The whole circumstances were strange to me. The dust, the din, the work, the hissing and roaring of one person to another, the obscene language uttered, even by the youngest, and the imperious commands harshly given by those 'dressed in a little brief authority', struck my young country heart with awe and astonishment. At that time the twelve hours' factory act had not come into operation, and spinning mills were in their glory as huge instruments of demoralization and slavery. Mercenary manufacturers, to enable them to beat more upright employers in the markets, kept their machinery and hands active fifteen, and, in many cases, seventeen hours a–day, and, when tender children fell asleep under the prolonged infliction of 'work! work! work!,' overseers roused them with the rod, or thongs of thick leather burned at the points. The lash of the slave driver was never more unsparingly used in Carolina on the unfortunate slaves than the canes and 'whangs' of mill foremen were then used on helpless factory boys. When I went to a spinning mill I was about seven years of age. I had to get out of bed every morning at five o'clock, commence work at half-past five, drop at nine for breakfast, begin again at half-past nine, work until two, which was the dinner hour, start again at half-past two, and continue until half-past seven at night. Such were the nominal hours; but in reality there were no regular hours, master and managers did with us as they liked. The clocks at the factories were often put forward in the morning and back at night, and instead of being instruments for the measurement of time, they were used as cloaks for cheatery and oppression. Though this was known amongst the hands, all were afraid to speak, and a workman then was afraid to carry a watch, as it was no uncommon event to dismiss any one who presumed to know too much about the science of horology. In country mills, a more horrific despotism reigned than in Dundee. There, masters frequently bound the young by a regular contract, which gave them a more complete control over their labour and liberties than taking them from week to week. In one establishment in the vicinity of Dundee, the proprietor, a coarse-minded man, who by accident had vaulted out of his natural element into the position of a 'vulgar rich' man, practised the contract system, and had bothies where he lodged all his male and female workers. They were allowed to cook, sleep, and live in any dog and cat manner they pleased, no moral superintendence whatever being exercised over them. His mill was kept going 17 and frequently 19 hours per day. To accomplish this all meal hours were almost dispensed with, and women were employed to boil potatoes and carry them in baskets to the different flats [floors]; and children had to swallow a potato hastily in the interval of putting up 'ends'. On dinners cooked and eaten as I have described, they had to subsist until half-past nine, and frequently ten at night. When they returned to their bothies, brose, as it is a dish that can be quickly made, constituted their suppers, for they had no time to wait the preparation of a different meal. They then tumbled into bed; but balmy sleep had scarcely closed their urchin eyelids, and steeped their infant souls in blessed forgetfulness, when the thumping of the watchman's staff on the door would rouse them from repose, and the words, 'Get up; it's four o'clock,' reminded them they were factory children, the unprotected victims of monotonous slavery. At this mill, and indeed all mills, boys and girls were often found sleeping in stairs and private places, and they have been seen walking about the flats in a deep sleep, with cans of 'sliver' in their hands. When found in this state, they were caned or kicked according to the mood of their superiors. One poor boy, who is still alive, and who, by force of mind, great persistency and rectitude, rose to be a mercantile clerk in Dundee, and now fills a responsible situation on one of the principal railways in England, was for some time in this factory. One day he was carrying an armful of bobbins from one flat to another. When ascending the stair, he sat down to rest himself, as his legs were sore and swollen by incessant standing. In a few moments he was fast asleep. Whilst enjoying this stolen repose, the master happened to pass. Without the least warning he gave him a violent slap on the side of the head, which stunned and stupefied him. In a half-sleeping state of stupefaction he ran to the roving frame, which he sometimes attended, and five minutes had barely elapsed when his left hand got entangled with the machinery, and two of his fingers were crushed to a jelly, and had to be immediately amputated.

His unfeeling taskmaster gave him no recompense – in fact never asked after him; he was left to starve or die, as Providence might direct . . .

Myles quotes a witness before a House of Commons Committee, who had worked at Duntroom Mill, to describe the savagery of treatment.

Was excessive working accompanied with excessive beating? – Yes, very frequently they were beaten. Children were not able to stand the work, and if they had made the least fault, they were beaten excessively.

Did you ever hear of anyone attempting to escape from that mill? – Yes, there were two girls that made their escape from the mill through the roof of the house, and left nearly all their clothes behind them.

What became of them? – They were not brought back during the time I was there.

They finally escaped? – Yes.

Do you know any body that escaped and was brought back again? – At the time I was in that mill there was a young woman who had been kept seven months in Dundee jail for deserting, and she was brought back after having been in the jail for seven months, to make up for her lost time and the expenses incurred. One day I was alarmed by the cries of 'murder' from the lowest flat [floor], and when I went there she was lying on the floor, and the master had her by the hair of the head, and was kicking her on the face, and the blood was running down.

Was that at Duntroom Mill? – Yes.

How long ago? – About eleven years.

What was the consequence of that? – I understood it would break her engagement, and after the master had retired from the flat, I opened the door and let her out, and told her to run; and the master came back, and missing her, began cursing and swearing at me for letting her out, and ordered me to run after her, which I refused to do. I state that, owing to the ill treatment she had received, I never would be the man that would run after her to bring her back to the torture, and therefore he and I separated.

★

Was she brought back? – No.

Was she in a situation to get any other employment? – No, she became a prostitute, and was tried at the Circuit of Perth, and transported to Van Dieman's Land for stealing.

Do you think she was very anxious to get a situation if she could have done so without resorting to those courses? – Yes, she had tried to get into service several times; but when they knew she had been at mills they would have nothing to do with her.

Do you think that that severity of treatment has not unfrequently a similar effect in driving females to improper courses? – Undoubtedly.

The Recipe for Haggis, 1826

MEG DODS

With haggis, a melange of offal tied up in a sheep's stomach, Scottish peasant cuisine reached its apotheosis. This delicacy had been on the menu for centuries, but in her comprehensive guide for housewives, Meg Dods, the stern landlady of Cleikum Inn near Peebles (whom Sir Walter Scott immortalized in his novel St Ronan's Well), recorded a method that until then many had learnt only by word of mouth.

Sheep's pluck [lights, liver and heart] and paunch, beef-suet, onions, oatmeal, pepper, salt, cayenne, lemon or vinegar.

Clean a sheep's pluck thoroughly. Make incisions in the heart and liver to allow the blood to flow out, and parboil the whole, letting the windpipe lie over the side of the pot to permit the discharge of impurities; the water may be changed after a few minutes' boiling for fresh water. A half-hour's boiling will be sufficient; but throw back the half of the liver, and part of the lights, trimming away all skins and black-looking parts, and mince them together. Mince also a pound of good beef-suet and four or more onions. Grate the other half of the liver. Have a dozen of small onions peeled and scalded in two waters to mix with this mince. Have ready some finely-ground oatmeal, toasted slowly before the fire for hours, till it is of a light brown colour and perfectly dry. Less than two teacupfuls of meal will do for this quantity of meat. Spread the mince on a board and strew the meal lightly over it, with a high seasoning of pepper, salt, and a little cayenne, first well mixed. Have a haggis bag (i.e. a sheep's paunch) perfectly clean, and see that there be no thin part in it, else your whole labour will be lost by its bursting.

Some cooks use two bags, one as an outer case. Put in the meat with a half-pint of good beef gravy, or as much strong broth as will make it a very thick stew. Be careful not to fill the bag too full, but allow the meat room to swell; add the juice of a lemon or a little good vinegar; press out the air and sew up the bag, prick it with a large needle when it first swells in the pot to prevent bursting; let it boil slowly for three hours if large.

The Search for the Sugar Pine, 1826

DAVID DOUGLAS

David Douglas was one of the most intrepid of Scotland's small army of plant hunters, combining botanical passion with the physical strength and courage of an explorer. Born in Scone in 1799, he went to North America on behalf of the Horticultural Society of London, where he covered over 10,000 miles by foot, horseback and canoe between 1825 and 1827. He was a man of extraordinary hardiness, although he admitted that he got 'fretful' if he had to go to sleep wet and without supper. As he crossed the Rockies, he collected such specimens as the Douglas fir, that took his name, and the sitka spruce, whose cultivation was to change the face of the Scottish Highland economy in the twentieth century. He was intrigued by discovering enormous pine seeds, and went in search of an as yet undiscovered species, Pinus lambertiana, or the Sugar Pine, the largest of the ninety-six known pines. Douglas came to a mysterious end in Honolulu in 1834 in a pit for trapping wild bulls, which may have been an accident, or may have been murder.

September 25th, 1826
Last night was one of the most dreadful I ever witnessed. The rain, driven by the violence of the wind, rendered it impossible for me to keep any fire, and to add misery to my affliction my tent was blown down at midnight, when I lay among bracken rolled in my wet blanket and tent till morning. Sleep of course was not to be had, every ten or fifteen minutes immense trees falling producing a crash as if the earth was cleaving asunder. . . . My poor horses were unable to endure the

violence of the storm without craving of me protection, which they did by hanging their heads over me and neighing. Toward day it moderated and before sunrise clear, but very cold. . . . Started at ten o'clock, still shivering with cold although I rubbed myself with my handkerchief before the fire until I was no longer able to endure the pain . . . took my course southerly towards a ridge of mountains, where I hope to find my pine. The night being dry I camped early in the afternoon, in order to dry the remaining part of my clothing. Travelled eighteen miles.

Thursday 26th
Weather dull and cloudy. When my people in England are made acquainted with my travels, they may perhaps think I have told them nothing but my miseries. That may be very correct, but I now know that such objects as I am in quest of are not obtained without a share of labour, anxiety of mind, and sometimes risk of personal safety. I left my camp this morning at daylight on an excursion, leaving my guide to take care of the camp and horses until my return in the evening, when I found everything as I wished; in the interval he had dried my wet paper as I desired him. About an hour's walk from my camp I was met by an Indian, who on discovering me strung his bow and placed on his left arm a sleeve of racoon-skin and stood ready on the defence. As I was well convinced this was prompted through fear, he never before having seen such a being, I laid my gun at my feet on the ground and waved my hand for him to come to me, which he did with great caution. I made him place his bow and quiver beside my gun, and then struck a light and gave him to smoke and a few beads. With my pencil I made a rough sketch of the cone and pine I wanted and showed him it, when he instantly pointed to the hills about fifteen or twenty miles to the south. As I wanted to go in that direction, he seemingly with much good-will went with me. At midday I reached my long-wished *Pinus* (called by the Umpqua tribe *Natele*), and lost no time in examining and endeavouring to collect specimens and seeds.

New or strange things seldom fail to make great impressions, and often at first we are liable to over-rate them; and lest I should never see my friends to tell them verbally of this most beautiful and immensely large tree, I now state the dimension of the largest one I could find that was blown down by the wind: Three feet from the ground, 57 feet 9 inches in circumference; 134 feet from the ground, 17 feet 5 inches; extreme length, 215 feet. The trees are remarkably straight; bark uncommonly smooth for such large timber, of a whitish or light brown colour;

and yields a great quantity of gum of a bright amber colour. The large trees are destitute of branches, generally for two-thirds the length of the tree; branches pendulous, and the cones hanging from their points like small sugar-loaves in a grocer's shop, it being only on the very largest trees that cones are seen, and the putting myself in possession of three cones (all I could) nearly brought my life to an end.

Being unable to climb or hew down any, I took my gun and was busy clipping them from the branches with ball [shooting them down] when eight Indians came at the report of my gun. They were all painted with red earth, armed with bows, arrows, spears of bone, and flint knives, and seemed to me anything but friendly. I endeavoured to explain to them what I wanted and they seemed satisfied and sat down to smoke, but had no sooner done so than I perceived one string his bow and another sharpen his flint knife with a pair of wooden pincers and hang it on the wrist of the right hand, which gave me ample testimony of their inclination.

To save myself I could not do by flight, and without any hesitation I went backwards six paces and cocked my gun, and then pulled from my belt one of my pistols, which I held in my left hand. I was determined to fight for life. As I as much as possible endeavoured to preserve my coolness and perhaps did so, I stood eight or ten minutes looking at them and they at me without a word passing, till one at last, who seemed to be the leader, made a sign for tobacco, which I said they should get on condition of going and fetching me some cones. They went, and as soon as out of sight I picked up my three cones and a few twigs, and made a quick retreat to my camp, which I gained at dusk. The Indian who undertook to be my last guide I sent off, lest he should betray me.

Wood of the pine fine, and very heavy; leaves short, in five, with a very short sheath bright green; cones, one 14½ inches long, one 14, and one 13½, and all containing fine seed. A little before this the cones are gathered by the Indians, roasted on the embers, quartered, and the seeds shaken out, which are then dried before the fire and pounded into a sort of flour, and sometimes eaten round. How irksome a night is to such a one as me under my circumstances! Cannot speak a word to my guide, not a book to read, constantly in expectation of an attack, and the position I am now in is lying on the grass with my gun beside me, writing by the light of my Columbian candle – namely, a piece of wood containing rosin.

Travelling Conditions for Emigrants, 1827

A HUNTER, W.S. [WRITER TO THE SIGNET]

The mass emigration that the Highlands and Islands witnessed as the clearances gathered pace was made even more painful because of the way some were treated. Here the official charged with organizing the emigration of the people of Rum shows how little concern was given to their conditions.

If government think seriously of being at any expense in sending out emigrants, I think it can be done a great deal cheaper than it has hitherto been done. . . . According to the present rate of freight to Cape Breton, or any of these places, New Brunswick or Nova Scotia, a ship could be freighted for 25s. per ton; at present two tons are allowed for every adult passenger, and the crew are included; but if government, for so short a voyage, would allow the crew not to be included, but let them go extra, it would be a very considerable saving of expense; and for so short a voyage, the captains of ships in that trade, who have gone with emigrants, and with whom I have conversed, say it would not be the least inconvenience. There is also the additional expense of a surgeon for so short a voyage, which is a very great additional expense. Then there are the provisions according to the Act of the Parliament, a certain quantity of beef; now by substituting what the Rum people were allowed by government, oatmeal instead of beef, the expense would be greatly reduced, and they are not accustomed to beef, they live altogether on oatmeal; in fact, on potatoes principally. In this way I make the expenses per adult 4l. 14s. 6d. I am allowing the twelve weeks provision in this calculation, because when they land they must have some provisions to maintain them until they raise a crop.

The Sale of a Wife, 1828

Popular broadsheets, the tabloid papers of their day, were sold by pedlars and chapmen on the streets. The event described here clearly made such a stir that it reached Newcastle, where this account was published.

SALE OF A WIFE

A full and particular Account of the Sale of a Woman, named Mary Mackintosh, which took place on Wednesday Evening, the 16th of

July,1828, in the Grass Market of Edinburgh, accused by her Husband of being a notorious Drunkard; with the Particulars of the bloody Battle which took place afterwards.

On Wednesday evening last, in the Grass-market, Mary Mackintosh was brought down about six o'clock by her husband, for the purpose of being sold. Her crime was drunkenness and adultery. She was held by a straw rope tied round her middle, and the words, 'To be sold by public auction' in front of her bosom. Several thousand spectators were assembled to witness this novel occurrence. John F—n, a pensioner, and knight of the hammer, commenced business, but the acclamations of the people were so great, that no one could get a hearing for ten minutes, to bid for the unfortunate woman.

When the crowd got a little quiet the people began to examine the countenance of the woman; a Highland Drover stepped through the crowd and pulled out his purse, and said, 'She be a good like lassie, I will gi'e ten and twenty shillings for her.' This caused great cheering among the crowd – then a stout Tinker made a bolt into the crowd, and said she should never go to the Highlands – he then bid sixpence more for her. At this time, one of the KILLARNEY PIG JOBBERS, with his mouth open as wide as a turnpike gate, and half drunk, cried loudly, FAUGHAHOLLICE, I will give two shillings more, for she is a pretty woman. A Brogue maker, from Newry, coming out of a public house, as drunks [sic] as 50 cats in a wallet, came up to the Killarney man, and hits him in the bread bag, and he lay there for the space of ten minutes, which made the woman for sale laugh heartily, and the cheers of the crowd at this time was long and incessant. – The Brogue-maker being a supposed friend to the woman, went up to the auctioneer, and told him there were three bidders: he was so enraged, he knocked the auctioneer down, and made his claret flow desperately. Great cheering among the people, at the expense of the knight of the hammer.

The women of the neighbourhood gathered to the number of 700, and armed themselves with stones, some threw them, and others put them in their stockings and handkerchiefs, and made a general charge through the mob, knocking every one down that came in their way, until they go up to the auctioneer, when they scratched and tore his face in a dreadful manner, in consequence of the insult the fair sex had received. One resolute woman came up with a stone and knocked down

Thomas M'Guisgan, husband to the woman who was exposed for sale. This woman, a true female hero, and a SWEEP'S WIFE, displayed great courage in favour of her sex, and said I will learn you to auction your wife again, you contaminated villain. Tom returned the blow, and hit her between the eyes, and made them like two October cabbages. The sweep seeing his wife struck, made a sally with his bag and scrapper; the women all took the sweep's part and cried with a loud voice, mill him the old boar, a general battle ensued, and only for the interference of the police, there would have been lives lost.

After the disturbance was quelled, the husband insisted she should be sold. She was brought up again, and the auctioneer declared that if he could not be protected, he would have no more call to her. Some young fellows shouted he should, and the sale began again. An old pensioner, a Jack tar, stepped forward, saying, damn my tarry top-lights and chain plates she is a tight little frigate, and well-rigged too, and I will give half a crown more than the last bidder. Well done, cried the mob to the sailor, you are a spirited fellow, and you must get her; when a farmer, who was a widower, bade two pound five shillings for her, he being a friend to the sex, and the auctioneer knocked her down. The farmer took her up behind him on his horse, and away they went amidst the cheers of the populace.

W. BOAG, PRINTER, NEWCASTLE

Sutherland after the Clearances, 1828

DONALD MACLEOD

More than a decade after witnessing the brutal clearing of the Sutherland estate, Donald MacLeod returned to see how things had changed.

After a considerable interval of absence, I revisited my native place in the year 1828, and attended divine worship in the parish church, now reduced to the size and appearance of a dove-cot. The whole congregation consisted of eight shepherds, with their *dogs*, to the number of between 20 and 30, the minister, three of his family, and myself! I came in after the first singing, but, at the conclusion, the 120th psalm was given us, and we struck up to the famous tune Bangor; when the four-footed hearers, became excited, got up on the seats and raised a most infernal chorus of howling. Their masters then attacked them with their crooks, which only made matters worse; the yelping and howling continued to the end of the service. I retired, to contemplate the shameful scene, and compare it with what I had previously witnessed in the large and devout congregations formerly attending in that kirk. What must the worthy Mr Campbell have felt while endeavouring to edify such a congregation!

The Trial of Burke and Hare, 24 December 1828

WILLIAM HARE

In the space of a year or so, William Burke, an Irish cobbler, and William Hare, an Irish navvy, lured sixteen people into their Edinburgh tenements and murdered them. They then sold the corpses to the anatomist Dr Robert Knox, a surgeon at Edinburgh University. Their final victim, who proved their downfall, was an old woman called Madgy Docherty, a beggar who went by several names, including Campbell and M'Gonegal. Falling into their company, she was murdered on the night of 31 October 1828. At their trial, Hare turned King's Evidence, and got off without even a sentence. Burke, meanwhile, was hanged. The people of Edinburgh, who had packed the court at Christmas to attend the sensational trial, were so pleased to see the back of Burke that 30,000 filed past his dissected corpse, which had been used for a two-hour anatomy lecture by the surgeon Dr Monro. Burke's corpse was then skinned, and his skin tanned and sold in strips. Hare's testimony gives a flavour of what the pair's other victims probably suffered.

LORD JUSTICE-CLERK – You will understand that you are called here as a witness regarding the death of an elderly woman, of the name of Campbell or M'Gonegal. You understand that it is only with regard to her that you are now to speak? *To this question the witness replied, by asking, 'T'ould woman, Sir?'*
LORD JUSTICE-CLERK. – Yes . . .
Interrogated by the LORD ADVOCATE – How long have you been acquainted with William Burke? About a twelvemonth.
You have been ten years in Scotland, and you have been a resident in Edinburgh? Yes.
You are a married man, and your wife is here? Yes.

When did you become acquainted with the prisoner Burke? About a twelvemonth ago.

And you became acquainted with the other prisoner Macdougal [Nelly MacDougal, Burke's partner] about the same period? Yes.

She lodged with him then, and since? Yes.

Your house is near his? On the same side of the street.

Were you in a public house on the 31st of October last, kept by a person of the name of Rymer? Yes.

How much did you drink? A gill.

Was any body with you? No.

Did he tell you about any person being in his house? Yes.

About what o'clock was it? I could not say; it was in the fore part of the day. He took me to this house, and he told me to go down to his house, and said that there was an *ould* woman in the house that he was going to murder, and for me to see what they were doing; that he had left some whisky in the house; that he got the woman off the street; and that he thought she would be a good *shot* to take to the Doctors . . .

Did he use the word murder; or did you understand it from the *shot* for the Doctors? To see what they were doing.

Did he use the word murder? No.

What did you understand by the word *shot* for the Doctors; did you understand the meaning of it? Yes.

What was it? That he was going to murder her.

Well, did you go down? Yes, Sir, I went down.

Alone? Yes.

You went to Burke's house? Yes, I went to his house.

Who did you find there? A strange man and woman in the house; Nelly M'Dougal, and the old woman, – and she was washing her gown . . .

What colour was it? White and reddish colour, – striped.

Was it like that there? *the gown was handed to the witness,*
Yes, that is it.

Did you remain long there? About five minutes.

And then went away home? Went home.

Were you in Mrs Connoway's after that? No, I was not in there till after night.

You know that woman? Yes.

Were you in her house that night at all? Yes, between eight and nine o'clock.

Then you came back from that to your own house? Yes.

Now, who was in Connoway's when you was there? John Connoway and his wife; and there was William Burke, John Brogan, and another *chap* – I don't know his name.

Did William Burke remain with you? He went away with the two chaps, Brogan, and the one I don't know.

Who else were there? That old wife, and Nelly M'Dougal, and my wife.

Had you some drink when you was there? Yes.

Did you remain there till pretty late? We remained there till between 11 and 12 o'clock. I could not say just directly.

Where did you go to? Nelly M'Dougal asked me and my wife to take a dram in her house.

And you left the old woman there? Yes, we left the old woman sitting at the fire, and John Connoway.

Well, when you were in Mrs Burke's house, did Burke come in? Yes, and the old wife with him.

Had you any more drinking? Yes; there was a *soup* of whisky in the bottle, and we all drank it out. We were all pretty hearty.

Was the old woman that way too? Yes . . .

At this time, did you expect that any mischief was to happen to this old woman? Not that night.

Now, after this, had you any quarrelling or fighting with Burke? He asked me what I was doing there, in his house: I told him that Nelly M'Dougal asked me in to get a dram; and he struck me then.

Did you strike again? Yes, I did.

Had you a fight? Yes.

And her there? Yes, we had.

Now, where were the women during this? They were *redding* us.

They came betwixt you to separate you? Yes; he pushed me down twice on the bed, and the last time I lay on the bed.

How long did you lie there? I could not say.

LORD JUSTICE-CLERK. – You were twice down on the bed? Yes.

LORD ADVOCATE. – Now, when you were fighting, where was this old person? She was sitting at the fire, – and she got up and desired Burke to sit down, and she said that she did not want to see Burke abused.

Did she run out? Yes, she ran out twice to the entry, and cried out for the police.

She went twice to the passage? Yes.

What did she call out? It was either murder or police, I could not say which, but it was some of them.

Well, how was she brought back again? It was Nelly M'Dougal that fetched her back.

Both times? Yes.

Did she then get any push, or fall over on the ground? Yes she did; – when we were struggling, I pushed her over a little stool.

And you continued to struggle while she lay there? Yes; she raised herself on her elbow, – she was not able to rise, being drunk, – and called on Burke to be quiet.

LORD JUSTICE-CLERK. – You mean quiet from fighting with you, or you with him? Yes.

LORD ADVOCATE. – Did he quit you at last? After he threw me the second time on the bed, he then quit, and I lay still in the bed.

What did he do? He stood on the floor; – he then got stride-legs on the top of the woman on the floor, and she cried out a little, and he kept in her breath.

Did he lay himself down upon her? Yes, he pressed down her head with his breast.

She gave a kind of a cry, did she? Yes.

Did she give that more than once? She moaned a little after the first cry.

How did he apply his hand towards her? He put one hand under the nose, and the other under her chin, under her mouth.

He stopped her breath, do you mean? Yes.

Did he continue this for any length of time? I could not exactly say the time; ten or fifteen minutes.

Did he say anything to you when this was going on? No, he said nothing.

Did he then come off her? Yes; he got up off her.

Did she appear dead then? Yes; she appeared dead *a wee*.

Did she appear to be quite dead? She was not moving; I could not say whether she was dead or not.

What did he do then? He put his hand across her mouth.

Did he keep it there for any length of time? He kept it two or three minutes . . .

What was you doing all this time? I was sitting on the chair.

What did he do with the body? He stripped it of the clothes.

Where did he put them? Under the bed.

What did he do with the body? He took it and threw it at the foot of the bed, doubled her up, and threw a sheet over her; he tied her head to her feet. He tied her head and feet together, and covered her up with straw.

Now, during this time this man was lying on her, where was M'Dougal and your wife? When they heard the first screech, they left the foot of the bed and went into the passage.

Did they both run to the passage? Yes.

Did they come in again when this was going on? They did not come in till this was all over, and her covered over with straw . . .

Did you see the blood? I did not observe any at that time.

No blood on the floor? Not any at that time.

Any blood on the woman's face? I did not see any at that time.

Did you hear these women cry any thing after they went into the passage? I did not take heed.

Nobody came in at that time? None.

Before the women sprang up, had you seen Burke turn the woman round, or do any thing at all to her? He was on the top of her when they sprung out of the bed.

Was he long in that position before they went away? A minute or two; whenever he catched her, she gave a screech, and they ran away.

None of them laid hold of Burke, and tried to screen the woman? None at all . . .

Neither of them made any attempt to save this woman, or to take Burke off her? Not that I saw . . .

Well, did Burke go out then? Yes, Burke went out.

Immediately after this old woman was laid in the straw? Yes; he immediately went out.

Was he long absent? About ten minutes.

When the women came back, did they say anything? Did they ask no questions? No.

Did you say anything? No.

What did you do then? They went to their beds again.

Did neither of them ask for the woman Docherty when they came back? They did not.

Then you say Burke went out, and returned in about ten minutes; did any body come back with him? Mr Jones.

Was it not Mr Paterson? It was the Doctor's man . . .

Do you know where this man lived? He lives down on the other side of the street, in the West Port.

Well, when he came back with Burke, what did Burke say to him? He asked him to look at the body he had got; he said it would do well enough; to get a box and put it into.

Did he point to the straw where it was? Yes, and he wanted him to look at it; but he would not look at it.

Mendelssohn Visits Scotland, 1829

FELIX MENDELSSOHN BARTHOLDY

Scotland made a lasting impression on Mendelssohn's imagination when he visited on a walking tour with his friend the poet Karl Klingemann. He kept his family apprised of his impressions through regular letters. Writing from England sometime after he left Scotland, he noted: 'since Scotland is a place I shall never forget, since I have never been able to regard times when I felt cheerful and invigorated as wasted time (and whenever I was lazy I was never cheerful), especially since some new things were coming together in my head which proved to me that I had survived the cold-bloodedness of London society and people, and that I had to start composing again . . .' The result was the 'Hebrides' Overture and the 'Scottish' Symphony.

To Abraham Mendelssohn Bartholdy
Blair Atholl, August 3, 1829

Evening, August 3, Highland inn at the bridge of Tummel.
A wild affair. The storm is howling, blustering, and whistling around outside, causing the doors to slam shut down below and blowing the shutters open, but we can't tell whether the sounds of water are from the rain or from the blowing spray, since both are raging. We're sitting here calmly around the burning hearth, which I poke a bit from time to time, making it flare up. Otherwise, the room is large and empty, water is dripping down along one of the walls; the floor is thin, and the conversation in the servants' quarters can be heard echoing up from below; they're singing drunken songs and laughing – dogs are barking as well. Two beds with purple curtains, on our feet Scottish wooden shoes instead of English slippers, tea with honey and potato cakes, a narrow winding wooden staircase, which the maid made use of to bring us whisky, a dismal procession of clouds in the sky, and in spite of all the wind and water noises, in spite of the servants' conversation and the banging doors it seems quiet! Quiet and very lonely. I should like to say that the quiet resounds even through the noise. Just now the door opened by itself. It's a Highland ale house. The little boys with their plaids and bare knees and colourful caps, the waiter in his tartan, old people with their periwigs, all speaking a jumble of incomprehensible Gaelic. The countryside is broad and wide, covered with dense vegetation, from all sides cascades of water are rushing under the bridges, there is little corn but much heather with brown and red flowers, ravines, passes, crossroads;

everywhere beautiful green, deep blue water – but everything is stern, dark, and very lonely . . .

The weather is discouraging. I have invented my own method of drawing it, and today rubbed in some clouds, and drew gray mountains in pencil; Klingemann is rhyming cheerfully, and I carry out more of the details when it rains. But it had better not rain tomorrow, for if possible we are to see Loch Tay, Kenmore, and Killin tomorrow. Today is almost an autumn day. I'll tell you all about today soon; I don't lack for material to make me an important figure at Leipziger Str. No. 3 . . . When I think of how this piece of paper will be carried out to the garden house, and how yesterday at the waterfall the beginning of the letter blew out of my sketchbook and went fluttering down onto the gravel (we scrambled after it and retrieved it, though), and how just now the innkeeper's wife is singing her child to sleep with a sweet melody in a minor key, and how all of this is on its way to you. So things will still pass back and forth a few times. But then when the late autumn weather sets in, I'll put on my coat for the last day of the journey home, and walk in one evening. It will be merry. But now I am still in Scotland, and the winds are blustering wildly. Good night. I'm going to my bed inside the red curtains. Sleep well. Felix MB

To Abraham Mendelssohn Bartholdy
On one of the Hebrides, August 7, 1829

In order to make clear what a strange mood has come over me in the Hebrides, the following occurred to me:

Glasgow, August 11

How much has passed in the meantime. The most horrible seasickness, Staffa, scenery, travels, people; Klingemann can describe them, for in the first place he didn't have to make the London mail, as I did today, for which I had to write several letters, and second he hasn't been plagued as I have been by severe headaches all evening, which make it hard for me to even think, let alone write. Then take into account that it's already midnight, and we've already filled a whole day of our Highlands journey with boat travel, galleries, churches, steam, people, and smokestack funnels, and you will excuse me for being so brief. I can't go on today. Also, the best thing I have to report can be found in the above lines of music, and I'll gladly spare you descriptions of my illness, the thoroughly unaccommodating, damp weather, and so on. So please forgive me this time. I am drawing assiduously, and Klingemann's poems are coming along splendidly, and I also think that several of my pictures were more successful than usual. And expenditures have been more moderate than I thought. We've only spent twenty-four pounds so far. Tomorrow we're going to Loch Lomond and Ben Lomond, to Loch Katrine, the Trossachs, Aberfoyle, Stirling, and Lanark; we'll be back here at the end of this week, and you will receive our last joint letter from here; my own half should be better by then . . .

F.

Reminiscences of Edinburgh Life, Early 1800s

HENRY COCKBURN

The advocate Henry Cockburn was one of the most colourful recorders of life in early and mid-nineteenth-century Scotland, Edinburgh in particular. His posthumously published memoir danced through his life with startling and strongly opinionated digressions into the habits, manners and abilities of his fellow citizens. It begins with his childhood, and ends with inevitable repining for a better age.

The High School in Edinburgh

Out of the whole four years of my attendance there were probably not ten days in which I was not flogged, at least once. Yet I never entered the class, nor left it, without feeling perfectly qualified, both in ability and preparation, for its whole business; which, being confined to Latin alone, and in necessarily short tasks, since every one of the boys had to rhyme over the very same words, in the very same way, was no great feat. But I was driven stupid. Oh! the bodily and mental weariness of sitting six hours a day, staring idly at a page, without motion and without thought, and trembling at the gradual approach of the merciless giant. I never got a single prize, and once sat *boobie* at the annual public examination. The beauty of no Roman word, or thought, or action, ever occurred to me; nor did I ever fancy that Latin was of any use except to torture boys . . .

As mere school years, these six were very fruitlessly spent. The hereditary evils of the system and of the place were too great for correction even by Adam; and the general tone of the school was vulgar and harsh. Among the boys, coarseness of language and manners was the only fashion. An English boy was so rare, that his accent was openly laughed at. No lady could be seen within its walls. Nothing evidently civilized was safe. Two of the masters, in particular, were so savage, that any master doing now what they did every hour, would certainly be transported.

On valiant attempts to prevent the New Town's rise as the heart of genteel society

In my youth the whole fashionable dancing, as indeed the fashionable everything, clung to George Square; where in Buccleuch Place (close by the south-eastern corner of the square) most beautiful rooms were erected, which, for several years, threw the New Town piece of presumption entirely into the shade.

Here were the last remains of the ball-room discipline of the preceding age. Martinet dowagers and venerable beaux acted as masters and mistresses of ceremonies, and made all the preliminary arrangements. No couple could dance unless each party was provided with a ticket prescribing the precise place in the precise dance. If there was no ticket, the gentleman, or the lady, was dealt with as an intruder, and turned out of the dance . . .

Tea was sipped in side-rooms; and he was a careless beau who did not present his partner with an orange at the end of each dance; and the oranges and the tea, like everything else, were under exact and positive regulations. All this disappeared, and the very rooms were obliterated, as soon as the lately raised community secured its inevitable supremacy in the New Town. The aristocracy of a few predominating individuals and families came to an end; and the unreasonable old had nothing for it but to sigh over the recollection of the select and elegant parties of their youth, where indiscriminate public right was rejected, and its coarseness awed.

On dining

The prevailing dinner hour was about three o'clock. Two o'clock was quite common if there was no company. Hence it was no great deviation from their usual custom for a family to dine on Sundays '*between sermons*' – that is, between one and two. The hour, in the course of time, but not without groans and predictions, became four, at which it remained for several years. Then it got to five, which, however, was thought positively revolutionary; and four was long and gallantly adhered to by haters of change as 'the good old hour.' At last even they were obliged to give in. But they only yielded inch by inch, and made a desperate stand at half-past four. Even five, however, triumphed, and continued the average polite hour from (I think) about 1806 or 1807 till about 1820. Six has at last prevailed, and half-an-hour later is not unusual. As yet this is the farthest stretch of London imitation, except in country houses devoted to grouse or deer, where the species called sportsmen, disdaining all mankind except themselves, glory in not dining till sensible people have gone to bed. Thus, within my memory, the hour has ranged from two to half-past six o'clock; and a stand has been regularly made at the end of every half hour against each encroachment; and always on the same grounds – dislike of change and jealousy of finery.

On laxer days on the Bench

At Edinburgh, the old judges had a practice at which even their age used to shake its head. They had always wine and biscuits *on the Bench*, when the business was clearly to be protracted beyond the usual dinner hour. The modern judges – those I mean who were made after 1800, never gave in to this; but with those of the preceding generation, some of whom lasted several years after 1800, it was quite common. Black bottles of strong port were set down beside them on the Bench, with glasses, carafes of water, tumblers, and biscuits; and this without the slightest attempt at concealment. The refreshment was generally allowed to stand untouched for a short time, as if despised, during which their Lordships seemed to be intent only on their notes. But in a little, some water was poured into the tumbler, and sipped quietly as if merely to sustain nature. Then a few drops of wine were ventured upon, but only with the water.

But at last patience could endure no longer, and a full bumper of the pure black element was tossed over; after which the thing went on regularly, and there was a comfortable munching and quaffing to the great envy of the parched throats in the gallery. The strong-headed stood it tolerably well, but it told, plainly enough, upon the feeble. Not that the ermine was absolutely intoxicated, but it was certainly sometimes affected. This however was so ordinary with these sages, that it really made little apparent change upon them. It was not very perceptible at a distance; and they all acquired the habit of sitting and looking judicial enough, even when their bottles had reached the lowest ebb.

Cholera Epidemic, 1832

THE *GREENOCK ADVERTISER*

Cholera was one of the scourges of the industrial era, helped in its spread by the dreadful living conditions and squalor of overpopulated and poverty-stricken quarters. A fierce epidemic broke out in Greenock in 1832, in which about 2,000 died. Doctors grew increasingly anxious to understand the root of the disease. Some, it seems, were more anxious than others.

For the purpose of endeavouring to set all doubt at rest respecting the contagious or non-contagious nature of Cholera a medical gentleman on Wednesday last made the following experiment. Immediately after the death of a Cholera patient in the Hospital, he undressed, went into the same bed, and covered himself with the same clothes which had the moment before been occupied by the person who died. He remained for two hours and a half in bed, thus exposing himself as much as possible to the risk of imbibing the disease, if it be really contagious. He was in excellent health at the time he made the experiment and up to this hour, we have much pleasure in stating, he continues to remain so. So convinced were some of his medical brethren that he would fall a victim, that next day numerous enquiries were made at the Hospital of the hour when he died.

(To our weak thinking, this valorous feat proved no more than the hero of the tale 'went into the bed' a fool, and came out no wiser – for which he may thank his stars. To add to the wonderment, we are informed that 'he was in excellent health at the time he made the experiment' – but this is a condition to which, of all others, we should imagine he was most indebted for his security. Had he been infirm with age, and broken down from bodily disease, would he have made the attempt? We suspect not. Moreover, we cannot let him off with the idea that he has performed a feat second only to that of precipitating himself down the crater of mount Vesuvius with the small chance of being vomited forth again in a whole skin; for it appears that he took care to have the body of the patient removed before he nestled himself in the blankets, and in this case made but half an experiment. Yet we do not advise him to perform the other moiety; that we conceive he should prudently leave to some one of his sage companions, who called to enquire if he were still alive next morning. – Editor, G.A.)

Testimony of Coal Workers, 1840

JANET CUMMING, JANET ALLEN, JANE JOHNSON, ISABEL HOGG, JANE PEACOCK WATSON, KATHARINE LOGAN, HELEN READ AND MARGARET WATSON

The Children's Employment Commission of 1840 was one of the most shocking documents of its time. Its inspectors, who had been sent out to investigate whether the provisions of a series of factory acts limiting the working hours of apprentices and children were being implemented, decided also to examine conditions in the mines. In mining towns baby girls were disparagingly described as 'a hutch of dross', while boys were 'a hutch of coal'. Even so, girls and women were enormously useful in the mines, partly because they could make themselves helpful at a younger age, and thus start work earlier, and partly because of their willingness to crawl into the most uncomfortable areas without complaint. Although the Commission's focus was the conditions of children, the report unexpectedly threw up voices of women as well as girls. It was illustrated with sketches showing the nature of work underground, and so horrified the public that a law was passed making it illegal for women and children to go down the pits. This legislation heightened the misery for those women for whom the pit was their only source of income. To evade the law, some disguised themselves as men; their co-workers turned a blind eye. Here are a few comments recorded in the 1840 Commission:

The foreman at Ormiston colliery: 'In fact women always did the lifting or heavy part of the work and neither they nor the children were treated like human beings where they are employed. Females submit to work in places where no man or even lad could be got to labour in; they work in bad roads, up to their knees in water, their posture almost double. They are below till the last hour of pregnancy. They have swelled ankles and haunches and are prematurely brought to the grave or, what is worse, to a lingering existence.'

Janet Cumming, 11, coal bearer: 'I gang with the women at five and come up at five at night; work all night on Fridays and come away at twelve in the day. The roof is very low; I have to bend my back and legs and the water is frequently up to the calves of my legs. Have no liking for the work. Father makes me like it.'

Janet Allen, 8, who pushed tubs: 'It is sair, sair work, would like to be playing about better.'

Jane Johnson: 'I was seven and half years of age when my uncle yoked me to the pit as father and mother were both dead. I could carry two hundredweights when fifteen but now feel the weakness upon me from the strains. I have been married ten years and had four children, have usually wrought till one or two days of birth. Many women get injured in back and legs and I was crushed by a stone some time since and forced to lose one of my fingers.'

Isabel Hogg, 53, retired coal bearer: 'Been married thirty seven years; it was the practice to marry early, when the coals were all carried on women's backs, men needed us. I have four daughters married and all work below till they bear their bairns. One is very badly now from working while pregnant which brought on a miscarriage from which she is not expected to recover. Collier people suffer much more than others – my guid man died nine years since with bad breath, he lingered some years but was entirely off work eleven years before he died.'

Jane Peacock Watson, 40, coal bearer: 'I have wrought in the bowels of the earth thirty three years; have been married twenty three years and had nine children; six are alive, three died of typhus a few years since, have had two dead born, think they were so from oppressive work; a vast women have dead births. . . . I have always been obliged to work below till forced to go home to bear the bairn, and so have all the other women. We return as soon as we are able, never longer than ten or twelve days, many less if we are needed.'

Katharine Logan, 16, coal carrier, who was put in a harness: 'drawing backward with face to tubs. The ropes and chains go under pit clothes, it is o'er sair work, especially when we crawl.'

Helen Read, 16: '[I work] from five in the morning till six at night and carry two hundredweight on my back. I dinna like the work but think I'm fit for none other. Many accidents happen below ground. I've met with two serious ones myself. Two years ago the pit closed on thirteen of us and we were two days without food and light. Nearly one day we were up to our chins in water. At last we picked our way to an old shaft and were heard by people working above.'

Margaret Watson, 16: 'We often have bad air, had some a short time since and lost brother by it. He sunk down and I tried to draw him out but the air stopped my breath and I was forced to gang.'

Streets of Sewage, 1842

DR W. L. LAWRIE

As part of the Chadwick Report of 1842 examining the living conditions of the poor, this eye-watering account was submitted by W. L. Lawrie, a doctor in Greenock, describing life in this notoriously filthy town.

The great proportion of the dwellings of the poor are situated in very narrow and confined closes or alleys leading from the main streets; these closes end generally in a *cul-de-sac*, and have little ventilation, the space between the houses being so narrow as to exclude the action of the sun on the ground. I might almost say there are no drains in any of these closes, for where I have noticed sewers, they are in such a filthy and obstructed state, that they create more nuisance than if they never existed. In those closes where there is no dunghill, the excrementitious and other offensive matter is thrown into the gutter before the door, or carried out and put in the street. There are no back courts to the houses, but in nearly every close there is a dunghill, seldom or never covered in; few of these are cleaned out above once or twice a-year; most of them are only emptied when they can hold no more: to some of these privies are attached, and one privy serves a whole neighbourhood. The people seem so familiarized with this unseemly state of things, and so lost to all sense of propriety, that it is a matter of no small difficulty, in some of the back streets, to make your way through them without being polluted with filth.

Behind my consulting rooms, where I am now sitting, there is a large dunghill with a privy attached; to my knowledge that dunghill has not been emptied for six months; it serves a whole neighbourhood, and the effluvium is so offensive that I cannot open the window. The land is three stories high, and the people, to save themselves trouble, throw all their filth out of the stair-window, consequently a great part of it goes on the close, and the close is not cleaned out till the dunghill is full: the filth in the close reaches nearly to the sill of the back window of a shop in front, and the malarious moisture oozes through the wall on the floor . . .

There is one poor man who was under my care in the hospital with asthma for six months, he was dismissed an incurable, and is now living with his wife and seven children in a dark room on the ground-floor, more fit for a coal-cellar than a human being; it is lighted by a fixed window about two feet square; the breadth of the room is only four feet, and the length eight. There is only one bed for the whole family, and yet the rent of this hole is 5*l.*

As I was passing one of the poorest districts not long ago, a little girl ran after me and requested me to come and see her mother as she could not keep her in bed; I found the mother lying in a miserable straw bed with a piece of carpet for a covering, delirious from fever; the husband, who was a drunkard, had died in the hospital of the same disease. There was no fire in the grate; some of the children were out begging, and the two youngest were crawling on the wet floor; it was actually a puddle in the centre, as the sewer before the house was obstructed, and the moisture made its way to the middle of the floor by passing under the door. Every saleable piece of furniture had been pawned during the father's illness for the support of the family. None of the neighbours would enter the house; the children were actually starving, and the mother was dying without any attendance whatever . . .

The first question I generally put when a new case of fever is admitted is as to their abode. I was struck with the number of admissions from Market-street; most of the cases coming from that locality became quickly typhoid and made slow recoveries. This is a narrow back street; it is almost overhung by a steep hill rising immediately behind it; it contains the lowest description of houses built closely together, the access to the buildings being through filthy closes; the front entrance is generally the only outlet; numerous foci for the production of miasma lie concealed in this street, I think I could point out one in each close.

In one part of the street there is a dunghill, yet it is too large to be called a dunghill. I do not mistake its size when I say it contains 100 cubic yards of impure filth, collected from all parts of the town. It is never removed; it is the stock in trade of a person who deals in dung; he retails it by cartfuls: to please his customers he always keeps a nucleus, as the older the filth is the higher is the price. The proprietor has an extensive privy attached to the concern. This collection is fronting the public street; it is enclosed in front by a wall; the height of the wall is about 12 feet and the dung overtops it; the malarious moisture oozes through the wall and runs over the pavement. The effluvium all round about this place in summer is horrible; there is a land of houses adjoining, four stories in height; and in the summer each house swarms with myriads of flies; every article of food and drink must be covered, otherwise, if left exposed for a minute, the flies immediately attack it, and it is rendered unfit for use from the strong taste of the dunghill left by the flies. But there is a still more extensive dunghill in the street, at least, if not so high, it covers double the extent of surface; what the depth of it is I cannot say. It is attached to the slaughter-house, and belongs, I believe, to the town authorities. It is not only the receptacle for the dung and offal from the slaughter-house, but the sweepings of the streets are also conveyed and deposited there. It has likewise a public privy attached. In the slaughter-house itself (which is adjoining the street) the blood and offal is allowed to lie a long time, and the smell in summer is highly offensive . . . I believe it to be a rare occurrence when fever is not to be found in [here] during any time of the year.

The Disruption of the Church of Scotland, 1843

REVEREND MCLEAN

After years of growing discontent, over a third of the clergy of the Church of Scotland (474 of 1,203) signed a Deed of Demission, left their manses and charges, and formed their own church, the Free Church of Scotland, under the leadership of Thomas Chalmers. They were an evangelical band who resented the legal right of landowners to choose the minister for a parish, regardless of parishioners' wishes. As Argyllshire minister Mr McLean below makes clear, it was a highly emotional and anxious time. Seceding ministers were turning their backs on a secure income and were now dependent on the financial support of their new congregations. While some dissenters were firebrands, many were mild and unconfrontational men who were driven to join the Free Church on a point of principle. In 1929 the rift was healed, leaving only a few diehards in the Free Church.

When that now memorable event, the Disruption, began to cast its shadow before it, I was the happy pastor of a peaceful Highland parish. The population did not exceed a hundred families . . . Grouped prominently together, in this pleasant field of ministerial labour, are seen the manse with its garden, and the Church with its grave-yard. On every side, hills rise abruptly to a considerable height; while above, the blue vault seems to rest all round on their summits, and to roof in the whole scene . . .

Such were the external attractions of this quiet retreat, while, not less peaceful, and still more endearing, were the relations between pastor and people, from the highest to the humblest. And in these circumstances, so pleasing to my tastes, suited to my capacity, and satisfactory to my ambition, with a numerous family besides, all of us literally dependent on the benefice as our sole means of support, to imperil all, hastily or on light grounds (as we are sometimes accused of having done), to sacrifice it from any motive short of the inexorable constraint of conscience, would have been a folly, a sin, and a shame.

Such a constraint did, in the sovereign providence of God, unmistakably come. . . . I spared no pains from the first in publicly plying the people with week-day lectures on the great question at issue; but I could never bring myself to deal privately and personally with them, never asking even my elders what part they purposed to take in the approaching

Disruption.... And so it was, that even so late in the day as the 'Convocation,' I did not know, on going to that meeting, of a single individual prepared to take the step to which I then pledged myself. The lowest ebb, however, was the turning point of the tide; and it flowed from that time forward. It was known what I had done, and it was not doubted that I would redeem my pledge. On my return home, a written assurance was sent me from *all* my elders ... that, come what might, the session would remain unbroken. The great mass of the people, too, adhered.... All now gave good promise that, under God's blessing, these principles had taken deep root in the land ...

The gentleman, whom I may call the author and manager of the persecution in the Glen, the proprietor of more than one-half of the parish, called on me on the eve of the Disruption, and asked me, seemingly much affected, if there was no alternative, but that I must 'go out.' Nothing, he said, had ever so grieved him as the thought that such might be the case. He was on all sides congratulated on its being a model parish, educationally, as well as otherwise, under my auspices, and he had hoped for himself and his children long to enjoy the blessing of my ministry. He was pleased to say so, and much more which I will not repeat. But, finding that he had failed in the main object of his visit, he forgot all this; and from that day forth he exerted himself to the very utmost when we became houseless to keep us so, and have us exterminated altogether as a nuisance from the district. Even on his own showing, however, he could 'find no occasion against us, except concerning the law of our God.' ...

I pass on to the period of the Disruption in which I had the honour of bearing my humble part as a member of Assembly [General Assembly of the Church of Scotland]. So confident was I of that event being inevitable, that ... I had, before leaving home, sold off all the stock and implements of a valuable glebe; and now, on my return, with those things out of the way, we at once set about packing furniture and preparing for instant removal. We had just finished our heavy task by Saturday evening. On Sabbath the church was to be preached vacant, while I was to address my flock on the green in front of the manse. On Monday morning we were to bid a final farewell to the sweet spot, and proceed to a temporary home, mercifully opened to us in a neighbouring parish, when unexpectedly (at this hour) a deputation of the heritors was announced. They found me pondering all these things in a dismantled apartment, and amid the heart-sickening desolations of an uprooted home. Without one softening word of sympathy, to their object they went hard and straight. And it was this – that either I should not preach at all on the morrow, or go away somewhere out of sight and hearing, lest I should disturb the feelings of the reverend gentleman who was to preach in the church and declare it vacant! This modest request, though little careful of my feelings, was certainly most considerately tender towards his. He had inducted me to the charge, introduced me to the congregation, held our principles all along till he must needs suffer for them, solemnly pledged himself to them at the Assembly of 1842, and at the Convocation of the same year; and now, having deserted the cause, he was the man whom its enemies delighted to honour in dealing the *coup de grace* to an old friend!

Many a solemn and touching scene did those trying times make us acquainted with. I am not sure, however, but that the Sabbath meeting on the green was the most trying of all in my experience. Not only did most trying circumstances, inseparable from such a meeting, concur to impart to it a deep and painful interest, but special care was taken to produce the impression among the people that, if I ventured to preach, measures were all ready and constables at hand for my forcible removal. . . . Entirely disregarding the threats, I felt it to be my duty to take my stand there; and there, accordingly, in the presence of my persecutors, who kept walking round about us, speaking loudly within earshot, and with significant looks, I conducted public worship, with such emotions as I may never feel again; while my poor flock, apprehensive every moment of what might happen, sat closer and closer together, like a fluttered covey when the hawk sails overhead . . .

I shall not dwell on our 'quitting the manse.' Monday came, with all the dreary accompaniments of such a 'flitting' as ours. Nearly twenty carts mustered on that morning – not all actually needed, perhaps, but not the less tokens of their owners' sympathy and respect. In silence and with subdued air, like men on solemn and affecting duty, each took his allotted share of the *disjecta membra* of our home, and formed into line. Our six children, the oldest just eight . . . took their places in the rear; and all things being now ready, we quenched our hearth, took a last look through the deserted apartments . . . and, having turned the key in the door of our once happy but now desolate dwelling, slowly and sadly the long procession moved on. Immediately, by the hands of a messenger-at-arms, a farewell shot was fired after us in the shape of a very formidable interdict, which, fortunately for me, would not, as I have said, go off till after the Sabbath . . .

Shortly previous to the crisis, with no prospect of accommodation in the district for my family, I fully expected to be separated from them by a long distance and for a considerable time, when, unsolicited, a farm-house, providentially vacant for a season, was placed at my disposal by a noble-minded benefactor of the cause. More than that, he gave me not only a house, but a church also, which he had built for his tenantry in that neighbourhood; and they welcomed me to be their pastor with a cordial call. Nor was this all. In the Glen, which still engaged my chief interest, a suitable site was obtained, and steps taken for the erection of a church. An elder of mine possessed a small property, completely surrounded by wide territories, on which we dared not have set foot for God's worship, no, not even on their lone heathery fells; and there, in a spot suggestive of the sweet description of the Psalmist, 'We found a place for the Lord, we found it in the fields of the wood.' There, till we could 'go into His tabernacles,' we worshipped on His footstool, the green earth, heaven alone our canopy, and He whose throne it is, our glory and defence. These my two congregations being ten miles apart, and it being desirable, for a time at least, that they should have regular supply, in Gaelic and English, I travelled twenty miles and preached four sermons every Sabbath for two summers. My hearers had increased in numbers, instead of being diminished, by the Disruption; while a mere handful was left in both parishes in connection with the now Erastianized Establishment.

The Origins of Photography, 1845

DAVID OCTAVIUS HILL

The painter David Octavius Hill went into partnership with photographer Robert Adamson from St Andrews in 1843, thus forging a hugely influential artistic pairing that resulted in over 1,800 photographic portraits of extraordinary quality that some believe carried on the tradition of artists such as Henry Raeburn. Here Hill describes to a fellow member of the Royal Scottish Academy the perfecting of the technique that allowed the young art of photography to flourish. He is quick to acknowledge the collaborative nature of this new procedure, citing the work of Fox Talbot, who had pioneered the calotype, and Adamson, who had learnt from the work of St Andrews University scientists Dr David Brewster and Dr John Adamson.

To David Roberts
Inverleith Place, Edinburgh

12 March 1845

. . . I cannot fail to be more than gratified by the intelligence I received from you this morning as to the manner in which the portfolio of our Calotypes had been received by yourself, by Stanfield, and the distinguished guests of Lord Northampton. Your flattering opinions have been shared by Etty, Allan, Leitch and many artists and a few who know what art is, and these I have used as a warm blanket, to restore me to my natural heat, after a few cold bucketings of ignorant criticism, which my desire to foster and improve this hand maiden of Fine Art, has exposed me to. Most welcome therefore and highly prized by me are Stanfield's and your own cordial approval of our labour. Accept of my gratitude both of you . . .

The art is the invention of Mr Fox Talbot who is the sole patentee: his patent extends in England only. About three years ago this said process was chemically and artistically speaking a very miserable affair. Dr Adamson of St Andrews – brother of my friend R. Adamson whose manipulation produced the pictures now with you, took up Mr Talbot's process as an amateur. You are aware how jealous some scientific men are, as to their rights in the paternity of inventions or improvements, therefore I say *entre nous* that I believe Dr Adamson & his brother to be the fathers of many of these parts of the process which make it a valuable and practical art. I believe also from all I have seen that Robert Adamson is the most successful manipulator the art has yet seen, and his steady industry and knowledge of chemistry, is such that both from him and his brother much new improvements may yet be expected . . .

Railway Mania, 1847

JOSEPH MITCHELL

The industrial Victorian era offered lucrative opportunities to those with money or vision. Some ventures, however, were not as secure as they first appeared, and could have disastrous results. Engineer Joseph Mitchell witnessed the moneyed classes' rash love affair with railways, which came to a bitter end in 1847.

In 1845 the whole country was in fever heat regarding railways. The frenzy continued in 1846. However absurd the scheme, the public rushed at it, and every stock ran up to a premium; in fact, there was a mania which resembled the insanity of the South Sea Bubble. Many thousands of people, who could pay a deposit of £2 10s. expecting to get a premium and then sell out, were involved in obligations for thousands of pounds, and he was a fortunate speculator whose project Parliament rejected and the Provisional Committee were required to wind up.

Apart from speculators, for whom there may be less sympathy, thousands of respectable people, believing railways an advantageous investment for their savings, were ruined by the fluctuation in the value of their property, mainly from the opposition lines and the uncertain actions of the Legislature.

In 1847 came the railway crash, consequent on the wild schemes and speculation of former years, and which spread ruin and dismay throughout the country.

Directors who had their Bills passed entered on their works, and had to struggle through excessive difficulties. Some became involved in heavy responsibilities to the extent of their whole fortunes. Notable cases of this occurred in the Caledonian and Scottish Central, and other Northern lines.

Shareholders were prosecuted for calls to their absolute ruin. Stocks were unsaleable. Some railway companies suspended operations.

The Caledonian and Scottish Central contractors, Messrs. Brassey, Mackenzie, and Stephenson, who had upwards of 20,000 men engaged, could not get funds to pay their workmen for a time; and Mr Stephenson, who had the management of the works, in his distress and excitement, lost his reason and died.

The South Aberdeen Railway had to suspend operations, and our opponents, the Great North of Scotland Railway Company, who had got their Bill passed, were unable to proceed with their works.

When this company was formed, instead of issuing their stock to the public, the promoters distributed the greater part of it among themselves, calculating, as many did, that when they obtained their Bill the stock would run up to a premium, as was then common. Hence the law agents of the company had allotted to them 2,130 shares, upon which they deposited £75,850. The secretary was liable for £25,000; the Edinburgh agents, £20,000; two other agents, £15,000; while eight directors subscribed for £170,000 of the stock.

The deposits had been apparently advanced by the banks, chiefly the North of Scotland Bank; but unfortunately the crash came before the calculations of the promoters were realized.

Then came a long period of monetary depression, so that not only had they no capital, as I have said, to carry on their works, but the banks got uneasy regarding the deposits they had advanced, and insisted on payment and security.

The unfortunate promoters of the Great North of Scotland Railway were thus involved in much pecuniary difficulty; some of the directors, it was said, were ruined. At last it was resolved before their power expired to go on with the works, but limit their efforts to the forty miles of line between Aberdeen and Huntly.

The works were contracted for; and with the aid of contractors who took stock in part payment, they with great difficulty succeeded in completing that portion of the railway, thus giving little hope to the northern counties of obtaining railway communication even by Aberdeen.

Experimenting with Chloroform, 1847

JAMES SIMPSON

The father of gynaecology, James Simpson, was a prodigy whose work transformed medicine. Appointed Professor of Midwifery at the University of Edinburgh in 1835 at the age of twenty-four, he worked on finding a safe means of anaesthetizing patients. His early attempts with sulphuric ether were not a success, but in this letter he describes how early in November 1847 he discovered the effectiveness of chloroform (which he had not actually invented) by experimenting on himself. Simpson's use of chloroform was initially criticized by some for interfering with God's intention for women to suffer in childbirth, but he persevered with its use. When in 1853 he used it on Queen Victoria when she gave birth to Prince Leopold, it gained general acceptance.

To Mr Waldie

Edinburgh 14 November 1847

My Dear Sir

[. . .]

I had the chloroform for several days in the house before trying it, as, after seeing it such a heavy unvolatile-like liquid, I despaired of it, and went on dreaming about others.

The first night we took it Dr Duncan, Dr Keith and I all tried it simultaneously, and were all 'under the table' in a minute or two.

I write in great haste, as I wish to scribble off several letters.

Be so good as say what you think may be the ultimate selling price of an ounce of it? Duncan and Flockhart charge 3s for the ounce.

There has been great demand for the pamphlet yesterday at the booksellers' here.

Yours very truly
J. Y. Simpson

PS By the bye, Imlach tells me Dr P. is to enlighten your medical society about the 'morality' of the practice. I have a great itching to run up and pound him. *When* is the meeting?

The true moral question is, 'is a practitioner justified by any principle of humanity in not using it?' I believe every operation without it is just a piece of the most deliberate and cold-blooded *cruelty*.

Rioting in Caithness, 1847

THE *INVERNESS COURIER*

The dreaded potato blight that devastated Ireland also hit Scotland, in 1845–6, leaving the Highland and Islands population, which depended particularly heavily upon the potato crop, in desperate straits. Although in comparison with Ireland relatively few died, thousands were reduced to abject poverty and illness, and found themselves sinking under debts that were to dog them for years thereafter. For those suffering, the thought of food being sent out of Scotland was unbearable. When word got out that a ship filled with grain was to leave from the port in Wick, for instance, there was trouble.

We regret to say that the excitement so general throughout the north with respect to the shipment of grain has, in Wick, resulted in a collision between the populace and the military. On Tuesday, last week, two companies of the 76th regt, consisting of 104 men, commanded by Capt. Evans Gordon, were landed at Ackergill, and the same day marched into Wick . . . Sheriff Thompson having obtained intimation of an intention on the part of the mob to scuttle a small vessel lying at the wharf at Wick loading with grain, Captain Gordon was ordered to put a guard on the vessel for her protection. The guard consisted of an officer, Lieutenant Brett, and twenty men. Captain Gordon accompanied Lieutenant Brett to the wharf, where an immense mob had collected, manifesting the most violent and hostile feelings. To avoid being hemmed in the military cleared the pier, and then formed a line across it. At this time a party of sailors and others – about twenty men – . . . rushed suddenly behind the soldiers with a cable, and had the men not been instantly thrown back against a wall, some of them must have been hurled into the water. . . . Captain Gordon crossed the harbour in a boat (the passage to the pier being closed up by a dense crowd), and brought down the Sheriff with a reinforcement of troops. On arriving at the opening of the pier they found a formidable barricade of large boats obstructing the passage, and Lieut. Brett was prevented from joining them. The position of this officer was extremely critical. The mob was furious, and stones were thrown with great violence, striking Lieut. Brett and several of the men. The policeman who was with the military calculated that not less than 2,000 persons were present in the space between them and the barrier of boats (150 yards), which was one dense mass of men and boys. Lieut. Brett found it necessary to force the mob before him by slow degrees. At the point of the bayonet . . . On the arrival of fresh troops the Riot Act was read, and a position in front of the barrier taken up. For one hour the soldiers were exposed to every insult that can be imagined. The men were pelted, spat upon, struck with stones. . . . An order was then given to Captain Gordon by the Sheriff to clear the streets, which was done with the bayonet. . . . Some prisoners were taken, and on conveying them to the jail the soldiers were assailed from a hill with a volley of stones that rattled on the soldiers' accoutrements like hail. Several of the men were severely hurt, and the Sheriff and Provost were both struck. Captain Gordon was then ordered to fire. . . . The fire, we are happy to say, was not productive of fatal results. Two persons, a man and a woman, were wounded. The report of the shot had an instantaneous effect upon the mob. The utmost quietness was restored. This may be said to have terminated the melancholy proceedings. The feeling of the populace, however, is reported to be very bad, and nothing but force prevents them again from breaking out into outrage. . . . The detachment under Captain Gordon has since proceeded to Thurso, where similar insubordination has been manifested.

Victoria and Albert at Balmoral, 1848

QUEEN VICTORIA

Queen Victoria and Prince Albert felt an instant affinity with the Highlands and established a royal connection with Scotland that subsequent generations of royalty have continued. They rented then bought the estate at Balmoral, and spent the first of many visits there in 1848. The castle was built in 1853. These occasions were probably the happiest times of Victoria's life. After Albert's death in 1861 she took comfort from the memories she had of him at Balmoral and in the gillie John Brown's steadfast support. He became her personal attendant, and proved such a good friend that she disregarded all gossip about their relationship. In the diary she kept faithfully from childhood, she describes a particularly memorable expedition a couple of years before Albert's death.

October 7, 1859

Breakfast at half-past eight. At ten minutes to nine we started, in the sociable [open carriage], with Bertie and Alice and our usual attendants. Drove along the opposite side of the river. The day very mild and promising to be fine, though a little heavy over the hills, which we anxiously watched. At Castleton we took four post-horses, and drove to the Shiel of the Derry, that beautiful spot where we were last year – which Albert had never seen – and arrived there just before eleven. Our ponies were there with Kennedy, Robertson, and Jemmie Smith. One pony carried the luncheon-baskets. After all the cloaks, etc. had been placed on the ponies, or carried by the men, we mounted and began our 'journey'. I was on 'Victoria', Alice on 'Dobbins'. George McHardy, an elderly man who knew the country (and acts as a guide, carrying luggage for people across the hills 'on beasts' which he keeps for that purpose), led the way. We rode (my pony being led by Brown most of the time both going up and down) at least four miles up Glen Derry, which is very fine, with the remnants of a splendid forest, Cairn Derry being to the right, and the Derry Water running below. The track was very bad and stony, and broken up by cattle coming down for the 'Tryst'. At the end of the glen we crossed a ford, passed some softish ground, and turned up to the left by a very rough, steep, but yet gradual ascent to Corrie Etchan, which is in a very wild rugged spot, with magnificent precipices, a high mountain to the right called Ben Main, while to the left was Cairngorm of Derry. When we reached the top of this very steep ascent (we had been rising, though almost imperceptibly, from the Derry Shiel), we came upon a loch of the same name, which reminded us of Loch-na-Gar and of Loch-na-Nian. You look from here on to other wild hills and corries – on Ben A'an, etc. We ascended very gradually, but became so enveloped in mist that we could see nothing – hardly those just before us! Albert had walked a good deal; and it was very cold. The mist got worse; and as we rode along the stony, but almost flat ridge of Ben Muich Dhuie, we hardly knew whether we were on level ground or the top of the mountain. However, I and Alice rode to the very top, which we reached a few minutes past two; and here, at a cairn of stones, we lunched, in a piercing cold wind.

Just as we sat down, a gust of wind came and dispersed the mist, which had a most wonderful effect, like a dissolving view – and exhibited the grandest, wildest scenery imaginable. We sat on a ridge of the cairn to take our luncheon, – our good people being grouped with the ponies near us. Luncheon over, Albert ran off with Alice to the ridge to look at the splendid view, and sent for me to follow. I did so; but not without Grant's help, for there were quantities of large loose stones heaped up together to walk upon. The wind was fearfully high, but the view was well worth seeing. I cannot describe all, but we saw where the Dee rises between the mountains called the Well of Dee – Ben-y-Ghlo – and the adjacent mountains, Ben Vrackie – then Ben-na-Bhourd – Ben A'an, etc. – and such magnificent wild rocks, precipices, and corries. It had a sublime and solemn effect; so wild, so solitary – no one but ourselves and our little party here.

Albert went on further with the children, but I returned with Grant to my seat on the cairn, as I could not scramble about well. Soon after, we all began walking and looking for 'cairngorms', and found some small ones. The mist had entirely cleared away below, so that we saw all the beautiful views. Ben Muich Dhuie is 4,297 feet high, one of the highest mountains in Scotland. I and Alice rode part of the way, walking wherever it was very steep. Albert and Bertie walked the whole time. I had a little whisky and water as the people declared pure water would be too chilling. We then rode on without getting off again, Albert talking so gaily with Grant. Upon which Brown observed to me in simple Highland praise, 'It's very pleasant to walk with a person who is always "content".' Yesterday, in speaking of dearest Albert's sport, when I observed he never was cross after bad luck, Brown said, 'Everyone on the estate says there never was so kind a master; I am sure our only wish is to give satisfaction.' I said, they certainly did.

By a quarter-past six o'clock we got down to the Shiel of the Derry, where we found some tea, which we took in the 'shiel', and started again by moonlight at about half-past six. We reached Castleton at half-past seven – and after this it became cloudy. At a quarter-past eight precisely we were at Balmoral, much delighted and not at all tired; everything had been so well arranged, and so quietly, without any fuss. *Never* shall I forget this day, or the impression this very grand scene made upon me; truly sublime and impressive; such solitude!

Andrew Carnegie Shows an Early Interest in Libraries, 1853

ANDREW CARNEGIE

The renowned philanthropist Andrew Carnegie emigrated with his family from Dunfermline to Pittsburgh in 1848 when he was twelve. Through immense industry, self-discipline and astuteness, he went on to make a fortune in the iron and steel industries. He was to become famous in his homeland as well as in America for many charitable endowments, but above all for his championing of public libraries, the first of which he founded in Dunfermline in 1881. (He established 2,508 libraries in all, and gave away approximately $350 million in his lifetime.) As a teenager living in Allegheny he was frustrated by the lack of books. He was delighted when a library of 400 books owned by a Colonel Anderson opened on Saturday afternoons, purely for the use of local working boys. When the library was expanded and moved to new premises, the librarian asked Carnegie to pay a subscription fee since he was no longer an apprentice but a salaried employee of the telegraph company. Carnegie was incensed, arguing that he believed the Colonel would want those who had previously enjoyed his library to continue to do so for free. He wrote to the Pittsburgh Dispatch *to complain, and won the day.*

Allegheny, May 9th, 1853
Mr Editor:
Believing that you take a deep interest in whatever tends to elevate, instruct and improve the youth of this county, I am induced to call your attention to the following. You will remember that some time ago Mr Anderson (a gentleman of this city) bequested a large sum of money to establish and support a Library for working boys and apprentices residing here. It has been in successful operation for over a year, scattering precious seeds among us, and although fallen 'by the

wayside and in stony places,' not a few have found good ground. Every working boy has been freely admitted only requiring his parents or guardian to become surety. But its means of doing good have recently been greatly circumscribed by new directors who refuse to allow any boy *who is not learning a trade and bound* for a stated time to become a member. I rather think that the new directors have misunderstood the generous donor's *intentions*. It can hardly be thought that he meant to exclude boys employed in stores merely because they are not bound.

A Working Boy
though not bound.

Thomas Carlyle's Tax Return, 21 November 1855

JANE CARLYLE

The marriage of dour but brilliant historian Thomas Carlyle and the spirited Jane Baillie Welsh was a meeting of minds, if not temperaments. While Carlyle made his name as the foremost historian of his generation, Jane acted as a behind-the-scenes administrator, secretary and hostess. Her letters and other writing show her abundant talent for description and wit. Here she describes doing battle with the tax inspectors in London on her husband's behalf.

Mr C. said 'the voice of honour seemed to call on him to go himself.' But either it did not call loud enough, or he would not listen to that charmer. I went in a cab, to save all my breath for appealing. Set down at 30 Hornton Street, I found a dirty private-like house, only with Tax Office painted on the door. A dirty woman-servant opened the door, and told me the Commissioners would not be there for half an hour, but I might walk up. There were already some half-score men assembled in the waiting-room, among whom I saw the man who cleans our clocks, and a young apothecary of Cheyne Walk. All the others, to look at them, could not have been suspected for an instant, I should have said, of making a hundred a year . . .

'First-come lady,' called the clerk, opening a small side-door, and I stept forward into a *grand peut-être*. There was an instant of darkness while the one door was shut behind and the other opened in front; and there I stood in a dim room where three men sat round a large table spread with papers. One held a pen ready over an open ledger; another was taking snuff, and had taken still worse in his time, to judge by his shaky, clayed appearance. The third, who was plainly cock of that dung-heap, was sitting for Rhadamanthus – a Rhadamanthus without the justice.

'Name,' said the horned-owl-looking individual holding the pen.

'Carlyle.'

'What?'

'Carlyle.'

Seeing he still looked dubious, I spelt it for him.

'Ha!' cried Rhadamanthus, a big, bloodless-faced, insolent-looking fellow. 'What is this? why is Mr Carlyle not come himself? Didn't he get a letter ordering him to appear? Mr Carlyle wrote some nonsense about being exempted from coming, and I desired an answer to be sent that he must come, must do as other people.'

'Then, sir,' I said, 'your desire has been neglected, it would seem, my husband having received no such letter; and I was told by one of your fellow Commissioners that Mr Carlyle's personal appearance was not indispensable.'

'Huffgh! Huffgh! what does Mr Carlyle mean by saying he has no income from his writings, when he himself fixed it in the beginning at a hundred and fifty?'

'It means, sir, that, in ceasing to write, one ceases to be paid for writing, and Mr Carlyle has published nothing for several years.'

'Huffgh! Huffgh! I understand nothing about that.'

'I do,' whispered the snuff-taking Commissioner at my ear. 'I can quite understand a literary man does not always make money. I would take it off, for my share, but (sinking his voice still lower) I am only one voice here, and not the most important.'

'There,' said I, handing to Rhadamanthus Chapman and Hall's account; 'that will prove Mr Carlyle's statement.'

'What am I to make of that? Huffgh! We should have Mr Carlyle here to swear to this before we believe it.'

'If a gentleman's word of honour written at the bottom of that paper is not enough, you can put me on my oath: I am ready to swear to it.'

'You! you, indeed! No, no! we can do nothing with *your* oath.'

'But, sir, I understand my husband's affairs fully, better than he does himself.'

'That I can well believe; but we can make nothing of this' – flinging my document contemptuously on the table. The horned owl picked it up, glanced over it while Rhadamanthus was tossing papers about and grumbling about 'people that wouldn't conform to rules'; then handed it back to him, saying deprecatingly, 'But, sir, this is a very plain statement.'

'Then what has Mr Carlyle to live upon? You don't mean to tell me he lives on *that*?' – pointing to the document.

'Heaven forbid, sir! but I am not here to explain what Mr Carlyle has to live on, only to declare his income from literature during the last three years.'

'True! true!' mumbled the not-most-important voice at my elbow.

'Mr Carlyle, I believe, has landed income?'

'Of which,' said I haughtily, for my spirit was up, 'I have fortunately no account to render in this kingdom and to this board.'

'Take off fifty pounds, say a hundred – take off a hundred pounds,' said Rhadamanthus to the horned owl. 'If we write Mr Carlyle down a hundred and fifty he has no reason to complain, I think. There, you may go, Mr Carlyle has no reason to complain.'

Second-come woman was already introduced, and I was motioned to the door; but I could not depart without saying that 'at all events there was no use in complaining, since they had the power to enforce their decision.' On stepping out, my first thought was, what a mercy Carlyle didn't come himself! For the rest, though it might have gone better, I was thankful it had not gone worse.

Fish Gutters, 1859

CHARLES RICHARD WELD

The English traveller Charles Richard Weld spent two months in the Highlands in 1859, and recorded his experiences in detail. Here he encounters fisherwomen in the thrumming harbour at Wick, carrying on one of the country's most lucrative but vulnerable seasonal trades.

On leaving our hotel we bent our steps to the harbour. Wick, at any time, cannot be a lovely town; but during the herring fishing it is odious. The stationary population of 6,722 souls is increased during the fishing season to upwards of 16,000, and as the houses do not increase in the same proportion, and the sanitary arrangements are not of the highest order of excellence, you may imagine that this great influx of population is not calculated to improve the appearance of Wick.

But as we walk through the fishy streets, there is no sign of an overflowing population; the thoroughfares are nearly peopleless, and, with the exception of children making dirt pies here and there, and old crones airing themselves at open doors, there is no one to be seen.

The explanation is easy; the men are in bed, the women at work among the herrings, as we shall soon see. We pass through more streets, the population of which is sunk in slumber, and emerging on the harbour, we are amidst a world of women.

The harbour is full of fishing-boats, as close as they can pack; no room for a punt. You wonder how they ever got in, and equally how they ever get out. This is not the commercial port. Ships trading with Wick lie in the more commodious harbour of Staxigo, belonging to the adjacent village of that name.

Wick harbour is surrounded on the land side by hundreds of erections, looking like abortive attempts at building wood houses, some twenty feet square, for the walls are only about three feet high. These are the gutting troughs. Round them stood rows of what close inspection led you to conclude were women, though at first sight you might be excused for having some doubts respecting their sex. They all wore strange-shaped canvas garments, so bespattered with blood and the entrails and scales of fish, as to cause them to resemble animals of the ichthyological kingdom, recently divested of their skin, undergoing perhaps one of those transitions set forth in Mr Darwin's speculative book 'On the Origin of Species.' And if a man may become a monkey, or has been a whale, why should not a Caithness damsel become a herring? Here you may see, during the fishing season, the transition process going on before your very eyes. Skin becoming scaly – as to metempsychosis, surely there can be no paradise for a Caithness gutter where herrings are absent. I was sceptical respecting mermaids, ranking them among the creations of mythical zoology, and with Caithness gutters before you, mermaids, and mermans too, you will say, may exist.

Badinage apart, the women do cast their skins. Work over, they don gay dresses, and, flaunting in colours, you would not know the girls that you meet in the evening to be those whom you saw in the morning coated with blood and viscera . . .

Let us watch the operations. First, the herrings are carried as fast as possible in baskets from the boats to the gutting-troughs until the boats are emptied of their scaly treasures. Then, the women, familiarly called *gutters*, pounce upon the herrings like a bird of prey, seize their victims, and, with a rapidity of motion which baffles your eye, deprive the fish of its viscera. The operation, which a damsel not quite so repulsive as her companions obligingly performed for me at slow time, is thus effected. The herring is seized in the left hand, and by two dexterous cuts made with a sharp short knife in the neck an opening is effected sufficiently large to enable the viscera and liver to be extracted. These with the gills are thrown into a barrel, the gutted fish being cast among his eviscerated companions. Try your hand, as I did, at this apparently simple process, and ten to one but your first cut will decapitate the herring. If this does not happen, you will mangle the fish so seriously in your attempts to eviscerate it that you will render it entirely unworthy the honour of being packed with its skilfully gutted companions. And even if you succeed in disembowelling herring artistically, you will probably spend many minutes in the operation, whereas the Wick gutters – I timed them – gut on an average twenty-six herrings per minute.

The herrings undergo successive packings at various intervals of time before the barrels are finally closed. At each packing more salt is added, and at the final packing great care is taken to dispose the herrings in even layers. The viscera is deposited in barrels and sold to farmers for manuring purposes, at the average price of 1*d.* per barrel . . .

As may be supposed, considerable drunkenness and immorality prevails at Wick during the fishing season. Much of this is due to the indiscriminate herding together of sexes. The ministers complain that while great pains are taken to promote the success of the fishers of herrings, little care is taken to promote that of the fishers of men. Temperance societies have, however, been highly beneficial. A few years ago, I am assured that during the herring fishing season five hundred gallons of whisky were consumed daily. Now the quantity is much less.

When the weather is unfavourable and the boats cannot venture out, broils arising from drink and clanship occur, though they rarely attain the magnitude of a riot. Last year, however, was an exception; a quarrel, commenced by a couple of boys wrangling over an apple, was taken up by the idle fishers. Ancient clan feuds broke out between Highlanders, Lowlanders and Islanders. Knives were drawn and blood flowed so fast that the riot act was obliged to be read, and military brought from Edinburgh, at great expense to the country. I happened to be visiting Sir John Sinclair, at Barrock House, near Wick, when the riot occurred, and had a good opportunity of hearing accounts of the outbreak. As usual, these differed greatly, but sufficiently agreed in two respects to lead the impartial hearer to the conclusion that the fierce dissensions of clanship which formerly raged are not yet extinct.

Scavenging, May 1859

THE *ARGYLLSHIRE HERALD*

Smuggling, wrecking and scavenging were a way of life in certain parts of Scotland, an engrained habit dating back even before the very first taxes and duties were levied on desirable goods. Far from the comic or romantic activity they're often portrayed as, these could be vicious and even murderous trades. The following incident on Islay shows how avidly people would fall on free gifts and how fiercely they would defend them.

The brig *Mary Ann*, of Greenock, now lying a wreck at Kilchoman Bay, Islay, is fast breaking up, and portions of the cargo floating ashore. Up to Saturday there had been about 200 boxes saved, containing bottled brandy, whisky, and gin, and upwards of six puncheons of whisky, brandy, and wine; but the wildest scenes of drunkenness and riot that can be imagined took place.

Hundreds of people flocked from all parts of the neighbourhood, especially the Portnahaven fishermen, who turned out to a man. Boxes were seized as soon as landed, broken up, and the contents carried away and drunk. Numbers could be seen here and there lying amongst the rocks, unable to move, while others were fighting like savages. Sergeant Kennedy and Constable Chisholm, of the County Police, were in attendance, and used every means in their power to put a stop to the work of pillage.

They succeeded in keeping some order during the day of Thursday, but when night came on the natives showed evident symptoms of their disapproval of the police being there at all, and on the latter preventing a fellow from knocking the end out of a puncheon, in order, as he said, to 'treat all hands', they were immediately seized upon by the mob, and a hand to hand fight ensued, which lasted half an hour, and ended in the defeat of the police, of whom there were only two against from 30 to 40 of the natives.

The police beat a retreat to Cuil Farm – about a mile from the scene of action – closely pursued by about 30 of the natives, yelling like savages. Mrs Simpson of Cuil, on seeing the state of matters, took the police into the house and secured the doors, at the same time placing arms at their disposal for their protection. The mob yelled two or three times round the house, but learning that the police had got fire-arms, they left and returned to the beach.

Next morning the scene presented was still more frightful to contemplate. In one place there lay stretched the dead body of a large and powerful man, Donald M'Phayden, a fisherman from Portnahaven, who was considered the strongest man in Islay; but the brandy proved to be still stronger. He has left a wife and family. Others apparently in a dying state were being conveyed to the nearest houses, where every means were used to save life. Mrs Simpson, who is a very kind and humane person, supplied every remedy, but there was no medical man within fifteen or sixteen miles of the place. Mr James Simpson got a coffin made for M'Phayden, and had him interred on Friday. At the time when the corpse was being taken away, some groups could be seen fighting, others dancing, and others craving for drink, in order, as they said, to bury the man decently. Up to Saturday there was only one death, but on Monday it was reported that two more had died.

The Glorious Twelfth, 1859

CHARLES RICHARD WELD

Charles Richard Weld was typical of well-heeled visitors to Scotland, keen to enjoy the sport offered by a richly stocked Scottish estate. For many like him, 12 August – the Glorious Twelfth – the start of the grouse shooting season, was the best time to visit Scotland. For some it was the only incentive that could lure them north.

We spring from our bed, keenly alive to the fact that another 12th of August has dawned, rush heroically beneath a shower bath, which seems to flog our back with icicles, leave the bath-room red as a boiled lobster and braced as a drum, dress, and sit down to a breakfast. . . . No chance of starving here. No trifling with infinitesimal portions – we eat of all, and leave such a wreck behind that a dog would fare badly which came after us . . .

And now for filling the liquor flasks – flasks, did I say? – barrels rather, those pretty modern inventions with glass ends through which you see the beverage. Tantalizing contrivances doubtless to the very thirsty gilly, who, if you have securely locked the bung-hole, cannot even wet his lips with the coveted liquor. But our gillies were not tantalized, for although we had imported from Tunbridge a cask of rare bitter ale, and had various wines and spirits, we preferred filling the barrels with tea without milk or sugar, having found from considerable experience that this is the most refreshing beverage during a long and fatiguing day's shooting.

The gillies did not, of course, approve this decision, for your Scotch or at all events, Caithness gilly, has not yet acquired the knowledge that a pound of tea that may be had for three shillings and sixpence is capable of giving far more comfort than a gallon of whisky that costs sixteen shillings. So we, or rather they, carried supplementary flasks filled with fiery whisky, which they drank with the same unconcern that a child would drink a cup of milk. Indeed, I thought that the stronger the spirit the more was it esteemed . . .

The dog-carts are at the door, the dogs, after a world of trouble, stowed in the wells, the gillies up – nothing, we believe, forgotten, and we are off to the moors. We have a long drive before us, for our moors are not near Brawl; some of the beats are ten miles distant, the nearest four. The day is glorious; sky dappled with clouds, and a pleasant breeze blowing from the west. At the end of the avenue our party separate; good luck to each, and away we speed to heather-land. . . . On, still on, through the vast wilds till we come to the hamlet of Dale. Here we leave our dog-cart, and in a few minutes are in grouse-land . . .

As may be supposed, our shooting was not all *couleur de rose*. Are you a weak-limbed man? Then think not of shooting on the Brawl moors. For there are 'hags' that stand up like islands, and mosses in which you might disappear, to be exhumed, perhaps, in unborn ages, a fossil, the wonder of the species occupying the place now filled by man.

Nowhere, I venture to say, will you be made more aware of the truth of the adage, 'union is strength,' than on the Caithness moors. For nowhere are those little animated miracles, gnats or midges, more abundant than there. Talk of solitude on the moors! – why, every square yard contains a population of millions of these little harpies, that pump the blood out of you with amazing savageness and insatiability. Where they come from is a puzzle. While you are in motion not one is visible, but when you stop a mist seems to curl about your feet and legs, rising, and at the same time expanding until you become painfully sensible that the appearance is due to a cloud of gnats . . .

And now the sporting reader will be impatient to know the nature of our bags; for this is the true test of the quality of preserves, whether land or water. Well, our chief, who kept the game books very accurately, tells me that our sport averaged fifteen brace of grouse per day per gun, but besides grouse the bags always contained snipe and hares, and occasionally wild ducks and plover. These figures look, it is true, very insignificant by the side of those startling returns which the Scotch papers love to parade of the slaughter perpetrated on certain moors. But I agree with Christopher North in not admiring any shooting ground which resembles a poultry-yard, preferring that requiring skill and good dogs to discover the latent riches . . .

Of course many more grouse were killed than we could consume. The greater portion were purchased from us by Mr Dunbar, but we sent a large number to friends in England. And it may be worth stating that by packing fresh birds in boxes made to hold six and ten brace, without heather or compartments, they always reached their destination, though this was generally as distant as London, in excellent condition.

An Edinburgh Detective at Work, 1861

JAMES MCLEVY

Edinburgh may have been the birthplace of Sherlock Holmes, but it had very real sleuths of its own. The Victorian detective James McLevy had an impressively high conviction rate, and made the most of his exciting career by publishing accounts of his most dramatic cases.

One day . . . a gentleman came to the head-office late in the afternoon. There were several detective officers present, ready for any emergency. He was much excited. . . . He stated, that in the morning of that same day he and his wife had left his house in Haddington Place (a flat) to go to the country, where they intended to sojourn for some time. Their children, and the care of their house, they left to the sympathy and trustworthiness of the servant, a young girl, in whom, for her gentleness, religious feelings, and general good conduct, they had the most unbounded confidence. For some reason which, I think, he did not state, he returned himself in the afternoon, and, to his horror, found the door locked, and no trace of the key. He knocked, but all that he heard was the weeping and wailing of his children, all very young, and one, indeed, only newly weaned. Even amidst this very eloquent evidence of something being wrong, he could not at the instant, nor for some time, suspect any foul play on the part of the gentle Helen, but after waiting longer, he heard one of the young creatures sobbing behind the door, and crying out that Nelly had gone out long ago. And that they had got nothing to eat. He was now satisfied that there was something very wrong, and, hurrying for a blacksmith, he got the lock picked, and, the door opened.

On getting inside he observed an extraordinary scene. The newly-weaned child had been laid in the cradle, where it had wept itself nearly blind – its eyes swelled, and its face all wet with its tears. Another was lying on the ground, in a perfect agony of fear; a third was sitting looking wistfully out of the window, which it could not open, and where it had been knocking and crying to the passers-by for hours, without having been responded to; and two others were running backwards and forwards, not knowing for what object, but just in obedience to an impulse that would not permit of rest. But what was more strange, they had, from sheer hunger, got hold of a loaf of bread, no doubt to eat it ravenously; and yet there was the loaf untouched, as if the desire to eat had been overcome by their fear, so that, while the stomach craved, the muscles of the mouth disobeyed even this primary instinct. But he had not yet seen everything. On examining further, under the suspicions excited by the sobbing, weeping words of the poor young creatures, he found that the bureau where he kept his money had been broken up with a poker, and sixteen pounds extracted. He now understood everything too well, and having got a neighbour to attend to the children, and give them something to eat, he hurried up to the office. Captain Stewart having heard the strange story, questioned the gentleman in the ordinary way.

'What like is the girl?'

'Rather pretty, about nineteen years of age, dark eyes, aquiline nose, small mouth, and a mole on the left cheek.'

'How was she dressed?'

A more difficult question – rather befitting the gentleman's wife. He could scarcely answer.

'This beats me,' replied he; 'but I have a notion she has red ribbons on a white straw bonnet. I could not say more; and if it had not been that Mrs B— had remarked to me, on the previous day, that Nelly was a little too gaudy (and consequently she probably thought giddy) about the head, with these glaring red ribbons of hers, I would not have been able to condescend even upon this particular, so little attention do I pay to these things.'

Captain Stewart noted, and several officers were sent right and left, while I sat meditating a little. 'All good-enough marks, these,' I thought; 'but the girl may have got out of town.' Going up to the gentleman, I whispered (for I wanted the answer to myself – not that I lacked faith in Captain Stewart's tact, but that sometimes I found it more convenient to take my own way, and report afterwards) –

'Is she an Edinburgh girl?'

'No,' said he, in a similar under-tone, from probably mere sympathy.

'Then where does she come from?' was my next question.

'Glasgow.'

'You will find me turn up, perhaps, in the morning,' I said to the Captain, who had confidence in me, and did not wish to lay open my intentions, whatever they were, to those alongside.

'Very well,' cried he. 'I only hope you will catch the mole.'

'I have caught as deep a moudiewart [mole] before,' said I, as I prepared to depart. But I wanted an answer to another question.

'Have you any reason,' I inquired further, 'to suppose that the girl suspects you know her friends' whereabouts in Glasgow?'

'No,' replied the gentleman; 'because I never knew that, neither does my wife.'

'Of what bank were the notes?'

'British Linen Company.'

'Enough;' and with an idea in my head – a very easy to be found one, and no other than that most animals, whether moles, or mud-larks, or men, (and far more women,) generally, when pursued, seek their old holes and lurking-places – I set out. I knew that the afternoon coach to Glasgow would leave about this very hour, and expected to be all in good time; but on arriving at the office, I found that it had left only a few minutes before. I knew that I could not make up with it on foot, and therefore hailed a cab. In the meanwhile, and while it was coming up, I made out, from a few rapid questions at the clerk, – whether there were any young girls among the passengers, what like they were, and so forth, – that there was one coming near my mark, not of the mole, or of the dark eyes, or aquiline nose, but of the red ribbons.

'I can't be wrong about the red ribbons on the bonnet,' said he; 'only I think there are two – one inside and one out.'

'Did any of the girls change a note?'

'Yes, one of them.'

'Let me see it.'

'British Linen Company,' said the clerk, handing it to me.

'The changer inside or out?' said I.

'Outside.'

'All right,' said I; and, mounting the cab – 'Now, cabby, you are to overtake the Glasgow coach *at any rate*, if you should break your horse's wind, your own neck, and my collar-bone.'

And the man, knowing very well who I was, set out at a gallop at once, and so furious a one, that it almost put me out of a study – no other than the examination of all the bonnets I could see in Princes Street; for I had, for the nonce, become a student of the *beau monde*, at least of the *beaux* of the world of bonnets; – in short, I was curious to know the proportion, in a hundred colours, of my new favourite one of red; – and so furious, moreover, was his driving, that the eyes of the whole street were turned upon us – those under the shadow of red ribbons being, fortunately, unconscious that I was doing all I could to reduce the renown of their favourite colour. We soon passed the Hay-weights, and were fairly on the high-road to Corstorphine. Nor was it long till I could see the red badge waving very proudly on the top of the coach, just as the clerk had told me; nay, it even appeared to me that the cabman's ambition was roused by the pennant, for he drove harder and harder, till at length the coach stopped, no doubt in obedience to the conviction of the driver that he was to get a too-late fare.

'Make haste,' cried the coachman, as I got alongside and was getting out. 'We have room for one, but not time for parley.'

'Room for one,' said I, as I looked up into the face of the gentle Nelly, where the mole was, and where there rose upon the instant something else, first a blush as red as her ribbons, and then a pallor as white as the bonnet. 'Rather, I think you've got one too many.'

'No, the Act of Parliament says we are entitled to carry –'

'Not that girl with the red ribbons,' said I, producing my baton. 'You come down, Miss Helen N—.' (I forgot to say I got her name from her master.) 'I want to give you a ride back to town.'

She wouldn't though, and seemed inclined to resist to the uttermost; but the passengers seeing she couldn't, for want of will, come of herself, took her by force, and handed her down to me, who thanked them for so pretty a charge. Having got her into the cab, I next got out her box, and, placing that alongside of her, I drove her direct up to the office. Captain Stewart, recollecting the red ribbons and the mole, and casting his eyes over her head-gear and the face, smiled in spite of his usual gravity. We soon found that the gentle Nelly wanted to prove as untrue to us as she had been to her master, for she absolutely swore that she was not only not guilty of doing anything against the laws, but that she was not even Helen N— at all, notwithstanding of the ribbons, the mole, and the black eyes, and the really fine aquiline nose; so it did actually seem necessary that we should prove, to her own satisfaction, who she was. After searching her, we thought that the exact sum of £15, 14s. found on her – which, with the 6s. for her fare, made up the £16 – would have removed her scepticism as to her identity; but even this was insufficient, and the resolute Nelly might have remained in utter ignorance of herself till doomsday, had it not been that Mr B— called at the office, and satisfied her that she was herself. And not only was she then convinced, but she had reason not to relapse again into her ignorance; for, during the six months she was doomed to remain in prison, she was so much by herself, with seldom another to confound her notions of who she was, that she could not have avoided herself, however willing.

Abbotsford, the Tourist Trap, 1863

EDWARD BRADLEY

Sir Walter Scott bought the farm of Cartley Hole or Clarty Hole in 1811, and renamed it Abbotsford, an old name for the river crossing there. He renovated the farmhouse into a magnificent mansion that incorporated as many elements of Scottish history and architecture as was possible. Within a few years of his death in 1832 it had become a major tourist attraction. Edward Bradley, an artist with Punch, *calculated the cost of a visit.*

Abbotsford is the Mecca of the Scotch tourists, and during the summer months the stream of pilgrims is incessantly flowing towards Scott's shrine. The cost to each one, coming by rail from Edinburgh, and returning thither within the day, can scarcely be less than thirty shillings; and a statistician may therefore calculate the wealth that is made to filter through Melrose through 'the magic of a name.' Carriages for Abbotsford form a summer institution in Melrose, that must be exceedingly remunerative to the landlord of The George Hotel, especially when taken in connection with luncheons, and, above all, with that terrible item in a hotel bill, 'apartments,' which appears to be 'a noun of multitude, signifying many' curious additions to the normal necessities of a traveller. A one-horse carriage to Abbotsford will cost you five shillings, with eighteen-pence for the driver, and a sixpence for a turnpike. When you are there, Black's valuable 'Guide,' with some hesitation in pronouncing an opinion on so delicate a point, says that with regard to 'the gratuity payable to domestics, the amount will necessarily vary between prince and peasant, but 1s. for a single individual, and 2s. 6d. for parties not exceeding six, may be regarded as fair medium payments.' Regarded by whom? There's the rub. Try the gentleman's gentleman who trots you through the show suite of rooms with a shilling for a single individual, and half-a-crown for parties not exceeding six, and note the expression of his features (which might be overlooked), and (which is more to the purpose) his consequent conduct. *Experto crede.* He was barely satisfied with half-a-crown from my wife and myself; but he turned upon a French family (with whom we had formed that confluent concourse of atoms which was necessary to make up the 'party' to view the rooms) and rejected their offerings with contempt. A scene thereupon followed, in which pantomime had to explain dialogue, and which terminated, as a matter of course, in the victory of the gentleman's gentleman, and the tax-paying of his opponents. Their intense delight, while going through the rooms, whenever they lighted upon any of the French presents to the illustrious novelist, must have been in strong contrast to the chagrin with which their tour of inspection was terminated by their enforced and involuntary present to that illustrious novelist's showman.

A Missionary Visits Greenock, 1865

WALTER GUNN

The missionary Walter Gunn went knocking on doors in the backstreets of Greenock, in order to prove to the authorities that despite years of agitation to improve conditions for the poverty-stricken, their situation was still dire. The area he visited was known, rather ominously, as The Burrows. He was appalled to report that it offered 'twenty houses of ill-fame', but the real horror, as he shows, was the conditions in which people were living. His examples are drawn only from those who worked at home, which explains why they are all women.

The cases we shall mention are merely a few out of hundreds we have met with, but they will afford a very fair estimate of the whole:

CASE I Is an old widow who lives by bruising sandstone, which she obtains from buildings in the course of erection; and is able to carry from 40lb to 50lb. Bringing the burden home, she sets to work with a bit of iron as a pestle, and a piece of hard stone as a mortar, and reduces the lumps to powder. Having done this, she goes out to sell the result of her labour, trudging from door to door; some days selling none, other days perhaps from *fourpence to sixpence worth*, which is considered a good day's sale. She is sixty years of age, yet in this way her days are spent, and her bread obtained.

CASE II Is likewise an old widow, who lives by gathering whelks and tangle [coarse seaweed]. To obtain this she is up at day-break, and walks a mile beyond Inverkip; making a distance of *seven* miles, or, including the return, *fourteen*. Having gathered them, she carries home the load; or, if willing to lose half the profit, pays a carter to let herself and her burden into his cart. On getting home, the whelks are boiled and the tangle washed, and set upon a tray and taken to the quay, where she sits until her stock-in-trade is disposed of to chance passers-by; thus contriving to make a sixpence or a shilling a day. She is on the borders of seventy; and the last time we saw her she was drenched to the skin with rain, having just returned from a fruitless errand, the sea being too rough to admit of her procuring a supply of her usual stock-in-trade.

CASE III Is a married woman; her husband, like hundreds more, is given to drink; she must, therefore, work to sustain herself and her children; the husband – shall we call him so? – for such as he deserve not that name – getting a share by the way. She lives by teasing oakum [untwisting ropes] . . .

CASE IV Is a woman who makes her living by giving whiting in exchange for rags and bones.

CASE V Is another woman who earns a livelihood by cutting grass from the wayside in summer, and seeking sand in winter. In other cases some contrive to eke out a living by begging: the meat and meal they get being sold at a profit to certain shops, who buy the goods thus obtained and retail them again to the public . . .

Although the inhabitants of this place are so degraded, and the majority unable to read, yet such as can do so have a strong relish for a certain kind of literature; but not of the highest class. Religious publications cannot be found, yet the *Penny Post* and *Sporting News* are most abundant;

while in the way of fiction, the *Halfpenny Magazine, Reynolds's Miscellany, Dick Turpin*, and such-like, seem to enjoy the greatest popularity.

Although everyone cannot participate in these pleasures, yet all seem to appreciate the fine arts, judging from the pictures which adorn the walls. On those of the labouring classes may be seen prints of race horses, swimmers, runners, and pugilists, who appear the most favoured. These are cut from the *Sporting News* and stuck on the wall, in many cases, perhaps, more to keep out the wind, or prevent their neighbour from seeing through the partition, than from a love of the beautiful. In other cases, however, they are pasted up from real admiration of the hero, or to break the dreariness of a bare stone wall. The houses of open vice have pictures of a finer appearance, but in workmanship only they are of the German stamp, and the subject in numerous cases such as ought not to be drawn, much less exhibited upon a wall. Occasionally a person's taste may be found developed in another direction. On entering a house one day, the window of which happened to be open, we were quite surprised to see on the outside a neat box, full of earth, with many flowers just beginning to bud. This was such a noteworthy object that we complimented the woman on her taste for flowers, but felt rather crestfallen when she said, 'Oh, sir, they are not flowers, but some onions which my husband put there to keep, and the tails are begun to sprout.'

The First Scottish Football Match, 1868

ROBERT GARDNER

Who knows how long football has been played in Glasgow? Millennia, possibly. The earliest reported account of it, however, dates from 1590, but it was not until 1867 that the first organized team was arranged. They were called Queen's Park. A year later they suggested a match with Thistle (not Partick Thistle). This letter is written by the Queen's Park secretary, arranging the first official game between Scottish sides.

Dear Sir

I duly received your letter dated 25th inst. on Monday Afternoon, but as we had a Committee Meeting called for this evening at which time it was submitted, I could not reply to it earlier. I have now been requested by the Committee, on behalf of our Club, to accept of the Challenge you kindly sent, for which we have to thank you, to play us a friendly Match at Football on our Ground,

Queen's Park, at the hour you mentioned, on Saturday, first proximo, with Twenty players on each side. We consider, however, that Two-hours is quite long enough to play in weather such as the present, and hope this will be quite satisfactory to you. We would also suggest that if no Goals be got by either side within the first hour, that Goals be then exchanged, the ball, of course, to be kicked of [sic] from the centre of the field by the side who had the original Kick-off, so that both parties may have the same chance of wind and ground, this we think very fare [sic] and can be arranged on the field before beginning the Match. Would you also be good enough to bring your ball with you in case of any break down, and thus prevent interruption. Hoping the weather will favour the Thistle and Queen's.

I remain,
Yours very truly,
(Sgd.) Robt. Gardner
Secy.

Mayhem at Musselburgh Golf Match, 22–23 April 1870

THE *SCOTSMAN*

In its early days golf was far from the bourgeois and restrained game it has since become. Musselburgh golfer Willie Park, who won the first Open Championship, was a rival of Tom Morris, from St Andrews, with whom over the years he played a series of challenge matches. The Musselburgh match described here was the concluding game of four, the others played previously at St Andrews, Prestwick and North Berwick. The crowd, who were on Park's side, were said to have moved Morris's ball whenever they could, but their excess enthusiasm rebounded on their hero. The high-handed referee is the publisher Robert Chambers, himself a keen golfer.

April 22
The great golf match between Tom Morris (St Andrews) and Willie Park (Musselburgh) for £200, which has excited so much interest during the past fortnight, has unfortunately terminated in a dispute. The deciding section of the match was fixed to take place over Musselburgh Links yesterday, and accordingly the two champions appeared on the green at the appointed hour. The weather was most unpropitious for a grand display of golf. A high south-west wind blew in strong gusts across the

links, and during the day there were several heavy showers of rain. About six or seven thousand spectators assembled on the course to witness the play, and it was said that such a large number of persons had never before been present at a golf match. It is a matter for regret, however, that the onlookers behaved in the most disgraceful manner. Very fair order was maintained during the first two rounds of the links, but as the crowd increased, and the excitement over the result intensified, the players were pressed in upon in a very rude manner, and were scarcely allowed room to wield their clubs freely. An appeal was made by the referee, Mr Robert Chambers, jun., to the crowd to keep better order and to stand further back from the players. This had some effect for a time, but as the spectators again became somewhat unruly, action was taken by the referee and one of the players, which led to the unfortunate dispute detailed in the sequel.

Considering the inauspicious circumstances under which the game took place, the play was first-class. Both men played cautiously, especially when it came to the short game, but this only rendered the match more interesting. In the first round, Park showed in form going out, but Morris headed him coming in. The latter won four holes, Park three, and two were halved. Some splendid play was exhibited in the second round – five holes being halved and two secured by each representative. In the third round, Park won three holes, Morris two, and four were halved; and this left them to commence the last round in the same position as at the start – Morris one hole ahead on the match. The first hole of the final round was halved, and Park won the next two, giving him one of a majority on the main. Both players then retired for refreshment.

In a short time, Park appeared at the teeing-ground; but the St Andrews champion not putting in an appearance, the excitement amongst the crowd became great. It was shortly ascertained that the referee had decided that the play in the remaining six holes of the match should be postponed till this (Saturday) forenoon, at eleven o'clock. Park protested against this, the more especially as he had not been consulted, and stated that if Morris did not come forward and finish the round, he would do so by himself and claim the stakes. Morris abided by the decision of the referee, who stated that his reason for postponing the play was, 'That notwithstanding all exertions, no means were practicable for keeping back the onlookers, some of whom by their conduct rendered fair play an impossibility.' Park maintained that the referee had power only to decide disputes as to balls, that he could not postpone the play without the consent of both combatants, and that the articles under which the match was being played distinctly stated that it should be finished that day. He therefore played the remaining six holes of the round himself, and sent a letter to the stakeholder (Mr Robert Dudgeon) claiming the stakes. Mr Dudgeon, we understand, refused to pay over the stakes, and the matter stands in this unsatisfactory position.

April 23
On Saturday morning at eleven o'clock, the hour appointed by Mr Robert Chambers, jun., for playing off the six holes left unplayed on Musselburgh Links in the great golf match between Tom Morris and Willie Park, Morris and a few spectators appeared at the eighth hole. Park was present, but he adhered to the view he had taken of the referee's duties; maintaining that he had played out the match on the day fixed by the articles viz., the 22nd April; that no man had any power to stop the play in the middle of the game; that as Morris had refused to play out the last six holes when called on by him, he had done so by himself, and therefore won the match. He accordingly refused to play the six holes with Morris on Saturday morning unless a new match were made. Mr Chambers directed Morris to walk the course, which he did, holing out the six holes from Mrs Forman's in 4,4,5,5,6, and 4 strokes respectively. At the conclusion Morris was loudly hissed by the partisans of the Musselburgh's champion, as was the referee, who gave the following written decision in the course of the forenoon: 'As referee in the match between Morris and Park on Musselburgh Links, I have to certify that the first thirty holes were played on April 22, and, in terms of my decision, the remaining six holes were played by Morris this day. I therefore declare Morris to be the winner. (Signed) R. Chambers, Jun – Musselburgh April 23 1870.'

Dr Livingstone Is Found by Henry Morton Stanley, November 1871

DAVID LIVINGSTONE

The missionary David Livingstone is said to have converted only two people in his proselytizing career. By far his greater legacy is as one of the most intrepid explorers of all time, who was not only one of the first white men to journey to the heart of Africa, but in doing so heightened awareness of the slave trade being practised there, thus leading eventually to its abolition in 1873, the year of his death. An addictive journal keeper, when he ran out of ink he would make a substitute from plant juice. When paper supplies dwindled, he used scraps of paper, or wrote over old writing, making it extremely difficult to decipher his words. His late journals, written during his nerve-racking expeditions to the Great Lakes, make painful reading. Still lonely after the death of his doughty wife Mary in 1862, he was in very poor health and low spirits, his mood worsened by the tribal violence he witnessed. In the days preceding these entries, he and his party had almost been killed on a couple of occasions, by spear and ambush. Here he gives an account of events running up to his famous meeting at Ujiji by Lake Tanganyika with American journalist Henry Morton Stanley, who had been sent to find out if he was still alive. Livingstone's dates do not match those of Stanley, who said they met in November, not October.

23rd September 1871

We now passed through the country of mixed Barua and Bagaha, crossed the River Loñgumba twice and then came near the great mountain mass on west of Tanganyika. From Mokwaniwa's to Tanganyika is about ten good marches through open forest. The Guha people are not very friendly; they know strangers too well to show kindness: like Manuema, they are also keen traders. I was sorely knocked up by this march from Nyañgawé back to Ujiji. In the latter part of it, I felt as if dying on my feet. Almost every step was in pain, the appetite failed, and a little bit of meat caused violent diarrhoea, whilst the mind, sorely depressed, reacted on the body. All the traders were returning successful: I alone had failed and experienced worry, thwarting, baffling, when almost in sight of the end towards which I strained.

3rd October

I read the whole Bible through four times whilst I was in Manyuema.

8th October

The road covered with angular fragments of quartz was very sore to my feet, which are crammed into ill-made French shoes. How the bare feet of the men and women stood out, I don't know; it was hard enough on mine though protected by the shoes. We marched in the afternoons where water at this season was scarce. The dust of the march cause ophthalmia . . . this was my first touch of it in Africa. We now came to the Lobumba River, which flows into Tanganyika, and then to the village Loanda, and sent to Kasanga, the Guha chief, for canoes. The

Loñgumba rises, like the Lobumba, in the mountains called Kabogo West. We heard great noises, as if thunder, as far as twelve days off, which were ascribed to Kabogo, as if it had subterranean caves into which the waves rushed with great noise, and it may be that the Loñgumba is the outlet of Tanganyika: it becomes the Luassé further down, and then the Luamo before it joins the Lualaba: the country slopes that way, but I was too ill to examine its source.

23rd October

At dawn, off and go to Ujiji. Welcomed by all the Arabs, particularly by Moenyegheré. I was now reduced to a skeleton, but the market being held daily, and all kinds of native food brought to it, I hoped that food and rest would soon restore me, but in the evening my people came and told me that Shereef [the chief Arab in Ujiji] had sold off all my goods, and Moenyegheré confirmed it by saying, 'We protested, but he did not leave a single yard of calico, out of 3000, nor a string of beads out of 700 lbs.' This was distressing. I had made up my mind, if I could not get people at Ujiji, to wait till men should come from the coast, but to wait in beggary was what I never contemplated, and I now felt miserable. Shereef was evidently a moral idiot, for he came without shame to shake hands with me, and when I refused, assumed an air of displeasure, as having been badly treated; and afterwards came with his 'Balghere,' good-luck salutation, twice a day, and on leaving said, 'I am going to pray,' till I told him that were I an Arab, his hand and both ears would be cut off for thieving, as he knew, and I wanted no salutations from him. In my distress it was annoying to see Shereef's slaves passing from the market with all the good things that my goods had bought.

24th October

My property has been sold to Shereef's friends at merely nominal prices. Syed bin Majid, a good man, proposed that they should be returned, and the ivory be taken from Shereef; but they would not restore stolen property, though they knew it to be stolen. Christians would have acted differently, even those of the lowest classes. I felt in my destitution as if I were the man who went down from Jerusalem to Jericho, and fell among thieves; but I could not hope for Priest, Levite, or good Samaritan to come by on either side, but one morning Syed bin Majid said to me, 'Now this is the first time we have been alone together; I have no goods, but I have ivory; let me, I pray you, sell some ivory, and give the goods to you.' This was encouraging; but I said, 'Not yet, but by-and-bye.'

I had still a few barter goods left, which I had taken the precaution to deposit with Mohamad bin Saleh before going to Manyuema, in case of returning in extreme need.

But when my spirits were at their lowest ebb, the good Samaritan was close at hand, for one morning Susi came running at the top of his speed and gasped out, 'An Englishman! I see him!' and off he darted to meet him. The American flag at the head of a caravan told of the nationality of the stranger. Bales of goods, baths of tin, huge kettles, cooking pots, tents, &c., made me think 'This must be a luxurious traveller, and not one at his wits' end like me.' (28th October) It was Henry Moreland [sic] Stanley, the travelling correspondent of the *New York Herald*, sent by James Gordon Bennett, junior, at an expense of more than 4,000l., to obtain accurate information about Dr Livingstone if living, and if dead to bring home my bones.

The news he had to tell to one who had been two full years without any tidings from Europe made my whole frame thrill. The terrible fate that had befallen France, the telegraphic cables successfully laid in the Atlantic, the election of General Grant, the death of good Lord Clarendon – my constant friend, the proof that Her majesty's Government had not forgotten me in voting 1,000l. for supplies, and many other points of interest, revived emotions that had lain dormant in Manyuema. Appetite returned, and instead of the spare, tasteless, two meals a day, I ate four times daily, and in a week began to feel strong.

I am not of a demonstrative turn; as cold, indeed, as we islanders are usually reputed to be, but this disinterested kindness of Mr Bennett, so nobly carried into effect by Mr Stanley, was simply overwhelming. I really do feel extremely grateful, and at the same time I am a little ashamed at not being more worthy of the generosity.

The Invention of the Telephone, 1875

ALEXANDER GRAHAM BELL

Few innovations have had a greater cultural impact than Alexander Graham Bell's invention of the telephone. A man whose interest in the voice was sparked originally by teaching the deaf, he was living in America as Professor of Vocal Physiology at Boston University when he made his world-changing discovery. His work on finding a means of communicating speech electronically was painfully slow and frustrating. In the first letter here he writes to his parents describing his conversation with the American physicist Professor Joseph Henry, Secretary of the Smithsonian Institute in Washington, in which he explained the sound response he had achieved from an empty electric coil. In the second, he writes to the Electric Telephone Company to tell them of his extraordinary invention.

To Mr and Mrs Melville Bell   Boston 18 March 1875
. . . He started up, said, 'Is that so? Will you allow me, Mr Bell to repeat your experiments and publish them in the world through the Smithsonian Institute, of course giving you the credit of the discoveries?' I said it would give me extreme pleasure and added that I had the apparatus in Washington and could show him the experiments at any time . . .

He said he thought it 'the germ of a great invention' and advised me to work at it myself instead of publishing. I said that I recognized the fact there were mechanical difficulties. . . . I added that I felt I had not the electrical knowledge necessary to overcome the difficulties. His laconic answer was 'GET IT'.

I cannot tell you how much these two words encouraged me . . .

Three months later, in June 1875, Bell communicated by telegraph wire with his assistant, in the immortal words: 'Come here, Mr Watson, I want to see you.'

To the capitalists of the
Electric Telephone Company   Kensington 25 March 1878

. . . The great advantage it possesses over every other form of electrical apparatus is that it requires no skill to operate. . . . The simple and inexpensive nature of the Telephone . . . renders it possible to connect every man's house or manufactory with a Central Station so as to give him the benefit of direct Telephonic Communication with his neighbours at a cost not greater than that incurred for gas or water.

At the present time we have a perfect network of gas pipes and water pipes throughout our larger cities. We have main pipes laid under the streets, communicating by side pipes with the various dwellings enabling the inmates to draw their supplies of gas and water from a common source.

In a similar manner it is conceivable that cables of Telephonic wires could be laid underground or suspended overhead communicating by branch wires with private dwellings, counting houses, shops, manufactories etc. etc. uniting them through the main cable with a central office where the wires could be connected together as desired establishing direct communication between any two places in the City. Such a plan as this though impracticable at the present moment will, I believe, be the outcome of the introduction of the Telephone to the Public. Not only so but I believe that in the future wires will unite the head offices of Telephone Companies in different cities and a man in one part of the country may communicate by word of mouth with another in a distant place . . .

'Saxpence in ma claes, ninepence in ma skin', 1876

JOHN LAVERY

John Lavery, a member of the renowned Glasgow Boys School of Art, was to become one of the most sought-after portraitists of his age, his commissions including the state visit to Scotland of Queen Victoria to the Glasgow International Exhibition in 1888. It took many years to establish himself, however, and here he describes some of the exigencies of his early career.

In the School of Art I made the acquaintance of a fellow-student whose father had a furniture shop on the island of Islay. McTaggart, the great Scottish painter, when he was young held exhibitions there, and my picture was included in one of these. Then at long last for the first time I saw my name in print in the two-page catalogue. When the exhibition opened I bought the local newspaper, the *Glasgow Herald*, the *Scotsman*, and others, expecting to read long articles on the exhibition, more especially on the discovery of a young genius, myself. Armed with half a dozen papers I could not wait until I got home to my lodgings, and yet was ashamed to be seen reading them in public because I felt sure that everyone would know who I was and what I was looking for. I found a quiet corner in a backyard and went through every page, even the advertisements, without finding any mention of the show. Today to be ignored is not as painful as it then was . . .

In those days in Glasgow the existence of the artist's model was made known by advertisements in the *Herald*, which brought forth all kinds of applicants for the post. One morning I found sitting at the studio door a ragged, barefooted child of about seven or eight. 'Would you be wanting a model, sir?' 'Have you been sitting?' 'A wus sitting to Rattray.' Her reply indicated a familiarity with the profession that was surprising. Mr Rattray was a stained-glass painter and I inquired what she had been posing for. 'A wus posing for an angel, and he gave me saxpence an oor in ma claes and ninepence in ma skin.'

She compared favourably to the girl who came to pose as Marguerite for a picture of the garden scene in *Faust*. She was terribly upset when

Faust got a bit familiar in the greenhouse that was being used as a dressing-room. She rushed out and refused to let him near her. Faust was a hussar that I had got from the barracks close by. She was very refined in her appearance and genteel in her choice of language. She would not pose again, saying to her friends, 'I would not have went if I had knew.'

Sitting at dinner one afternoon in the house of a friend, we heard a loud knock on the front door and a strange voice in the hall wanting to know if Lavery were there. A burly Highland policeman entered the dining-room, looked hard at me and said, 'Are you Lavery?' 'Yes,' I answered with some anxiety. 'Weel, ye're gutted.' It was his delicate way of breaking the news that my studio had been burnt to the ground and my first masterpiece, 'Tis better to have loved and lost,' had gone with the rest of my belongings.

I cannot remember ever feeling so happy. I was insured for £300. At the moment I could not pay my rent long overdue, and my present sitter, a busy city man, had got tired of sitting for his portrait. On the morrow he was giving me my last sitting, and I was in a terrible mess as I knew I could not possibly finish it. I had pawned everything I could get money on, literally my shirt, for food. I met with much sympathy, even from people who did not like me, and it was difficult to hide my joy at the thought of getting £300, a larger sum than I had ever had before.

Mary Slessor's Campaign to Save Babies, Late 1870s/1880s

MARY SLESSOR

Mary Slessor started work in a jute factory in Dundee at the age of eleven to help support a large family whose father was a drunk. After years of studying while at her weaving machine, she became a missionary and in 1876 was sent to Calabar in Nigeria. Once there she was horrified by the widespread custom of killing twins at birth and of leaving the infants of mothers who had perished in childbirth to die. Greatly admired and loved by the tribespeople, she became known as 'the Ma who loves babies', not only because she campaigned against these cruelties, but because she adopted children who would otherwise have been killed. This letter, written to the Sunday School children in Dundee, describes the day the tribe decided to outlaw these practices.

Just as it became dark one evening I was sitting in my verandah talking to the children, when we heard the beating of drums and the singing of men coming near. This was strange, because we are on a piece of ground which no one in the town has a right to enter. Taking the wee twin boys in my hands I rushed out, and what do you think I saw? A crowd of men standing outside the fence chanting and swaying their bodies. They were proclaiming that all twins and twin-mothers could now live in the town, and that if any one murdered the twins or harmed the mothers he would be hanged by the neck. If you could have heard the twin-mothers who were there, how they laughed and clapped their hands and shouted, 'Sosoño! Sosoño!' ('Thank you! Thank you!'). You will not wonder that amidst all the noise I turned aside and wept tears of joy and thankfulness, for it was a glorious day for Calabar.

A few days later the treaties were signed, and at the same time a new King was crowned. Twin-mothers were actually sitting with us on a platform in front of all the people. Such a thing had never been known before. What a scene it was! How can I describe it? There were thousands of Africans, each with a voice equal to ten men at home, and all speaking as loudly as they could. The women were the worst. I asked a chief to stop the noise. 'Ma,' he said, 'how I fit stop them woman mouth?' The Consul told the King that he *must* have quiet during the reading of the treaties, but the King said helplessly, 'How can I do? They be women – best put them away', and many *were* put away.

The Mental Asylum, 1878

CHRISTIAN WATT

Christian Watt was born in 1833 into a fishing family in Buchan and wrote a vivid memoir of her eventful and difficult life while she was a patient in a mental asylum. She married a sailor who became a fisherman, and as the mother of nine made the best of the physically exhausting life of those who made their living from the land and sea. A spirited, intellectually questioning woman, she was seen by some as lofty and stuck up. She refused to consider the gentry as in any way superior to her or others. This account describes her struggle to make ends meet after her husband drowned, and the desperate mental state it reduced her to. His was the last in a line of bereavements, following the loss of four of her seven brothers, her mother and father and two of her children. The following extract records the first episode of a condition that worsened until she was declared insane and put permanently in the asylum in Aberdeen, where she lived for the last forty-seven years of her life.

My elder son was at sea, but I had still seven bairns to feed and clad. I wore myself out with hard work. In buying fish at the Broch market I could not compete with the Fishermerchants, so got little to barter for food in the country. I was sick with worry, neither eating nor sleeping, for I had no money except my son's allowance of 4/–. I know now I should have gone to the Parish for help, but I was far too proud. It may be wrong but that was how we were brought up; and selling your possessions is a degrading game.

Eppie Buchan, a St Combs woman who lived up the New St at Broadsea, commented on my growing so thin. I said, 'It is hard to be provider'. She gave me a bag of tatties which were most welcome, for I had been raking in the sea for everything edible for us to eat. When the bairns had gone to school and the little one was still asleep, I would put my arms round Ranger the doggie and break my heart crying . . .

There is a time to laugh and a time to weep, a time to mourn and a time to dance. These were the second great tears in my life. How I missed my mother, who had also known grief. Sixty years have passed and I see her now, resting her heavy creel on a dyke to get her breath. Both my parents are safe within the veil of salvation, but how I wished I still had them when I lost my man.

[. . .]

For the doctor had asked me to go for a rest to Aberdeen Royal Mental Asylum. After a great deal of thought I consented, for something must break. I worried so much about my hungry children and who would look after them. My sister-in-law had no room, and her mother was over seventy. My cousin Mary said she would keep an eye on the bairns, as my daughter Isabella was only ten – but she kept the house, washed and baked, cooked and put the young ones to school clean while I was in the Asylum. Charlotte the youngest was not quite two, but past the worst stage . . .

I boarded the train at Fraserburgh. My cousin Mary and her daughter Annie saw me off, also my daughter Isabella. It was a sad day in my life. We passed Kirktoun Kirkyard. The tall lums [chimneys] of Philorth House [where she had worked as a maid from the age of eight] stood above the trees, I could see the kitchen and parlour ones reeking . . .

Then Cornhill was on the outskirts of the City of Aberdeen amid a large garden. Forbes, the Laird of Newe, had generously donated ten thousand pounds towards the building of the new asylum. I entered by a small gate set in a high granite dyke, and was admitted. The nurse who gave me a bath commented on how clean I was. We went through endless corridors, and in each section I noticed the door was firmly locked behind us which gave an eerie feeling. Finally I went to bed tired after my journey.

We were washing our faces at five o'clock in the morning for breakfast was at six. Not even the pangs of sheer hunger could have forced me to eat in the diningroom. That was a sight the King and Queen should go and witness, for if you are not humble before, once you have seen it you will be, and value good health and every other blessing you have got from the depth of your heart. Patients were gulping and stomaching their porridge in such a slovenly and distasteful manner . . . when I feigned some excuse to skip dinner, the sister said, 'If you work in the kitchen you can eat there.' The Physician Superintendant was . . . a kindly, skeely man, genuinely interested in his patients. I spoke with him for an hour, and then I was fixed up with a job in the kitchen. I did not want any of my children to visit me, for it is not the sort of place bairns should see, especially if they are very young . . .

Being in the asylum is a terrible stigma. . . . When I came home I found folk constantly trying to shun me as if I had leprosy. The usual pattern was to smile and be pleasant for a moment, then make some kind of excuse they were in an awful hurry to do something. I went to the farms in the country, and in many places where they could see me coming I found the door barred in my face, once it got around I had returned from the asylum. It was a terrifying experience . . .

I was told at both Philorth and Strichen House, in my absence somebody else had taken their custom. I have gone as far as New Deer selling hardly anything. It was a sad defeat to have to return with a full heavy creel and a heavy heart. I could see it was not going to be easy to make a living, and it seems impossible for the public to be sufficiently educated to the fact that a mental disorder is an illness . . .

So now so many doors were closed to me it was hardly worth my while going to the country, but I plodded on. Though I was 'sodger clad' I was 'Major minded'. It seems that under great mental stress insanity takes over. The odd thing in many cases, the patient knows all that is going on. I called at Witchill House, as I usually did, by the back door. . . . I asked the housekeeper if she wanted fish, she said, 'I must ask Madam,' whom they call her Ladyship. . . . In Witchell a long lobby like a street ran the whole length of the interior. The housekeeper had to consult Madam in the drawingroom at the far end. I had tip-toed in to hear Lady Anderson's reply which was so loud I heard it all, 'Tell her we are supplied by a Rosehearty merchant since she went off the round and it is not necessary to come back.' She added, 'Under no circumstances give her tea or anything that might encourage her. We can't have a mad woman coming about the place.' I retreated to the back door. They were none the wiser. The housekeeper delivered her message and I thanked her with a courteous smile, just as if nothing had happened. I had a strong urge to go back and hit the wifie.

The Tay Railway Bridge Disaster, 28 December 1879

WILLIAM MCGONAGALL

The Tay Railway Bridge opened in 1878, to great public fanfare, including a eulogy from Dundee's self-appointed laureate, William McGonagall. The following year, on the night of 28 December, the bridge collapsed during a severe storm as a train was crossing. Seventy-five passengers and crew died. It was later discovered that the engineer, Thomas Bouch, had miscalculated the effects of wind pressure, and the contractor had used defective materials for the job. McGonagall again recorded the event. Although his facts are inaccurate and his tone unintentionally comic, one cannot doubt the sincerity of his distress.

The Tay Bridge Disaster

Beautiful Railway Bridge of the Silv'ry Tay!
Alas! I am very sorry to say
That ninety lives have been taken away
On the last Sabbath day of 1879,
Which will be remember'd for a very long time.

'Twas about seven o'clock at night,
And the wind it blew with all its might,
And the rain came pouring down,
And the dark clouds seem'd to frown,
And the Demon of the air seem'd to say –
'I'll blow down the Bridge of Tay.'

[. . .]

It must have been an awful sight,
To witness in the dusky moonlight,
While the Storm Fiend did laugh, and angry did bray,
Along the Railway Bridge of the Silv'ry Tay.
Oh! ill-fated Bridge of the Silv'ry Tay,
I must now conclude my lay
By telling the world fearlessly without the least dismay,
That your central girders would not have given way,
At least many sensible men do say,
Had they been supported on each side with buttresses,
At least many sensible men confesses,
For the stronger we our houses do build,
The less chance we have of being killed.

Among the Residents of Black Houses, c. 1880

JOHN WILSON

A school inspector from the mainland can hardly conceal his amazement at the primitive living conditions he encountered in the Hebrides.

Lewis

The bulk of the natives could not be described as of cleanly habits. The children often wore their scanty clothing till it was literally in rags. Almost all were barefooted in both summer and winter. It was customary to see women crossing the moors barefooted, but a man was rarely seen without boots on his feet. To save her husband the trouble of taking them off, when a stream had to be forded his wife transported him in her creel. Seeing this, I often wished that the *ithish* or straw rope across her breast would snap and let the unmanly burden drop into the water.

Let me now describe a Lewis crofter's home, or 'black house' as it was appropriately called at least half a century ago. It consisted of two tiers of dry stone walls, with a padding of earth between them. On the top of the four feet thick walls grass generally grew, sometimes so profusely that I have seen a woman hoisting a lamb to feed on it. The roof consisted of rough cabers covered with a thick layer of straw held down by ropes or rapes of twisted heather, with big terminal stones to keep it from being blown off. Rarely was any sort of chimney seen by which the thick peat smoke could make its exit. As a rule there was a hole near the bottom of the thatch for the convenience of the poultry. The smoke from the peat fire in the middle of the floor percolated through the thatch, which in time became laden with a good deposit of soot. Annually the thatch was carefully stripped off by the men and carried in creels by the women to the potato patches, where it was laid alongside the drills for the nourishment of the sprouting tubers. The Lewis crofter would rather endure cold than part with his soot. The Gaelic proverb bears this out: Is fhearr an toit na' ghaoth tuath (The smoke is better than the north wind).

At different ends of these black houses the family and the cattle, generally separated by a low wall, shared the accommodation. In such circumstances sanitation and cleanliness could not be expected. To remove the manure at a certain time of the year the end wall of the house had to be taken down. It was then that scarlet fever became prevalent, and sometimes carried off whole families. But what disgusted the Inspector most was the occasional verminous condition of the children. I have seen a pretty little girl so tormented that in the midst of her reading she tossed the book on the floor and vigorously scratched herself, the while eyeing first me and then her teacher with a troubled expression of uncertainty as to how this departure from good behaviour would be received.

Sometimes the animals also made themselves comfortable in the fire end of the house. One day after the examination of a school on the west side I visited a crofter's house across the road. When I opened the door the volume of smoke almost blinded me. This explained the prevalence of ophthalmia amongst the children. Entering, I could just distinguish in the distance the subdued glow of a peat fire in the middle of the floor. I made in that direction, and as I neared it I saw beyond the fire a girl that had just arrived home from the school. When I drew near her she stepped back over some object at her feet. This I was amused to discover was a full-grown pig, which was lying comfortably by the side of the fire at her heels.

The Eyemouth Fishing Disaster, 14 October 1881

GEORGE COLLIN AND GEORGE PATERSON

The annals of Scotland are full of shipwrecks, but the Eyemouth fishing disaster of 1881 is one of the most harrowing. In one day, 129 men and boys drowned off the Berwickshire fishing port of Eyemouth in a storm likened by newspapers to the one that brought down the Tay Bridge two years earlier. It was not until several days later, however, that the extent of the losses became clear. What makes this tragedy particularly awful was that many of the ships sank within sight and sound of the fishermen's relatives who were watching from the pier and shore.

George Collin, Jun, skipper of the *White Star*:

We went out with the rest of the fleet on Friday morning. We were about fifteen miles off when the storm came. . . . Our first indication of the approach of the storm was some craft on the weather side of us taking down their sails. The hurricane had great strength. We were unable to haul in more than a quarter of a line, as the boat would not lie alongside. There was great smoke, and rain accompanied the wind, so that we could not see 500 yards around us. It was also very dark. We put about for Eyemouth, and the *Myrtle* ran alongside of us. We both stopped to endeavour to discover where we were, and at that time the boats were lying broadside on the wind.

It was very dark and we lay about twenty minutes in this position. As it did not clear, the heads of the boats were turned eastward. While in this position a heavy sea struck the *White Star* and almost swamped her. Ten minutes later the *Myrtle* was struck and overturned. From the *White Star* we saw her twice afterwards, but none of the men ever rose to the surface. We were several hundred yards from her. The sea getting heavier, we put the head of the boat to the sea and bore away out. We came upon a second boat bottom up. It had a new mast, from which the rigging was floating about. We saw no one.

On the air clearing, we discovered that we were about five miles off the harbour, to leeward, and as it was impossible to beat up, we lifted the ballast to the front of the boat, so as to put her in a better position to meet the waves, and decided to 'have the sea for our friend for the night' rather than venture near the land. The night was cold, but we had both provision and fuel on board; and it was not necessary that more than one should remain on deck at a time.

At daylight on Saturday we got up sail and made for the land, being then south of the Fern Islands, and we ran on to Tynemouth. During the whole of Friday the sea was dreadfully high, especially in the evening. Every wave looked as if it would engulf our craft. We could see them far above us coming on breaking and with a loud noise, but Providence seemed to cut a path for our boat. When we came to them we either mounted safely over, or seemed to get through between the different breakers in a remarkable way.

I have had great experience at sea, but I never saw such a storm, nor do I think in my recollection a gale continued to blow so hard for so long a time. I may say it blew twenty-five hours before it could be said to have abated. We were forty-four hours in the open.

George Paterson, of the *Enterprise*:

We left Eyemouth about eight o'clock on Friday morning, and were about four miles out when the squall struck us. It came like the clap of a hand, accompanied by sudden darkness and bringing rain. We cut our lines, and, as our only chance of escape, kept the boat away to the sea, having managed to get the sails reefed. When we were about six miles out I was washed overboard and thought I was clean gone, but had the presence of mind to grip the mizzen-sheet when the boat dipped and was, with great difficulty, hauled on board by comrades.

About ten minutes afterwards, the boat took another sea, and washed James Windram overboard. It was impossible to do anything to save him. After the sea broke the water was quite calm for a minute or two, and we saw Windram swimming bravely in the wake of the boat, but in the course of two or three minutes he became exhausted, hung his head, and sank.

The sea still ran very high, and every man on board gave up all hope of ever seeing land again. We continued to stand east and off, trying to make a better offing, till about four o'clock in the morning. We were then 30 or 40 miles from the Fern Island light. The gale having by this time moderated considerably, we wore the boat round and endeavoured to make for the land. We succeeded in weathering the storm, and were taken in tow by a tug off North Shields, arriving there about two o'clock.

Such a storm I never experienced, and I have been going to sea now for about thirty years.

The Battle of the Braes, 18 April 1882

ALEXANDER GOW

Highlanders and Islanders may have felt beleaguered by the seemingly endless hardships they faced in the nineteenth century, but they did not lose their spirit. In 1881, as pressure on land increased, Skye crofters from the Braes demanded the restoration of rights to pasturage on Ben Lee that had been reappropriated by the MacDonald estate some years before. Since they protested by withholding their rents, eviction notices were served upon them. The officer from Portree who delivered the notices was set upon and the eviction notices burned. Several days later, fifty police were despatched to bring the rent evaders and troublemakers to justice. In their company were a handful of journalists. What followed was dubbed the Battle of the Braes, and went down in local legend as one of the most significant confrontations of what was known as the Crofters' War. Thanks to the publicity the newspaper accounts roused, the men who had been arrested were dealt with leniently and the old pasturage rights were quietly retaken, albeit for a fee.

Here we were, then . . . in weather that for sheer brutal ferocity had not been experienced in Skye for a very long time. . . . Arrived at the boundary of Balmeanach, we found a collection of men, women, and children, numbering well on to 100. They cheered as we mounted the knoll, and the women saluted the policemen with volleys of sarcasms about their voyage from Glasgow . . .

At the base of the steep cliff on which we stood, and extending to the seashore, lay the hamlet of Balmeanach. There might be about a score of houses dotted over this plain. From each of these the owners were running hillward with all speed. It was evident they had been taken by surprise. . . . While we were watching the crowds scrambling up the declivity, scores of persons had gathered from other districts, and they now completely surrounded the procession. The confusion that prevailed baffles description. The women, with infuriated looks and bedraggled dress – for it was still raining heavily – were shouting at the pitch of their voices, uttering the most fearful imprecations, hurling forth the most terrible vows of vengeance against the enemy . . .

The authorities proceeded at once to perform their disagreeable task, and in the course of twenty minutes the five suspected persons were apprehended. A scene utterly indescribable followed. The women, with the most violent gestures and imprecations, declared that the police should be attacked. Stones began to be thrown, and so serious an aspect did matters assume that the police drew their batons and charged. This was the signal for a general attack. Huge boulders darkened the horizon as they sped from the hands of infuriated men and women. Large sticks and flails were brandished and brought down with crushing force upon the police – the poor prisoners coming in for their share of the blows.

One difficult point had to be captured, and as the expedition approached this dangerous position, it was seen to be strongly occupied with men and women armed with stones and boulders. A halt was called and the situation discussed. Finally it was agreed to attempt to force a way through a narrow gully. By this time a crowd had gathered in the rear of the party. A rush was made for the pass, and from the heights a fearful fusilade of stones descended. The advance was checked. The party could neither advance nor recede. For two minutes the expedition stood exposed to the merciless shower of missiles. Many were struck, and a number more or less injured. The situation was highly dangerous.

Raising a yell that might have been heard at a distance of two miles, the crofters . . . rushed on the police, each person armed with huge stones, which, on approaching near enough, they discharged with a vigour that nothing could resist. The women were by far the most troublesome assailants. . . . The police charged, but the crowd gave way scarcely a yard. Returning again, Captain Donald gave orders to drive back the howling mob, at the same time advising the Sheriffs and the constables in charge of the prisoners to move rapidly forward . . .

Hundreds of determined looking persons could be observed converging on the procession, and matters began to assume a serious aspect. . . . Cheers and yells were raised. 'The rock! the rock!' was taken up, and roared out from a hundred throats. The strength of the position was realized by the crofters; so also it was by the constables. The latter were ordered to run at the double. The people saw the move, and the screaming and yelling became fiercer than ever. The detachment reached the opening of the gulley. Would they manage to run through? Yes! No! On went the blue coats, but their progress was soon checked. It was simply insane to attempt the passage. Stones were coming down like hail, while huge boulders were hurled down before which nothing could stand. These bounded over the road and descended the precipice with a noise like thunder.

An order was given to dislodge a number of the most determined assailants, but the attempt proved futile. They could not be dislodged. Here and there a constable might be seen actually bending under the pressure of a well-directed rounder, losing his footing, and rolling down the hill, followed by scores of missiles. This state of matters could not continue. The chief officials were securing their share of attention. Captain Donald is hit in the knee with a stone as large as a matured turnip. A rush must be made for the pass, or there seems a possibility that Sheriff Ivory himself will be deforced. Once more the order was given to double. On, on, the procession went – Sheriffs and Fiscals forgetting their dignity, and taking to their heels.

The scene was the most exciting that either the spectators or those who passed through the fire ever experienced, or are likely ever to see again. By keeping up the rush, the party got through the defile, and emerged triumphantly on the Portree side, not however, without severe injuries . . .

The crofters seemed to have become more infuriated by the loss of their position, and rushing along the shoulder of the hill prepared to attack once more. This was the final struggle. In other attacks the police used truncheons freely. But at this point they retaliated with both truncheons and stones. The consequences were very serious indeed. Scores of bloody faces could be seen on the slope of the hill. One woman, named Mary Nicolson, was fearfully cut in the head, and fainted on the road. When she was found, blood was pouring down her neck and ears . . . Another woman, well advanced in years, was hustled in the scrimmage on the hill, and, losing her balance, rolled down a considerable distance, her example being followed by a stout policeman, the two ultimately coming into violent collision. The poor old person was badly bruised, and turned sick and faint. Of the men a considerable number sustained severe bruises, but so far as I could ascertain none of them were disabled . . .

Treasure Island, *1882*

ROBERT LOUIS STEVENSON

Treasure Island is one of the world's most popular novels for children. Its author, Robert Louis Stevenson, was struggling to make a living as a writer when circumstances finally conspired to bring him the success he had longed for.

In the fated year [1882] I came to live with my father and mother at Kinnaird, about Pitlochry [and then at the Castleton of Braemar]. . . . There it blew a good deal and rained in a proportion. My native air was more unkind than man's ingratitude; and I must consent to pass a good deal of my time between four walls in a house lugubriously known as 'the late Miss M'Gregor's cottage.' And now admire the finger of predestination. There was a schoolboy in the late Miss M'Gregor's cottage, home for the holidays, and much in want of 'something craggy to break his mind upon.' He had no thought of literature; it was the art of Raphael that received his fleeting suffrages, and with the aid of pen and ink and a shilling box of water-colours, he had soon turned one of the rooms into a picture-gallery. My more immediate duty towards the gallery was to be showman but I would sometimes unbend a little, join the artist (so to speak) at the easel, and pass the afternoon with him in a generous emulation, making coloured drawings. On one of these occasions I made the map of an island; it was elaborately and (I thought) beautifully coloured; the shape of it took my fancy beyond expression; it contained harbours that pleased me like sonnets; and with the unconsciousness of the predestined, I ticketed my performance Treasure Island . . .

No child but must remember laying his head in the grass, staring into the infinitesimal forest, and seeing it grow populous with fairy armies. Somewhat in this way, as I pored upon my map of Treasure Island, the future characters of the book began to appear there visibly among imaginary woods; and their brown faces and bright weapons peeped out upon me from unexpected quarters, as they passed to and fro, fighting and hunting treasure, on these few square inches of a flat projection. The next thing I knew, I had some paper before me and was writing out a list of chapters. How often have I done so, and the thing gone no farther! But there seemed elements of success about this enterprise. It was to be a story for boys; no need of psychology or fine writing; and I had a boy at hand to be a touchstone. Women were excluded. I was unable to handle a brig (which the *Hispaniola* should have been), but I thought I could make shift to sail her as a schooner without public shame. And then I had an idea for John Silver from which I promised myself funds of entertainment: to take an admired friend of mine (whom the reader very likely knows and admires as much as I do), to deprive him of all his finer qualities and higher graces of temperament, to leave him with nothing but his strength, his courage, his quickness, and his magnificent geniality, and to try to express these in terms of a culture of a raw tarpaulin. Such psychical surgery is, I think, a common way of 'making character'; perhaps it is, indeed, the only way . . .

On a chill September morning, by the cheek of a brisk fire, and the rain drumming on the window, I began *The Sea Cook*, for that was the original title. I have begun (and finished) a number of other books, but I cannot remember to have sat down to one of them with more complacency. It is not to be wondered at, for stolen waters are proverbially sweet. I am now upon a painful chapter. No doubt the parrot once belonged to Robinson Crusoe. No doubt the skeleton is conveyed from Poe. I think little of these, they are trifles and details: and no man can hope to have a monopoly of skeletons or make a corner in talking birds. The stockade, I am told, is from *Masterman Ready*. It may be, I care not a jot. These useful writers had fulfilled the poet's saying: departing, they had left behind them

> Footprints in the sands of time;
> Footprints that perhaps another –

and I was the other! It is my debt to Washington Irving that exercises my conscience, and justly so, for I believe plagiarism was rarely carried further. I chanced to pick up the *Tales of a Traveller* some years ago, with a view to an anthology of prose narrative, and the book flew up and struck me; Billy Bones, his chest, the company in the parlour, the whole inner spirit and a good deal of the material detail of my first chapters – all were there, all were the property of Washington Irving. But I had no guess of it then as I sat writing by the fireside, in what seemed the springtide of a somewhat pedestrian inspiration; nor yet day by day, after lunch, as I read aloud my morning's work to the family. It seemed to me original as sin; it seemed to belong to me like my right eye. I had counted on one boy; I found I had two in my audience. My father caught fire at once with all the romance and childishness of his original nature . . . in *Treasure Island* he recognized something kindred to his own imagination; it was *his* kind of picturesque; and he not only heard with delight the daily chapter, but set himself actively to collaborate. When the time came for Billy Bones's chest to be ransacked, he must have passed the better part of a day preparing, on the back of a legal envelope, an inventory of its contents, which I exactly followed; and the name of 'Flint's old ship,' the *Walrus*, was given at his particular request. And now, who should come dropping in, *ex machina*, but Doctor Japp, like the disguised prince who is to bring down the curtain upon peace and happiness in the last act, for he carried in his pocket, not a horn or a talisman, but a publisher; had, in fact, been charged by my old friend, Mr Henderson, to unearth new writers for *Young Folks*. Even the ruthlessness of a united family recoiled before the extreme measure of inflicting on our guest the mutilated members of *The Sea Cook*; at the same time we would by no means stop our readings, and accordingly the tale was begun again at the beginning, and solemnly redelivered for the benefit of Doctor Japp. From that moment on I have thought highly of his critical faculty; for when he left us, he carried away the manuscript in his portmanteau.

Here, then, was everything to keep me up – sympathy, help, and now a positive engagement . . . It seems as though a full-grown, experienced man of letters might engage to turn out *Treasure Island* at so many pages a day, and keep his pipe alight. But alas! This was not my case. Fifteen days I stuck to it, and turned out fifteen chapters; and then, in the early paragraphs of the sixteenth, ignominiously lost hold. My mouth was empty; there was not one word more of *Treasure Island* in my bosom; and here were the proofs of the beginning already waiting me at the *Hand and Spear*! There I corrected them, living for the most part alone, walking on the heath at Weybridge on dewy autumn mornings, a good deal pleased with what I had done, and more appalled than I can depict to you in words at what remained for me to do. I was thirty-one; I was the head of a family; I had lost my health; I had never yet paid my way, had never yet made two hundred pounds a year; my father had quite recently bought back and cancelled a book that was judged a failure; was this to be another and last fiasco? I was indeed very close on despair; but I shut my mouth hard, and during the journey to Davos, where I was to pass the winter, had the resolution to think of other things, and bury myself in the novels of M. du Boisgobey. Arrived at my destination, down I sat one morning to the unfinished tale, and behold! it flowed from me like small talk; and in a second tide of delighted industry, and again at the rate of a chapter a day, I finished *Treasure Island* . . .

Treasure Island – it was Mr Henderson who deleted the first title, *The Sea Cook* – appeared duly in the story paper, where it figured in the ignoble midst without woodcuts and attracted not the least attention. I did not care. I liked the tale myself, for much the same reason as my father liked the beginning: it was my kind of picturesque. I was not a little proud of John Silver also, and to this day rather admire that smooth and formidable adventurer. What was infinitely more exhilarating, I had passed a landmark; I had finished a tale, and written 'The End' upon my manuscript, as I had not done since the *Pentland Rising*, when I was a boy of sixteen, nor yet at college. In truth it was so by a set of lucky accidents: had not Doctor Japp come on his visit, had not the tale flowed from me with singular ease, it must have been laid aside like its predecessors, and found a circuitous and unlamented way to the fire. Purists may suggest it would have been better so. I am not of that mind. The tale seems to have given much pleasure, and it brought (or was the means of bringing) fire and food and wine to a deserving family in which I took an interest. I need scarce say I mean my own.

The Origins of Sherlock Holmes, 1891

SIR ARTHUR CONAN DOYLE

Sherlock Holmes, one of the most famous literary characters ever created, both liberated and trapped his Edinburgh-born author. Arthur Conan Doyle recalls his early career as an oculist in London, when he first began writing seriously. His future career as a writer was to prove enormously successful, thanks to the fortunes of his fictional detective.

Every morning I walked from the lodgings at Montague Place, reached my consulting-room at ten and sat there until three or four, with never a ring to disturb my serenity. Could better conditions for reflection and work be found? It was ideal, and so long as I was thoroughly unsuccessful in my professional venture there was every chance of improvement in my literary prospects. Therefore when I returned to the lodgings at tea-time I bore my little sheaves with me, the first-fruits of a considerable harvest.

A number of monthly magazines were coming out at that time, notable among which was 'The Strand'. . . . Considering these various journals with their disconnected stories it had struck me that a single character running through a series, if it only engaged the attention of the reader, would bind that reader to that particular magazine. On the other hand, it had long seemed to me that the ordinary serial might be an impediment rather than a help to a magazine, since, sooner or later, one missed one number and afterwards it had lost all interest. Clearly the ideal compromise was a character which carried through, and yet instalments which were each complete in themselves, so that the purchaser was always sure that he could relish the whole contents of the magazine. I believe that I was the first to realize this and 'The Strand Magazine' the first to put it into practice.

Looking round for my central character I felt that Sherlock Holmes, whom I had already handled in two little books, would easily lend himself to a succession of short stories. These I began in the long hours of waiting in my consulting-room. Greenhough Smith [the editor of *The Strand*] liked them from the first, and encouraged me to go ahead with them. My literary affairs had been taken up by that king of agents, A. P. Watt, who relieved me of all the hateful bargaining, and handled things so well that any immediate anxiety for money soon disappeared. It was as well, for not one single patient had ever crossed the threshold of my room.

I was now once more at a crossroads of my life, and Providence, which I recognize at every step, made me realize it in a very energetic and unpleasant way. I was starting off for my usual trudge one morning from our lodgings when icy shivers passsed over me, and I only got back in time to avoid a total collapse. It was a virulent attack of influenza, at a time when influenza was in its deadly prime. Only three years before my dear sister Annette, after spending her whole life on the family needs, had died of it at Lisbon at the very moment when my success would have enabled me to recall her from her long servitude. Now it was my turn, and I very nearly followed her. I can remember no pain or extreme discomfort, and no psychic experiences, but for a week I was in great danger and then found myself as weak as a child and as emotional, but with a mind as clear as crystal. It was then, as I surveyed my own life, that I saw how foolish I was to waste my literary earnings in keeping up an oculist's room in Wimpole Street, and I determined with a wild rush of joy to cut the painter and to trust for ever to my power of writing. I remember in my delight taking the handkerchief which lay upon the coverlet in my enfeebled hand, and tossing it up to the ceiling in my exultation. I should at last be my own master. No longer would I have to conform to professional dress or try to please any one else. I would be free to live how I liked and where I liked. It was one of the great moments of exultation of my life. The date was in August 1891.

Presently I was about, hobbling on a stick and reflecting that if I lived to be eighty I knew already exactly how it would feel. I haunted house-agents, got lists of suburban villas, and spent some weeks, as my strength returned, in searching for a new home. Finally I found a suitable house, modest but comfortable, isolated and yet one of a row. It was 12 Tennison Road, South Norwood. There we settled down, and there I made my first effort to live entirely by my pen. It soon became evident that I had been playing the game well within my powers and that I should have no difficulty in providing a sufficient income . . .

I settled down with a stout heart to do some literary work worthy of the name. The difficulty of the Holmes work was that every story really needed as clear-cut and original a plot as a longish book would do. One cannot without effort spin plots at such a rate. They are apt to become thin or to break. I was determined, now that I had no longer the excuse of absolute pecuniary pressure, never again to write anything which was not as good as I could possibly make it, and therefore I would not write a Holmes story without a worthy plot and without a problem which interested my own mind, for that is the first requisite before you can interest any one else. If I have been able to sustain this character for a long time and if the public find, as they will find, that the last story is as good as the first, it is entirely due to the fact that I never, or hardly ever, forced a story. Some have thought there was a falling off in the stories, and the criticism was neatly expressed by a Cornish boatman who said to me, 'I think, sir, when Holmes fell over that cliff, he may not have killed himself, but all the same he was never quite the same man afterwards.' I think, however, that if the reader began the series backwards, so that he brought a fresh mind to the last stories, he would agree with me that, though the general average may not be conspicuously high, still the last one is as good as the first.

Keir Hardie Elected as First Labour MP, 3 August 1892

KEIR HARDIE

Former pit-worker turned trade union activist, Lanarkshire-born Keir Hardie formed the first party dedicated to workers' rights. He stood unsuccessfully as Labour candidate for Mid-Lanark, but was luckier when, standing for West Ham, South he benefited from the death of the Liberal candidate, and thus became the first Labour MP. His inauguration at Westminster was greeted with derision by some of the press, who used as much imagination in disparaging this working-class Scot as Hardie had used in founding this historic party. In a letter to the Guardian *some years later, Hardie dispelled some of the myths surrounding that day.*

The 'brass band' of which so much has been heard in connection with my first entry to the House of Commons in 1892, and of which I have seen pictorial illustrations including the big drum, consisted of one solitary cornet. The facts are these. The dockers of West Ham had decided that I should go to Parliament in a 'coach' like other MPs, and had actually raised money for the purpose. When, however, I declined their offer they resolved to have a 'beano' on their own. Whereupon they hired a large-sized waggonette to drive to Westminster in, from which to give me a cheer as I entered the gates, and, good honest souls, invited me to a seat therein. Only a churl could have said them nay. The cornet-player 'did himself proud' on the way up from Canning Town, and the occupants of the brake cheered lustily as I was crossing Palace Yard. The cornet may also have been used, though I cannot now for certain recall. The incident was no scheme of mine – in fact, I knew nothing about the arrangements till asked to occupy a seat. It was the outcome of the enthusiasm, and warm-hearted enthusiasm, of my supporters, for which I honoured them then, even as I do now.

So much for the 'brass band.'

The statement that I perambulated the floor of the House in my offensive cap until recalled to orderliness by the 'awful tones' of Mr Speaker Peel is without any foundation in fact. I was walking up the floor to take the oath in conversation with Sir Charles Cameron, then one of the members for the city of Glasgow, who, with hands plunged deep in his trousers pockets, *was* wearing his hat. He did not realize that it was against him that the Speaker's call was directed until I called his attention to the fact that he was wearing his hat, which he at once re-moved. It sufficed for some of the more imaginative gentlemen in the Press Gallery that I was there, and next day there were long descriptions of the 'truculent' way in which I had defied the conventions and of the stern rebuke which Mr Speaker administered. All pure fiction! In fact, Mr Speaker Peel himself, in his own room next day, expressed to me personally his surprise and regret at the injustice which the press had done.

Unknown Comedian Tries His Luck in London, March 1900

HARRY LAUDER

Diminutive music-hall comedian Harry Lauder, born in Portobello, near Edin-burgh, started out as a mill-worker and pit-boy in the mines, but through indefatigable hard work and self-belief became one of the most popular comedians of his day. Dressed in a parody of Scottishness with a plaid, crook and Highland dance shoes, he specialized in droll and sentimental songs. His brand of tartan humour appealed particularly to the overseas expat community. Here he describes trying to find work in London, the first step in what was to become an international career.

Next morning, the 19th of March, 1900, I packed my 'props' into two Gladstone bags, took twenty pounds in golden sovereigns from the 'stocking' we kept in a secret spot beneath the kitchen bed, kissed Nance half a dozen times and set off to the Central Station [Glasgow], booking there a third–class single ticket for London . . .

The first evening I spent at a cheap hotel in the Euston Road. My bed and breakfast cost three and sixpence – a lot more than I had been in the habit of paying while on tour in Scotland, and I resolved that I would have to economize in other directions. So I walked all the way down to Cadle's Agency. This firm had given me some 'dates' in the provinces and I felt sure they would be able to get me a show in London. But the head of this firm – I forget his name at the moment – only smiled pityingly when I said that I wanted to get work as a Scotch comedian in one or other of the big West End halls.

'Harry, my boy,' he said, 'you haven't an earthly. We have had one or two of your kidney down here before and they have all been dead failures. If you have any money saved up for this trip get away back again before you do it all in!'

This was a most disheartening start. But there were other agents in London, hundreds of them, and I resolved to call on every blessed one of them before I caved in. Late that afternoon I met an old variety agent named Walter Munroe, whom I had met in Glasgow. I offered to buy him a refreshment. Like all good professionals he accepted with alacrity and I could see he was most powerfully impressed by the fact that I paid for it with a golden sovereign. Walter took me round several offices but with no result – the agents were all averse to handling the unlucrative business of an unknown Scottish comedian. Late in the afternoon we were walking rather mournfully along the Strand when we ran into Mr Tom Tinsley, the manager of a little hall known as 'Gatti's-in-the-Road.' The 'road' referred to was the direct thoroughfare leading south from Westminster Bridge. Tinsley was the first actual manager I met in London. We adjourned to a public house and again I 'flashed' a sovereign for publicity purposes. Once more it had a good effect, Tinsley opening his eyes in palpable amazement at a Scots 'comic' being in such affluence. But whenever I mentioned that I was looking for a job his geniality dried up on the spot.

'It's no good, me lad,' he assured me, 'my patrons at the "road" would eat me alive if I put you on. I tried a Scot last year and he had to fly for his life. You're in a foreign country and the sooner you realize it the better!' Tom had another drink at my expense and left us, but before taking his departure he noted my 'town address' (I had fixed up a third-floor room in the Lambeth Road at fifteen shillings a week), and said he would let me know if anything fell out of his bill at any time within the next week or two. Walter Munroe took me to several more agencies, but we met with the same reception at them all. 'Luv-a-duck, 'Arry,' said Walter Munroe in his most lugubrious tones, 'it ain't no bleedin' good. You ain't wanted up 'ere and that seems the finish!' And then Walter went his way.

I spent a very cheerless night in my back-third at the Lambeth Road, but was up bright and early tackling more agents and more managers. I must have walked ten or twelve miles in that weary search for work. But everywhere the result was nil – a blank wall of discouragement. When I got home I asked the landlady, 'Any letters, messages, or telegrams?' Had I stopped for a minute to consider I would never have put so stupid a question, for it was a million to one against any communications awaiting me. My wife did not know of my address in London yet, and Tom Tinsley was the only person who had taken a note of it. To my amazement the landlady replied, 'Yes, there's a telegram up in your room!' I dashed upstairs two steps at a time – had my legs been longer than they are I would have tackled three – rushed into the room and there, sure enough, was a telegram addressed Harry Lauder, Comedian. It read as follows: –

One of my turns ill. Can you deputize at ten o'clock tonight? Reply at once – Tinsley, Gatti's.

Inside two minutes I was in a grocer's shop near by appealing for the use of his telephone. I was so excited that the grocer was constrained to ask me if anybody was dead. 'No,' said I, 'but I've just got my first London job an' it's awfu' important to me!' 'That's the worst of you Scotties,' dryly observed the grocer, 'you always take your work too d—d seriously. But you'll find the 'phone round the end of the counter there.' Tinsley was in his office. I assured him that I would be on hand in good time the same evening, and I thanked him profusely for keeping his promise. From the grocer who had been so kind to me in the matter of the 'phone I bought a fivepenny tin of salmon and went home and ate the lot to the acccompaniment of a pot of tea and some bread and butter. Feeling pretty chirpy after the repast I began to debate within myself what songs I would sing to the hard-baked lot of Londoners whom I would have to face that night at Gatti's-in-the-Road . . .

I was in the dressing-room an hour and a half before I was due to go on the stage. I took immense pains with my make-up. When it was finished and I was ready for my call I found I had fully half an hour to wait. It was dreadful. I couldn't sit, I couldn't stand still; my nerves and emotions were in a state of tempest. My memory of what happened in the next hour is completely blurred. But I have a hazy recollection of dashing on the stage, my crook stick thumping the floor to give the orchestra the correct time – an almost unconscious habit to which I have been prone for many years – of starting my first song in dead silence before a rather sparse audience, of suddenly hearing a snigger or two all over the house, and of finishing 'Tobermory' amid an outburst of applause. Down came the curtain. Evidently the stage manager was under the impression that one number was quite enough for an extra turn. But the applause and laughter continued. 'Can you give 'em something else, young Scottie What's Yer Name?' asked the stage manager. 'Yes, number four in my music-books – "Killiecrankie!"'

I excitedly replied. 'Kill a what?' asked the stage manager. 'Never mind,' I replied, rapidly changing in the wings while we were speaking. 'Ye'll ken a' aboot it when I've finished.'

'The Lass' went even better than 'Tobermory.' The audience went mad over the unknown Scot who was making them laugh and they raised the roof for another song. 'Calligan, Call Again' left them still unsatisfied, but I had taken up far more time than the programme permitted and the only thing left for me to do was to go on and make a speech of thanks. I assured the audience that although this had been my first appearance in London it would not be my last. My name, I told them, was Harry Lauder, and I asked them to come and hear me whenever they saw the name on a music-hall bill in London.

'Sure we shall, 'Arry,' shouted a cockney voice from the fourth row of the stalls. 'You've made my ol' woman 'ere laugh for the first time since I married 'er!'

This sally put the house into a fit of merriment and I made my exit from the stage the most successful extra turn that ever descended on London from the fastnesses of Caledonia, stern and wild.

Down the Mine in Fife, 1900

KELLOGG DURLAND

In a spirit of anthropological research, American writer Kellogg Durland spent several months in the Fife mining community of Kelty. His descriptions of miners' work and lives read like an explorer's revelations.

One morning the gaffer met me at the bottom and told me that I must go on to the drawing. Drawing was the hardest work in the pit according to the men, so that I received my orders with a slight qualm. On long wheel braes, where there is a distinct gradation, the endless cable system is used for running the hutches back and forth, up and down, and on long levels where it is possible ponies draw the loaded hutches in long trains or races. Drawers push the hutches one at a time from the face where they are filled to the main levels or wheel braes where they are formed into races and sent to the bottom.

There were forty ponies in the Aitken pit, and wonderfully intelligent beasts they were. Many of them came from Norway. Once taken into the pit some of them spend all their lives in the darkness. They become accustomed to the roads they travel, and in a very short time are able to go trotting over the roughest places at a smart pace which occasionally breaks into a gallop. When they near the bottom they are trained to leap aside at the moment they are freed from the hutches and let the heavy load rumble past at a rate that would mean death to the animal that delayed the fraction of a moment in stepping over the rails. But most wonderful of all are the thieving ponies, that show their fondness for food and drink by learning to open the piece boxes of the men and eating the bread and jam or cheese; or the still cleverer ones that uncork the flasks and drain them to the last drop. When I first heard these stories I was sceptical but it was not long ere I was convinced of their truth. One man lost his piece box, and after accusing his neighbours of playing him a mean, practical joke, went home hungry. The next morning a pony was seen to leave his stall with an empty piece box which was duly dropped at the very spot where on the previous day the victim had left his breakfast.

It was to a part of the pit that was new to me that I was directed for the drawing – a walk of ten minutes through a much used level where long races of hutches rattled from one end to the other, the ponies guided by reckless boys who delight in shouting their warning at the last moment and make the dismal passage ring with their piercing voices high above the clatter of the hoof-beats and the thunderous rumbling of the heavy hutches. At the point where I left the main level there was a blast of air so warm and for the moment overpowering, that it seemed vitiated. The man with whom I was to work appeared, and I followed toward the ever increasing heat for nearly two hundred yards where the men were working naked to the waist, their streaming bodies streaked and begrimed with coal dust which permeated all the atmosphere till they seemed little like men. Breathing was an effort in spite of the current of air that passed through the passage. The monotonous click of the picks against the resisting coal fell on the ear like sounds from an unreal world, while from a distance the men who crouched or knelt before the grim wall, which they attacked with the brutal force of automatons, looked like creatures damned for their sins, the muttered 'T-s-s-t—t-s-s-t, sish-s—sish-h, t-s-s-t' coming from between their half closed teeth with machine-like regularity.

An empty hutch weighs nearly five hundred pounds. In appearance it is like a small railway coal waggon. An average load is from half a ton to twelve hundred pounds of coal. Fourteen or fifteen hundred pounds is a fairish load for a muscular man.

I started on my first trip. First a dead level, followed by a slight rise, another short level then an abrupt fall, not sufficiently abrupt to be characterized as steep but so inclined that it would have sent an unrestrained or unbalanced car forward at so bounding a rate that it would have left the rails at the first bend, of which there were several. It took every particle of my strength to mount the first incline and with a sense of relief I felt the forward end drop as I gripped the other to hold it back. An uneven bit of rock caused my foot to trip over a sleeper, the hutch gained in speed till I was jerked off my feet. The hot air cooled as I was dragged on with quickly increasing speed, faster and faster. I struggled with might and main to hold back, but it was useless. The thing had gained a terrible headway, by great leaps and bounds I went stumbling into the nothingness ahead at a mad pace; my lamp was blown out before twenty yards had been covered and there flashed a picture of the one hundred and sixty or more yards to go; clinging desperately as if for my life, my weight hanging all too loose on the end of the runaway hutch barely balanced it to the rails. If I rose to three quarters my height I knew I would crash against the stone roof with terrific force, if I let go, a hard tumble would be inevitable. Not knowing what was in front was terrible, and the thought of reaching the end of the level where men, ponies and long races were passing with every few seconds, was sickening, as with crouching leaps we – hutch and I – went careering on, till with a joyous thrill I found it coming more and more under my control and at last it rolled gently on to the switch as if the whole run had been just as usual. Every muscle in my body felt pulled out and my tongue was cleaving to the roof of my mouth like dry leather. There was naught to do but relight my lamp, get behind an empty hutch, and laboriously push it back to the face. How my legs stiffened and ached under the strain! My breath came in wheezes and every pore seemed a tiny spring. With greater determination I started upon the second trip, when to my unaffected horror it was the same madcap rush over again, only worse. My fingers would not act, my strength seemed to be running like the sweat from every limb. How the hutch kept the rails throughout that breathless, perilous run I shall never know. The heat was cruel. With violently trembling hands I grasped my flask and swallowed a mouthful of tea, lukewarm but refreshing. My lips were like blotting paper.

Until now my mate, a broad shouldered fellow with Herculean biceps and chest had not spoken a word, but as he passed he said lightly: 'After my first shift on this job I thought I was dead.'

The Opening of Peter Pan, December 1904

MAX BEERBOHM

Peter Pan opened in December 1904 at the Duke of York's Theatre in London, and was warmly received by critics and public alike. Within days it had become a family Christmas outing, a tradition that has endured for a century and more. Writer and caricaturist Max Beerbohm, who was drama critic of the Saturday Review, *considered it the best thing Barrie had written, though he attributed its cleverness to far from flattering aspects of Barrie's persona.*

Peter Pan; or, adds Mr Barrie, *The Boy Who Wouldn't Grow Up*. And he himself is that boy. That child, rather; for he halted earlier than most of the men who never come to maturity – halted before the age when soldiers and steam-engines began to dominate the soul. To remain, like Mr Kipling, a boy, is not at all uncommon. But I know not any one who remains, like Mr Barrie, a child. It is this unparalleled achievement that informs so much of Mr Barrie's last work, making it unique. This, too, surely, it is that makes Mr Barrie the most fashionable playwright of his time.

Undoubtedly, *Peter Pan* is the best thing he has done – the thing most directly from within himself. Here, at last, we see his talent in its full maturity; for here he has stripped off from himself the last flimsy remnants of a pretence to maturity. Time was when a tiny pair of trousers peeped from under his 'short-coats', and his sunny curls were parted and plastered down, and he jauntily affected the absence of a lisp, and spelt out the novels of Mr Meredith and said he liked them very much, and even used a pipe for another purpose from that of blowing soap-bubbles. But all this while, bless his little heart, he was suffering . . .

Time passed, and mankind was lured, little by little to the point where it could fondly accept Mr Barrie on his own terms . . . Now, at last, we see at the Duke of York's Theatre Mr Barrie in his quiddity undiluted – the child in a state of nature, unabashed – the child, as it were, in its bath, splashing, and crowing as it splashes . . .

Our dreams are nearer to us than our childhood, and it is natural that *Peter Pan* should remind us more instantly of our dreams than of our childish fancies. One English dramatist, a man of genius, realized a dream for us; but the logic in him prevented him from indulging in that wildness and incoherence which are typical of all but the finest dreams.

Credible and orderly are the doings of Puck in comparison with the doings of Peter Pan. Was ever, out of dreamland, such a riot of inconsequence and of exquisite futility? Things happen in such wise that presently one can conceive nothing that might not conceivably happen, nor anything that one would not, as in a dream, accept unhesitatingly. Even as in a dream, there is no reason why the things should ever cease to happen. What possible conclusion can inhere in them? The only possible conclusion is from without. The sun shines through the bedroom window, or there is a tapping at the bedroom door, or – some playgoers must catch trains, others must sup. Even as you, awakened, turn on your pillow, wishing to pursue the dream, so, as you leave the Duke of York's, will you rebel at the dream's rude and arbitrary ending, and will try vainly to imagine what other unimaginable things were in store for you. For me to describe to you now in black and white the happenings in *Peter Pan* would be a thankless task. One cannot communicate the magic of a dream. People who insist on telling their dreams are among the terrors of the breakfast table. You must go to the Duke of York's, there to dream for yourselves.

The fact that Mr Barrie is a child would be enough, in this generation which so adores children, to account for his unexampled vogue. But Mr Barrie has a second passport. For he, too, even pre-eminently, adores children – never ceases to study them and their little ways, and to purr sentimental paens over them, and finds it even a little hard to remember that the world really does contain a sprinkling of adults . . .

The strange thing is the preoccupation itself. It forces me to suppose that Mr Barrie has, after all, to some extent, grown up. For children are the last thing with which a child concerns itself. A child takes children as a matter of course, and passes on to more important things – remote things that have a glorious existence in a child's imagination . . . A little girl does not say 'I am a little girl, and these are my dolls, and this is my baby brother', but 'I am the mother of this family'. She lavishes on her dolls and on her baby brother a wealth of maternal affection, cooing over them, and . . . stay! that is just Mr Barrie's way. I need not, after all, mar by qualification my theory that Mr Barrie has never grown up. He is still a child, absolutely. But some fairy once waved a wand over him, and changed him from a dear little boy into a dear little girl. Some critics have wondered why among the characters in *Peter Pan* appeared a dear little girl, named in the programme 'Liza (the Author of the Play)'. Now they know. Mr Barrie was just 'playing at symbolists'.

The Early Adventures of Toad, May 1907

KENNETH GRAHAME

Kenneth Grahame was born in Edinburgh in 1859 and brought up in Inverary until his mother died and he was sent to live with relatives in Berkshire. He was Secretary to the Bank of England when he and his wife sent their four-year-old son Alastair to spend the summer in Littlehampton with his nanny to escape the heat of London. Perhaps to assuage his guilt at parting with his son, whom he called Master Mouse, Grahame wrote him fifteen letters in the space of seven weeks. It was in these letters that he first began to describe the Adventures of Toad.

11 Durham Villas, London

10 May 1907

My Darling Mouse,

This is a birthday letter to wish you very many happy returns of the day. I wish we could have been all together, but we shall meet again soon and then we will have *treats*. I have sent you two picture-books, one about Brer Rabbit, from Daddy, and one about some other animals, from Mummy. And we have sent you a boat painted red, with mast and sails to sail in the round pond by the windmill – and Mummy has sent you a boat-hook to catch it when it comes ashore. Also Mummy has sent you some sand-toys to play in the sand with, and a card game. Have you heard of the Toad? He was never taken prisoner by the brigands at all. It was all a horrid low trick of his. He wrote that letter himself – the letter saying that a hundred pounds must be put in the hollow tree. And he got out of the window early one morning and went off to a town called Buggleton and went to the Red Lion Hotel and there he found a party that had just motored down from London and while they were having breakfast he went into the stable-yard and found their motor-car and went off in it without even saying Poop-poop! And now he has vanished and every one is looking for him, including the police. I fear he is a bad low animal.

Good-bye from

Your loving Daddy.

Force-feeding Suffragettes, 1909

MEDICAL OFFICERS OF PERTH AND BARLINNIE PRISONS

Suffragette activity in Scotland gathered pace between the late nineteenth and the early twentieth centuries. By 1909, the authorities were having to consider how to deal with their increasingly troublesome charges. The following letter to the Prison Commissioners for Scotland gives a glimpse of what the protesters were prepared to endure for their cause. Despite the horrors of imprisonment, suffragette activism reached its peak in 1913. Among a plethora of almost daily criminal acts were arson at Ayr racecourse, an attempt to smash the windows of the King's car, and an ambush on the Prime Minister at Lossiemouth golf course. A political ceasefire was called during the First World War, and in 1918 women – though only those over the age of thirty – were finally given the vote.

1909, 15 November

Prison Commissioners,

The Secretary for Scotland asks for full information as to the conduct of the operation of artificial feeding. This information has been fully supplied in the Reports of the Medical Officers of Perth and Barlinnie prisons, and their experience as well as that of Medical Officers of Asylums and other institutions may be epitomized as follows: –

There are three methods in use; (1) by means of a feeding cup; (2) by means of an oesophageal catheter, and (3) by means of a nasal tube.

(1) Feeding by means of a feeding cup consists of introducing the mouthpiece of a feeding-cup between the teeth and pouring the contents into the patient's mouth. For prisoners who offer resistance it is a method attended with considerable risk of injury.

(2) For feeding by means of an oesophageal catheter, it is necessary that the movements of the patient be carefully and fully controlled, and for that purpose five assistants may be required. The ordinary method of controlling the patient is to put the patient into bed; one assistant sits on the bed at the pillow end and steadies the patient's body with his-or-her knees and steadies the patient's head by pressing the head against his or her chest; an assistant is required to control each of the patient's limbs. The patient being under control, the medical officer inserts a gag into the mouth and leaves the subsequent charge of the gag to another assistant. The medical officer then introduces the catheter, previously smeared with oil or Castile Soap into the upper part of the gullet and when

there reflex involuntary contractions of the gullet carry the end down into the patient's stomach. A risk in this method of feeding is the introduction of the catheter into the windpipe instead of into the gullet; but this is an exceedingly rare accident and the effects of the accident can be obviated by observation after the introduction, for if the catheter happens to be in the windpipe respiratory movements of air would take place through the catheter, while if the catheter be in the gullet and stomach there are no such respiratory movements. The medical officer being satisfied that the catheter is properly in the stomach, connects the catheter with the feeding funnel, and then introduces a small quantity of warm water, which is a further precaution against introduction into the windpipe; and when he observes that the water enters the stomach, he gradually introduces the food, which generally consists of thin custard or a strained mixture of milk and eggs, or broth. After administering the food, the medical officer passes a little more warm water through the catheter; he then pinches the catheter to prevent entrance of the food into it at the stomach end and withdraws it in that condition. The operation should be completed in from two to three minutes. It may produce discomfort but is not painful.

(3) For feeding by means of the nasal tube, similar control to the above is necessary and the proceedings are generally the same, excepting that the tube, which is smaller in calibre than an oesophageal catheter, is introduced through the nose. The advantage of this method over that of the oesophageal catheter is that the gag can be dispensed with, but it is slower in operation on account of the narrowness of the tube, and it is not entirely free from inconvenience of the tube accidentally entering the windpipe.

It appears to me that feeding by means of a cup is altogether unsuited for prisoners who purposely resist artificial feeding, as by it considerable damage might be done to the prisoner's mouth.

In regard to oesophageal feeding, it is attended with the objections inseparable from the forcible insertion of a gag, whereby the opportunities for resistance on the part of the prisoner are increased and may result in accidents such as the breaking of teeth and the production of superficial wounds of the mouth with bleeding. Its chief advantage is that a somewhat shorter period of time is required for the passage of the food than is the case with nose-feeding, but the difference is immaterial.

Nose feeding is not attended with any of these drawbacks or slight risks, and its easy application is only rarely interfered with by an exceptional narrowing of the nose passages.

I am, accordingly, of the opinion that when artificial feeding is adopted, the nasal method should be preferred. At the same time, seeing that the difference in risk between nasal and oesophageal feeding is only slight, this risk amounting to but little in either method, I would recommend that when the medical officer has had special or exclusive experience of oesophageal feeding, it should be optional for him to adopt that method.

The Secretary for Scotland also raises the question of how long it is safe for a prisoner to remain without food. Deprivation of food, while liquids are being freely drunk, may be continued for many days in healthy and normal persons, without immediate danger to life. It commences, however, to be detrimental to health in a few days, when the individuals are weakly and untrained for deprivation, and this is especially so in women of high-strung nervous suscepti-bilities. In the latter, also, the chances of deterioration in health would be increased if, when strength had already been lost by deprivation of food, they were subjected to the emotional incidents inseparable from mental and physical resistance to artificial feeding.

I am therefore of the opinion that artificial feeding should always be employed in from forty-eight to sixty hours after food has last been taken and in women of weakly constitution nearer forty-eight than sixty hours.

It would be advisable to convey definite instructions to this effect to the officials of H.M. Prisons.

(Sgd.) Thomas R Fraser
15/xi/09

Life at the Front in France, 1915–1918

DAVID SMITH

David Smith was a fourteen-year-old apprentice painter in Edinburgh when the First World War began. He and some friends tried to enlist, but were quickly detected as underage. 'To the public we were Bantams, to ourselves Goliaths,' he wrote. Desperate to join the Seaforth Highlanders, he tried again and after being told to come back the next day and say he was nineteen and not eighteen, he succeeded in joining up. He was sent to France in 1915, where he was in the front line until he was taken prisoner in 1918. His hectic account of these years shows how raw the memories remained. (Note: All spelling and grammar oddities are as in his account.)

After being disappointed at not getting home I settled down to see the end of the war, or the war to see the end of me, the only other alternative being wounded or as the soldier called it 'A Blighty'! We finished our month's rest, and about February 1916, we relieved the French Troops in the trenches at a place called the Labarinth, which was fairly quiet, except for the only thing of any incident was our battalion, the 5th Seaforths, was relieved by our 6th Battalion one night, and in the morning the Germans blew up a mine, but by the sharpness of our Artillery which was the Edinburgh Lowland the Germans suffered heavier casualties from our 6th Batt, although the 6th was heavy, after a few months at the above place we were removed to Vimy Ridge, this is where we began to get heavy bombardments and also heavy casualties with shells and snipers. We were relieved about June 1916 after serving spells of 21 days at a time in the trenches, then about the end of June we were taken in Motors to the worst place I have ever been in my service in France, namely High Wood July 1916. My God! how I wished for home 18 years old and nearly a year in France – I thought it was a bloody shame having young boys in France at that age, of course there was more than me, but as I am writing my memories, I leave others to write there's. 1914 I thought I was a man (High Wood 1916 – I thought I was a boy) and ought to be home – Delvil Wood shelled night and day like buggery, dead lying all over, this was the first time I had seen so many dead – Burning hot weather. Dead horses – oh what a smell no drinking water and by this time I was the Company Captains Runner Oh! how I was wishing I had been sent home with Rupture like Jock my pal, but I didn't grudge him his luck as I know he would rather have been with me at Delvil Wood, did the people at home know the true facts about this hellish place, of course not. They were all mad in France to carry on like this, and I was one of them, well if I didn't kill I would be killed so I had to bang away too, eight days Sunday included we were hemmed and hammered in the wood – my God! don't they ever take a rest here, or is it three eight hour shifts, we were doing 24 hours, of course sleep was out of the question, at times we got restless – and fearless, wishing to God we got killed as we were fed up with it, at last we went over the top, and glad to go, to get out of the wood, as a wood makes a fine target for Artillery, after doing another three days in attacking, we had to be relieved as our Battalion was depleted with the amount of dead, and the second day on rest I was sent down to the base hospital with Malaga fever, of course it was a God-send in a sense, as it gave me a good bed, food and a rest, although the Battalion was on rest at the time . . .

We entered the trenches on Nov. 12th Midnight ready to go over the top on the 13th (unlucky 13th for Jock) at day break, – day did break and I thought so did the earth, mines, shells and every dam thing went up and over we went, Jock and I and a Sergent Cameron quite close to each other. I stuck in mud (this was a hellish place for mud), but after a minute or two was free, and just as I got free Jock, my pal of all pals, got covered with shrapnel, from a bomb. What could I do – nothing, there was stretcher-bearers for that job I was told, so I had to carry on, but not for long, I saw Sergent Cameron – a hero if ever there was one, but his body was found riddled with bullets, a VC never honoured was what was said about him, – now one of the 'Forgotten heroes' to some only, but not to me for one.

I will now take the privilage to write a few lines about my dearest Pal which may not interest some, but whose memory I cherish. After I had left Jock badly wounded, I got knocked out myself, by shell concussion, and partly buried and when I came to, I was in Hospital thanking God I was away from it for the time being, but as I have found out Jock my pal lay for 24 hours before being picked up he was in Hospital in France, so serious that his father had to go over to France to his bedside, and after going through a large number of operations, he was discharged with his leg useless, through which he died in the year 1920. So ended a great friendship one could not wish for better.

I returned to the Battalion about the middle of Jan, 1917, and after doing a spell in the trenches, we went back on rest to Abbeville, from where I went on leave home to Edinburgh. What a fine feeling, home again, since 1915 playing in mud and Soldiering just as I wanted but I had realized now what it was and had had enough, and hoping it would be over before my leave was over, but to be candid I did not think there was an end to it.

Back from leave oh! how I felt leaving mother, no one at home, and I had never seen my father since 1914 my brother I had met in France, and those dam Zepps were beginning to frighten her, often I thought if there's a God cant he finish it, then again I would say if they cant obey God's words then let them carry on. 'Thou shalt not kill'. We were not obeying, so blame ourselves.

Back from leave seven days late. What the hell did I care I had a good time in London with a Canadian Soldier, it was a glorious war for that seven days, so when I arrived back up in front of the CO, but he said as you are going over the top at Arras, I will give you no sentence as you can take your chance; which meant I might get knocked out or I might not.

I was wishing to hell I had been fourteen days late but still if I had been up to time I would of had to take my chance, so it was all the same. . . . After getting a good issue of rum from my officer, who I was servant to, I fell fast asleep, not giving a dam what was in store for me the next morning, of course the rum was doing the thinking. Zero-hour – what a hell of noise, I am in my senses now, Smith I hear the officer calling for me, a proper toff, keep by my side, for I will have to take back a message when we get our objective, at last we go over, the usual sight dead, and dying moaning and groaning, oh! what a hell of a life will this bloody war finish, however we plod on, the Germans are fleeing back like hell and we reach our objective, with few casualties considering the ground we have taken, we go no further as we are not allowed, my God, what a chance we are missing to chase them, but we are still living so to hell with Jerry, let him run, we all releived at night and in a few days all shifted to the right to a place called Roun, where we get battered to hell, attacking and counter-attacking, we get chased back to a canal, where an order is given to jump in and cross to the other side Thank God it is not deep as most of us cant swim, but who the hell invented the kilt, I wish I was in a trouser regiment now . . .

We eventually got to the Somme canal where we joined the rest of the Brigade, as the Seaforths were fighting as a rear guard for the rest of the Brigade, I was wishing to hell I was on a horse or in the Motor Transport.

By this time I had picked up a Sandbag of rations as we were setting fire to all our dumps and canteens not to let them fall in German hands.

The 24th March after having a piece of bread and a drink of Ideal Milk (scrounged from a Transport which had been shelled and the Driver and horses killed) the Germans got up on us again, here he gave us very heavy casualties, as it was here we lost our last officer. We retired to a ridge and as we had no officers a South African officer gathered what men he could; all regiments were represented, his order was to hold on at all costs, I wondered if this bugger had a home to go back too, no doubt he was a hero, but were we not all heroes? every man in the Trenches deserved a VC but I myself would rather of been home than have all the bloody medals made, well we were told to hold on as we had no artillery, so as soon as the Germans showed face we let blaze inflicting severe causualties on them, but at the same time our numbers were getting smaller.

This was a hell of a day of heat, and we were beginning to get exhausted and day of all days it was a Sunday, how I wished for my Sunday School days.

We retired to shell holes of the 1914 days as we were now retiring over that ground, we lay in the shell holes in fours and five's etc, there being five of us all told in the hole I was in, his aeroplanes came over swooping down on us, and rattling his machine gun at us, one of our five a Seaforth fell back dead, Oh! God is my turn coming, but alas; we were surrounded – my God – A Prisoner of War – out in France in 1915 and then being taken Prisoner in 1918, I could hardly realize it, but there were thousands captured, and when we saw the Germans there seemed to be tens of hundreds of thousands, Russia had packed up by this [time] and all the German Troops had been drafted to our front. Would I ever see home again, would my mother ever know, would they do me in, these were the thoughts that passed through my head, I wanted to be a soldier, I was one now, but the war was ended as far as I was concerned. The Germans who captured me took my wristlet watch and a few Photos I had, and also a half-a-loaf of bread, and a tin of jam I carried in my pack, to be just he was fairley decent, but one of the few I met (later on while in prison camp) he shared the bread and jam along with the other three captured along with me, and then he took us over to the chap who got killed he was a terrible sight, an explosive bullet got him in the stomach. This was war – what for I dont know.

Glasgow Rent Strike, September–October 1915

THE *GLASGOW HERALD*

Steep rises in rents and the threat of evictions for non-payment, issued in Glasgow early in 1915, led to collective action among the city's womenfolk, who felt obliged to protect their homes while their men were away at the Front. The protests were coordinated by the influential Scottish and Co-operative Women's Guild, leading to strikes and marches, where banners carried such slogans as 'Defence of the Realm: Government must protect our Homes from Germans and landlords or the Public Will protect Themselves'. This revolt was so effective that late in 1915 a Rent Restrictions Act was passed which appeased the protesters.

28 September

The occupants of a number of tenement houses in the Partick district are resisting a proposal of the factor of the properties to increase their rents. They received intimation about a fortnight ago that the rents were to be increased, and they sent a protest to the factor with a statement that they declined to pay the advance. In reply the tenants were served with notices to leave the houses to-day. Several meetings of the tenants have been held, and they have decided to remain in the houses. They are displaying small Union Jacks over their doors and windows, in which they also show a placard with the words: 'Rent Strike against Increases; we are not removing.' Altogether 130 tenants are involved, and the houses, which are of one and two apartments, are situated in Rosevale Street, Hozier Street, Clyde Street, and Exeter Drive. Last night about 100 of the tenants remitted their rents at the present rates to the factor by postal order . . .

29 September

A deadlock has been reached in the relations between the factor of the properties in Partick involved in the 'rent strike against increases' and the tenants. As has been explained already, 130 tenants refuse to pay increases, which in the majority of cases are 1s per month on rentals of £15 per annum. Notices were served some time ago on the protesting tenants to leave the house yesterday, but these notices were ignored, and the tenants reaffirmed their determination not to pay the increases and to remain in the houses. The factor is equally determined that the increases shall be paid, or, if they are not, that the resources of the law shall be used to evict those in revolt. He states that he will apply to the Sheriff Court for warrants to take possession of the houses. It will be three or four days before this procedure is completed.

Until yesterday there was no rowdiness in the agitation, but when the factor called at several of the houses in the afternoon in order to return postal orders for the value of the rents under the old scale, which had been posted to him, he got a very hostile reception. He was pelted with bags of peasemeal and chased from one of the streets by a number of women, who upbraided him vociferously.

29 October

The first attempt to put into force the ejectment warrants which have been issued against Glasgow tenants who are participating in the 'Rent Strikes' was made yesterday afternoon in Merryland Street, Govan. The householder is a widow. As has been the custom since the beginning of the movement against increased rents, a demonstration of the 'strikers' was held at the time when the warrant became operative. While Mrs

Barbour of the Glasgow Women's Housing Association, was addressing those who had assembled, two sheriff officers arrived and endeavoured to gain admission to the house. As soon as it was known that it was proposed to eject the tenant the demonstrators determined to resist. Most of them were women, and they attacked the officers and their assistants with peasemeal, flour, and whiting. A woman was arrested on a charge of assaulting one of the officers. She was taken to the Govan Police Office, but was not detained.

A consultation took place between Mrs Barbour and the officer, after which the latter entered the house without molestation. It was pointed out that the tenant was ill, and the officer decided not to proceed with the enforcement of the warrant.

A Hospital on the Western Front, July 1916

MISS V. C. C. COLLUM

The idea of hospitals run entirely by women, which could be set up near the battlefront, was the inspiration of the pioneering Scottish surgeon Elsie Inglis, who, among other ventures, founded three military hospitals in Serbia. She helped with the campaigning and organizing of another remarkable all-woman outfit, a group of Scottish doctors, nurses, cooks and cleaners, who established a hospital in the French abbey of Royaumont, on the Western Front. The hospital was operational from 1915 until the end of the war, but one of its most severe challenges came in the early days of the Battle of the Somme, which began on 1 July, when tens of thousands of men were wounded and killed in a matter of days. The following account comes from the radiographer, Miss V. C. C. Collum, who herself had been seriously wounded a few months earlier when her ship was torpedoed.

On the first [July] we waited, full of tense, suppressed excitement. The Great Push had begun – how were the Allies faring? Our hospital had been evacuated almost to the last man. Our new emergency ward of 80 beds had been created in what had once been as big as an English parish church – our theatre and our receiving rooms had been supplied with a huge reserve of bandages and swabs, of lint and gauze and wool; our new x-ray installation had been fitted up to the last connection; our ambulances were waiting ready to start at a moment's notice in the garage yard. The incessant thunder and boom of the great guns had never been silent for days. This day, at dawn, the thunder had swelled to an orgy of terrific sound that made the whole earth shiver; then, a few hours later, had ceased, and we could hear once more the isolated reports of individual cannon. Those of us who had been at the hospital through the attacks of June 1915, and the more serious push in Artois on September 25, went early to bed. If the call came in the night we could always be summoned – meanwhile we slept when we could. The late-comers marvelled at our lack – our apparent lack – of anticipation and excitement, and waited up long into the night.

[Finally, the casualties began to arrive.] Their wounds were terrible . . . many of these men were wounded – dangerously – in two, three, four and five places. That great enemy of the surgeon who would conserve life and limb, gas gangrene, was already at work in 90% of cases. Hence the urgent need for immediate operation, often for immediate amputation. The surgeon did not stop to search for shrapnel and pieces of metal: their one aim was to open up and clean out the wounds, or to cut off the mortifying limb before the dread gangrene had tracked its way into the vital parts of the body. The stench was very bad. Most of the poor fellows were too far gone to say much . . .

[We] had accommodation for 400, and for weeks we worked, once we were filled, with never a bed to spare. Our operating theatre was hardly ever left vacant long enough to be cleaned during the small hours and it became a problem how to air the x-ray rooms during the short hours of dawn that stretched between the ending of one day's work and the beginning of another's. We were fighting gas gangrene and time was the factor that counted most. We dared not stop work in the theatre until it became physically impossible to continue. For us who worked, and for those patient suffering men, lying along the corridor outside the x-ray rooms and the theatre, on stretchers, awaiting their turn, it was a nightmare of glaring lights, of appalling stenches of ether and chloroform, and violent sparking of tired x-ray tubes, of scores of wet negatives that were seized upon by their respective surgeons and taken into the hot theatre before they had even had time to be rinsed in the dark room. Beneath and beyond the anxiety of saving men's lives, there was the undercurrent of anxiety of the theatre staff as to whether the boiling of instruments and gloves could be kept level with the rapidity with which the cases were carried in and put on the table, as to whether the gauze and wools and swabs would last! – and with us it was anxiety for the life of the tubes, anxiety to get the gas gangrene plates developed first, to persuade them to dry, to keep the cases of the six surgeons separate, to see that they did not walk off with the wrong plates – for we had pictures that were almost identical, duplication of names, and such little complications. And it all had to be done in a tearing hurry, and at the end of a day that had already lasted anything from 10 to 18 hours, and no mistakes to be made. I do not think we lost a case from delay in locating the trouble and operating in all that first terrible week of July. The losses were due to delay in reaching the hospital.

Red Clydeside Erupts, 31 January 1919

THE STRIKE BULLETIN

Industrial unrest which had been fomenting during the First World War came to a head early in 1919. With the threat of mass unemployment as hundreds of factory workers were being paid off, just as demobbed troops were about to return home, anxieties were running high. Agitating for a forty-hour week, 40,000 shipyard workers went on strike on 27 January, a number that doubled within a day. On 31 January 100,000 strikers gathered in Glasgow's George Square while their leaders met in the City Chambers to press their case to the government. Alarmed by the crowds, which raised fears of the sort of revolutionary behaviour that had lately terrified Russia and Germany, the authorities overreacted and the police attacked the crowd. By the time the following report was published 12,000 English troops, 100 army trucks and six tanks had been rushed to Glasgow to protect the citizens, it was said, from what was believed to be a 'Bolshevist rising'. In the presence of tanks, with machine-gun posts in the city centre and patrolling soldiers, there was no chance of the strikers getting a reasonable hearing. They soon melted away and with it their hopes for a reduced working week.

Henceforth January 31, 1919, will be known in Glasgow as Bloody Friday, and, for the crime of attacking defenceless workers, the citizens will hold the authorities responsible. The police have once more been used as hirelings to bludgeon the workers. The workers will not forget.

The outrage looks like a prearranged affair by the master class. As arranged on Wednesday, a deputation from the Joint Committee, composed of [Emanuel] Shinwell, [David] Kirkwood, Neil MacLean, [Harry] Hopkins, and other delegates, waited on the Lord Provost in the City Chambers to receive the reply from the Prime Minister and the Minister of Labour, in response to his Lordship's *own* appeal for Government intervention. While the deputation were kept waiting for twenty minutes, and, while there, the police were ordered to draw their batons and forcibly disperse the crowd of strikers who were standing in George Square until the deputation returned.

On hearing the sound of conflict, Shinwell and Kirkwood rushed out to help in restoring order; but instead of listening, the police made an attack on them, too, and Kirkwood was felled to the ground. The strikers covered Shinwell successfully, and got him clear away without injury. Those who appealed for order were also clubbed, as were other strikers who were quietly inclined, as was shown by their defenceless condition.

The bludgeon attack on the strikers in front of the City Chambers was deliberately ordered by the officers, *and was unprovoked*. The attack was sheer brutality by the police to satisfy the lust of the masters for broken skulls. The masters, afraid to do their own dirty work, employ the police to do it for them.

The meeting in front of the City Chambers was quiet and orderly, and was being addressed by members of the Strike Committee until the deputation returned from the interview with the Lord Provost. Shinwell, before the deputation entered the City Chambers, appealed to the crowd to be of good behaviour, and this appeal was endorsed by the other speakers. The audience, which was turned towards the Gladstone statue, on which the speakers were perched, overflowed into the street fronting the Chambers, and, in this avenue the police allowed two motors to run into the crowd, with the result that two men were knocked down and injured. This annoyed the strikers, who appealed to the police to turn the vehicular traffic by another street – a not unreasonable request.

The reply was: a police attack on the strikers, who stood their ground, and the police withdrew after an appeal from the speakers. The mounted police then arrived, and, in a display of trick riding, two of them allowed their horses to fall, which caused the crowd to chaff the bulky Tod Sloans. This chaff was an awful violation of the sacred dignity of the police, who apparently lost their reason, and made a mad rush with drawn batons on the defenceless crowd. The infuriated men in uniform struck wherever they saw a head. . . . The strikers put up the best defence possible with bare fists, but, being unarmed, they were gradually forced back, retreating in order and without panic. The strikers did nobly against big odds, and if they had not been without the means of defence, there would have been a different story to tell.

The affair looks like a plot to smash the strike by force. Threats of that nature have been made in the employers' press. Then the attack

was made while the deputation was kept waiting inside the City
Chambers. Think it over.

The Scuttling of the German Grand Fleet at Scapa
Flow, 21 June 1919

JAMES TAYLOR

*At the end of the First World War, the German High Seas fleet, consisting of
seventy-four warships, was interned at Scapa Flow in Orkney, awaiting the
negotiation of the details of armistice. On the morning of 21 June, when the ships
and their skeleton crews had been corralled for six months, a party of 400
schoolchildren was given a sightseeing tour of the fleet onboard an Admiralty tug,
the* Flying Kestrel. *James Taylor, who was fifteen at the time, recalls the
extraordinary spectacle as the German fleet began to sink before their eyes. It was
the first time anyone had ever sunk a navy. Only recently has it been revealed
that the Imperial Navy's commander, Rear-Admiral Ludwig von Reuter, ordered
the scuttling because of a misunderstanding.*

At long last we came face to face with the German Fleet, some of them
huge battleships that made our own vessel look ridiculous. [The sailors
thumbed their noses.] Our teacher tried anxiously to explain that perhaps
we would do the same if we were prisoners of war being stared at by a
crowd of gaping school-children. We ought to feel sorry for those poor
men who could no more help being Germans than we could help being
Orcadians. Rognvald St Clair, who was always so smart, said he only
felt sorry he hadn't brought his catapult. . . . Some of the Germans sat
. . . playing mouth organs . . .
    [And later, when in sight of the capital ships] Suddenly, without any
warning and almost simultaneously, these huge vessels began to list over
to port or to starboard; some heeled over and plunged headlong, their
sterns lifted high out of the water and pointing skywards; others were
rapidly settling down in the ocean with little more showing than their
masts and funnels, while out of the vents rushed steam and oil and air
with a dreadful roaring hiss, and vast clouds of white vapour rolled up
from the sides of the ships. Sullen rumblings and crashing of chains
increase the uproar as the great hulls slant giddily over and slide with
horrible sucking and gurgling noises under the water. The proud vessels
slowly disappear with a long-drawn-out sigh.

On the surface all that remains is a mighty whirlpool dotted with dark objects swirling round and round, many of them drawn inwards until they too sink from sight. Now the sea is turning into one vast stain of oil which spreads gradually outwards as if the life-blood of some ocean monster mortally wounded was oozing up from the seabed. And as we watched, awestruck and silent, the sea became littered for miles round with boats and hammocks, lifebelts and chests, spars and matchwood. And among it all hundreds of men struggling for their lives . . . Suddenly the air was rent by the lusty cheering of long lines of sailors drawn up on the deck of one of the largest German ships. They were bidding farewell to a sister-ship whose decks were now under water.

Churchill on the Eve of Defeat, 14 November 1922

WINSTON CHURCHILL

As MP for Dundee, Winston Churchill knew he was facing a desperate challenge to his seat in 1922. Believing he was being traduced by the press, on the night before the election he gave an outspoken speech to constituents in Broughty Ferry. In typically robust style he castigated Mr D. C. Thomson, the local newspaper owner who was managing director of twelve Scottish papers, for setting his face 'against the free expression of opinion'. His outburst won him few friends, and the following day he was trounced at the polls by the teetotal Dundonian candidate, Mr Scrymgeour.

You have the Liberal and the Conservative newspaper owned by the same man and produced from the same office on the same day. Here is one man, Mr Thomson, selling Liberal opinions with his left hand and Conservative opinions with his right hand. . . . That is an extraordinary spectacle. . . . If such conduct were developed in private life or by politicians in public life every man and woman in the country would say 'That is very double-faced. You cannot believe the two.' What would be said, I would like to know, of a preacher who preached Roman Catholicism in the morning, Presbyterianism in the afternoon, and then took a turn at Mohammedanism in the evening? He would be regarded as coming perilously near a rogue. It would be said of a politician who made Socialist speeches in Scotland, Conservative speeches in England, and Radical speeches in Wales – you would say he was downright dishonest . . .

Here we get in the morning the Liberal Mr Thomson through the columns of the liberal 'Dundee Advertiser' advising the Liberals of Dundee to be very careful not to give a vote to Mr Churchill because his Liberalism is not quite orthodox. This is the Mr Thomson, the same Mr Thomson, who failed to get elected as chairman of the Conservative Party, telling the Liberals to be very careful of the company they keep, warning the Liberal Association that they have strayed from the true fold, and that by any attempt to stretch a friendly hand to progressive Conservatives they are running perilously in danger of jeopardizing their political soul.

At the same time, the same moment, you have the Conservative, the 'Die-Hard' Mr Thomson, through the columns of the Conservative 'Dundee Courier', advising the Conservative electors of Dundee to be very careful lest in giving a vote to Mr Churchill they should run the risk of building opposition to the new Conservative Government; and you get the same man behind these two absolutely differently served up dishes, hot or cold, roast or boiled, seasoned or unseasoned, according to taste, and both brought out by the same cook from the same kitchen. Behind those two, I say, you get the one single individual, a narrow, bitter, unreasonable being eaten up with his own conceit, consumed with his own petty arrogance, and pursued from day to day and from year to year by an unrelenting bee in his bonnet.

Sectarian Anxieties, 1923

THE GENERAL ASSEMBLY OF THE CHURCH OF SCOTLAND

In a shameful episode in the career of the Church of Scotland, one of its committees, led by the Rev. Dr John White – who later became Moderator – argued for restrictions on Irish immigration in order to quell the rising tide, as they saw it, of Roman Catholicism. This outburst of intolerance sparked years of sectarian trouble in previously peaceful parts of the country. The report below is from the debate on the subject held during the General Assembly of the Church of Scotland.

The Rev. William Main, Edinburgh, presented the report of the Committee to consider overtures from the Presbytery of Glasgow and from the Synod of Glasgow and Ayr on Irish Immigration and the Education

(Scotland) Act 1918. The report, he should say, was the work of the Rev. Duncan Cameron, Kilsyth. As a result of their inquiries they had found that the fears and anxieties expressed at last General Assembly were well grounded. It was not possible to prove that their facts and statements were either inaccurate or exaggerated in any way. The Irish population in Scotland during the past forty years had doubled itself, and in the last twenty years the increase of the Irish population was six and a half times as great as that of the Scottish population. This was not because of the greater fertility of the Irish race. It was not a matter of the birth-rate at all; but for the most part, if not entirely, it was due to the emigration from Ireland, and as the Irish settled in an area the Scots departed from it. The two races could not fuse. The political influence of the immigration was seen already in the West. It was very largely due to that fact that they had in the House of Commons at the present time men who were supposed to represent constituencies in Glasgow and the west, but who did not represent them really. (Applause.) They had been elected members of Parliament by the fact that they had this enormous Irish Roman Catholic population in these areas. Hence the type of men sent from these areas to Parliament, bringing disgrace and scandal into the House of Commons. (Applause.) He was not afraid of proselytism by the Roman Catholic priests, but increased Roman Catholic populations brought with them a certain power, and in educational, municipal, and Parliamentary elections they held the balance. It was very easy to state the problem, but much more difficult to solve it. He thought, however, they had adduced a sufficient number of facts and figures to warrant the General Assembly calling upon the Government to institute an inquiry into the condition of matters, which, to say the least of it, was a menace to their Scottish nationality. (Applause.) Touching on the second part of the report Mr Main said what had happened under the Education Act of 1918 in the Roman Catholic schools which had been transferred to the Education Authorities throughout the land was that they were just the same as they were when they were under the full direct control of the authorities of the Roman Catholic Church. In name they were national schools. In reality they remained Catholic. Religious instruction and religious observation could go on all day, while according to the Act of 1872 religious instruction must be given at the beginning or at the end of a school period. They should call on the Government to amend the Act so that the right to impart religious instruction should be accorded to all public schools as was accorded in transferred schools. He moved approval of the deliverance.

The Rev. Duncan Cameron, Kilsyth, seconded. Under present conditions, he said, there was a great danger that the Scottish nationality would be imperilled and Scottish civilization subverted. He quoted official figures which showed that in 1920 the number of Scottish people leaving the Clyde for other parts was 24,179, while the number of Irishmen leaving was 341; in 1921 Scots were 20,810 and Irish 296; and in 1922, the respective numbers were 22,427 and 219. On the other hand, if they went to the clerk of the Parish Council in Glasgow they would hear that of the total numbers applying for the 'dole' last year no fewer than between 60 and 70 per cent were Irish, though the proportion of Irish in Glasgow to the total population was between 25 and 30 per cent. Charity organizations would also tell them that no less than 70 per cent of the applicants for relief were of Irish origin.

It was time that the people of Scotland realized the situation. The complexion and the spirit of our Scottish civilization were being altered by a large alien race in our midst, people of different ideals and faith and blood. Professor Phillimore had written that within a generation the Roman Catholic Church in Scotland would be more predominant than in the Eastern States of America – which implied that the power of that Church in the Eastern States was so great that it was impossible for any politician to do anything that might be remotely antagonistic to its people. The time might come when political parties would not touch this question, when men in positions of public authority and power would be afraid to speak, to see this land passing into strange hands. (Applause.) . . .

The Rev. Dr White, Glasgow, remarked that the problem was very difficult, but it was also very urgent. That was specially felt in the West. The question was not one between Roman Catholicism and Protestantism; it was a question of how to safeguard the Scottish nationality. Our civilization differed from that of those immigrants; the spirit of our institutions was widely different. The problem was how to regulate the incoming of those new forces from Ireland, Italy, and Jewry so as to be a strength and not a menace – how to fuse those heterogenous elements into one essential whole so that they should be Scottish and not foreign. The need was for regulation of emigration, as every other nation did. (Applause.) The main purpose of the report was to bring before the community and the attention of statesmen an urgent problem which called for solutions . . .

The Rev. G. W. Mackay, Killin, suggested that it was exceedingly dangerous to use the word 'alien' in this connection. Were the great majority of the English an alien race? Was the great mass of Protestants in Ulster an alien race? ('No.') He agreed that immigration should be regulated, and that it was in a wise, statesmanlike regulation that to a large extent a solution of this problem lay. He deprecated Mr Main's references to the Labour members in Glasgow. (Hear, hear.)

Eric Liddell Wins Gold at the Olympics, 11 July 1924

THE *EDINBURGH EVENING NEWS*

At the Olympics in Paris in 1924, the Edinburgh-born runner Eric Liddell refused to take part in the heats for the 100 metres race he was a hot favourite to win because they were held on a Sunday, on which day as a devout Christian he was unable to run. Instead, he competed for the 200 metres, for which he won bronze, and the 400 metres, which he went on to win with spectacular speed, breaking the world record with a time of 47.6 seconds. 'The secret of my success over the 400 metres,' he later said, 'is that I run the first 200 metres as hard as I can. Then, for the second 200 metres, with God's help, I run harder.' Liddell later became a missionary in China, and died from a brain tumour in a prison-of-war camp in Japan in 1945. The story of his Olympic victory was told in the film Chariots of Fire *(1981).*

It was Liddell who first caught the eye as they came round the first bend. The Scot set up a terrific pace. He ran as if he were wild with inspiration, like some demon. And as he flew along to the accompaniment of a roar, the experts wondered whether Liddell would crack, such was the pace he set out to travel. 'Liddell' was shrieked, 'Imbach' was thundered by the Swiss, 'Taylor' was shouted by a finely drilled American clique; 'Butler', 'Fitch' in turn were yelled. Liddell, yards ahead, came round the bend for the straight, and as he did so he pulled harder at himself, for Fitch was getting nearer. There was Butler too, and Imbach to be reckoned with. It was the last fifty metres that meant the making or breaking of Liddell. Just for a second it was feared that he would kill himself by the terrible speed he had got up, but to the joy of the British camp, he remained chock full of fight. Imbach, perhaps fifty yards from the tape, fell. It was then Liddell or Fitch. The Scotsman had so surely got his teeth into the race that the American could not hold, and Liddell got home first by what, considering the formidable opposition, was almost a remarkable finish. Butler was third, Johnson next, and then Taylor, who had the bad luck to stumble a yard or two from the finish.

The Invention of Television, October 1925

JOHN LOGIE BAIRD

John Logie Baird, the son of a Helensburgh minister, was an irrepressible inventor from a young age, starting with a telephone exchange that cut the electricity supply to Helensburgh, and later bringing electric light to the oil-lit manse. He first conceived the notion of television in 1903, when he was about fifteen, but it was not until he was in his thirties that he had the time to devote to experimenting. Prior to that his most successful innovation had been heated socks. Using a collection of scrap materials, and working from a garret in London, he finally succeeded in transmitting the first televized images.

In spite of every effort . . . I could not get anything like enough light to operate the photoelectric cells available and I decided to try either to make a new cell or to find some way of using the selective selenium cell. Two devices sensitive to light were known, the selenium cell and the photoelectric cell. The photoelectric cell of those days was so extremely insensitive to light that no detectable signals could be got from it, except by shining a powerful light directly into it. It could be used to show the difference between total darkness and the light from a powerful arc lamp beam, so that it was possible by interposing simple shapes in the path of an arc lamp beam, to send their shadows; but to use it for true television where all the light available would be relatively infinitesimal light thrown back from, say, a human face, was utterly out of the question.

The selenium cell was enormously more sensitive, but it had what all writers on the subject agreed was an insurmountable objection to its use – a time lag; that is it took some little time to respond to light.

I made a number of efforts to increase the sensitivity of the photo-electric cells and to find other materials which would give greater reactions to light. The light sensitivity of the human eye, according to Eldridge, Green and certain others, resides in a purple fluid found in the retina of the eye, and called the visual purple.

I decided to make an experimental cell using this substance, and called at the Charing Cross Ophthalmic Hospital, and asked to see the chief surgeon. I told him I wanted an eye for some research work I was doing on visual purple. He thought I was a doctor and was very helpful.

'You've come at an appropriate time,' he said, 'I am just taking out an eye, and will let you have it, if you will take a seat until the operation is over.'

I was handed an eye wrapped in cotton wool – a gruesome object. I made a crude effort to dissect this with a razor, but gave it up and threw the whole mess into the canal. My efforts to produce a sensitive cell without time lag proving abortive, I decided to try selenium cells and see what could be done – if anything – to overcome the time lag. The first thing I tried was to use interrupted light, by passing the light rays through a serrated disc, which acted as a light chopper. The time lag did not enter into the matter. The cell had to distinguish only between interruptions and no interruptions. With this I could use selenium but the light chopper split the picture into crude bars, so nothing could be sent but coarse outlines. I discarded the chopper and concentrated on the problem of overcoming the time lag.

I used, as the object for my experimental transmission, a ventriloquist's dummy's head. This came out on the screen as a streaky blob. What was happening was this: When the light fell on the cell, the current, instead of jumping instantly to its full value, rose slowly and continued rising as long as the light fell on it. Then when the light was cut off the current did not stop instantly, but only stopped increasing and began falling, taking an appreciable time to get to zero. While watching this effect, it occurred to me that it could be cured or mitigated if I superimposed a curve representing the rate of change of the current with time upon the curve of current with time.

By putting a transformer in the circuit I could, in effect, accomplish this. The moment the light fell upon the cell there would be a change from no current to current. And although the current would be small the rate of change would be great; again at the time when the current changed from increasing to decreasing, the rate of change would be maximum, so that I would get a big up kick and a big down kick when required. My amplifier was a DC battery coupled amplifier (and a source of infinite worry). Now I decided to build a second amplifier, battery coupled but with one transformer coupled stage, so that one amplifier could give me the time/current curve, and the second the time/rate of current curve. I would then mix the two until the time lag was corrected. And this I proceeded to do. I was on the right track.

Funds were going down, the situation was becoming desperate and we were down to our last £30 when at last, one Friday in the first week of October 1925, everything functioned properly. The image of the dummy's head formed itself on the screen with what appeared to me almost unbelievable clarity. I had got it! I could scarcely believe my eyes, and felt myself shaking with excitement.

I ran down the little flight of stairs to Mr Cross's office and seized by the arm his office boy William Taynton, hauled him upstairs and put him in front of the transmitter. I then went to the receiver only to find the screen a blank. William did not like the lights and the whirring discs and had withdrawn out of range. I gave him 2/6 and pushed his head into position. This time he came through and on the screen I saw the flickering, but clearly recognizable, image of William's face – the first face seen by television – and he had to be bribed with 2/6 for the privilege of achieving this distinction.

The Origins of Miss Jean Brodie, 1929

MURIEL SPARK

Miss Jean Brodie, the schoolteacher created by novelist Muriel Spark, has become an immortal literary character. Spark, who was born in 1918, went to Gillespie's School for Girls in Edinburgh. Even at that age she was known as the school's 'poet and dreamer'. She went on to become one of the finest writers of her generation, living most of her life away from Scotland, in Africa, London, New York, Rome and latterly Tuscany. She never, however, forgot her homeland, or the influence it exerted on her writing and her imagination. Here she describes the origins of her beloved but sinister schoolmistress.

The walls of our classrooms had hitherto been covered with our own paintings and drawings, records of travels, pages from the *National Geographic*, portraits of exotic animals and birds. But now I come to Miss Christina Kay, that character in search of an author, whose classroom walls were adorned with reproductions of early and Renaissance paintings, Leonardo da Vinci, Giotto, Fra Lippo Lippi, Botticelli. She borrowed these from the senior art department, run by handsome Arthur Couling. We had the Dutch masters and Corot. Also displayed was a newspaper cutting of Mussolini's Fascisti marching along the streets of Rome.

I fell into Miss Kay's hands at the age of eleven. It might well be said that she fell into my hands. Little did she know, little did I know, that she bore within her the seeds of the future Miss Jean Brodie, the main character in my novel, in a play on the West End of London and on Broadway, in a film and a television series.

I do not know exactly why I chose the name Miss Brodie. But recently I learned that Charlotte Rule, that young American woman who taught me to read when I was three, had been a Miss Brodie and a schoolteacher before her marriage. Could I have heard this fact and recorded it unconsciously?

In a sense Miss Kay was nothing like Miss Brodie. In another sense she was far above and beyond her Brodie counterpart. If she could have met 'Miss Brodie' Miss Kay would have put the fictional character firmly in her place. And yet no pupil of Miss Kay's has failed to recognize her, with joy and great nostalgia, in the shape of Miss Jean Brodie in her prime.

She entered my imagination immediately. I started to write about her even then. Her accounts of her travels were gripping, fantastic. Besides turning in my usual essays about how I spent my holidays, I wrote poems about how she had spent her various holidays (in Rome, for example, or Egypt, or Switzerland). I thought her experiences more interesting than mine, and she loved it. Frances [Niven], too, fell entirely under her spell. In fact, we all did, as is testified by the numerous letters I have received from time to time from Miss Kay's former pupils.

I had always enjoyed watching teachers. We had a large class of about forty girls. A full classroom that size, with a sole performer on stage before an audience sitting in rows looking and listening, is essentially theatre.

From my first days at school I had been far more interested in the looks, the clothes, the gestures, of the individual teachers than I was in their lessons. With Miss Kay, I was fascinated by both. She was the ideal dramatic instructor, and it is not surprising that her reincarnation, Miss Brodie, has always been known as a 'good vehicle for an actress'.

It was not that Miss Kay overacted; indeed, she never acted at all. She was a devout Christian, deeply versed in the Bible. There could have been no question of a love-affair with the art master, or a sex-affair with the singing master, as in Miss Brodie's life. But children are quick to perceive possibilities, potentialities: in a remark, perhaps in some remote context; in a glance, a smile. No, Miss Kay was not literally Miss Brodie, but I think Miss Kay had it in her, unrealized, to be the character I invented.

Years and years later, some time after the publication of *The Prime of*

Miss Jean Brodie, Frances Niven (now Frances Cowell), my dear best friend of those days, observed in a letter:

Surely 75% is Miss Kay? Dear Miss Kay! of the cropped iron grey hair with fringe (and heavy black moustache!) and undisputable admiration for Il Duce. Hers was the expression 'crème de la crème' – hers the revealing extra lessons on art and music that stay with me yet. She it was who took us both (who were especial favourites of hers –? – part of the as yet unborn Brodie Set) to see Pavlova's last performance at the Empire Theatre. Who took us for afternoon teas at McVities.

The Evacuation of St Kilda, 29 and 30 August 1930

THE *GLASGOW HERALD*

By 1930 only thirty-eight people were left on the once thriving island of St Kilda, and many of them were old. For decades the population had been finding its marginal way of life increasingly gruelling, and after the First World War, which gave a few the opportunity to see something of the outside world, discontent with an almost medieval way of life spread. As the number of able-bodied islanders dwindled and crops failed, so hardship heightened for a society dependent on climbing cliffs to catch its staple food of fulmar and puffin. When the final evacuation came, there was little regret among those leaving. Many were wholly unsentimental about selling their distinctive spinning wheels and oil cruses to those desperate for relics from this unique outpost of civilization. One put a sign in the window of an abandoned house: St Kildan Relics for Sale. Apply Within.

OBAN, Friday, 29 August

A rugged little man with his jacket buttoned up to his throat to half conceal a red 'kerchief, and wearing well-patched blue trousers, stood with a melancholy mongrel beside a turf cleit at the base of Ruival and looked steadily out to sea between the Point of Coll and Levenish towards a blur of eastern horizon. On his left rose the towering green cone of Conachair, grey with screes and steaming with mist, at the base of which are the tin-roofed cottages of the village, held back from the rocky shore by pastured croftlands. On his right the sun shone out of the sea on steep green slopes which come to sharp pinnacles black as the Coolin tops.

Under his gaze and ahead was the village bay, or Loch Hirta as some call it, the only landing-place on the island. . . . The sentinel on the cliff and the wet-haired dog had stood vigil on the cliff from after dawn, patient and unwearying. Many of his kind had done the same thing before him, but few would do it again. The rain swept down in fierce squalls, but still he stood, the moisture sparkling on his dark eyebrows. The white vapours draped Levenish and sea and sky melted into one, but still he stayed.

For two days now the islanders had been waiting. Then suddenly he straightened. A way out on the waters to where the Sound of Harris lay behind the cloud of mist was the spectred shape of a narrow steamer. He rose, tapped the dog with his stick, and lumbered along the ledge towards the village with the news.

His look-out was ended. The last landing ship to call before the islanders deserted their wild volcanic rock in the Atlantic had been sighted.

The *Dunara Castle*, that was to carry away the sheep of the hills and the simple goods and chattels of the population before the Admiralty vessel would come to remove them too and complete the story, was swinging between the headlands as man and dog crossed the dyked pastures towards the village.

This was the beginning of the end of St Kilda as a human habitation. The episodes of the watcher belong to Wednesday. On Thursday the fishery cruiser *Harebell*, commissioned to clear the island, came over by Levenish and dropped anchor beside the *Dunara Castle* . . .

The evacuation was suddenly dramatized by the advent of the navy. Bugles sounded on the deck. Presently a boat was lowered from the davits. Three braided officers were pulled away to the shore by navymen in white ducks . . .

Soon the waters of the bay were churned with traffic. The black flat-bottomed boats of the St Kildans, sea water over the floor-boards, were in strange contrast to the gleaming enamel and glistening brass of the naval craft.

All morning between quay and steamer they plied with sheep, cows, dresser, tables, and canvas bags to be lodged on the *Dunara Castle*.

The embarkation of the shaggy Highland cattle was extraordinary. The great tan beasts followed in the wake of the boats which towed them from shore to ship until, alongside, they were hoisted aboard by a noose around the horns, their big eyes bulging and their necks taut with the bellying weight below.

Before the morning sun had melted the mists on Conachair, the pens between decks on the *Dunara Castle* were packed with the hill sheep, Blackfaced and cross bred soays, that look like Nubian goats, while the holds were stowed with the frugal household goods of a unique race . . .

The last black boat rocked away before midday. The *Dunara Castle* closed her hatches, hauled up her anchor, swung round, and steamed towards the entrance of the bay. Her siren shrieked out its farewell blasts, which echoed to the very summit of Conachair.

From two cottage doors white sheets fluttered. One felt a catch in the throat . . .

The people of St Kilda, the last of the sea-girt Hebrides, perched on the edge of the great Atlantic plateau just before the ocean dips to unfathomable depths, have been calmly preparing for evacuation from Monday, four days ago. The *Dunara Castle* was expected on Monday night or thereabouts. All depended upon the weather . . .

The packing and parcelling were begun in the village. . . . The women worked at packing from the hour the sun climbed over the speckled slopes of Conachair. The men were out on Mullack and Carn Mohr, peaks of the mountainous island, with the shepherds and dogs from the Outer Isles, chasing the sheep that had taken refuge on crag and ledge . . .

I went in the dark to visit one of the cottages. . . . I was greeted in Gaelic, which is the language used, English being spoken imperfectly. Through the little lobby filled with laden boxes I passed into the living room.

The St Kildans are not a forgotten people, living in black houses. The cottages, by many standards in the isles, are comfortable. There is nothing here to resemble the hovel I once saw in Skye, so low-roofed that one crawled into it, and which had yet produced two Metropolitan policemen.

As I sat down in the St Kildan cottage the father and three sons in the blue fisher jerseys and patched and repatched trousers, just returned from inhospitable hills, were steaming in the warmth. A single oil lamp lit the deep shadows on the boarded walls, which were plastered with newspaper illustrations and lithographs. A stock pot sat by the open fireplace. It contained the household supper of salted mutton, a staple dish, with porridge, syrup, baked scones, dried ling, and the exclusive dishes of the islanders – salted fulmar and roasted puffin, the food of a race of expert fowlers.

In a corner rested a broom of gannet's wings used for sweeping the stone floor. This broom, the St Kildan mother told me, is far superior to a heather switch, but it belongs to the hygiene of a later day, for once the St Kildans allowed the refuse to gather deep on the floor of their dwellings, and cleared it out for manure once a year.

The women, as always, worked as they talked, the mother sitting at her spinning wheel and a daughter of 13 with glorious hair – a rarity among the St Kildans – adroitly carding wool with hand implements.

Yesterday morning I was awakened early by the next phase of the Exodus. Through a sound sleep on the floor of the schoolhouse . . . I heard the steady tramp of feet and of quick jabbering in the Gaelic. Usually it has been the bleating of half a thousand head of sheep awaiting shipment that has called me in the morning.

I rose and looked through the window into the white mist that swept coldly over the slopes of the Oiseval and blotted out the bay. Across the glebe towards the school, which is attached to the church buildings, came a chain of St Kildans from the village bearing boxes and furniture on their backs . . . Now they were ready and waiting for the approach of the *Dunara Castle*, men were out on the slopes of the Ruaival scanning the horizon like Cortes on his peak in Darien . . .

Perhaps the *Dunara Castle* will come this day, perhaps it won't. We wait for a sail, like Robinson Crusoe. As we wait there is plenty of time for reflection. We are about to leave an island that has been inhabited since the second century. . . . Within a few short hours, as time is rated in this island, where the clock is given the same short shrift as all things mechanical, the hearths will be stone cold, and the people will be gone and scattered to places unfamiliar.

Two of them, Ewan Macdonald and his sister . . . have never before left St Kilda. They will see roads, horses, and trains for the first time, but to what end?

The transplantation from the island, with its distinctive life and habits, to the routinized mainland will be salutary. No longer will turfs be cut on the Mullack Mhor to be stored in the drystone cleits. No more will barefooted St Kildans descend fearlessly that dreaded 1,000 feet fall of Conachair to the frothed sea far below in search of the fulmar, that skunk of birds whose flesh, oil, and feathers once sustained life. The 60-fathom manila ropes will go into the limbo where the salted cowhide and horsehair strands of their fathers went.

August is now nearly over. The young fulmar is undisturbed. September is nearly here, but the nests of the gong, or tender solan goose, are not raped. The last trip has been made in the lug sailboat to Boreray where the shearing kept the men for long summer months. The women have ended their task of snaring the puffins or 'Tammie Norrie,' the sea pigeons that look like parrots and taste like kipper.

The churns are curios and the handmills are with the collectors. St Kilda is of the historied past. The play is ended.

Burns's Halo Is Tarnished, 1930

CATHERINE CARSWELL

The publication of Catherine Carswell's seminal biography of Burns, which was serialized in the Daily Record, *caused a sensation among the Burns Federation and other Burns idolizers, who were deeply offended at her portrayal of him as a less than saintly, carousing and womanizing genius.*

This morning (through the newspaper where it was serialized) I had an anonymous letter containing a *bullet*, which I was requested to use upon myself that the world might be left 'a brighter cleaner and better place'. So evidently the fun has started. Oh Scotland, oh my country!

The Loch Ness Monster, 1933

LT-COMMANDER R. T. GOULD RN (RETIRED)

The Loch Ness monster first appeared in print in Adamnan's Life of St Columba, *in which the missionary apparently persuaded a fierce sea creature to close its fearsome jaws and go in peace, rather than devour Columba's fellow monk. It was not until 1933, however, that the first newspaper account of a sighting of the beast was published in the* Inverness Courier, *after which a flurry of reported sightings filled the papers. Such was the excitement the monster aroused that the authorities posted policemen around the Loch to prevent anyone harming the creature should it reappear. The reports drew the attention of an amateur marine naturalist who considered himself something of an expert on sea serpents. He conducted his own scrupulous survey of the facts by talking to fifty-one witnesses.*

When I went North my mental attitude towards the Loch Ness 'monster' was one of detachment, not untinged with pity for a number of honest but misguided persons who (so I judged) were making much unnecessary fuss about a goose which they took for a swan. Of all possible or conceivable eventualities the one farthest from my mind was that I should be confronted with a mass of testimony demonstrating that a sea creature, in whose existence the vast majority of educated persons do not believe, was domiciled in a fresh water loch. Still, 'facts are stubborn chiels . . .' and only a totally unscientific mind will dismiss a statement of fact as impossible a priori, without investigating the evidence upon which that statement is based.

Within the limits of an article it is impossible to give even an adequate summary of the first-hand evidence which I collected, and which I hope to publish in full at an early date. But a few specimens will indicate its nature.

The most striking feature of the Loch Ness 'monster' – one which differentiates it, in type, from all other known living creatures – is a very long and slender neck, capable of being elevated very considerably above the water-level. The observations of Mr B. A. Russell, MA, the schoolmaster at Fort Augustus, were made, on October 1, 1933, in almost ideal conditions. He was on an eminence overlooking the south-western extremity of the loch, and about 100 ft above the water level. The day was brilliantly sunny, and the surface of the loch was as smooth as glass. There was no haze, and the creature was in view for 12 minutes (10.10 a.m. to 10.22 a.m.), moving slowly from left to right at a maximum distance of 800 yards and a minimum of 700.

What he saw, and subsequently sketched, was a serpentine head and neck, arched like a swan's, dark in colour, rising fully five feet out of the water and turning occasionally from side to side. He saw nothing of the body, but a V-shaped ripple spread off from the neck at the point where it met the water. The creature ultimately sank slowly, and disappeared. As he told me, he had previously been disposed to believe that some large creature (probably a big seal) had entered the loch – but he had never in the least expected to see anything of this 'prehistoric' kind.

A similar view of the head and neck, with occasional glimpses of the body, was obtained from the Halfway House, Alltsigh, by (among others) Miss J. S. Fraser and Miss M. Howden, on September 22, about 11 a.m. In this case also (as in nearly all) the conditions of visibility, etc., were practically perfect. Miss Fraser noticed two frill-like appendages at the junction of the head and neck . . .

Later in the same day the creature was seen off Balnafoich, which is considerably further up the Loch towards Inverness. Its speed on the surface was then estimated at 15 knots – as also, it may be recalled, was that of the Daedalus creature (1848) and of that seen by the SS *Umfuli*, Captain R. J. Cringle, in 1893 . . .

The majority of the witnesses, however, have not seen the head and neck elevated above water. The creature has more often presented the appearance of a large dark hump, or humps, moving through the water with considerable commotion at the rear, and occasionally also at the sides. The number of the humps varies; the aspect most frequently noted has been that of one large hump – resembling the back of a 'killer' whale minus its dorsal fin – but two humps, the large one and a smaller in front, with a water-space between, have also been seen by several witnesses.

Light is thrown upon this point by the evidence of three ladies – Miss Rattray, Miss A. Rattray, and Miss M. Hamilton, MA – who saw the creature off Dores on August 24. It appeared to be following astern of a drifter going towards Inverness, and looked like a line of five dark humps, the second (counting from the front) being notably larger and higher out of the water than any other, while the fourth and fifth were somewhat shorter and lower than the first and third. The humps (which, as sketched by Miss Rattray, most strikingly recall the creatures seen off Gloucester, Mass., in 1817, and in Loch Hourn, 1872) rose and fell slightly, with an undulating motion, while, at times, all rose or sank on an even keel. In consequence of this there were sometimes five humps visible, sometimes three (the two rear ones being submerged), and sometimes only the largest (second) hump.

Incidentally, the conventional 'school of porpoises' theory is not applicable here; the motion was quite different, and no dorsal fins were seen. The mean of three independent estimates of the lengths of the line of humps, as compared with that of the drifter, was that the former was at least three-quarters of the latter. The drifter, I have since ascertained, was the *Grand Hay* of Lossiemouth, whose length is 88 ft.

One witness of the 'single-hump' aspect (Mr Shaw of Whitefield) noticed underwater and some little distance in front of the hump something undulating up and down, but never quite breaking the surface, and another (Miss C. McDonald) observed, on either side of the hump, continuous splashing – apparently made by two objects 'moving like oars' . . .

A preliminary analysis of my data suggests the following conclusions. The 'monster' has a length of at least 50 feet or so, with a maximum diameter of some 5 feet. The neck and tail are long and tapering. The head is comparatively small, not much larger than the neck – which can be elevated to a considerable height above the water. The colour of the body, under strong sunlight, is indeterminate, something between dark brown and dark grey. The skin is rough, presenting a granulated (but not scaled) appearance. A small ridge, darker in colour, runs along the crest of the back. The body appears to be flexible to some extent, both laterally and vertically. There are small appendages, possibly gills, at the sides of the head where it joins the neck. Finally there are at least two, and possibly four, propelling fins or paddles.

On the whole, despite the advocates of the 'surviving plesiosaurus,' this and other 'sea-serpent' cases, suggest to me nothing so much as a vastly enlarged, long-necked marine form of the common newt. However, that is a matter for a qualified zoologist with an open mind.

There can, at all events, be little question that Loch Ness contains at least one specimen of the rarest and least known of all living creatures. Unless it comes and goes – as it may do – it has been there some years; I have first-hand evidence of its having been seen in 1932 and 1931, as well as second-hand accounts of several earlier appearances. Presumably it made its way up the Ness by night during a spate, and has found the loch an admirable refuge from its natural enemies, the sperm whale and the 'killer'.

The Queen's Governess, 1933

MARION CRAWFORD

At the age of twenty-four, a shy young woman from Kilmarnock became governess to Princesses Elizabeth – known as Lilibet – and Margaret Rose at their home at 145 Piccadilly. Marion Crawford was a much loved member of the family until, after her retirement, she published a memoir of her young charges. The Royal Family was outraged, and severed all contact with her. From her house on the road between Aberdeen and Balmoral the disconsolate Crawford would watch the royal cars pass without a head turning in her direction. Some believe she had been persuaded into publishing this anodyne and affectionate biography by her husband, who had resented being kept waiting for several years to marry because the timing of his fiancée's engagement did not suit the Royal Family's requirements. After his death, Crawford attempted to commit suicide. Some years later she died, still unforgiven by her employers.

It was a homelike and unpretentious household I found myself in. It was a home the centre of which was undoubtedly the nurseries. They were on the top floor, comfortable, sunny rooms that opened on to a landing beneath a big glass dome. Round the dome stood some thirty-odd toy horses about a foot high on wheels.

'That's where we stable them,' Lilibet explained, and she showed me that each horse there had its own saddle and bridle, which were kept immaculate and polished by the little girls themselves. . . . Stable routine was strictly observed. Each horse had its saddle removed nightly and was duly fed and watered. No matter what else might be going on, this was a must-be-done chore. The obsession for toy horses lasted unbroken until real horses became important some years later, and even then the old friends were not forgotten. They stood in a row along one of the corridors at Buckingham Palace, their grooming basket at the end of the row, for many a year.

One of Lilibet's favourite games that went on for years was to harness me with a pair of red reins that had bells on them, and off we would go, delivering groceries. I would be gentled, patted, given my nosebag, and jerked to a standstill, while Lilibet, at imaginary houses, delivered imaginary groceries and held long and intimate conversations with her make-believe customers.

Sometimes she would whisper to me, 'Crawfie, you must pretend to be impatient. Paw the ground a bit.' So I would paw.

Frosty mornings were wonderful, for then my breath came in clouds, 'just like a proper horse,' said Lilibet contentedly. Or she herself would be the horse, prancing around, sidling up to me, nosing in my pockets for sugar, making convincing little whinnying noises.

Besides the toy horses there were other four-legged friends in the world outside. A brewer's dray with a fine pair often pulled up in Piccadilly just below, stopped by the traffic lights. There they would stand, steaming, on winter nights. The little girls, their faces pressed to the nursery window, would watch for them fondly, anxious if they were late. On wet streets anything might happen to big dray horses. And many a weary little pony trotting home at the end of the day in its coster's cart little dreamed of the wealth of royal sympathy it roused, from that upper window.

Edinburgh and Its Street Girls, 1934

EDWIN MUIR

In 1934–5 writer Edwin Muir travelled the breadth of Scotland to take the temperature of his country in what proved to be a rather dyspeptic analysis. Here he records his impressions of the capital.

Within a stone's throw of one end of Princes Street begins a promenade quite different in character. This is Leith Street and its continuation Leith Walk, a long spacious boulevard containing some fine old houses, which have with time sunk to the status of working-class tenements. Here, instead of the cosy tea-rooms and luxurious hotel lounges of Princes Street, one suddenly finds oneself among ice-cream and fish-and-chip bars and pubs. At one point the two different streams of promenaders are brought within a few yards of each other; yet they scarcely ever mingle, so strong is the sense of social distinction bred by city life. They turn back when they reach this invisible barrier, apparently without thought or desire, as if they were stalking in a dream; and if, through necessity or whim, an occasional pedestrian should trespass for a little on enemy ground, he is soon frightened and scurries back as fast as he can. The prostitutes are the sole class who rise superior to this inhibition. They live, as members of the proletariat, in the poorer districts, but their main beat is Princes Street, and it has in their eyes the prestige and familiarity of a business address. But their occupation seems to be the sole remaining one in modern society which acts as a general dissolvent of all social distinctions; and that in reality is because they are tacitly outlawed by all society, in which the principle of class distinction is constantly operative. The ordinary crowds, not possessing this classless power, turn back at a certain point. The upper and lower middle classes, the men about town, clerks, commercial travellers, students, patrol Princes Street, because, without being conscious of it, they look upon that walk as a preserve where they can be at their complete ease, and where nobody will ever intrude upon them. And this calculation is justified. Their seclusion is as perfect as if they were behind locked doors.

The Hungry Prostitute, 1935

RALPH GLASSER

Ralph Glasser was brought up in the Jewish quarter of the Gorbals between the First and Second World Wars, and began work in a garment factory at the age of fourteen. After years of studying at night he won a scholarship to Oxford University. He went on to become a psychologist, economist and notable memoirist. This is a record of a conversation he had with a fellow factory worker as they walked home one night through the Saltmarket, a particularly desolate and ill-lit district renowned as the haunt of prostitutes.

We were walking home from the factory late one night, about ten o'clock, the streets stilled. Something in his [Alec's] mood suggested he wanted a cue to talk.

I said: 'Have you ever had one of them?'

'Aye, a few times,' he replied in assumed indifference, 'when ah've been hard up for ma hole. That wis where ah had ma first hoor, when ah was aboo' fifteen. Ah wis jist this minute thinkin' aboo' 'er! In fact she comes tae mind many a time. She wis ma first proper fuck!' He fell silent. 'But that's no' the reason. She wis, ah don't know how tae put i'. She wis warm an' understandin' an', well, she was genuine. She wanted me tae be happy! She made me feel ah wisnae jist *anybody*. Ah'll never ferrget it. Never. A wee thin-faced lassie wi' red hair, verry pale, shiverin' in the cauld wi' a thin coat an' skirt on. A guid bi' older than me she was, aboo' twenty-five. An' wi' a weddin' ring on.'

He pushed his lips out: 'It wis one payday, an' it wis snowin' an' cauld, an' ah wis comin' away frae the workshop late at night dog tired an' for some reason ah don't remember ah wis gaun hame through the Saltmarket an' no' thinkin' aboo' anythin'. An' suddenly there was this lassie beside me an' caught haud o' ma hand sayin': "C'mon ah'll show ye somethin' wonderful!" An' she pulled me intae a big dark archway an' before ah knew anythin' she'd put ma haun' up 'er skirt – Jesus ah can feel it this minute – an' she'd got haud o' me an' a couldnae stop masel!' Christ wis ah ashamed! Bu' she said, quiet an' soft: "Never yew mind. Ah'll wait. An' ye'll be fine wi' me in a wee while." And she held me tight, an' kissed me as if she really meant i'. An' efter a minute she shivered and said: "Ah'm sae cauld! Ah'm tha' hungry. Will ye gie me a sixpenny piece an' ah'll go an' ge' a bag o' fish an' chips?"'

He snorted. 'If a hoor said that tae me the noo ah widnae trust her tae come back! Bu' ah wis ony a boy. An' she'd been sae warm and gentle wi' me. She looked sae peaked ah wanted 'er tae have somethin' tae eat. Ah gave her a whole shillin'. Ah'd have tae tell ma mither ah'd lost it on ma way hame. In a way that wis true! She took tha' shillin' in baith 'er hauns it could've been a gold sovereign! An' she said: "Yew jist wait here an' rest yersel'. Ah'll be back in a wee minute."

'An' ah wis left standin' there all flustered an' lonely an' wonderin' whit was happenin' tae me. Ah felt ah wis seein' this wurrld fer the verry furrst time. Aye, seein' a lo' o' things fer the furrst time. Ah thought of 'er walkin' aboo' hungry in tha' God forsaken place, through piles o' rubbish an' horse shit dirty white wi' the snow left lyin'. A' the emptiness an' loneliness. And the bitter cauld that had driven a' the ither hoors hame. An' her sae desperate. Grabbin' hold of a boy tae ge' a shillin' aff of, for a bag o' fish an' chips an' pennies fer the gas an' the price o' a pint o' milk! An' *her* bein' nothin' tae me, and *me* bein' nothin' tae her. An' the next minute ah thought: "No. That's wrong! I' *is* somethin'! If it wis nothin' ah wouldnae be carin' at a'! It's *got* tae mean somethin'!" Ah started shiverin', standin' there under the arch, the freezin' cauld creepin' up ma legs frae the pavement. Ah wanted tae feel 'er warm body pressin' against me again, an' 'er gentleness, sayin' nothing', jist *bein'* there wi' me. An' then ah started wonderin' if it wid be different fuckin' her than blockin' ma sister.'

I should not have been shocked but I was, and I must have shown it, or at least that I was surprised, perhaps by the slightest shift in my step or a questioning turn of the head, for he looked at me in astonishment. 'Yours've done it wi' yew surely?'

I shook my head, not sure what words would fit.

'Come on!' he said, disbelieving, 'Yewr sisters must've shown ye whit's what? Ah'll lay ye odds o' a hundred tae one ye'll no' find a feller, who's go' an older sister, who's no' been intae 'er – aye many, many times, sleepin' in the same bed night efter night! Hiv ye really no' done i'? Ah'll no' tell on ye mind!'

'No. It really is true.' I searched for a bland excuse. 'Maybe it was because they were so much older than me.'

Most Gorbals parents, trying to instil the standard prohibitions, fought against impossible odds. Girls and boys were not even supposed to undress in each other's presence after a certain age, but in most families they had to share bedrooms and as often as not beds, and so the rules were dead letters . . .

Alex paused for only a moment: 'Aye, ah see whit ye mean. Maybe that's it.' He dismissed it. 'Anyway, *ma* sister went at i' wi me fer years. She used tae play wi' ma prick in oor bed even before ah'd go' any hair on me; an' after ah grew ma bush an' started comin', she go' me tae take 'er maidenhied.'

The memory jolted him: 'Christ tha' wis a night an' a half! Wonderin' whit tae do aboot the big bloodstain in the bed. Though at first when she saw it she was sae overjoyed – no, ah mean light-hieded like she wis drunk. Ah couldnae understand it . . .

'Well, anyway, in the end we decided she'd pretend she'd had a freak early monthly! An' ah'm no sure tae this day if ma mither believed 'er! Still an' a', nothin' wis said. Efter tha' she go' me tae block 'er over an' over again, nearly every night sometimes! But it wis never a proper fuck 'cos she never let me come inside 'er. She always knew when ah wis goin' tae come an' pulled me oo' jist before. Well, she stopped a' tha' when ah was aboo' sixteen. Ah've go' an idea tha' Father Millan, seein' ah was gettin' tae be a big lad, had a quiet word wi' 'er one day in Confession, an' tellt 'er it was bad for her immortal soul! An' mine too. How 'e knew, well, ye can guess. Them priests! Aye, them priests. They're on tae everythin' that's goin' on. Too bliddy much.'

I wondered if he was about to branch off into that familiar pastime, scurrilous talk about priests and female parishioners. Not this time. The encounter in the Saltmarket long ago, shining within him over all the years, needed to have its say.

'Anyway, as ah wis sayin', ah stood there under the arch freezin'. It wis snowin' again. There wisnae a soul aboo'. Every single hoor must a' given i' up that night. An' ah did begin tae wonder if she'd come back. An' then ah heard the quick steps muffled in the snow, an' ah smelt the chips an' vinegar, an' the next minute she was pressin' against me there in the dark. Shiverin' an' movin' against me tae get the warmth. An' d'ye know? She'd waited till she was back wi' me afore she started to eat any! Ah could tell she wis real hungry 'cos she ate them fish an' chips as if she hadnae had anythin' tae eat fer days. Ah hadnae the herrt tae take a chip frae the bag. Bu' after she'd had most of i', she stood there leanin' close an' put chips in ma mooth on a' a time till the bag was finished . . .'

We walked on for several minutes in silence and I thought he would reveal no more. He needed to, but couldn't.

At last he did, quietly, sombrely: 'Well, as she'd said, ah' wis fine wi' her in the end. She showed me many things. Aye, many things. An' then she came! She really did. A lo' o' hoors jist pretend tae come so's tae make ye feel great. Aye an' tae make ye think they're enterin' intae the spirit o' things an' no' jist standin' there thinkin' aboo' the gas meter! Anyway ah'd never felt anythin' like i'. I' made me feel – ah don't know how tae say it – I' made ma herrt feel full tae burstin' an' then she went very quiet an' hung on tae me all limp an' said: "Haud me up dear ah cannae stand."'

It had all been said sadly. . . . He might have been pouring out his heart for a long lost love. His silence could have been of mourning, and reverence, for the lost bounty of innocence and revelation . . .

'Did you see her again?' I asked.

'Whit did ye say?'

He had fallen into reverie once more.

'Did you ever see that hoor again?'

'See her? Ah wish ah could've stayed wi' 'er fir ever!' The words rushed out. He stopped and looked at me, in wonder at himself . . .

'Ah never fucked 'er again if that's whit ye mean. Bu' ah've seen 'er plenty o' times. She's lived a' the time in the next close tae us! Married wi' two kids. Her man's on the booze, an' knocks 'er aboo' regular. He's given 'er that many black eyes she cannae see tae wurrk. She used tae be a button hole hand. *They* always ge' bad sight, bu' getting' a' them black eyes as well must've buggered up 'er sight good an' proper! She cannae see tae thread the needle any more. Come tae think of i', if 'er eyes'd been be'er she'd 'ave recognized me in the dark that night afore she'd got hold o' me. An' maybe left me alane? Anyway, bein' hungry an' cauld, whit can ye say? She needed that shillin'.'

The Spanish Civil War, May 1937

ETHEL MACDONALD

An anarchist from Bellshill in Glasgow, a city renowned for nurturing passionate left-wing political views, Ethel Macdonald joined the flood of foreigners offering solidarity to the Republicans in the Spanish Civil War, even though when she arrived she could speak scarcely a word of Spanish. Before she left, she urged British workers to act swiftly against 'the unchallenged use of German and Italian troops to aid Franco in Spain'. Here, she describes the outbreak of violence in Barcelona, known as the May Days, in which the Communists turned on the anarchists. Shortly after this Macdonald was imprisoned briefly for her activities, before being escorted back to Britain, severely disillusioned. Her activities earned her the title of the Scots Scarlet Pimpernel.

News reached Jenny and I as we were having after lunch coffee in a little anarchist restaurant not far from our headquarters in the Via Durruti. The messenger told us that three lorry loads of police had made use of the peaceful siesta hour when shops and offices are closed, to launch their attack. They had no difficulty in seizing the ground floor (of the telephone building) but our comrades in the building barricaded the stairways and swept them with machine gun fire thus preventing further assault.

Immediately, crowds gathered outside the building and the streets were filled with anxious men and women. Suddenly the cry was raised – 'To the barricades! To the barricades!' It echoed through the streets and in a very short time firing had broken out all over the city.

It seems that the police had used sandbags and bricks, originally intended to repel Franco's attack, to build complete fortifications round all areas controlled by the Government. Opposite each barricade our anarchist comrades tore up the loose paving stones from the streets to build their own barricades.

Hurrying back to headquarters, Jenny and I passed groups of men and women running, rifles in hand, to their appointed places behind the barricades or in the buildings that we controlled. The roar of traffic had died down and the only sounds were the heavy firing and the screaming of ambulances rushing to and from the hospitals.

Our headquarters were preparing for attack. While men barricaded windows and doors, women dragged out cases of ammunition. Machine guns were mounted and we waited for what we knew was coming. Jenny and I went back to our hotel, the Oriente, that night. We had little difficulty, but we had to be very careful. Actually, the firing had died down when we set out but we were stopped every few yards and searched for arms.

Next morning we decided that our places were with our comrades at headquarters, and at seven we set out. At that hour Spanish women go to market and, knowing this, both sides look out for them and cease fire to allow them to move about.

We mingled with these women, some of whom carried little white flags in their hands. We would slink along a street, hugging a wall. At every corner where we knew there was a barricade, one of the women would poke her flag round.

At this signal firing would stop and we would scurry across. Some-times, though, firing went on above our heads (it was aimed at windows) and showers of plaster would fall about our ears. Behind every tree and every lamp post there was a soldier on one side or the other, and they would scowl at us or smile, waving us on.

In this way, and by all the back streets, we eventually reached the Via Durruti where we chatted with a comrade while we waited for a lull. Five minutes later, looking out of a window in headquarters, we saw him fall, seriously wounded. Once inside we went up to the roof to see if we could see anything. As soon as we stuck our heads outside a burst of firing made us duck quickly and we had to crawl back to safety on our stomachs.

By this time it would have been impossible to put a nose into the Via Durruti. A little bit away from us was the police station. Looking at it from a sheltered window we saw puffs of smoke coming out of every window – for all the world like a wild and woolly west picture. It was the same from another Government building on our other side.

All that day we busied ourselves filling cartridge clips for the soldiers and preparing meals for them. At meal times we felt that all the food we had was needed for them, and that we might try to have our meals in a little restaurant a few streets away at the back which had remained open for us.

It lay in an area under our control. Still it was funny to see the men lay down their arms and hustle through those few streets, have their lunch and then hustle back and start firing again. If they had taken their arms with them, they ran a risk of being stopped by the police who might have broken through.

This was our life for the next three days. We could not get back to the hotel so at nights we dragged mattresses under the windows of our rooms (the safest part of the rooms) and tried to get what sleep we could.

At seven in the morning we always made use of the lull in the firing to have a little walk. We would go up past the police station, or down by the other government building, just to see if we could find out anything of importance.

Of course we were stopped every few minutes, but as we carried no arms and were women, we were allowed to pass. At the barricades we watched the soldiers and police drag easy chairs out of the nearby buildings and sit – smoking till it was time to start firing again. They seemed to take things as coolly as that. Sometimes we were able to take some food to them.

When we did that we had to creep up to the barricades with it, crouching on the ground. If we had showed a head above, it would have been a signal for the firing to start again. From our windows we saw a motor car being shot at by our enemies. We did not know who was in it. Actually there were three men who managed to get out and take cover in a doorway where they were stuck.

One man kept firing to draw the others off, and we sent an armoured car out to bring the men in. When the car stopped beside them it was struck by a bomb, and a comrade was injured but we saved the men. On another occasion twelve comrades were dragged from their car shot. When the ambulance people tried to go to them they were ordered back and told that if they went to the men they would be fired upon. Our comrades did not want to kill people and they withheld their fire as much as possible. They never attacked, contenting themselves with defence.

Dead and wounded lay between the barricades. Wrecked cars were in every other street. Hardly a pane of glass was left in a window and all street lamps were shattered. Walls were wrecked by bombs. Altogether 300 of our comrades were killed during those three days and I have no idea how many were wounded. As soon as the fighting stopped, wives and mothers hurried through the streets searching for their loved ones. Some, hearing that they had been wounded rushed from hospital to hospital. The streets were filled with fear-stricken and frenzied women.

Benny Lynch Retains His Triple Crown, 12 October 1937

THE *SCOTSMAN*

Benny Lynch, the Glasgow boxer, was one of the most talented but tragic figures in Scottish sporting legend. The first Scot to hold a world title, he was undisputed world champion from 1937 to 1938. The following match, however, was one of his last moments of glory. Thereafter, his life began to crumble, and he was more in the headlines for personal problems, drinking high among them, than for his fighting prowess. Even so, in his career he won eighty-two out of 110 bouts, an astonishing record. He died in 1946, at the age of thirty-three.

Benny Lynch (Glasgow) successfully defended his World, European, and British Fly-Weight Boxing Championships at Shawfield Park,

Glasgow, last night against Peter Kane (Liverpool), the Scot winning by a knock-out in the 13th round.

The fight was fought at a furious pace, but from the sixth round it was evident that the Champion was the stronger.

The big fight was preceded by an even bigger fight outside the ground. Only the humour of the thousands who clamoured for admission, and the good-natured handling of them by scores of police on foot and on horse-back, prevented an ugly scene. There were insufficient entrances to allow ticket-holders to get in, and when people did get past the first barriers, they found themselves unable to enter the arena itself.

Police had to be called to the scene to pacify ringside ticket-holders, a minority of whom were adopting a threatening attitude to the officials, owing to their inability to gain admittance. Many holders of the dearer tickets made a rush for the only apparent entrance available – to the cheaper parts of the ground – and, in the middle of it all, Peter Kane arrived with his fiancée, Miss Margaret Dunn. They were separated in the struggle, and Miss Dunn was one of those left on the fringe of the huge crowd.

At one of the 'popular' sides of the ground the railings were torn down, and a policeman who sprang to the breach was stoned.

In many cases it took well over an hour and a half for a ringside ticket-holder to travel between the main gate and the enclosure. This long wait had to be endured in pouring rain, and with the ground underfoot rapidly churning to mud . . .

The fight, which had many sensational moments, must rank amongst the finest title bouts ever seen. The opening rounds were especially brilliant, the boxing, hard-hitting and speed of the encounter being without parallel in Scotland.

Lynch proved to be a great and confident champion, and Kane an almost equally great challenger, who withstood terrific punishment and rallied time and again in an effort to gain a knock-out. The champion, however, was always stronger, and apart from one bad round, was the master of his opponent from the first gong.

It was with the first punch of the contest that there was the first sensation. Both boxers rushed from their corners, and Lynch as he did repeatedly throughout the fight, beat his rival to the punch, and shook him with a right swing, and followed so quickly with his deadly left hook that Kane toppled back against the referee and onto the floor.

In face of that devastating onslaught the Lancashire boxer did marvels to weather the opening rounds. Not only so, but he boxed cleverly, and helped to make the early exchanges amongst the best ever seen in a title fight. For three rounds champion and challenger fought at a furious pace, with never a hold or clinch, and after the pace had slowed for a round or two, they rallied to further fierce exchanges.

Lynch, however, was supremely confident. From the moment he stepped into the ring there was never any doubt about his fitness. This was the old Lynch. While Kane smiled quite happily to the cheers of partisan followers, he appeared to be a little drawn and nervous.

It was amazing how Lynch could always open the rounds with the first punch, and only in the seventh, when Kane made his most magnificent rally, was the champion in real difficulty. That bad spell, however, proved that Lynch still had the stronger punch, and thereafter there were occasions when he not only took what appeared to be risks, but deliberately enticed his opponent by leaving himself open. It was an amazing display by both boxers, culminating actually in the twelfth round, when the deadly left hook of Lynch completed its work. Kane was 'out' on his feet but tottered around the ring, instinctively avoiding a knock-out. He appeared to be a beaten man in his corner, and he was sent to the floor in the next round, first for a count of seven and then for a full count, after as plucky a display as anyone could have given.

Not another fly-weight could be named who could have survived the opening onslaught by the champion, who fought within himself at other periods but always weakened his opponent with quick and severe cross punches.

Lynch was given a great ovation at the finish. While he jumped about the ring for joy, his supporters swarmed towards the ringside, and outside the ground the streets were lined with crowds acclaiming him.

A Glasgow Orange March, 1938

J. R. ALLAN

One of the most controversial events in Scottish civic life, annual Orange Marches by members of the Protestant Orange Order have acted as touchpapers for violence. Journalist J. R. Allan looked on with some amusement as events took a predictable turn one night in Glasgow.

Once on a November afternoon I was walking along Buchanan Street about half-past four o'clock. It was a busy day: hundreds of fashionable women were trafficking among the shops and the business men were returning from or going to the coffee-rooms. There was an atmosphere of money and well-being, the sort of thing that makes you feel pleased with yourself as long as you have a few shillings in your own pocket. Then a procession came up the street, with blood-red banners, that swayed menacingly under the misty lights. These should have driven the women screaming into the basements of the shops for they bore legends in praise of Moscow, warnings about the wrath to come. 'Communists,' the word flew along the pavements. But no-one screamed. The men that carried the flags were broken beyond violence by the prolonged misery of unemployment and could not sustain the menace of the legends. The ladies in the fur coats could look without fear on the procession, for it was not the first stroke of revolt but another triumph of law and order. A dozen constables were shepherding the marchers, and they were such fine big men and stepped along with such manly dignity that they themselves were the procession. The unemployed seemed to have no community with such defiant banners, such splendid constables, and they may have known it, for they walked without any spirit, as if they realized they had no place in society, not even in their demonstrations against it. The procession turned into George Square. The unemployed dismissed and went home wearily to their bread and margarine. The constables eased their uniform pants and went off to the station with property and privilege resting securely on their broad shoulders. It was just another Glasgow afternoon.

Then some months later I was looking out from the window of a coffee-house in Argyle Street about seven o'clock of a Saturday evening. I heard fife music; then a procession came out from St Enoch's Square. It was a company of Orangemen, or some such Protestants, in full uniform, back from an excursion in the country. They passed, an army terrible with banners, and comic, as men that have a good excuse for dressing up. They had just gone by when a new music came up to us and a new procession appeared, coming from Queen Street Station. They were Hibernians, or some other Catholic order, also returning from a day in the country; terrible and comic also, after the fashion of their kind. Orangemen and Hibernians! we said to ourselves. What will happen if they forgather? Being wise youths and having some pleasure on hand, we did not follow to see. But we met a man some time later that night who swore he had been present. The Hibernians, he said, discovered that the Orangemen were in front, so they quickened their pace. The Orangemen, hearing also, slackened theirs. Some resourceful and sporting policemen diverted both parties into a side street and left them to fight it out. After half an hour, when all the fighters had thoroughly disorganized each other, bodies of police arrived, sorted the wounded from the winded and despatched them to their proper destinations in ambulances and plain vans. That is the story as it was told to me and I cannot swear that it is true in every detail; but it might have happened in Glasgow that way, and I doubt if it could have happened in any other town. Such incidents give Glasgow afternoons and evenings their distinctive flavour.

Rape, Late 1930s

ISA PORTE

Isa Porte had been orphaned when she was seven, and was brought up in Glasgow by a harsh uncle. A passionate member of the Young Communist League, she went to work in her home county of Fife when she was offered a job at the United Mineworkers office. A promising future, however, was blighted because of a night of bad luck.

I had to leave my job in the United Mineworkers at Dunfermline because unfortunately I met a young man at a dance. I discovered that he wasn't from Fife, he had a Lanarkshire accent and he started to dance with me. I went out in the middle of the dance at the interval and it was more or less a case of – you would now call it rape. But they didnae call it that in those days. I had just got myself into a situation that I couldn't get out of. And from that I became pregnant. When I went to the doctor he gave me a medical examination and he discovered what I was saying was true, and that I had been forced. And the doctor said, 'It's a difficult thing for you to tell your boss.' He was Mrs Moffat's [her boss's wife] doctor. And he said he would tell them, to save me having to tell them myself. So I went to the UMS office trembling, waiting on Mr Moffat saying something. Then one morning he said, 'Well, I've had very bad news about you. I'm very disappointed,' you know. He said, 'Because we liked having you here and you did your work to our satisfaction.' Miss Morton, the bookkeeper, said to me, 'I don't care if you work till the day before you have your baby. It's nobody's business as long as you do your work.' But Mr Moffat had to put it to the committee and they said, well, if I went home to my friends in

Cambuslang and had the baby they were quite happy to have me return and get my job back.

And I left and came to Cambuslang. By that time I was about six months' pregnant. And I was unemployed. Then of course when it became obvious, my money was stopped and I had to get what they called a Court of Referees. And that was no money till that happened. Well, I knew according to the regulations that I was considered fit for work till eight months of pregnancy. They asked all the details about me. They said, 'Where was the young man?' And 'Why was I in Cambuslang when I had been living in Fife?' I said I had only friends in Cambuslang. I had no other friends. Where was I born? And had I relatives? They made very intensive enquiries about relatives. I had no closer relatives than cousins, and I said I had no connection with them. And they said, 'All right, then come back on Friday.' When I went back on Friday, they said, 'Sorry, we have no money for you. We can't give you anything.' So I got really very angry. I felt like pulling the man over the counter. I said, 'Look, I've got no relatives. I have strangers to feed and clothe me.' When I went home to my friends I was suggesting going to the workhouse, which was up in Hamilton, and asking to be taken in there. But my friends wouldn't allow it in case something happened and the baby was born in the workhouse. So I stayed with my friends and they kept me till I got my money. I won my Court of Referees, got my few shillings a week back, and was able to repay them.

I had the baby. It was a little boy. When I had the baby I did odd days working. And at the time that I went to the Parish they suggested I take court proceedings against the father. Well, what I did, I did instigate proceedings with a lawyer. But I didn't take it as far as the courts, because you were put on trial – it was the girl who was put on trial, not the father. You were put on trial. All your morals and everything else was examined in court, and I didn't want to go that far.

But the young man was in Lochgelly and my landlady who I had lived with in Lochgelly told me about him, gave me his address, and I wrote. He came through to Cambuslang to see me. By that time I was about eight month pregnant. He came through and said he would marry me after the baby was born. And I said, 'Now or not at all. If you can't marry me before I have the child it's not on.' And he went off and I never saw him again. So I didn't take the proceedings as far as court.

When the child was born I had to go to the registrar and he suggested that I postpone registering till I got the father. I said, 'No, just carry on.' So the boy got my name. And, well, you're classified of course as illegitimate. I had to support him myself. I managed to get odd days' typing. . . . While I was working my friend looked after him. She was married and would have adopted him because she had no children by that time. But I didn't fancy the idea of looking on and seeing my own child with somebody else and being at so close quarters. So I decided against that and I worked to support him. The money that I got – I got fifteen shillings for myself, and three shillings for the baby. Three shillings then didn't even buy the child's milk when he was a baby getting bottles of milk. But the few shillings I earned helped to supplement that. I made application for what you would now call a one-off payment to Social Security, to get clothes so that I could be decently dressed to apply for a job, because looking for a job in an office they expect you to be tidy. And I made an application for help. First of all I asked for an extra allowance for the child. They said if I got a certificate that he was malnourished I would get something. And I was turned down. And then of course I applied for help with clothing. One of the gentlemen in the office in Rutherglen where I applied was considerate, and when I was applying for that and getting the small allowance he got me a job. He put me in touch with someone and I got a job, which helped a lot. That was one kind person.

The Sinking of the Arandora Star, 2 July 1940

THE TIMES

In 1940, when Mussolini declared war on Britain, Scotland's cities saw violent riots against their hitherto welcomed Italian communities. Shortly after, all Italian men between the ages of seventeen and sixty were interned or transported out of the country. In July 712 Italians were shipped off to Canada from Liverpool on board the Arandora Star, *which carried 1,500 'enemy aliens'. When it was torpedoed by a German U-boat, 450 Italian internees drowned, most of them shopkeepers and café workers. In all, 805 internees, crew and guards on the ship died.*

Further interviews with survivors of the liner *Arandora Star*, which was sunk by a German U-boat in the Atlantic, indicate that but for the disgraceful panic by the Germans and Italians on board many more lives could have been saved.

When the Germans made a wild rush for the lifeboats and fought with the Italians for precedence, scores were forced overboard in the struggle. British troops and British seamen had to waste valuable time that might have been devoted to rescue work in forcibly separating the aliens. Some British seamen actually went down with the liner while they were still working feverishly to get some of the aliens off.

The hostility between the Germans and Italians was so fierce that even after they had been landed at a Scottish port they continued to attack each other and had to be put in separate buildings.

Martin Verinder, of Romford, an 18-year-old steward of the *Arandora Star*, said that but for attempts to keep the Germans and Italians under control hardly anybody would have escaped.

'As they rushed the boats with the idea of every man for himself,' he said, 'soldiers and crew had to threaten them. I even saw one German sailor, who seemed to have a lot more sense than the rest, take a rifle and club his compatriots. In the lifeboat the internees were selfish, too, and when an aeroplane dropped bread and bully beef, they grabbed it and a few started to wolf it as fast as they could. Soldiers had to seize it from them before it could be shared evenly.

'The last I saw of the captain was when he coolly asked one man to fetch him a glass of water. The man brought him a coat as well. The captain was standing on his bridge giving orders; the bridge was protected with barbed wire and I knew as I saw him standing there that the captain would never get away. I saw the ship's doctor, apparently wounded in the leg, stand up and salute the ship and the captain as the vessel sharply turned half over and sank within two minutes at about 7 a.m. A cloud of steam rose 100 ft into the air and the suction dragged rafts and men under with the ship.'

Another survivor said that in some of the lifeboats the internees, both German and Italian, refused to let members of the crew who were swimming in the water get into the boats. As the Englishmen tried to clamber on board there were shouts of 'No room in here,' and many of the crew were beaten as they tried to climb in . . .

The Travelling Family, 1941

DUNCAN WILLIAMSON

Traveller and story-teller Duncan Williamson enjoyed a very different upbringing from most, one that made him and his kind a target for ancient prejudice. Here he recalls an epidemic of diphtheria that heightened tensions between settled and shifting communities.

Life was very hard for us as a travelling family living on the Duke of Argyll's Estate in Furnace in Argyll, because it was hard to feed a large family when times were so hard. We ran through the village and we stole a few carrots, stole a few apples from the people. Some of the local people respected us, some didn't want their children to play with us. We were local people too, but we were tinkers living in a tent in the wood of Argyll. And of course we did a lot of good things forbyes, because we helped the old folk. My brothers and I sawed sticks and we collected blocks along the shore for their fires and we dug a few gardens. If there was a little job for a penny or two, we would do it for them. We did things for the people that the other children would not do. And we gained a good respect from some of the older folk where we lived. As the evening was over boys would get together, and we'd climb trees and do things, but we never caused any trouble or damage. But some of the people in the village actually hated us.

I went to the little primary school in Furnace when I was six years old. It was hard coming from a travelling family. You went to school with your bare feet wearing cast-off clothes from the local children that your mother had collected around the doors. And of course you sat there in the classroom and the parents of the children who were your little friends and your little pals in school had warned them, 'Oh, don't play with the tinker children. You might get beasts off them, you might get lice.' You were hungry, very, very hungry in school. You couldn't even listen to your school teacher talking to you, listen to her giving you lessons you were so hungry. But you knew after the school was over you had a great consolation. You were looking forward to one particular thing: you would go home, have any kind of little meal that your mother had to share with you, which was very small and meagre, but she shared it among the kids. Then you had the evening together with your granny and your parents. The stories sitting by the fire, Granny lighting her pipe and telling you all those wonderful stories. This was the most important thing, the highlight of your whole life.

We were the healthiest children in the whole village. We ran around with our bare feet. We lived on shellfish. We didn't have the meals the village children had, no puddings or sweet things. We were lucky if we saw one single sweet in a week. But we hunted. If we didn't have food, we had to look for it, and looking for food was stealing somebody's vegetables from somebody's garden or guddling trout in the river or getting shellfish from the sea. We had to provide for ourselves. Because we knew our parents couldn't do it for us. Mammy tried her best to hawk the doors, but you couldn't expect your mother to go to the hillside and kill you a hare or a rabbit. And you couldn't expect your mammy to go and guddle trout. So, from the age of five-six-seven-year-old you became a person, you matured before you were even ten years old. And therefore you were qualified to help raise the rest of the little ones in the family circle. You could contribute. Because you knew otherwise you wouldn't have it. You didn't want to see your little brothers and sisters go hungry, so you went to gather sticks along the shore, sell them to an old woman and bring a shilling back to your mother.

The epidemic of diphtheria hit the school in 1941. Diphtheria then was deadly. Now you had to pay a doctor's bill in these days. And by this time there were nine of us going to the single little school, all my brothers and sisters going together. But because there were so many children actually sick with diphtheria, they closed the primary school. Now we ran through the village with our bare feet. 'Little raggiemuffins' they called us in the village. Our little friends, five of them went off to hospital with diphtheria. Two of my little pals never came back.

My mother had good friends in the village, but some people wouldn't even talk to us. One particular woman, a Mrs Campbell, had two little boys. She was one who wouldn't even look at you if you passed her on the street. She wouldn't give you a crust. After the school had been closed, I walked down to the village this one day in my bare feet. She stepped out of the little cottage.

And she said, 'Hello, good morning.' I was amazed that this woman should even speak to me. She said, 'How are you?'

I said, 'I'm fine, Mrs Campbell. I'm fine, really fine.'

She said, 'Are you pleased? Are you enjoying the school closure?'

I said, 'Well, the school's closed. We're doing wir best to enjoy wirsels.'

She said, 'Are you hungry?'

I said, 'Of course I'm hungry. We're always hungry. My mother cannae help us very much.'

She said, 'Would you like something to eat?' Now I didn't know, I swear this is a true story, that her two little boys were took off with diphtheria and sent to Glasgow to hospital. She said, 'Oh, I have some nice apples. Would you like some?' Now an apple to me was a delight. She said, 'Come in, don't be afraid!' and she brought me into that house for the first time in my life, into the little boy's bedroom. And there was a plate sitting by his little bed full of apples. He was gone. And she took the apples from that plate and gave them to me, three of them. She said, 'Eat this, it'll be good for you.' I didn't know what she was trying to do. Because I was too young, only thirteen. And she was trying to contaminate me with the diphtheria because her two little boys were taken away. Because none of Betsy Williamson's children ever took diphtheria. And that school was closed for five weeks. And everyone was saying, 'Oh, have you got a sore throat?'

Then they began to realize, why were the travelling children so healthy? And they used to say, when my mother walked round the doors of the village, 'What was Betsy Williamson – oh, Betsy Williamson must have superior powers. She must be collecting herbs or something in the woods and looking after children.' You see what I mean? And some would say, 'Oh, she must be some kind of a witch.' And things were never the same after that, never the same.

The Clydebank Blitz, 13 March 1941

THE *GLASGOW HERALD*

Scotland was relatively unscathed by the German bombing that English cities suffered, but the blitz on Clydebank and Glasgow on the night of 13 March 1941 gave a taste of the horrors London was suffering. The raid was so severe that the townsfolk escaped to the nearby moors for safety. Only seven of the houses in Clydebank were untouched, and 35,000 were made homeless overnight. The following report was one of several incidents in which the trapped were finally rescued, although few had lain undetected, and alive, for so long.

After being entombed in the wreckage of a bombed tenement in the Glasgow area since last Thursday night, two men, one of them a War Reserve Policeman, were rescued alive yesterday.

The policeman, weakened by his severe ordeal, died in the early evening, some five hours after he had been released from the mass of debris. The other man, discovered in the course of the evening – almost eight days after the raid – now lies in the Glasgow Western Infirmary in a serious condition.

Hopes were raised last night that a girl might be found alive, and rescuers were working with all speed to trace her. At a late hour, however, their efforts had been unrewarded.

The two men concerned in the remarkable rescues, whose endurance aroused the admiration of the rescue workers, were Frederick Clark (32), War Reserve Policeman, and John Cormack (22).

Cormack was found lying in a bed, where he was resting when the tenement was bombed. A big beam lay above him, and only his face and arms were visible. His arms were folded across his breast.

The rescue workers who discovered him were astonished when he feebly waved his hand to them through the debris. Quickly they cleared the way to him.

'Could you go a cup of tea?' Dr Mackay, who had been summoned to the scene, asked Cormack while he was still a prisoner in the wreckage. 'Aye, Ah could fine,' was the reply.

'I gave him a cup of tea and some brandy, and put a cigarette in his mouth,' said the doctor. Cormack was quite warm. Apparently, he had been in bed when the tenement collapsed, and this saved him from dying of cold.

'He was able to help us to get him out, and explained how a beam was protecting him. He also told us there was a young girl, somewhere near, and that she had spoken to him about a day before.'

Describing the discovery of Cormack, Jack Coughlin, a Dublin-born man, who was one of the rescue squad, said – 'I had a hunch that there was somebody else still alive in the wreckage in the same corner where we had found the other man earlier in the day. I went on working at that spot, and there, when I lifted up some boards, I saw a man lying below. He looked like a statue, lying on a bed with his arms folded. But in a moment I found that he was alive. We called other rescue workers to the spot, and very soon managed to release the man.'

Mr D. Barr, who had been bombed from his home in the same street, and was on his way to salvage some of his belongings, was passing when he heard some one shout, 'A man alive! Get a doctor and an ambulance quickly!'

Mr Barr ran at once to the surgery of Dr Mackay near-by. The doctor went at once to the bombed tenement and stood by in shirt sleeves as the workers extricated Cormack. As soon as he could reach him he went to his aid.

When Clark was rescued he was still able to speak. As he was removed on a stretcher to a waiting ambulance, he told his rescuers – 'I'm all right.' Before he was taken to the Western Infirmary Clark was able to drink a cup of tea and eat a biscuit.

Demolition and rescue workers who have been working side by side since last week's blitz, and with decreasing hope of removing trapped victims alive, were astonished yesterday forenoon to hear a moan come from among the debris. They had just removed a body when they were startled by the sound.

With the utmost speed they excavated a tunnel through the mess of twisted wreckage as a woman doctor hastened to the scene from a near-by clinic.

Dr Annie Thomson, of an Outdoor Medical Services Clinic, was the first person to reach the imprisoned man. She crawled through the improvised tunnel, no more than 18 inches wide, and administered an injection. 'That wasn't so bad, was it?' she asked the man, still pinned beneath the weight of debris. She was surprised when she found that he was able to reply. 'No,' he said.

As the rescuers worked feverishly and grimly to release him, jacking up wreckage to free his feet, they discovered that a chest of drawers had apparently fallen over Clark's body, thus protecting him from the mass of stone and timber that had crashed above him. He was lying at full length on top of a fallen door in a passage-way many feet below street level . . .

The successful and unexpected rescue effort was described by Mr Norman Manson, a joiner, who was in charge of the rescue squad. 'We had,' he said, 'to smash in a floor and crawl underneath to locate the trapped constable. I estimate that we had to remove seven tons of wreckage before we were able to break a way through to him.'

The rescue operations were in two distinct stages. When the tunnel was driven through to reach Clark it was discovered that he could not be freed until a weight of stone pinning a leg beneath a chest of drawers had been removed.

It was seen that to remove this stone would cause a downfall of more wreckage, and it was decided to dig another passage in the foundation ground of the building below where Clark was lying. While this was being done, warm blankets and hot-water bottles were placed round Clark, who was also given stimulants.

As the under-tunnelling proceeded, Clark's leg dropped clear, while the chest of drawers holding up the wreckage above remained in position, and eventually, after three hours' work, the rescuers were able to free the imprisoned man.

Colleagues at the police headquarters where Clark was stationed said that he was actually on night shift last week, but had left the station for his night off when the raid occurred. He was lodging with a Mr and Mrs Docherty, who, with their two daughters, are believed to be still trapped in the partially wrecked building.

A Conscientious Objector, 1941

NORMAN MACCAIG

Poet and teacher Norman MacCaig was a conscientious objector, and between brief spells in Winchester prison and Wormwood Scrubs spent the war farming and gardening. Later in life he wondered if his pacifism had cost him promotion as a teacher. He bore the thought with equanimity.

It was the violence in the world that really made me think about questions of peace and war and pacifism. But that had nothing to do with me becoming a conscientious objector. I keep on repeating: I was just not going to kill people, whether it was in Abyssinia or anywhere else. I just refused to kill people: simple as that . . .

In the 30s an awful lot of people were certain there was a war coming – particularly, as usual, the writers. They've got a nose for such things – the poets and all that, you know, that are looked down on as being illogical, etc. They are not a bit. And we were all perfectly sure the war was coming. But there weren't writers who influenced me in that way. I wasn't influenced. My mind was made up – consciously made up when I was about twelve. And I wasn't influenced by anything whatever, except myself. I sound very aggressive and selfish but that's the way it was.

Well, I was actually called up in the winter of 1941, because I remember there was heavy snow on the ground that winter. I must have been 31. And I told my parents that I wasn't going to kill anybody, of course, and I think they thought, 'This is joking'. None of my relatives, nor even my friends, were pacifist. And my father, who was a wage slave in a chemist's shop and was an intelligent man with a lot of interests, thought I was just being a cheeky young man when the letter came. He was very disturbed indeed. He lost his temper. But that was only that morning. After six weeks or so it was totally accepted by both my parents. So that I had an easy journey compared with a lot of young men.

At the Tribunal I told them: 'You can't put a label on me. I'm not refusing to fight in the war for religious reasons or political reasons or anything like that. It's just that I refuse to murder people – kill people.' And I said, 'I am very willing to join the Royal Army Medical Corps or the Red Cross or the Quakers. But I'm not going to kill anybody.' And since I'd said I was willing to join the RAMC they couldn't write me off as a hundred percent conshie. And they put me in the Non-Combatant Corps, a collection of people that nobody seems to have heard about, a Corps made up of people like myself. The NCC were linked to the Pioneer Corps in order to have corporals, sergeants, captains, majors. All the officers and NCOs were Regular army people. But all the privates, as it were, were just like myself.

Well, when I was told to go to Ilfracombe in Devon to the Pioneer Corps, I wrote to the commanding officer and said, 'I'm no comin. You'll generally find me home after midnight if you want me.' Eventually two coppers appeared after midnight and took me up in the black maria to the High Street police station. I think it was a Friday and there was no Police Court on the Saturday. So I stayed in the cell there over the weekend. I didn't get bail but the policemen were very nice to me. I said, 'I can't sleep. Is there anything I can read?' and a policeman went off and came back with half-a-dozen paperbacks. Then I was brought before the beak in the Police Court on Monday. He said, 'This is a matter for the army. Just go back into your cell.'

Two soldiers came down from Edinburgh Castle and took me up to the Castle. I was put in jankers – to use the old fashioned word. I was there for several days. Most interesting it was. I was put into a room – it was the guardhouse – with a great lot of soldiers under arrest. They were held there until they were brought before a military court. And most of them, I think, were up for absence without leave, that sort of thing. I was the only pacifist in the place. And they all knew I was a conshie. Because the first question they asked was, 'What regiment are you in?'

Anyway a big shot – the Commanding Officer in the Castle – came round to inspect us in the guardhouse. Everybody had their beds tidy and their boots in the proper place. I'd just made up mine as if I were at home. In he came. We were all shouted at to 'Stand to attention!' They all sprang to attention. And I didn't. I was sitting on the edge of my bed and I just stayed sitting. I didn't get up. And the Commanding Officer flushed crimson and started shouting and bawling at me. I said, 'You don't realise I'm not in the army. I'm a pacifist. They've summoned me to the army but I'm not going because I'm a pacifist. I've resigned.' He nearly exploded. I thought he was going to burst. But I didn't get up on my feet. The rest of the soldiers hearing a major general or whatever he was being talked to like that, sitting on the end of my bed, 'Oh, no, I'm not standing up. I'm not in the army' – wonderful! So what they thought of me in that tough place suddenly rose. I was their lily-white boy after that.

Our lunch in the guardhouse was laid on a table and you just piled in – which I wouldn't or couldn't. They just swarmed like bees. And out of that dense mass an arm emerged from this tough guy – and he was a real toughie – handing me something to eat, and this fellow mutters, 'There ye are, chum.' To a conshie! Well, this tough guy was on his way to Barlinnie I think for the sixth or seventh time. . . . And yet it's he whose arm came out of that mob and handed me my lunch: 'There you are chum.' He was a soldier, not a conscientious objector. But again, you see, they had no resentment, no resentment at all.

Rudolf Hess Crash-lands in Scotland, 13 May 1941

THE *GLASGOW HERALD*

In one of the most unlikely episodes in the war, Rudolf Hess, Hitler's deputy and one of his closest companions, left Augsburg and flew 1,000 miles in his Me-110, before crash-landing near Glasgow. Discovering his disappearance, the Nazi Party issued a statement in which they said Hess was suffering from a 'mental disorder', and that they feared he was a 'victim of hallucinations'. The following description by a farm worker suggests he was wholly sane.

Darkness was falling when Hess made his parachute landing on a Renfrewshire farm on Saturday night. The crash of his 'plane was heard over a wide area. People rushed to the spot, but were kept at a safe distance by members of the Home Guard, who little suspected the distinguished nature of their first parachute haul.

When Hess arrived over the area where he intended to land, his machine was heard circling for some time. Soon afterwards it dived to the ground, falling on a field of the farm. The airman came down on a near-by field, landing almost at the door of a ploughman's cottage. The ploughman, David McLean, rushed to the door and found the airman busily divesting himself of his parachute gear.

In an interview Mr McLean said that the airman was limping badly, his left leg seemed to get a wrench when he landed. 'He was a thorough gentleman,' Mr McLean said. 'I could tell that by his bearing and by the way he spoke. He sat down in an easy chair by the fireside. My mother got up out of bed, dressed, and came through to the kitchen to see our unusual visitor.'

When Mr McLean and his mother were visited last night they had just heard the news of the German radio broadcast of the disappearance of Hess. 'We were wondering if it was Hess,' they said. 'There was some excitement in the kitchen when the military people came to take him away, but he was the coolest man of the whole lot.'

Mr McLean said that the German airman had a slight scar on the neck. When he smiled he revealed several gold teeth. The clothing showing below his flying kit was of good quality, and according to Mrs McLean he wore boots made of fine leather 'just like gloves.' On one wrist he wore a gold watch and on the other a gold compass.

Mr Mclean said there was no sign of his suffering from hallucinations such as the German wireless spoke about Hess. 'He was perfectly composed though tired. He spoke like any sane man.' He gave his age as 46.

He was completely unarmed when he baled out – and his 'plane also carried no bombs, nor had his guns been fired. Petrol was running low, and as a landing seemed impossible he resolved that there was nothing else for it than to bale out and let the 'plane crash into a field. Seconds after he had jumped from the 'plane by parachute the machine crashed with a roar on a field – killing a young hare. He was rolling on his back on the ground, extricating himself from the parachute gear when Mr David McLean suddenly stood over him and said – 'Who are you? What are you doing here?'

Without showing any signs of fright or anxiety to escape the airman spoke to him in almost perfect English. 'He was limping badly. His left leg seemed to have got a wrench when he landed,' said Mr McLean when recounting the experience. 'He was a thorough gentleman. I could tell that by his bearing and by the way he spoke. He sat down in an easy chair by the fireside and my mother got out of bed, dressed, and came through to the kitchen to see our unusual visitor.'

'Will you have a cup of tea?' Mrs McLean asked him. 'No,' he replied, 'I do not drink tea at night, thank you.' He then asked for water and two young soldiers who had been attracted to the farm by the sound of the 'plane crashing, jocularly remarked – 'It's beer we drink in Britain.' Hess replied – 'Oh yes, we drink plenty of beer too in Munich where I come from.'

The 'plane, the wreckage of which was strewn around a field not far from the ploughman's cottage, was guarded all day yesterday, and sight-seers had to be kept at a distance.

Prisoner of War, 1944–5

ROBERT GARIOCH

Poet Robert Garioch was captured at Tobruk in June 1942 while serving in 201 Guards Motor Brigade Headquarters. He spent the rest of the war in prisoner-of-war camps in Italy and Germany. The following account is from his period in a camp called Chiavari on the Italian Riviera.

The weather began to be uncomfortably hot. Every day, the sun became stronger, and the nights were warm and stuffy. Though we wore hardly any clothing, we could not keep cool. The air became filled with flies: each man walked about, attended by a cloud of these insects. Whilst we were having a meal, we had to keep the food covered up, reaching under the cloths when we wanted to take a bit. Even then, we could hardly keep them out of our mouths. A camp like ours, crowded with people, must have seemed a paradise specially prepared for flies with all kinds of sweet and nasty things on which they could feed and breed in enormous quantities. The cook-house was full of them, and so was the stew. Each little globule of olive oil which floated on the surface of our ration of stew was sure to have a little fly stuck in it. The more fastidious of us used to pick the flies out of each spoonful, which would take practically the whole evening. The other way of approach was to shut your eyes and gobble it up: probably it would not do us any harm, but the thought of the thing was not pleasant.

We used to kill flies all day, but it seemed to make no difference to their numbers, possibly because we did not do it systematically enough. So the Camp Welfare Committee organized a Grand Fly-swatting Contest. Each man was to collect the corpses of his fallen enemies into tins, and the man who could produce the most evidence of his zeal would receive a handsome prize. We started swatting for all we were worth. We made weapons out of cardboard and pieces of wood, and laid about us with a will. There was no need to go out to seek our prey; we simply stayed in one place and banged repeatedly at the same patch of sunlit wall. One stroke would often yield a dozen flies. We filled tin after tin and took them to the welfare office, where the day's bag was credited to our name, and the heaps of corpses were disposed of in some manner into which we did not enquire.

Fly-swatting slogans were posted up everywhere, in English and Afrikaans, to stimulate us to further effort. An alluringly gruesome poster depicted a seductive-looking female fly perched upon a heap of eggs, with statistics of the number of offspring she was capable of producing in a season. We swatted away, and hoped that our victims were females. There were pessimists amongst us, who said that all these efforts were simply a waste of time, but after some weeks of intensive swatting it did seem as though there were not quite so many flies as before.

Another trouble, however, began to afflict us, which we could not cope with, whatever we tried to do. There were many wooden bunks in each hut, and each bunk harboured its permanent society of bedbugs. When the weather became really hot, those bugs multiplied so fast that they beat us altogether. The trouble with those things was that they hid away during the daylight in all the cracks in the walls and in the bunks. As soon as the lights went out, they emerged for their nightly activities, and drove us nearly mad. Each of their bites raised a blister on our skin; and they were such big dirty creatures that even the thought of them kept us from sleeping. When we caught them, by groping about in the darkness, they squashed messily, and gave off a disgusting smell. There was nothing that we could do to get rid of them. Our efforts must have made some difference, but they still managed to make our nights miserable.

It became a matter of routine to carry out a systematic debugging, every forenoon. We got thin strips of steel from packing-cases, and poked into the crevices of our bunks. They would come out, stained with blood, and bugs would scatter in all directions. We would take all the movable parts of the beds outside, and deal thoroughly with every crack, every day: we must have killed thousands of the creatures, but still they bred too fast for us. We organized days of thorough cleansing, when we took the bunks entirely to pieces, and washed them with strong disinfectant. We used to think that the nights following these campaigns were always the worst of all. Perhaps the bugs were making up for having had a bad day of it.

One man, of a mathematical turn of mind, had the curiosity to take his bed apart, and to count the bugs which he found in several of the places where one piece of wood was joined to another. He found an average of about twenty-five in each place; and as there were one hundred and thirty-two bug-cracks in each double bunk, he calculated that he and his mate shared three thousand three hundred bugs between them.

We even took the bunks outside, and burned all the cracks by holding them over the flames of blowers: but this had no apparent effect. Then a few men began to take their palliasses outside, to sleep under the stars. This was one of the things which we were not supposed to do, unfortunately; and the Carabinieri used to go round in the middle of the night to make the men go back to their huts. We persisted, however, and protested, till at length the Commandant, who generally did all he could to help us, gave permission to sleep outside. This Commandant had been a prisoner in the last war, and sympathized with us to some extent. The regulations prevented him from doing very much, but he did make it possible for this to be a decent camp. So we abandoned the huts to the bugs, leaving them in possession, and took our bedding outside. Fortunately, the bugs, being a conservative race, went on living in the cracks as all their forebears had done, and did not think of lurking on the blankets. One or two did sometimes follow us outside: but these were easily dealt with.

It was pleasant to sleep beneath the sky on those warm summer nights, to wake up sometimes and see the stars, the same constellations that our people could see at home; and it seemed only a little way over the world's rim to where they were still living and thinking about us, or so we hoped. Sometimes a dew would come down in the early morning, and we would wake in the midst of a mizzling mist; but it did us no harm. We went inside only for air-raids, during which we were not allowed out of the huts. We used to wake on hearing the bugle, to find that all the lights in the camp were out. Then the Carabinieri would come and move us inside among the bugs. We would hear the planes coming over, and sometimes bombs would explode a long way off, usually in the direction of Genoa. As soon as the lights came on again, and the bugle sounded, we moved outside. These raids became more and more frequent, till they happened nearly every night, so some of the men took to sleeping beneath the huts, where they could not be seen. It was not very comfortable there, however; and bugs were liable to fall on them through cracks in the floor, so most of us preferred to sleep in the open, and to come inside during the raids.

The Second Edinburgh Festival, 1948

TYRONE GUTHRIE

The first Edinburgh International Festival was held to great acclaim in 1947, injecting a badly needed dose of artistic life into drab post-war Britain. The only criticism was that it hadn't included enough Scottish work. Notably missing, said novelist E. M. Forster among others, were the playwrights J. M. Barrie and James Bridie. So for the festival of 1948 it was agreed that theatre director Tyrone Guthrie would produce The Thrie Estates, *by Sir David Lyndsay, which hadn't been performed in Scotland since the sixteenth century. Guthrie reckoned it was three times the length of* Hamlet; *certainly it was a huge challenge theatrically as well as logistically. He discussed the difficulties he faced with James Bridie, who said he knew someone who might be able to help find a venue.*

A few weeks later, over drinks, Bridie introduced me to Robert Kemp. I remember him coming in, out of the Edinburgh drizzle, with a thick tweed overcoat, a tweed cap of a kind which went 'out' when my father was a lad, with a thick ashplant in his hand, much more like a cattle dealer than an author. We discussed *The Thrie Estates*, got on fine and have been the best of friends from that instant.

Next day in downpours of rain we set out to find a suitable place to stage the play. Bridie, Kemp, William Graham of the festival office and myself, in a noble old Daimler with a noble old chauffeur, lent by the municipality. We visited big halls and wee halls. Halls ancient and modern, halls secular and halls holy, halls upstairs and halls in cellars, dance halls, skating rinks, lecture halls and beer halls.

The rain continued to pour. We got extremely wet and Bridie, as our physician, advised, as a precaution against the cold, that we sample the demon rum. We looked at several more halls, and several more rums. The quest waxed hilarious. Bridie and the noble old chauffeur began to sing, as our Daimler careered wildly from a swimming bath, which we were assured could be emptied, in the extreme east of the city, to the recreation hall of a steam laundry in the city's extreme west. Darkness was falling; the street lamps were reflected in the puddles. The repertoire of our singers was nearly exhausted: the limousine was out of petrol; William Graham was asleep on its flyblown cushions; I was beginning to be acutely conscious that I had led them all a wild-goose chase. Then spake Kemp in the tone of one who hates to admit something unpleasant: 'There *is* the Assembly Hall.'

The minute I got inside I knew that we were home. It is large and square in the Gothic style of about 1850. It has deep galleries and a raked floor sloping down to where, in the centre, the Moderator's throne is set within a railed enclosure. The seats have sage-green cushions; there are endless stone corridors. Half-way up the steep black approach – it stands on one of the precipitous spurs of the Castle Rock – is a minatory statue of John Knox. There are endless portraits of departed pillars of the Kirk, including, as I was afterwards to discover, a very nice one by Harvey of my great-grandfather preaching al fresco in the Highlands.

None of the others thought the Hall particularly suitable; but they were impressed by my enthusiastic certainty and it was agreed that the Kirk authorities be approached as to its use for a play. The Scottish Kirk, with its austere reputation, might have been expected to take a dim view of mountebanks tumbling and painted women strutting before men in its Assembly Hall. On the contrary, no difficulties were raised; no one suggested censoring the bluer portions of the text or issued fussy interdicts about tobacco, alcohol or dressing-rooms. There was a single stipulation: no nails must be knocked into the Moderator's throne.

Stealing the Stone of Destiny, 25 December 1950

IAN HAMILTON

Since the time of Alexander III, the Stone of Scone, known popularly as the Stone of Destiny, had played a symbolic role in the assumption of royal power. It was removed from Scone Abbey in Perthshire by Edward I's men in 1296 and placed in Westminster Abbey, where it became a focus for nationalist resentment. Many dreamt of returning it to its rightful place at Arbroath Abbey. With due ceremony it was finally returned to Scotland in 1996, but a valiant and briefly successful attempt was made early on Christmas Day in 1950 by Ian Hamilton and three fellow students.

We vaulted the railings, and crossed the patch of light, and stood crucified by the rays of the lamp, against the shining door. At least we should not work in darkness.

Gavin put his shoulder against the door. 'The jemmy!' he hissed. I turned to Alan. 'The jemmy!'

'What!' said Alan, 'I thought you had it.'

Sheepishly I returned to the car and retrieved it from under the seat where I had hidden it during the skirmish with the detective.

At first we made little impression on the door, for the two halves met closely, and the join was covered with a lath of wood which ran from top to bottom. We were desperately afraid of noise, and with the sharp end of the jemmy chewed away sufficient wood to enable us to prise the blade between the two sections of the door. Then the three of us put our weight on the end of the jemmy, and the door began to give a series of creaks which sounded like minute guns. At each creak we expected a police car, summoned by the watchman, to sweep up the lane. Let it come; at least we were going down fighting.

I could now put my fingers through and feel the hasp on the inside. It was slack. We prised up the bottom of the door, and it came clear of the ground, bringing the bolt with it. Our gap widened to three inches. We could see into the Abbey. There was no watchman waiting there.

We put the blade of the jemmy close behind the padlock, and together we all wrenched mightily. With a crash, the door flew open. In the car Kay heard the noise and shuddered, but the way to the Abbey was open.

We swept into the Abbey. I returned and pulled the doors close behind me. I had rehearsed that part.

A light glowed dimly at the west end of the nave, but the rest was in black darkness. We went down the transept in silent hurry, and found that the gate in the metal grill was open. We crept through and round and up into the Confessor's Chapel. We did not listen for the watchman, for we might have heard him coming. At least, we would touch the stone.

The chapel was in darkness. The glimmer from my torch showed the glass doors into the sanctuary as black sheets, and I hastily turned it to the side where it shone wanly on the green marble tomb of Edward I, whose dead bones Bruce had feared more than he feared any living Englishman.

The other two had already lifted aside the rail which kept the public from the Chair. The Stone was before us, breast high, in an aperture under the seat of the Coronation Chair, which was raised three feet from the floor on a kind of trestle. We gently prised at the bar of wood which ran along the front of the Chair as a retainer for the Stone. It was dry with age, and it cracked and splintered, and I felt sorry, for it did not belong to us.

The Stone should now theoretically have slipped out, but it was a very close fit and its weight made it unwieldy. I got to the back and pushed, and it moved a little. The chains on its sides kept catching on the carved sides of the Chair, and since the three of us were working in a sweating fever, not one of us had the patience to hold the light. At last we saw that brute strength and black darkness would not budge it, so we called a halt. Then one man holding the torch, one prising at the sides with the jemmy, and one pushing at the back, we started afresh. It moved. It slid forward. We had moved the Stone. The English Chair would hold it no longer.

We were sweating and panting. It was coming. The plaque saying 'Coronation Chair and Stone' fell from the Chair. I caught it in mid-air and thrust it into my coat pocket. They would not need that now. It was almost free. One last heave. 'Now!' said Gavin. I pushed from the back. It slid forward and they had it between them. I rushed forward to help them and we staggered a yard. We had to put it down. It was too heavy.

'A coat!' said Alan deep in his throat.

'Mine is the strongest,' I said. It was the strongest, but also I wanted the honour for my coat. I slipped the jemmy out of my pocket. We would come back for that later. I struggled out of my coat and laid it on the ground; one hasty heave and the Stone was on the coat.

I seized one of the iron rings, and pulled strongly. It came easily – too easily for its weight, and I felt something uncanny had happened. 'Stop!' I said and shone my torch.

I shall not forget what the faint light revealed, for I had pulled a section of the Stone away from the main part, and it lay in terrifying separation from its parent.

I was going to be sick. Everything was now turned to a new purpose which was not good. Better to howl and bring the watchman and have it repaired than carry away a broken Stone.

'We've broken Scotland's luck,' came Alan's awful whisper.

I shone the torch on the break. Suddenly I saw that the greater area of the break was much darker than the thin wafer round the top edge. The Stone had been cracked for years, and they had not told us.

'No we haven't!' I said. 'They did it. They've cheated us, and kept it from us.'

'Quit talking and get moving!' said Gavin.

I picked the small part up like a football, and opened the door into the sacrarium. The light still burned at the far end of the nave, but of the watchman there was no sign.

I stepped hurriedly past the altar, down the steps, and round into the transept. That part of the Stone weighed almost a hundred pounds, yet I might have been on the sports field for all the hindrance the weight was. I came out into the light at the Poets' Corner door, and plunged again into the darkness of the masons' yard. Alan had taken the precaution of opening the doors before he entered the Abbey, so that I had little difficulty. Kay had seen me coming and had the car halfway down the lane. She opened the door, and I rolled the piece of Stone into the back.

'It's broken,' I said. 'Get back into cover.' I don't know what she thought, but by the time I was back in the Abbey the car was once more in position at the top of the lane.

The other two had made good progress. The steps leading down from the altar are wide and shallow, and they presented little difficulty to us. We grasped the coat and slung it down, step by step, between us. Except for our gasps for breath and an occasional grunt of effort, we made little noise. Now and again there was a rending sound from the coat as the weight told on it.

We reached the foot of the steps and dragged it across the nave. Sweat blinded us and we were breathless. . . . Suddenly and miraculously we were at the door. We stopped for a breather, for we were all at the end of our strength. 'One more pull,' said Alan. 'We're not going to be beaten now.' I opened the door, and as I did so I heard the car start up. It moved forward into the lane, whence it was clearly visible from the road. We still had to drag the Stone down the masons' yard. It was far too early to move forward yet. 'The fool,' I said, and dashed through the line of sheds to tell Kay to get back into cover.

The car was standing outside the gap in the hoarding. I opened the car door. 'Get the damned car back into cover,' I spat. 'We're not ready yet.' Kay looked at me coolly. 'A policeman has seen me,' she said. 'He's coming across the road.'

I got into the car beside her and silently closed the door. I reached forward, and switched on the lights. I fought breath into myself and wiped the dust of the Abbey off my hands on to Kay's coat. I put one hand over the back of the seat, and groped for Alan's spare coat. Carefully I draped it over the fragment of the Stone. Then I took her in my arms.

It was a strange situation in which we found ourselves, yet neither of us felt perturbed. Kay was as cool and calm, as though we were on our way home from a dance, and for a couple of minutes I was so immersed in the task at hand that I completely forgot the approach of the policeman. It was our third night without sleep, and I think we were both so drugged with tiredness that we would have accepted any situation as normal. Our minds were cold as ice, and we had thrashed our bodies so hard and worked for so long in the shadow of our ultimate aim that fear or panic played no part with us.

The policeman loomed in front of us. 'What's going on here?' he thundered. It was perfectly obvious what was going on. Kay and I did not fall apart until he had plenty of opportunity to see us.

'It's Christmas Eve, you know, officer,' I explained.

'Christmas Eve be damned!' he answered. 'It's five o'clock on Christmas morning.'

'Ochtone! Ochtone!' I said. 'Is it that time already?'

'You're sitting on private property here,' he told us. 'And why did you move forward when you saw me coming?'

'I know,' I said humbly. 'I knew we shouldn't be here. We put on the lights to show you that we were quite willing to move on.'

'But where can we go?' asked Kay, vamping at him. 'The streets are far too busy.'

'You should be off home,' he told her, and looked at her severely.

We explained to him that we were down from Scotland on tour, and that we had arrived in London too late to get a bed. We sat and held hands in front of him, and tried to give him the impression that we were too much in love to go to a hotel and be parted.

He began to warm to us. To my horror, he took off his helmet, and laid it on the roof of the car. He lit a cigarette and showed every sign of staying, till he had smoked it.

'There's a dark car park just along the road,' he said, smacking his lips contemplatively. We knew that car park. The other car was there.

'Och, well,' said Kay, thrusting her head into the lion's mouth, 'if we're not comfortable there we can always get you to run us in and give us a bed in the cells.'

'No! No!' said the PC knowingly. 'There's not a policeman in

London would arrest you tonight. None of them want to appear in court on Boxing Day to give evidence against you.' Kay gave my hand a squeeze.

'A good night for crime!' I said, and we all laughed.

All this time I had been conscious of a scraping going on behind the hoarding. Why on earth didn't they lie low until the policeman had gone? It transpired that they had no idea that we were entertaining the police, and they were calling my parentage in question to the tenth generation for sitting in the car while they did all the work.

Kay heard the noise, too, and we engaged the constable in furious conversation. He thought us excellent company. His slightest sally brought forth peals of laughter, and when he essayed a joke we nearly had convulsions. Surely they would hear our laughter and be warned.

There was a muffled thud from behind the hoarding. The constable stopped speaking, tensed, listening. My heart sank to my boots. Kay's hand became rigid in mine. Then the constable laughed and said, 'That was the old watchman falling down the stairs.' Furiously and hysterically, Kay and I laughed at the idea of the watchman falling down the stairs. Surely they heard us now.

'I wish it was six o'clock,' said the policeman. 'And then I would be off duty.'

Out of the corner of my eye, I saw the door in the hoarding slowly opening. Gavin's face appeared, followed by his head and shoulders. Suddenly he froze. He had seen the policeman. His lips formed an amazed oath. Inch by inch he edged back, and the door closed behind him. The policeman finished his cigarette and put on his helmet. 'You'd better be going now,' he said.

'We had indeed!' I said, wiping the sweat out of my eyes.

'Will you show us the way?' asked Kay, trying to get him off the premises.

'Oh, you can't miss the car park,' he said, and redirected us.

Kay started the engine. She is, although she will be annoyed that I said so, a very bad driver, but that morning her bad driving was designed and not incompetence. Never has a clutch been let in so jerkily; never has a car veered from side to side so crazily. I looked back and waved to the constable. As Kay had expected, he was following down behind us – too amazed at the crazy driving to pay attention to anything else. We reached Old Palace Yard and Kay put her toe down.

Jimmy MacBeath, King of the Cornkisters, 1951

HAMISH HENDERSON

The pioneering folklorist Hamish Henderson played a crucial role in recording, collecting and preserving the great ballad tradition of Scotland. A songwriter and poet, he began travelling in search of balladeers in the early 1950s. His work was then archived in the newly formed School for Scottish Studies in Edinburgh, for whom he was an inspirational figurehead. Here he describes one of his earliest trips. A Cornkister is a bothy balladeer.

Jimmy learned the 'bothy style' – the way of life of the farm servants of the pre-First World War North-East – the hard way. He left school at thirteen and was fee'd at Brandane's Fair to a farm in the parish of Deskford, south of Cullen in Banffshire. . . . His most vivid memory of that first year was a savage beating with the back chain of a cart for not being in proper control of his horses: 'Ye ca'd oot muck wi' your pair at that time ye used your pair at that time. The foreman went oot first, and of course I was oot ahin', man; I happened til miss my hin'-sling, o' my cairt like – and the horse gaed agley, dae ye see. H [the foreman] pulled me oot-ow'r the cairt and thrashed me we' a back chain – richt ow'r the back wi' a back chain. An' the fairmer was passin' at the time, and never lookit near hand.'

. . . No wonder Jimmy MacBeath later described the North-East farm servants of that period as 'a very sad-crushed people, very sair crushed doon'. Conditions of work, living accommodation and the food (generally brose) provided for the lads were all the subject of outspoken complaint in bothy ballads, and when Jimmy sang 'Drumdelgie' to audiences far outside the North-East, he was able to communicate more of the immediate reality of a farm labourer's life in the old days than a hundred Government papers or bureaucratic reports could possibly have done.

The outbreak of World War I did at any rate provide a chance of a break from this 'hard slavery work'. Jimmy enlisted in the Gordons, and saw service in the trenches of France and Flanders. . . . When he was demobilized, he was faced with the depressing prospect of re-entering farm service, but fate – in the shape of Geordie Stewart of Huntly, a wealthy travelling scrap dealer. . . . – willed otherwise. Geordie was a connoisseur of ballad singing, and it was he who put the idea into

Jimmy's head that he might be better employed using his by-ordinar voice, with its unique gravely tone, as a street singer than meekly submitting to the necessity of a return to the bothy life. Geordie not only assured Jimmy that fame, money and a great lyric future lay before him on the road; he also taught him two or three dozen of the songs which he was afterwards to make famous, including the best version collected to date of 'Come a' ye Tramps and Hawkers' . . .

The time of the year when Jimmy really came into his own was Aikey Fair . . . When Jimmy MacBeath turned up, he at once became the centre of a lively group of farm servants, who urged him on to sing 'The Banks o' Ross-shire', 'Torn a', rippit a'', 'The Ball o' Kirriemeer' and other colourful items from his repertoire . . .

Afterwards Jimmy would repair to a hotel bar in Old Deer, and the fun would continue. I remember well seeing him in his glory in that same bar in the evening of the Fair Day in 1953; one of the young farm servants, who had obviously formed a strong attachment to him, was sitting and listening attentively, while Jimmy taught him 'Airlin's Fine Braes' verse by verse. I felt it was a real privilege to witness the actual act of oral transmission, especially when the transmitter was none other than the reigning 'King o' the Cornkisters'.

Jimmy also used to sing at 'Turra Market' (Porter Fair), and it was in Turriff that Alan Lomax and I made our first recordings of him in 1951. The lead that carried us to Jimmy came from 'Lordie' Hay, a veteran bothy singer whom I had met on an earlier tour . . . We recorded a number of songs from him in the Commercial Hotel in Turriff; in addition, he provided a graphic account of the career and personality of Jimmy MacBeath, and obligingly told us where we would probably find him; this turned out to be the North Lodge, a model lodging-house in Elgin.

The following day we drove west from Turriff, via Banff and Buckie. Alan dropped me off at Jessie Murray's house in Buckie and drove on alone to Elgin to pick up Jimmy. Jessie, a great ballad singer, was in rare fettle and I hardly noticed the two hours go by, when suddenly I heard Alan's car draw up in front of the house. A moment or two later, Jessie and I had a simultaneous first vision of Jimmy's beaming, rubicund, booze-blotched face as he walked into the kitchen, followed by Alan. There was a moment of silence. Then Alan said: 'Hamish . . . Jessie . . . I want you to meet Jimmy MacBeath.'

Half an hour later we were *en route* for Turriff, and Jimmy was singing in the back of the car. . . . When he learned that we were heading for

'Turra toon', Jimmy was none too confident of his reception. The last time he had been there, he had been slung out of the town by the local police, who had told him never to set foot in Turriff again. However, Alan assured him that this was a 'special case' – as indeed it was – and Jimmy rode back into Turra in triumph. He was shortly taking his ease, and a royal dram, in the best hotel in the town.

Indeed, Jimmy, who was never slow to claim descent from the Macbeth who 'stabbed King Duncan through the mattress' – and, given any encouragement, from the best-looking of the three Weird Sisters too – was quick to realize that here, in the shape of two wandering folklorists, was fate in a Ford Anglia, and that his reappearance (against all the odds) in Turra toon signified a qualitative change in more than his own personal picaresque career. Those early recording sessions in the Commercial marked the intersection in space and time of the old world of Aikey Fair and the new world of the as yet undreamed-of Keele Festival of the future, with its hundreds of youthful enthusiasts from all over Britain gathered to hear Flora MacNeil, Ewan MacColl, Margaret Barry, Felix Doran, Bell and Alex Stewart – and Jimmy MacBeath himself, the symbolic unifying factor in the whole clanjamfrie.

The Flodden of Football, 15 April 1961

DENIS LAW

The annihilation of the Scottish football team, 9–3, by the English at Wembley was the worst defeat they had ever suffered, and a humiliation that has never yet been forgotten. In the aftermath, the goalkeeper, Frank Haffey, emigrated to Australia.

England were on a roll when we met them. Earlier in the season they had already beaten Northern Ireland 5–2, Luxembourg 9–0, Spain 4–2 and Wales 5–1. Their form continued after they had played against us as they went on to beat Mexico 8–0. If it seems that I am reluctant to get round to talking about the match, those who recall the game will probably understand why . . .

Bobby Robson set the ball rolling for England when he scored after nine minutes. The Tartan Army fell silent. This was not how it was supposed to be. There were almost 100,000 at Wembley that day and the Scots were the loudest as usual, but the English fans found their voices after Robson's goal and the atmosphere, which had already been intense, now became electrifying. It was almost as if something special was expected. Jimmy Greaves – who else? – made it 2–0 after 20 minutes and then, nine minutes after that, he scored again. I don't know why England did not score a lot more before half-time. We were there for the taking but the scoreline remained the same.

Our dressing room was more than a little animated during half-time. We were not just in disarray on the pitch, for those few minutes we were in a state off it as well. Blame was being handed around as if it was a grenade with the pin removed. We managed to pull ourselves together, though, and some team spirit began to spread through the camp. We realized that all was not lost and that we could get back into the game if we were prepared to give it a real shot. By the time we went back on to the pitch we were much more fired up than we had been at the start of the match.

The second half was not very old when Dave Mackay sent in a flying long shot which left Ron Springett in the England goal floundering. The ball thumped into the back of the net and the Tartan Army leapt to its feet as one. We gained a lot of confidence from that and it was not long before Davie Wilson scored our second with a terrific diving header. England were reeling and the scene was set for one of the greatest comebacks in the history of the game.

It didn't happen. England stormed back and were awarded a free-kick near our penalty area. To this day it seems to us that Jimmy Greaves gained an unfair advantage by taking the free-kick several yards nearer to the goal than he should have done. The referee must have had some mud in his eye for a moment and, from that kick, the ball found its way to Bryan Douglas, who made it 4–2. We were very disappointed because it seemed such an injustice.

We fell apart after that and England took full advantge of the situation. Bobby Smith made it 5–2 with 18 minutes left and, even when Pat Quinn scored for us, it didn't seem to matter any more. Johnny Haynes scored twice in less than two minutes, Jimmy Greaves completed his hat-trick, and Bobby Smith made it 9–3. It was a result that went down in history for all the wrong reasons from a Scottish viewpoint. While Johnny Haynes, the England captain, was being carried off the pitch shoulder-high and their goalkeeper Ron Springett was hurrying away to see his newborn daughter, Frank Haffey was in tears. I think we were all close to tears in our morgue of a dressing room, but Frank gave way to his. He never played for Scotland again.

Petition for Women to Become Ministers in the Church of Scotland, 26 May 1963

MARY LUSK

Mary Lusk (later Levison), a deaconess of the Church of Scotland, made history by petitioning the General Assembly of the Church of Scotland to be allowed to be ordained as a minister. This led the way to the decision, five years later, to allow women to be ordained as ministers. Although Levison was not subsequently the first woman to be ordained, she is regarded as the most influential campaigner for the right of women to be employed in any post of the Church. One newspaper believed that Levison's achievement put her on a par with two other great champions of women's rights, Sophia Jex-Blake and Nancy Astor. Her revolutionary petition came in the form of a fifteen-minute speech to the General Assembly. It was so enthusiastically received the Assembly had to be reminded that applause was not permitted.

The fact that as a woman I should be required to show special cause why I should be ordained appears to me a curious situation; for my plea is that as a person I may share in the whole ministry of the Church, and may therefore be eligible to be ordained to any particular ministry within the Church . . .

I would submit that there is to be found in Scripture no theological ground for denying ordination to women. If one takes the New Testament as a whole one sees that women played a full part in the service of the whole body, being accepted fully as persons by Christ Himself and then by His followers. Paul is often considered to be the stumbling-block here, with his injunctions to silence; but these should surely be taken against the background of far more general evidence of his acceptance of women in the Church – as his fellow workers and as leaders in prayer and prophecy in public worship – and all this based on the theological ground that in Christ there is no difference as to male and female.

Of course the Order of Redemption in Christ does not contradict the Order of Creation. Of course, men are still men, and women women, and we glory in it. There can be no question of women wanting to be like men and to take on anything that is shown to be a male function. But I have yet to be convinced that to preach the Word is to do something specifically masculine – if I were so convinced I should stop doing it; I fail to see how the ministry of the Sacraments belongs to men exclusively in virtue of their maleness; and if it be the exercise of discipline which is objected to in the case of a woman, then we have to remind ourselves that the only kind of government rightfully exercised within the Church is the authority of the Servant, and surely that kind of authority can never be held to be the prerogative of the male sex.

Prince Charles and the Cherry Brandy, 20 June 1963

THE *DAILY TELEGRAPH*

The year after Prince Charles was sent to Gordonstoun School he created a furore when a journalist caught him ordering a cherry brandy in a public bar while on a trip to Stornoway. The Palace at first issued a denial but later was forced to admit the truth.

The Prince's private detective, Donald Green, was immediately removed from royal duty and the prince was punished by his headmaster by being demoted in his rank at school. Charles later commented of these seemingly comic events, 'I thought it was the end of the world.'

Palace Withdraws its Denial: He Did Buy Cherry Brandy

The Prince of Wales, who is 14, did have a drink in a hotel cocktail bar at Stornoway, Lewis, on Monday. Buckingham Palace yesterday withdrew a denial of reports that he had bought himself a cherry brandy for 2s 6d. Mr F. R. G. Chew, headmaster of Gordonstoun, where the Prince is a pupil, said later that boys at the school were forbidden alcoholic drink. He added: 'If, after investigation, the reports prove correct I shall consider if disciplinary action is necessary. At present I don't know the full details. I shall be interviewing the boys when they return to school on Sunday.' He declined to say what form disciplinary action could take.

Nudity at the Edinburgh Festival, September 1963

THE *SCOTSMAN*

In the same summer that Britain was gripped by the Profumo–Keeler scandal, the Edinburgh Festival was besmirched by its own flurry of moral outrage when a drama conference, organized by impresario John Calder, flaunted a naked woman on a trolley. The boundaries of good taste, it was felt, had been pushed too far. Front-page headlines in the Scotsman *confirmed what some had feared when the Festival was proposed for Edinburgh, that its citizens were too straitlaced for such an event. Despite the disapproval that greeted Calder's conference, however, Edinburgh quickly adjusted to a new climate of artistic experimentation and provocation, and soon proved virtually unshockable.*

Commenting last night on the surprise appearance of a nude woman at the final session of the Drama Conference in the McEwan Hall on Saturday, the Earl of Harewood, artistic director of Edinburgh Festival, said he believed the incident had sabotaged the chances of another conference of a similar nature in next year's Festival. He regarded the whole incident as extremely silly and pointless.

The incident brought an end to the Festival in a loud explosion of indignation. Anna Keseler (19), an Edinburgh model, was wheeled across the organ gallery for 30 seconds as part of an 'action theatre' display staged by Kenneth Dewey (21), avant-garde director from Los Angeles. It was part of a 'Play of Happenings', organized by Mr Dewey, which was designed to get the audience involved in the conference . . .

Mr John Calder, London publisher and organizer of the drama conference, thought the whole thing 'very funny'. Not so Edinburgh's Lord Provost, Duncan M. Weatherstone. 'It is quite a tragedy that three weeks of glorious Festival should have been smeared by a piece of pointless vulgarity,' he said in an indignant statement issued yesterday . . .

After the first startled gasp which followed Miss Keseler's nude appearance in the McEwan Hall, the audience were further shaken by the sound of a piper playing and marching in the top tier. Someone hung a sheep's skeleton on the platform, men hung from windows 70 feet up, to the background noises of tape recorded gibberish and murmurs of apprehension from the paying public.

As if that was not enough, American film actress Carroll Baker slipped off her marmalade mink with a queenly air, revealing figure-hugging silver trousers and tunic. Then, for no apparent reason, she jumped down from the platform and made her way out of the hall – not by the aisle, but by jumping over the seats without a 'by-your-leave' or an 'excuse me'.

At his country home in Kinross, Mr John Calder had his Sunday morning peace shattered by the loud reports of Press and Provost. 'I saw the whole thing,' he said, 'and it was all in very good taste. The girl was wheeled through very quickly and no one in the audience could have seen very much of her.' . . .

At her Portobello home yesterday, Miss Keseler described her appearance as 'a bit of a giggle'.

Gordonstoun School, 1965

WILLIAM BOYD

Novelist William Boyd's memories of his schooldays at the remote boarding school of Gordonstoun, on the Moray Firth, deflate the myth that public school education is innately superior to comprehensive. Far from home in Africa, the convivial Boyd fitted in well, yet his experience of the bigotry, snobbishness and squalor of dorm life appears to have left him with simmering resentment.

The living quarters of your average public schoolboy are at best functional and soulless, and at worst utterly disgusting. If Borstals or remand homes were maintained in similar conditions, there would be a public outcry. I recently visited several famous public schools, and nothing I saw there made me so depressed as the dormitories and the thought that for so many years I had slept so many nights in such dismal and depressing circumstances.

It is, I think, a retrospective revulsion. Adolescent boys are not much preoccupied with personal hygiene, let alone the care and maintenance of their living quarters. But now, when I recall the concrete and tile washrooms and lavatories, the pale-green dormitories with their crude wooden beds, I form a new respect for the resilience and fortitude of the adolescent spirit . . .

When I arrived at the school, aged thirteen, in 1965, everything about the house was functional and anonymous. . . . Only in the studies was individual decoration permitted, but as this consisted almost entirely of pictures of women scissored from lingerie and swimwear advertisements, they too had a homogenous air.

The house was large, but it felt curiously constricted. In the summer one could get outside, but during the winter there was nowhere else to go. . . . We had a succession of popular and ineffectual housemasters. There was no discipline. A new housemaster was strenuously trying to impose his authority. But when he retired to his flat at the end of the day the old regime established itself. The source of the problem was a group of boys in the sixteen-to-seventeen age bracket. They were 'bad' in the sense that they had no interest in promotion. In the evenings they terrorized juniors with a kind of candid ruthlessness that I still find chilling to recall. They would roam the junior studies, four or five of these roughs, and beat people up at random, extort money or food, rifle letters and lockers in search of diversion. One felt in a way rather like a medieval peasant during the Hundred Years War: one never knew when another marauding army might march by, randomly distributing death and destruction. It was comparatively short-lived, this period of capricious thuggery, but it provided me with a full catalogue of the resourceful cruelties of the adolescent mind . . .

Our school was in Scotland, was in almost every respect a Scottish public school, and yet a strong Scottish accent was a real stigma. Indeed, any regional accent was parodied mercilessly. When people spoke with a strong Scottish accent we would make harsh retching sounds in the base of our throats or emit loose-jawed idiot burblings. Anyone with a Midlands or north of England accent heard nothing but a barrage of 'Eeh bah goom' and 'Trooble at t' mill'. We all found mocking of accents endlessly amusing. This was part snobbery, part self-defence. All public schoolboys have an intensely adversarial relationship with the local population, especially with the local youths. To us the locals were 'yobs', 'oiks', 'plebs', 'proles', 'peasants' and 'yokels'. It now seems to me astonishing to recall the patrician venom we would express, like aristocrats faced with imminent revolution – a curious mixture of contempt, fear, guilt and jealousy. They lived, after all, in the real world beyond the school grounds, and however superior we congratulated ourselves on being, there was no escaping the fact that they were freer than we were – and that grated. I am sure that we in our turn were looked on as revolting, arrogant, nasty snobs. By no means a harsh judgement.

We longed to get out of the school, but the outside world was both a lure and a taunt. It possessed everything that school denied us and at the same time was a constant reminder of the constraints and abnormalities of the society in which we were confined. Strenuous attempts were made to escape it.

The easiest way to get there was to be selected for a school team. Because the school was situated so far north a considerable amount of travelling was involved in order to find reputable opponents. Rugby and hockey would take you to Inverness or Aberdeen two or three times a term, and often there were matches in Dundee, Glasgow, and Edinburgh. Edinburgh occupied a place in our imaginations rather as Berlin did for poets in the 1930s. It seemed to our impoverished eyes unfailingly sinful and glamorous. To be selected for a rugby tour to Edinburgh meant happy hours in Thistle Street pubs rather than eager sporting challenges . . .

The outside world was a welcome source of contraband – pornography, drink, cigarettes – and also, in a sense, fair game. When boys went into towns the shoplifting rate rose alarmingly. In the local Woolworth's two store detectives used to follow one particular boy around. He was the most accomplished kleptomaniac and used to take orders for his Saturday visits. We exulted in our delinquency and bandied legends of epic thefts: a souvenir shop in the Highlands left almost empty when a busload of boys cleaned it out; a boy who dug up copper wires on a nearby RAF station, at one stage blacking out the control tower when he sank his axe into a crucial cable. We would return gleefully to the safety of school, clutching our booty. And yet within the school itself theft was regarded as the most serious and antisocial of crimes – any thief could expect years of excoriation. Two worlds, two sets of standards . . .

We were obsessed with sex. I know this is true of all adolescent experience, but when I think now of the energy and relentless focus of our interminable discussions about the subject a sort of retrospective lassitude descends upon me, as well as a retrospective anger. *Of course* we talked about sex – we lived in a freakish, monosexual society. There was a parallel world out there in which the two sexes mingled and interacted and to which entry was denied us. No wonder our curiosity was so febrile and intense – and so destructive. The sexual apartheid to which we were subjected all those years utterly warped our attitudes and precluded us from thinking about girls and women in any way but the most prurient and lubricious. The female sex was judged by one criterion – fanciable or non-fanciable, to put it rather more delicately than we did . . .

The people who bore the brunt of our lewd interest were the maids. These were local girls, I think, and were hired – so public-school rumour famously has it – solely on the grounds of their ugliness. It made little difference. Their encounters with the boys, three times a day at meals, were characterized by a one-sided traffic of sexual banter of the vilest and coarsest sort. Given the opportunity, more daring boys actually molested them – squeezing, pinching, feeling. The girls were remarkably tolerant. I never heard of any boy disciplined as a result of a complaint made by one of them. I think our attitudes to them brought out the very worst in our natures: it was male lust at its most dog-like and contemptuous, tarnished further by a brand of wilful class disdain and mockery that was almost dehumanizing . . .

There was also, it is true, a brand of passionate romanticism about our sexual curiosity that was slightly more amusing. Nobody ever admitted to being a virgin. By tacit consent conversation about the great day was always rather vague and woolly – it was just taken as read that everybody was, well, pretty experienced. There was one boy who made the mistake of confessing, at the age of seventeen, that he had still to lose his virginity. He became the laughing stock in the house. Little boys of fourteen would howl, 'Virgin! Virgin!' at him. He came back the next term claiming to have lost it in the holidays, but it was too late. His greatest mistake was to have admitted it – the only honest man among shameless liars . . .

The school dance was little more than a meat market. By the time the girls arrived all the boys were well-fortified with alcohol. At the first slow number they pounced. The occasion degraded everybody. The Gilbert and Sullivans were more fun and more decorum reigned. We were meant to be rehearsing and we saw the girls quite regularly over a period of a month. Courtship rituals were rather primly observed, and the alliances that were struck up remained for a good while on a rather chaste level – one was often invited to the girl's house for tea on Sunday afternoons to meet her parents, for example. This more sustained contact usually provoked the dormant, romantic side of our nature, and many of us fell deeply in love as a consolation for being denied any physical release. That came, eventually, usually as the dates of the performances approached, a sense of time running out – as with soldiers due to return to the front – affecting both boy and girl. These wistful encounters were not so shaming. They were like any adolescent affair – cute, thrilling, melancholic – a brief foray into real life. They ended after the show as the barriers of the single-sex boarding school were reimposed. The only real victim was the Gilbert and Sullivan, in my memory always appalling, for the simple reason that none of the chorus had joined for the singing.

A Glasgow Gang, 1966

JAMES PATRICK

Gang warfare in Glasgow escalated severely in the 1960s, leading to fears of American-style gangster activity. A youthful teacher at an approved school wanted to observe what motivated the boys and men in these gangs. He enlisted the help of one of his pupils, Tim Malloy, who was leader of one of the more notorious gangs, the Young Team. Tim introduced him as a newly approved gang member and James Patrick (which was not his real name) spent four months as part of the Team, between October 1966 and January 1967.

The main outlet for the Young Team's aggression and hatred was its traditional enemy, the Calton Tongs; by all accounts, the most hated gang in Glasgow. Early on in our relationship, Tim's attitude towards his main rivals was expressed as follows: 'If Ah saw wan o' thae Tongs lyin' in the gu'er bleedin' tae death, Ah'd stab him again. Ah'm swearin' it. Ah'd run a *right* psychey. Nae Kiddin'! Ah wid.' Such phrases were uttered almost in a scream, with his teeth grinding together in tension. At the same time, all manner of actions were performed; the word 'stab', for example, was accompanied by a flashing stroke of his arm . . .

The variety of weapons I saw was manifold, the types I heard of legendary. Hatchets, hammers, knives, meat cleavers, meat hooks, bayonets, machetes, open razors, sharpened tail-combs, all these were the regular chibs. Bottles of all sorts and tumblers and bricks and sticks were employed in emergencies. Berettas, double-barrelled shot-guns, swords, scimitars, and hand-grenades were lovingly described, but mercifully never appeared in my presence.

The sources for these arms were also various. The home provided such items as the bread knife, the coal hammer and the poke. Antique shops were 'screwed' and their armouries raided. A military store was reputed to have been emptied. . . . But apart from the home, the place of employment seemed to be the main supply depot. One job above all others was coveted in this respect. The butcher's boy had access to the most terrifying weapons both for his own use and for sale to his mates. The approved schools continue unwittingly to place boys, known to be gang members, in the meat trade.

To be more particular, Dougie, the borstal boy I never met, had always been attached to hatchets. Convicted of carrying an offensive weapon, and having served his term of detention, he bought a new hatchet on his release and went out at night 'tae break it in'. He walked into the centre of the city, claiming a total of thirty-three windows on his way, and was finally arrested 'fir a daft wan doon the toon'.

'Big M', whom I found myself calling 'wan o' oor big boays', dreamed up the following ruse to trick the police. His weapon was a claw-hammer, carefully wrapped in brown paper and string, so that, if stopped, he could pretend to have just bought the tool for his work. I do not know what ironmonger's he could have cited as being open at three o'clock on a Sunday morning.

The Malloy brothers had earned the revered title of 'chib-men'. This was no honorary title, but one accorded few members of any gang. Not everyone 'kerried' by any means, and even amongst those who did, some used their weapons mainly on property, while others carried them only intermittently. Those who carried chibs or malkies (i.e. any kind of weapon) more often than not, and who had used them 'successfully' on people, were 'chib-men'. The Malloys boasted of being able to outwit any policeman who searched them; Tim, for instance, claimed to have been 'raked' one night while 'kerryin'' and to have escaped arrest for possessing an offensive weapon. The trick he had picked up from his elder brothers, none of whom had ever been caught in pos-session. Before leaving the house, John used to tie a short blade to his wrist with a piece of string; he then concealed it by rolling down his shirt sleeve over the knife which rested alongside his forearm. Tim adopted the same technique, but in addition, was fond of carrying his favourite weapon – an open, lock-back razor . . .

I asked Tim how he kept his parents from knowing about his weapons. Mick and he shared a room, the door of which was always locked – 'ma Maw wouldnae dare go in.' The guns and knives were hidden in the dresser in this bedroom. Bill, the oldest son, had been in the habit of leaving his favourite malky, the coal hammer, in the fireplace and had thus been hoist with his own petard. For, climbing in the window one Saturday night, 'steamin' he wis', he had been hit on the leg by his own weapon. His future brother-in-law had been sitting in the front room, 'winchin'' in the dark with one of the Malloy girls. Thinking someone was breaking into the house, he had hurled the hammer at the intruder and broken Bill's leg . . .

When Jack Martin chibbed Marty, the leader of the Barnes Road, during the Christmas holidays, the Young Team had known that this meant open war. But, as the Barnes Road were inferior in numbers and had never ventured much beyond their boundaries before, Tim had felt the initiative lay with him. So he had been surprised to hear one night that the Barnes Road were on the move and heading along Maryhill Road. The pub in which the Young Team were sitting had cleared in a frenetic rush, as boys ran to collect their chibs and rouse the neighbourhood. I am not sure whether the Barnes Road and the Young Rolland Boys advanced deep into Young Team territory by chance or lack of foresight, or whether they were allowed to do so by design; in any case, within fifteen minutes of their vanguard being spotted, the Wild Young Team, numbering 'over a hundred', were on the streets, armed and 'ready to go *right* ahead'. The Barnes Road and their allies were attacked from all sides; bottles and bricks were showered upon them; and Tim, Dave Malloy and others of the in-group led the charge which scattered and routed the opposition. 'The streets wir black wi' boays, runnin' aw ower the place. It wis a laugh,' commented Tim. 'Ye go mad. Ye slash aboot at oaneywan. And that's aw aboot it.'

Big Fry, the boy 'wi' aw the answers', who was easily the most fluent and effusive member of the gang, described the sensation as follows: 'See the feelin' in yir belly goin' intae battle, it's like the feelin' ye have when Rangers are attackin' the Celtic goal. Yir heart's racin', ye feel sick; it's better'n sex.' The others agreed that gang fighting was what really mattered to them; sex came a poor second in their list of priorities.

Considering the number of boys reputed to have been involved, the list of casualties was infinitesimal. . . . Benny of the Barnes Road 'goat twelve boatels ower his nut', and two or three others were said to have been slashed, before Marty yelled to his team: 'Get oan yir sannies' (i.e. 'Get off your marks'). The order was unnecessary, as the invaders were already pouring from the field, diving through closes, and dodging through traffic. The most frightening aspect of the whole affair had been the arrival of the team, moving across the city like a storm cloud, terrifying pedestrians with their weapons and chants, and totally out of the control of the constables on the beat. When the police reinforcements arrived in the shape of the riot squads, the Young Team had also dispersed, with the exception of Dave Malloy, who was 'huckled' while still screaming full-throated challenges in the middle of the street to the 'fuckin' shit-bags' to stand and fight. He had tackled the first few policemen as if they were members of the opposing gang; perhaps his irrational behaviour is explicable in terms of a desperate effort to recover status and position within the gang. Harry Johnstone ended the discussion with a remark, loaded with meaning for me: 'There hid been too many square-goes. *We aw* goat right intae it. An' if ye shit yirsel' in a ba'le, the boays get intae yir heid – wi' weapons.' Honour demanded that the Barnes Road should be invaded for reprisals. I began to prepare Tim for my imminent departure. I had had enough.

Scotland Beats the English World Cup Team, 15 April 1967

JOHN RAFFERTY

When the Scotland football team became the first to beat England after their World Cup victory in 1966, their jubilation was extreme. Their success also vindicated those who had disparaged the tactics of the England players' manager, Sir Alf Ramsay. The score was 3–2.

Bobby Brown beamed and grinned and made no affectation of coldness. We liked him for that, for Scotland's victory was one to be relished. His team had subdued, tormented and outclassed Sir Alf Ramsay's tattered World Cup champions on their own Wembley turf that they were so shy of leaving last summer, and his were the tactics. This was a manager's victory, and one which gives him massive authority at the start of his reign.

He explained: 'I planned for the team to take control of the mid-field. The mistake I made against the English League was in not being strong enough there, and I think I rectified the deficiency with the energy of Bremner, the elegance of Baxter, and with this new boy, McCalliog, who did so well. I wanted him to flit about much in the way of the late John White, making space and linking the play, and this he did to perfection. He was the discovery of the match: our superiority in mid-field the decisive factor.'

Indeed, Bobby Brown was right. Baxter, Bremner and McCalliog won the vital mid-field battle, and no one can accuse him of being wise after the event, for on the morning that he announced his team he explained to me the pattern he had in mind, and the team did play to it, and the results were glorious.

The victory was exciting, too, for those, and there were many, who had not liked the footballing methods of Sir Alf Ramsay with which England won the World Cup. They had deplored their willingness to concede the mid-field, and put their faith in a tight defence and a hectic break-away.

Such made for dull, tedious football, of the sort that England played up to the World Cup final, and which they played on Saturday. Bobby Brown is the new champion of those who want good football players used right throughout the length of the field.

We have struggled to deal with these serious academic matters, for it is still so near the frenzy of Saturday, so near the wild excitement, when the twinkling feet of Law scored the first goal, when a solid sweep of Lennox's foot made the second, so near that thrilling instant when the new hero, McCalliog, planted the ball so solidly in the English net.

We would write off England's two as irritating freaks that have distorted the picture for those who were not there.

Then there was the second Wembley victory, which we report without commending, elated Scots supporters defeating the police and spilling on to Wembley's turf in their thousands and kissing it, and howking out souvenir clods. They had been grievously annoyed by the arrogant writing in the London newspapers, which had slashed contemptuously at the poor footballing cousins from north of the Border – so, too had the Scots players.

When little Billy Bremner told me: 'That was a good one to win,' he hissed the words, and in the venom of them was the pent-up feelings of the exile who had been sorely tried.

There was the wild frolicking in the West End at night, and the great Lion Rampant flags being paraded perilously in the swirl of the traffic in Piccadilly Circus. The taxi driver said: 'They should play it in Scotland every year. They're mad.' We saw his point.

Celtic Win the European Cup, 25 May 1967

HUGH MCILVANNEY

When Celtic beat Inter Milan 2–1 in Lisbon they become the first British team to win the coveted European Cup.

Today Lisbon is almost, but not quite, back in Portuguese hands at the end of the most hysterically exuberant occupation any city has ever known.

Pockets of Celtic supporters are holding out in unlikely corners, noisily defending their own carnival atmosphere against the returning tide of normality, determined to preserve the moment, to make the party go on and on. They emerge with a sudden burst of Glasgow accents from taxis or cafés, or let their voices carry with an irresistible aggregate of decibels across hotel lounges. Always, even among the refugees who turn up at the British Embassy bereft of everything but the rumpled clothes they stand in, the talk is of that magical hour-and-a-half under the hot sun on Thursday in the breathtaking tree-fringed amphitheatre of the national stadium.

At the airport, the impression is of a Dunkirk with happiness. The discomforts of mass evacuation are tolerable when your team have just won the greatest victory yet achieved by a British football club, and completed a clean sweep of the trophies available to them that has never been equalled anywhere in the world. They even cheered Helenio Herrera and his shattered Inter when the Italians left for Milan yesterday evening. 'Inter, Inter, Inter.' The chant resounded convincingly through the departure lounge, but no one was misled. In that mood, overflowing with conquerors' magnanimity, they might have given [Rangers manager] Scot Symon a round of applause.

Typically, within a minute the same happily dishevelled groups were singing: 'Ee Aye Addio, Herrora's on the Buroo'. The suggestion that the most highly paid manager in Europe is likely to be queueing at the Labour Exchange is rather wild but the comment emphasized that even the least analytical fan had seen through the hectic excitement of a unique performance to the essential meaning of the event. *Mundo Desportivo* of Lisbon put it another way: 'It was inevitable. Sooner or later the Inter of Herrera, the Inter of *catenaccio*, of negative football, of marginal victories, had to pay for their refusal to play entertaining football.' The Portuguese rejoiced over the magnificent style in which Celtic had taken retribution on behalf of the entire game.

A few of us condemned Herrera unequivocally two years ago after Inter had won the European Cup at their own San Siro Stadium by defending with neurotic caution to protect a luckily gained one-goal lead against a Benfica side with only nine fit men. But he continued to receive around £30,000 a year for stifling the flair, imagination, boldness and spontaneity that make football what it is. And he was still held in awe by people who felt that the statistics of his record justified the sterility of his methods. Now, however, nearly everyone appreciates the dangers of his influence. The twelfth European Cup final showed how shabbily his philosophy compares with the dynamically positive thinking of Jock Stein. Before the match Stein told me: 'Inter will play it defensively. That's their way and it's their business. But we feel we have a duty to play the game our way, and our way is to attack. Win or lose, we want to make the game worth remembering. Just to be involved in an occasion like this is a tremendous honour and we think it puts an obligation on us. We can be as hard and professional as anybody, but I mean it when I say we don't just want to win this cup. We want to win it playing good football, to make neutrals glad we've done it, glad to remember how we did it.'

The effects of such thinking, and of Stein's genius for giving it practical expression, were there for all the football world to see on Thursday. Of course, he has wonderful players, a team without a serious weakness and with tremendous strengths in vital positions. But when one had eulogized the exhilarating speed and the bewildering variety of skills that destroyed Inter – the unshakable assurance of Clark, the murderously swift overlapping of full-backs, the creative energy of Auld in midfield, the endlessly astonishing virtuosity of Johnstone, the intelligent and ceaseless running of Chalmers – even with all this, ultimately the element that impressed most profoundly was the massive heart of this Celtic side. Nothing symbolized it more vividly than the incredible display of Gemmell. He was almost on his knees with fatigue before scoring that thunderous equalizer in the 63rd minute but somehow his courage forced him to go on dredging up the strength to continue with the exhausting runs along the left-wing that did more than any other single factor to demoralize Inter.

Gemmell has the same aggressive pride, the same contempt for any thought of defeat, that emanates from Auld. Before the game Auld cut short a discussion about the possible ill-effects of the heat and the firm ground with a blunt declaration that they would lick the Italians in any conditions. When he had been rescued from the delirious crowd and was walking back to the dressing-rooms after Celtic had overcome all the bad breaks to vindicate his confidence, Auld – naked to the waist except for an Inter shirt knotted round his neck like a scarf – suddenly stopped in his tracks and shouted to Ronnie Simpson, who was walking ahead: 'Hey, Ronnie Simpson! What are we? What are we, son?' He stood there sweating, showing his white teeth between parched lips flecked with saliva. Then he answered his own question with a belligerent roar. 'We're the greatest. That's what we are. The greatest.' Simpson came running back and they embraced for a full minute.

In the dressing-room, as the other players unashamedly sang their supporters' songs in the showers and drank champagne from the huge Cup ('Have you had a bevy out of this?'), Auld leaned forward to Sean Fallon, the trainer, and asked with mock seriousness: 'Would you say I was the best? Was I your best man?'

'They've all got Stein's heart,' said a Glasgow colleague. 'There's a bit of the big man in all of them.'

Certainly the preparation for this final and the winning of it were impregnated with Stein's personality. Whether warning the players against exposing themselves to the sun ('I don't even want you near the windows in your rooms. If there's as much as a freckle on any man's arm he's for home') or joking with reporters beside the hotel swimming-pool in Estoril, his was the all-pervading influence.

Despite the extreme tension he must have felt, he never lost the bantering humour that keeps the morale of his expeditions unfailingly high. The impact of the Celtic invasion on the local Catholic churches was a rewarding theme for him. 'They're getting some gates since we came. The nine o'clock and ten o'clock Masses were all-ticket. They've had to get extra plates. How do they divide the takings here? Is it fifty-fifty or in favour of the home club?'

It was hard work appearing so relaxed and the effort eventually took its toll of Stein when he made a dive for the dressing-rooms a minute before the end of the game, unable to stand any more. When we reached him there, he kept muttering: 'What a performance. What a performance.' It was left to Bill Shankly, the Scottish manager of Liverpool (and the only English club manager present), to supply the summing-up quote. 'John,' Shankly said with the solemnity of a man to whom football is a religion, 'you're immortal.'

An elderly Portuguese official cornered Stein and delivered ecstatic praise of Celtic's adventurous approach. 'This attacking play, this is the real meaning of football. This is the true game.' Stein slapped him on the shoulder. 'Go on. I could listen to you all night.' Then, turning to the rest of us, 'Fancy anybody saying that about a Scottish team.' . . .

The SNP Take Their Second Seat at Parliament, 17 November 1967

WINNIE EWING

In November 1967 Winnie Ewing swept to victory at the Hamilton by-election, thus winning the SNP's second seat at Westminster. This sent a frisson through the political establishment and seemed to herald a new era of politics, in which nationalists would be a force to be reckoned with. Two weeks after the election, Ewing travelled to Westminster on an overnight train from Glasgow, along with 300 supporters, who stopped off at Newcastle at three in the morning, and entertained the porters with an impromptu eightsome reel on the platform.

Bookings were taken for what would be an overnight journey on the night of 16 November 1967 (returning the following night) to see the honourable member for Hamilton safely sworn in at Westminster, two weeks after the by-election itself. The travellers included fiddlers, pipers, accordionists, tin-whistlers and, of course, singers. The only people with sleeping berths were the Ewing family, and we were all there – myself, my husband Stewart, and my children Fergus, Annabelle and Terry, aged ten, seven and three. I think the children got a good night's sleep but there wasn't much sleep for the rest of us . . .

The send-off, I was later told, resembled that given to the Red Clydesiders when they went to the House of Commons after the 1922 election. My father had actually been there and had described it to me many times. During that event Jimmy Maxton had climbed onto a luggage wagon and had said, 'Before six months are over we will return with a Scottish parliament.' Of course, it took a bit longer – in fact seventy-seven years . . .

Amid the mixed emotions of pride and victory and the feeling of gratitude to all who achieved the remarkable result at Hamilton, I myself knew that I was taking part in a moment in history. Yet my strongest emotion was that of fear. How would I stand up to the strains of a political life in the House of Commons? How would my children be affected by the inevitable separation? Would my friends and family stand by me in the hard moments, which were bound to come? Would I – could I – live up to the huge and widespread Scottish aspirations that Hamilton had brought to the surface in Scotland? . . .

Eventually the train arrived at Euston and there, too, were vast crowds, complete with several pipers. I was lifted shoulder-high by Angus McGillveray and Hugh McDonald. The photo of me on the shoulders of Angus and Hugh went right round the world.

We went first to the Rembrandt Hotel, to get ourselves organized. Then it was on to the House of Commons to meet my sponsors, Gwynfor Evans, MP for Carmarthen, and Alistair Mackenzie, MP for Ross and Cromarty. We met in a splendid tearoom. Of course I had met Gwynfor before, at the Plaid Cymru conference in July 1967. I had also shared a platform with him in Aberdeen later in the year, when he had generously given up three days of his time to hold public meetings in Glasgow, Aberdeen and Edinburgh. There was a very sad downside to that Plaid conference, though. At the event I had given a big bowl of white heather to Gwynfor, saying, 'Before the blooms on this heather fade, I'll be sitting beside you in Westminster to speak up for Scotland as you do for Wales.' The presentation was photographed by, of all papers, the *Sunday Post*. At the same time, unknown to me, my father had felt very ill and signed himself into the Victoria Infirmary where he was diagnosed with pneumonia. By the time I got back to Scotland he was dead. The ward sister in the hospital told me she had shown the photo of me with Gwynfor in the *Sunday Post* to my father in what was probably his last conscious moment. I was always very sad that he never lived to see me take my seat in the House of Commons . . .

Before going to the House to be formally sworn in I collected Stewart, Betty Nicholson [the nanny] and the children. They were escorted to the Speaker's Gallery, which has the best seats in the House, while I was accompanied to the bar of the House with Gwynfor on my right and Alistair on my left. The Chamber was packed and all the galleries full. By this stage I was very nervous and keen to get the oath-taking over with. Unfortunately – for me as well as the country – the pound had just been devalued, so instead of the Speaker calling out his question, there was a statement followed by what seemed an age of debate. I think we had to stand there for an hour and a half and I was very conscious, as time went on, of the increasing pain from my rather tight new shoes . . .

Then, finally, the Speaker called out his question. I moved forward and took the oath. Then I stepped up to shake the Speaker's hand – it was Horace King at that time – and there was a huge noise in the Chamber behind me, which I took to be friendly, although I am not so sure now. Horace King was very kindly, gave me warm words of welcome and said he would make sure I was fairly treated. Someone heckled, 'Give her a kiss', which caused great amusement, though he didn't do it. And that was it.

Prison, November 1967

JIMMY BOYLE

On 3 November 1967, Jimmy Boyle was sentenced to life imprisonment for a murder he insisted he did not commit. One of Scotland's most feared criminals, from the Gorbals in Glasgow, he enjoyed a career of violent theft, money racketeering and gang fights, with regular spells in prison. His autobiography, A Sense of Freedom, *written from Barlinnie prison and smuggled out for publication, was shocking not only for his unflinching portrait of gangland life but, even more, for its depiction of the brutality of prison conditions.*

I lay on the dark floor in a terrible state. I cried that first night, my heart and my eyes cried. I was so angry at myself and the world that I couldn't think straight. Internally I was a raging storm, but to anyone peering through the Judas hole of the cell door I would look calm, as though I was just dozing. Without that façade I would have broken into a million little pieces. For some reason it was very important that I cling to this and make it see me through till I recovered from this inner blitz. I was a walking time-bomb, primed and ready for exploding, all it needed was one wrong word and there would have been such a holocaust that they wouldn't have believed it. That inner something that seemed to take over the minute the verdict was given stayed with me. By some miraculous means or other I managed to get through the first night and the next few days, though they were very hazy and I can only remember pieces of them.

The press were giving it big licks and I covered the pages with the same old crap of being the super baddie. It seemed to keep up for the first week or so and guys showed me what they were saying but by now I was sick of it. For the first time in my life I became revolted at the sight of my name in the papers whereas all the other times it had been a prestigious thing and I had enjoyed it. The press were keeping on about the moneylending rackets and saying that they would have to be clamped down on, so the cops reacted and went round the pubs in the Gorbals lecturing to the customers and telling them to come forward and give evidence and they would be guarded. There were stories printed saying that some of us had 'crucified' a non-paying customer to the wooden floor of a house. This was a statement reported to have been issued by the police. Most of what they printed was nonsense.

My hopes during the first few days automatically lay with the Appeal Court and I applied to the prison authorities, saying I wanted to appeal against the conviction. I began to think it out very carefully as this was my last chance in life and I had no intention of putting it into the hands of anyone else. This time when I went to court I wanted to speak for myself . . .

Prison being what it is, one has to go to the Governor for permission to obtain what are known as Appellant visits. These are special visits over and above the normal quota for an appellant to gather material for his case. I went to my hall governor to get a special visit from a Mr Davidson. I told him the circumstances about wanting to speak on my own behalf and the need for a visit to get certain information. He began to hum and haw and stretch the whole thing out telling me he would give me an answer later in the day. That was it. I could take no more. Didn't he realize what this meant to me? The anger came up from my toes and I swung a blow that knocked him from his chair and put him on the floor. I lifted a wooden inkwell but was pounced on from behind and put into the cell next door. I tore a piece of wood from the book shelving and stood with it in my hand, as they carried the Governor out. They waited some time allowing me to cool off and then cautiously opened the door, there was a mob of them. The screws said that everything was all right and I would be okay, that there would be no brutality handed out. I told them to remember that if there was brutality it wouldn't end here, as I was now in for the rest of my life and would remember anyone who laid a finger on me. I was put into a solitary confinement cell and left alone without any harm done to me.

A short time later I heard the sound of heavy boots and the cell door opened. There stood the heavy mob all wearing coloured overalls and they told me to take off my clothes. I refused, saying that if they wanted to fight why didn't they get on with it? I was told that there would be no brutality, all they wanted was my clothes for the cops. I thought this over and accepted that they were telling the truth as there were enough of them to beat me up with my clothes on. No sooner had I stripped off than some of them moved in punching and kicking me. I tried to hit back, calling them cowardly lumps of shit. There were shouts of anger, but they beat me to the floor, leaving me in a pool of blood. There is something totally humiliating about being brutalized when naked. Nakedness leaves a feeling of helplessness, and even though I was returning blows it felt as though they couldn't hurt the person they landed on. There was this feeling of impotence. I lay on the floor in an absolute rage, hating myself for being such a bloody fool as to trust them.

Being a Life prisoner meant looking at prison in a totally different perspective. This experience resulting from my assault on the Governor meant that I had to rethink everything. It was obvious to me that my life style would have to change in order to survive in this jungle. Certainly I had lost my life, but not my will to live, to fight. The whole of my thought processes were undergoing a dramatic change. It dawned on me for the first time that my life sentence had actually started the day I left my Mother's womb. Strangely enough I now found a new sense of freedom, which I had never experienced before; it was important to me. I decided that I would now live by my laws, not giving one fuck for society or the laws of society. Their very representatives, the media, were labelling me 'Animal', 'Maniac' and lots of other names. From now on I would totally reject everything and everyone and label them the 'Dangerous Majority' and the 'Perpetuators of Fascism'. Who was society? I described them as being like every para-military organization on the government payroll, and all those silly ignorant bastards who would be brainwashed by the media, accepting their every word as being gospel. From now on the world could go to fuck. I hated everyone and distrusted everyone. They made it plain that they felt the same about me, so we all knew where we stood.

The Ibrox Disaster, 2 January 1971

THE *GLASGOW HERALD*

One of the worst tragedies in modern Scottish history took place at Ibrox stadium in Glasgow shortly before the end of the traditional New Year derby between Rangers and Celtic. As spectators surged to leave, a stairway collapsed, sending people crashing down upon those behind them. Sixty-six were killed by asphyxiation or crushing. As the following report testifies, it was some time before the rest of the stadium realized what had happened.

In the press box we had all been commenting on how well behaved the crowd had been and thinking that Rangers' equalizer in the closing seconds had restored the good nature of their fans, ensuring that there would be no subsequent trouble

Then, across the field at the north-east corner – Section 13 – there were four or five policemen standing on the track looking up into the terracing. Someone said: 'Fighting must have started there.' But this seemed inexplicable because one had been able to sense the entire good humour of the crowd after the thrilling end to the game.

Then, across the floodlight mist, the distant sounds of shouts and screams could be heard. Two of us rushed down the spiral staircase from the top of the stand. We pushed our way through the cheerful fans on the pavement, through another entrance and ran across the bone-hard frosted pitch onto which only minutes before, Colin Stein had brought so much happiness by scoring that equalizing goal.

In the deserted ghostly atmosphere of the playing pitch we had thoughts of fantasy, such as 'So this is what it is like to play at Ibrox.' Thoughts of disaster had still not penetrated.

Even when we reached the track at the far corner there was still no indication of the enormity of what had happened. Two or three people were being carried or helped down the terracing. Then, as dozens of police and ambulancemen converged and ran up the terracing, we felt the first real chill of the situation.

There was a numb silence now, broken only by shouts for stretcher bearers. We started to make our way to the top of the terracing, but several times went back with injured spectators who asked, 'Can you give us a hand?' Willing hands abounded to assist injured boys and men down to the track.

Eventually, at the top of the terracing, the true horror of the situation became apparent. Half a dozen lifeless forms were lying on the ground. Rescuers were tripping over the dead and injured as they struggled back with more victims.

A wedge of emptiness had been created part of the way down the long steep flight of steps leading to the Cairnlea Drive exit. In it were the twisted remains of the heavy steel division barriers. They had been mangled out of shape and pressed to the ground by the weight of bodies.

Lying all over the steps were scores of shoes that had been ripped off in the crush. Beyond, the steps were still dense with groaning people. We helped another of the injured back down the terracing. Then Sir Donald Liddle, the Lord Provost, who had watched the game from the directors' box, walked across the pitch. He climbed over the wall into the terracing and moved around, trying to comfort the injured. He knelt beside one man who had had a pillow of beer cans made for his head and had coats and jackets placed over him. But he was dead. The Lord Provost was in tears when he left.

On the exit steps, Sir James Robertson, the chief constable, was directing the activity. Bodies were now lying everywhere. One man was still lying halfway down the steps, a jacket over his face. There was almost complete shocked silence at this stage. Occasionally one could hear the noise of coins falling from the victims' pockets as they were lifted away.

Back on the field a row of bodies on stretchers was reaching from the corner flag position to the goalposts. Ambulances and police cars, their emergency lights flashing, were speeding round the track. Mr William Waddell, Rangers' manager, and Mr William Thornton, his assistant, together with Mr Jock Stein, Celtic's manager, were directing stretcher bearers to the team dressing rooms which had been set up as casualty stations.

Dozens of policemen, nurses, and ambulancemen were working desperately and mostly in vain to bring life back to the crushed victims.

When two hours later, there were only officials left on the terracing and steps of Section 13, one young nurse was being helped away, crying. She kept repeating – 'I felt so helpless.'

The Upper Clydeside Shipyards' Work-in, 18 August 1971

JIMMY REID

Through the summer of 1971 and into 1972, the shipyards of Glasgow, once the pride of Scottish industry, came under threat of massive redundancies. Instead of going on strike, the workers staged a work-in protest. On the day that they announced this strategy, Jimmy Reid, convener of the shop stewards, made history for telling the men, in no uncertain terms that: 'There will be no hooliganism, there will be no vandalism, there will be no bevvying, because the world is watching us.' In the months ahead, Reid played a leading role in defending the shipyards, although it eventually proved to be an unwinnable battle. This is the speech he made at Glasgow Green to a crowd of 30,000 demonstrators, eight weeks into the work-in.

Today Scotland speaks. Not the Scotland of Edward Heath, Gordon Campbell, Sir Alec Douglas Home – of the Lairds and their lackeys. They have never represented Scotland, the real Scotland, the Scotland of the working people. No title, no rank, no establishment honour can compare with the privilege of belonging to the Scottish working class.

That is what I want to say on behalf of UCS workers to our brothers and sisters who have responded so magnificently to our call for help and solidarity. Government action has projected us into the front rank of the battle against the policies of redundancies and closure. THEY PICKED THE WRONG PEOPLE. We stood firm and refused to retreat. We were prepared, of necessity, to stand on our own and fight alone.

But we were not alone.

Confident in our belief in our fellow workers, we told Heath and his government that this was the breaking point for the Scottish working classes . . . indeed for the Scottish people.

There were those – and they were few – who counselled against a precipitate appeal to the workers. But the shop stewards believed that time was of the very essence. That for too long the fight against redundancies and closures had been confined to the morass of high-level negotiations. Meanwhile workers whose livelihoods were at stake stood waiting outside closed doors to be told at second hand whether they might work, or whether they would sign on at the Labour Exchange. AND THE ANSWER, INVARIABLY, WAS THE DOLE QUEUE.

This time the workers and the shop stewards of UCS were determined this would not happen. This time we took appropriate action and appealed over the heads of government and institutions. We appealed to the highest authority in this land . . . TO THE PEOPLE. Already there was pent-up anger and frustration. Hopes had been dashed. There was despair at our apparent inability to influence and determine our own destiny. There were creeping redundancies.

It needed only a spark to ignite those feelings. To give them positive expression. We suggest that the workers of UCS have themselves provided that spark. We are witnessing an eruption not of lava but of labour. The labour of working men and women.

Let Mr Heath take note. Unless he and his colleagues are prepared to meet the urgent social needs of the people then this eruption will engulf both him and his government. It is incredible, but the Downing Street mentality seems to be: this government has lost confidence in the people – let's change the people.

Edward Heath, I tell you this. We are going to fight and we are not going to change. Either you will change, or we will change the government.

The Big Yin, 1975

GEORGE ROSIE

Billy Connolly, the raucous comedian from the Clydeside shipyards, epitomized perceptions of the rough working-class Scot. Dubbed the Big Yin as much for his flamboyant personality as for his stature, his unholy brand of humour travelled well, and by the mid-seventies he had become the darling of the London comedy scene.

There is a man in Glasgow called Billy Connolly who has been putting forward a new representation of Christ – head man of a squad of Glasgow tearaways. It goes something like this; the scene is a well-known hostelry in the Gallowgate. 'The door opens . . . crash! And in he comes. The Big Yin . . . With the long dress and the casual sandals . . .' It is, of course, the King of Kings, the Messiah, the Man himself, but with a terrible thirst on. 'Oot a' mornin' daein' thae miracles. I'm *knackered*! Gie's a glass o' that wine. Nae kiddin' son, I'm knackered . . . Take a look oot that door. There's nuthin' but deid punters walkin' up and doon, wi' their beds under their airms . . .'

As the Last Supper gets underway, the Big Yin makes a prophecy. 'Wan o' you is goin' tae shop me . . . and two big Roman polis is goin' to wheech me right oo' o' here, and into the jail. And ah'm goin' tae dae a wan-night lie-in, me with the good dress on tae. And I'm going to get up in the mornin' and say, first offence, ah'm on to probation nae bother. But a big Roman is going to come into my cell and say "Probationum my arsium". . . .'

It is a *tour de force*, a stunning and relentless piece of near-blasphemy which can, and regularly does, reduce every variety of Christian – from the fiercest of Protestants to the most devout of Catholics – to helpless, hysterical mirth. And the whole piece is delivered in harsh, uncompromising Glasgow dialect, a racy, demotic and brutal argot which bears no resemblance to music-hall 'Scotch'!

Connolly's version of the Last Supper and the Crucifixion goes some way to explaining his amazing, runaway success. Because over the last year, Billy Connolly has become *the* man in Scotland, the only one with the ability to pack every theatre in the country five times over, and with a following which includes old-age pensioners from Gorbals and Drumchapel, to the Edinburgh intelligentsia. And the word is getting out to the enormous Scottish diaspora; in January he sold every seat at the London Palladium, and the sales of his latest LP record are expected to top 200,000 copies.

In most ways Connolly is the antithesis of the Scots comic, a species usually composed of dapper little men in neat suits, with patent leather hair or a penchant for sporrans, kilts and bow ties. Connolly is big, glamorous, wears his auburn curls down to his shoulders, sports a long wizard's beard, and likes to trick himself out in gaily-coloured silks and brocades. He has all the stage arrogance of, say, the lead guitarist in a good rock-and-roll band. But he works hard at his stagecraft; he moves well, is an excellent banjo-player, a decent guitarist, possesses a fair if unspectacular singing voice, pens a nice song, and has developed a neat way with his hecklers, 'You should get an agent, pal. Why sit there in the dark handlin' yersel' . . .'

But it is his stories that the punters pay to hear, long, rambling, crude, blasphemous and raw, packed with incident and character, full of the clang of the shipyards and the echoes of the back close. A running commentary on the intricate, hot-tempered culture of the Scottish working class. Reports from a world peopled by meandering musical drunks, street-fighting heavies, slatternly mothers and snotty kids, inept teachers, no-hope scholars, whores, shipyard gaffers and wily apprentices. At its root, Connolly's work is kindly and deeply nostalgic. But it is laced with a sly wit, a caustic intelligence, a sense of menace, and a cunning eye for just the right detail. It is a rich and heady mixture.

Connolly was born 31 years ago into a respectable, working-class Catholic family. Although his father was a time-served engineer and never without a job, home was two rooms in a 'right bummer' of a close in Anderston. When young, Connolly moved in with two of his father's sisters in the dockside area of Partick . . . School was the local RC primary. 'I hated every minute,' he says. 'I used to stand outside the door greetin' until I was pulled in by the teacher, or shoved in by my father.' Secondary school was better. St Gerard's RC, across the Clyde in Govan. But even then he was the joker in the pack. 'There was always one and I was it. I was the funny guy, the patter merchant.'

It was a talent which gave him a vague ambition to be a comedian. He was a regular attender at the famous *Five Past Eight* shows which flourished in Glasgow, and used to feature almost every variety of Scots funny man. He recalls watching Jimmy Logan dressed up as a coal-man singing 'What do you want if you don't want briquettes', and thinking, 'I'd love to do something like that'.

In the event young Connolly's career got off to an inauspicious start; messenger boy in a bookshop to be promptly sacked for stealing books. 'Thing wis . . . I didnae dae it.' That was followed by a spell as a van boy for Bilslands bread, a job he loved, and then at the age of 16, into Stevens shipyard at Lindhouse as an apprentice welder.

Connolly talks about his years in the Clyde shipyards in the way that some literati conjure up their golden days at Eton or Oxford or Cambridge. 'I was *so* happy there,' he says. 'I fell right into it. Loved it. As soon as that gate shuts, a shipyard becomes a complete wee town. You could buy shoes, cigarettes, transistor radios, cheap booze. It was an amazing place.' . . .

For reasons that he is still not too clear about, Connolly joined the Parachute Regiment, Territorial Army. 'It just sounded great,' he says. 'And I liked the red beret and that. I thought, Christ, I'm guaranteed a woman in this gear. But not this joker . . .' Surprisingly, perhaps, Connolly was a fairly enthusiastic paratrooper, with 23 jumps to his credit, and spent three or four years travelling about, firing off his rifle, and generally enjoying himself. But the radical traditions of the Clyde were seeping through, and the pointlessness of the whole business came to him in the Kyrenia Mountains in Cyprus. 'We were supposed to be chasing the Green Howards,' he says. 'After about a fortnight we captured one. It turned out he worked in the same shipyard as me. So I said to myself, Christ, I could have got him any day in the canteen. What the hell am I doin' in the Kyrenia Mountains wi' nae arse in my trousers.' . . .

At that stage Connolly's musical tastes were simple enough. 'I liked country and western, and I liked traditional jazz, but nothing out of the ordinary.' A few years previously he had bought a banjo for fun. 'I just wanted to make that picking noise.' But he found that his interest was sharpening, so he bought a guitar as well. Because someone had told him about it, he turned up at a folk club in Clydebank, and was immediately converted. 'I thought, Oh-ho . . . This is it. All the women looked like Joan Baez, and the guys were all hairy. All I'd known was suits, ties, and Perry Como haircuts.'

Before long he was getting to sing, and enjoyed it all so much that he gave up his job at Stevens, and started to eke out a very small living singing in the folk clubs and pubs. 'They were places where you could go and *learn* in front of an audience.' He was a natural, and gradually began to pick up something of a reputation. He ventured into England with a little group called The Skillet-lickers, then got together with an ex-rock guitarist called Tam Harvey and started The Humblebums. Later Connolly met, and was enormously impressed by, Gerry Rafferty (later to found Stealers Wheel), and the Humblebums duo became a trio. After a short time (and with some acrimony) Tam Harvey left, leaving Connolly and Rafferty to make a couple of reasonably successful LPs and become, probably, the most popular folk duo in Scotland. But it fell apart. 'Gerry was a better musician than me, but I was better at stage craft,' he explains. 'It couldn't work any more. I just had to get funny.' . . .

So Connolly packed it in, put together a solo act, and flopped miserably when he tried it out on Musselburgh. He then took off on a short tour of the clubs in the North of England where, he says, 'I grew up, entertainment-wise'. Then came a show at Cumbernauld called *Connolly's Glasgow Flourish*, which he took to The Close theatre in Glasgow where he teamed up with Tom Buchan the poet. Together they scripted *The Great Northern Welly Boot Show*, a UCS [Upper Clyde Shipyards]-inspired political rock-musical which did great business at the 1972 Edinburgh Festival, and turned out nicely when transferred to the Young Vic in London. After that, a series of increasingly successful tours (including the US), a fast-growing word-of-mouth reputation, and then early in 1974 a watershed show at the Glasgow Pavilion, after which everything fell into place for Connolly, and he proceeded to pack out every theatre in every city in Scotland. At the same time his records began to take off, the old Humblebum albums were re-released and his new LP *Cop Yer Whack For This* broke all kinds of records. The whole thing culminated (perhaps) in January this year when Connolly hit the London Palladium, generated a thriving black market in tickets, and was given a five-minute standing ovation at the end of the show . . .

But it is the eerie psychopaths and murderers of the 'Nutcracker Suite', Barlinnie's famous Special Wing, with whom he finds most rapport. 'Look. These guys are condemned. They're in there for an awful long time, if not forever. They've come through bad times – maybe the worst there is – and they're standing upright. They know exactly who they are and what they are. Which is a great thing. Giving a guy like that a laugh is a big thing to be doing with yourself.' . . .

And Connolly is prepared to speak the unspeakable. His Crucifixion piece is the most obvious example, but there are others. He will, for instance, register the constituents of a pool of vomit and conclude, 'It's no' the 18 Guinnesses that does it, it's the diced carrots.' And Connolly's drunks do not just walk funny and have problems articulating; they also have vomit down their jackets and their trouser legs are soaked in urine.

But if that is the way that the Scots choose to get drunk – and large numbers of them do – then that is the way Billy Connolly will represent them. As he says: 'The basic charm of my stuff is its honesty. That's all.'

The Death of Hugh MacDiarmid, 9 September 1978

ALAN BOLD

When Hugh MacDiarmid died the country lost a robust champion of Scots language and Scots nationalism who had challenged writers to wake up, take courage, and be heard. A poet and political grenade, his immoderate and often persuasive views ignited a renaissance in the literary community. Alan Bold, a prolific man of letters, was MacDiarmid's friend and biographer.

Christopher Murray Grieve was eighty-six when he died in Chalmers Hospital, Edinburgh, on 9 September 1978. He had outlived not only his mentors but most of his colleagues and contemporaries. . . . Though he advanced the ideal of being 'self-universal', MacDiarmid was aware of his identity as a witness to a particular period. He had no desire to live on into another era as an invalid.

As news of his death was announced to the public, the name Grieve was mentioned only by way of explaining that this was the actual identity of Scotland's greatest modern poet who was internationally known by the pseudonym he adopted in 1922: Hugh MacDiarmid. I remember sitting at home and listening to the lunchtime news. MacDiarmid was dead and, as if in defiance of that fact, the poet's voice was reproduced through a recording. That he maintained a living presence was evident. Shortly after the announcement there was a knock on my door. The actor Henry Stamper, my near neighbour, had also heard. 'Chris,' said Henry, 'was a great man. Now we'll see how he is remembered.'

On Wednesday, 13 September, my wife and I were driven down to Langholm, for the funeral, by our close friend Trevor Royle, then Literature Director of the Scottish Arts Council. It was a dreich day and umbrellas were out to protect heads against the drizzle. There were distinguished heads at the gathering of several hundred admirers. Most of them were bowed down, grieving for MacDiarmid.

As the mist settled on the hillside of Langholm Cemetery tears were shed unashamedly by the graveside. Alex Clark, MacDiarmid's election agent in his campaign against Sir Alec Douglas Home, spoke about MacDiarmid's political commitment: 'Having been greatly influenced by the Russian Revolution, and by Marxism, he wanted to see Socialism here in Scotland and believed that given full recognition of Nationhood, Scotland would lead Britain to Socialist change.' Norman MacCaig, poet and one of the closest friends during MacDiarmid's final years, delivered a more subjective statement. 'He would,' said MacCaig, 'walk into my mind as if it were a town and he a torchlight procession of one, lighting up the streets of my mind and some of the nasty little things that were burrowing into the corners.' MacCaig described MacDiarmid as 'a gregarious, genuinely friendly, and most courteous man, who savaged hypocrisy and fought for the enlargement of life'.

A piper, Seamus MacNeill of the Glasgow College of Piping, played the pibroch 'Lament for the Children'. Valda Grieve, the poet's widow, placed white roses on the coffin. Christopher Murray Grieve was thus laid to rest in his native Langholm. The restless spirit of Hugh MacDiarmid could not be similarly confined.

After the funeral the mourners gathered for a drink in Langholm. Valda expressed her opinion that it was appropriate that her husband should be buried in the Muckle Toon so 'those who rejected him will now have to live with him'. Many of us got drunk and, this being Scotland, there were discussions that turned into fierce arguments. Norman MacCaig had anticipated, in his poem 'After His Death', that MacDiarmid's death would be observed by two minutes' pandemonium. Doubtless MacDiarmid would have liked it that way.

Allan Wells Wins Olympic Gold, 25 July 1980

THE *SCOTSMAN*

In the Olympics, held at Moscow, long-jumper turned runner Allan Wells became the first Scot to win a medal on the Olympic track since Eric Liddell in 1924 by taking gold for the 100-metre sprint.

Allan Wells dipped his head to win the closest Olympic 100 metres final for 28 years, in the Lenin Stadium in Moscow last night.

The 28-year-old Scot, who had been more strongly favoured to win a Gold medal in the 200 metres, stunned everyone by taking the premier sprint title in a photo-finish from the Cuban, Silvio Leonard.

It was so close that neither Wells nor Leonard was sure who had taken the Gold until the race was replayed on the screen high above the stadium. Both men were given identical times of 10.25 seconds.

The announcer, the television cameras and the photographers had all gone for the 25-year-old Cuban, but the big silver screen showed without doubt that the Edinburgh marine engineer had dipped in front of his upright rival.

'It was very close,' said Wells afterwards. 'I thought I had got it, but I wasn't sure until I saw that replay, and then I knew it.'

Wells, normally so cool and collected, suddenly set off round the track on a lap of honour while the bewildered Leonard stood there, a lonely figure, as the cameramen realized their error and set off after the fastest man in the Olympic Games.

His wife and coach Margo, herself an international sprinter, said: 'I thought Leonard had beaten him until the replay.'

The difficulty was that the two were separated by the full width of the track, with the Cuban in lane 1 and Wells in lane 8.

'Allan was running with tunnel vision,' said Margo. 'There was just no one there to help him. But we did it, thank God.'

Even in this moment of glory, Wells was annoyed at the way he had been treated by the seeding committee which pitched him in with three other heat winners in the quarter-finals, when he was forced to run a British record time of 10.11, and again yesterday at being isolated in the lane nobody wants.

'Russia is not the easiest place to do it,' he said. 'Leonard had all the favours by being in the inside lane, and I had no one to pull me through.

I only saw him in the last 20 metres, and knew then that I had to do something special to get it.'

But the Scot, a failed long-jumper until he took up sprinting, has always been noted for his powerful finish. His problems this time were accentuated by the fact that he was forced by the International Athletics Federation rules to abandon his normal free start and use the electronic starting blocks.

In spite of this drastic change to his style, he produced four marvellous runs to win the title that every sprinter wants. Wells said: 'As I settled in my blocks, the thought went through my mind that I needed my best ever start. Maybe it wasn't the quickest, but it was good enough.'

The Pope Visits Scotland, June 1982

CHRIS BAUR

The first ever visit from a Pope to Scotland was an emotional occasion for the Catholic community in Scotland. Pope John Paul II spoke to adoring crowds in Edinburgh and Glasgow, who braved sunstroke and dehydration to hear him. This historic visit was followed in 1994 by the appointment of Thomas Winning, Archbishop of Glasgow, as only the third Cardinal from Scotland since the Reformation.

Under a furnace summer sun yesterday more than 250,000 people gathered at the feet of Pope John Paul to hear him deliver his sermon on a Scottish hillside. In those joyful and solemn moments, the Catholic flock of St Andrew was at last embraced by the successor of St Peter. He did it with timeless simplicity. Gently, he enfolded them with his own sense of their story: 'It was Andrew, the heavenly patron of your beloved Scotland, who introduced Peter to Jesus . . . today we are bound to one another by a supernatural brotherhood stronger than that of blood.'

He allowed himself to compare it to the Sermon on the Mount. But in truth it cannot have been anything like this. He had flown to them – the largest crowd ever assembled north of the Border – in a huge Sikorsky helicopter made in America.

It came low over the trees and every move was watched on a gigantic Mitsubishi screen made in Japan. For some on the edges of the vast crowd – fully half-a-mile away – even the Japanese screen was not visible . . .

There was no-one, in those times, to tell them over 100 loudspeakers that 'the Holy father is now approaching sections F21 to F28' as they did when they drove the Pope for almost an hour through the 280 corrals in which the faithful were penned.

There were no pibrochs to welcome him in those days. Nor did they play the fiddle faster and faster as he approached until *Kate Dalrymple* had become a frenzy too quick to dance.

Nor did they have a thousand priests, then, each shaded with a white-and-gold umbrella to walk through the throng, slowly administering to communicants, many of them stripped to the waist on this the hottest day of the year.

Did they have first aid, then, to help the victims of heart attacks (there were six yesterday), or cases of suspected appendicitis (there were three of those yesterday), or the thousands who collapsed with sunburn and dehydration in the heat, or the lady who began to have her baby?

Did they have any of that? . . . They did not. But what does that matter? They had not come for such things. They had come for their Pope to tell them from his own lips about the 'complete transformation of Catholic life that has come about in Scotland' since the black days four centuries ago when the medieval church had been shattered and all but lost in a Scotland isolated on the outer edge of Europe.

Now, he said, Scots Catholics were 'assuming their legitimate role in every sector of public life and some of them were invested with the most important and prestigious offices of this land.' . . . He told them simply to be Christians by example – 'the world still recognizes genuine goodness for what it is.'

Then he addressed himself 'to that larger community of believers in Christ, who share with my Catholic brothers and sisters the privilege of being Scots sons and daughters alike of this ancient nation.' . . . And then, as the children had done in Edinburgh the night before, they stopped him. Long before he had said 'Let Scotland flourish' they had for a little while imposed their will on him as they sang to him and called for him in the midst of his address . . .

It became a game between them. As the people became still and saw him on that huge screen moving to speak again, another wave of cheers and singing would detain him. He let them do it over and again – finally taking his own private joy from those 'several moments,' he said, 'when the Pope became silent and you became preachers.'

Munro-bagging, 1980s

MURIEL GRAY

Broadcaster and writer Muriel Gray gritted her teeth and climbed her first mountain as a teenager so she could impress her boyfriend. From that day she was hooked, going on to become an unlikely proselytizer for one of the country's most distinctive sports and obsessions, climbing mountains above 3,000 feet. This pursuit is known as Munro-bagging.

Sometimes even the easiest of mountains can defeat you. There is nothing particularly difficult about Creag Meagaidh, unless it comes up in a spelling test, yet it took me three attempts to get to the top of the damned thing.

It's only in recent years that I've learned to use the weather forecast before contemplating a hill-walk. Millions of pounds spent on satellite technology is wasted when people like me ignore Michael Fish yelling on television from behind some sandbags, 'For God's sake take cover!' as we set off to claim a Munro with a song in our hearts.

It was just such foolhardy behaviour that enabled me continually to miss the summit of Creag Meagaidh. The first attempt was in winter, precisely at that dark, depressing period when the sun can barely be bothered rising for more than 20 minutes before it packs in and hands over to nightfall. The weather on this occasion seemed ideal. A heavy snowfall left the hills deliciously inviting and the sky was clear and bright.

Two of us set off up the long path from Aberarder at the mind-bogglingly stupid time of 11.30 a.m. . . . We reached Lochan a' Choire at 3 p.m. when the sun was starting to remember it was needed elsewhere. Simple arithmetic told us that even if we gained the summit we would be stumbling back down in the dark like late cinema-goers trying to find their seats.

As we sat at the loch eating a cold lunch, deciding who could first pin the blame on the other for messing up the day, we heard voices from the cliffs surrounding the lochan. A third of the way up a vicious-looking ice-climb were two men, slowly hacking an unenviable route with axes and crampons. By this time it was past 3.30, the light was fading fast, and the blizzard that the ignored weatherman had warned would sweep the Highlands was whipping into action. That's odd, we thought. Perhaps they're going to spend the night on the mountain. Maybe they're top mountaineers training for a Himalayan expedition that requires constant overnight bivvying on icy rock faces. So we ignored them and went home. Unfortunately they turned out to be two fools who didn't realize the time, and brought Mountain Rescue out combing the hill for them next morning. Luckily, they had survival gear and were found alive and well, albeit a trifle sheepish, at the top of the climb.

I felt rather guilty after that episode. When should you tell Mountain Rescue that you think there might be somebody in danger? After all, if those two boys had died, it would have been on our consciences that we saw them get into difficulty and did nothing. On the other hand, imagine the embarrassment of calling a full-scale search out for somebody who is not only not in peril, but is mightily cheesed off to be awoken from a deep sleep by an RAF Sea-King helicopter blowing the filling out of their sleeping-bag? . . . I live in fear of calling out the rescue team for a solitary figure glimpsed high on a darkening summit, only to find it's Hamish McInnes nipping back up to fetch a dropped mitten.

That was the first attempt at Creag Meagaidh. The second, on a blustery Sunday in October, was more frustrating. Ignoring the weather forecast yet again, a number of us packed our rucksacks and headed up that interminable path to Coire Ardair. Meanwhile, canny Munroists who paid attention to satellite technology, which indicated a depression deeper than Christmas in Barlinnie, were sitting at home by the fire eating cheese on toast. This, however, was a determined pack and we were not going to be put off by small obstacles like being unable to stand up or walk forward. This time I at least got past the lochan and up on to the boulder field that leads to the window. The window is a coll neatly dividing Creag Meagaidh and another Munro, Stob Poite Coire Ardair but, more significantly, it acts as a highly efficient wind tunnel. As we lurched up the soaking, slimy boulders towards it, like a team of wet-look mime artists walking against the wind, one of our party stopped and said, 'Let's go back.'

At least we all hoped that's what he said. In the gale it sounded like, 'Ehh . . . oaaah . . . aaack.' We were back in the car with the heater on before you could say 'Who finished the soup?' and another attempt was foiled.

The last failure was human. I made the mistake of telling two non-hill-walking friends that they could easily manage Creag Meagaidh. The day was perfect. A crisp winter morning greeted us with snow quilted in twinkling ice crystals. The time was 9 a.m., the sky was clear and blue, and nothing was going to stop me this time. What I failed to realize was that to those who never walk up mountains, visiting the bank, the post office and the dry cleaners on the same day is considered a triathlon. My friends had to have their first sit-down in sight of the car. I was heart-broken. By 12.30 we had just made the birch wood and had to admit defeat. Friendship is more important than mountaineering, and so for their sakes I told them they'd done very well and we turned back to the prospect of a more leisurely Sunday afternoon, with colour supplements, cats, coffee and carpets to lie on. I cast one longing glance up at the cliffs of Coire Ardair, where the sun was glancing off the icy tips of gleaming rock, and I knew that next time I'd get the sucker.

The Miners' Strike, March 1984 to March 1985

MICK MCGAHEY

The miners' strike of 1984–5 signalled the beginning of the end for the industry in Britain. It was followed by such widespread pit closures that the mining trade was shortly as good as dead. The year-long strike was a time of heavy-handed picketing, police aggression, and hardship. The strike saw a period of high solidarity in the mining community, who had many supporters. Those few who continued to work were considered traitors and never forgiven. As a spokesman, Mick McGahey, from Bilston Glen colliery in East Lothian, was one of the loudest voices of protest during the strike.

I was born in Glasgow and moved through to Edinburgh in 1967/68, left the school at fifteen, went to Bilston Glen and started working in . . . April 1971, and worked there for thirteen years, eight months until I was sacked during the miners' strike . . .

The start of the strike was quite a traumatic time but it was interesting, it was good. The thing that stands out is the solidarity, particularly the first six months wi' all the workers that were involved and the solidarity that came from other trade unions, particularly SOGAT (Society of Graphical and Allied Trades). No' just the money but the practical things that they gave to strike centres like foodstuffs, but also toiletries and stuff like that that women would use. It wasnae just about men being on strike, it was about women and men and their families and a lot of the unions reflected that in the type of stuff that they gave and in the way that they gave it.

The one thing that happened was that I got arrested nine times during the strike, well it was five times and nine charges, and out of that it was four I was convicted o' and five I wasnae. . . . At that particular time it didnae have that much effect getting the sack. To a certain degree it was like earning your stripes, you know . . .

We did pit head collections every Friday and the main problem was that, at the end o' the strike, you started off wi' thirty or forty people standing outside Bilston Glen and various other pits, but by the second year it was only two or three. It was after the first six months, though, that it really started to affect people. People really realized that they wernae going to take you back . . .

But right up until the time where Bilston Glen was shut, and that was a few years after the strike, my intentions were that I was going back working in the pit. But when Bilston Glen was shut that was the bubble burst for me . . . I miss the pit, I miss the work. I don't miss the shifts but I certainly miss the people I worked with, even the ones that scabbed. Some of them.

Glasgow's Cultural Credentials Are Recognized, 1986

BILLY CONNOLLY

When Glasgow was nominated in 1986 as European Capital of Culture for 1990, comedian Billy Connolly raised a cheer. His sentiments were felt by many, who were not only keen to see Glasgow recognized for its merits, but wanted to score a point in the city's long-standing rivalry with the capital, which had grown keener since the advent of the Edinburgh Festival.

An actor friend of mine told me once of how he returned home to Glasgow after some success on the London stage and decided to visit the Italian café where he frittered away his youth. The owner, Tony, was still there, hidden behind the whooshing and grinding cappuccino machine. He gave my friend a warm welcome and, drying his hands with his ever-present tea towel, asked him what he thought of the place. Had it changed much while he had been away pursuing fame?

My friend cast an eye around the sea of Fablon and Formica and found it much the same. There was one obvious addition, though: a horrendous painting covering one wall, in gaudy colours unknown in nature, depicting a shortbread-tin Highland scene, a loch with mountains, complete with unlikely looking wildlife – eagles, deer, badgers, pheasant and haggis. Below the painting sat the café's only other customer, a dishevelled individual, his head in the soup, snoring and bubbling furiously between mumbled swear words.

The owner then asked my friend the question he had been dreading. Pointing to the garish wall, Tony said, 'Well, what do you think of my muriel?' The best response my friend could manage was a blurted, 'Eh it's very nice, Tony.' No sooner had the words left his lying lips than the soup drinker in the corner uttered his judgement: 'Very nice, ye say? Very nice? Ye call that a muriel? Christ, Venus de Milo would turn in his grave if he'd seen that!'

Thus goes the best piece of artistic criticism I have ever heard; a thumping piece of honesty which the Sunday review pages would do well to emulate. Of course, it was uttered in the midst of that cultural centre of Western civilization, Glasgow. What is this I hear you say in the cultural deserts of London, Birmingham, Bristol and Manchester – tish, bah, pooh, bosh and figs?

The reason for my bout of civic pride in my old home town is that, in an unusual display of wisdom, Richard Luce, the arts minister, has nominated Glasgow as a centre of cultural excellence, and not before time.

For too long Glasgow has languished under the shadow of Edinburgh. In the minds of those who award prizes and tributes to cities and the like, Edinburgh has held a sort of franchise on the beauty department of Scotland's cultural heritage; a fact that has caused a great deal of sand to lodge in the collective Glasgow craw.

Glasgow, this city of 70 (yes, 70) parks and open spaces, has long resented its image as the blackspot of Europe. For many years it has been a victim of documentary film-makers who, when short of evidence of marauding gangs terrorizing the wide-eyed and innocent populace, were not above slipping some unemployed youths a couple of bob to imper-sonate the same.

To deny Glasgow's violent past would, of course, be less than sensible. However, it seems to me the right approach would be to build on the more positive side of Glasgow's character.

Glasgow scored a cultural dropkick a few years ago when it refurbished the Theatre Royal – a great Victorian music hall which had been sliced up, groaning all the way, into a television studio eventually wrecked by fire – and made it the home of Scottish Opera. In a world that seems obsessed with building car parks and high-rise office blocks this came as a real shock . . .

My own love of things cultural arises from a mistake of geography, really. I was born and spent my formative years in Partick, most famous I suppose for Partick Thistle, a football team of somewhat mixed fortunes – an English friend once remarked on hearing the result Partick Thistle 2, Motherwell 1: 'My goodness, I always thought that they were called Partick Thistle Nil'.

At the front of Kelvingrove Park in Partick is the Kelvingrove Art Gallery and Museum, where, on many a Sunday, my sister Flo and I would go for an afternoon's cultural absorption and a slide on the highly polished floor.

Some talented buyer in the Glasgow council had purchased Salvador Dali's *Christ of St John of the Cross*, causing quite a furore at the time. I have always been grateful to that person, for I spent many happy hours looking at that painting. It has instilled in me a love of Salvador Dali and, more important, surrealism in art and in life in general that has pleased and fortified me many times in my travels.

As a special treat, I would be taken every couple of years to the People's Palace, a truly great folk museum at Glasgow Green. This, the most alive museum I have experienced, is dedicated to Glasgow's history and life-style, without denying the humour of the place. It suffers greatly at the hands of the press and the less enlightened members of the council because of the shadow thrown over it by its wealthier cousin, the Burrell Collection, affluently housed in Pollok Estate.

Personally, I preferred the Burrell Collection when it was in boxes in various warehouses, disused schools, and abandoned churches. My father would point out one of these schools solemnly. 'That building holds treasures,' he would say, and I would stare at the sooty, grimy place, suitably impressed.

The culture of my Glasgow is a living, working, singing and laughing culture. It is a culture of a city renowned for toughness and born of adversity. If this type of toughness upsets you, I would advise you to stay clear of Glasgow.

It is a culture that has been fought for and won by dedicated men and women, not always citizens of Glasgow. People like Giles Havergal of the Citizens' Theatre, John Cunningham and Sandy Goudie in art, Alasdair Gray and Carl MacDougall in literature, Liz Lochhead in poetry, Elspeth King in the museum department, and Sir Alexander Gibson and Bill McCue in music.

My only hope, when an honour has been placed on such richly deserving shoulders, is that the louder and more shrill trumpet-blowers of the Scottish press can be blanketed by the calmer members. The time for trumpet-blowing and naïve pleas for recognition has long gone. If you are lucky enough to have been born there, or smart enough to wish to be there, then the time has come to be quietly pleased.

The Lockerbie Disaster, 22 December 1988

BARCLAY MCBAIN

When a PanAm flight bound from London to New York exploded over the small town of Lockerbie in the Scottish Borders, the full horror of international terrorism hit Scotland. The 259 crew and passengers died, and forty Lockerbie homes were destroyed, killing eleven townspeople. The following report was filed the morning after the plane fell on the town.

All day long the good folk of Lockerbie walked up their High Street to their town hall and on the public notice board scanned the list containing the names of more than 200 people who were friends, neighbours, relatives, acquaintances, or just fellow citizens.

The etiquette of relationships did not matter. Those who read the list and those whose names appeared on it had both been touched by the awful consequences of international terrorism.

Lockerbie is a friendly market town whose western spine leans against the A74, the main artery between Scotland and the south. Yesterday this accommodating little place laid bare its wounds, its wounded, its dead, and the hundreds who it had been decided would die on its gentle fields to the world.

Those named on the list were the lucky ones. They had been evacuated from their houses, many of which were exposed in the bright sunshine yesterday as mere blackened shells, but had now all been safely accounted for. Stripped of its civic functions, the town hall now served as an emergency morgue. By last night crew and passengers from the PanAm Jumbo and local people lay dead. Dumfries and Galloway police estimated that more than 150 bodies lay in six acres within a 10-mile radius.

Yesterday morning I went to The Main Farm and looked over a dyke at the remains of the cabin of the Jumbo jet. It lay, distressed, on its side like a giant toy discarded by a spoiled child. But this mindless fit of pique had the bloody hand of the callous zealot on it. I walked along the lane towards the farm to speak to the farmer, Mr Jim Wilson. As I passed the old churchyard I saw sheep grazing in the field to my left. Something, which I took to be a motionless, possibly dead, sheep with a gash in its side, caught my eye. It was the naked body of a middle-aged man. A pole stuck into the ground with a piece of cloth fluttering at the top marked the spot. On my right a small bundle, which can only have been the body of a child, lay wrapped in plastic sheeting. Looking up the hill I saw more poles and more bundles. It was a terrible massacre.

Mr Wilson was speaking to the postman outside his front door. If you took away the calamitous toy, the bundles, and the body it was an idyllic scene. Mr Wilson said there were between 50 and 60 bodies on his land. He had discovered many of them himself. 'You would not know what age they were. They were battered beyond recognition. Some hit the earth with such force that you could almost bury them in the indentations they made in the ground. I have never seen anything like this before and I never want to see anything like it again in my lifetime.'

Mr Wilson said that most of the bodies were naked, apart from socks. He had been told that the effects of decompression had pulled off their clothes. In one appallingly macabre incident a falling body had killed one of his sheep.

When the plane came down and cut an apocalyptic swathe from west to east across the south of Lockerbie Mr Wilson thought it was an electrical storm. The noise he took to be thunder. When the power in his house went off he blamed lightning. When he went outside to fetch his son-in-law, Mr Kevin Anderson, who lives in the cottage nearby, he knew there had been no natural storm. Another falling body had brought down his power lines. The local doctor took one look at the futile scene and returned to Lockerbie to tend the wounded. Mr Luciano Dovesi, one of Mr Wilson's neighbours, tried to find the pulse of a stewardess but there was no life in this field.

On the way down the hill into town I passed the golf course which contained about another 60 bodies. More sticks, more bundles, more wreckage. Back in Carlisle Road glaziers, slaters and joiners wanted to repair damaged houses. Under their ladders bits of the plane lay where they had fallen.

The wife of a former chairman of Lockerbie Community Council told me: 'Everyone seems to be going about in a daze. Everything is off on a tangent.' Mr Robert Riddett, the present chairman, said, 'Everyone I have spoken to, everyone in the town, is affected in one way or another. I saw it myself and got a terrible shock. Everyone is in the same state. We have had a terrible devastation. I have spoken to as many people as I can and I still do not know who has gone. The whole town is shattered.'

Mr Tom Corrie, from Galashiels, searched until 2.30 a.m. yesterday for his 82-year-old aunt Miss Jean Murray. All that is left standing of her house in Sherwood Crescent is one wall. Sherwood Crescent bore the brunt of the devastation. Mr Corrie's wife Maureen said the family had had conflicting reports about Miss Murray. One stated that she was missing presumed dead but according to another she had been evacuated.

Porridge, 1990

GEORGE MACKAY BROWN

For centuries porridge has been one of the staple foods of the country, but as Orcadian poet George Mackay Brown records, it can take a lifetime even for a Scot to learn to love it.

Chief o' Scotia's Food

Porridge on a cold winter morning – I suppose northerners have been comforting themselves with porridge of one kind and another for centuries. And of course, in the days before cornflakes, porridge was an important part of our childhood diet. And of course we didn't like it much; together with mince, stew, soup and boiled fish it was a thing to be endured rather than enjoyed. The only food we seemed to enjoy was ham-and-eggs, sausages, kippers, and especially cakes, chocolate and sweeties.

As cows munched hay we took our spoonfuls of porridge, mechanically, and 'because it's good for you' . . . We often wondered, I'm sure, how the things that were good for us were on the whole unpleasant.

But anyway, we grew out of porridge, weaned away in large part by the 1930s craze for corn-flakes, which swept our generation like a prairie fire. For one thing, there were no lumps in corn-flakes. For another, there was no sticky smudgy pot to be cleaned. For decades thereafter, porridge was a food of which we had only theoretical knowledge. 'The halesome parritch, chief o' Scotia's food'; even Burns' mother had told him it was good for him.

Last summer, I had to spend a while in hospital in Aberdeen. Porridge was on the menu, among other items, every morning. I must say I enjoyed my first plate of Foresterhill porridge so much, that thereafter I had it nearly every morning. I was able to tell the sister-in-charge: 'Foresterhill porridge is really good.' . . . So when I eventually got home, I thought seriously of making porridge every morning first thing. Three things held me back: the thought of steeping the stuff, the probability of 'lumps', and the certainty of a mucky, sticky pot to clean afterwards.

For my birthday, a friend gave me a small non-stick pot, along with two wooden stirring spoons. I bought a packet of porridge, and found out that no steeping was required. A little five-minute stir and simmer, and there on the table was a plate of most delicious hot nourishment, laced with cold milk. Now I have it nearly every morning.

How the locusts have eaten all those years of grain-rich cold-defying corn. Now I see clearly what Burns meant. And I'm sure many an ancient Celtic bard before him has sung the praises of porridge.

Scotland Win the Grand Slam, 17 March 1990

IAIN ANDERSON

There was more than a hint of ancient antagonism in the way the Scottish rugby team faced down their English opponents to take a 13–7 victory and win the Grand Slam.

> The tumult and the shouting dies:
> The captains and the kings depart

So wrote the great English poet of Empire, Rudyard Kipling. But if in these former, halcyon days the playing fields of Eton were primarily charged with the responsibility of forming character and firing that kind of resolution which would ultimately yield other fields in other countries, so also the contemporary catchment area has produced stalwart yeomanry from Bath and Bristol, Gloucester and Nottingham, Leicester and London.

Certainly, they had done England proud on French and foreign soil. But at Murrayfield yesterday afternoon they were given a glimpse of rugby immortality.

It was, however, only a glimpse – for on this occasion the Empire was to strike back. The little white rose of Scotland – that smells so sweet and breaks the heart – is basking in a little deserved glory today and for some time to come as her native sons collected the spoils of a war of attrition and a battle of wills which, for sheer endeavour, fitness, commitment and courage is now and forever writ large in the chronicles of sporting history.

The preliminaries themselves spoke volumes in the psychological hostilities that were immediately apparent. As England shed their imperial purple tracksuits on a March day softened by a fitful southerly wind and bright sunshine, Scotland walked out of the tunnel with a measured, dignified, yet curiously ominous pace to signal the most passionate rendition of *Flower of Scotland*. The torch remained to be lit.

With England kicking off, apparently into the wind, the ferocity of the Scottish onslaught was immediately intimidating as the visitors reeled under a pressure from which they had been mercifully oblivious over their three previous games.

Within the first eight minutes, Craig Chalmers had kicked at goal three times and Scotland led by six points. But more than this, English confidence had been seriously breached as, from the opening line-out, the home tactics of variety and disruption were immediately apparent.

Chalmers' first successful penalty followed productive work at the ruck after an impressive scrimmage shunt in four minutes, and the second came when the touch-judge, Derek Bevan, indicated to referee David Bishop that Jeff Probyn was guilty of illegal footwork on David Sole. The kick was in front of the posts and there were eight minutes on the clock.

The Scottish line-out was enjoying a most profitable opening with Gray, Cronin and Jeffry denying the twin threat of Dooley and Ackford.

However, England fashioned a delightful try after 14 minutes. It had its origins in good scrimmage ball which Teague held as Jeffrey detached and, rolling to the open side, the big Gloucester No. 8 committed Finlay Calder's tackle, enabling Richard Hill to deliver such a pass as to allow Andrew to evade Sean Lineen on the outside and serve Jeremy Guscott.

The centre's momentary hesitation as he looked to Rory Underwood invited a Gavin Hastings tackle on the wing, but the covering Gary Armstrong was too late to prevent the Bath centre from scoring England's first try at Murrayfield since 1980.

England were now to sustain their best period of the game with a series of scrimmages close to the home line. But they could not score –

just as the Welsh had found the dark blue jerseys impenetrable two weeks ago.

In this torrid and punishing confrontation Derek White suffered ligament damage which forced him to leave the field after 27 minutes, with John Jeffrey moving to No. 8 and Derek Turnbull taking up position on the flank. It would take a brave man to suggest a more suitable replacement for such a contest.

The ease and facility with which Jeffrey assumed his club role in an international jersey, and his telepathic liaison with Gary Armstrong, were now to bear fruit as Gavin Hastings' intrusions began to worry the English. Six minutes from half-time, Chalmers kicked his third penalty from 40 metres after Ackford was penalized at a line-out which Scotland had swept superbly.

However, if there was a moment when the English recognized intuitively that theirs was a lost cause, it was in the opening moments of the second period when Scotland scored a superb try.

Jeffrey and Armstrong once again set up copybook scrimmage possession for the little Jed scrum-half to break and find the omnipresent Gavin Hastings with a pass which the full-back held almost by instinct. Hastings' chip up the touchlines reduced the English defence to shreds and tatters, and Tony Stranger, stretching for the bounce, was over in the corner.

Chalmers could not convert, but no matter, the psychological damage done was immense and the visitors grew desperate in their attempts to salvage something from a game which was slipping from their grasp.

That they succeeded in committing Scotland to a rearguard action owed much to the precision of Rob Andrew's kicking and to the tireless efforts of Will Carling to inject some penetration into his three-quarter line. On more than one occasion the captain was swept to the perdition of a Scottish ruck, while an escaping Underwood was magnificently tackled by the best defender in British rugby – Scott Hastings.

England's only score in the second half came from a Simon Hodgkinson penalty goal after 15 minutes, but their hearts and hopes were dashed by the iron discipline of the Scottish scrimmage, its backrow cover and the mighty, relieving boot of Gavin Hastings.

At the whistle, several members of the English pack were close to exhaustion but John Jeffrey sprinted 50 metres in exultation for the tunnel.

Thus ended the greatest rugby show on earth. Thus England failed to meet their rugby destiny and thus Scotland once more realized their highest aspirations. Thus triumph and disaster were wrought at Murrayfield – imposters both in the eyes of Rudyard Kipling. Is rugby, after all, on such a day only a game?

Trainspotting, *August 1993*

KENNY FARQUHARSON

Novelist Irvine Welsh arrived on the literary scene in 1993 like a pugnacious gatecrasher. His mercilessly grim but funny account of a group of no-hope Leithers ushered in a new age of fiction. This original take touched a nerve in readers and spawned a thousand imitators, most far less able than himself. In one of the earliest interviews he gave, Welsh was keen to paint a portrait of the artist as an only partially reformed reprobate.

Should we kick off with Irvine Welsh's life as a punk, when he collected dogshit to wear on his clothes and screamed abuse at strangers on buses? Or his criminal record, which includes a suspended sentence for smashing up a north London community centre in a whisky-crazed frenzy? Maybe we should begin with his heroin experiences and current enthusiasm for ecstasy. Or I suppose there is always his book.

It has to be said that *Trainspotting* is a bum title for a would-be bestseller – just try asking for it in Waterstone's and watch the funny looks from other customers. Undaunted, PR people from Welsh's London publisher, Secker & Warburg, are waging a campaign of hype unprecedented for a debut Scottish author, enthusing breathlessly that the book will be huge and that Irvine is 'just a lovely man'. A Secker executive makes known his belief that Welsh will 'do for Edinburgh what Jim Kelman did for Glasgow'. Jeff Torrington, winner of the Whitbread prize, calls the debut novel 'wickedly witty . . . a bad day in Bedlam'. This month's *Literary Review* hails a 'wonderfully sordid depiction of how the other half dies and why it matters'.

All this flannel usually has self-respecting journalists reaching for the vitriol. But not this time – *Trainspotting* turns out to be a genuine wonder. In a nutshell, it is the *Sunday Post* reader's worst nightmare, an everyday story of drug-taking folk with invaluable advice on injecting heroin into your genitals, using a glass ashtray as a pub weapon and scoring with opium pessaries while suffering from diarrhoea. The book has swearie words, a heart and a smidgin of hope. Peopling its pages are characters with names like Second Prize, Rent Boy, Jam Rag, Sick Boy and The Swan. Imagine Jim Kelman with a sense of humour and six cans of superlager, and you will be close. It is revolting, funny, scary and deeply affecting. Best of all, it destroys the myth that the only Scottish urban working-class culture worth a damn can only be found a pub crawl's distance from Parkhead and Ibrox: the east coast keelie has arrived.

Irvine Welsh, in the kitchen of his second-floor flat overlooking Leith Links, offers a can of export (13% extra free) and talks about a friend of his who tentatively suggested including a glossary so that posh people could understand words like barry, rage, swedgin, shan, biscuit-ersed, skaggy-bawed, shunky, spawny and donks. 'No way,' he says. 'One thing I can't stand is these Merchant City yuppies with a copy of Michael Munro's *The Patter* next to their Filofax. The last thing I want is all these fuckers up in Charlotte Square putting on all the vernacular as a stage-managed thing. It's nothing to do with them.'

Welsh is tall and thin with receding black hair, cut short and gelled spikey. He is wearing a black jumper, drainpipe blue jeans and black boots. His face has a beery, asymmetical look about it, and he speaks in an even monotone, almost without moving his lips. Every now and again he breaks into a grin that takes 10 years off him, and his eyes gleam. We zip through a condensed life story:

Born in Leith. Father was a docker and then a carpet salesman. Mother was a waitress. Moved to a maisonette in Muirhouse, a pretty rough Edinburgh housing scheme. Got drunk for the first time at 14 while camping in Arran. First took speed at 17. Worked as apprentice TV repairman. Went to London, blind drunk on a bus, to be a punk. Lived the punk life, sleeping in Green Park by day, pogoing to bands like 999, Chelsea and Slaughter and the Dogs at the Vortex and Marquee at night. Played in bands with names such as The Pubic Lice, always getting ditched because he was a talentless guitarist. Lived in seedy shared flats and not-so-sleazy squats. Threw rocks at police at Wapping picket line and miners' strike barneys. Had short-term jobs as dish-washer, road-digger, clerk. Took lots of heroin, speed and alcohol. Got arrested frequently. Then found decent job in local government, married, flitted to Croydon and tried to settle down – his first really bad move.

'I was more worried about myself then than I was at any other time of my life,' he says. 'You've fallen into something that's so ugly and horrible. Instead of My Drugs Hell, it's My Suburban Hell. That's not being flippant. One thing I really fear is living that whole kind of home/

garden/kids kind of suburban existence. DIY and all that. I'd much rather be selling my arse in King's Cross than living that kind of life. It's sick and sordid that people have set such limitations on themselves, thinking that's all they'll get.'

These days, with a middle-class job in staff training in local government and a comfortable home, you could be forgiven for believing he has at last succumbed. 'I'm basically Mr Straight from nine-to-five during the week. Maybe every other weekend I'll go to a rave. My finger isn't jammed on the self-destruct button any more – but I'll give it a wee flick every now and then just for a bit of intrigue. Maybe once in about six months I'll go through a miniature breakdown and I'll disappear for a few days at a time; I'll vanish into this labyrinth of places in Edinburgh I never knew existed, and come out of the other end.' . . .

Asked how bad his drug-taking became, Welsh looks thoughtful for a full 15 seconds. 'I can't really say I've had a great deal of personal problems with drugs,' he says eventually. 'The problems were caused by the procurement rather than the effects. In your teens and your twenties you're not really aware of your mortality, you're just steaming in.' He thinks it would be hypocritical simply to condone or condemn drugs. Heroin, he says, always causes problems. If you want to take a class A drug, he advises, go for ecstasy instead. 'There's a tension when you write a book like this, that you are some kind of middle-class voyeur looking in and writing an exploitation book about other people's misery, which equally I don't think I am. Probably you could point to people in my past and they'd say: "Oh, he was never into anything like that to that extent." Or get people saying: "That bastard was much worse than any of the characters in the book."'

The Flying Scotsman Breaks the World Hour Record, 17 July 1993

GRAEME OBREE

Known as the Flying Scotsman, Kilmarnock policeman's son Graeme Obree set several world cycling records in one of the most unconventional sporting careers yet seen. He first astonished the cycling community with his home-made bicycle, Old Faithful, which he had made partly from bits of an old washing machine, before demonstrating equally unconventional cycling techniques that were frequently banned. He came to international attention in July 1993 when he attempted unsuccessfully to break the World Hour Record held by Francesco Moser. The following day, he made another attempt.

I remember striding over to the waiting crowd like Butch Cassidy, before putting on my helmet and going straight up onto the track. I was careful to say almost nothing and to not catch anyone's eye, as a matter of keeping my momentum. It was now almost 9 a.m., and I was right on time. I did three laps of the track and pulled up to the starter, who grabbed the back of my saddle to steady me at the tie. At this moment, I had no sweaty hands, no tightness of breathing and no sense of fear or anxiety. Instead I had a 'blitzkrieg', arrogant impatience to 'bring it on', and I knew that I would succeed with this mood. What I did not want was the starter to utter the same words that he had done the afternoon before. I was afraid, deep down, about thinking about the greatness of the record or how taking a deep breath to humble myself to it would break through my thin veneer of arrogant aggression and reduce me to a cowering, tired and beaten athlete before the start.

I was having none of it, and just as he was about to speak, I got there first with a loud and clear, 'Are you ready?' Now, that is normally the question that the starter asks, and to hear it from the athlete must have taken him aback, but in any case, he instantly replied 'yes'. Such was my fighting spirit that I attacked from the line there and then, and such was the unexpected nature of my start that I could see the timekeepers fiddling with watches from the first banking, while out of the saddle.

I gave myself four laps to settle into the time-trial-type rhythm with Old Faithful that I could not find the afternoon before. Andy – the schedules guy – had suggested the evening before at dinner that I use a schedule for Moser's record itself, and I agreed, as it seemed to make good sense. On that schedule, I was up from the start, and I was into a flow that I was gradually building a margin over the record, and the more ground I gained over the record, the more gung-ho I became.

The ride was no easier than before, and it was a full-on effort to maintain my pace and my rhythm. Where it had been a battle against the black line, it was now a battle against myself not to lose my rhythm, as the effort needed to sustain my ride got greater and greater. The vocal support from the team and supporters was greater than it had been the previous day, and a lot of people spread out along the inside of the track so that I could pick out individual voices, hearing their message as I sped around. [My wife] Anne and her mum stood on the apex of a banking so I could glance at them as well as hear them every time I came round.

By halfway, it felt like hell, as my effort from the previous day started to tell on me. Minutes seemed like hours, and lap after lap, it got harder, like going up a steeper and steeper incline. Many times, I thought about how nice it would be to stop and end the agony. I was up on the record, though, and I would go on and on, no matter what – even if I had to ride to death by exhaustion like a horse – and every lap I thought about the failure. For a little while, I imagined I was that horse, galloping on and on and on to its oblivion.

I was in agony by the last quarter of the ride, my feet, ankles, genitals, hands, face and scalp had all gone completely numb. Every muscle in my legs was on fire, and I had to think about how each muscle moved individually to keep them pedalling on some sort of rhythm. My eyes were a flickering blur now, though I could still see my line, and my lungs were rasping air in and out like bellows. Still, it was a beautiful feeling to be breaking the record, and when I got the 'ten minutes to go' shout, I knew I could hold on, no matter what – I would ride through any misery now to grasp my prize.

Misery it was, but just before my time was up, I heard what was – and always will be – the most beautiful sound in the world. A pistol shot rang out to mark the point where I completed Moser's distance, and there and then I was the record holder. I had an extra half minute or so to add distance to the old record, but in my head I was celebrating already and I had an official finishing distance of 51.596 km.

The Poll that Put Gordon Brown out of the Leadership Race, 26 May 1994

THE *SCOTSMAN*

The untimely death of John Smith, leader of the Labour Party, in May 1994 sparked a furious behind-the-scenes struggle for the leadership of the party. Until Smith's death it had been thought that in the event of such a crisis, Tony Blair would step aside for his more experienced friend Gordon Brown, rather than split the vote. Within hours of Smith's death, however, at his wife's urging Blair was considering running for the position. It has been widely rumoured that Brown finally agreed to step aside during a dinner with Blair at the Granita restaurant in London on 31 May. The truth, according to his biographer Paul Routledge, is that this decision was announced instead at a meal the night before, dubbed the Last Supper, held by Brown for his closest friends and advisors. According to

Brown's brother John, the deciding factor for this momentous move was the publication of the following poll in the Scotsman: *'Gordon said to me that was the finish.'*

Gordon Brown, the shadow chancellor, cannot count on the automatic endorsement of Scottish Labour MPs in his struggle to become the next Labour leader. Scots MPs are split between Mr Brown and Tony Blair, the shadow Home Secretary, in the battle for the leadership according to a poll conducted by the *Scotsman*. The failure of Mr Brown to secure an overwhelming majority in his Scottish heartland will heighten the dilemma over which of the two close friends should stand.

In a survey of 42 of Scotland's 48 Labour MPs, 15 were firmly in favour of Mr Brown becoming the next Labour leader. Six supported Mr Blair outright, but crucially, six others said that though they felt an obligation of loyalty to vote for Mr Brown, they hoped he would stand aside so that they could back Mr Blair. Several said they would be pressing Mr Brown not to stand because they believed Mr Blair is more likely to win the next election for Labour. One, who has been agonizing over the decision, said: 'My heart is with Gordon but my head is with Blair.'

Five MPs supported John Prescott, the employment spokesman, three backed Robin Cook, the trade and industry spokesman, one was for Margaret Beckett, the acting leader, and six would not reveal their thinking. . . . All but a handful of the MPs contacted by the *Scotsman* wanted to remain anonymous but there was a high level of anguish about how they would vote.

Much of Mr Brown's support came from traditional left-wingers. But other left-wingers such as George Galloway (Hillhead) and John McAllion (Dundee East) backed Mr Prescott. Tommy Graham, the MP for Renfrew West, who is supporting Mr Brown, said: 'He is in the best tradition of socialism that comes out of Scotland . . . there is no doubt the trust the nation placed in John Smith would be safe in the hands of Gordon Brown.'

Mr Blair is also being helped by anti-Scottish sentiment among some English MPs. As one put it: 'We have had a Welsh leader, a Scottish leader, let's try an English one'. Another said it was time to 'ditch the Scottish mafia'.

James Kelman Wins the Booker Prize, 11 October 1994

SIMON JENKINS

Novelist James Kelman was the first Scot to win the prestigious Booker Prize in its twenty-five-year history, with his mesmerizing stream-of-consciousness depiction of a Glaswegian blind man, How Late It Was, How Late. *The decision split the judging panel, with Rabbi Julia Neuberger volubly expressing her disgust that a book she couldn't understand had taken the prize. Journalist Simon Jenkins rallied intemperately to her cause.*

The award of the Booker Prize to James Kelman is literary vandalism. 'My culture and my language have the right to exist and no one has the authority to dimiss that!' So said James Kelman, Booker prizewinner for 1994, at a dinner on Tuesday night. He duly received the accolade of 'genius' from the chairman of the judges, John Bayley, formerly Warton Professor of English Literature at Oxford.

Each year I read the Booker winner in a ritual obeisance to the gods of civilization. The experience is sometimes uplifting, sometimes perplexing. This year it was unpleasant. I am glad Mr Kelman is a cultural pluralist. We have that in common. I too believe in the right to culture and language, which in my case is what he calls 'colonial' Standard English. I believe something more. If it comes to war my English will win as long as Mr Kelman and the Booker judges are in the enemy camp.

First the book, lyrically entitled *How Late It Was, How Late*. I once found myself alone in a no-smoking compartment of a corridor train to Glasgow. An ambassador for that city lurched into the compartment and crashed down opposite me. He took out a bottle of cider, rolled himself a cigarette, leant across to me and belched, 'Ye git a light, Jimmy?' For almost an hour I humoured him, chided him, remonstrated with him, fearful for the safety of the Indian conductor who I knew was coming down the train (and who wisely passed us by). My reeking companion demanded attention like a two-year-old. He told me his so-called life story, requested money with menaces, swore and eventually relieved himself into the seat.

Reading Mr Kelman's book was a similar experience. I refuse to play his 'colonialist' game by dismissing the work out of hand. He is welcome to transcribe the rambling thoughts of a blind Glaswegian drunk, though my drunk had more humour than his. In the book's first half, the hero Sammy fights some policemen, finds himself blind in a cell, goes home, makes a cup of tea and takes a bus to the DSS office to claim benefit. I am reluctant to cheat readers of the excitement of the second half. Suffice to say that Sammy comes back from the DSS office, returns to the police station, goes home, has an overdue bath and, in a rare moment of embourgeoisement, gets into a taxi.

Sammy may win some passing sympathy from readers as they stumble along at his side. Encounters with a social worker, a neighbour, a lawyer and a son scatter shafts of sentiment among the ordure. Somewhere may even be a pastiche of a 'kitchen-sink' short story trying to get out. But I cannot convey the literary barrenness of this book except by quoting a typical passage. Even using the old newspaper safeguard of the asterisk, I would not inflict it on readers of *The Times* if the gods of literary criticism had not starred it with the mark of genius. To this is the Booker reduced: 'It couldnay get worse than this. He was really ft now. This was the dregs; he was at it. He had fg reached it now man the fg dregs man the pits, the fg black fg limboland, purgatory, where all you can do is think. Think. That's all you can do. Ye just fg think about what ye've done and what ye've no fg done; ye cannay look at nothing ye cannay see nothing it's just a total fg disaster area, yer mind, yer fg memories, a disaster area. Ye wonder about these things. How come it happened to you and nay other c? He wasnay ordinary, that's the thing man, Sammy, he wasnay ordinary, cause if he was fg ordinary it wouldnay be fg happening.'

This passage, spelling and so-called punctuation retained, does not appear as a single, pseudo-virile outburst. The book continues relentlessly like this for 374 pages. The literary editor of the *Independent on Sunday* has forestalled a dozen doctoral theses by counting 4,000 uses of the Anglo-Saxon expletive and its conjugations in the book. They stand proxy for very, hell, nothing, depart, exhausted, finished and what the dictionary rightly calls an 'empty intensifier'. Mr Kelman is totally obsessed with the word. He sometimes writes it over and over again when he cannot think of anything else with which to fill a line. His language is not Older Scottish, or Scots English, or Lallans, or any dialect of Burns's 'Guid Scots Tongue'. The *Guardian* called it 'the authentic voice of Glasgow', a libel on that city. I would call the language merely Glaswegian Alcoholic With Remarkably Few Borrowings.

I try to envisage the Booker judges tittering in the corner of my railway compartment. 'Oh, isn't he naughty,' says the Professor of Literature with a seraphic smile as Mr Kelman gobs on the floor. 'Oh, but I think he's really sweet,' says another judge, hugging his knees. 'Mightn't he be just a teeny weeny bit of a genius?' pipes a third. A string of expletives from Mr Kelman sends a thrill down their rubbery spines. They huddle together. Booker judges seek safety in numbers except the admirable Julia Neuberger, who ran from the compartment in horror.

This book is literature's answer to the Turner Prize. It is a pair of old gym shoes, a sheep's head in formalin, a house turned inside out. It was greeted by those guardians of culture, the fiction reviewers, with the sort of breathy notices art critics used to give 'conceptual art' before the galleries rumbled it. One spoke of the book's 'subcutaneous throb of language', another of its 'acoustics of domination', another of Mr Kelman's 'deliberately restricted palette'. Comparisons were drawn with Proust, Joyce, Beckett and Pinter. The *Times*'s critic spoke of 'Kafka on the Clyde'. A dozen Henry Higginses queued up to pat the head of the new Eliza Dolittle. Mr Kelman, I must say, had the measure of them. He failed to attend an earlier Booker dinner, fearing defeat. Scenting better luck this time, he turned up having paid as much attention to his dress as Liz Taylor at a Hollywood premiere. He eschewed the notorious dinner jacket and made his 'statement' in the form of a pinstriped suit and tie, in which garb, I gather, his friends had never seen him before. Much care went into this. The double-breasted jacket was left carefully open, thus diminishing its capitalist content. But how could the tie not signify English cultural domination? Mr Kelman's solution was to undo the top shirt button and lower the tie knot just one inch. That inch was rebellion superbly controlled. Lear's Fool knew the measure of his licence.

The award of the Booker Prize to Mr Kelman is literary vandalism. Professor Bayley must have known in his heart that a dozen authors this year were more merit-worthy, among them Brookner, Mantel, Amis, McWilliam, Ackroyd, Carey, Gordimer, Mount, none of whom even made the shortlist. I can only assume that the judges were aspiring to some apogee of political correctness. They greeted Mr Kelman as an inversion of the norm, a Jilly Cooper of the gutter, a Barbara Cartland of the Gorbals. They wanted to give awfulness a break. Here was a white European male, acceptable only because he was acting the part of an illiterate savage. Booker contrived both to insult literature and patronize the savage.

Philip Larkin asked four questions in judging a novel: 'Could I read it? If so, did I believe it? If so, did I care about it? Finally, if so, would

I go on caring about it?' In the case of this book, I defy anybody to get beyond Larkin's first question. Any fool can defend Mr Kelman's 'right' to write English in his own way. It is a free world. But to give him the Booker Prize? What lunacy has seized English literature?

The Dunblane Massacre, 13 March 1996

FORDYCE MAXWELL

There have been few darker days in Scotland than when former Scout master Thomas Hamilton walked into the gym at Dunblane Primary School holding two guns, and shot a class of twenty-nine five- and six-year-olds, killing sixteen pupils and their teacher. The world's press went into overdrive, but few were in a better position to write about the impact of a child's death than Scotsman columnist Fordyce Maxwell, whose own daughter had been murdered fourteen years before.

Hundreds of thousands of words have now been written about Dunblane. Here are a few more. Not because I want to, but because nothing else will do, not hope for the future, but a bleak warning which I hope, perversely, will help. Writing it is difficult, reading it will bring little comfort to anyone, least of all the families of the murdered children.

So why write it? The slaughter has already been dealt with by journalists and columnists in almost every conceivable way, with Sunday's coverage still to come. Most have dealt with it well, some wonderfully well, with only a few slipping into instant-emotion, instant-solution, noble rhetoric, mode. . . . But no matter how hard they try they are not on the receiving end. They and the bereaved families don't know that it is now downhill for some time, for some perhaps for ever. It might be hard to believe after the events of this week, but the suffering has only started.

Instant religion, instant counselling, instant memorial funds, and turning the gym into a shrine won't help. Within weeks the present apparent astonishing self-possession of some involved will disintegrate and they will then suffer even more than those who screamed and raged and cried immediately.

In the next few months the world will move on, stressed out counsellors will be debriefed by specialist debriefing counsellors and the bereaved will be left on their own. They will find that to hang on to their own sanity some of their best friends and relatives cannot talk about the murder. Some will cross the road to avoid them because they can't face the emotion. Others will visit or stop to chat, but talk about anything and everything except the one subject bereaved parents want to talk about – their murdered child.

There will be bickering and muttering about any money raised or funds started. Remember the long aftermath of Aberfan. Even in the most close-knit community, a time comes, and much sooner than bereaved parents expect, when the most sympathetic have to get on with their own lives, handle their own problems and, in many cases, their own family agonies.

Some parents will avoid the school. Others will haunt it. They live in two worlds – one, where they know a child is dead, the second where they still expect her to come out of the school gate with a smile. Go to the school gate often enough and one day, one day, she'll be there.

At home the crying and arguments and screaming fits will get worse. Other children in the family will be told they are lucky to be alive, followed by instant remorse. The most difficult thing to do will be to bring them up normally, trying not to spend too much on them, trying not to panic if they are five minutes late. Parents not blaming each other, but trying to destroy themselves by taking responsibility for a horror for which no one is to blame except the man who carried it out.

Already commentators are talking about 'coming to terms' with what happened. My wife Liz said yesterday: 'If I hear coming to terms with one more time I'll scream. You never, ever, come to terms with it.' All you do for the rest of your life is keep on keeping on, one of the few things I can write with certainty since our daughter, Susie, was abducted and murdered at the age of 11. She would have been 25 this month.

I write because I must. For the Dunblane parents, facing the future will be worse than they now think possible. But if they accept that, they can begin to try to live with it. There is naught for anyone's comfort in that warning, because there is no comfort to be had. Strictly speaking, for the bereaved it doesn't matter what Thomas Hamilton was, or how he became like that, any more than it matters to us how Susie's murderer, Robert Black, became the twisted pervert he is.

What matters is that a child is dead and that parents will never come to terms with it, only at best learn to keep going in a world where even those of us who think we're normal live on two planes – the cheerful, hard-working, outward one, and the inner one where the pain is.

All you can do is never forget how much joy a child gave you in the years they were with you. Or the satisfaction of helping their brothers and sisters grow and develop. Or the knowledge that the surviving children recover. And even forget.

Dolly the Sheep, 5 July 1996

PROFESSOR IAN WILMUT

The first-ever successful cloning of an animal from an adult cell took place at the Roslin Institute near Edinburgh. A Finn Dorset lamb called Dolly, her birth marked a pivotal advance for science. Dolly's unveiling the following spring sparked unprecedented attention, including references on The Simpsons *and cover photos on magazines. She also created high anxiety among ethicists and legislators, who feared that human cloning would soon follow. Others believed that medical science was about to take a quantum leap forward in the cure of disease, while the most radical began to wonder if human cloning was such a terrible idea after all. Head of the Roslin Institute team Professor Ian Wilmut, who became known as 'the father of Dolly', describes one of the most remarkable pregnancies and births yet seen.*

In the first tranche of experiments, we used cells from a nine-day-old embryo, differentiated skin cells from a twenty-six-day-old foetus and frozen udder cells. The first ultrasound scans, at around eight weeks, showed that only one-third of the ewes had foetuses. Much to our surprise and delight, however, one ewe was pregnant with a clone from an adult cell. Ultrasound revealed an apparently normal foetus. Karen Mycock recorded the scan on a video with maternal pride and felt a thrill of anticipation that a lamb could result from this supposedly impossible experiment.

That day, 20 March 1996, was when we first began to think seriously about clones from adult cells. Keith Campbell [pioneer of nuclear transfer in the cloning process] and I became nervous, particularly as the pregnancies continued to fail. Except, that is, the one that should not have been: Dolly. We shared a mixture of excitement and concern because we knew that a milestone would be passed if the lamb survived. We knew from previous experience that many of the foetuses die, sometimes late in pregnancy or even at birth. As we fretted over Dolly the foetus, the Princeton professor Lee Silver was writing a popular book on reproduction technology in which he was patiently explaining why cloning from adults was a biological impossibility.

That May, around 110 days into pregnancy, four foetuses were found to have perished, all clones of embryos. Of the 29 embryos that we had created from 277 udder cells, one foetus continued to thrive in her Scottish Blackface surrogate mother. We constantly monitored her well-being. Every time John Bracken used ultrasound, it always took a few seconds to get the whole image in view. You could usually see the head, legs and ribs at first. There would also be some movement. Most important of all was the moment when we could see a heart beating. Then we all felt a great sense of relief and satisfaction.

To ensure that our nails were bitten to the quick, Dolly's gestation, like that of other clones, took longer than normal. In most British breeds of sheep the average duration of pregnancy is 147 days. Experience now tells us that pregnancy sometimes drags on up to 155 days for clones. They usually die if the pregnancy goes beyond day 153. The labour of the ewe carrying a clone is also slow and sluggish, as we now know also to be the case in other species. Just before the onset of labour, a ewe having a normal pregnancy will often leave the rest of the flock and make a 'nest' by pulling grass or straw together to form a hollow in a quiet corner of a field, an ancient reflex to create a defence against predators. For reasons we don't understand, nesting was less likely to be triggered by a cloned embryo. The wait continued.

We did everything we could to keep the ewes and the clones safe, and placed the animals under twenty-four-hour observation. We wanted to leave nature to take its course, but if the pregnancy went beyond 153 days we would induce birth with an injection of the same hormones that the foetus normally releases to signal that it is ready for the outside world. The lambing pen at Roslin had seen great excitement and satisfaction, but more often than not with clones it has also witnessed death and deformity. But that was not the case on 5 July 1996. A healthy lamb was born that day, one that would become the talking point of paupers and presidents.

Dolly entered the world head and forelegs first in a shed on the Roslin farm late in the afternoon. Her arrival was a muted affair. She weighed 6.5 kilograms, surprisingly large for a normal lamb but not for a clone; we now know that animals cloned by nuclear transfer are often oversize. In attendance were a local vet and a few staff members from the Roslin. John Bracken was in charge. Even though I am often called the father of Dolly the sheep, I was an old-fashioned father and was not present at her birth. Her expected arrival was the cause of a great deal of excitement among the team, and I gave the instruction that only those who had to be present should be there. At the time of the birth I was digging in the vegetable garden in the grounds of the institute. One thing her mother did not need was stress brought on by too many people being present . . .

[After the birth] I did not hand out cigars or go for a celebratory drink in the local pub. No one took photographs. Nor could my wife remember me coming home and performing cartwheels of joy. Roslin was not painted red. Dolly's creation had been so long coming, so protracted, so difficult and such hard work that we were too fatigued to cry 'Eureka!'

The Day They Buried Princess Diana, 6 September 1997

JAMES ROBERTSON

The tragic death of Princess Diana in a Paris underpass on 31 August 1997 held unexpected significance for Scotland, since it coincided with the run-up to a highly charged referendum on devolution. Some said that voting should be postponed out of respect, others that even if it went ahead as scheduled, a yes verdict would be jeopardized since campaigners had to cram their work into a mere 100 hours. Novelist James Robertson captures the political and emotional mood of the country on the day of Diana's funeral.

The door was open, just a wee bit. I could see light through the frosted glass. Hope rose in me. I pushed the door, just a wee bit further, and stepped half-in.

'Are you open?'

'Aye we're open. Of course we're open,' said the barman. There were two other men and a woman, sitting or standing at the bar.

I'd been up and down the street for half an hour, looking for a pub that would serve me. Most had posted signs saying that, out of respect, they would not be opening till one, or two, or five. The shops were the same. I imagined managers and owners had spent some time weighing up how much respect they needed to show before they could start running their businesses again. A bus had gone by, with a few folk on the top deck looking like they were trying to get home before a curfew. The bus was going pretty fast: there was no traffic and no one waiting at the stops.

But in Robbie's Bar the man was saying, 'Of course we're open.' I stepped inside, relieved. I could taste the IPA on my lips already. The place, it seemed to me, was an island of common sense in a sea of insanity.

One of the drinkers said, 'And we've got fucking cartoons on the telly as well.' . . .

Saturday 6th September 1997. I'd been determined not to be part of it, succumb to it. I was angry that you were expected to be silent, that at a moment when the country was supposed to make a crucial decision about its future the future was effectively put on hold by a media-induced hysteria over the death of an unfortunate, incredibly wealthy young divorcee. Before the television coverage got under way I was off, up Leith Walk to see if I could find a shop open, or a pub where I could sit the thing out. I walked towards the city centre but it was soon obvious that there was not much chance of browsing in a bookshop or trying on a new pair of shoes. The only shops still trading on the Walk were a couple of fishmongers, with their shutters half-down. Fish, I thought, stay fresh for no one, however famous, especially on a Saturday. And I remembered the words of Maggie Mucklebackit the fishwife in Scott's *The Antiquary*, chiding Jonathan Oldbuck for haggling over the price of a bannock-fluke and a cock-paidle: 'It's no fish ye're buying – it's men's lives.'

Jim Farry of the Scottish Football Association had been castigated in the media for refusing to postpone a Scotland international. He'd eventually had to bow to the pressure. Various sanctimonious shits had been offended by his question, Does the world come to a stop on Saturday? – a question which outraged them chiefly because there was only one obvious answer to it, as the crowded supermarkets and shopping centres that afternoon would testify: most of them would have kicked off by three o'clock, and some would stay open late for extra time, to make up for the sales lost when they and their customers were mourning Diana. The not altogether strange thing about Farry's crucifixion in the press was that I had yet to meet anyone who didn't agree with him.

Another refugee came into the bar when I was halfway through my pint, watching Donald Duck instead of Diana's funeral, and started telling Diana jokes. They weren't very funny but we laughed, a little. I thought of the taxi driver, who in the small hours of the previous Sunday had first given me the news of the car-crash in Paris. Stupidly, I'd said, 'You're kidding.' 'No,' he said, 'I'm no. I mean, I'm no royalist, but I wouldnae joke about a thing like that.' In Robbie's Bar, after seven days in which there had been non-stop, wall-to-wall coverage of Diana's death to the exclusion of virtually everything else – Mother Teresa died the same week and was lucky to get a passing mention – it felt like we'd earned a bad joke or two. We were a wee knot of protestors, with nothing to protest against except that we shouldn't have to feel like strangers in a strange land. We were in our own place, yet out of place. Or were we, really?

There was, I believe, a silent majority who thought that the Diana thing was so over the top as to be on another planet. One has to be careful with terms like 'silent majority' – a phrase coined by Richard Nixon in 1969, when, in appealing for support for the war in Vietnam, his ploy was to persuade his fellow Americans that most of them, out there in front of their TV sets, were just as decent, honest, courageous and fully prepared to do the right thing as he was. Nevertheless, I was sure at the time, and as time passes I become even surer, that a sizeable majority of people in Scotland thought that the rest of the 'nation', led or at least encouraged by the newly elected Labour government, had taken leave of their senses. The world was going up in flowers again, but the trail of cellophane and wilting stems thinned out rapidly the further north one got. But this is probably a false impression in one sense: I suspect a major percentage of people in England, Wales and everywhere else also thought they were the only ones for whom all four wheels were still on the trolley of life. But it was virtually impossible to say so, and for those working for a yes vote in the referendum campaign, it was unbelievably frustrating to be forced to take a week off. It was, however, necessary: there were elements in the media who would have slavered over the opportunity to taint the pro-parliament campaign with images of Scotland Forward workers out on the street, refusing to suspend their politicking while a nation, the nation, mourned.

However, maybe the hiatus was not, in the end, detrimental to the cause. On the Monday, when things were allowed to happen again, I was leafleting tenements and tower-blocks in Leith. At the first inter-com I buzzed to get entry to a stair, a disembodied voice demanded angrily why I wanted in. When I explained, the voice exploded in my ear, 'Oh thank Christ for that! Back to bloody reality.' I think it was at that point, as the lock was released, that I knew everything was going to be all right.

The Scottish Parliament Reconvenes, 12 May 1999

IAN BELL

The reopening of the Scottish Parliament, 292 years after it was dissolved on the Union of Scotland and England in 1707, can be largely attributed to the indefatigability of Labour politician Donald Dewar. During many long, hard years of diplomacy and argument his credo had never faltered: 'There shall be a Scottish Parliament,' he vowed. And so it proved.

'The Scottish Parliament, adjourned on the 25th day of March, 1707, is hereby reconvened.'

David Steel could not resist it. Five years to the day since the death of John Smith, nobody thought that he should. It was, said Sir David, Presiding Officer of Scotland's first democratic parliament, the start of a new song. That and more.

Dr Winifred Ewing, sixty-nine, mother of the house, had already reminded us of what was being done. In the capital's grey Assembly Hall, just after 9.30 a.m., to a half-empty chamber, she uttered the simple, astonishing truth: 'The Scottish Parliament, adjourned on the 25th day of March, 1707, is hereby reconvened.'

History is memory. This moment was memory reclaimed, a right restated, a truth reaffirmed. The nation of Scotland, with all its thrawn suspicions, numberless confusions, apathy, clumsy rivalries and disparate hopes, had remembered.

We began again on a May morning in Edinburgh, high on the Mound, with thirty-five white roses, a clenched fist, 129 members sworn in with a measure of honest dissent, a Labour Party honouring John Smith's promise and a strange kind of ease. This, said the language of ritual, is what we do, ours by right, and this is how we do it. The fact was woven in neat, white letters into the very uniforms of the hall's polite, patient staff: 'Scottish Parliament'.

But then, suddenly, many strands came together. The clenched fist was Tommy Sheridan's, affirming on behalf of the Scottish Socialist Party a long tradition for a democratic socialist republic. The white roses were on the lapels of the Scottish National Party. The power was with Donald Dewar's Labour, the novelty with Britain's first Green parliamentarian, the democratic question with the Liberal Democrats, the new argument with the new Scottish Tories. Whatever else home rule may come to mean, it has already given articulacy to Scotland's diversity. We have not been here, or anywhere like it, before.

Hence, perhaps, the sense of relaxation. Whatever the tensions over pacts and deals, whatever the storms to come, the bitterness and the arguments, Scotland's parliamentarians seemed content yesterday just to celebrate, to be themselves.

Mr Dewar entered the forecourt of the Assembly Hall and, as usual, failed to co-operate with the photographers. Alex Salmond of the SNP was as ebullient as nature intended. By lunchtime David McLetchie of the Tories was in a pub in the Royal Mile close listening hard, as promised, to the people, in this case some young men from an Edinburgh housing scheme.

This is what we are; this is what we do. Mr Salmond spoke for the collective strength of the SNP when he said, before swearing the oath: 'For the Scottish National Party parliamentary group, loyalty is with the people of Scotland, in line with sovereignty of the people.'

Before that, Mr Dewar, following Dr Ewing, had seemed almost to efface himself, he whose creation this parliament had been. Jim Wallace of the Lib Dems took his place after Mr Salmond, but made no objection to monarchy or ordained allegiances. But then came Dennis Canavan, the socialist from Falkirk West that 'new' Labour could not silence, recording that he owed a duty first and above all to the people of Scotland.

It became what the glib call a defining moment: almost one-third of Scotland's first democratic parliamentarians put on record their belief that sovereignty resides, as old doctrine and the Claim of Right once supported by Labour says, with the people of Scotland, not with the Crown. Mr Canavan said it; the SNP said it; Robin Harper of the Greens said it; Mr Sheridan of the SSP said, loud and clear, that he took his oath under solemn protest.

The maker's label in Mr Sheridan's dapper suit says 'Candidate'. Yesterday the democratically elected socialist amended the prescribed ceremony by affirming his vision, as he called it, of a democratic socialist republic. An open palm was raised towards him as he recited the oath to 'bear true allegiance to Her Majesty Queen Elizabeth, Her Heirs and Successors, according to Law'. In return, Mr Sheridan offered a clenched fist.

An antique gesture from another Scotland, in some books, but yesterday there seemed nothing odd in that. The reconvened parliament, for all the blond wood and desktop computers, the twenty-first-century procedures, the pagers and the mobile telephones, was itself an antique revived. The idea, if not the entity, had proved unkillable. Scottish Labour, under orders, male and female, to dress with due sobriety, finally seemed proud of itself. The SNP at last seemed a reality rather than a rhetorical device.

It was a haphazard day, nonetheless. The journalist Dorothy Grace Elder, the SNP MSP for Glasgow region, upset the parliamentary lawyers by infiltrating a mention of the people into the formalities involving the Queen and was obliged to say her piece again. Fergus and Margaret Ewing, Nationalist spouses and MSPs for Inverness East and Moray, made their declarations simultaneously.

When Mr Dewar trooped his parliamentarians *en masse* up the High Street after lunch, in an interval between showers of rain, it seemed more than symbolic that Mr Canavan followed, as though tracking them, twenty yards behind.

But business, such as it was, was conducted. After the MSPs had made their oaths and settled into their blue chairs, Sir David Steel was found to have won the Presiding Officer's job over the SNP's George Reid by eighty-two votes to forty-four. Mr Reid, a friend of Sir David's for more than four decades, duly became one of the PO's deputies. This is, was, remains, a small country – and what of it?

Yesterday in the Royal Mile the bewildered tourists wanted to know what was going on, and if it might be worth a souvenir snap. The journalists wanted to know whether the Lib Dems and Labour had reached an accommodation, and what it might be. A few local people looked on diffidently, with honest curiosity at this parliament suddenly reborn in its temporary home beneath the standing rebuke of John Knox's statue. If a historic thing can be done casually, without much fuss, this had become the Scottish way.

There were clues for that. Refusing Mr Canavan's considered and dignified demand that there be an open vote rather than a secret ballot for the post of Presiding Officer, for example, Dr Ewing confounded centuries of Westminster practice by calling a parliamentarian by his first name. In the Assembly Hall's black-and-white corridor, so called, that instantly became the parliament's lobby, political rivals mingling freely. The absence of pomp was almost disconcerting.

This was a small parliament in a small country, and none the worse for it. The spin-doctors were conspicuous, if not by their absence then at least by their silence. How to enlarge or diminish what was taking place? It may be sullied in the months and years to come but Scotland's parliament pledged itself into existence with what seemed, in the measure of these things, honest intent.

Mr Dewar is there for the sake of his own belief and for John Smith's promise. Mr Canavan is there for his principles, Mr Sheridan for his people, Mr Salmond for a new nation, Mr Harper for the planet, Mr McLetchie for the Union. Scotland is represented, male and female, from a sixty-nine-year-old to a twenty-five-year-old. In the closes, wynds and pends off the Royal Mile, new politics, a new democracy, came to an old city and an old country.

It is too easy, now, to be cynical. On the Mound yesterday something new did happen, just for once, without self-consciousness, from beneath the weight of history, with a sense of honest purpose. This process will take us only where we want to go. Just for once, we cannot say that we have seen it all before. Yesterday, for a moment, Edinburgh was the only place in the world to be.

Under the television lights, the SNP's white roses had a yellowish hue, and we could not all remember every word they were meant to invoke. No matter. The flowers were a nationalist gesture that might, just once, have done for all. Hugh MacDiarmid (Christopher Murray Grieve) wrote of the little blossom sixty-five years ago, in another Scotland, in the same Scotland:

> The rose of all the world is not for me. I want for my part
> Only the little white rose of Scotland
> That smells sharp and sweet – and breaks the heart.

Sean Connery: a Lifetime's Perspective

RICHARD DEMARCO

Sean Connery, the Edinburgh milkman who became a movie star, made his name with his superbly sardonic role as James Bond. Latterly he has become a rallying figure for the political aspirations of the Scottish National Party. He is a lifetime friend of artist and cultural impresario Richard Demarco.

I first knew him over sixty years ago, as Tommy Connery, an Edinburgh schoolboy, a month younger than myself. We were born not far from each other near the West End of Edinburgh. I was the eldest of three sons born to my parents, Carmino and Elizabeth Demarco, known to their friends as Car and Cissy. He was the elder of the two sons born to his parents, Joseph and Euphemia Connery, known to their friends as Joe and Effie. I was born in a private nursing home and brought back to the comfort of my parents' new bungalow with a bedroom prepared specially for me in the fashionable suburb of Ravelston, with a nanny to help my mother recover from the breach birth which brought me into the world.

Tommy Connery was born in a two-room flat in one of the tenement buildings which characterized Fountainbridge, an industrial area beside the Union Canal Basin. This was the part of Edinburgh associated with the pungent smells of the Scottish and Newcastle Breweries, mixed with that of the North British Rubber Works. Euphemia Connery placed her new-born child in the safety and warmth provided by the top drawer of her bedroom cupboard.

The Connerys lived in Fountainbridge throughout the childhood and young adult years, a fact which strongly influenced Tommy Connery's idea of himself, having to cope with the disadvantage of making a premature ending of his schooldays at Darroch Junior Secondary School. His parents suffered, as did mine, during the years of the Depression, so they had no means of sending him to one of the city's secondary schools or paying the tuition which might have helped him enjoy his schooldays.

Both our fathers were obliged to work excessively long hours for their hard-earned weekly wages; Joseph Connery, working for the Co-op in Fountainbridge, and my father for Maison Demarco in a family-run Parisian-style café in Portobello. Portobello had a reputation as Edinburgh's Riviera, attracting tens of thousands of Glasgow Fair holidaymakers. It also attracted the teenager, Tommy Connery, not only because Portobello's public baths offered the luxury of well-equipped shower rooms but also because he could find employment as a life guard in the Art Deco sophistication of Portobello's outdoor swimming pool. I well remember the eye-catching handsome figure he made patrolling the poolside.

When my father acquired his own business in the form of The Ralleye Café, Tommy Connery was a regular customer because its location on Edinburgh's Lothian Road was within walking distance of his parents' house. In my third year at Edinburgh's College of Art, I cemented my friendship with Tommy Connery. We met in one of the life rooms, the one where he played the demanding role of an artist's model and I played the role of an aspiring painter in oils. He was a natural model with the ability to hold a pose for extended periods to give the students the opportunity to make not only drawings, but also paintings in oils.

Artists' models were not allowed to fraternize with the students so at the lunch break, the students would disappear into the College refectory and the models would lunch elsewhere. Tommy Connery had solved the problem of his lunch break by bringing sandwiches and a bottle of milk. He invited me to share his lunch. Why was milk his favourite drink, I wondered. He explained he was drinking it to help him cure the pain of the stomach ulcers he had suffered which had caused him to be invalided out of The Royal Navy.

We talked in general about his hopes for a purpose to our lives. At this time in his early twenties, Tommy Connery had a guardian angel in the form of Anna Neagle, then among the most popular icons of British film and theatre worlds. It was she who changed the course of his life and gave him his first true experience of being on the actor's side of the footlights. She gave him the opportunity to earn what he considered 'easy money', to stand on the stage of The Empire Theatre with a half-dozen other would-be actors. The qualifications required were very basic. Firstly, you had to be a six foot tall young man and secondly be prepared to look like a soldier on guard duty at Buckingham Palace as a loyal member of the Brigade of Guards protecting the Imperial figure of Queen Victoria.

Anna Neagle had devised a 'musical' play together with her husband, Herbert Wilcox, which was inspired by the successful film she had made on the life of Queen Victoria. The play had come to Edinburgh on tour. In each city, Anna Neagle interviewed local young men who would be asked to stand on stage without uttering a word. The musical was entitled *Sixty Glorious Years* and when it ended its run in Edinburgh, Anna Neagle took with her the most handsome of the guardsmen, Tommy Connery. I recorded this historic departure in my diary with the simple entry: 'Today Tommy Connery left Edinburgh as an actor'. My words had more than a tinge of regret and a hint of admiration mixed with relief that, at long last, Tommy Connery had freed himself from the restrictions imposed upon him in the life he had lived within the confines of Fountainbridge.

I was sad, not just because I knew I would miss him as a friend, but as someone I knew should be regarded as an artist. I had a feeling that, having escaped, he would not return. To my surprise and delight, he returned to Edinburgh as an actor with a small speaking part in the touring production of *South Pacific*. Making the most of the role of a

US Navy radio operator, he also made his mark in the chorus singing with gusto 'There is nothing like a dame'.

He returned once again not long afterwards in a play starring opposite a popular starlet, Heather Sears, and I was pleased to see that the Edinburgh evening newspaper publicized the play with a photograph of 'Sean' Connery introducing his stage partner to one of his favourite parts of Edinburgh beside the estuary of the River Almond at Cramond.

It seemed inevitable that not long afterwards he would be chosen against the odds to play James Bond, Ian Fleming's personification of the British super spy more than able to cope with the world-threatening forces which would endanger the British way of life. Of course, I saw every film in which Sean Connery starred as James Bond. When he made his occasional visits to Edinburgh, he contacted me at the Traverse. In 1966, The Demarco Gallery was born out of the spirit of the Traverse Theatre and so it provided us with our place of meeting, particularly in the seventies when Sean invited me to become the first Director of The Scottish International Education Trust.

The Trust came into being in 1970 because Sean Connery had become involved in the struggle of the Clydeside shipbuilders to save their industry from total collapse. He forged friendships with those stalwart figures defending the beleaguered position of the shipbuilders' unions, led by Jimmy Reid. The actor who portrayed James Bond was seen to be a supporter of the workers' cause when he made a film highlighting their preparedness to run the shipyards by themselves. The aims and objectives of the Trust were simply defined. They were to give support to various projects which would encourage Scots with initiative and ideas to remain in Scotland. It also intended to stimulate a deeper interest in Scotland by Scots who had been obliged to settle in other countries.

In the eighties, Murray and Barbara Grigor, as the directors of VIZ Films, made a film on Sean Connery's Edinburgh and, at the same time, an hour-long film for Channel Four television entitled *Art in a Cold Climate*. This focussed on the involvement of many artists and actors who had contributed to the life of The Demarco Gallery. Among them was Sean Connery. The sequence in which he and I were filmed together gave me the opportunity to congratulate him on the occasion when he stood resplendent in the academic robes of St Andrews University, having just received an Honorary Doctorate. The thought struck me as we spoke that his headmaster at Darroch Junior Secondary School should have lived to see the day when one of his students was being referred to as Dr Connery.

I see him at one and the same time as an artist's model par excellence in the splendour of his youth like a young Greek athlete and as the wise old monk who dominated the screen version of Umberto Eco's novel *The Name of the Rose*. I remember fondly the day when he invited me to meet his beautiful mother when, as a widow, she lived in the Edwardian terraced house he had bought for her far from Fountainbridge. She had extraordinary dignity and acute awareness and pride in the achievements of her son. He could not persuade her to leave Edinburgh so she lived modestly into her old age, in no way desirous of living the glamorous life.

Edinburgh will always be an important factor in the life of Scotland's most famous son and he well deserved the day when he became a Freeman of the city of his birth, an example to anyone wishing to live their life as a Scot on an international stage.

The Death of Donald Dewar, 11 October 2000

TREVOR ROYLE AND ALAN TAYLOR

With the sudden death of Donald Dewar, father of the new Scottish Parliament, the country lost a statesman of rare ability who had worked steadfastly throughout his career on behalf of Scotland. Many felt it as a personal loss, and feared for the future of the infant parliament. Those who had imbibed Dewar's optimism about their country, however, clung to his vision and determined to make a success of his legacy.

'Now I know what it feels like to be a horse,' declared Donald Dewar. He was speaking at a lunch in Glasgow in May last year, less than a week before the people of Scotland went to the polls to elect its first parliament for 292 years. He paused just long enough to let the words sink in before he delivered the punchline: 'Because these days I'm constantly being groomed.'

The audience of hardbitten hacks and New Labour apparatchiks dissolved in laughter. Here was Dewar in his element, a stand up comedian in the Chick Murray mould 'arms flailing like a combine harvester out of control,' as one friend has described his speaking technique, he was the warm-up man for none other than Tony Blair, his former roommate at Westminster. It is a side of Dewar which was rarely allowed to surface in public. Wry, witty, laconic, dry as a rusk, deadpan as the

Rev. I. M. Jolly, he had the personality to charm even the most cynical of crowds. His vanity, he once said, was 'an incurable delusion that people like me'. But clearly it was not a delusion; people really did like him, for himself and – not least – for his obvious aversion to being 'groomed'.

Substance not style was his priority. In that sense, he was a politician from a bygone age, to whom a soundbite was an alien language not worth learning. He preferred the unglamorous routine of constituency surgeries and the hard slog of the streets of Garscadden and Anniesland to Saatchi and Saatchi slogans and appearances on *This Morning with Richard and Judy*. It was as if he was always wary of getting above himself, of giving himself airs and graces, a peculiarly Scottish trait. He knew his roots and remained loyal to them throughout his life.

Famously, he never indulged in holidays. While some of his colleagues last week took the opportunity of the parliamentary recess to take an autumn break, for Dewar, who recently had major heart surgery, it was the usual round of greetings, meetings and briefings. Such a punishing schedule would have left much younger and fitter men peching in his wake, let alone a 63-year-old with a history of heart complaint. Married to politics as many have suggested, he was driven by an insatiable desire to make the parliament, for which he had worked all his political life, succeed and live up to the expectations of those who had fought for the 'unfinished business' to be completed. Donald Dewar was under no illusion on that score and was impatient to move things on. In doing so, he probably hastened his death, a price which plunged the nation into mourning and produced heartrending, hypocritical headlines in news-papers which only a few days before he died had been virulent in his denunciation.

How he would have savoured the irony. No one appreciated better than he the Scottish tendency to lambast the living and hero-worship the dead. Only on the night that the Scottish parliament was reconvened after a hiatus of almost three centuries did he allow himself to enjoy a moment of glory, strolling the streets of Edinburgh as night fell enjoying the celebrations, a proud grin fixed on his face as his back was slapped to bruising. 'It was certainly the most satisfying moment of my life,' he said later, the apotheosis of a career which had many highs and indelible lows. Throughout it all, though, the remarkable thing about him was how little he changed.

He was the only child of elderly parents, which he did not rec-ommend. However, he was at pains to stress that his childhood was generally happy, if unusual. Both his parents suffered from serious illness. His father, who was a well-to-do Glasgow dermatologist, had tuberculosis, while his mother developed a brain tumour. Donald Campbell Dewar was born in August 1937 as portents of war reverberated around the globe and he was sent at the age of two and a half to a small boarding school in Perthshire which was run by friends of his parents. Two years later he went south to another boarding school, Beverley, at Bonchester Bridge near Hawick, which was used to house refugees from the London blitz. 'I have memories of the shrubberies, of the pets in the stable block, particularly a black and white rabbit,' he recalled last year. 'I suffered from the delusion that I owned it.' But when he was nine he returned to Glasgow and went to Mosspark Primary School, where he spent a miserable year. 'I remember being puzzled by that,' he said, 'very forlorn and lost because of the sharp change from a small, closed, rural environment. There was a certain amount of teasing because of my accent, which was part Hawick part non-English because of my previous classmates.'

Dewar may have hated his time at Mosspark Primary School – he recalled rushing for the bus at four o'clock 'and it was not just because I thought it was leaving' – but there were occasional glimpses of Eden. In the summer of 1945, as war-time Scotland started getting used to the brave new world of the welfare state, he and his parents went on the first of several never-to-be-forgotten holidays to the north-east. He stayed on the farm of their friends, the Allans, near the small Aberdeenshire town of Methlick. Dewar was [sent to] Glasgow Academy. It was a school which championed sporting excellence, leaving Dewar, who had Harry Potter-ish tendencies, cold.

His flowering, however, came when he went to Glasgow University, which brought him into contact with a group of men who were to influence him throughout his life. There was John Smith, already a political animal but also a great party-goer. His death in 1994 devastated Dewar but it galvanized him, too. Like Smith, he subscribed to the view that we are not put on this world simply to enjoy. A Scottish sense of duty impelled both of them, as did the idea that there could be no privilege without responsibility.

His was by any standards an outstanding generation. As well as Dewar, Smith and [Angus] Grossart, there were Menzies Campbell, the Liberal Democrat MP, Jimmy Gordon, now Lord Gordon of Strathblane, Ross Harper, the lawyer, broadcaster Donald McCormack, Cameron Munro, until recently the European Union's representative in Edinburgh, and

Derry Irvine, the Lord Chancellor, who was to cause Dewar huge emotional upheaval when he had an affair with his wife, Alison.

Dewar first did a history degree, then law, which would give him a career to fall back on. But of more significance was the milieu of the university and the role it played in transforming the geeky, bookish, bespectacled teenager into a confident and accomplished student, which he later confirmed. 'I came up to university remarkably inhibited and limited in my social experience and all that kind of changed, which was a great thing. I discovered in the debating society that I could, in a staccato kind of way, string together words and phrases. It wasn't the debates that were important, frankly, it was what was built around them. In those days there was a tremendous social structure, drinking structure, social experience in every sense.' The hub was the union where, he said, 'you could eat, drink and find yourself a lumber for the night, or whatever'.

You can almost hear the smile in his voice as he said that. There can be few more incongruous notions than Donald Dewar on the prowl for female prey. It was also at the university that he acquired the nickname 'Gannet', on account of his gargantuan appetite. It stuck with him, as did his friends.

The image of the endearing eccentric is in danger of overshadowing the immense achievement of a man driven by a passion to eradicate inequality and poverty. Menzies Campbell was spot on when he said that Donald Dewar and Scotland were made for each other. With his knowledge of his country's literature and history and his respect for artists, particularly the Scottish Colourists, Dewar had the kind of hinterland once common in cultivated Scots.

But it was not just book learning which provided fodder for the mind and clutter for his flat in the West End. Scotland helped form him in many other untold ways. Not only was he a product of his Glasgow middle-class roots, the lace-curtain respectability celebrated by the novelist Guy McCrone, which gave him his early education and his collection of Peploes, Fergussons and McTaggarts, but his training in history and law helped form the radical inside the anonymous – if crumpled – suit.

Partly, he was affected by Scottish Labour history with its totemic figures of Keir Hardie and the more recent Red Clydesiders, the Wheatleys and Maxtons who vowed to export the revolution to Westminster. But these connections are too obvious. There was always the touch of the Covenanter about Dewar that even his best friends could not ignore

– not the mood of religious exaltation which took fanatics such as James Renwick to the scaffold, but the calmer and more considered views of Robert Baillie, who struggled with his conscience before signing the National Covenant in 1638. In the late 1980s, when it seemed that devolution was as far away as it ever would be, Dewar once confessed to a Scottish historian that he felt many affinities with Baillie, also a Glasgow graduate. It took time and much soul-searching before the young minister of Kilwinning agreed to throw in his lot with the Covenanters, because he realized that in so doing he might be violating his loyalty to the Crown. His heart told him that the National Covenant had been produced to protect Scotland's interests and was a statement of the country's intent. But he also knew that it might be construed as a threat to the authority of King Charles I. 'That's the beauty or the terror of Scottish history,' Dewar said. 'We are all affected by it and its influences are never far away.'

The comparison with his own position on the devolution issue was left unsaid but its shadow hovered uneasily over the conversation. Now he has sculpted his own place in the country's story. His modesty would doubtless have it otherwise but there is no denying it. 'I am asked what I am,' he said in Dublin at the end of September. 'I am a Scot, a citizen of the United Kingdom, and someone who has a very real interest in the future of the European Union.'

It was a brilliant speech, casually erudite, humourful, urbane and broadranging. But to those present it was clear the heart surgery had had a profound physical effect. He told the historian Tom Devine that in the next few months he would have to reappraise the situation if there was no surge of the energy of old. Sadly, he never got the chance. But he leaves a legacy which cannot be easily ignored. It can be summed up in the six sonorous words he himself wrote and which will be his epitaph: 'There shall be a Scottish parliament.'

The SNP Come to Power, 4 May 2007

ALEX SALMOND

Seven years after Donald Dewar's death, the Scottish Parliament faced its most serious test of mettle and proved just how fluid history is. The Holyrood elections in May 2007 were dogged not only by the bitter rivalry common to any election but by a growing disaffection with the Labour Party across Britain as a whole.

The election fell at a time of widespread and deepening condemnation of Prime Minister Tony Blair and his Labour Party's role in taking Britain into the Iraq War, and some commentators speculated that the Scottish National Party would make significant gains at Labour's expense. In the event, the SNP won by the smallest possible margin, taking 47 seats to Labour's 46. Even so, it represented a seismic shift in the country's political axis.

This unprecedented result was tarnished for all parties by a huge number of spoiled ballot papers, an estimated 140,000 of which were discarded because, some suggested, the voting papers were too complicated. Taking a long view, however, historian Tom Devine opined in the Sunday Herald *that the SNP's win was 'a very welcome development. I think the national result shows the voter has been prudent by giving the SNP a chance at power. The electoral level was becoming moribund . . . Giving SNP a chance is a powerful critique of Labour's sins in UK government.' Of the 'shambles' of the election itself with regard to spoiled ballot papers, he considered that 'in the long run that won't matter'.*

Unable to negotiate a coalition with other parties, who objected to their desire to hold a referendum on independence during their term, the SNP who were 18 seats short of a majority in the 129-member Parliament, opted to run a minority administration. May 16 was a momentous day in modern Scottish politics, when Alex Salmond was sworn in as First Minister. Indicating the new climate he was hoping to create, he told MSPs that he wanted to develop 'a new and fundamentally more reflective' model of democracy in Scotland. Almost two weeks earlier, on May 4, in the nail-biting minutes before the SNP's win was confirmed, he had reflected on the dramatic and historic surge in the SNP's popularity:

I think it's much more than a new Scotland struggling to be born. It's much more a change in people's attitude, a growing confidence. It's more than a party thing, it's more than just giving the other chaps a go. It's much more than that. It's not just the Labour Party's worst result since 1922 in Scotland; it's our best result ever, full stop, in history.

You see, eight years of devolution has done two things. They're apparently contradictory but when you really think deeply about it they're not contradictory at all. The first thing it's done is to instil a sense of impatience – disappointment – that more has not changed. But secondly, it's reassured people that the roof hasn't fallen in, that the 10 plagues of Egypt have not descended upon our benighted country and, you know, that the grass is still getting cut and the rain falls occasionally and the sky is still blue.

So simultaneously, it's increased people's appetite for change while reassuring them that change is not as apocalyptic a concept as some people try to present it. Basically, you've got a classic case of rising political expectations. And what you're sensing is the impatience and the conclusion that currently people think that something better must be done, and I intend to see it done.

Those watching this wholly new administration taking power could have been forgiven for feeling trepidation as well as excitement at what the future held. Campaign-hardened journalist George Rosie spoke with relish, in the Scottish Review of Books, *of the thrilling rollercoaster of constitutional politics. 'Hold on tight,' he advised, 'It looks like being a bumpy ride.'*

Appendices

Original Texts

APPENDIX I

The Battle of Flodden, 9 September 1513

THOMAS RUTHALL

. . . for on the 9th daie of this instante monethe of Septembere after a mervelouse greate conflicte and terrible bataille the King of Scotes with the greatest parte of the lordes and nobles of his ream wer in playn bataille venquyshed, overthrowen and slayne. At whiche bataille my Lorde Tresourere like a noble, valiaunte and puysaunt capitain, by his greate wisdome, hardiesse and experience, with the assistance, goode conduyt and actyvenesse of his sonne the Lorde Haworde, Admiralle of Englande, so acquitted hym self that for this moste famouse acte dedounding to the inestimable honour, comforte, commoditie and sueritie of the Kinges Grace, this his reame and subjectes of the same, they deserved asmoche lawde, renomme and thankefull remembraunce as ever anny noble men did. Specially remembering the multitude of theire enmyes, being ferre in nombre above the Kinges armye, conscidering also the grete nombre of mervelouse large peces of orynaunce as courtaldys, culverins, sacres and serpentyns amounting in the hole to 17 greate peces, besides moche other smale ordynaunce. Regarding also the greate and strong personages of the Scotes being aswelle fournesched with goodely harneys, wepons and other abilimentes of werre as ever men were, with their abundaunce of vitails, wynes of all sortes, brede, bere and ale, tentes and pavilions ferre above our estimacion and not lightely credible ooneles it had bene seen, tasted and vewed by our folkes to their greate refreshing, and over that the hardinesse and sharp setting on of the said Scotes with the discomforte and feblenes of our people being destitute of vitails and having no thing to drinke but oonely watere by the space of thre daies and moche scarcitie of that, with the mervelous greate payn and laboure that they toke in going 8 myles that daye on fote by daungerouse and paynefull passages over hilles and dales and yet, moste daunger of all, in ascending and clymyng an highe and stipe hille to encountre and geve bataill to the said King of Scotes being there campyd and his ordynaunce set to his moste advauntage and annoysaunce of our armye. And the said Scotes having the hill, the wynde and the sunne with thaym ayeinst our folkes, all whiche impediments, daungers and perells well consciderde, it is to be thought this vitorye procedethe more by the veray hande of God, with the helpe and merites of the gloriouse Confessour Seint Cutbert, thenne by anny strenghte or power of menne, how be it after so greate payn and labour there lakked no goode courage, strenghte and herte in our folks as it well appered by their actes.

For besides the King of Scotes all the lordes of Scotlande, excepte five, and the moste parte of the noble men of the same which that day dyed, there were 10 thousande Scotes slane, and as summe of thaym afferme they lacke 15 thousande in the hoole to the utter confusion of all Scotlande.

The said Scotes wer so surely harnessed with complete harneys, jackes, almayn, ryvettes, splentes, pavices and other habiliments that shote of arrowes in regarde did theim no harme, and whenne it comme to hande strokes of billes and halbardes they wer so myghtie, large, strong and grete men that they wolde not fall whenne 4 or 5 billes strake on oon of thaym at oonys; how be it our billes qwite them veray welle and did more goode that day thenne bowes for they shortely disappointed the Scotes of their long speres wherin was their greatest truste and whenne they came to hande stroke, though the Scotes faght sore and valiauntlye with their swerdes, yet they coude not resiste the billes that lighted so thicke and sore upon theym.

There were that day many goode and towarde capitains which did their partes righte welle, how be it the Lorde Howard was the firste setter on and toke moste payn in counduyting the vawarde of our armye to whome joined Seint Cutbertes banner with the hoole retynewe of the bisshoprike; and al be it the Scotes had moste dispecte to the said banner and set moste feresly upon it, yet what by the grace of God, the assistence of Seint Cutbert to his banner, and the valiauntnesse of the capitains and others being under the same, there gate they noon advauntage but greate losse and damage of their folks, and yet fewe or noon being under the same banner wer slayn thoughe many hurte. This with grete honour is Seint Cutberts banner returned againe to his churche, bringing with it the King of Scotes banner which for a memorial now standeth besides the shryne there. And the sayd Kyng was not farre from hys baner when he was slayne. And besides this all the grete ordinaunce of Scotlande is taken and resteth at Berwike with diverse prisoners, but not many, for our folks entending to make all thing sure, toke little regarde in taking of prisoners, but rid all that came to hande, bothe King, bisshopes, lordes, knyghtes, nobles, or others what so ever came which wer not so soon slayn but forthewith despoiled out of their harnais and array and lefte lying naked in the felde where men moughte have seen a mervelouse nombre of many goodely men well fedde and fatte, among which nombre was the King of Scotes bodye founde, having manye woundes and naked, and the same was broughte to my Lorde Tresourer thenne being in Berwike in whose keping the same bodye yet restethe.

And yet whenne our capitains and folks had thus welle acquitted them self, greate displeasure was done unto theym, for in their absence from their tentes, they being occupied with the Scotes, all their goodes, horses and necessaries wer clerely taken awaye. But whether it wer doon by Scottes or bordourers

I canne not saye, but the brute is that the borderours did full ill. I pray God amende theyme for by this dealing our folks wer wars discouraged at their departing thenne by all the harmes doon to them by the Scottes, and suche dealing hath and shall cause thame to have the wars wille to retourne thider again if necessite require.

APPENDIX II

The Burning of George Wishart, 1 March 1546

JOHN KNOX

When that he came to the fire, he sat down upon his knees, and rose again; and thrice he said these words, 'O Thou Saviour of the world, have mercy upon me: Father of Heaven, I commend my spirit into Thy holy hands.' When he had made this prayer, he turned him to the people, and said these words: 'I beseech you, Christian brethren and sisters, that ye be not offended at the word of God for the affliction and torments which ye see already prepared for me. But I exhort you, that ye love the word of God, your salvation, and suffer patiently, and with a comfortable heart, for the word's sake, which is your undoubted salvation and everlasting comfort. Moreover, I pray you, show my brethren and sister, which have heard me oft before, that they cease not nor leave off to learn the word of God, which I taught unto them, after the grace given unto me, for no persecutions nor troubles in this world, which lasteth not, and show unto them that my doctrine was no wives' fables, after the constitutions made by men; and if I had taught men's doctrine, I had not greater thanks by men. But for the word's sake, and true Evangel, which was given to me by the grace of God, I suffer this day by men, not sorrowfully, but with a glad heart and mind. For this cause I was sent, that I should suffer this fire for Christ's sake. Consider and behold my visage, ye shall not see me change my colour. This grim fire I fear not; and so I pray you for to do, if that any persecution come unto you for the word's sake; and not to fear them that slay the body, and afterward have no power to slay the soul . . .

Then, last of all, the hangman, that was his tormentor, sat down upon his knees and said, 'Sir, I pray you, forgive me, for I am not guilty of your death.' To whom he answered, 'Come hither to me.' When he was come to him he kissed his cheek and said, 'Lo! Here is a token that I forgive thee. My heart, do thine office.' And then, by and by, he was put upon the gibbet, and hanged, and there burnt to powder. When that the people beheld the great torment-ing of that innocent, they might not withhold from piteous mourning and complaining of the innocent lamb's slaughter.

APPENDIX III

The Murder of Cardinal David Beaton, 29 May 1546

JOHN KNOX

Many purposes were devised how that wicked man might have been taken away. But all failed, till Friday, the 28 of May, Anno 1546, when the foresaid Norman [Leslie] came at night to Saint Andrews; William Kirkcaldy of Grange, younger, was in the town before, awaiting upon the purpose; last came John Leslie foresaid, who was most suspected. What conclusion they took that night, it was not known but by the issue which followed.

But early upon the Saturday, in the morning, the 29 of May, were they in sundry companies in the Abbey kirk-yard, not far distant from the Castle. First, the yetts being open, and the drawbrig let down, for receiving of lime and stones, and other things necessary for building (for Babylon was almost finished) – first, we say, essayed William Kirkcaldy of Grange, younger, and with him six persons, and getting entrance, held purpose with the porter, 'If My Lord was walking [awake]?' who answered, 'No.' . . . While the said William and the porter talked, and his servants made them to look the work and the workmen, approached Norman Leslie with his company; and because they were in no great number, they easily got entrance. They address them to the midst of the close, and immediately came John Leslie, somewhat rudely, and four persons with him. The porter, fearing, would have drawn the brig; but the said John, being entered thereon, stayed, and leapt in. And while the porter made him for defence, his head was broken, the keys taken from him, and he cast in the fosse [ditch]; and so the place was seized. The shout arises: the workmen, to the number of more than a hundred, ran off the walls, and were without hurt put forth at the wicket yett. The first thing that ever was done, William Kirkcaldy took the guard of the privy postern, fearing that the fox should have escaped. Then go the rest to the gentlemen's chambers, and without violence done to any man, they put more than fifty persons to the yeyt: The number that enterprised and did this, was but sixteen persons. The Cardinal, awakened with the shouts, asked from his window, What meant that noise? It was answered, That Norman Leslie had taken his Castle. Which understood, he ran to the postern; but perceiving the passage to be kept without, he returned quickly to his chamber, took his two-handed sword, and gart [made] his chamber child cast kists [chests], and other impediments to the door. In this meantime came John Leslie unto it, and bids open. The Cardinal asking, 'Who calls?', he answers, 'My name is Leslie.' He re-demands, 'Is that Norman?' The other says, 'Nay; my name is John.' 'I will have Norman,' says the Cardinal, 'for he is my friend.' 'Content yourself with such as are here; for other shall ye get none.' There were with the said John, James Melville, a man familiarly acquainted with Master George Wishart, and Peter Carmichael, a stout gentleman. In this meantime, while they force at the door, the Cardinal hides a box of gold under the coals that were laid in a secret corner. At length he asked, 'Will ye save my life?' The said John answered, 'It may be that we will.' 'Nay,' says the Cardinal, 'swear unto me by God's wounds, and I will open unto you.' Then answered the said John, 'It that was said, is unsaid'; and so cried, 'Fire, fire,' (for the door was very stark); and so was brought a chimney full of burning coals. Which perceived, the Cardinal or his chamber child, (it is uncertain), opened the door, and the Cardinal sat down in a chair and cried, 'I am a priest; I am a priest: ye will not slay me.' The said John Leslie (according to his former vows) struck him first, once or twice, and so did the said Peter. But James Melville (a man of nature most gentle and most modest) perceiving them both in choler [temper], withdrew them, and said, 'This work and judgment of God (although it be secret) ought to be done with greater gravity'; and presenting unto him the point of the sword, said, 'Repent thee of thy former wicked life, but especially of the shedding of the blood of that notable instrument of God, Master George Wishart, which albeit the flame of fire consumed before men, yet cries it a vengeance upon thee, and we from God are sent to revenge it: For here, before my God, I protest, that neither the hetterent [hatred] of thy person, the love of thy riches, nor the fear of any trouble thou could have done to me in particular, moved, nor moves me to strike thee; but only because thou hast been, and remains an obstinate enemy against Christ Jesus and his holy Evangel.' And so he struck him twice or thrice through with a stog sword; and so he fell, never word heard out of his mouth, but 'I am a priest, I am a priest: fye, fye: all is gone.'

APPENDIX IV

John Knox Apologizes to Queen Elizabeth I, 1559

EDINBURGH 1559

... As your Grace's displeasure against me, most unjustlie conceaved, hath beene, and is to my wretched hart a burthein grievous, and almost intollerabill; so is the testimonie of a cleene conscience to me a stay and uphold, that in desperation I sink not, how vehement that ever the temptation appear: for in Goddis presence, my conscience beareth me record, that maliciouslie nor of purpose I never offended your Grace, nor your realme; and, therefore, howsoever I be judged of man, I am assured to be absolved by Him who onelie knoweth the secreates of hartes. I cannot denie the writting of a booke against the usurped Authorities and unjust Regiment of Women; neyther yit am I mynded to retreate or to call backe anie principall point, or propositioun of the sam, till truthe and veritie doe farther appear. Bot why, that eyther your Grace, eyther anie such as unfainedlie favour the libertie of England, sould be offended at the author of suche a worke, I can perceive no just occasioun: For, first, my booke tuichest not your Grace's person in especiall, neyther yit is it prejudiciall to anie libertie of the realme, if the time and my writing be indifferentlie considered. How could I be enemie to your Grace's person, for deliverance quahairof I did more study, and interprised farther, than anie of those that now accuse me? And, as concerning your regiment, how could I, or can I, envy that which most I have thirsted, and the which (als oblivion will suffer) I render thanks unfainedlie unto God? That is, it hath pleased Him of his eternall goodnes to exalt your head there (who sometime was in danger), to the manifestatioun of his glorie, and extirpatioun of idolatrie?

. . . God is witnesse, that unfainedlie I both love and reverence your Grace; yea, I pray that your raigne may be long prosperous, and quiet; and that for the quietnes which Christ's members, before persecuted, have received under you . . .

APPENDIX V

James Melville's Schooldays, 1560s

My father put my eldest and onlie brother, David, about a yeir and a half in age above me, and me togidder, to a kinsman and brother in the ministerie of his, to school, a guid lernit, kynd man, quham for thankfulness I name, Mr Wilyame Gray, minister at Logie Montrose. He had a sister, a godlie and honest matron, reular of his hous, quha often rememberit me of my mothir, and was a verie loving mothir to me indeid. Thair wes a guid nombir of gentil and honest mennis bairnis of the countrey about, weill trainit up baith in letteris, godliness, and exerceis of honest gamis. Thair we lernit to reid the Catechism, Prayeris, and Scripture; to reherse the Catechism and Prayeris par coeur; also notis of Scripture eftir the reiding thairof; and thair first I fand (blissit be my guid God for it!) that Spreit of Sanctificatioun beginning to wark sum motiounis in my hart, evin about the aucht and nynt yeir of my aige; to pray going to bed and rysing, and being in the feildis alane to say ower the prayeris I haid lernit, with a sweit moving in my hairt; and to abhor sweirin and rebuik and complein upoun sic as I herd sweir. Quhairunto the exempil of that godlie matron, seiklie and giffen to reid and pray in hir bed, did mekil profit me; for I lay in hir chalmer and herd hir exerceisis. We lernit thair the Rudimentis of the Latin grammair, with the vocablis in Latin and French; also divers speichis in French, with the reiding and richt pronounciatioun of that toung. We proceidit furder to the Etymologie of Lillius and his Syntax, as also litil of the Syntax of Linacer; thairwith wer joynit Hunter's Nomenclatura, the Minora Colloquia of Erasmus, and sum of the Eclogis of Virgil and Epistolis of Horace; also Cicero his Epistolis ad Terentiam. . . . Thair also we had the air guid, and feildis reasonabil far, and be our maistir wer techit to handil the bow for archerie, the glub for gowff, the batons for fencing, also to run, to loup, to swoom, to warsel, to preve pratticks [test, by competition], everie ane haiffing his matche and antagonis, baith in our lessounis and play.

A happy and goldin tyme indeid, gif our negligence and unthankfulness haif noct movit God to schorten it, pairtlie be decaying of the number, quhilk causit the maister to wearie, and pairtlie of a pest quhilk the Lord, for sin and contempt of His Gospel, send upoun Montrose, distant from Over Logie bot two mylis; sa that school skailit, and we wer al sent for an brocht hame. I was at that school the space of almost fyve yeiris, in the quhilk tyme, of publict newis, I remember I herd of the mariage of Hendrie and Marie, King and Quene of Scottis, Seignour Davies slauchtir, of the Kingis murdour at the Kirk of Feild, of the Quenis taking at Carberi, and the Langsyde feild. . . . Also I remember weill how we passit to the heid of the muir to sie the fyre of joy burning upoun the stepil heid of Montrose at the day of the Kingis birth.

APPENDIX VI

Mary, Queen of Scots, Arrives in Scotland, 19 August 1561

JOHN KNOX

The nineteenth day of August, the year of God 1561, betwixt seven and eight hours before noon, arrived Marie Queen of Scotland, then widow, with two galleys forth of France. . . . The very face of heaven, the time of her arrival, did manifestly speak what comfort was brought unto this country with her, to wit, sorrow, dolour, darkness, and all impiety. For, in the memory of man, that day of the year was never seen a more dolorous face of the heaven than was at her arrival, which two days after did so continue; for, besides the surface wet, and corruption of the air, the mist was so thick and so dark that scarce might any man espy another the length of two pair of boots. The sun was not seen to shine two days before, nor two days after. That fore-warning gave God unto us; but alas, the most part were blind.

APPENDIX VII

The Murder of Riccio, 9 March 1566

SIR JAMES MELVILLE

Now ther cam heir in company with the ambassadour of Scavoy, ane David Ricio, of the contre of Piedmont, that was a merry fallow and a gud mucitien; and hir Maieste had thre varletis of hir chamber that sang thre partis, and wanted a beiss to sing the fourt part; therfor they tald hir Maieste of this man to be ther fourt marrow [mate], in sort that he was drawen to sing somtymes with the rest; and eftirwart when the ambassadour his maister retournit, he stayed in this contre, and wes retiret in hir Maiestes service as ane varlet of hir chamber. And efterwart when hir French secretary retired him self till France, this David obtenit the said office, and therby entrit in greter credit, and occupied hir Maiesteis ear of tymes in presens of the nobilite, and when ther was gretest conventions of the estates; quhilk maid him to be sa invyed and hated . . . that some of the nobilite wald glown [frown] upon him, and some of them wald schulder him and schut hym by, when they entrit in the chamber, and fand him always speaking with hir Maieste. . . . Not without some fear, therefore, he lamented his estait unto me, and askit my counsaill, how to behave hym self. I tald him, that strangers wer commonly envied when they medlit over far in the affaires of forren contrees . . . I said again, that it wes thocht that the maist part of the affaires of the contre past throw his handis; and advysit him, when the nobilite were present, to gif them place, and prey the Quenis Maieste to be content therwith. . . . Quhilk he did, and said unto me efterwart, that the Quen wald not suffer him, bot wald nedis have him to use him self in the auld maner. . . . Efterwart, seing the invy against the said David still increase, and that be his wrek hir Maieste mucht incure displesour, I . . . tok occasion . . . to enter with hir Maieste, and in maist humble maner schew her what advyse I had geven unto Seigneur David, as is above specified. Hir maieste said, that he medlit na farther bot in hir French wretingis and affaires, as hir uther Frenche secretary had done of before; and said, that wha ever fand falt therwith, sche wald not leave to do hir ordinary directions. . . . Sche thankit me for my continuell cair, and promised to tak sic gud ordour ther intill as the cause required . . .

The K. [the King, Darnley] wes wone to geve his consent over facely to the slauchter of seigneur David, quihilk the Lordis of Mortoun, Ruthven, Lindsay and uthers had devysit; that way to be masters of the court, and to stay the parlement. The King was yet very yong of yeares, and not weill experimented with the nature of this nation. It was supponit also that the Erle of Lenox knew of the said enterprise, for he had his chamber within the palice; and sa had the Erles of Atholl, Bothewell, and Huntly, wha baith eschaiped be louping down out of a window, towardis the litle garding wher the lyns are lugit. This vil act was done upon a Satterday [9th] of [March] in the year [1565] about sex houres. When the Quen was at hir supper in hir cabinet, a number of armed men entrit within the closs before the closing of the yetis, and tok the keyes from the porter. And part of them passit up throw the Kingis chamber, conducted be the Lord Ruthven and George Douglas the postulat [postulate bishop]; the rest remanit in the close, with drawen swerdis in ther handis, crying 'a Douglas, a Douglas,' for ther slougern; for it was in the glomyng of the venyng. The King was past up to the Quen of before, and was leanin upon hir chair, when the Lord Ruthven entrit with his knappisca [headpiece] upon his head, and George the postulat entrit in with him and dyvers uther, sa rudly and unreverently, that the burd [table] fell, the candelis and meat and plaitis fell. Sr David tok the Quen about the waist, and cryed for marcy; bot George Douglas pluckit fourth the Kingis dager that wes behind his bak, and strak him first with it, leaving it sticking within him. He giving gret skirlis and cryes, wes rudly reft from the Quen, wha culd not get him saif, nother for boist [threat] nor fairness. He wes forceably drawen fourth of the cabinet, and slain in the utter hall, and her Maieste keped as captive.

APPENDIX VIII

Act against Luxury, 1581

THE PARLIAMENT OF SCOTLAND

The kingis maiestie and estates of this present parliament considering the greit abuse standing amang his subiectis of the meane estate presuming to conterfait his hines and his nobilities in the use and wearing of coistlie cleithing of silkis of all sortis, layne, cameraige, freinyeis and pasmentis of gold, silver and silk and wollin claith maid and brocht from uthir foryne cuntreis quhairthrow the prices of the same is groun to sic exorbitant derth as it is nocht abill to be langer sustenit without greit skayth and inconvenient of the commone weill quhowbeit god hes grantit to this realms sufficient commodities for cleithing of the inhabitantis thairof within the self gif the pepill were verteouslie employit in working of the same at hame, quhairby gret numberis of pure folkis now wandering in beging mycht be releissit alsweill to the honestie and welth of the cuntrie, for remeid quhairof it is statute and ordanit . . . that nane of his hines suiectis man nor woman being under the degrees of duikis, erlis, lordis of parliament, knichtis, or landed gentilmen, that hes or may spend of fre yeirlie rent twa thowsand merkis or fiftie chalderis victual at leist or thair wyffis, sonnes, or dochteris sal eftir the first day of Maii nixtocum use or weir in thair cleithing or apparel or lyning thairof onie clayth of gold or silver, welvet, satyne, damas, taffateis or onie beggaries, freinyeis, pasmentis or broderie of gold, silver or silk, nor yit layne, cameraige or wollin clayth maid and brocht from onie foryne cuntreis under the pane of an hundreth pundis of everie gentilman landit, an hundreth pundis of everie yeman man for everie day that his wyff, sone or dochter trangressis this present act. . . . A alsua that the puir pepill may be the bettir haldin in werk throw the laboring of the woll of the cuntrie within the same, thairfoir it is statut and ordanit . . . that na maner of wollbe transportit furth of this realme in tyme cuming under the pane of confiscation of the same woll and of all the remanent guides moveabill of the personis awneris and transportis thairof to oure soverane lordis use . . .

APPENDIX IX

No Pipe-playing on Sundays, 1593

THE PRESBYTERY OF GLASGOW

The Presbiterie of Glasgow statutis and ordainis that gif Mungo Craig sal play on his pypes on the Sonday fra the sun rising quhill the sun going to, in onie place within the boundis of the Presbiterie, that he incontinent thaireftir sall be summarilie excommunicat.

APPENDIX X

Grammar School Mutiny, 1595

ROBERT BIRREL

The 15 of September, Johne Macmorrane slaine be the schott of ane pistole out of the school. This Johne Macmorrane being Baillie for the tyme, the bairns of the said grammar school came to the tounes counsel conforme to yair yeirlie custome, to seek the priviledge, quha wes refusit; upon the qlk, ther wes ane number of schollaris, being gentelmens bairns, made ane mutinie, and came in the night and tooke the school, and provydit yameselfis wt meit, drink and hagbutis [ancient firearms], pistolet, and suord: they ranforcit the dores of the said school, sua yat yai refusit to let in yr mr. [master] nor nae uthir man, wtout they wer grantit ther privilege, conforme to yr wontit use. The Provost and Baillies and Counsell heiring tell of the same, they ordeinit John Macmorrane Baillie, to goe to the grama school and take some order yrwt. The said Johne, with certain officers, went to the school, and requystit the schollaris to opin the dories: yei refusit. The said Baillie and officers tooke an geast [beam of wood] and rane at the back dore with the geast. Ane scholar bad him desist from dinging up the dore, utherways, he vouit to God, he wald shute ane pair of bulletis throw hes heid. The said Baillie, thinking he durst not shute, he, with his assisters, ran still wt the geast at the said dore. Ther came ane scholar callit William Sinclair, sone to William Sinclair chansler of Catnes [Caithness], and with ane pistolet shott out at ane window, and shott the said Baillie throw the heid, sua yat he diet. Pntlie [shortly after] the haill tounesmen ran to the school, and tuik the said bairns and put yame in the tolbuith: bot the haill bairns wer letten frie wtout hurte done to yame for the same, wtin ane short tyme yairafter.

APPENDIX XI

Border Reivers Defy Capture, 14 April 1596

THE LORD TREASURER OF ENGLAND

I thought it my duty to acquaint you with 'the proude attempte' which the Scots have made on this her Majesty's castle and chief strength here, praying you to move her Majesty for such redress as may stand with her liking. The ground of it proceedeth from the cause which I formerly advertised, and will now be imparted to you by my Lord Treasurer, to whom to avoid tediousness, I refer you.

'Yesternighte in the deade time therof, Water Scott of Hardinge, the cheife man aboute Buclughe, accompanied with 500 horsemen of Buclughes and Kinmontes frends, did come armed and appointed with gavlockes and crowes of iron, handpeckes, axes and skailinge lathers, unto an owtewarde corner of the base courte of this castell, and to the posterne dore of the same – which they undermined speedily and quietlye and made them selves possessors of the base courte, brake into the chamber where Will of Kinmont was, carried him awaye, and in their discoverie by the watch, lefte for deade two of the watchmen, hurt a servante of myne one of Kynmontes keperes, and were issued againe oute of the posterne before they were descried by the watche of the innerwarde, and ere resistance coulde be made. The watch, as yt shoulde seeme, by reason of the stormye night, were either on sleepe or gotten under some covert to defende them selves from the violence of the wether; by meanes wherof the Scottes atcheived theire enterprise with lesse difficultie. The warding place of Kinmonte, in respect of the manner of his takinge, and the assurance he had given that he woulde not breake awaye, I supposed to enforce in the suretie, and litle looked that any durst have attempted to enforce in the tyme of peace any of her Majesty's castells, and a peece of so good strength. Yf Buclugh him selfe have bin therat in person, the capten of this proud attempt, as some of my servantes tell me they hard his name called upon (the trueth wherof I shall shortly advertise), then I humblie beseech, that her Majesty wilbe pleased to send unto the Kinge, to call for and effectually fynde that the quality of his offence shall demirite, for yt wilbe a dangerous example to leave this highe attempt unpunished . . . in revenge whereof, I intend that somethinge shalbe shortly entreprised against the principalles in this accion for repaire therof . . .

APPENDIX XII

The First New Year's Day, 1600

THE PRIVY COUNCIL

The Kingis Majestie and Lordis of his Secreit Counsall, undirstanding that in all uthiris weill governit comoun welthis and countryis the first day of the yeir beginnis yeirlie upoun the first day of Januar, comounlie callit New Yeiris Day, and that this realm onlie is different fra all uthiris in the compt and reckoning of the yeirs, and His Majestie and Counsall willing that thair sall be na disconformitie betwixt His Majestie his realm and liegis and uthiris nichtbour countreyis in this particular, bot that they sall conform thaimselffis to the ordour and custom observit be all uthiris countreyis, especiallie seing the course and sesoun of the yeir is maist propir and ansuerabill thairto, and that the alteratioun theirof importis na hurt nor prejudice to onie pairtie: thairof His Majestie, with advice of the Lordis of his Secreit Counsall, statutis and ordainis that in all tyme coming, the first day of the yeir sall begin yeirlie upoun the first day of Januar, and thir presentis to taik execution upoun the first day of Januar nixt to cum, quhilk sall be the first day of them and six hundreth yeir of God . . .

APPENDIX XIII

The National Covenant, 1638

JOHN LIVINGSTONE

All the Summer 1637 I had as much work in preaching in publick & exercises in privat as any time before partly in Lanerk & partly in the west, & at Communions at divers places, & in the Stewartry of Kircudbright & the presbyterie of Stranrawer while I was waiting at the port for my wifes coming out of Ireland. This Summer severall ministers of Scotland were charged wth letters of horning to buy & receive the Service book wch stirred up great thoughts of heart through ye Land, beside a tumult in Edinburgh begun by some of the common people at the first reading of the Service book the true rise of that blessed reformation in Scotland began wth two petitions against the Service book the one from the west and the oyz [other] from ffife wch mett together at the Councell door in Edz [Edinburgh] the one now knowing the other, after that the 20 of Septz [September] a great many petitions from severall parts were presented against the Service book, these being denyed by the king the number of the petitioners & their demands increased for they desired not only exemption from the Service book but from ye five ceremonies of Perth & the high Commission Court, & these things being denyed they at last desired also freedom from episcopacy and a free parliment & generall Assembly; when these things were still denyed; & their number had so increased yt in some sort they were the whole body of the land and considering yt the lords controversy with them was ye breach of Covenant they did in the beginning of March 1638 renew the nationall Covenant wch had formerly by authority of king and parliament severall times been sworn, I was immediatly sent to go post to London wth severall copies of the Covenant & letters to friends at Court of both nations; to avoid discovery I rode in a gray coat and a gray Montero cape.

One night riding late, the horse & I fell to the ground where I lay about a quarter of an hour as dead, ye first thing I discerned when I came to myself I found the guide sitting under me & crying & weeping, yet it pleased ye Lord I recovered, & got to fferrybriggs where after a day or two's stay I came to London, but one of my eyes and part of my cheek being bloodshot I did not go to the Street, but mz Eleasar Borthwick delivered the letters for me, some friends & some of the english nobility came to my chamber to be informed how matters went, & told yt the Marquess of Hamilton had sent him to me to show he had overheard the king saying, I was com'd but he would endeavour to put a pair of fetters about my feet, wherefore fearing to be way laid on the post way, I bought a horse, & came home by St Albans and the wester way.

I was present at Lanerk and at severall other parishes when on a Sabbath after the forenoon Sermon the Covenant was read & sworn, & may truly say yt in all my life except one day in the kirk of shotts I never saw such motions from the Spirit of God, all the people generally & most willingly concurring where I have seen above a thousand persons all at once lifting up their hands, and the tears dropping down from their eyes, so yt through the whole land except the professed papists & some few who for base ends adhered to the prelates, the people universally entered into the Covenant of god for reformation of religion against prelates and the ceremonies.

APPENDIX XIV

The Run-up to the Union of the Scottish and English Parliaments

STIRLING TOWN COUNCIL, 1706

To His Grace Her Majesties high Commissioner and the Estates of Parliament. The Address of the provost Baillies Town Councill and other Inhabitants of the Burgh of Stirling.

Humbly Sheweth

That having had our most deliberat thought upon the great affair of the Union of the two Nationes, as Contained in the printed Articles, wee judge it our Indispensable duety to the Nation to this place, yea to posterity, with all Imaginable defference to your Grace and Honourable Estates of parliament humbly to represent, That though we are desirous that true peace and freindship be perpetually Cultivat with our neighbours in England, Up on Just and honourable termes consisting with the being, Soveraignitie & Independencie of our Natione and parliaments as defenders therof, Yet we judge your goeing into this Treaty as it now Lyes before you, will bring ane Insupportable burden of Taxationes upon this Land, which all the Grants of freedome of Trade will never Counterballance being so uncertain and precarious while still under the regulations of the English in the parliament of Brittain, who may if they please discourage the most Considerable Branches of our Trade, if any way apprehended to interfeir with their own. That it will prove, ruining to our manufactores, That it will be ane expossing of our Religione, Church Government as by Law Established, our Claime of Right, Lawes, Liberties & consequently all that's valuable. To be incroached upon, yea wholly Subverted by them, whose principles does, & Suposed Interests may Lead yr Unto, That it will be a depryving of us and the rest of the royall burghs in this Natione, in a great measure of our fundamentall right and propertie of being represented in the Legis Lative power, That therby one of the most ancient nations so long and so gloriously defended by our worthie patriots will be supprest. Our parliaments the very hedge of all that is dear to us, Extinguished and we and our posterity brought under ane Lasting yoke which we will never be able to bear, The fatal consequences of which we tremble to think upon . . .

Personal Acknowledgements

Grateful thanks to all the family, friends and colleagues who have provided invaluable advice, in particular Chris Dolan, Allan Hunter, Angela Laurins, Barclay McBain and Hugh MacDonald. The staff of the Edinburgh Room and Scottish Department of Edinburgh Central Library have been unfailingly helpful, as have the staff of the National Library of Scotland, Haddington's local history department, and the British Golf Museum. Thanks also to Andrew Marr for pointing me towards Agnes Mure Mackenzie's books, to Richard Demarco, Jan Leman, Conrad Wilson, Stuart Allan of National Museums Scotland, and to James Robertson for introducing me to Zachary Macaulay. Judy Moir, my editor, has been a constant source of enthusiasm, ideas and sound advice, and copy editor Helen Campbell has been elegantly meticulous. And thanks above all to Alan Taylor.

Sources and Permissions

The author gratefully acknowledges permission to reproduce copyright material in this book. If any material has been inadvertently included without permission, please contact the author c/o the publishers.

Acts of Parliament ('Act against Luxury'), Acts of Parliaments of Scotland, iii, 220, c.18, quoted in *Source Book of Scottish History*, vol. I, ed. W. Croft Dickinson, Gordon Donaldson, Isabel A. Milne (Thomas Nelson and Sons Ltd, Edinburgh, 1958)

Adamnan ('Death of St Columba'), from Adamnan's *Life of Columba*, quoted in *Early Sources of Scottish History AD 500–1286*, collected and translated by Alan Orr Anderson, vol. 1 (Paul Watkins, Stamford, 1991)

Ailred of Rievaulx ('English Invective against the Scots'), from Richard of Hexham, *De Gestis Stephani*, in *Chronicles of Stephen*, vol. III, quoted in *Scottish Annals from English Chroniclers, AD 500–1286*, collected and translated by Alan Orr Anderson, vol. 1 (Paul Watkins, Stamford, 1991)

Allan, J. R. ('A Glasgow Orange March'), from J. R. Allan, 'Sketches for a Portrait of Glasgow', in *Scotland – 1938* (1938), quoted in *Glasgow Observed*, ed. Simon Berry and Hamish Whyte (John Donald, Edinburgh, 1987)

Anderson, Iain ('Scotland Win the Grand Slam'), *Scotland on Sunday*, 18 March 1990. Copyright © The Scotsman Publications Ltd.

Anglo-Saxon Chronicle ('Battle between the Saxons and Northmen'), from verse passage MSS, a,b,c,d, s.a.937, quoted in *Scottish Annals from English Chroniclers, AD 500–1286*, collected and translated by Alan Orr Anderson (Paul Watkins, Stamford, 1991)

Annals of Dunstable ('The Burning of a Bishop'), from Annals of Dunstable in *Annales Monastici*, vol. III, quoted in *Scottish Annals from English Chroniclers, AD 500–1286*, collected and translated by Alan Orr Anderson, vol. 1 (Paul Watkins, Stamford, 1991)

Anonymous ('The Death of the Maid of Norway'), Anonymous, from *The Golden Treasury of Scottish Poetry*, ed. Hugh MacDiarmid (Canongate, Edinburgh, 1993)

Anonymous ('The Declaration of Arbroath'), The Declaration of Arbroath, translated from Latin by Sir James Fergusson (Edinburgh, 1970), quoted in *Scotland, an Unwon Cause*, by P. H. Scott (Canongate, Edinburgh, 1997)

Anonymous ('The Execution of William Wallace'), Anonymous, translated by J. Russell from *Documents Illustrative of Sir William Wallace, His Life and Times*, ed. Joseph Stevenson, Maitland Club, 1841. Quoted in Louise Yeoman, *Reportage Scotland* (Luath, Edinburgh, 2005)

Anonymous ('The Massacre of Glencoe'), by A Gentleman in Scotland, from *Gallienus Redivivus, or Murther Will Out, &c*, 1695, reprint ed. by Ed Edmund Goldsmid (Edinburgh, 1885); letter extracts from *Source Book of Scottish History*, ed. W. Croft Dickinson, Gordon Donaldson, Isabel A. Milne, vol. I (Thomas Nelson and Sons Ltd, Edinburgh, 1958)

Anonymous ('The Murder of James I'), quoted in Agnes Mure Mackenzie, *Scottish Pageant*, vol. I (Oliver & Boyd, Edinburgh, 1946)

Anonymous ('The North Berwick Witches'), *News from Scotland*, anonymous, c.1591, quoted in *Witchcraft in Early Modern Scotland*, ed. Lawrence Normand and Gareth Roberts (University of Exeter Press, Exeter, 2000)

Anonymous ('The Sale of a Wife'), from National Library of Scotland archive.

The *Argyllshire Herald* ('Scavenging'), the *Argyllshire Herald*, 27 May 1859, quoted in Gavin D. Smith, *The Scottish Smuggler* (Birlinn, Edinburgh, 2003)

Baird, John Logie ('The Invention of Television'), from *Television and Me: the Memoirs of John Logie Baird*, ed. Malcolm Baird (Mercat Press, Edinburgh, 2004). Reprinted with kind permission of the publishers

Balcarres, Colin, Earl of ('The Battle of Killiecrankie'), The Earl of Balcarres, *Memoirs Touching the Revolution in Scotland, M. DC. LXXXVIII – M. DC. XC*, ed. Alexander W. C. Lindsay (Bannatyne Club, Edinburgh, 1841)

Bald, Robert ('Conditions in the Mines'), from Robert Bald, *A General View of the Coal-Trade of Scotland, chiefly that of the River Forth and Mid-Lothian, to which is added an inquiry into the condition of these women who carry coals under ground in Scotland* (Edinburgh, 1808)

Barbour, John ('The Battle of Bannockburn'), John Barbour, *Barbour's Bruce: 'A fredome is a noble thing'*, ed. Matthew P. McDiarmid, James A. C. Stevenson (Scottish Text Society, 1980)

Baston, Robert ('The Battle of Bannockburn: an Englishman's View'), from *Metrum de proelio apud Bannockburn*, translated from Robert Baston's Latin by Edwin Morgan (The Scottish Poetry Library with Akros Publications and Mariscat Press, Edinburgh, 2004). Reprinted by permission of the publishers

Baur, Chris ('The Pope Visits Scotland'), the *Scotsman*, 2 June 1982. Copyright © The Scotsman Publications Ltd

Beerbohm, Max ('The Opening of *Peter Pan*'), from the *Saturday Review*, 7 January 1905, quoted in Rupert Hart-Davis, *Around Theatres, London* (Granada Publishing Ltd, London, 1953)

Bell, Alexander Graham ('The Invention of the Telephone'), from Helen Elmira Waite, *Make a Joyful Sound* (Macrae Smith Company, 1961), quoted in *A Scottish Postbag*, ed. George Bruce and P. H. Scott (W. & R. Chambers, Edinburgh, 1986)

Bell, Ian ('The Scottish Parliament Reconvenes'), Ian Bell, in *What a State! Is Devolution for Scotland the End of Britain?*, ed. Alan Taylor (HarperCollins, London, 2000). Copyright © The Scotsman Publications

Birrel, Robert ('Grammar School Mutiny'), Robert Birrel's diary, quoted in *Scottish Diaries and Memoirs, 1550–1746*, ed J. G. Fyfe (Stirling, 1927)

Blind Harry ('The Rise and Fall of William Wallace'), Blind Harry, *The Wallace*, ed. Anne McKim (Canongate, Edinburgh, 2003)

Bold, Alan ('The Death of Hugh MacDiarmid'), from Alan Bold, *MacDiarmid* (John Murray, London, 1988). Reproduced by permission of the publisher

Boswell, James ('A Scot Meets Voltaire'), from James Boswell, *Boswell on the Grand Tour*, ed. Frederick A. Pottle (1953), quoted in *The Oxford Book of Literary Anecdotes*, ed. James Sutherland (OUP, Oxford, 1975)

Boswell, James ('Dr Johnson Arrives in Scotland'), from James Boswell, *Journal of a Tour to the Hebrides with Samuel Johnson LLD, 1786*, ed. Peter Levi (Folio Society, London, 1990)

Boyd, William ('Gordonstoun School'), from William Boyd, *Bamboo: Non-fiction 1978–2004* (Hamish Hamilton, London, 2005). Reprinted with permission by Penguin

Boyle, Jimmy ('Prison'), from Jimmy Boyle, *A Sense of Freedom* (Pan/Canongate, London/Edinburgh, 1977). Reprinted with permission by Pan Macmillan

Bradley, Edward ('Abbotsford, the Tourist Trap'), from Cuthbert Bede [Bradley's pseudonym], *A Tour in Tartan-Land* (Richard Bentley, London, 1863)

Brereton, Sir William ('A Visitor's Impression of Edinburgh'), from Sir William Brereton's account of Edinburgh in 1636, quoted in *Early Travellers in Scotland*, ed. P. Hume Brown (Edinburgh, 1892)

Brown, George Mackay ('Porridge'), from George Mackay Brown, *Rockpools and Daffodils: An Orcadian Diary 1979–1991* (Gordon Wright, Edinburgh, 1992). Copyright © George Mackay Brown 1992. Reprinted with permission by Steve Savage Publishers Ltd

Buchanan, George ('The Habits of Highlanders'), George Buchanan, found in *Early Descriptions of Scotland*, from *Rerum Scoticarum Historia, 1582*, trans. James Aikman (Blackie, Fullarton & Co., Edinburgh, 1827)

Campbell, Colonel Archibald ('The American Independence War'), from J. P. Maclean, *A Historical Account of the Settlements of Scotch Highlanders in America, prior to the peace of 1783* (John Mackay, Cleveland and Glasgow, 1900)

Carey, Robert ('The Union of the Crowns'), from *The Stirring World of Robert Carey: Robert Carey's Memoirs, 1577–1625* (*www.RippingYarns.com*, 2005)

Carlyle, Reverend Alexander ('The Porteous Riot', 'The Battle of Prestonpans', 'Taking a Play to London'), from *The Autobiography of Dr Alexander Carlyle of Inveresk 1722–1805*, ed. John Hill Burton (1990, Thoemmes Antiquarian Books Ltd, Bristol)

Carlyle, Jane ('Thomas Carlyle's Tax Return'), from *Letters and Memorials of Jane Welsh Carlyle*, ed. J. A. Froude (1883), quoted in *The Oxford Book of Literary Anecdotes*, ed. James Sutherland (OUP, Oxford, 1975)

Carnegie, Andrew ('Andrew Carnegie Shows an Early Interest in Libraries'), from Joseph Frazier Wall, *Andrew Carnegie* (OUP, Oxford, 1970)

Carswell, Catherine ('Burns's Halo Is Tarnished'), from letter, 23 September 1930, British Library Add. MS 48975, no. 174, quoted in *Opening the Doors:*

The Achievement of Catherine Carswell, ed. Carol Anderson (Ramsay Head Press, Edinburgh, 2001)

Childe, Professor Vere Gordon ('Discovering Skara Brae'), the *Glasgow Herald*, 17 August 1929

The Chronicle of Lanercost ('Church Corruption' and 'The Death of Alexander III'), *Chronicle of Lanercost*, translated by Sir Herbert Maxwell, from *Scottish Historical Review*, vol. VI (Glasgow, 1909)

Churchill, Winston ('Churchill on the Eve of Defeat'), quoted in Martin Gilbert, *World in Torment, Winston S. Churchill 1917–1922* (William Heinemann, London, 1975)

Cockburn, Henry ('The Historical Novel Is Born', 'The *Scotsman* Is Launched', 'Reminiscences of Edinburgh Life'), from Henry Cockburn, *Memorials of His Time* (Robert Grant & Son, Edinburgh, 1856, revised and abridged edn 1945)

Collin, George ('The Eyemouth Fishing Disaster'), the *Scotsman*, 17 October 1881

Collum, Miss V. C. C. ('A Hospital on the Western Front'), quoted in Eileen Crofton, *The Women of Royaumont: A Scottish Women's Hospital on the Western Front* (Tuckwell Press, Edinburgh, 1997). Extract reproduced by permission of Birlinn Ltd (*www.birlinn.co.uk*)

Connolly, Billy ('Glasgow's Cultural Credentials Are Recognized'), from Billy Connolly, 'I'm telling ye, we're the Big Yin of arts', in the *Sunday Times*, 26 October 1986, quoted in *Glasgow Observed*, ed. Simon Berry and Hamish Whyte (John Donald, Edinburgh, 1987)

Craig, James ('Highland Emigration'), from *Eight Letters on the Subject of the Earl of Selkirk's Pamphlet on Highland Emigration, by Amicus (James, Gordon of Craig, advocate), as appeared in one of the Edinburgh Newspapers* (Edinburgh, 1806)

Crawford, Marion ('The Queen's Governess'), from Marion Crawford, *The Little Princesses, The Story of the Queen's Childhood, by Her Governess* (Orion, London, 2002)

Creech, William ('Twenty Years of Dramatic Change'), from *The First and Second Statistical Accounts of Edinburgh* (West Port Books, Edinburgh, 1998)

Cromwell, Oliver ('The Battle of Dunbar'), from Oliver Cromwell, *Cromwell's Letters and Speeches, with elucidation by Thomas Carlyle* (Chapman & Hall, London, 1889–91)

Cumming, Janet; Allen, Janet; Johnson, Jane; Hogg, Isabel; Watson, Jane Peacock ('Testimony of Coal Workers'), from Children's Employment Commission, 1840, quoted in Lillian King, *Sair, Sair Wark: Women and Mining in Scotland* (Windfall Books, Kelty, 2001)

Cunningham, Allan ('Henry Raeburn'), from John Brown, MD, *Horae Subsecivae*, 3rd series (Adam and Charles Black, Edinburgh, 1882)

The Daily Telegraph ('Prince Charles and the Cherry Brandy'), the *Daily Telegraph*, 20 June 1963

Defoe, Daniel ('The Run-up to the Union of the Scottish and English

Parliaments'), from Paul H. Scott, *Daniel Defoe, Defoe in Edinburgh and Other Papers* (Tuckwell Press, Edinburgh, 1995); Stirling Town Council, Perth and Kinross Council Archives, Perth Burgh Records, B 59/34/17/3, quoted in *Modern Scottish History 1707 to the Present: Vol. 5 Major Documents*, ed. Anthony Cooke, Ian Donnachie, Ann MacSween, Christopher A. Whatley (Tuckwell Press, Edinburgh, 1998); and George Lockhart of Carnwath, memoir, quoted in Agnes Mure Mackenzie, *Scottish Pageant*, vol. III (Oliver & Boyd, Edinburgh, 1949)

Defoe, Daniel ('The Aftermath of the Union of Parliaments'), from Daniel Defoe, *A Tour through Scotland*, in *A Tour through the Whole Island of Great Britain* (London, 1724–7)

Demarco, Richard ('Sean Connery: a Lifetime's Perspective'), by Richard Demarco, a memoir written for this book.

Devine, Professor Tom, quoted in the *Sunday Herald*, 6 May 2002

Dickson, Sergeant-Major ('The Battle of Waterloo'), from 'Account by Sergeant-Major Dickson', from *Chambers's Journal*, 6th series, 19 January 1907

Dods, Meg ('The Recipe for Haggis'), from Mistress Margaret Dods of the Cleikum Inn, St Ronans, *The Cook and Housewife's Manual*, 1826, quoted in F. Marian McNeill, *The Scots Kitchen* (Blackie & Son Ltd, London, 1929)

Douglas, David ('The Search for the Sugar Pine'), from *Douglas of the Forests: The North American Journals of David Douglas*, ed. John Davies (Paul Harris Publishing, Edinburgh, 1980)

Doyle, Sir Arthur Conan ('The Origins of Sherlock Holmes'), from Arthur Conan Doyle, *Memories & Adventures* (OUP, Oxford, 1989)

Drummond, William of Hawthornden ('Ben Jonson Walks to Scotland'), William Drummond of Hawthornden, from R. F. Patterson, *Ben Jonson's Conversations with Drummond of Hawthornden* (Blackie & Son Ltd, London, 1923)

Durland, Kellogg ('Down the Mine in Fife'), from Kellogg Durland, *Among the Fife Miners* (Sonnenschein, London, 1904)

The *Edinburgh Evening News* ('Eric Liddell Wins Gold at the Olympics'), the *Edinburgh Evening News*, quoted in Sally Magnusson, *The Flying Scotsman* (Quartet, London, 1981)

Ewing, Winnie ('The SNP Take Their Second Seat at Parliament'), from *Stop the World, The Autobiography of Winnie Ewing*, ed. Michael Russell (Birlinn, Edinburgh, 2004). Extract reproduced by permission of Birlinn Ltd (*www.birlinn.co.uk*)

Farquharson, Kenny ('*Trainspotting*'), *Scotland on Sunday*, 8 August 1993. Copyright © The Scotsman Publications Ltd

Forbes, Robert ('The Aftermath of Culloden'), from Robert Forbes, *Jacobite Memoirs of the Rebellion of 1745*, ed Robert Chambers (Edinburgh, 1834)

Froissart, Jean ('The Auld Alliance'), Froissart's Chronicle, ii, chs 2,3, in P. Hume Brown, *Early Travellers in Scotland*, quoted in *Source Book of Scottish History*, vol. I, ed. W. Croft Dickinson, Gordon Donaldson, Isabel A. Milne (Thomas Nelson and Sons Ltd, Edinburgh, 1958)

Gardner, Robert ('The First Scottish Football Match'), quoted in *Glasgow Observed*, ed. Simon Berry and Hamish Whyte (John Donald, Edinburgh, 1987)

Garioch, Robert ('Prisoner of War'), from Robert Garioch, *Two Men and a Blanket: A Prisoner of War's Story* (Southside, Edinburgh, 1975)

Gervase of Canterbury ('Religious Houses'), from *Mappa Mundi*, vol. II, quoted in *Scottish Annals from English Chroniclers*, collected and translated by Alan Orr Anderson, vol. 1 (Paul Watkins, Stamford, 1991)

The *Glasgow Herald* ('Glasgow Rent Strike', 'Sectarian Anxieties', 'The Evacuation of St Kilda'), from the *Glasgow Herald*, 28 and 29 September; 29 October 1915; 30 May 1923; 30 August, 1930

The *Glasgow Herald* ('The Clydebank Blitz'; 'Rudolf Hess Crash-lands in Scotland'; 'The Ibrox Disaster'), from the *Glasgow Herald*, 22 March and 13 May 1941; 3 January 1971. The *Glasgow Herald*, copyright © Newsquest (Herald & Times)

Glasser, Ralph ('The Hungry Prostitute'), from Ralph Glasser, *Growing Up in the Gorbals* (Chatto & Windus, London, 1986). Permission granted by Black & White Publishing, Edinburgh

Gould, Lt-Commander R. T., RN (Retired) ('The Loch Ness Monster'), *The Times*, 9 December 1933

Gow, Alexander ('The Battle of the Braes'), from the *Dundee Advertiser*, in Donald MacLeod, *Gloomy Memories of the Highlands*, Letter VII, quoted in Alexander Mackenzie, *The History of the Highland Clearances* (Mercat Press, Edinburgh, 1991)

Grahame, Kenneth ('The Early Adventures of Toad'), from Patrick R. Chalmers, *Kenneth Grahame: Life, Letters and Unpublished Work* (Methuen, London, 1933)

Gray, Muriel ('Munro-bagging'), from Muriel Gray, *The First Fifty: Munro-bagging without a Beard* (Mainstream, Edinburgh, 1991). Reproduced by permission of the publisher

The *Greenock Advertiser* ('Cholera Epidemic'), the *Greenock Advertiser*, 9 March 1832

Gunn, Walter ('A Missionary Visits Greenock'), from Walter Gunn, Missionary, *Sketches of the Sanitary and Social Condition of Greenock* (Greenock 1865)

Guthrie, Tyrone ('The Second Edinburgh Festival'), from Tyrone Guthrie, *A Life in Theatre* (Columbus, London, 1987). Reproduced by kind permission of the Wylie Agency (UK) Ltd

Hamilton, Ian ('Stealing the Stone of Destiny'), from I. R. Hamilton, *The Taking of the Stone of Destiny* (Lochar, Colonsay, 1991). Reproduced with permission of the author

Hardie, Keir ('Keir Hardie Elected as First Labour MP'), from *Keir Hardie's Speeches and Writings from 1888 to 1915*, 4th edn, ed. Emrys Hughes (Forward Printing and Publishing Company, Glasgow, 1927)

Hare, William ('The Trial of Burke and Hare'), from *Edinburgh Courant*, quoted in *Burke & Hare: the Resurrection Men*, ed. Jacques Barzun (The Scarecrow Press, Metuchen, NJ, 1974)

Henderson, Hamish ('Jimmy MacBeath, King of the Cornkisters'), from Hamish Henderson, *Alias MacAlias: Writings on Songs, Folk and Literature* (Polygon, Edinburgh, 1992). Extract reproduced by permission of Polygon, an imprint of Birlinn Ltd (*www.birlinn.co.uk*)

Hill, David Octavius ('The Origins of Photography'), from NLS MS Acc 7967/1, quoted in *A Scottish Postbag*, ed. George Bruce and P. H. Scott (W. & R. Chambers, Edinburgh, 1986)

Hume, David ('*The Wealth of Nations*'), from *The Correspondence of Adam Smith*, ed. Ernest Campbell Mossner and Ian Simpson (Oxford, 1977)

Hunter, A. ('Travelling Conditions for Emigrants'), from Testimony of A. Hunter, WS on 10 April 1827, Report of the Select Committee appointed to inquire into the Expediency of encouraging Emigration from the United Kingdom, Parliamentary Papers V 1826–291–2, quoted in *Modern Scottish History, 1707 to the Present: Vol. 5, Major Documents*, ed. Anthony Cooke, Ian Donnachie, Ana Macsween, Christopher A. Whatley (Tuckwell Press, Edinburgh, 1998)

Hutton, James ('The Age of the Earth Is Proved by James Hutton'), quoted in Donald B. McIntyre and Alan McKirdy, *James Hutton: The Founder of Modern Geology* (NMS Publishing, Edinburgh, 2001)

The *Inverness Courier* ('Rioting in Caithness'), *Inverness Courier*, 3 March 1847, found in H. Noble, *The Potato Famine in the Highlands, 1846–49* (pamphlet)

James I, James II and James III ('Acts of Parliament'), quoted in *Scotland Before 1700 from Contemporary Documents*, ed. P. Hume Brown (David Douglas, Edinburgh, 1893)

James VI and I ('The Evils of Tobacco'), James VI, *Counterblaste to Tobacco*, 1604, quoted in Agnes Mure Mackenzie, *Scottish Pageant*, vol. II (Oliver & Boyd, Edinburgh, 1948)

Jenkins, Simon ('James Kelman Wins the Booker Prize'), *The Times*, 15 October 1994

John of Fordun ('Bird Flu, or Similar' and 'The Black Death'), from John of Fordun, *Chronicle of the Scottish People*, translated from Latin by Felix J. H. Skene, from *Historians of Scotland*, vol. VI (Edinburgh, 1872)

Johnson, Samuel ('A Visitor's Impressions of Scotland'), from Samuel Johnson, *Journey to the Western Islands of Scotland* (1775), ed. Peter Levi (Folio Society, London, 1990)

Ker of Gradyne, Colonel ('The Battle of Culloden'), Colonel Ker of Gradyne quoted in Robert Forbes, *Jacobite Memoirs of the Rebellion of 1745*, ed. Robert Chambers (Edinburgh, 1834)

Knox, John ('The Burning of George Wishart', 'The Murder of Cardinal David Beaton', 'John Knox Apologizes to Queen Elizabeth I', 'Mary, Queen of Scots, Arrives in Scotland'), from John Knox, *A History of the Reformation*, vol. II, quoted in *Source Book of Scottish History*, vol. I, ed. W. Croft Dickinson,

Gordon Donaldson, Isabel A. Milne (Thomas Nelson & Sons Ltd, Edinburgh, 1958)

Lauder, Harry ('Unknown Comedian Tries His Luck in London'), from Harry Lauder, *Roamin' in the Gloamin'* (1928). Reproduced by kind permission of Elizabeth Hamilton.

Lavery, John ('Saxpence in ma claes, ninepence in ma skin'), from Sir John Lavery, *The Life of a Painter* (1940), quoted in *Glasgow Observed*, ed. Simon Berry and Hamish Whyte (John Donald, Edinburgh, 1987)

Law, Denis ('The Flodden of Football'), from Denis Law, with Bernard Bale, *The Lawman: an Autobiography* (Andre Deutsch, London, 1999). Copyright © Denis Law

Lawrie, Dr W. L. ('Streets of Sewage'), from Reports of the Sanitary Condition of the Labouring Population of Scotland (London, 1842)

Levison (née Lusk), Mary ('Petition for Women to Become Ministers in the Church of Scotland'), from Mary Levison, *Wrestling with the Church* (Arthur James, London, 1992)

Livingstone, David ('Dr Livingstone Is Found by Henry Morton Stanley'), from *The Last Journals of David Livingstone, in Central Africa, from 1865 to his Death*, Vol II (London, 1880)

Livingstone, John ('The National Covenant'), from John Livingstone, *The Diary of a Covenanting Minister 1626–1667* (Wigtown District Museum Service, 1993)

Lockhart, John Gibson ('George IV Visits Scotland'), quoted in *The Oxford Book of Literary Anecdotes*, ed. James Sutherland, (OUP, Oxford, 1975)

The Lord Treasurer of England ('Border Reivers Defy Capture'), from *Calendar of Border Papers*, ed. Joseph Bain (HM General Register House, Edinburgh, 1894)

Macaulay, Zachary ('A Jamaican Sugar Plantation'), from *Life and Letters of Zachary Macaulay*, by his granddaughter Viscountess Knutsford (London, 1900)

McBain, Barclay ('The Lockerbie Disaster'), the *Herald*, 23 December 1988. The *Herald*, copyright © Newsquest (Herald & Times)

MacCaig, Norman ('A Conscientious Objector'), quoted in *Voices from War: Personal Recollections of War in Our Century by Scottish Men and Women*, ed. Ian MacDougall (Mercat Press, Edinburgh, 1995). Reprinted by kind permission of the publishers

Macdonald, Ethel ('The Spanish Civil War'), from *Barcelona Bulletin*, quoted in Rhona M. Hodgart, *Ethel MacDonald: Glasgow Woman Anarchist* (Kate Sharpley Library, London, 1995). Reproduced with kind permission of Rhona Hodgart and the publisher

Macdonald, John ('Jacobite Orphans'), from John Macdonald, *Memoirs of an Eighteenth-century Footman* (Century, London, 1985)

McGahey, Mick ('The Miners' Strike'), quoted in *Miners 1984–1994: A Decade of Endurance*, ed. Joe Owens (Polygon, Edinburgh, 1994). Reproduced by permission of Polygon, an imprint of Birlinn Ltd (*www.birlinn.co.uk*)

McGonagall, William ('The Tay Railway Bridge Disaster'), from William McGonagall, *Poetic Gems* (Duckworth, London, 1989)

McIlvanney, Hugh ('Celtic Win the European Cup'), from Hugh McIlvanney, *McIlvanney on Football* (Mainstream, London, 1994). Copyright © Guardian Newspapers Limited, 1967

Mackenzie, Henry ('Robert Burns Is Hailed as a Genius'), from *The Lounger*, quoted in Agnes Mure Mackenzie, *Scottish Pageant*, vol. 3 (Oliver & Boyd, Edinburgh, 1949)

McLean, Reverend ('The Disruption of the Church of Scotland'), from Rev. Thomas Brown, *Annals of the Disruption* (Macniven & Wallace, Edinburgh, 1876–84)

MacLeod, Donald ('The Sutherland Clearances' and 'Sutherland after the Clearances'), from Donald MacLeod, *Gloomy Memories of the Highlands*, Letter VII, quoted in Alexander Mackenzie, *The History of the Highland Clearances* (Mercat Press, Edinburgh, 1991)

McLevy, James ('An Edinburgh Detective at Work'), from James McLevy, *McLevy Returns: Further Disclosures of the Edinburgh Detective* (Mercat Press, Edinburgh, 2002)

Major, John ('A Paen to Oatcakes'), from John Major, *A History of Greater Britain as well England as Scotland*, 1521, translated from Latin by Archibald Constable (Scottish History Society, Edinburgh, 1892)

Martin Martin ('A Gael's View of the Islands'), from Martin Martin, *A Description of the Western Islands of Scotland circa 1695*, ed. Donald Monro (Mercat Press, Edinburgh, 1999)

Mary, Queen of Scots ('Mary, Queen of Scots, Appeals to Elizabeth I for Help' and 'The Morning of Mary, Queen of Scots's Execution'), quoted in Agnes Mure Mackenzie, *Scottish Pageant*, vol. II (Oliver & Boyd, Edinburgh, 1948)

Maxwell, Fordyce ('The Dunblane Massacre'), Fordyce Maxwell, the *Scotsman*, 16 March 1996. Copyright © The Scotsman Publications Ltd

Medical Officers of Perth and Barlinnie prisons ('Force-feeding Suffragettes'), from National Archives of Scotland, HH55/327

Melville, James ('Schooldays'), Memoirs of James Melville, quoted in Agnes Mure Mackenzie, *Scottish Pageant*, vol. II (Oliver & Boyd, Edinburgh, 1948)

Melville, Sir James ('The Murder of Riccio'), Sir James Melville, quoted in *Scottish Diaries and Memoirs 1550–1746*, ed. J. G. Fyfe (Stirling, 1927)

Mendelssohn, Felix Bartholdy ('Mendelssohn Visits Scotland'), from *Felix Mendelssohn: A Life in Letters*, ed. Rudolf Elvers, translated from German by Craig Tomlinson (Fromm International Publishing Corporation, New York, 1986)

Mill, Reverend John ('Superstition and Punishment'), from *The Diary of the Reverend John Mill, minister of the parishes of Dunrossness, Sadwick and Cunningsburgh in Shetland, 1740–1803* (Edinburgh, 1889)

Mitchell, Joseph ('Law and Justice in the Highlands' and 'Railway Mania'), from Joseph Mitchell, *Reminiscences of My Life in the Highlands*, vols I and II (London, 1883–4)

Moryson, Fynes ('The Scottish Diet'), Fynes Moryson, in *Early Travellers in Scotland*, ed. P. Hume Brown (David Douglas, Edinburgh, 1891)

Muir, Edwin ('Edinburgh and Its Street Girls'), from Edwin Muir, *Scottish Journey* (Mainstream, Edinburgh, 1979). Reprinted with permission by the publisher

Muir, Thomas ('The Trial of "the Pest of Scotland" '), from *The Trial of Thomas Muir, younger, of Huntershill, Before the High Court of Justiciary, at Edinburgh, on the 30th and 31st Days of August, 1793* (London, 1793)

Myles, James ('Child Worker in a Dundee Factory'), from James Myles, *Chapters in the Life of a Dundee Factory Boy* (Dundee, 1850)

Nithsdale, the Countess of ('A Jacobite Escapes from the Tower of London'), from Genuine Account of the Escape of Lord Nithsdale written by the Countess of Nithsdale, to her sister, Lady Lucy Herbert, Abbess of the Augustine Nuns, of Bruges (National Library of Scotland, manuscript archive)

Obree, Graeme ('The Flying Scotsman breaks the World Hour Record'), from Graeme Obree, *Flying Scotsman, the Graeme Obree Story* (Birlinn, Edinburgh, 2003). Extract reproduced by permission of Birlinn Ltd (*www.birlinn co.uk*)

Owen, Robert ('An Experiment in Humanity'), from Report of Minutes of Evidence Taken by the Select Committee on the State of the Children Employed in the Manufactories of the United Kingdom (Parliamentary Papers, vol. 3, 1816), quoted in *Scottish Voices, 1745–1960*, eds. T. C. Smout and Sydney Wood (William Collins and Sons, London, 1990)

Paris, Matthew ('Viking Invaders'), from Matthew Paris, *Chronica Majora*, vol. 1, quoted in *Scottish Annals from English Chroniclers, AD 500–1286*, collected and translated by Alan Orr Anderson (Paul Watkins, Stamford, 1991)

Park, Mungo ('African Exploration'), from Mungo Park, *Travels in the Interior Districts of Africa* (London, 1799), quoted in *The Oxford Book of Exploration*, ed. Robin Hanbury-Tenison (OUP, Oxford, 1993)

Patrick, James ('A Glasgow Gang'), from James Patrick, *A Glasgow Gang Observed* (Eyre Methuen, London, 1973)

Petrie, Reverend Adam ('Manners'), from *Rules of Good Deportment, or of Good Breeding for the Use of Youth* (Edinburgh, 1720), in *The Works of Adam Petrie, the Scotish [sic] Chesterfield* (Edinburgh, 1877)

Playfair, John ('The Age of the Earth Is Proved by James Hutton'), quoted in Donald B. McIntyre and Alan McKirdy, *James Hutton: The Founder of Modern Geology* (NMS Publishing, Edinburgh, 2001)

Pollock, Thomas ('Smallpox'), from *The Statistical Account of Scotland 1791–1799*: Vol. VI *Ayrshire* (parish of Kilwinning), ed. Sir John Sinclair quoted in *Modern Scottish History 1707 to the Present: Vol. 5 Major Documents*, ed. Anthony Cooke, Ian Donnachie, Ann MacSween, Christopher A. Whatley (Tuckwell Press, Edinburgh, 1998)

Porte, Isa ('Rape'), quoted in *Voices from the Hunger Marches*, ed. Ian MacDougall (Polygon, Edinburgh, 1990). Extract reproduced by permission of Polygon, an imprint of Birlinn Ltd (*www.birlinn.co.uk*)

The Presbytery of Glasgow ('No Pipe-playing on Sundays'), the Presbytery of Glasgow, Kirk Session of Glasgow, 1573, quoted in Agnes Mure Mackenzie, *Scottish Pageant*, vol. II (Oliver & Boyd, Edinburgh, 1948)

Rafferty, John ('Scotland Beats the English World Cup Team'), the *Scotsman*, 17 April 1967. Copyright © The Scotsman Publications Ltd

Register of the Privy Council ('The First New Year's Day'), the Privy Council of Scotland, 1599, quoted in Agnes Mure Mackenzie, *Scottish Pageant*, vol. II (Oliver & Boyd, Edinburgh, 1948)

Register of the Privy Council ('A Good Use for the Plantations'), Register of the Privy Council, 3rd series, ii, quoted in *Source Book of Scottish History*, vol. I, ed. W. Croft Dickinson, Gordon Donaldson, Isabel A. Milne (Thomas Nelson and Sons Ltd, Edinburgh, 1958)

Reid, Jimmy ('The Upper Clydeside Shipyards' Work-in'), from 'The UCS Campaign', in Jimmy Reid, *Reflections of a Clyde-Built Man*, ed. Ruth Wishart (Souvenir Press, London, 1976). Reprinted by permission of the publisher

Robertson, James ('The Day They Buried Princess Diana'), an extract from his essay 'Six Deaths, Two Funerals, a Wedding and a Divorce', first published in *Scotland into the New Era* (Canongate, Edinburgh, 2000). Reproduced by permission of the author

Rosie, George ('The Big Yin'), George Rosie, 'King Billy', in the *Sunday Times*, 23 February 1975

Rosie, George, quoted in the *Scottish Review of Books*, Vol. 3, No. 2, 2007

Royle, Trevor and Taylor, Alan ('The Death of Donald Dewar'), the *Sunday Herald*, 11 October 2000. *Sunday Herald*, copyright © Newsquest Ltd (Herald & Times)

Russell, James ('Murder of Archbishop Sharp'), in James Kirkton, *Secret and True History of the Church of Scotand*, ed. C. K. Sharpe (Edinburgh, 1817), Appendix: Russell's Account of the Murder of Archbishop Sharp

Ruthall, Thomas ('Battle of Flodden'), from Facsimiles of National MSS [of Great Britain], 11. nos 4 and 5, quoted in *Source Book of Scottish History*, vol. I, ed. W. Croft Dickinson, Gordon Donaldson, Isabel A. Milne (Thomas Nelson and Sons Ltd, Edinburgh, 1958)

St Fond, B. Faujais ('A Bagpipe Competition'), quoted in *The Land Out There, a Scottish Land Anthology*, ed. George Bruce, with Frank Rennie (AUP, Aberdeen, 1991)

Salmond, Alex ('The SNP Come to Power'), quoted in the *Sunday Herald*, 6 May 2007

Scotichronicon ('English Fashion'), from Walter Bower, *Scotichronicon*, c. 39, ii, 34–83, quoted in Walter Bower, *A History Book for Scots, Selections from Scotichronicon*, ed. D. E. R. Watt (Mercat Press, Edinburgh, 1998). Reprinted by kind permission of the publisher

The Scots Magazine ('The New Town Is Conceived'), from *The Scots Magazine*, August 1767

The *Scotsman* ('Mayhem at Musselburgh Golf Match'), from the *Scotsman*, 23 and 25 April 1870

The *Scotsman* ('Benny Lynch Retains His Triple Crown'; 'Nudity at the Edinburgh Festival'; 'Scotland Beats the English World Cup Team'; 'Allan Wells Wins Olympic Gold'; 'The Poll that Put Gordon Brown out of the Leadership Race'), from the *Scotsman*, 13 October, 1937; 9 September 1963; 26 July 1980; 26 May 1994. Copyright © The Scotsman Publications Ltd

Scott, Sir Walter ('Robert Burns Meets Walter Scott'), quoted in *From Scenes Like These: Scottish Anecdotes and Episodes*, ed. David Ross (Birlinn, Edinburgh, 2000)

Scott, Sir Walter ('The Ossian Fraud'), from *The Letters of Sir Walter Scott*, vol. IX, ed. H. J. C. Grierson (London, 1932–7), quoted in *A Scottish Postbag*, ed. George Bruce and P. H. Scott (W. & R. Chambers, Edinburgh, 1986)

Scottish Ecclesiastical Statutes ('Guidelines for the Clergy'), from *Ecclesiae Scoticanae Statuta tam Provincialia quam Synodalia quae Supersunt*, quoted in *Scotland before 1700 from Contemporary Documents*, ed. P. Hume Brown (David Douglas, Edinburgh, 1893)

Simpson, James ('Experimenting with Chloroform'), from J. Duns, *Memoir of Sir James Y. Simpson, Bart* (Edinburgh, 1873)

Slessor, Mary ('Mary Slessor's Campaign to Save Babies'), from W. P. Livingstone, *The White Queen* (Hodder & Stoughton, London, 1931)

Smellie, William ('The *Encyclopaedia Britannica*'), from *Encyclopaedia Britannica, or, a Dictionary of Arts and Sciences, compiled upon a new plan*, vol. 1, 1773

Smith, Adam ('Death of David Hume'), from *The Correspondence of Adam Smith*, ed. Ernest Campbell Mossner and Ian Simpson (Oxford, 1977)

Smith, David ('Life at the Front in France'), from 'Memories of my life as a soldier and prisoner of war during the Great War 1914–1918', the unpublished diary of Private David Smith, 5th and 7th Battalions Seaforth Highlanders, National Museums Scotland, M. 1969. 19. Courtesy of the trustees National Museums Scotland

Somerville, Alexander ('Radicals in the Playground'), from Alexander Somerville, *The Autobiography of a Working Man* (1848)

Spark, Muriel ('The Origins of Miss Jean Brodie'), from Muriel Spark, *Curriculum Vitae* (Constable, London, 1992)

Stevenson, Robert ('Building the Bell Rock Lighthouse'), from Robert Stevenson, *An Account of the Bell Rock Lighthouse* (Constable, London, 1824)

Stevenson, Robert Louis ('*Treasure Island*'), from Robert Louis Stevenson, 'My First Book', in Robert Louis Stevenson, *The Lantern Bearers and other essays*, ed. Jeremy Treglown (Chatto & Windus, London, 1988)

Stobo, Reverend Archibald ('The Darien Venture'), Rev. Archibald Stobo, Darien Letters, from the Spencer Collection, Glasgow University Library (Glasgow College Press, 1971)

The Strike Bulletin ('Red Clydeside Erupts'), from *The Strike Bulletin, Organ of the 40 Hours Movement*, 1 February 1919

Tacitus ('Agricola Sails around Scotland'), from Tacitus's *Life of Agricola*, quoted in Agnes Mure Mackenzie, *Scottish Pageant* (Oliver & Boyd, Edinburgh, 1946)

Taylor, James ('The Scuttling of the German Grand Fleet at Scapa Flow'), quoted in Dan van der Vat, *The Grand Scuttle: the Sinking of the German Fleet at Scapa Flow in 1919* (Birlinn, Edinburgh, 1997)

The Times ('The Sinking of the *Arandora Star*'), *The Times*, 4 and 5 July 1940

Victoria, Queen ('Victoria and Albert at Balmoral'), from *Queen Victoria's Highland Journals*, ed. David Duff (Webb and Bower, Exeter, 1980)

Walker, Patrick ('Famine'), from Patrick Walker, *Biographia Presbyteriana*, ii, quoted in *Source Book of Scottish History*, vol. I, ed. W. Croft Dickinson, Gordon Donaldson, Isabel A. Milne (Thomas Nelson and Sons Ltd, Edinburgh, 1958)

Watt, Christian ('The Mental Asylum'), from *The Christian Watt Papers*, ed. David Fraser (Paul Harris, Edinburgh, 1983)

Watt, James ('The Invention of the Steam Engine'), from *Partners in Science: Letters of James Watt and Joseph Black*, ed. Eric Robinson and Douglas McKie (Constable, London, 1971)

Weld, Charles Richard ('Fish Gutters' and 'The Glorious Twelfth'), from Charles Richard Weld, *Two Months in the Highlands* (London, 1860)

William of Malmesbury ('The King of Scots Insults the English King'), from William of Malmesbury, *Gesta Regum*, vol. I, quoted in *Scottish Annals from English Chroniclers, AD 500–1286*, collected and translated by Alan Orr Anderson, vol. 1 (Paul Watkins, Stamford, 1991)

William of Newburgh ('Capture of William I by the English'), from *Historia Rerum Anglicarum*, in *Chronicles of Stephen*, vol. I, pp. 183–5, quoted in *Scottish Annals from English Chroniclers*, collected and translated by Alan Orr Anderson, vol. 1 (Paul Watkins, Stamford, 1991)

Williamson, Duncan ('The Travelling Family'), from Duncan Williamson, *The Horsieman: Memories of a Traveller* (Canongate, Edinburgh, 1994)

Wilmut, Professor Ian ('Dolly the Sheep'), from Ian Wilmut and Roger Highfield, *After Dolly: The Uses and Misuses of Human Cloning* (Little, Brown, London, 2006). Reproduced by permission of Little, Brown

Wilson, John ('Among the Residents of Black Houses'), from John Wilson, *Tales and Travels of a School Inspector: In the Highlands and Islands at the End of the Nineteenth Century* (reprinted 1998 and 2006, Acair Ltd, Isle of Lewis).

Wingfield, Robert ('The Execution of Mary, Queen of Scots'), in the Hon. Mrs Maxwell Scott, *The Tragedy of Fotheringay* (Edinburgh, 1905), quoted in Agnes Mure Mackenzie, *Scottish Pageant*, vol. II (Oliver & Boyd, Edinburgh, 1948)

Select Bibliography

Anderson, Alan Orr, *Early Sources of Scottish History AD 500–1286*, vol. 1 (Paul Watkins, Stamford, 1991)

Anderson, Alan Orr, *Scottish Annals from English Chroniclers, AD 500–1286* (Paul Watkins, Stamford, 1991), pp. 71–3

Baird, Malcolm, ed., *Television and Me: the Memoirs of John Logie Baird* (Mercat Press, Edinburgh, 2004)

Balcarres, Colin, Earl of Balcarres, *Memoirs Touching the Revolution in Scotland* (Bannatyne Club, Edinburgh, 1841)

Bald, Robert, *A General View of the Coal-Trade of Scotland* (Edinburgh, 1808)

Barzun, Jacques, ed., *Burke & Hare: the Resurrection Men* (Scarecrow Press, Metuchen, NJ, 1974)

Bede, Cuthbert, *A Tour in Tartan-Land* (Richard Bentley, London, 1863)

Berry, Simon and Whyte, Hamish, eds., *Glasgow Observed* (John Donald, Edinburgh, 1987)

Bold, Alan, *MacDiarmid: Christopher Murray Grieve, A Critical Biography* (John Murray, London, 1988)

Boswell, James, *The Journal of a Tour to the Hebrides* (Folio Society, London, 1990)

Bower, Walter, *A History Book for Scots, Selections from* Scotichronicon, ed. D. E. R. Watt (Mercat Press, Edinburgh, 1998)

Boyle, Jimmy, *A Sense of Freedom* (Pan and Canongate, London and Edinburgh, 1977)

Brodie, Alexander, ed., *The Scottish Enlightenment, An Anthology* (Canongate, Edinburgh, 1997)

Brown, George Mackay, *Rockpools and Daffodils: An Orcadian Diary 1979–1991* (Gordon Wright, Edinburgh, 1992)

Brown, Peter Hume, ed., *Scotland before 1700 from Contemporary Documents* (David Douglas, Edinburgh, 1893)

Brown, P. Hume, *Early Travellers in Scotland* (David Douglas, Edinburgh, 1891)

Brown, Thomas, ed., *Annals of the Disruption* (Macniven & Wallace, Edinburgh, 1876–84)

Bruce, George, and Scott, Paul H., eds, *A Scottish Postbag: Eight Centuries of Scottish Letters* (W. & R. Chambers, Edinburgh, 1986)

Buchanan, George, *Rerum Scoticarum Historia, 1582, The History of Scotland*, trans. James Aikman (Blackie, Fullarton & Co., Glasgow, Archibald Fullarton & Co., Edinburgh, 1827)

Burton, John Hill, ed., *The Autobiography of Dr Alexander Carlyle of Inveresk 1722–1805* (London, 1910)

Carey, Robert, *The Stirring World of Robert Carey, Robert Carey's Memoirs, 1577–1625* (*www.RippingYarns.com*, 2005)

Carlyle, Thomas, ed., *Oliver Cromwell's Letters and Speeches* (Chapman & Hall, London, 1847)

Chalmers, Patrick R., ed., *Kenneth Grahame: Life, Letters and Unpublished Work* (Methuen, London, 1933)

Cockburn, Henry Cockburn, Lord, *Memorials of His Time* (1856, revised and abridged edn, R. Grant, Edinburgh, 1945)

Cooke, Anthony, Donnachie, Ian, MacSween, Ann, Whatley, Christopher A., eds, *Modern Scottish History 1707 to the Present: Vol. 5 Major Documents* (Tuckwell Press, Edinburgh, 1998)

Darien Letters, from the Spencer Collection, Glasgow University Library (Glasgow College Press, Glasgow, 1971)

Davies, John, ed., *Douglas of the Forests: The North American Journals of David Douglas* (Paul Harris Publishing, Edinburgh, 1980)

Defoe, Daniel, *A Tour thro' the Whole Island of Great Britain, 1734* (London, 1734)

Devine, Tom, *Scotland's Empire 1600–1815* (Penguin, London, 2003)

Devine, Tom, *The Scottish Nation 1700–2000* (Penguin, London, 1999)

Dickinson, W. Croft, Donaldson, Gordon, Milnes, Isabel A., eds, *Source Book of Scottish History*, vol. I (Thomas Nelson and Sons Ltd, Edinburgh, 1958)

Doyle, Sir Arthur Conan, *Memories & Adventures* (OUP, Oxford, 1989)

Dunn, Jane, *Elizabeth and Mary: Cousins, Rivals, Queens* (HarperCollins, London, 2003)

Duns, J., *Memoir of Sir James Y. Simpson, Bart* (Edinburgh, 1873)

Durland, Kellogg, *Among the Fife Miners* (Sonnenschein, London, 1904)

Elvers, Rudolf, ed., *Felix Mendelssohn: A Life in Letters*, trans. from German by Craig Tomlinson (Fromm International Publishing Corporation, New York, 1986)

Ewing, Winnie, *Stop the World, The Autobiography of Winnie Ewing*, ed. Michael Russell (Birlinn, Edinburgh, 2004)

The First and Second Statistical Accounts of Edinburgh (West Port Books, Edinburgh, 1998)

Forbes, Robert, *Jacobite Memoirs of the Rebellion of 1745*, ed. from the manuscripts of the Late Right Rev. Robert Forbes, A. M. Bishop of the Scottish Episcopal Church, by Robert Chambers (Edinburgh, 1834)

Fordun, John of, *Chronicle of the Scottish People*, in *Historians of Scotland*, vol. VI (Edinburgh, 1872)

Fraser, Antonia, *Mary Queen of Scots* (World Books, London, 1970)

Fraser, David, ed., *The Christian Watt Papers* (Paul Harris Publishing, Edinburgh, 1983)

Froude, J. A., *Letters and Memorials of Jane Welsh Carlyle Prepared for Publication by Thomas Carlyle* (London, 1883)

Fyfe, J. G., ed., *Scottish Diaries and Memoirs 1550–1746* (Stirling, 1927)

Fyfe, J. G., ed., *Scottish Diaries and Memoirs 1746–1843* (Stirling, 1942)

Garioch, Robert, *Two Men and a Blanket: A Prisoner of War's Story* (Southside, Edinburgh, 1975)

Glasser, Ralph, *Growing Up in the Gorbals* (Chatto & Windus, London, 1986)

Grierson, H. J. C., *The Letters of Sir Walter Scott*, vol. IX (London, 1932–7)

Gunn, Walter, *Sketches of the Sanitary and Social Condition of Greenock* (Greenock, 1865)

Hamilton, Ian R., *The Taking of the Stone of Destiny* (Lochar, Colonsay, 1991)

Hughes, Emrys, ed., *Keir Hardie's Speeches and Writings from 1888 to 1915* (Forward Printing and Publishing Company, Glasgow)

Johnson, Samuel, *A Journey to the Western Islands of Scotland* (Folio Society, London, 1990)

King, Lillian, *Sair, Sair Wark: Women and Mining in Scotland* (Windfall Books, Kelty, 2001)

Knutsford, Viscountess, *Life and Letters of Zachary Macaulay* (London, 1900)

Laing, D., ed., *The Works of John Knox*, vol. VI (Edinburgh, 1895)

Lauder, Harry, *Roamin' in the Gloamin'* (London, 1928)

Levison, Mary, *Wrestling with the Church* (Arthur James, London, 1992)

Lindsay, Ann, *Seeds of Blood and Beauty: Scottish Plant Explorers* (Birlinn, Edinburgh, 2005)

Livingstone, David, *The Last Journals of David Livingstone, in Central Africa, from 1865 to his Death*, vol. II (London, 1880)

Macdonald, John, *Memoirs of an Eighteenth-century Footman* (Century, London, 1985)

MacDougall, Ian, ed., *Voices from War: personal recollections of war in our century by Scottish men and women* (Mercat Press, Edinburgh, 1995)

McIlvanney, Hugh, *McIlvanney on Football* (Mainstream, Edinburgh, 1994)

McIntyre, Donald B. and McKirdy, Alan, *James Hutton, The Founder of Modern Geology* (NMS Publishing, Edinburgh, 2001)

Mackenzie, Agnes Mure, ed., *Scottish Pageant*, 4 vols (Oliver & Boyd, Edinburgh & London, 1946–9)

MacLeod, Donald, *Gloomy Memories of the Highlands* (Mercat Press, Edinburgh, 1991)

McLevy, James, *McLevy: The Edinburgh Detective* (Mercat Press, Edinburgh, 2001)

McLevy, James, *McLevy Returns: Further Disclosures of the Edinburgh Detective* (Mercat Press, Edinburgh, 2002)

McNeill, F. Marian, *The Scots Kitchen* (Blackie & Son Ltd, London, 1929)

Major, John, *A History of Greater Britain as well England as Scotland* (Scottish History Society, Edinburgh, 1892)

Martin, Martin, *A Description of the Western Islands of Scotland circa 1695* (Mercat Press, Edinburgh, 1999)

Maxwell, Sir H., ed., *The Chronicle of Lanercost*, in *Scottish Historical Review*, vi (Glasgow, 1909)

Mitchell, Joseph, *Reminiscences of My Life in the Highlands*, vols 1 and 2 (Chilworth, London, 1883–4)

Morton, H. V., *In Scotland Again* (Methuen, London, 1933)

Mossner, Ernest Campbell and Simpson, Ian, eds, *The Correspondence of Adam Smith* (Clarendon Press, Oxford, 1977)

Muir, Edwin, *Scottish Journey* (Flamingo, London, 1935)

Myles, James, *Chapters in the Life of a Dundee Factory Boy* (J. Myles, Dundee, 1850)

Noble, H., *The Potato Famine in the Highlands, 1846–49* (Highland Environmental Link Project, 1987)

Normand, Lawrence, and Roberts, Gareth, eds, *Witchcraft in Early Modern Scotland* (University of Exeter Press, Exeter, 2000)

Obree, Graeme, *Flying Scotsman: The Graeme Obree Story* (Birlinn, Edinburgh, 2003)

Owens, Joe, ed., *Miners 1984–1994: A Decade of Endurance* (Polygon, Edinburgh, 1994)

Paterson, George, 'The Eyemouth Fishing Disaster', the *Scotsman*, 17 October 1881

Patrick, James, *A Glasgow Gang Observed* (Eyre Methuen, London, 1973)

Patterson, R. F., *Ben Jonson's Conversations with Drummond of Hawthornden* (Blackie & Son Ltd, London, 1923)

Petrie, Adam, *The Works of Adam Petrie, the Scotish [sic] Chesterfield* (Edinburgh, 1877)

Reid, Jimmy, *Reflections of a Clyde-Built Man*, ed. Ruth Wishart (Souvenir Press, London, 1976)

Robinson, Eric and McKie, Douglas, eds, *Partners in Science: Letters of James Watt and Joseph Black* (Constable, London, 1971)

Ross, David, *From Scenes Like These: Scottish Anecdotes and Episodes* (Birlinn, Edinburgh, 2000)

Scott, Hon. Mrs Maxwell, *The Tragedy of Fotheringay* (Sands, Edinburgh, 1905)

Scott, Paul H., *Defoe in Edinburgh and Other Papers* (Tuckwell Press, Edinburgh, 1995)

Scott, P. H., *Scotland: An Unwon Cause* (Canongate, Edinburgh, 1997)

Sharpe, C. K., ed., *James Kirkton, Secret and True History of the Church of Scotland* (Edinburgh, 1817)

Smith, Gavid D., *The Scottish Smuggler* (Birlinn, Edinburgh, 2003)

Smout, T. C., *A History of the Scottish People 1560–1830* (Collins, London, 1969)

Smout, T. C., *A Century of the Scottish People 1830–1950* (Collins, London, 1986)

Smout, T. C. and Wood, Sydney, *Scottish Voices, 1745–1960* (Collins, London, 1990)

Somerville, Alexander, *The Autobiography of a Working Man* (London, 1848)

Stevenson, Robert, *An Account of the Bell Rock Lighthouse* (Constable, London, 1824)

Stevenson, Robert Louis, *The Lantern Bearers and other essays*, by RLS, ed. Jeremy Treglown (Chatto & Windus, London, 1988)

The Trial of Thomas Muir, younger, of Huntershill, Before the High Court of Justiciary, at Edinburgh, on the 30th and 31st Days of August, 1793 (London, 1793)

Victoria, Queen, *Queen Victoria's Highland Journals*, ed. David Duff (Webb and Bower, Exeter, 1980)

Wall, Joseph Frazier, *Andrew Carnegie* (OUP, New York, 1970)

Weld, Charles Richard, *Two Months in the Highlands* (London, 1860)

Williamson, Duncan, *The Horsieman: Memories of a Traveller* (Canongate, Edinburgh, 1994)

Wilmut, Ian and Highfield, Roger, *After Dolly, The Uses and Misuses of Human Cloning* (Little, Brown, London, 2006)

Wilson, John, *Tales and Travels of a School Inspector: In the Highlands and Islands at the End of the Nineteenth Century* (Acair Ltd, Stornoway, 1998)

Yeoman, Louise, ed., *Reportage Scotland* (Luath Press, Edinburgh, 2000)

Index